Elbridge Gerry Spaulding

A resource of war

The credit of the government made immediately available

Elbridge Gerry Spaulding

A resource of war
The credit of the government made immediately available

ISBN/EAN: 9783744739344

Printed in Europe, USA, Canada, Australia, Japan

Cover: Foto ©ninafisch / pixelio.de

More available books at **www.hansebooks.com**

Yours Truly
E. G. Spaulding

A RESOURCE OF WAR—THE CREDIT OF THE GOVERNMENT
MADE IMMEDIATELY AVAILABLE.

HISTORY

OF THE

LEGAL TENDER PAPER MONEY

ISSUED DURING THE

GREAT REBELLION.

BEING A

Loan without Interest and a National Currency.

PREPARED BY

Hon. E. G. SPAULDING, Chairman,

OF

THE SUB-COMMITTEE OF WAYS AND MEANS, AT THE TIME
THE ACT WAS PASSED.

In such a nation as this, there is one and only one RESOURCE for loans sufficient to carry hrough the expenses of a GREAT WAR, namely, fundable Treasury Notes fitted for circulation as money, and based upon adequate taxation.

"That in the interval between war and war, all the outstanding paper should be called in *coin permitted to flow in again*, and hold the field of circulation, until *another war* should re quire its yielding place again to the NATIONAL MEDIUM."—JEFFERSON.

BUFFALO.
EXPRESS PRINTING COMPANY, 14 EAST SWAN STREET,
1869.

INDEX TO THE NEW INTRODUCTION—1875.

	PAGE
Secretary Chase's first mistake in rejecting the bank check in 1861,	1
Antagonism of the Sub-Treasury act and its suspension—Mr. Chase refuses to recognize its suspension,	2
[See also historical letters of Geo. S. Coe and J. E. Williams, Appendix, pages 89 to 99.]	
The Banks and Sub-Treasury suspend specie payments—Mr. Chase in breaking the banks, at the same time broke the Sub-Treasury, and both were discredited together,	3—4
Legal tender act introduced by Mr. Spaulding, Dec. 30, 1861,	4
The primary object of the act was to *fund* the debt,	5
It was a "temporary *war measure*,"	5
Title of the act was to "fund the greenbacks and floating debt" into 6 per cent. gold bonds—First legal tender notes issued March 10, 1862, with endorsement on the back to fund in 6 per cent. gold bonds,	7
Second $150,00,000 legal tenders authorized,	8
Second great mistake of Secretary Chase—Abrogation of the right to fund the greenbacks in 6 per cent. gold bonds,	8—9
$900,000,000 loan act,	9—10
Secretary Chase resigns—Gold, 2.85,	10
Mr. Chase to Mr. Spaulding, July 15, 1869,	11
W. P. Fessenden, Secretary of Treasury, July 5, 1864,	11
Hugh McCulloch, Secretary of Treasury, March 4, 1865,	11
Secretary McCulloch not supported by Congress,	11
$830,000,000 of 7-30 Treasury notes issued to pay the army, and which were funded in three years into 6 per cent. gold bonds,	11—12
Geo. S. Boutwell, Secretary of Treasury, March 11, 1869,	12
Third mistake of Treasury Department,	12
New engraved plates and new issue of greenbacks, four years after the close of the war,	13
Wm. A. Richardson, Secretary of Treasury, March 17, 1873—$26,000,000 inflation of the currency,	14

Several decisions of the U. S Supreme Court on the legal tender act—
    Only justified as a temporary war measure, to be dispensed with as
    soon as possible after the close of the war, - 15—16
Justice Strong's letter on our early return to a "*normal condition*," 16
Atty.-Gen. Hoar's letter on our early return to a "*normal condition*," 17
A tender of the new emission of greenbacks not valid (unconstitutional), 17
President Grant's veto of inflation bill, 17
Assorting Bureau for redemption of national currency, 18
President Grant's plan for resuming specie payments, 19
Senator Sherman's law for resuming specie payments, January 1, 1879, 20
When the gold standard is reached, the surplus of paper currency will
    be retired, 23
New York to resume Jan. 1, 1879, Treasury sales of gold to pay current
    expenses, because the revenue is insufficient, is discreditable to the
    government, -' 24
Secretary Bristow not sufficiently supported by Congress, 25
Conclusion, 26
Hon. W. H. Seward's letter, - 27
Hon. Horace Maynard, 27
Charles Sumner, E. Corning, S. Hooper, 28
Senator Sherman, Secretary Stanton, and H. Hamlin, 29
Benson J. Lossing, W. W. Corcoran, - 30
Senator Morrill and Samuel Hooper, - 31
Horace Greeley, New York Tribune, 32

SECOND EDITION.

INTRODUCTION.

THE LEGAL TENDER ACT.—FUNDING ITS ORIGINAL OBJECT.—
HOW IT HAS BEEN ABUSED AND PERVERTED.—
RESUMPTION OF SPECIE PAYMENTS.—
SUB-TREASURY ACT, &c.

In the publication of a further edition of the "Financial History of the War," prepared by me in the winter of 1869, I may be indulged in a few words in vindication of the Legal Tender act as originally passed, and some criticisms on the general management of the Finances, especially the mistakes of the Treasury department in its administration of that act, and of other laws authorizing the issue of bonds and treasury notes.

As chairman of the sub-committee of ways and means, having charge of this subject, I became very much identified with this legislation, as well as with the bank bill passed during the second year of the war.

The first material mistake in the management of the finances, occurred when Secretary Chase discarded the use of the bank check, and the clearing house, in the fall of 1861. The Secretary of War might, with the same propriety, have rejected the railroad, the locomotive, and the telegraph. The modern invention of the bank check and the clearing house for the transaction of large financial operations with facility, are quite as useful as are railroads and telegraphs in carrying on military operations with success. The Secretary of War did not fail to make use of the railroads and the telegraph, but the Secretary of the Treasury, by sticking to the sub-treasury, and rejecting the bank check and clearing house, committed a great blunder at the commencement of the war. This mistake occurred under the following circumstances:

Two important loan acts were passed at the extra session of Congress in July and August, 1861. The first act was approved July 17th, and the second August 5th. By section six of the last mentioned act, the sub-treasury act passed in 1846, was so far suspended as to allow the Secretary of the Treasury

"To *deposit* any of the moneys obtained on any of the loans now authorized by law, to the credit of the Treasurer of the United States, in such solvent specie paying banks as he may select; and the said moneys, so deposited, may be withdrawn from such deposit, for deposit with the regular authorized depositories, *or for the payment of public dues*, or paid in the redemption of the notes authorized to be issued under this act, or the act to which this is supplementary, payable on demand, as may seem expedient to, or be directed by the Secretary of the Treasury."

The primary object, which Mr. Appleton and myself had in view, in preparing this section, was to relax the rigid requirements of the sub treasury act, in regard to the receipt and disbursement of coin, and instead of paying solely from *coin deposits* in the treasury, to allow all the money obtained on these loans to be deposited in solvent banks; the United States Treasurer to draw his checks directly on such deposit banks in payment of war expenses, which checks would be paid in state bank notes then redeemable on demand in gold, or in the ordinary course of business, to a large extent, they would pass through the New York clearing house, and the clearing houses of other cities, and be settled and cancelled by offset, without drawing large amounts of specie. This mode of payment would have enabled the Secretary more easily to effect such loans, and make his large disbursements, without materially disturbing the coin reserves held by the banks, which were then well protected by these reserves in their vaults.

This mode of making the disbursements for the large war expenses was regarded by me at that early period of the war as of vital consequence to the stability of the finances of both government and people; hence the preparation and adoption of the sixth section of the act of August 5, 1861, giving the Secretary of the Treasury discretionary power to suspend the sub-treasury law in respect to these loans.

After the battle of Bull Run, which occurred on the twenty-first of July, of that year, the necessities of the government in clothing, arming and feeding troops—in providing munitions of war and building a navy—became so urgent that the banks in New York, Boston and Philadelphia most patriotically came forward and made arrangements in several negotiations with Secretary Chase, to loan to the government $150,000,000 under the provisions of the two loan acts passed at the extra session. Of this sum $105,000,000 was apportioned to the associated banks in the city of New York payable by instalments. The banks were then in good condition, transacting their business on a specie basis, and paid coin for all balances at the clearing house, and redeemed their circulating notes in coin, and the loan to the government was made with the expectation that the money would be deposited in the banks, and be checked out under the direction of the Secretary, in pursuance of the sixth section above referred to. The Secretary of the Treasury refused to use the discretionary power conferred upon him by that section, and would not check on the banks for the expenses of the war, so that current bank notes could be paid or balances settled through the clearing house, but insisted that the banks should pay the money loaned into the sub-treasury in gold or gold treasury notes, and from thence it was distributed for war purposes and scattered in different parts of the country. By far the greater part of this loan was paid in gold coin, taken from the reserves of the banks commencing on the nineteenth of August, 1861. This unnecessary mode of requiring the payment of the loans, so weakened the banks, that it brought on a general suspension of specie payments, during the last days of December, 1861. Notwithstanding the banks commenced making advances to the government about the nineteenth of August, 1861, yet none of the securities to be issued by the government for the loans were turned over to them until the fourteenth of January, 1862.

The banks having been committed to making the loans, and having made partial advances on account of the same, were obliged to complete the loan notwithstanding the Secretary of the Treasury deemed it incompatible with his views of duty, and the traditions of the sub-treasury law, to use such banks as disbursing agents of the government, even under the extraordinary exigency under which the loans were made. The call upon the banks for payment into the government depository of the remaining instalments of the loan, either in coin or gold treasury notes, was persistently urged by the Secretary until the final closing of the transaction on the third of February, 1862. This was the first material mistake of the Secretary of the Treasury, and was the first step in the wrong direction, which, combined with other important events, led to the necessity of passing the legal tender act. The Secretary in breaking the banks, at the same time broke the sub-treasury, and both were discredited together. Under the policy pursued, the state bank bills which were local in character and credit, became uncurrent money, and the available gold in the country was wholly inadequate to meet the gigantic expenses of the war.

"A meeting of bank officers was held at the American Exchange Bank in the city of New York, December 28, 1861. One of the bank Presidents in a well considered speech delivered on that occasion, criticising the course of Secretary Chase in regard to those loans, said that

" 'He (Secretary Chase) was urged to draw directly on the banks. Coin being the basis of credits it was only in that way the increased financial operations of the government could be conducted; for it is impossible to maintain the superstructure of credit when the basis is withdrawn, for in destroying the basis the superstructure is also swept away. He refused to draw directly upon the banks for the proceeds of the loan taken by each. We are informed that the act of Congress was passed expressly for the purpose of authorizing him to do so, but he gave it a different interpretation which may be the correct one, although I do not think so.' "

The failure of the Secretary to recognize the suspension of the sub-treasury law, fully demonstrates the truthfulness of the remark made by Disraeli, that "upon a perfect knowledge and right appreciation of details the settlement of great questions mainly depends." The Secretary was intent upon having the gold for disbursement, without fully comprehending the effect this large drain was to have upon the banks and the general finances of the country.

LEGAL TENDER ACT.

The suspension of specie payments by the banks and the treasury of the United States occurred on the twenty-eighth of December, 1861, and two days later, on the thirtieth of the same month, I prepared and introduced the legal tender act, into the House of Representatives. The history of this measure in its passage through both houses is fully set forth in the text. The speeches and votes of members on both sides of the question are given in detail in this book, commencing at page six. The measure was prominently discussed before the people and in Congress for more than six weeks. It passed both houses and received the approval of President Lincoln February 25, 1862.

It is a fundamental principle, which I think I fully comprehended when I introduced this act into Congress, that not one dollar of paper money ought ever to be issued by the government, or by any bank, without at the same time, making ample provision for its prompt redemption, on demand. The best redemption, and the best attainable standard of value, is gold coin, and the only admissible standard in time of peace. It was an utter impossibility for our government at that time to redeem the legal tender notes in gold, because it could not be had on any terms; it was not in the country in sufficient amount to meet the great emergency; but the government could redeem (fund) the legal tender notes in six per cent. twenty years gold bonds. And here I may say, most emphatically, that if these six per cent. bonds could then have been negotiated for any funds available, and in adequate amount, for war expenses, not one dollar of legal tender notes would have been issued. This could not be done, and the act was framed with the express agreement that the legal tender notes issued under it should be redeemed in the six per cent. gold bonds. The second section of the act authorized the issue of $500,000,000 bonds for that purpose.

The leading object of the legal tender act, was to create a currency national in character, which could be used for liquidating war expenses, and, to prevent any plethora or redundency of such currency, provide at the same time for funding it in the six per cent. bonds. The leading object was to *fund* the debt. This provision for funding, also, in a great measure, relieved the act of the apparent injustice of compelling people, by the legal tender clause, to receive this currency on ordinary debts and invested securities when they could immediately upon its receipt, convert it into six per cent. gold bonds at par.

In the opening speech which I made soon after I presented the bill to the House, (see History, page 29) I said

"The bill before us is a war measure, a measure of *necessity*, and not of choice, presented by the committee of Ways and Means to meet the most pressing demands upon the treasury to sustain the army and navy until they can make a vigorous advance upon the traitors and crush out the rebellion. These are extraordinary times and extraordinary measures must be resorted to, in order to save our Government and preserve our nationality."

After a full presentation of the scope and object of the bill, and an argument in favor of its constitutionality, as a war measure, and as a means of carrying into full effect the war power, granted in the constitution, substantially as has since been decided by the U. S. Supreme Court, I closed my first presentation of the bill to the House as follows:

"It is plainly within the scope of the constitution that the government should maintain itself; that the army should be supported; that the navy should be maintained. The ways and means of doing this are left to Congress to provide. Congress may do this entirely by taxation. It may provide by law to levy and collect taxes enough every year to pay the whole expenses of the war, during each current year, and so 'pay as we go.' It may issue six per cent. bonds and sell them on the market for what they will bring—even if they will not sell for over fifty cents on the dollar—to raise money to carry on the war. It may issue treasury notes payable on demand, and make them a legal tender in payment of debts. Either one or all of these modes of paying the expenses of the government is left to the discretion of Congress. Either mode is constitutional; and it is left to the *sound discretion* of Congress to decide which mode it will adopt, or whether it will adopt a part of each, as being the best in the present crisis. My own impression is, that it will be best for us to adopt, in part, all of these modes for providing the means:

"1. Raise by taxation, the current year, over and above the amount received from duties on imports, the sum of $150,000,000.

"2. Issue $100,000,000 of demand treasury notes in addition to the $50,000,000 authorized in July, making them legal tender in payment of debts, and exchangeable at any time for six per cent. twenty years' bonds; with a further issue of demand notes, if Congress shall hereafter deem it necessary.

"3. Provide for the issue of all the twenty years' six per cent. bonds that may be necessary to fund the demand treasury notes, and other fundable treasury notes, that may be issued (say $500,000,000 six per cent. twenty years' coupon bonds), and pledge $30,000,000 of the annual taxes to pay the interest half-yearly thereon, and pledge $25,000,000 more as a sinking fund to redeem the principal in twenty years.

"4. This tax of $150,000,000 would afford an ample basis on which to rest the credit of the government for this large issue of treasury notes and bonds, and would insure the punctual payment of the interest to the capitalists who might hold them.

"The demand notes put in circulation would meet the present exigencies of the government in the discharge of its existing liabilities to the army, navy and contractors, and for supplies, materials and munitions of war. These notes would find their way into all the channels of trade among the people; *and as they accumulate in the hands of capitalists they would exchange them for the six per cent. twenty years' bonds.*

"These circulating notes in the hands of the people would enable them to pay the taxes imposed, and would facilitate all business operations between farmers, mechanics, commercial business men and banks, and be equally as good as, *and in many cases better, than the present irredeemable circulation issued by the banks.*

"The $500,000,000 six per cent. twenty years' bonds in the hands of the Secretary of the Treasury ready to be issued would afford ample opportunity for *funding the treasury notes* as fast as the capitalists might desire to exchange treasury notes, not bearing interest, for coupon bonds of the United States, bearing six per ceent. interest, and amply secured by a tax upon the people and all their property.

"In this way the government will be able to get along with its immediate and pressing necessities without being obliged to force its bonds on the market at ruinous rates of discount; the people, under heavy taxation, would be shielded against high rates of interest; and the *capitalists will be afforded a fair compensation for the use of their money during the pending struggle of the country for national existence.*"

From this brief statement of the inception of the legal tender act, it will be seen that it was a temporary war measure; that this greenback currency was receiveable for internal taxes and all other dues, except customs duties and interest on the funded debt; that a sinking fund was provided of one per cent. each year of the entire debt of the United States after July 1, 1862, and the whole of this temporary currency and all the floating debt of the United States was, by the second section of the act, fundable (redeemable) in six per cent. gold bonds. The title of the act was very expressive. "An act to authorize the issue of United States notes *and for the redemption or funding thereof*, and for funding the floating debt of the United States." The government could not redeem in gold, but could redeem in bonds issued on its credit. These legal tender notes were in substance and effect, certificates of debt given for war expenses redeemable on demand in these bonds. Thus, the fundamental principal, that no paper currrency should ever be issued, without providing at the same time, for its prompt redemption, was provided for in the best mode in which, under the unparalled emergency, the government was able to provide for it.

The first legal tender notes issued under the act bore date March 10, 1862, and had printed on the back of them these words:

"This note is a legal tender for all debts public and private, except duties on imports and interest on the public debt, *and is exchangeable for U. S. six per cent. bonds redeemable at the pleasure of the United States, after five years.*"

These notes in the form of greenback currency were immediately issued by Secretary Chase and disbursed for war expenses, and the treasury of the United States was very soon relieved of the pressing demands that were made upon it. The army and navy were paid, and supplies and materials of war obtained on these paper promises in sufficient quantity to prosecute the war with vigor.

The first edition of legal tender notes were by the gigantic war expenses very soon exhausted. On the seventh of June, 1862, Secretary Chase sent an official communication to the Committee of Ways and Means asking for a further issue of $150,000,000 of legal tender notes, and that a part of this emission should be in one dollar notes, the previous emission having all been issued in notes of five dollars and upwards. (Legal tender History, page 154.) In this communication Mr. Chase urged in favor of small bills, and said "it may further be properly observed *that since the United States notes are made a legal tender and maintained at near the par of gold by the provision for their conversion into bonds bearing six per cent. interest payable in coin*, it is not easy to see why small notes may not be issued as wisely as large ones."

This quotation is made for the purpose of showing how important it was deemed at that time, that all the greenback currency should be redeemable in gold bonds.

I made the opening speech on the bill in favor of this further issue of the legal tender notes. In the course of my remarks I said:

"The soldiers and sailors give their services, risk their lives and endure all the hardships, sickness and privations of the campaign, and cheerfully take these notes in payment. Supplies, subsistence and material of war of every kind is eagerly furnished, and these greenbacks taken in exchange for the same. This kind of loan is so popular with the people, and being without interest, is so advantageous to the government, it is desirable that it should be extended so far as it can be done safely, and without unduly stimulating speculations to such an extent as to cause an unfavorable reaction to the legitimate business of the country. *But when bonds can be negotiated at par I think it will be safer to have bonds negotiated than to issue legal tender notes.*"

The act for this additional issue of greenback currency was passed and approved by President Lincoln, July 11, 1862. It provided that the notes should be redeemed on demand in the six per cent. gold bonds.

SECOND MISTAKE.

The great mistake—greater than all other mistakes in the management of the war—was the abrogation of the right to fund the greenback currency in gold bonds, as provided for in the two preceeding acts.

All the other mistakes, civil and military, which occurred during the war were of slight consequence when compared with the mischievous and grave consequences resulting from this one mistake. Taking away from the holder of this paper money the right to have it redeemed on demand in gold bonds, besides being manifestly unjust to the holders, let the government and the whole country—banks and people—down into the *slough* of an irredeemable paper currency, where we have remained for over eleven years. From 1864 to 1875 it has been a dead weight on the business and industry of the country, without elasticity, and without any provision whatever being made for its redemption or payment. Its redundency and consequent depreciation has operated very injuriously to the legitimate business of the country. It was an instrument of expenditure representing the waste of war, and not possessing the essential elements of a commercial currency. A majority of the people, however, have been deluded into the belief that those broken promises, representing the waste of war, were money, and a proper standard of value as a basis for doing business, and have plunged headlong into all sorts of speculations, unprofitable enterprises, extravagance in living general abuse of credit, idleness, and consequent demoralization.

If the right to fund the greenbacks into the six per cent. gold bonds had not been abrogated, no financier or practical business man, whose opinion is worth quoting, can doubt that we would have gone to specie payment within two or three years after the close of the war, in spite of ourselves. The individual indebtedness at the close of the war in 1865 was small. Every one was comparatively free from debt. The six per cent. gold bonds were sought for as an investment. They soon appreciated to par in gold, and if the right to fund had been continued, the greenback currency would have appreciated to par in gold along with bonds. The legal tender act would have served its purpose as a war measure, and we would have returned to the specie standard without material detriment to the legitimate business of the country. In this way we would have avoided a large part of the extravagance and demoralization that has been so reckless since the close of the war.

The circumstances leading to this mistake are fully set forth in the Financial History of the War, pages 188 to 198, but I will briefly recapitulate the facts. The $900,000,000 loan act was passed and approved by the President March 3, 1863. At the urgent request of Secretary Chase a clause was inserted in the act, taking away the absolute right of the holders of greenbacks to fund them into six per cent. gold bonds after July 1, 1863, and leaving it *discretionary* with the Secretary to allow them to be funded or not, as he might deem best for the public interest. Under this discretionary power the Secretary allowed them to be funded up to January 21, 1864. The legal tender act had worked well and all of the $500,000,000 six per cent. bonds authorized by the first act had been taken up at par. The Secretary then decided that he would not allow any more funding in the six per cent. bonds, but would allow the holders of the greenbacks to fund them in a five per cent. bond. This mistake of the Secretary arrested the funding of the greenbacks into bonds, and materially depreciated and lowered the standard of this currency.

This attempt of the Secretary to *float* five per cent. bonds made it necessary, in order to meet the enormous war expenses, to issue and keep out large amounts of currency in the form of greenbacks, interest bearing notes, certificates of indebtedness, fractional currency and national bank notes, besides the irredeemable currency issued by state banks. Gold and commodities continued to advance in price. On the fifteenth of January, 1864, gold was $1.55, on the fifteenth of April, $1.78, on the fifteenth of June, $1.97, and on the twenty-ninth of June, $2.35 to $2.50, which showed that the legal tender notes were then only worth forty cents on the dollar in gold. The next day, the thirtieth of June, 1864, Mr. Chase resigned the office of Secretary of the Treasury. At this time the inflating paper issues outstanding were over $1,100,000,000, and in a few days thereafter gold reached its highest quotation, $2.85, or more accurately speaking greenbacks depreciated until they were only worth in gold thirty-five cents on the *promised* dollar, at the Board of Brokers, in the city of New York. (History, page 198.)

Secretary Chase and myself differed materially in regard to the points herein stated in managing the finances. When the Financial History of the War was published, I sent him a copy, and received from him the following reply :

"WASHINGTON, July 15, 1869.

"MY DEAR SIR: This morning I have received your book on the Financial History of the War, promised in your letter, which came several days ago. I have had time to give only a very hasty glance at the contents. *You adhere, I perceive, to your old views on the points where we differed; and I can-*

not say I have changed mine. But I shall read your connected account of what transpired both while and since I was Secretary of the Treasury, with attention and interest, and will write you by-and-by more in detail. Meantime, I remain with that sincere regard and respect, which your abilities most honorably devoted to the welfare of our country inspired in me.

"Faithfully yours,   "S. P. CHASE.
"HON. E. G. SPAULDING."

No further communication was ever received from Mr. Chase on the subject. He commenced his administration of the Treasury in 1861, as a believer in hard money, and a firm advocate of the Sub-Treasury law, and without much practical knowledge of the credit machinery by which the great financial transactions of the country are carried on. He left the office with twice as much inflating paper outstanding as ought ever to have been issued, and with the *promised* dollar printed on the face of the greenback worth only from 35 to 40 cents in gold.

Hon. Wm. Pitt Fessenden was appointed Secretary of the Treasury in place of Mr. Chase, and entered upon the duties of the office July 5, 1864, and continued in the office performing the duties very acceptably about eight months, and until the second inauguration of President Lincoln, March 4, 1865, when Mr. McCulloch was appointed in his place.

Secretary McCulloch was one of best practical financiers in the country, and managed the Treasury Department with marked prudence and ability. His annual reports were based upon correct principles, and were very clear and able expositions of the financial situation. If Congress had continued to give him proper support, instead of repealing the law for retiring greenbacks, it is my firm belief that he would have conducted us back to the specie standard during the four years of his administration of the Treasury Department, and without materially affecting, in an unfavorable manner, the legitimate business of the country. The controlling majority in Congress was weak and vacillating in its course, and utterly failed to make any provision for redeeming the greenback currency.

After the surrender of the rebel armies to Gen. Grant and Gen. Sherman the volunteer army was mustered out of the service, and had to be paid in full. Secretary McCulloch obtained the means to pay them chiefly by the issue of 7.30 treasury notes. The amount required for that purpose was very large, and the amount of these notes outstanding in October, 1865, was $830,000,000, which were, by law, expressly fundable within three years into six per cent. gold bonds. The right to fund them was not abrogated, and within three years they were all taken off the market and funded in those bonds. This shows conclusively how treasury notes may be retired from circulation by an efficient system of funding. The greenbacks would have been funded in the same way if the original contract for funding them had not been abrogated.

Upon the inauguration of President Grant on the fourth of March, 1869, Hon. George S. Boutwell was made Secretary of the Treasury, and entered upon the duties of the office March 11. The President, in his inaugural address, expressed himself favorable to a return to specie payments at the earliest practicable moment, and in his annual message, he said in reference to an irredeemable currency, "It is an evil which I hope will receive your most earnest attention. It is a duty, and one of the highest duties of the government to secure to the citizen a medium of exchange of fixed and unvarying value. This implies a return to a specie basis, and no substitute for it can be devised. *It should be commenced now.* * * * I earnestly recommend to you such legislation as will insure a gradual return to specie payments, and put an immediate stop to fluctuations in the value of the currency." The first act of Congress approved by President Grant after his inauguration, contained an express promise in these words: "The United States solemnly pledges its faith *to make provision,* at the earliest practicable period, for the redemption of the United States notes in coin."

This promise on the part of Congress to *make provision* for the redemption of the greenback currency in gold, has been about as badly broken as was the promise made in the first legal tender act February 25, 1862, to redeem it in six per cent. gold bonds.

It is true that by the acts of Congress the revenues derived from custom duties and internal taxes were ample, in 1869, to pay the annual expenses of the government and interest on the public debt, and leave a surplus, and consequently an accumulation of gold in the treasury which would, in due time, have been an ample fund "to redeem the United States notes in coin" in accordance with the above promise.

Here commenced the third mistake on the part of the Treasury Department in the management of the finances. Secretary Bout-

well did not regard this surplus as at all necessary to the support
of the credit of the greenbacks, or as a reserve by which they
could ultimately be redeemed in coin. He therefore proceeded to
pay off and take up the bonded debt not yet due for ten to fifteen
years, leaving the past due greenbacks (badly broken promises)
still in the slough of irredeemable currency, without any provision
whatever for their payment. In this way he reduced the public
debt including three per cent. notes about $368,000,000 during the
four years of his administration, but did not redeem any of the
greenbacks, or keep any reserve for that purpose.

He also went further and committed an act which I have always
regarded as a violation of the spirit and intent of the original
legal tender act, in procuring new engraved plates to be made
and the printing and paying out of a new emission of legal tender notes in time of peace, four years after the close of the war,
when the public interests did not require, at that time, any such
forced loan to be made. The clause in the original legal tender
act in regard to the re-issue of the greenback currency is as follows: "Such United States notes shall be received *the same as coin
at their par value* in payment of any loans that may hereafter be
sold or negotiated by the Secretary of the Treasury, and may be
reissued from time to time as the *exigences of the public interests*
shall require." (History legal tender act, p. 149.) The only
ground on which, by any possibility, the legal tender notes could
be constitutionally issued was that it afforded a means by which
the war powers of the government could be carried into full effect
in the prosecution of the war. But four years after the close of
the war, it was not constitutional to reissue them, and it was very
clear that no legitimate "public interest" required that this new
emission should be reissued. On the contrary, it was manifestly
for the "public interest" that as fast as these notes were returned
to the treasury they should be held there, or cancelled, until the
balance outstanding were on a par with gold. The forcing into
circulation of a new emission of broken promises so long after
the close of the war was not only a violation of the constitution,
but was manifestly contrary to the spirit and intent of the legal
tender act as originally passed. Secretary Boutwell's policy of
using his surplus revenues to pay off a funded debt not due, instead of redeeming the broken and past due promises, was based
on the fallacious idea put forth by him on many occasions that

the country would "grow up" to the situation, and that the greenback currency would ultimately all appreciate to par with gold by the increased population, and the enlarged demands of the business of the country without making provision for redeeming it.

Hon. William A. Richardson succeeded Mr. Boutwell as Secretary of the Treasury, on the seventeenth day of March, 1873. He was assistant Secretary under Mr. Boutwell, and upon assuming the duties of Secretary continued the same mistaken policy in regard to the finances which had been carried out by his predecessor. Both of them went so far as to claim that the greenbacks withdrawn from circulation during Mr. McCulloch's administration of the treasury, were still a *reserve*, and that they had a right to reissue them in case of an emergency. During the great financial panic which occurred in the fall of 1873, and with a view to stop it, Secretary Richardson did actually reissue and pay out in the purchase of bonds, not due, the sum of $26,000,000 of greenbacks, which Mr. McCulloch in a recent letter says, " was as powerless to stop the panic as bread pills would be to check the progress of the cholera or yellow fever."

The general policy of both Mr. Boutwell and Mr. Richardson was, to pay a debt not due, and leave neglected and unpaid the broken promises of the government, which had remained unpaid for several years. During their administration of the treasury the amount of greenbacks outstanding was increased from $356,000,000 to $382,000,000. Subsequently Congress, by act of June 20, 1874, fixed that sum as the maximum amount of the greenback currency, "and that no part thereof should be used as a reserve," which effectually cut off the pretense that the previously redeemed greenbacks were a reserve to be used by the Secretary of the Treasury at his discretion. Thus leaving the greenback currency $26,000,000 more in 1874 than it was in 1869, when Mr. Boutwell became Secretary of the Treasury.

The Supreme Court of the United States, in the case of Lane County vs. The State of Oregon, decided, that the greenback currency was not a legal tender in the payment of *taxes* levied by that State. 7 Wallace R., 71. Also in the case of Brousen vs. Rhodes, 7 Wallace, 229, that where the contract *in express terms* is payable in gold coin of the United States it cannot be satisfied by a tender of the greenback currency. These two cases are regarded as good law, and have not been overruled.

In the case of Hepburn vs. Griswold, 8 Wallace, 604, the Court (opinion of Chief Justice Chase), decided that a contract made payable in dollars before the passage of the legal tender act, could not be satisfied by a tender of greenbacks; that such act, so far as it applied to debts contracted *before* its passage, is unconstitutional.

Hon. J. W. Wallace, the official reporter of the United States Supreme Court, in a letter written by him March 9, 1770, says of this decision, "that notes of the United States when tendered in payment of a contract made previously to the passage of the legal tender act of February, 1862, was no lawful tender, was concurred in by *five* judges, not by *three* as assumed in the paragraph quoted. These five judges were the Chief Justice, and Justices Nelson, Grier, Clifford and Field. Judge Grier had left the bench before the *opinions were delivered*, but he was on it when the case was argued in conference; and when the judgment of affirmance of the Court of Appeals of Kentucky which had decided the tender bad, was irrevocably and perfectly agreed upon."

Subsequent to the decision in the above case of Hepburn vs. Griswold, the Supreme Court was filled up by the appointment of new judges, and consisted of nine judges—Chief Justice Chase and Associate Justices Nelson, Clifford, Swayne, Miller, Davis, Field, Strong and Bradley. This court thus constituted decided to hear a full argument on all the points raised in the cases of Knox vs. Lee, and Barker vs. Davis. The argument was heard at the December Term, 1870.

The court, after mature deliberation, decided, five to four, that a tender of United States notes on debts contracted previous to the passage of the legal tender act, February 25, 1862, was a valid tender in payment of such debts, thereby overruling the previous decision of the court in the case of Hepburn vs. Griswold.

Mr. Justice Strong delivered the opinion of the majority of the court, and Mr. Justice Bradley read an opinion on the same side. On the other side of the question very elaborate opinions were read by Chief Justice Chase and Justices Clifford and Field, all of which are published in 12 Wallace Reports, 457.

Hon. Reverdy Johnson, in a recent communication reviewing this case, comes to the conclusion that Justice Strong did not intend to go so far as to decide that such an act would be constitutional if passed in time of peace. In that part of the opinion which appears at page 540 (12 Wallace), Justice Strong says the inquiry is whether such laws "were, *when enacted*, appropriate instrumentalities for carrying into effect or executing any of the known powers of Congress, or of any department of the government. Plainly to this inquiry, a consideration to the time *when they were enacted*, and of the *circumstances* in which the government *then* stood is important." He then states, in glowing but not exaggerated terms, what was the overwhelming *necessity* for the passage of the legal tender act in February, 1862, and adds "it is not to be denied that acts may be adapted to the exercise of lawful power, and appropriate to it in seasons of exigency which would be inappropriate at other times." Judge Bradley, the other new member, expressed the same idea of necessity even more emphatically. Said he: "It follows as another corollary from the views which I have expressed, that the power to make treasury notes a legal tender, whilst a mere incidental one to that of issuing the notes themselves, and to one of the forms of borrowing money, is nevertheless a power *not to be resorted to* except on extraordinary and pressing occasions, *such as war or other public exigencies of great gravity and importance;* and should *be no longer continued than all the circumstances of the case demand.*" This very plainly indicates that the majority of the court would not have decided the legal tender act constitutional if it had been passed while the government was on a peace footing.

LETTER FROM JUSTICE STRONG OF THE U. S. SUPREME COURT, IN FAVOR OF RETURNING TO OUR NORMAL CONDITION.

"PHILADELPHIA, March 8, 1870.

"Hon. E. G. SPAULDING: My Dear Sir: I received a short time since through your politeness, a copy of your 'Financial History of the War.' I have not hitherto acknowledged the receipt, and returned the thanks I owe, because I wished first to read the book, and my engagements have been such of late, that I could not find the necessary time. I have now read it, and have been both instructed and interested. The financial history of the country during the war is quite as remarkable as the war itself, and I am glad you have spread it before the public so intelligently. There were doubtless some mistakes, but it is wonderful that there were no more, and no greater. *Now if we can soon return to our normal condition, the scars of the war will soon be obliterated, and we shall have remaining only the blessings achieved.*

"I should be glad to discuss with you some subjects brought forward in your book, but I have not now the time, I can only say that your book, as a whole, is, in my opinion very valuable, and that you deserve the gratitude of the country not only for your history, but for the part you acted during the war in sustaining the power of the government.

I am, yours truly,

W. STRONG.

If a *tender* of the new emission of greenbacks put out by Secretary Boutwell in 1869-70, should be made on an existing contract, it is doubtful whether such tender would be valid, because, four or five years after the close of the war, there did not exist any public necessity for such a forced loan. The revenues were then ample to pay all expenses and leave a surplus, which, under a mistaken policy was used to *unfund* the public debt, leaving the over due debt unpaid.

LETTER FROM ATTORNEY-GENERAL HOAR ON THE FINANCES.

WASHINGTON, Oct. 15, 1869.

HON. E. G. SPAULDING:

MY DEAR SIR:— I have the honor to acknowledge the receipt of your letter of the 6th inst., and with it a copy of your Financial History of the War, for which I desire to return my thanks.

The constant pressure upon my time has prevented me from giving the book more than a cursory inspection, but it seems to be a valuable acquisition to our financial history, and throws considerable light upon the important question of a return to specie payments. I am one of those who believed that it was for the interest as well as the duty of the nation to return at once to the true and solid standard of value as soon as active hostilities had ceased; *that we should have treated the currency as we did our armies*—REGARDING THE VOLUNTEERS AND THE GREENBACKS ALIKE AS NECESSITIES OF WAR, TO BE DISPENSED WITH AS FAST AS POSSIBLE ON THE RETURN OF PEACE. I think we made a great mistake in not doing so; that the shortest method was the shortest and best; that the only way to reach the object is by a steady and persistent contraction of the currency—a painful process whenever it comes, no doubt, but harder and worse for us the longer it is delayed.

I hope that Congress will address itself with courage and constancy to the solution of the problem as soon as it meets; and will feel assured that the American people have intelligence enough to support those who do it. My views on the subject are of little importance to anybody, but, as an American citizen, I should be sorry and ashamed to find my country unable and unwilling, in a time of peace and prosperity, *to provide for its over-due paper*.

Very respectfully,

E. R. HOAR.

PRESIDENT GRANT'S VETO.

In 1874, Congress passed an inflation act authorising a large increase of the greenback currency and containing other mischievous provisions. This act was submitted to President Grant, and extraordinary efforts made by the inflationists in and out of Congress, to have him approve it. He refused to do so, and on the 22d of April vetoed the act in a message to the Senate condemning this measure of inflation in unqualified terms. He says "the theory, in my belief, is a departure from the true principles of finance, national interest, national obligation to creditors, congressional promises, party pledges by both political parties, and of the personal views and promises made by me in every annual message sent to Congress and in each inaugural address." This veto is regarded as one of the most important and useful acts of President Grant's administration. It had an important influence in checking the clamor for more irredeemable currency.

Secretary Richardson, after holding the office about fourteen months and a half, resigned, and on the 4th of June, 1874, Hon. Benjamin H. Bristow was appointed Secretary of the Treasury, and entered upon the duties of the office.

ASSORTING HOUSE.

In pursuance of the provisions of the act of Congress passed June 20, 1874, an Assorting Bureau has been established in the Treasury Department for the redemption of National Bank currency. This assorting and redeeming process serves a very useful purpose in taking out of circulation all the worn, dirty, mutilated and defaced notes, and replacing them with clean ones. All this is done in a satisfactory manner, and by an equitable assessment, the Banks pay all the expenses of this Assorting Bureau; but in so far as it seeks to be an efficient redemption of the National Bank notes, it utterly fails to give that vitality and elasticity which ought to attach to a commercial currency. The greenbacks and National Bank notes circulate on a par with each other, and each kind of notes possess about the same purchasing power. Both kinds are worth about 85 cents on the promised dollar. The consequence is that there has not been, and there cannot be, any efficient redemption of bank notes in the present condition of the currency, because there is neither object nor motive to prompt it. This, so called, redemption simply resolves itself into the swapping one kind of irredeemable paper for another kind of no higher value. But, inasmuch as it renovates the paper circulation, whether we call it redemption, or a process by which clean notes are furnished, is not material. This redemption bureau will, however, become very important as soon as there is a general resumption of specie payments.

PRESIDENT GRANT'S PLAN.

On the 24th of June, 1874, President Grant published his further views in regard to resuming specie payments:

"First—I would like to see the legal-tender clause, so-called, repealed, the repeal to take effect at some future time, say July 1, 1875. This would cause all contracts made after that date, for wages, sales, &c., to be estimated in coin. It would correct our notion of values. The specie dollar would be the only dollar known as the measure of equivalents. When debts afterwards contracted were paid in currency, instead of calling the paper dollar and quoting gold at 20 per cent. premium, we should think and speak of paper at so much discount. This alone would aid greatly in bringing the two currencies nearer together at par.

Second—I would like to see a provision that at a fixed day, say July 1, 1876, the currency issued by the United States should be redeemed in coin on presentation to any Assistant Treasurer, and that all the currency so redeemed should be cancelled and never reissued. To effect this it would be necessary to authorize the issue of bonds, payable in gold, bearing such interest as would command par in gold, to be put out by the Treasury only in such sums as should from time to time be needed for the purpose of redemption. Such legislation would insure a return to sound financial principles within two years, and would in my judgment, work less hardship to the debtor interest than is likely to come from putting off the day of final reckoning. It must be borne in mind, too, that the creditor interest had its day of disadvantage also, when our present financial system was brought in by the supreme needs of the nation at the time. * * * *

ECONOMY AND TAXATION.

"Again, I would provide an excess of revenue over current expenditures. I would do this by rigid economy and by taxation, where taxation can best be borne. Increased revenue would work a reduction of debt and interest, and would provide coin to meet demands on the Treasury for the redemption of its notes, thereby diminishing the amount of bonds needed for that purpose. All taxes after redemption begins should be paid in coin or United States notes. This would force redemption on the national banks. With measures like these, or measures which would work out such results, I see no danger in authorizing free banking without limit."

CONGRESSIONAL PLAN OF RESUMING SPECIE PAYMENTS.

Senator Sherman, who was the most efficient member in procuring the original legal tender act to be passed through the Senate in 1862, introduced into the Senate at the last session of Congress, "An act to provide for the resumption of specie payments." This bill after being very fully discussed and criticised in the Senate and House, was passed and approved by the President, January 14, 1875.

The first section requires the Secretary of the Treasury, as rapidly as practicable, to cause to be coined at the mints of the United States, silver coins of the usual denominations, above five cents, and redeem all the fractional currency of similar denominations outstanding, amounting to about $40,000,000.

The third section removes the monopoly feature of the Bank act, and allows *free banking* in all parts of the United States. Whenever bank notes are issued for circulation under this new law, eighty per cent. of greenbacks are to be redeemed by the Secretary of the Treasury, for all the new bank notes issued, and he is to continue such redemption *pari pasu* with new issue of bank notes, until there shall be outstanding $300,000,000 of greenbacks, and no more. And on and after January I, 1879, the Secretary of the Treasury shall redeem the greenbacks in coin, and to enable him to "*prepare* and provide for the redemption authorized or required in this act, he is authorized to use any surplus revenues from time to time in the Treasury not otherwise appropriated, and to issue, sell *and dispose of*, at not less than par, in coin, either of the description of bonds of the United States, described in the act of Congress approved July 14, 1870, entitled 'An act authorizing the refunding of the national debt,' with like qualities, privileges, and exemptions, to the extent necessary to carry this act into effect, and to use the proceeds thereof for the purpose aforesaid, and all the provisions of the law inconsistent with this act are hereby repealed."

This act for the resumption of specie payments is quite mandatory in its terms, and if Congress is not weak and vacilating enough to repeal or modify the law, and the yearly revenues are kept up to a proper amount, it will prove to be much more effective to bring about resumption than is generally supposed. The first section of the act "authorizes and *requires*" the Secretary of the Treasury to have enough silver coins struck at the mints to redeem all the fractional currency now outstanding, and Secretary Bristow, in obedience to the requirements of the act, is now coining the silver at the mints, as fast as possible, with a view to calling in all the fractional currency and have it replaced by the small silver coins like those in common use before the war. This will not be contraction, for the reason that the silver will take the place of paper.

The third section of the act is equally mandatory in requiring the Secretary to redeem all the greenback currency, in gold coin, on and after January 1, 1879. Preliminary to this important step, it is provided as before stated, that under the free banking feature of the law, for every $100 of bank notes issued, $80 of greenbacks shall be withdrawn from circulation. In this way it is believed that there will be quite a large reduction of greenbacks before January 1, 1879, and possibly it may be reduced to $300,-000,000, which is the maximum amount fixed by the act for the legal tender circulation. This amount, and whatever amount above that sum is outstanding on the first of January, 1879, is to be redeemed in gold on demand, when presented in sums of $50, and upwards. The object of the act is, by continued redemption in gold coin, to circulate $300,000,000 greenbacks on a par with gold. Can this be done under the provision of the act? If it can be done it will cause a general resumption of specie payments by the banks and people in all their business transactions. All business will then be done on a gold basis, and laborers and operatives will be paid in gold and silver, or its equivalent, and not in an irredeemable and depreciated paper currency.

What are the means provided by the act to enable the Secretary to resume specie payments at the time specified? All the necessary 5 per cent. gold bonds which can be disposed of at par for coin, are authorized by the act, and placed at the disposal of the Secretary. These bonds are now at par and above, and if they continue so to January 1, 1879, the Secretary will, if the revenues are kept up, have ample provision made for redeeming the greenbacks in gold coin at that time. If gold coin is paid out for greenbacks, the gold will take the place of greenbacks in the banking and business operations of the country, so that there will be only such contraction as is necessary to the stability of legitimate business. If a suitable gold reserve is retained in the Treasury against the greenbacks in circulation, there will be no loss of interest, because neither the gold nor the greenbacks bear any interest.

What is most to be feared is, that Congress will repeal the act, or so modify it as to prevent resumption at the time specified. With the known and expressed views of President Grant he would no doubt, veto any bill of that kind which may be passed during his term of office. The law will probably continue in force until 1877, and it is possible that further provision may be made to aid in causing resumption to take place January 1, 1879. But if only the present law remains on the statute book to that time, it will be found to be more efficient than is generally supposed, in bringing about the desired result, especially if the 5 per cent. gold bonds continue to sell at par for gold.

It is the general impression that the act ought to have authorized more extended *preparation* for resumption, and I am free to say that I have shared this feeling. If, however Congress gives proper support to the measure, by keeping up the revenues, it is by no means certain that the Secretary by a judicious administration of the act, will not be able to resume specie payments by January 1, 1879. The Treasury must be well supplied with gold, and an ample yearly revenue provided, in order to resume and *maintain* such resumption. If the reserve of gold is made ample, resumption will be easy. The greenbacks not having been issued upon commercial values, but for the waste of war, will require extraordinary support in order to maintain specie payments. At present there is too great a disparity between the reserve of gold in the Treasury and the amount of greenbacks to be redeemed. Whether resumption takes place in three, five or ten years, a larger reserve of gold will be necessary, or the greenbacks must be reduced. It is perfectly plain to every practical business man, that the greenback currency cannot be redeemed in coin until the Government is able to let coin flow into business channels and *again circulate as money*, the same as it did previous to the war. Coined money must resume its place in the business of the country simultaneously with the withdrawal of the greenbacks, so that there shall be no material disturbance to legitimate business, when resumption takes place. This can be accomplished if there is a continued surplus of gold received into the Treasury and retained there as a reserve against the greenback currency.* Every one hundred dollars set apart as a reserve against an equal amount of greenbacks, would be a practical payment of them, and as neither bears interest there would be no loss of interest. Every gold broker knows perfectly well that there can be no successful resumption until there is a much larger reserve of coin, and he accordingly asks $1.16 cents in greenbacks for a dollar in gold, but let him know that the Government holds an adequate reserve fund against the greenback currency, *and the National Banks a like fund*, the appreciation of greenbacks would be such that his occupation as a gold broker would be nearly gone, even if the gold did not pass out of the Treasury. This large reserve would be tangible evidence to him that the Government was master of the situation.

THE GOLD STANDARD.

When the business of the country is carried on upon a gold basis, and resumption is continued as an accomplished fact, all the greenbacks and National Bank notes which cannot be kept permanently on a par with gold, will necessarily have been retired from circulation, and either cancelled or held in the sub-treasury, or vaults of the banks. This surplus of paper currency, which is no doubt largely in excess of the requirements of legitimate business, ought to be cancelled and permanently kept out of circulation, so as not to hazard a continuance of specie payments.

A constitutional standard of value having been thus established, the Government, desiring to return to its legitimate function of coining money and regulating its value, will ultimately wish to rid itself of the trouble and risk incident to the issuing a paper currency and redeeming it in gold, and will finally repeal the legal tender act. This will leave the business of free banking where it belongs, open to all its citizens, to be carried on upon a gold basis, under proper legislative provisions. It would probably be better for all concerned if the legal tender act should be repealed at an earlier day, and at the same time provide for retiring the greenbacks by the issue of five or six per cent. compound interest notes, fundable in two and three years into a five per cent. ten years gold bonds. But the present resumption act has not been passed with that object in view, and for the present it will be best to support the law as it now stands, and if possible, add to its efficiency by further legislative provisions. The banks should be required to retain half the gold interest received on the bonds deposited as security for their circulating notes as a part of their reserve, preparatory to resumption, January 1, 1879.

NEW YORK TO RESUME JANUARY 1, 1879.

The State of New York at the last session of the legislature, passed a law, Chap. 73, which was approved by Gov. Tilden, March 22, 1875, "To establish specie payments on all contracts or obligations payable in this state after January 1, 1879." This law was passed in pursuance of the principles laid down in the case of Lane County vs. the State of Oregon, 7 Wallace R. 71, that the greenbacks are not a lawful tender in payment of *taxes* im-posed by state legislation   The text of this N. Y. law is as follows :

"Section 1. All taxes levied and confirmed in this State on and after January first, eighteen hundred and seventy-nine, shall be collected in gold, United States gold certificates or National bank notes which are redeemable in gold on demand.

2. Every contract or obligation made or implied after January first, eighteen hundred and seventy-nine, and payable in dollars, but not in a specified kind of dollars, shall be payable in United States coin of the standard of weight and fineness established by the laws of the United States at the time the contract or obligation shall have been made or implied."

This completes the statement of the measures now in force for resuming specie payments, which is the most important question now before the country.

TREASURY SALES OF GOLD.

The Treasury sales of gold at 16 per cent. premium, and the receipt of greenbacks in payment, and the immediate reissue of such depreciated greenbacks, at par, to pay the civil expenses of the Government, ten years after the close of the war, is an anomaly in any solvent government, and plainly shows the weakness and incompetency of Congress in not providing ample revenues to carry on the government in time of peace without resorting to any such discreditable means. The gold revenue is sufficient to keep up the sinking fund and pay the gold interest, but the currency revenues seem to be inadequate for ordinary expenses.

It is generally understood that Secretary Bristow continues his monthly sales of gold, (which ought to be husbanded for resumption in 1879,) to raise the money to pay the current expenses of the Government, because Congress has failed to provide sufficient means to carry on the Government in any other way. It is also generally understood that Secretary Bristow would not resort to this monthly "make-shift" of keeping these broken legal tender promises in circulation, if Congress provided the means of administrating the government in the old fashioned, honest way. Every reissue of these broken promises, backed by the legal tender provision, is a *forced loan* in time of peace, and is plainly in violation of the constitution.

These sales of gold at this time, when the act for the resumption of specie payments in 1879, is in full force, is not a good indication for resumption at that time. More revenue will be necessary, and it remains to be seen whether it will be provided to aid in carrying this very important measure into effect.

Secretary Bristow is believed to be sound on the main question. In his first annual report in December, 1874, he very clearly sets forth the evils of an irredeemable paper currency as follows:

"The history of the irredeemable paper currency repeats itself whenever and wherever it is used. It increases present prices, deludes the laborer with the idea that he is getting higher wages and brings a fictitious prosperity from which follow inflation of business and credit and excess of enterprise in ever increasing ratio, until it is discovered that trade and commerce have become fatally diseased, when confidence is destroyed, and then comes the shock to credit, followed by disaster and depression, and a demand for relief by further issues. The universal use of, and reliance upon, such a currency tends to blunt the moral sense and impair the natural self-dependence of the people, and trains them to the belief that the Government must directly assist their individual fortunes and business, help them in their personal affairs, and enable them to discharge their debts by partial payment. This inconvertible paper currency begets the delusion that the remedy for private pecuniary distress is in legislative measures, and makes the people unmindful of the fact that the true remedy is in greater production and less spending, and that real prosperity comes only from individual effort and thrift. When exchanges are again made in coin, or in a currency convertible into it at the will of the holder, this truth will be understood and acted upon."

Secretary Bristow is now making preparation to retire the fractional currency and replace it with silver coin, but, without any surplus revenue, he will not be able to accumulate gold in the Treasury, and must rely, at present, on the sale of the five per cent. bonds, authorized by the third section of the resumption act. It remains to be seen whether Congress will have the wisdom and courage to pass any further laws for increasing the revenue, or authorizing any further preparations for resuming specie payments on the first of January, 1879. This is the great question now before the people. I have a strong desire to witness a general and permanent resumption of specie payments. If I live to see it accomplished, I will write a concluding chapter on the "History of the legal tender paper money, issued during the Great Rebellion." Meantime I desire to repeat that if the legal right to fund the greenbacks in the six per cent. gold bonds, in accordance with the original legal tender act, had not been abrogated, we would have reached specie payments as early as 1868, seven years ago, and without very seriously injuring the legitimate business of the country.

The wit of man, during the last hundred years, has not been able to contrive any method by which a paper currency can be circulated on a par with gold, unless it can be conveniently converted into gold coin on demand. It is not enough that "the whole property of the country" is held liable to ultimately pay the greenbacks. Such security, though ample, is too general and intangible for the purpose. This "whole property" can only be reached and applied through the slow process of taxation. On this general theory the greenbacks have been greatly depreciated for over eleven years, and the government will continue in this discreditable condition, until some *specific provision* is again made for its redemption.

It was issued as a *redeemable* currency—it is now *irredeemable*, with no certain standard of value, and not possessing the requisites of a commercial currency. Congress ought to make ample preparation for its redemption in 1879—Will it do its duty ?

E. G. SPAULDING.

BUFFALO, Oct. 1, 1875.

TESTIMONIALS IN FAVOR OF THE LEGAL TENDER ACT AS A "WAR MEASURE."

FROM HON. WILLIAM H. SEWARD,
Late Secretary of State.

AUBURN, April 26, 1869.

My Dear Mr. Spaulding:

I thank you for a copy of your book. It is written without passion or prejudice, and makes it entirely clear that in adopting a legal tender currency, the government adopted a means not merely wise, but indispensible and effective. I always wonder at the resistance which the policy encountered.

With kind respect and esteem.

Faithfully your friend,
WILLIAM H. SEWARD.

The Hon. Horace Maynard, of Tennessee, was one of the few men of the South who remained in Congress during the war, and always supported the Union cause. Having been for many years a member of the Committee of Ways and Means, he is one of the most influential men in the House. He was a member of that Committee during the winter of 1861-2, when the Legal Tender Act, the Bank Bill, and other financial measures, were matured, and he still retains that position. The following letter from Mr. Maynard, on that question, will be read with interest.

KNOXVILLE, Tennessee, Nov. 3, 1869.

Hon. E. G. Spaulding:

DEAR SIR:—Thanks for the book, as well as the copy sent me. It is well-timed and much needed. So successful were the financial arrangements during the war that people incline to believe them as automatic, accomplished, with no special credit to anybody.

Of all who were concerned, you were the one to have prepared the book—entitled as you are, pre-eminently, to the credit of the great measures which carried the nation so triumphantly through the financial struggles. While I did not feel at liberty to participate very actively in the passage of acts which must affect other portions of the country far more seriously than that which it was my fortune to represent, it gratifies me to remember that both in the Committee of Ways and Means and in the House they received my unfailing support.

As a result we have now the best currency ever known in the nation. *Let it now be made convertible into coin at the pleasure of the holder, and nothing would be left to be discussed.* Why this has not been done, why it is not done, why it should not be done, I confess, after all I have read and heard, I am not able to see.

One of these days some bold man will take the step, and then everybody will wonder why it had not been taken years before. Would that you were again at your place in the House.

I am, very truly yours, HORACE MAYNARD.

FROM THE HON. CHARLES SUMNER.
On the Finances.

BOSTON, August 3, 1869.

MY DEAR SIR:—You have done a good service in preparing your book; nor is there anybody to whom this duty belonged more than yourself. In all our financial trials, while the war was most menacing, you held a position of great trust, giving you opportunity and knowledge. The first you used at the time most patriotically, and the second you use now for the instruction of the country.

I am not content with the long postponement of specie payments; I BELIEVE THAT THE TIME HAS COME FOR THIS BLESSING, and I begin to be impatient when I see how easily people find excuses for not accepting it.

Believe me, dear sir,
Very truly yours,
Hon. E. G. SPAULDING. CHARLES SUMNER.

FROM ERASTUS CORNING.
Also a member of the Committee of Ways and Means at the time the act was passed.

NEWPORT, August 30, 1869.

Hon. E. G. Spaulding, Buffalo:

DEAR SIR:—Your favor of the 14th ult. was forwarded from Albany to this place. Also a copy of your "Financial History of the War." I have read it with much interest, and can say that I consider it a fair and impartial history of the doings of the Committee of Ways and Means and of Congress while I was a member, and since as far as I understand their action. I am pleased that you have seen fit to place their doings on record. I thank you for the copy sent me. Yours very truly,

ERASTUS CORNING.

HOUSE OF REPRESENTATIVES.
Committee of Ways and Means.

WASHINGTON, D. C., Feby. 25, 1866.

DEAR SIR:—I have yours of the 23d inst., and have mailed to you to-day a copy of Mr. Sumner's speech on reconstruction, also the *Globe* which contains my own, on the Finance Bill. It seems to me that you have a right to be well satisfied with the part you took in initiating the financial measures which have carried the country so successfully through the war. We are somewhat excited here, but I have faith that everything will come right in a little time if we are discreet in our action in Congress.

Yours with great respect,
Hon. E. G. SPAULDING. S. HOOPER.

FROM SENATOR SHERMAN.

MANSFIELD, Ohio, June 14, 1869.

MY DEAR SIR:—I have received and partially read, with great interest, your Financial History of the War. It recalls many interesting events

almost forgotten, and is therefore like an old friend. I am much obliged to you for it, and will give it a careful reading and a place in my *selected* set of books. Very truly yours,
Hon. E. G. SPAULDING. JOHN SHERMAN.

FROM E. M. STANTON,
Late Secretary of War, a short time before his death.
WASHINGTON, November 28, 1869.

MY DEAR SIR:—I hasten to render my thanks for a copy of your "History of the Legal Tender Act," and the accompanying note, received this morning.

No one could more fully appreciate than I did, and still do, the vital importance of the financial measures adopted for maintaining the government during the war. On all occasions, in private conversation and in public assemblages, I have endeavered to do them justice and cause them to be estimated as I estimated them. *Without them I do not see how our armies could have been raised, equipped, clothed, fed, transported and kept in the field until the enemy were subdued.* But my attention was too closely absorbed by military affairs for me to discriminate between the several views discussed, or to observe to whose sagacity and energy the country was most indebted. A hasty glance through your History has enabled me to see that you have afforded means for correct judgment upon the interesting points involved.

With sincere regard, I am,
Truly your friend and obedient servant,
Hon. E. G. SPAULDING. EDWIN M. STANTON.

FROM HANNIBAL HAMLIN.
Late Vice-President, and President of the Senate at the time the Act was passed.
BANGOR, November 5, 1869.

MY DEAR SIR:—Please accept my cordial thanks for your "Financial History of the War Legal Tender" which you sent me. I have given it a hasty examination, but enough to see that it is a full and true history of the subject of which you treat, presenting the facts connected therewith in their chronological order. A work to set the public judgment right at this time, and for reference it will be truly valuable.

I am surprised to know that no one of the historians of the times has furnished the facts and evidence which you have so fully and clearly represented. Yours truly,
Hon. E. G. SPAULDING, Buffalo, N. Y. H. HAMLIN.

FROM HON. W. W. CORCORAN.
The Banker who negotiated the United States Loans during the war with Mexico in 1846-47.
WASHINGTON, September 13, 1869.

MY DEAR SIR:—Many thanks for your kind letter of the 9th, with a copy of your "Financial History of the War." I have only had time to glance over the index. It will be very valuable and interesting volume and I shall have pleasure in perusing it. *No one can doubt that the making the issues of the United States a legal tender was the great element of success. Without it the war could not have been carried on six months longer.* Again thanking you for thinking of an old friend,

I am very sincerely yours,
W. W. CORCORAN.

E. G. SPAULDING, Esq., Buffalo, N. Y.

FROM BENSON J. LOSSING,

Who published a valuable Illustrated History of the Military Operations during the Great Rebellion—in three volumes.

THE RIDGE, DOVER, N. Y., Dec. 27, 1869.

Hon. E. G. Spaulding :

MY DEAR SIR:—I cordially thank you for giving me the opportunity to peruse your valuable History of the Legal Tender Paper Currency issued during the late Rebellion—a measure which more than any other, contributed to the salvation of the Republic from great disaster. Without money suddenly and amply created, there could have been no army.

That measure was a novelty—a paradox in the history of nations—*a forced loan, with the cordial consent of the lenders!* The sterling common sense of the loyal people saw it was a necessity, and accepted it with cheerful acquiescence; and every man of common sense now sees that the everlasting good which the measure wrought, outweighs a thousand fold the temporary evils which it has occasioned.

It appeared to me at the time (and has never appeared otherwise) that the originating and perfecting of that measure was one of the wisest acts of true statesmanship that were displayed during the civil war, and will ever be regarded as a precedent of great value to the people of republics. The clamor against the measure, during the war and since, was and is simply the voice of selfish partizanship, and the cry of "unconstitutionality" was only the cry of disloyal politicians against the efforts for the salvation of the republic. Wisely did Madison declare that public necessity takes precedence of all Constitutions; and Mr. Lincoln as wisely said that the Union is older than the Constitution, and took measures outside the letter of the Constitution to save it.

The philosophic historian and statesman of another century, with vision unobscured by the smoke of conflict, will point to the Legal Tender Paper Money Act as one of the chief instrumentalities which preserved for themselves and their children the blessings of free institutions ; and among the names of the statesmen to whose wisdom and energy the nation is chiefly indebted for the measure, yours, sir will ever appear most prominent.

I am, dear sir, with gratitude for your public services,

Your friend and fellow citizen,
BENSON J. LOSSING.

HON. J. S. MORRILL,
One of the most effective men on the Committee of Ways and Means when
the Legal Tender Act was passed.

STAFFORD, Vt., June 9, 1869.

MY DEAR SIR:—Your favor of the 5th inst. came to hand yesterday, and your book on the Financial History of the War, has just arrived. Of course I have not yet had time to read it, but I have no doubt of its having received all the care necessary to make it valuable, and I know of no one who could more acceptably perform the service. You and I differed as to the policy of issuing the Legal Tender notes. Forecasting somewhat the train of difficulties in the way—such as increasing the ultimate debt—disorganizing trade and the final retirement, I then thought it possible to avoid their issue. Now I do not discuss the question because there are so many unpatriotic and discordant utterances on the subject, and I may be in error, but I have never had a doubt in my own mind that we could have furnished ample means to the Government and saved hundreds of millions of our public debt by reducing the discount on credit to the minimum final through some such course as that I advocated at the time. Your course then was patriotic and has been since, *and some of the errors since committed I know have not had the sanction of your judgment.* Others have gone further than you proposed, and there are yet others who even now do not propose to halt. But I am hopeful that we shall in due time emerge from our present unhappy condition and get our finances in a condition so that if another war was necessary, and I trust that day may be far off, we could bear our part without extreme trial. Please accept my thanks for the copy of your work.

Very truly yours,
Hon. E. G. SPAULDING, Buffalo, N. Y.   JUSTIN S. MORRILL.

HON. SAMUEL HOOPER,
A member of the Committee of Ways and Means.

BOSTON, September 5, 1869.

MY DEAR SIR:—Please accept my thanks for your book on the finances during the war, which has been received. I have not had time to read it, but have looked through it curiously, and saw that you had not departed from the principles which influenced us when we were striving so hard to get the financial bills through the Congress. I shall give the book a thorough reading before Congress meets. Specie payments seem as far off as ever. *Mr. Boutwell seems to believe the reduction of the debt, with the increase of business will bring about resumption in due time. He remarked to me a few days since that with the present tariff and internal revenue laws, the whole debt could be paid in twelve years.* I am curious to see what financial policy he will announce in his annual report to Congress. I have great distrust of the action of Congress unless the Government advocate measures to restore the value of the currency. A positive policy on the part of the Government strengthens public opinion, and that operates powerfully on the action of Congress.   *   *

Yours with regard,
Hon. E. G. SPAULDING.   S. HOOPER.

HORACE GREELEY,

In the New York *Tribune*, July 7, 1869.

"We render hearty thanks to the Hon. E. G. Spaulding, of Buffalo for his 'History of the Legal-Tender Paper Money issued during the great Rebellion.' It is the clearest and tersest account yet given of the origin of the Legal-Tender act, the views of those members of Congress who aided and of those who resisted its passage, the various modifications it underwent, closing with the text of the bill as finally passed ; the construction simultaneously given to it with regard to the medium wherein the Five-Twenty bonds were payable, etc., etc. The origin, tenor and and scope of the National currency act, and of the various acts by which our systems of finance and currency have since been modified, are also elucidated by extracts from speeches in Congress, by cotemporary letters, etc., etc. Mr. Spaulding was an active member both of the Committee of Ways and Means, and of its sub-Committee having charge of this subject, and is thus enabled to throw much light on the general subject. We advise any man who wants to cheat himself into the belief that the funded debt of the United States may lawfully be paid in greenbacks not to read this handy volume, unless he is anxious to *know* that he is a rascal and that everyone sees it."

The following additional letters will appear in the appendix to this edition:

Hon. Hugh McColloch, late Secretary of Treasury.
" Charles Francis Adams, Massachusetts.
" Geo. H. Pendleton, Ohio.
" C. L. Valandigham, Ohio.
President Woolsey, Yale College.
Prof. Perry, of Williams College.
Judge Noah Davis of New York.
Judge Fithian of New York.
Spaulding to J. S. Gibbons—Why the Banks Suspended in 1861.
J. S. Gibbons' reply. [Sub-Treasury Law.]
John E. Williams, Metropolitan Bank, New York.
Geo. S. Coe, American Exchange Bank, New York.
John P. Elton, Waterbury Bank, Connecticut.
The old United States Bank and National Banks.
President Grant's veto message, April 22d, 1874.
Hon. Samuel F. Miller, Justice of the United States Supreme Court.
" Samuel Nelson, late Justice of the United States Supreme Court.
" R. C. Grier, late Justice of the United States Supreme Court.
" Judge Swayne, Justice of the United States Supreme Court.
" David A. Wells, Political Economist.
" Joel T. Headly the Historian.
" R. E. Fenton, who voted for the Legal-Tender Act.
" Carl Schurz, late Senator for Missouri.
" H. L. Dawes, Senator from Massachusetts.
" A. M. Clapp, Public Printing, Washington.
" A. A. Low, of New York.
" J. P. Bradley, of the United States Supreme Court.
Prof. James P. White, Buffalo.
Major-General Sherman and Gen. B F. Butler, Massachusetts.
Hon. H. H. VanDyke, late Assistant Treasurer, N. Y.
" David Wilder, State Treasurer, Boston.
" J. F. D. Lanier, banker, New York.
" J. J. Knox, Comptroller of the currency.
" S. S. Cox, House of Representative.
" J. A Garfield, House of Representative
" A. H. Rice, Boston, House of Representative.
" John T. Heard, Boston.
" F. A. Conkling, New York.
" Amasa Walker, Political Economist.
" Geo. Walker, Springfield, Mass.
" Senator O. P. Morton.
" Senator T. O. Howe.
" Henry E. Davies, New York.
" J. O. Putnam, Buffalo.
" Martin J. Crawford, Georgia.

INDEX.

	PAGE
Introduction,	5
No National Currency at commencement of War,	5
War carried on upon credit and taxation,	5
Legal Tender act a War measure,	5—29
Loan of $150,000,000 by the Associated Banks,	7
Who composed the Committee of Ways and Means,	7
Sub-Committee, Messrs. Spaulding, Hooper and Corning,	8
Secretary Chase's financial plan, a bank and taxation,	8—11
Mr. Chase does not recommend legal tender,	10
Bank bill prepared by Mr. Spaulding,	11—12
Erastus Corning's letter on the Bank bill,	12
Origin of the Legal Tender act,	13
Legal Tender bill introduced by Mr. Spaulding,	14
Ways and Means divided on the bill,	15
Opinion of Attorney General Bates,	15
Ways and Means agree to report the bill,	16
Bill reported by Mr. Spaulding,	16
Mr. Spaulding's letter to Isaac Sherman, New York,	17
Isaac Sherman's letter,	18
The Press in New York opposed to the act,	19
Meeting of Bank Delegates in Washington to oppose the bill,	19
Meeting of Delegates and Committees at Treasury Department,	19
Their plan to raise money to carry on the War,	20
Secretary Chase modifies their plan,	21
Opposition to the Bank plan,	22
Letters of M. H. Grinell, L. F. Allen and Mr. Ganson,	23
Letters of J. W. Simonton, T. Denny & Co., J. E. Williams,	24—25
Section for $500,000,000 of 5-20 bonds,	26
Letter of Secretary Chase, January 22, 1862,	27
National Intelligencer, Col. Seaton, etc.,	28
Mr. Spaulding's opening Speech on the bill,	28
Value of the Real and Personal property, $16,159,616,068,	41
Mr. Vallandigham offers a substitute,	43
Mr. Pendleton's Speech on the bill,	43

Mr. Corning's resolution asking opinion of Secretary Chase,	45
Secretary Chase's opinion of the propriety and necessity of the bill,	45
Mr. Chase's letter to Mr. Spaulding, Jan. 30th,	46
Letters of John A. Stevens, George Opdyke and R. Morris,	47
Letters of Stephen Colwell, M. S. Hawley, J. H. Van Antwerp,	48—49
Letters of Robert Dennison, C. H. Russell, Mr. Lord, Mr. Prosser,	40—50
Letters of George B. Butler, T. W. Olcott and others,	51—52
Mr. Vallandigham's Speech,	52
Mr. Hooper's Speech,	54—55
Mr. Roscoe Conkling, Mr. Morrill, Stevens and Spaulding,	57—58
Mr. Conkling as to Secretary Chase's position,	58—59
Secretary Chase's letter in favor of bill,	59
Mr. Morrill's Speech against legal tender,	60
Mr. Roscoe Conkling's Speech against legal tender,	64
Mr. Bingham, of Ohio, in favor of the bill,	66
Mr. Sheffield, Crisfield and Pike,	68—69
Mr. Alley, of Massachusetts, in favor of the bill,	71
Letter of Secretary Chase urging immediate action,	71
Mr. Spaulding's motion to close debate opposed,	72
Mr. Horton and Mr. Wright oppose the bill,	73
Order to close debate passed,	74
Proceedings on the day the bill passed the House,	75
Mr. Kellogg's Speech,	75
Mr. Thomas and Mr. Edward's Speeches,	77
Mr. Riddle and Blake's Speeches,	78
Mr. Campbell's Speech,	79
Mr. Spaulding and Stevens' Speeches closing debate,	80—81
Five minute Speeches continued,	85
Mr. F. A. Conkling, Shellabarger, Hickman,	85—87
Mr. Lovejoy and Walton,	88—91
Motion to strike out legal tender clause lost,	91—92
Confusion and excitement on taking vote,	92
The substitute of Mr. Morrill, Conkling and others lost,	92, 93, 94
Bill passed; yeas 93, nays 54,	95—96
Copy of bill as passed the House February 6, 1862,	66—67
George Dawson's letter to Albany Journal,	98
Proceedings in Senate on the bill,	99—100
$10,000,000 demand notes for temporary relief,	99
Senate Finance Committee propose amendments,	100
Mr. Fessenden's opening Speech,	100
Speeches by Judge Collamer and Mr. Howe,	106—107
Speeches by Chandler, Wilson and Sherman,	109, 110, 111
Speeches by Cowan, Doolittle, Simmons, Bayard,	114, 115, 116
Speeches by Willey, Howard, McDougall,	117, 118, 119
Speech by Mr. Sumner,	121
Motion to strike out legal tender clause lost,	121—122
Speeches of King, Pearce, Salesbury, Powell,	122—123
Bill passed the Senate 30 to 7,	124
Letter of J. W. Simonton on the origin of legal tender act,	124

Objection in House to Senate amendments,	125—126
Mr. Spaulding's Speech opposing them,	127
Speeches by Pomeroy, Calvert, Morrill, Dunn, English,	133—138
Speeches by Pike, Diven, Windom, Pendleton,	139—140
Speeches by Hooper and Stevens close debate on amendments,	140—141
Yeas and nays to pay soldiers and sailors in coin,	144
Yeas and nays to pay interest in coin,	145
Yeas and nays to sell bonds at market value,	146
Yeas and nays to lay bill on table,	147
Conference Committee—bill passed,	148
Copy of legal tender act, February 25, '62,	149
Samuel Wilkeson's letter to N. Y. Tribune,	152
Temporary deposits in Sub-Treasury,	152
Certificates of indebtedness,	153
$60,000,000 more legal tender declared,	154
Secretary Chase asks for $150,000,000 more,	154
Secretary Chase asks for small bills less than $5,	155
Action of Committee of Ways and Means on this,	156
Mr. Spaulding's Speech upon it,	157
Mr. Colfax's Speech and Mr. Stevens',	161
Yeas and nays on passage of this bill,	162
Passed the Senate; yeas 22, nays 13,	163
Copy of second legal tender act,	163
Postage Stamps and Fractional Currency,	165
Shinplasters prohibited, 2d Section of the act,	165
Bank bill again recommended by Secretary Chase,	167
$900,000,000 loan bill reported from Committee,	167
Spaulding's opening Speech upon it,	167—168
Particulars of the National Debt, Jan. 2, 1863,	170
Constitutionality of a National Bank,	172
Constitutionality of State Banks,	172
Interest-bearing Treasury Notes,	178
Our only hope is in military success,	179
$100,000,000 legal tender to pay the army,	180—181
Mr. Gurly's Speech on market value of bonds,	181
Secretary Chase's special letter on Bank bill,	182
Special resolution passed to pay Soldiers,	182
President Lincoln's Special Message on the resolution,	183
Morrill, Ward and Amasa Walker's Speeches on the $900,000,000 Loan Act,	184
Substitutes of Hooper and Stevens lost,	185
$900,000,000 Loan Bill passed both Houses,	185
Synopsis of the bill as passed,	186
Bank bill passed; yeas and nays,	186—187
No National Currency issued until 1864,	187—188
The right to convert notes into bonds at par abrogated,	188
Jay Cook negotiates $500,000,000 of 5-20 bonds,	189
Mistake of the Secretary in not continuing funding,	189
Mr. Spaulding's two letters to Morris Ketchum on the subject,	190

Morris Ketchum's reply, March 21, 1864, - - - - - - 195
Second letter of Mr. Spaulding to Morris Ketchum, - - - - 195
Mr. Chase resigns—W. P. Fessenden appointed Secretary Treasury, - 198
Geo. Harrington Secretary of Treasury, *ad interim*, - - - 198
Gold $2.50 at the Board of Brokers, - - - - - - - 198
Great inflation of the currency, - - - - - - 198—199
Gold $2.85½—Gold bill in force only 15 days, - - - - 199
Legal tender U. S. notes limited to $400,000,000, - - - - 199
All bonds, notes and other obligations exempt from taxation, - - 200
How Secretary McCulloch paid the Army at close of the War, - - 200
$830,000,000 of 7-30 Treasury notes issued, - - - - - 200
Statement of Public Debt at the close of the War, - - - - 201
National Bank circulation, $185,000,000, - - - - - - 201
Tariff and Internal Revenue laws, - - - - - - - 201
Contraction of the currency, - - - - - - - 202
Secretary McCulloch on contraction, - - - - - 202
Mr. Alley's Resolution in favor of contraction, - - - - 202
Yeas and nays on Mr. Alley's resolution in the House, - 202
Contraction of the currency suspended, - - - - - 203
Public Faith—Debt to be paid in coin, - - - - - 203
Yeas and nays on this bill, - - - - - - - 204
U. S. Grant approves the bill, - - - - - - - 205
Decision of State Courts on the constitutionality of legal tender, - - 205
Coin contracts decided valid by U. S. Supreme Court, - - - 206
Conclusion—summing up, - - 208—213

APPENDIX.

Mr. Spaulding's Speech on the National Currency Bank bill, February
  19, 1863, - - - - - - - - - - 1—9
Letter of Mr. Spaulding to J. N. Orvis, Esq., - - - 9—13
Letter of Mr. Spaulding to Hon. H. R. Hubbard, Comptroller of
  Currency, - - - - - - - - - 13—17
Letter of Mr. Spaulding to Secretary McCulloch, - 18
Secretary McCulloch's reply, - - 18
National Debt—No repudiation, - - - 19—21
No State taxation of U. S. Bonds, - - - - - 22
Mr. Spaulding's letter to Senator Morgan, - - - 22—24
Letter of Fisk & Hatch to the Assistant Secretary of the Treasury, - 24
Assistant Secretary's reply, - - - - - - - 24
Mr. Spaulding's remarks, - - - 24—27
Secretary McCulloch's letter to L. P. Morton & Co., - 27
Mr. Spaulding's remarks, - - - 27
F. E. Spinner's letter to Mr. Spaulding, - - - - 28
National Currency—Legal Tender, - - - - 28—33
Mr. Spaulding's letter to Secretary McCulloch, 34—35
President Lincoln's Veto, - 36
Mr. Spaulding's Speech, May 3d, 1862, - 37—40

Mr. Spaulding to Mr. Adams—legal tender vindicated,	41
Vote of the Senate on the 4th $100,000,000 greenbacks,	42
Mr. Spaulding to Cincinnati Gazette—First mistake of Mr. Chase,	43
Old U. S. Banks and National Banks (Sub-Treasury),	45
Hon. Hugh McCulloch's letter, 1869,	48
Hon. Charles Francis Adams against legal tender,	49
Hon. Joel T. Headley's letter, 1869,	50
Mr. Spaulding to J. S. Gibbons on Sub-Treasury,	51
J. S. Gibbons' reply,	54
J. E. Williams, Metropolitan Bank, New York,	55
John P. Elton, Waterbury Bank, Conn.,	55
H. H. Van Dyck, Asst. Treasurer, New York,	57
H. F. Vail, Bank of Commerce, New York,	57
Judges Nelson and Grier, U. S. Supreme Court,	58
Judges Miller and Bradley, do	59
Judge Noah Davis, New York,	60
Judge Fithian, New York,	60
Judge Henry E. Davies, 27 N. Y. Reports,	62
President Woolsey, Yale College,	62
Prof. Perry, Williams College,	63
Prof. J. P. White, M. D., Buffalo,	63
John T. Heard, Esq., Boston,	64
C. L. Vallandigham, Ohio,	64
Geo. H. Pendleton, Ohio,	65
Martin J. Crawford, Georgia,	65
President Grant's veto of inflation bill,	65
Senator Timothy O. Howe, Wisconsin,	68
Senator O. P. Morton, Indiana,	69
Senator R. E. Fenton, New York,	69
Senator Carl Schurz's letter and speech,	69—70
E. W. Leavenworth's letter, 1869,	72
D. A. Wells and Amasa Walker,	72—73
Hon. A. H. Rice and J. A. Garfield,	74
Maj. Gen. Sherman and Gen. Butler,	74
Hon. Edward Haight, only Democrat that voted for legal tender,	75
Hon. J. O. Putnam, J. F. D. Lanier and A. M. Clapp,	75—76
Hon. H. L. Dawes, U. S. Senator,	77
French finances—Gold reserves	77
David Wilder, Boston,	79
H. Bowlby Wilson, New York,	80
Isaac Sherman, Esq., New York,	81
Hon. John J. Knox, Comptroller of Currency,	82
Hon. W. P. Fessenden, John Coburn, A. R. Eno,	83
Hon. F. A. Conkling's review from 1861 to 1875—Mistakes of Secretary Chase, etc.,	83—86
Hon. S. S. Cox against inflation and repudiation,	87

viii

A. A. Low, Esq., merchant, New York,	87
Gen. J. D. Cox, Secretary of the Interior,	88
Hon. J. S Morrill, Senate Finance Committee,	88
Hon. John J. Cisco, confirming facts stated	88
Geo. S. Coe, President of the American Exchange Bank—Early war finances — Mistakes of Secretary Chase — Sub-Treasury — Specie payments (able and historical),	89—96
John E. Williams, President of Metropolitan Bank, New York—Important historical letter to Sec'y Chase—First loans of $150,000,000 in 1861—Mr. Chase rejects the advice of experienced bankers,	96—99
Geo. Wm. Curtiss, Editor Harper's Weekly,	99
E. H. Stoughton, counsellor, New York,	99
Hon. Montgomery Blair, Postmaster General,	99
Senator Christiancy, gold and paper,	100
Senator Morgan,	100
Col. J. W. Forney, Washington Chronicle,	101
A. M. Clapp, Public Printer,	102
Gen. J. E. Hawley's speech,	103

HISTORY

OF THE

LEGAL TENDER ACT.

The United States, at the breaking out of the rebellion, had no national bank currency, and no gold or available means in the Treasury, or Sub-Treasury, to carry on the war for the Union, and consequently the means to prosecute the war had to be obtained upon the *credit* of the government, and by taxation. The fundable legal tender currency was the most available form of credit which the government could use in crushing the rebellion. It was at once a *loan* to the government without interest, and a *national currency*, which was so much needed for disbursement in small sums during the pressing exigencies of the war. It was indispensably necessary, and a most powerful instrumentality in saving the government and maintaining the national unity.

Experience has proved that, notwithstanding it was a forced loan, the end justified the means, and that no parties were materially injured by being compelled to receive this currency, so long as they could fund it at any time in six per cent. twenty years bonds. Although it was a war measure—a measure of *necessity* and not of choice, and could only be justified on that ground, it has, for many years, exerted a most decisive influence over the property and material interests of every individual in the United States. It has affected debtor and creditor, producer and consumer, and the price of labor and of every article consumed in every household. It still exerts a mighty influence socially, commercially and politically, over the people of this great nation, and all the ramified and extensive business in which they are engaged. Whether for good or evil, it has been and still is a most powerful element in all business affairs of the people, as well as the government, and the war debt of $2,500,000,000 incurred in maintaining the national union is more or less affected by the large volume of this currency still outstanding.

Having been requested to prepare a history of a measure of such transcendent importance as the legal tender act, and having in my possession a considerable number of documents, letters, and other materials relating to the subject, I have consented to put them into form, in order that the facts may be preserved for present and future reference, and which may be of some use in enabling the future historian to write a chapter on the financial history of the war. These facts will be presented in the form of a narrative of the circumstances and events, of the most grave and extraordinary character, occurring in rapid succession, which led finally to the issue of legal tender Treasury notes, and which were endowed with the attributes of money, so far forth as the Government had power under the Constitution and the pressure of the crisis to impart to a paper currency that high and most important attribute of sovereignty.

I was a somewhat prominent though humble actor in originating and maturing the measure, but I do not claim any particular merit or demerit for what I did in preparing and aiding to secure the passage of the bill. I was placed in a position where, if I performed my official duty, I must act, and must act with vigor and promptitude. The perilous condition of the country did not admit of hesitancy or delay. I endeavored, in the peculiar and responsible position in which I was placed, to do what I conceived to be my duty, and that is all I claim to have done. My associates performed their duty with equal fidelity and usefulness.

As chairman of the Sub-committee of Ways and Means, it became my duty, in connection with my associates, to devise an adequate plan for obtaining the necessary means for prosecuting the war to a successful issue. The rebellion, after the battle of Bull Run, had assumed most gigantic proportions. An Army and Navy of over half a million of men had been hastily brought into the service of the United States. The Capitol itself was guarded by a vast Army, under the command of General McClellan, which encircled it in all directions. The Army and Navy thus in the service had to be paid, fed, clothed and provided with ships, gunboats, monitors and all the necessary material of war to make them effective in crushing the rebellion. This required vast available means; where were those means to be obtained? It was plain that they must come from the loyal people themselves, and that, from whatever source these means were to come, they must be obtained, as before stated, upon the credit of the government, then assailed and weakened by armed rebellion.

The banks in New York, Boston and Philadelphia had, during the summer and fall of 1861, loaned to the government very nearly the sum of $150,000,000 in gold, which had so exhausted their resources that it was very difficult for many of them to pay the last instalments due on the last loan of $50,000,000. These banks, at the commencement of the war, possessed a large part of the available gold in the country, but in paying over to the Treasurer the gold on these loans, and in the disbursement of the same to sustain the Army and Navy, it became so scattered that it could not, to any considerable extent, be re-loaned to the government, nor could it any longer be made available as a reserve for the banks. The banks were consequently in great danger of suspending specie payments at the time Congress assembled at its regular session in December, of that year. Congress met on the 2d December, 1861. The House, having been organized at the Extra Session in July by the election of the Hon. Galusha A. Grow, Speaker, proceeded at once to business.

On the 5th, the vacancies in the Standing Committees were filled up. Hon. Samuel Hooper, of Mass., a new member, was appointed on the Committee of Ways and Means in place of Samuel Appleton, deceased; and Hon. Horace Maynard in place of Hon. John A. McClernand, who had been appointed a Brigadier General in the volunteer army. The Committee of Ways and Means then consisted of

           THADEUS STEVENS, of Pa.
           JUSTIN S. MORRILL, of Vt.
           JOHN S. PHELPS, of Mo.
           ELBRIDGE G. SPAULDING, of N. Y.
           VALENTINE B. HORTON, of Ohio.
           ERASTUS CORNING, of N. Y.
           SAMUEL HOOPER, of Mass.
           HORACE MAYNARD, of Tenn.
           JOHN L. N. STRATTON, of N. Y.

Owing to the pressure of business in the Treasury Department,

Secretary Chase did not get his Annual Report ready to submit to the House until the 10th, and it was not printed and laid on the table of the Committee of Ways and Means until near the middle of December.

Soon after the report of the Secretary of the Treasury was received, finding a large volume of business in the Committee room to be disposed of, the Committee agreed to the appointment of two Sub-committees, namely,

One Committee on the National Currency bank bill, making of loans, issue of Treasury notes, bonds, and the mode of raising the means to carry on the war, consisting of

    Mr. SPAULDING,
    Mr. HOOPER,
    Mr. CORNING.

The other Committee was appointed on the Tariff, Internal Revenue, and taxation generally, consisting of three or four members, Mr. Morrill of Vermont, being chairman. The appropriation bills were then in course of preparation, Mr. Stevens devoting a good deal of time in perfecting and passing them through the House, as chairman of the General Committee. Mr. Phelps was at this time absent in Missouri, and remained absent for several weeks, looking after public affairs in that State, which were then in a very disturbed condition.

The Committee of Ways and Means having thus divided the subjects before it, and having referred the papers and documents to these Sub-committees, the Committee was prepared for efficient work.

The Sub-committee, of which Mr. Spaulding was chairman, examined with care the report of the Secretary of the Treasury, to ascertain what measures he proposed for providing the ways and means to support the government and carry on the war. Here follows an extract from that part of the Secretary's report which was referred to this Sub-committee, viz:

"To enable the government to obtain the necessary means for prosecuting the war to a successful issue, without unnecessary cost, is a problem which must engage the most careful attention of the Legislature. The Secretary has given to this problem the best consideration in his power, and now begs leave to submit to Congress the result of his reflections.

The circulation of the banks of the United States on the 1st day of January, 1861, was computed to be $202,000,767. Of this circulation, $150,000,000, in round numbers, was in the States now loyal, including Western Virginia, and $50,000,000 in the rebellious States. The whole of this circulation constitutes a loan without interest from the people to the banks, costing them nothing except the expense of issue and redemption and the interest on the specie kept on hand for the latter purpose; and it deserves consideration whether sound policy does not require that the advantages of this loan be transferred, in part at least, from the banks, representing only the interests of the stockholders, to the Government, representing the aggregate interests of the whole people.

It has been well questioned by the most eminent statesmen whether a currency of bank notes, issued by local institutions under State laws, is not, in fact, prohibited by the National Constitution. Such emissions certainly fall within the spirit, if not within the letter, of the Constitutional prohibition of the emission of "bills of credit" by the States, and of the making by them of anything except gold and silver coin a legal tender in payment of debts.

However this may be, it is too clear to be reasonably disputed that Congress, under its Constitutional powers to lay taxes, to regulate commerce, and to regulate the value of coin, possesses ample authority to control the credit circulation which enters so largely into the transactions of commerce, and affects in so many ways the value of coin. In the judgment of the Secretary, the time has arrived when Congress should exercise this authority. The value of the existing bank-note circulation depends on the laws of thirty-four States, and the character of some sixteen hundred private corporations. It is usually furnished in greatest proportions by institutions of least actual capital, circulation, commonly, is in the inverse ratio of solvency. Well-founded institutions, of large and solid capital, have, in general, comparatively little circulation; while weak corporations almost invariably seek to sustain themselves by obtaining from the people the largest possible credit in this form. Under such a system, or rather lack of system, great fluctuations, and heavy losses in discounts and exchanges are inevitable, and not unfrequently, through failures of the issuing institutions, considerable portions of the circulation become suddenly worthless in the hands of the people. The recent experience of several States in the valley of the Mississippi, painfully illustrates the justice of these observations; and enforces, by the most cogent practical arguments, the duty of protecting commerce and industry against the recurrence of such disasters.

The Secretary thinks it possible to combine with this protection a provision for circulation, safe to the community and convenient for the government.

Two plans for effecting this object are suggested. The first contemplates the gradual withdrawal from circulation of the notes of private corporations, and for the issue, in their stead, of United States notes, payable in coin on demand, in amounts sufficient for the useful ends of a representative currency. The second contemplates the preparation and delivery, to institutions and associations, of notes prepared for circulation under national direction, and to be secured as to prompt convertibility into coin by the pledge of United States bonds and other needful regulations.

1. *The first* of these plans was partially adopted at the last session of Congress, in the provision authorizing the Secretary to issue United States notes, payable in coin, to an amount not exceeding $50,000,000. That provision may be so extended as to reach the average circulation of the country, while a moderate tax, gradually augmented, on bank notes, will relieve the national from the competition of local circulation. It has been already suggested that the substitution of a National for a State currency,

upon this plan, would be equivalent to a loan to the Government without interest, except on the fund to be kept in coin, and without expense, except the cost of preparation, issue and redemption; while the people would gain the additional advantage of a uniform currency, and relief from a considerable burden in the form of interest on debt. These advantages are, doubtless, considerable; and if a scheme can be devised by which such a circulation will be certainly and strictly confined to the real needs of the people, and kept constantly equivalent to specie by prompt and certain redemption in coin, it will hardly fail of legislative sanction.

The plan, however, is not without serious inconveniences and hazards. The temptation, especially great in times of pressure and danger, to issue notes without adequate provision for redemption; the ever-present liability to be called on for redemption beyond means, however carefully provided and managed; the hazard of panics, precipitating demands for coin, concentrated on a few points and a single fund; the risk of a depreciated, and depreciating, and finally worthless paper money; the immeasurable evils of dishonored public faith and national bankruptcy; all these are possible consequences of the adoption of a system of Government circulation. It may be said, and perhaps truly, that they are less deplorable than those of an irredeemable bank circulation. *Without entering into that comparison, the Secretary contents himself with observing that, in his judgment, those possible disasters so far outweigh the probable benefits of the plan, that he feels himself constrained to forbear recommending its adoption.*

2. *The second plan* suggested remains for examination. Its principal features are: first, a circulation of notes bearing a common impression, and authenticated by a common authority; second, the redemption of these notes by the associations and institutions to which they may be delivered for issue; and, third, the security of that redemption by the pledge of United States stocks, and an adequate provision of specie.

In this plan the people, in their ordinary business, would find the advantages of uniformity in currency; of uniformity in security; of effectual safe-guard, if effectual safe-guard is possible, against depreciation; and of protection from losses in discounts and exchanges; while in the operations of the Government, the people would find the further advantages of a large demand for Government securities, of increased facilities for obtaining the loans required by the war, and of some alleviation of the burdens on industry through a diminution in the rate of interest, or a participation in the profit of circulation, without risking the perils of a great money monopoly,

A further and important advantage to the people may be reasonably expected in the increased security of the Union, springing from the common interest in its preservation, created by the distribution of its stocks to associations throughout the country, as the basis of their circulation.

The Secretary entertains the opinion that if a credit circulation in any form be desirable, it is most desirable in this. The notes thus issued and secured would, in his judgment, form the safest currency which this country has ever enjoyed; while their receivability for all Government dues, except customs, would make them, wherever payable, of equal value as a currency in every part of the Union. The large amount of specie now in the United States, reaching a total of not less than $275,000,000, will easily support payments of duties in coin, while these payments and ordinary demands will aid in retaining this specie in the country as a solid basis, both of circulation and loans.

The whole circulation of the country, except a limited amount of foreign coin, would, after the lapse of two or three years, bear the impress of the nation, whether in coin or notes; while the amount of the latter, always easily ascertainable, and, of course, always generally known, would not be likely to be increased beyond the real wants of business.

He expresses an opinion in favor of this plan with the greatest confidence, because it has the advantage of recommendation from experience. It is not an untried theory. In the State of New York, and in one or more of the other States, it has been subjected, in its most essential parts, to the test of experiment, and has been found practicable and useful. The probabilities of success will not be diminished, but increased by its adoption under national sanction, and for the whole country.

It only remains to add that the plan is recommended by one other consideration, which, in the judgment of the Secretary, is entitled to much influence. It avoids almost, if not altogether, the evils of a great and sudden change in the currency, by offering inducements to solvent existing institutions to withdraw the circulation issued under State authority and substitute that provided by the authority of the Union. Thus, through the voluntary action of the existing institutions, aided by wise legislation, the great transition from a currency heterogeneous, unequal, and unsafe, to one uniform, equal, and safe, may be speedily and almost imperceptibly accomplished.

If the Secretary has omitted the discussion of the question of the Constitutional power of Congress to put this plan into operation, it is because no argument is necessary to establish the proposition that the power to regulate commerce and the value of coin includes the power to regulate the currency of the country, or the collateral proposition that the power to affect the end includes the power to adopt the necessary and expedient means.

The Secretary entertains the hope that the plan now submitted, if adopted with the limitations and safe-guards which the experience and wisdom of Senators and Representatives will, doubtless, suggest, *may impart such value and stability to Government securities that it will not be difficult to obtain the additional loans required for the service of the current and the succeeding year at fair and reasonable rates; especially if the public credit be supported by sufficient and certain provision for the payment of interest and ultimate redemption of the principal."*

Finding from the above extracts from the report of Secretary Chase that he forbore to recommend the issue of United States Treasury notes to circulate as money, and that he did recommend the National Currency bank bill, Mr. Spaulding, as chairman of the Sub-committee, addressed a note to the Secretary requesting him to furnish the draft of a bank bill for a national currency based on a pledge of public stocks, as recommended in his report, and received the following reply:

TREASURY DEPARTMENT, }
Dec. 18th, 1861. }

SIR:—I have the honor to acknowledge the note of the Committee of Ways and Means of this date, covering the note of yourself as chairman of the Sub-committee, requesting him to furnish the draft of a bill for a national currency based on the pledge of public stocks. The Secretary of the Treasury, who is now in New York, will give to your request his prompt attention on his return.

With great respect,
GEO. HARRINGTON,
Acting Secretary of the Treasury.

To Hon. E. G. SPAULDING,
Ch. of Sub-Com. of Ways and Means, H. R.

On the return of the Secretary from New York, it was ascertained that no National Currency bank bill had been prepared. The Secretary then requested Mr. Spaulding to prepare a bill at as early a day as possible. Mr. Spaulding, as chairman of the Sub-committee, immediately set to work at his rooms at the National Hotel in preparing the first draft of the bill, which was there copied by Mr. George Bassett, clerk of the Committee of Ways and Means. This was during the Christmas holidays; Congress adjourning over two or three days at a time, without doing much business, no quorum being present.

On the 24th inst. Mr. Spaulding wrote a letter to Mr. Corning, then at Albany, informing him that he was making a draft of the National Currency bank bill, and requesting that he would forward a copy of the New York Free Banking Law, passed in 1838, and amendments thereto, for the use of the Committee. Mr. Corning promptly complied with this request, and returned the following reply:

ALBANY, Dec. 26, 1861.

MY DEAR SIR—I am this morning in receipt of your favor of the 24th inst. I send you by this day's mail a copy of our Bank Laws, with amendments passed since 1856. *This matter, as recommended by Secretary Chase, will not, in my judgment, meet the approval of our State*, hence I think much care should be had in drawing up the bill.

Yours, very truly,
ERASTUS CORNING.
Hon. E. G. SPAULDING, Washington.

When the frame work of the bill was nearly completed, it was submitted to Mr. Hooper, the only other member of the Sub-committee then in Washington, Mr. Corning having gone to Albany. Mr. Hooper rendered valuable assistance in perfecting the bill. He incorporated into it some provisions which experience in his own State had shown to be valuable. The bill was finally completed soon after Christmas. A few days thereafter the National Currency bank bill, thus hastily prepared, was sent by Mr. Spaulding to the public printer, and two hundred copies printed for the use of the Committee of Ways and Means and the Secretary of the Treasury, with a view of having it more maturely considered in the General Committee, amended and corrected, and finally to be reported to the House. Copies of this printed bill are still in the possession of Mr. Spaulding, the chairman of the Sub-committee, which formed the basis of the bank bill which was finally adopted more than a year afterwards.

Mr. Spaulding, while preparing the national currency bank bill, upon mature reflection came to the conclusion, that it could not be passed and made available quick enough to meet the crisis then pressing upon the Government for money to sustain the Army and Navy. He therefore drafted a legal tender Treasury note section to be added to the bank bill, hoping, at first, that it might be made available by issuing legal tender notes direct from the Treasury, while the bank bill was put in operation throughout the country. In order to bring the subject of issuing legal tender fundable notes before the country, the section thus prepared by Mr. Spaulding was furnished to the New York Tribune, and published in the issue of the 31st December, 1861, and is as follows:

"That for temporary purposes, and until the circulating notes authorized by this act shall be issued and put in circulation by corporations and associations to the aggregate amount of $100,000,000, the Secretary of the Treasury be, and he is hereby authorized to issue $50,000,000 of Treasury notes on the faith of the United States, payable on demand, without specifying any place of payment, and of such denominations as he may deem expedient, not less than $5 each, which shall be receivable for all debts and demands due to the United States, and for all salaries, dues, debts and demands, owing by the United States to individuals, corporations and associations within the United States; and such Treasury notes shall also be a legal tender in payment of all debts, public or private, within the United States, and shall be exchanged at any time at their par value, the same as coin, at the Treasury of the United States, and the offices of Assistant Treasurers in New York, Boston, Philadelphia, St. Louis and Cincinnati, for any of the coupon or registered bonds which the Secretary of the Treasury is now, or may hereafter be authorized to issue; and such Treasury notes may be re-issued from time to time, as the exigencies of the public service may require. Such Treasury notes shall be signed by the Treasurer of the United States, or by some officer of the Treasury Department designated by the Secretary of the Treasury, and shall be countersigned by the Register of the Treasury, or by some officer of the Treasury Department designated by the Secretary of the Treasury for the Register. And all the provisions of an act entitled "An act to authorize the issue of Treasury notes, approved the 23d day of December, 1857," so far as the same can be applied to the provisions of this section, and not inconsistent therewith, are hereby revived and re-enacted."

Upon more mature consideration and further examination, Mr. Spaulding came to the conclusion that the bank bill, containing sixty sections, could not, with the State banks opposed to it, be passed through both Houses of Congress for several months, and that so long a delay would be fatal to the Union cause. The banks in New York, Boston and Philadelphia, had just suspended specie payments, which compelled a general suspension of coin payments by the Government, and all the other banks throughout the country. No more gold could be loaned to the Government, except in small and wholly inadequate amounts, because it was not to be had. State bank bills could still be obtained, but the banks having suspended specie payments, this currency was depreciated, and had only a local character and credit—not being much known out of the States where the banks were located. Hesitancy and delay, with the expenses of the war running on at an average of $2,000,000 per day, would have been fatal. Mr. Spaulding, therefore, changed the legal tender section, intended originally to accompany the bank bill, into a separate bill, with alterations and additions, and on his own motion introduced it into the House by unanimous consent on the 30th of December, 1861. It was read twice, and referred to the Committee of Ways and Means, and ordered printed (House Bill, No. 182), and is as follows:

Mr. Spaulding, on leave, introduced the following bill:

A BILL

To authorize the issue of treasury notes payable on demand.

Be it enacted by the Senate and House of Representatives of the United States of America in Congress assembled, That, for temporary purposes, the Secretary of the Treasury be, and he is hereby authorized to issue fifty millions of dollars of treasury notes, on the faith of the United States, payable on demand, without specifying any place of payment, and of such denominations as he may deem expedient, not less than five dollars each, which shall be receivable for all debts and demands due to the United States, and for all salaries, dues, debts, and demands owing by the United States to individuals, corporations, and associations within the United States; and such treasury notes shall also be a legal tender in payment of all debts, public and private, within the United States, and shall be exchangeable at any time at their par value, the same as coin, at the Treasury of the United States, and the offices of the assistant treasurers in New York, Boston, Philadelphia, St. Louis, and Cincinnati, for any of the coupon or registered bonds which the Secretary of the Treasury is now or may hereafter be authorized to issue, and such treasury notes may be re-issued from time to time as the exigencies of the public service may require. Such treasury notes shall be signed by the Treasurer of the United States, or by some officer of the Treasury Department designated by the Secretary of the Treasury, and shall be countersigned by the Register of the Treasury, or some officer of the Treasury Department designated by the

Secretary of the Treasury for the register; and all the provisions of the act entitled "An act to authorize the issue of treasury notes," approved the twenty-third day of December, one thousand eight hundred and fifty-seven, so far as the same can be applied to the provisions of this act, and not inconsistent therewith, are hereby revived and re-enacted.

As soon as the bill was printed, it was taken up in the Committee of Ways and Means, and duly considered. Mr. Hooper took active ground in favor of the bill. Mr. Stevens at first had some doubts about its constitutionality, but very soon decided to support the measure. Mr. Morrill, Mr. Horton, and Mr. Corning actively opposed the bill in the Committee and in the House. Mr. Maynard and Mr. Stratton took no active part in the discussions while the bill was under consideration in the Committee. It is believed, however, that Mr. Maynard was favorable to the bill from the start, while Mr. Stratton was very much in doubt what course he would take in relation to it, either in Committee, or in giving his vote in the House. Mr. Phelps was absent, and took no part while the bill was under discussion in the Committee.

Mr. Spaulding finding that the Committee were about equally divided, and that some members of the Committee had doubts as to the constitutional power of Congress to make treasury notes a legal tender, called upon the Attorney General, Hon. Edward Bates, for his opinion. He declined to give an official opinion, but consented to write an un-official note in favor of its constitutionality. The following is a copy of the opinion thus obtained:

MONDAY EVENING, Jan. 6, 1862.

Hon. E. G. Spaulding, M. C.,
    At the National Hotel:

DEAR SIR—Since you did me the honor of a call this afternoon, and propounded to me a question arising out of the pending bill "To authorize the issue of treasury notes payable on demand," I have given to the subject such attention as the very brief interval afforded, and proceed at once to answer.

In the first place, permit me to say, that my views of the place I hold forbid me to give your question a formal and official answer, but in proof of the high respect which I entertain for you and your honorable Committee, I, as a private man, and a professed constitutional legist, in all frankness will give you my opinion upon the point proposed, and this, with all brevity and without argument, for the time does not allow elaborate consideration.

The bill, after providing for the issue of treasury notes, contains i. e. this clause, "and which treasury notes shall be a *legal tender* in payment of *all* debts, public and private, within the United States," and you desire my opinion whether this clause is, or is not, constitutional.

Certainly the Constitution contains no direct verbal prohibition, and I think it contains no inferential or argumentative prohibition that can be fairly drawn from its expressed terms. The first article of the Constitution, section eight, grants to Congress specifically a great mass of powers. Section nine contains divers limitations upon Congress, upon the United States, and upon individuals; and section ten contains restrictions upon the several States. This last section is the only one that treats on *tender*. "*No State* shall make anything but gold and silver coin a tender in payment of debts." This applies to a State only, and not to the nation; and thus it has always been understood with regard to the next preceding clause in the same section—no State shall "emit bills of credit." The prohibition to emit bills of credit is quite as strong as the prohibition to make anything but gold and silver coin a legal tender; yet nobody doubts—Congress does not doubt its power to issue bills of credit. Treasury notes *are* bills of credit, and I think the one is just as much prohibited as the other—neither is forbidden to Congress.

The time is too short for argument, and so I remain, with all respect,
Your obedient servant,

EDWARD BATES.

Mr. Spaulding read this letter to the Committee of Ways and Means. The discussion on the bill had continued for several days, and when the vote was finally taken, it appeared that the Committee were at first equally divided—Mr. Spaulding, Mr. Hooper, Mr. Stevens, and Mr. Maynard voting in the affirmative, and Mr. Morrill, Mr. Horton, Mr. Corning, and Mr. Stratton in the negative. Mr. Stratton finally consented to vote for the bill, so as to allow it to be reported to the House. The bill was thus passed through the Committee of Ways and Means.

On the 7th of January, 1862, Mr. Spaulding reported the bill from the Committte to the House. It was read twice, committed to the Committee of the whole House on the state of the Union, and ordered to be printed. (House Bill No. 187.)

Mr. Spaulding, from the Committee of Ways and Means, reported the following bill:

A BILL

To authorize the issue of demand Treasury notes.

Be it enacted by the Senate and House of Representatives of the United States of America in Congress assembled, That, for temporary purposes, the Secretary of the Treasury be, and he is hereby authorized to issue, on the credit of the United States, one hundred millions of dollars of Treasury notes, not bearing interest, payable generally, without specifying any place or time of payment, and of such denominations as he may deem expedient, not less than five dollars each; and such notes, and all other Treasury notes payable on demand, not bearing interest, that have been heretofore authorized to be issued, shall be receivable for all debts and demands due to the United States, and for all salaries, dues, debts, and demands owing by the United States to individuals, corporations, and associations within the United States; and shall also be lawful money, and a legal tender in payment of all debts, public and private, within the

United States, and shall be exchangeable in sums not less than one hundred dollars, at any time, at their par value, at the Treasury of the United States, and at the offices of the Assistant Treasurers in New York, Philadelphia, St. Louis, and at the depository in Cincinnati, for any of the six per centum twenty years coupon bonds or registered bonds which the Secretary of the Treasury is now, or may hereafter be authorized to issue; and such Treasury notes shall be received the same as coin, at their par value, in payment for any bonds that may be hereafter negotiated by the Secretary of the Treasury; and such Treasury notes may be re-issued from time to time as the exigencies of the public service may require. There shall be printed on the back of the Treasury notes, which may be issued under the provisions of this act, the following words: "The within note is a legal tender in payment of all debts, public and private, and is exchangeable for the coupon or registered bonds of the United States bearing six per centum interest." Such Treasury note shall be signed by the Treasurer of the United States, or by some officer of the Treasury Department designated by the Secretary of the Treasury, and shall be countersigned by the Register of the Treasury, or some officer of the Treasury Department designated by the Secretary of the Treasury for the Register; and all the provisions of the act entitled "An act to authorize the issue of Treasury notes," approved the twenty-third day of December, one thousand eight hundred and fifty-seven, so far as the same can be applied to the provisions of this act, and not inconsistent therewith, are hereby revived and re-enacted; and the sum of one hundred and fifty thousand dollars is hereby appropriated, out of any money in the Treasury not otherwise appropriated, to enable the Secretary of the Treasury to carry this act into effect.

Soon after Mr. Spaulding introduced his bill proposing the issue of legal tender notes to circulate as money, he received many letters criticising the measure in rather severe terms. Among others, Mr. Isaac Sherman, of New York, an old friend, addressed a letter to him of this character, bearing date January 4th, 1862, and at the same time suggesting very *heavy taxation* in various forms, as the best plan for raising the money to carry on the war.

To this letter Mr. Spaulding made the following reply:

HOUSE OF REPRESENTATIVES,
WASHINGTON, Jan. 8, 1862.

Isaac Sherman, Esq., New York:

DEAR SIR—In reply to yours of the 4th inst., I would say that the Treasury note bill for $100,000,000 agreed upon in Committee yesterday is a measure of *necessity* and not one of *choice*.

You criticise matters very freely, and very likely you may be right in what you say.

We will be out of means to pay the daily expenses in *about thirty days*, and the Committee do not see any other way to get along till we can get the tax bills ready, except to issue temporarily Treasury notes. Perhaps you can suggest some other mode of carrying on the Government for the next one hundred days. You do not pretend that any considerable amount of taxes can be collected for the next three months, even under your plan. It is much easier to *find fault* than it is to suggest *practicable means or measures.*

We must have at least $100,000,000 during the next three months, or the Government must stop payment. With the navy and an army of 700,000 men in the field, we cannot say that we will *not pay.*

I will thank you to suggest a better *practicable* mode of getting $100,000,000 of paying means during the next three months. I would be glad to adopt it, and the Committee would be glad to adopt it. Let us have *your specific plan* for this purpose—one that will produce the money—and we will be very much obliged to you. In haste.

Yours truly,
E. G. SPAULDING.

P. S.—I am as impatient as you can be for an *early* and *successful* advance of the army, so important at this time to sustain the *credit* of the Government. Will it be done? You are just as well informed on that subject as any of us. I say to you privately that I could find fault more loudly than you do, but I will not do that without being able to suggest a *practicable remedy;* and I might say many things to you, personally, that I might not put on paper.

Confidentially yours,
E. G. S.

MR. ISAAC SHERMAN'S LETTER.

NEW YORK, Jan. 22, 1869.

Hon. E. G. Spaulding:

I have received your letter of the 20th, and inclosed I send a letter which you addressed me January 8th, 1862, and this letter fully explains your motives in advocating the legal tender act. I will add that I became fully satisfied that the immediate wants of the Government rendered it absolutely necessary that legal tender notes should be issued. It is possible that a good tax bill, passed and enforced in 1861, might have averted the necessity of the legal tender act; but in 1862 it was impossible to pay the expenses without an issue of Government paper as currency. I was shocked at first at the idea of issuing paper, but I have always since said that you finally convinced me of *the absolute necessity at the time* of the paper issue. I consider your letter historical, and after copying, I wish you would return it to me.

Yours truly,
ISAAC SHERMAN.

BANK DELEGATES IN WASHINGTON—MEETING AT THE TREASURY DEPARTMENT.

After the legal tender bill was reported from the Committee of Ways and Means by Mr. Spaulding, and published in the newspapers of the principal cities, opposition to it manifested itself in various ways. At first the New York city press were generally opposed to the legal tender clause. The *Times* and *Herald* early came into the support of the measure. The *Tribune* and *Commercial Advertiser* appeared to be in some doubt, but in their editorial columns opposed it. The *Evening Post, World,* and *Journal of Commerce* were decidedly hostile, and opposed the measure throughout. Delegates from some of the banks in New

York, Boston and Philadelphia, appeared in Washington to oppose the bill. The reporters of the New York press, at the time, preserved a tolerably accurate account of their doings, which may be summed up substantially as follows:

They organized by appointing Mr. Singleton A. Mercer, of Philadelphia, as chairman, and invited the Finance Committee of the Senate, and the Committee of Ways and Means of the House, to meet them at the office of the Secretary of the Treasury, on Saturday afternoon, January 11th, 1862. The invitation was accepted, and the Convention assembled accordingly at the Treasury Department.

Delegates from New York Banks.

Mr. COE, American Exchange Bank.
Mr. VERMILYE, Merchant's Bank.
Mr. MARTIN, Ocean Bank.
Mr. GALLATIN, National Bank.

Delegates from Philadelphia Banks.

Mr. ROGERS, Tradesman's Bank.
Mr. MERCER, Farmer's and Mechanics' Bank.
Mr. PATTERSON, Western Bank.

Delegates from Boston Banks.

Mr. HAVEN, Merchant's Bank.
Mr. WALLEY, Revere Bank.
Mr. BATES, Bank of Commerce.

Treasury Department.

SALMON P. CHASE, Secretary of the Treasury.

Finance Committee of the Senate.

Mr. FESSENDEN, of Maine.
Mr. SIMMONS, of Rhode Island.
Mr. SHERMAN, of Ohio.
Mr. HOWE, of Wisconsin.
Mr. PEARCE, of Maryland.
Mr. BRIGHT, of Indiana.
Mr. MCDOUGAL, of California.

House Committee of Ways and Means.

Mr. STEVENS, of Pennsylvania.

Mr. MORRILL, of Vermont.
Mr. PHELPS, of Missouri.
Mr. SPAULDING, of New York.
Mr. CORNING, of New York.
Mr. HORTON, of Ohio.
Mr. STRATTON, of New Jersey.
Mr. HOOPER, of Massachusetts.
Mr. MAYNARD, of Tennessee.

Some of the members of the above Committees of the Senate and House were not present, but there was a very full representation from each Committee. There were some other gentlemen present from Boards of Trade of different cities.

Mr. James Gallatin, of New York, made the principal speech against legal tender, and on behalf of himself and the Bank Committees from New York, Boston, and Philadelphia, and members from Boards of Trade associated with them, submitted the following plan for raising money to carry on the war, viz:

1. A tax bill to raise, in the different modes of taxation, $125,000,000, over and above duties on imports.
2. Not to issue any demand Treasury notes, except those authorized at the extra session in July last.
3. Issue $100,000,000 Treasury notes at two years, in sums of five dollars and upwards, to be receivable for public dues to the Government, except duties on imports.
4. A suspension of the sub-Treasury act, so as to allow the banks to become depositories of the Government of all loans, and to check on the banks from time to time as the Government may want money.
5. Issue six per cent. twenty year bonds, to be negotiated by the Secretary of the Treasury, *and without any limitation as to the price he may obtain for them in the market.*
6. That the Secretary of the Treasury be empowered to make temporary loans to the extent of any portion of the funded stock authorized by Congress, *with power to hypothecate such stock, and if such loans are not paid at maturity, to sell the stock hypothecated for the best price that can be obtained.*

These propositions having been read, the Secretary and Finance Committees of the Senate and House expressed themselves favorable to the first proposition to raise by taxation $125,000,000 a year, over and above duties on imports. It will be observed that this plan did not include the national currency bank bill, recommended by the Secretary of the Treasury in his Annual Report, and was not, therefore, in this respect, satisfactory to him.

The meeting was somewhat conversational in character, but there appeared to be a general dissent by the Secretary and Committees from all the other propositions. Mr. Hooper expressed very decidedly his dissent to them, and was in favor of the legal tender act as the best mode of providing the means. The only remarks I can find reported as being made by any member of the Committees of the Senate and House are in the New York *Tribune,* January 13, 1862, in substance as follows:

"The Sub-committee of Ways and Means, through Mr. Spaulding, objected to any and every form of 'shinning' by Government through Wall or State streets to begin with; objected to the knocking down of Government stocks to seventy-five or sixty cents on the dollar, the inevitable result of throwing a new and large loan on the market, *without limitation as to price;* claimed for Treasury notes as much virtue of par value as the notes of banks which have suspended specie payments, but which yet circulate in the trade of the North; and finished with firmly refusing to assent to any scheme which should permit a speculation by brokers, bankers, and others, in the Government securities, and particularly any scheme which should double the public debt of the country, and double the expenses of the war, by damaging the credit of the Government to the extent of sending it to 'shin' through the shaving shops of New York, Boston, and Philadelphia. He affirmed his conviction as a banker and legislator, that it was the lawful policy, as well as the manifest duty of the Government in the present exigency, to legalize as tender its fifty million issue of demand Treasury notes, authorized at the extra session in July last, and to add to this stock of legal tender, immediately, one hundred millions more. He thought that this financial measure would carry the country through the war, and save its credit and its dignity; at the same time we should insist upon taxation abundantly ample to pay the expenses of the Government on a peace footing, and interest of every dollar of the public obligation, and to give this generation a clear show of a speedy liquidation of the public debt."

This Conference did not result in devising any plan or arrangement which received the assent of either the Finance Committee of the Senate or the Committee of Ways and Means of the House, and the Conference adjourned.

The bank delegates and others had further consultations with Secretary Chase, continuing through two or three days, and which finally resulted in an arrangement with the Secretary alone, which was furnished to the agent of the Associated Press and published on the 15th of January, 1862, as follows:

"The results of the various conferences held in Washington by representatives from Boards of Trade, Chambers of Commerce, and Banking institutions, among themselves, and with the Secretary of the Treasury, may be summed up as follows:

1. The general views of the Secretary of the Treasury are assented to.
2. The banks will receive and pay out the United States notes (authorized by act of July last) freely, and sustain in all proper ways the credit of the Government.

3. The Secretary of the Treasury will, within the next two weeks, in addition to the current daily payments of $1,500,000 in United States notes, pay the further sum of at least $20,000,000 in 7-30 bonds to such public creditors as desire to receive them, and thus relieve the existing pressure upon the community.

4. The issue of United States demand notes not to be increased beyond the $50,000,000 authorized by the act of last July, but it is desired that Congress should extend the provisions of the existing loan acts, passed at the extra session in July, so as to enable the Secretary to issue in exchange for United States demand notes, or in payment to creditors, notes payable in one year, bearing 3.65 per cent. interest, and convertible into 7-30 three years bonds, or to borrow under the existing provisions to the amount of $250,000,000 or $300,000,000.

5. It is thought desirable that Congress should enact the national currency bank bill, embracing the general provisions recommended by the Secretary in his Annual Report.

6. It is expected that this action and legislation will render the making of the United States demand notes a legal tender or their increase beyond the $50,000,000 authorized in July last unnecessary."

The Committees of the Senate and House never gave any assent to this agreement made by Secretary Chase with the delegations above mentioned, for the reason that it was not deemed by them adequate to the crisis. A majority of the Committee of Ways and Means adhered to the legal tender bill, then pending in the House, as being a more available plan, and on a much larger scale. They believed it was necessary to authorize immediately an additional issue of $100,000,000 of United States fundable notes, to circulate as money, and be made a legal tender; and that $500,000,000 six per cent. twenty years bonds should be authorized, so as to enable the holders of the notes, when issued, to fund them at any time in these bonds.

As soon as the plan of the delegates from New York, Boston, and Philadelphia became fully known to the country, it was very generally disapproved. The press spoke out plainly against the Secretary being authorized to put United States bonds "on the market without any limitation as to the price he might obtain for them in the market," as proposed by Mr. Gallatin. Members of Congress generally opposed it and numerous letters were received by Mr. Spaulding from bankers, and other prominent citizens, in opposition to any such scheme, but at the same time expressing themselves in favor of the legal tender bill and urging its immediate passage.

The following is a sample of the letters received about this time by Mr. Spaulding:

LETTER OF HON. MOSES H. GRINELL TO MR. SPAULDING.

NEW YORK, January 30, 1862.

MY DEAR SIR—I thank you for your able speech, and can only say that nine out of twelve persons in this city agree with you. As for G———, and a few egotistical gentlemen that act with him, they should be driven out of Washington, as they only embarrass the Government; and it seems to me that their policy, if adopted, would soon ruin the Government credit, and break down the country.

Go a direct tax for one hundred and fifty or two hundred millions, and then issue one hundred and fifty millions Treasury notes *legal tender*, and we will go on without any trouble, and the Government credit will be saved from disgrace. There are not eight bank presidents that side with G———. He is an odd fish—has very little influence here. Some action must be had soon, or our country will be in a deplorable financial condition.

Yours truly,
M. H. GRINELL.

Hon. E. G. SPAULDING.

LETTER FROM HON. LEWIS F. ALLEN.

BLACK ROCK, January 31, 1862.

Hon. E. G. Spaulding:

MY DEAR SIR—I have just read, with great pleasure, your very able speech on the Treasury note bill you have introduced into Congress. The principle and plan are both right, and what the country demands; and I trust both Houses will *put it right along through*, regardless of what the New York note shavers and usurers may say, for they, and the like, in our large Atlantic cities, are the only ones who will oppose it, and that for the reason that they can not make their ten, twenty or fifty per cent., by buying in and selling out the *stocks* which they want passed by the Government, in place of the sound, available *Constitutional* currency which you propose. I see by my *Tribune* to-day, that there is good prospect that your bill will pass without material modification, if any. I hope so, and that speedily.

Truly yours,
L. F. ALLEN.

LETTER FROM J. M. GANSON, BANKER, OF BUFFALO.

NEW YORK, January 13, 1862.

Hon. E. G. Spaulding, Washington;

DEAR SIR—Your bill on Finance is received. I understand the *pulse* of the people. Now, then, put on a war tax of $200,000,000, issue $150,0000,000 demand notes, and ten, fifteen and twenty year bonds, seven per cent. "coupon bonds," redeemable at the pleasure of the Government within that time, and then go ahead. Put our Generals into the *saddle*, and all this fussing and fooling will come to an end in ninety days. One grand *rush* from all points of our armies will *cow* down the rebels. Send home the Bank Committee; their proposition is *awful*. Let a few leading minds, in connection with Chase, *nerve up*, and let the demand notes assume the place of specie in *every* particular. A tender for deposits in State banks, a tender for State bank notes, and receivable for *all* Government dues. We must have one terrible bloody battle, and must not shrink from the responsibility. Let members of Congress *cease* abusing our Generals. Put the right men in the right place. Have no proclamations issued by the Generals unless passed upon by Lincoln and McClellan jointly. Hard work, less pleasure-seeking, good financiering and energy, will wind up this war shortly, and nothing else will do it.

I remain yours truly, J. M. GANSON.

LETTER FROM JAMES W. SIMONTON, ESQ., OF N. Y. TIMES.

WASHINGTON, January 13, 1862.
Hon. E. G. Spaulding:

DEAR SIR—I failed to make myself clearly understood in our conversation last evening, or rather I failed to tell the *whole* story in suggesting payment of interest on demand notes.

What do you think of providing for the payment of interest on demand notes (at a *less* rate than that on loan bonds) from their date, the interest on such demand notes to be allowed and paid *only when they are presented to be converted* into bonds?

Would not the tendency of such an arrangement be to keep the current of demand notes steadily moving towards the loan office, and prevent any possible depreciation of either class of paper?

Of course, you could devise a means (if you desire) of preventing the payment of back interest on debts already accumulated. In haste.

Truly yours,
JAMES W. SIMONTON.

LETTER FROM THOMAS DENNY & CO., BANKERS AND BROKERS, WALL STREET, NEW YORK.

NEW YORK, January 13, 1862.
Hon. E. G. Spaulding, House of Representatives, Washington, D. C.:

DEAR SIR—Although not personally acquainted with you, we take the liberty of giving you, in few words, our views as to the most desirable measures to be adopted for the finances of the country at the present time. It will not do at all to crowd on the market at the present time Government stock fast enough to raise the amount of money needed to meet our wants. The price would run down so fast that people would become alarmed, and afraid to take it, except at a ruinous sacrifice, if at all. The best plan is that which, we understood, you propose to adopt. Issue $100,000,000 to $150,000,000 demand notes, and pay them out as the wants of the Government require; make them a *legal tender* in all transactions of business in our country; make them convertible at the pleasure of the holders into a 6 per cent. stock, or even into 7-30 three year notes, unless there is some serious objection on account of the previous negotiations of the 7-30 notes; pass a tax bill which will produce $100,000,000 to $150,000,000. The above plan will furnish abundant means to the Government, and will meet the approbation of the people. It will furnish an excellent circulation to the whole country, facilitate all business transactions among the people, make the money market easy, and raise the prices of Government stocks so that loans can be negotiated on favorable terms when more money if wanted, especially if, in the meantime, the rebellion is pretty well crushed down.

If the above plan is adopted, public sentiment will make it necessary for the banks to receive and pay out the demand notes, and the whole effect will be very salutary on our national affairs. The tax bill will

create a general demand for the Treasury notes and keep them at or near par. We write in great haste, as practical business men, and are, very respectfully
        Your obedient servants,
                THOAMS DENNY & CO.

LETTER FROM JOHN E. WILLIAMS, ESQ.

                METROPOLITAN BANK,
                NEW YORK, January 20, 1862.

DEAR SIR—I have your favor of 18th inst. I leave my bank affairs to write you at once, and congratulate you on the prospect of being able to effect a remedy for the fiscal malady. With a *leader* in the Treasury Department all these discordent financial schemes would disappear. A man of ability, of business talent and experience, even although he be not endowed with the creative genius of a Hamilton, or the statistical knowledge and general attainments of Albert Gallatin, would devise a plan sufficiently comprehensive, sensible, and wise, to satisfy the public that he knew whereof he wrote and spoke, and had no object in view but to restore confidence and replenish the Treasury. There is one point in reference to the demand legal tender notes to which I wish to call attention. It may seem small, but I think it important—that is, in reference to the *color* of the paper on which such notes are printed. I would have it different from that used for any other notes; and I would again suggest that that color be yellow. I would also have them payable one year after the close of the war. There is no risk of embarrassment from this clause, as we could sell our national bonds to-morrow if the war were closed to-day. I would also simplify the matter by having the amount one hundred and fifty millions, so as to absorb the present outstanding demand notes into the legal demand or yellow notes, which could easily be done, and yet leave you on this loan one hundred millions net. I think it would make these demand notes more valuable to insert this redemption feature one year after peace, for peace must come. As if William B. Astor should give his note for $100,000, payable one year after his death. He must die, and he has millions, consequently on a future day certain (though not yet fixed), his note would be paid in full.

    Please consider, then, before you finally decide, the *amount*, the *color*, and the *time* of payment of the legal tender notes. One other points Allow me to refer to the re-convertible feature of the six per cent. twenty years bonds. That is, I confess, a pet idea of mine, but I find it favorably regarded by others, though new. You will readily perceive that when this comes to be understood by the public the United States Government is going to pick up all the floating funds throughout the whole country, which the owners do not require to use in less than three, four, five or six months, whatever time you fix. Every business man seems to think this would be the means by which the Government would borrow, in the aggregate, a large amount. For who would not lend the United States his spare funds when he knew he could get a legal tender for it, with interest whenever he called for it? This would increase the value of the twenty years six per cent. bonds. Let the legal tender notes be convertible at any time into any unsold securities of the United States, in the hands of the Secretary of the Treasury, whether now authorized or hereafter to be issued. But only let the six per cent. bonds be reconvertible into legal tender Treasury notes.

Give my regards to Mr. Hooper.

Yours very truly,

J. E. WILLIAMS.

Hon. E. G. SPAULDING, Washington, D. C.

On the following Monday, January 20th, Mr. Spaulding, from the Sub-committee of Ways and Means, reported to the General Committee an additional section, and a new title to the legal tender note bill, which were adopted by the Committee of Ways and Means. The new section is as follows:

SECTION 2. "To enable the Secretary of the Treasury to fund the treasury notes and floating debt of the United States. he is hereby further authorized to issue on the credit of the United States coupon bonds, or registered bonds, to an amount not exceeding $500,000,000, in sums of $100, $200, $500, $1,000, $5,000, $10,000 and $20,000, and in such proportions of each as the exigencies of the public service may require, bearing interest at the rate of six per cent per annum, redeemable after twenty years at the pleasure of the United States, which bonds the Secretary of the Treasury is hereby authorized to deliver at their par value to any creditor or creditors having demands due against the United States, in payment thereof, and to deliver the same to officers, employees and individuals in payment for services rendered, for supplies, subsistence and materials furnished to the United States; and he may also exchange such bonds at any time for lawful money of the United States, or for any of the treasury notes that have been or may hereafter be issued under any former act of Congress, or that may be issued under the provisions of this act."

The new title to the bill adopted at this meeting of the Committee was as follows:

"An act to authorize the issue of United States Notes and for the redemption or funding thereof, and for funding the floating debt of the United States."

Soon after this additional section and new title were adopted by the Committee of Ways and Means, Mr. Spaulding submitted the bill and additional section to Secretary Chase and the Assistant Secretary, Mr. Harrington. At this interview the form of the bill and the manner of engraving, signing and issuing the legal tender notes was fully discussed, as well as the form and manner of exchanging them for the six per cent. bonds. The Secretary suggested that it would be necessary to limit the place for exchanging the notes for bonds to the Treasury at Washington instead of the Sub-treasuries at other cities, and that it would be necessary to have one or more penal sections to guard against counterfeiting. The original bill and additional section were finally left with the

Secretary to put into such form as he desired, incorporating the amendments which he had proposed, in order to enable him to execute the provisions of the bill with facility as soon as it should become a law.

On the 22d of January, 1862, Secretary Chase returned to Mr. Spaulding the bill as modified and amended by him, accompanied by the following letter:

TREASURY DEPARTMENT, Jan. 22, 1862.

MY DEAR SIR—I have carefully examined the bill and additional section which you left with me, and availing myself of the aid of the Assistant Secretary, have amended the bill, retaining the whole substance of yours, but introducing such modifications as the settled modes of business in the department and considerations of convenience and economy seem to suggest.

For example—the exchange of notes for bonds is confined to the course of business of the department, by limiting the power of Assistant Treasury and Depositories to the receipt of notes and issuing certificates, entitling the holder to bonds by which serious risks are avoided; and the denominations of bonds is left to the discretion of the Secretary, by which a considerable saving will probably be effected; as the demand for some denominations is so limited (for $20,000 for instance) that it may hardly be worth while to engrave a plate. These examples show the nature of the modifications.

The appropriation for expenses is put at three hundred thousand dollars. Should the act be fully executed by the issue of bonds to the amount of five hundred millions of dollars, this sum will not probably suffice. It has been usual in providing for the issue of bonds merely without notes, to allow a much larger proportion for expenses. I will send you, if desired, a statement which will make this clear.

Regretting exceedingly that it is found necessary to resort to the measure of making fundable notes of the United States a legal tender, but heartily desiring to co-operate with the Committee in all measures to meet existing necessities in the mode most useful and least hurtful to general interest, I remain, with great respect,

Very sincerely yours, S. P. CHASE.

Hon. E. G. SPAULDING.

The bill as amended by the Secretary was again submitted to the Committee of Ways and Means, and adopted; and thereupon, on the 22d of January, 1862, Mr. Spaulding again reported the bill to the House (Bill No. 240) in the nature of a substitute for Bill No. 187. It was read twice, and made the special order for the 28th inst., at one o'clock.

Each day's delay made it more and more apparent that the bill must pass in order to meet the overwhelming demands made upon the Treasury to sustain the army and navy. The end seemed to justify the means contemplated by the bill.

On the 23d inst. Secretary Chase directed his private Secretary,

H. G. Plants, Esq., to request Mr. Spaulding to furnish a copy of the amended legal tender note bill to the *National Intelligencer* for publication.

Up to this time Col. Seaton, the editor of that paper, had not been favorable to the bill, and it was deemed important that the old *National Intelligencer* should support the measure.

The following is a copy of the note received by Mr. Spaulding from Mr. Plants:

TREASURY DEPARTMENT, Jan. 23, 1862.

SIR—I am directed by the Secretary to ask you if you will be so good as to send a copy of the Treasury note bill to the *National Intelligencer*, in order that it may be printed to-morrow.

Very respectfully, H. G. PLANTS.
Hon. E. G. SPAULDING.

REPLY.

HOUSE OF REPRESENTATIVES, Jan. 24, 1862,

DEAR SIR—The note of Mr. Plants reached me this morning, and I have handed the U. S. demand note bill to Col. Seaton in person, to be published in the next issue of the *National Intelligencer*. It is important that there should be full co-operation on the part of Col. Seaton, the Cabinet, and all our friends on the financial measures pending in Congress, to overcome the opposition already developed and ensure success. My interview with Col. Seaton leads me to suppose that he will hereafter act in concert with us.

Yours truly, E. G. SPAULDING.
Hon. S. P. CHASE, Secretary of Treasury.

On the 28th inst., the bill being the special order in the House, Mr. Spaulding opened the debate upon it in the following

SPEECH.

The House being in Committee of the Whole (Mr. KELLOGG, of Illinois, in the chair) on the *Demand Treasury note* bill—

Mr. SPAULDING spoke as follows:

Mr. CHAIRMAN: This is an important measure, and I may be indulged for a few moments in explaining its objects, the situation of our finances, and the grounds upon which we rest this measure, and expect it to be adopted. In the first place, I will refer to the loan bills passed at the extra session of Congress, in July, in order to show how we obtained the means to carry on the Government from that time to the present, and to show how the Secretary of the Treasury has performed his duty. These bills were passed, the first on the 17th of July, and the other on the 5th of August. They gave the Secretary of the Treasury power to pledge the credit of the United States to the extent of $250,000,000. Reflections have been made by some gentlemen on the manner in which the Secretary of the Treasury had performed his duty in borrowing that money, and with some disposition to criticise his actions. As a general reply, I will say that the Secretary has acted in strict conformity with the law, and borrowed money at the rates authorized by Congress.

And, sir, I am disposed, upon this floor and elsewhere, to sustain the Secretary and all Departments of the Government where they have discharged their duties in accordance with the laws which have been passed by us.

The Secretary of the Treasury first borrowed $100,000,000, giving Treasury notes bearing seven and three-tenths per cent. interest, and he next issued United States bonds at six per cent. interest to the extent of $50,000,000, at the equivalent of par for seven per cent. bonds, and raised about $44,650,000; upon such loan, a discount of over $5,300,000 was sustained. These were the best terms that could be obtained, and were regarded at the time as very favorable to the Government.

But if he has borrowed the money at a high rate, it was authorized by the act of July. I am disposed to sustain the Secretary in what he has done. He has acted in good faith, and he should be sustained by us all.

I may be permitted to say, in explanation of some of the estimates which I shall introduce presently, differing, as they do, from the estimates of the Secretary of the Treasury in his annual report, that since his annual report, he has changed his own views as to what the expenses of the war will be up to July next, and what they will also be up to July, 1863, and that he substantially agrees with me now as to what those expenses will be.

In the discussion of this important measure, I desire, Mr. Chairman, to present the entire plan, with a view to enlist the co-operation not only of all Departments of the Government, but also the co-operation of all the members of the House, without regard to party distinctions. Hearty co-operation is desirable to the success of the important financial measures that will be presented.

Our finances deserve our most serious attention. The ways and means of carrying on the war should enlist the grave consideration of every gentleman on this floor who desires the preservation of this Government. We were never in greater peril than at this moment. It will require all our best energies to successfully meet the crisis through which we are passing. I am oppressed by the magnitude of the work before us. But, sir, I will not, I dare not—I trust we shall not any of us—shrink from the responsibility of performing every duty devolved upon us in this great crisis of our national affairs.

The bill before us is a war measure, a measure of *necessity*, and not of choice, presented by the Committee of Ways and Means to meet the most pressing demands upon the Treasury to sustain the army and navy, until they can make a vigorous advance upon the traitors, and crush out the rebellion. These are extraordinary times, and extraordinary measures must be resorted to in order to save our Government, and preserve our nationality.

This bill, in addition to the fifty million of demand notes authorized by the act of July last, authorizes the Secretary of the Treasury to issue, on the credit of the United States, one hundred millions of dollars of Treasury notes, not bearing interest, payable to the bearer at the Treasury, or at the office of the Assistant Treasurer in the city of New York, at the pleasure of the United States, and of such denominations as he may deem expedient, and not less than five dollars each; and such notes and all other United States notes payable on demand, not bearing interest, heretofore authorized, are made receivable for all debts and demands due to the United States, and for all salaries, debts, and demands owing by the

United States to individuals, corporations, and associations within the United States, and are also declared lawful money and a legal tender in payment of all debts, public and private, within the United States, making altogether $150,000,000 legal tender demand notes.

Provision is also made for the convenient exchange of such notes for six per cent. bonds of the United States redeemable in twenty years.

Further to enable the Secretary of the Treasury to fund the Treasury notes and floating debt of the United States, he is authorized to issue, on the credit of the United States, coupon bonds or registered bonds to an amount not exceeding five hundred millions dollars, and redeemable at the pleasure of the Government after twenty years from date, and bearing interest at the rate of six per cent. per annum, payable semi-annually; and the bonds thus authorized are to be of such denomination, not less than fifty dollars, as may be determined upon by the Secretary of the Treasury, or in sums not less than $2,500; for which, if requested, the Secretary of the Treasury, if he deem it expedient, may issue similar bonds, the principal and interest of which may be expressed in the currency of any foreign country, and payable there. The Secretary is authorized to issue said bonds at their par value to any creditor or creditors of the United States who may elect to receive them in satisfaction of their demands; provided that all such claims or demands shall have been first audited and settled by the accounting officers of the Treasury; and the Secretary of the Treasury may also exchange such bonds at any time for lawful money of the United States, or for any of the Treasury notes that have been or may hereafter be issued under any former act of Congress, or that may be issued under the provisions of this act.

The bill is simple and perspicuous in its terms, and easy of execution. It is a Government measure, and the officers of Government are required to execute its provisions.

By the time the Secretary of the Treasury can get these notes engraved, printed, and signed, ready for use, all other available means at his command, and in the Treasury, will be exhausted. This measure is therefore presented under the highest prerogatives of Government. The army and navy now in the service must be paid. They must be supplied with food, clothing, arms, ammunition, and all other material of war, to render them effective in maintaining the Government and putting down the rebellion. Having exhausted other means of sustaining the Government, this measure is brought forward as the best that can be devised in the present exigency to relieve the necessities of the Treasury; and I trust it will pass without delay.

At the extra session in July last, Congress authorized the Secretary of the Treasury to borrow $250,000,000, for which he was authorized to issue coupon bonds, or registered bonds, or Treasury notes, in such proportions of each as he might deem advisable. The bonds were to be issued for twenty years, at a rate not exceeding seven per cent. interest per annum, payable half-yearly; and the Treasury notes were to be issued in denominations of not less than $50 each, at three years, with interest at 7 3-10 per annum, payable half-yearly, and exchangeable at any time for twenty years six per cent. bonds. Or, at the option of the Secretary, he was permitted to issue $50,000,000 of the above loan in Treasury notes, on demand, in denominations of not less than five dollars each, without interest, and made receivable in payment of salaries or other dues owing by the United States; or, in his discretion, he was authorized to issue Treasury notes at one year, bearing interest at 3 65-100 per cent. per annum, exchangeable at any time in sums of $100, or upwards, for the three years Treasury notes bearing 7 3-10 per cent. interest; but in the aggregate not to exceed $250,000,000. A further provision was made, however, to wit: that the Secretary of the Treasury might negotiate any part of the loan for six per cent. twenty years' bonds, *at a rate not less than the equivalent of par, for bonds bearing seven per cent. interest per annum, half-yearly, payable in twenty years.*

Under these provisions, the Secretary of the Treasury has borrowed on the 7 3-10 per cent. Treasury notes, payable in three years	$100,000,000
On twenty years six per cent. bonds, reduced to the equivalent at par of seven per cent. per annum, half-yearly, say at 89½. ($44,661,230 97 actually received into the Treasury), for which six per cent. bonds were issued	50,000,000
Issued and put in circulation as currency (and to be put into circulation within a few days) all the demand Treasury notes authorized in July, not bearing interest	50,090,000
Borrowed on the loan bill of July	$200,000,000
Paid out to contractors and others 7 30-100 Treasury notes within the last few days, say	3,516,500
	$203,516,500

The total amount of the public debt up to the present time, and for which U. S. stock and Treasury notes have been issued, is as follows:

Up to July 1, 1861	$ 90,867,828 68
There was paid to creditors, or exchanged for coin at par, at different dates in July and August, six per cent. two years' notes to the amount of	14,019,034 66
There was borrowed, at par, in the same months, upon sixty days' six per cent. notes, the sum of	12,877,750 00
There was borrowed, at par, on the 19th of August, three years' seven and three-tenths per cent bonds, issued for most part to the subscribers to the national loan	50,000,000 00
There was borrowed on the 1st of October upon like securities	50,000,000 00
There was borrowed, at par, of seven per cent. on the 10th of November, upon twenty years' six per cent. bonds reduced to the equivalent of sevens, including interest	50,000,000 00
There have been issued and circulated of Treasury notes payable on demand	39,000,000 00
Making an aggregate debt in various forms, to January 15, 1862	306,764,613 34
I estimate that the amount required up to July 1, 1862, will be	343,235,386 66
Total debt estimated to July 1, 1862	650,000,000 00
I estimate for the fiscal year up to July 1, 1863, if the war continues to that time	550,000,000 00
Total indebtedness, liquidated and unliquidated, to July 1, 1863	$1,200,000,000 00

This estimate exceeds that of the Secretary of the Treasury by $300,000,000 to July 1, 1863. This, however, includes all indebtedness against the Government, whether funded or not, and all accounts in process of being audited, and such as are passing through the hands of the accounting officers.

There is now over $100,000,000 of accrued indebtedness, in different forms, that should be paid at an early day.

With this large accrued indebtedness, and with the prospect that (unless this bill is adopted) the Government will put on the market, to the highest bidder, still further issue of bonds, to the amount of $250,000,000 to $300,000,000, to pay current expenses to July next, it is not expected that even the present price of United States stocks can be maintained if forced on the market at this time. We have the alternative, either to go into the market and sell our bonds for what they will command, or to pass this bill, or find some better mode, if one can be devised, to raise means to carry on the war. The Secretary has the means of defraying the daily expenses required to be disbursed from the Treasury for only a few days longer. He has on hand about one-fifth of the loan made in November last, a small portion of the demand Treasury notes authorized by the act of July—say $10,000,000 not yet issued—and such of the remaining 7 3-10 and 3 65-100 Treasury notes authorized by that act as can be used in paying contractors, for supplies, and for salaries, and other Government dues to such persons as are willing to receive them. With the enormous expenditures of the Government, to pay the extraordinary expenses of the war, it requires no extended calculation to show that the Treasury must be supplied from some source, or the Government must stop payment in a very few days.

You cannot borrow of capitalists any more money on twenty years seven per cent. bonds, nor on your 7 3-10 Treasury notes at the rates fixed by the act of July last. If you offer to the people and put on the market $300,000,000 more, to the highest bidder, in the present aspect of affairs, they would not be taken, except at ruinous rates of discount. That policy would depreciate the bonds already taken by the banks and the people who are most loyal to the Government, and who came forward as your best friends, and furnished the means so much needed during the last few months to organize your army and navy; and, besides, depreciation would greatly increase the debt, by requiring a much larger amount of bonds to be issued than would be needed if your loans were taken at par. A loan put upon the market in the present depressed state of United States stocks, to be followed by other larger loans, is not regarded as a favorable mode of providing the means for maintaining the Government at the present time. If it had been adopted at first it might possibly have been the best mode; but it is now too late to essay that plan, and I believe it would be ruinous to adopt it. I fear the 20 years six per cent. bonds would, under the pressure, fall to 75, 70, 60, and even 50 cents. This would be a ruinous mode of raising the means to carry on the Government.

What, then, is to be done? The Secretary of the Treasury in his annual report does not recommend the issue of demand Treasury notes, although he points out many advantages that would result to the Government from the issue. He *suggests* two plans: first, the issue of demand Treasury notes; and second, a National currency, secured by a pledge of United States stocks, to be issued by banks and associations, with proper regulations for their redemption by the banks themselves. On the propriety of the issue of Treasury notes by the Government, to be put in circulation as money, the Secretary says:

"The first of these plans was partially adopted at the last session of Congress, in the provision authorizing the Secretary to issue United States notes, payable in coin, to an amount not exceeding fifty millions of dollars. That provision may be so extended as to reach the average circulation of the country, while a moderate tax, gradually augmented, on bank notes, will relieve the national from the competition of local circulation. It has been already suggested that the substitution of a National for a State currency, upon this plan, would be equivalent to a loan to the Government without interest, except on the fund to be kept in coin, and without expense, except the cost of preparation, issue, and redemption; while the people would gain the additional advantage of a uniform currency, and relief from a considerable burden in the form of interest on debt."

These remarks of the Secretary were made before the suspension of specie payments. The situation of the country is now very different from what it was two months ago. The circumstances have changed; and the Secretary and Congress, will find it necessary, in the present exigency, to conform their action to what *can* be done, and not to what they would *like* to do, were it otherwise practicable.

The second plan of the Secretary, and the one which he recommends for adoption, namely, a national currency, to be issued by banks, and secured by a pledge of United States stocks, the sub-Committee of Ways and Means have examined with considerable care. A bill has been prepared and printed for the use of the Committee, which may, after some modification, be reported to the House for its action. The Committee have come to the conclusion that, however meritorious this system may be in providing a way for funding the stocks of the United States, and however perfect the system may be made by Congress, it cannot, if adopted, be made available soon enough to meet the immediately-impending necessities of the Government.

This new system of banking would necessarily go into operation slowly. The existing circulation of bank notes in the loyal States is supposed to be about $140,000,000. This new currency, when issued, would come into competition with the existing circulation of the banks already established in the several States; and in the present embarrassed condition of monetary affairs, several months must necessarily elapse before any considerable amount of United States stocks would be absorbed by banks under this proposed new law. As an ultimate mode of funding some part of the large amount of Government stock which has already been issued, and which must from time to time be issued, it may be very valuable; and the national currency upon it would no doubt obtain a wide circulation, and greatly facilitate the payment of taxes and other dues to the Government. But with a navy and army of 600,000 in the field, requiring, with the other expenses of the Government, an average daily expenditure of more than $1,600,000, this new system of banking will not afford relief to the Treasury in time to enable the Secretary to meet the pressing demands that are made upon him.

The duties received at the different custom-houses, and the taxes levied at the extra session, or that may now be levied, will be wholly inadequate to meet the requirements of the Treasury in the present emergency during the next six months.

If you cannot borrow the money on the credit of the United States, except at ruinous rates of discount, and cannot make the new banking system available in time, and cannot realize the amount required from your tariff and tax bills, in what mode can the means be obtained, and the Government be carried on? It is believed that the only way in which it can be done is by issuing Treasury notes payable on demand, and making them a legal tender in payment of all debts, public and private, and by adequate taxation, to be imposed by new bills. This will bring into full exercise all the higher powers of Government under the Constitution. The Constitution confers on Congress the power (art. 1, sec. 8:)

"To lay and collect taxes, duties, imposts, and excises, to pay the debts and provide for the common defence and general welfare of the United States.

To borrow money on the credit of the United States.

To regulate commerce with foreign nations, among the several States, and with the Indian tribes.

To coin money, regulate the value thereof, and of foreign coins.

To raise and *support* armies.

To provide and *maintain* a navy.

To make all *laws* which shall be *necessary* and proper for carrying into execution the foregoing powers, and all other powers vested by the Constitution in the Government of the United States, or in any Department or officer thereof."

These are among the high powers of Government which must now be brought into full, ample play. The table which I have before me, procured from the Census bureau, shows that the true value of the property, real and personal, within the United States, is *sixteen billions, one hundred and fifty-nine millions, six hundred and sixteen thousand and sixty-eight dollars*, ($16,159,616,068,) and the assessed value to be $12,006,756,585. (See Appendix.)

The power in the Constitution to "lay and collect taxes, duties, imposts, and excises," is general and unlimited. Congress has the power to levy and collect any amount of taxes that may be necessary to preserve its existence and pay all its *debts*. Government has a claim, a mortgage in fact, on all this property, to that extent. Will Congress do its duty in passing bills to collect these taxes? This is the vital question. Will Congress have the firmness and the courage to impose the necessary taxation to sustain the credit of the Government? Direct taxation, excises, and internal duties, are new features within the United States. They will be heavy burdens on the people, but essential to sustain the circulation of demand Treasury notes. The tax-gatherer will be an unwelcome visitor to most people, but his face must soon be familiar.

Some members of Congress may hesitate to vote for the tax bills, fearing that they may not be in favor with their constituency at home. Under these circumstances, will members of Congress meet the question boldly and firmly? Here is the whole property of the country at the will of Congress. You have the power to tax it to an unlimited extent, if necessary to sustain the Government.

This is the *capital*, $16,000,000,000,000 in amount, on which your Treasury notes and bonds rest. This claim of Government, in the hands of Congress, is direct and specific on the banks throughout the United States, including the gold and silver in their vaults; on commerce; on all kinds of production and business; on railroads, steamboats, and their passengers; on gas companies; on manufacturing companies of all kinds; in short, all real and personal estate of every kind is held subject to the payment of the Treasury notes and bonds issued by the Government. Congress is clothed with this mighty power to sustain the nation at this time. Will you hesitate to do your duty? This is what the people, the capitalist, the merchant, and all who confide in your demand notes, want to know. If they take these notes, they want to know positively whether you will enforce the claim of the Government upon the property of the country, to the full extent necessary to redeem the Treasury notes, and pay punctually the interest on the bonds which they take of you to sustain the government. Unless you are prepared to satisfy the country on this point, it is in vain to issue bonds or notes, and expect them to pass currently among the people. Unless this is done they will depreciate, and they ought to depreciate; but with ample taxation, cheerfully voted by Congress, they will be the very best security in the country, because the whole property of the country is held for their redemption. Congress has a plain duty to perform. It has ample power. This power should now be enforced. Will Congress perform this duty?

I cannot doubt that it will. The emergency is great, and the exercise of this power is now an imperative necessity, in order to sustain the credit of the United States and justify the Government in issuing so large an amount of Treasury notes, to circulate as money and be made a legal tender in the payment of debts. Congress (as well as the Committee of Ways and Means) is of opinion that we must raise by direct taxes, excises, internal duties, and duties on imports, during the current year, at least $150,000,000. That was shown by the recent resolution passed by the Senate and House. This will pay the current ordinary expenses of the Government, and the interest on all the extraordinary war debt, and create a sinking fund for retiring annually a portion of the Treasury notes.

In carrying on the existing war, and putting down the rebellion, it is necessary to bring into exercise all the sovereign power of the Government to sustain itself. The war power must be exercised to its fullest extent. The money power of the Government must be brought into requisition. The power to tax must be availed of. All the energies of the nation must be aroused and brought into action. The power of the Government and the means of the people must all be devoted to this great work. The Government must be preserved, and this nation of thirty-four States must be perpetuated. The life of the nation is in peril; and all we have and all we hope for must be devoted to maintain its existence, until peace and quiet are restored in every part of our common country.

This bill is a *necessary means* of carrying into execution the powers granted in the Constitution "to raise and *support* armies," and "to provide and *maintain* a navy."

In the present *crisis* of our national affairs, it is necessary that the army should be "supported," and the navy "maintained." This necessity will not be questioned by any loyal member on this floor.

The Constitution provides that "*all the laws necessary and proper* for carrying into execution the foregoing powers" may be passed by Congress.

If the *end* be legitimate, and within the scope of the Constitution, all the *means* that are appropriate, which are plainly adapted to that end, and which are not prohibited, may be constitutionally employed to carry it into effect.

If a certain means to the exercise of any of the powers expressly given by the Constitution to the Government of the Union be an appropriate measure, not prohibited by the Constitution, the degree of its necessity is a question of *legislative discretion;* not of judicial cognizance.

The Government of the United States is not prohibited by the Constitution from issuing Treasury notes on demand, and making them a *legal tender* in payment of all debts within its jurisdiction. The Constitution (Art. 1, Sec. 10) prohibits the *States* from making any thing but gold and silver coin a legal tender in payment of debts; but this does not at all restrict the sovereign power of the United States. Congress has the power to coin money "regulate the *value* thereof, and of foreign coin." Gold and silver by long practice—a practice that has continued for centuries among all nations—has become the legal money of the world in all commercial transactions. Its real intrinsic value is not as great as that fixed upon it by Governments. All Governments fix the value of gold and silver, and without the Government stamp, gold and silver would be a simple commodity, like other things having intrinsic value. Some Governments fix the value of coin higher, and some lower, just as each, for itself chooses to determine. Any other metal or thing that should be stamped, and its value regulated by all the Governments of the world, would pass equally well in all commercial transactions as gold and silver, although not intrinsically as valuable. Exchequer bills or Treasury notes whose value is fixed by Government, and stamped as money, would pass as money in the payment of debts within the jurisdiction of the Government fixing such value.

In regulating the value of "coin," either foreign or domestic, Congress may provide that gold and silver shall be of no greater value in the payment of debts within the United States than the Treasury notes issued on the credit of this Government, which stamps such coin and fixes its value. These high powers of Government have been frequently exercised by Great Britain during her continental wars, in making the Bank of England notes receivable for public dues, and virtually a legal tender in payment of debts, by suspending the statutory clause requiring specie payments within the United Kingdom; and other Governments of Europe have exercised the same high prerogatives whenever necessary to preserve their existence. But we are not left to this argument alone for constitutional power to issue these demand notes and make them a legal tender in payment of debts, as I will endeavor hereafter to show.

The Constitution provides that Congress shall have power to pass "all laws necessary and proper" for carrying into execution all the powers granted to the Government of the United States, or any department or officer thereof.

The word necessary, as used, is not limited by the additional word "proper," but enlarged thereby.

"If the word *necessary* were used in the strict, rigorous sense, it would be an extraordinary departure from the usual course of the human mind, as exhibited in solemn instruments, to add another word, the only possible effect of which is to qualify that strict and rigorous meaning, and to present clearly the idea of a choice of means in the course of legislation. If no means are to be resorted to but such as are *indispensably* necessary, there can be neither sense nor utility in adding the word '*proper;*' for the *indispensable necessity* would shut out from view all consideration of the *propriety* of the means."—3 *Story's Commentaries*, sec. 122.

Alexander Hamilton, in discussing these high powers of the Constitution, says:

"The authorities essential to the care of the common defence are these: to raise armies; to build and equip fleets; to prescribe rules for the government of both; to direct their operations; to provide for their support. These powers ought to exist, WITHOUT LIMITATION; because it is impossible to foresee or define the extent and variety of national exigencies, and the correspondent extent and variety of the means necessary to satisfy them. The circumstances which endanger the safety of nations are infinite; and for this reason no constitutional shackles can wisely be imposed on the power to which the care of it is committed" * * * * "This power ought to be under the direction of the same councils which are appointed to preside over *the common defence*." * * * * "It must be admitted as a necessary consequence, that there can be NO LIMITATION of that authority which is to provide for the defence and protection of the community in any matter essential to its efficacy; that is, in any matter essential to the *formation, direction,* or *support* of the NATIONAL FORCES."

This statement, adds Hamilton—

"Rests upon two axioms, simple as they are universal: the *means* ought to be proportioned to the *end;* the persons from whose agency the attainment of the *end* is expected ought to possess the *means* by which it is to be attained."—*Federalist*, No. 23, pp. 95, 96.

Congress may judge of the necessity in the present exigency. It may decide whether it will authorize the Secretary of the Treasury to issue demand Treasury notes, and make them a legal tender in payment of debts, or whether it will put its six or seven per cent. bonds on the market, at ruinous rates of discount, and raise the money, at any sacrifice the money-lender may require, to meet the pressing demands upon the Treasury. In the one case the Government will be able to pay its debts at fair rates of interest; in the other, it must go into the streets *shinning* for the means, like an individual in failing circumstances, and sure of being used up in the end by the avarice of those who may exact unreasonable terms. The Government needs and should have, in her present peril, the aid and protection of all patriotic citizens.

But, sir, knowing the power of money, and the disposition there is among men to use it for the acquisition of greater gain, I am unwilling that this Government, with all its immense power and resources, should be left in the hands of any class of men, bankers or money-lenders, however respectable and patriotic they may be. The Government is much stronger than any of them. Its capital is much greater. It has control of all the bankers' money, and all the brokers' money, and all the property of the thirty millions of people under its jurisdiction. Why, then, should it go into Wall street, State street, Chestnut street, or any other street, begging for money? Their money is not as secure as Government money. All the gold they possess would not carry on the Government for ninety days. They issue only promises to pay, which, if Congress does its duty, are not half as secure as United States Treasury notes based on adequate taxation upon all the property of the country.

Why, then, go into the streets at all to borrow money? I am opposed, in our present extremity, to all shifts of this kind. I prefer to assert the power and dignity of the Government, by the issue of its own notes, pledging the faith, the honor, and property of the whole loyal people of the country to maintain their circulation and provide for their redemption.

On the question of constitutional power we are not left without the recorded opinions of the ablest jurists in the country.—1 *Kent's Com.*, 351–2; *McCulloch* v. *The State of Maryland*, 4 *Wheat,* R., 413—20.

Chief Justice Marshall, Daniel Webster, and Judge Kent lay down the doctrine as follows:

"The Government of the United States is one of enumerated powers, and it can exercise only the powers granted to it; but though limited in its powers, it is supreme within its sphere of action. It is the Government of the people of the United States, and emanated from them. Its powers were delegated by all, and it represents all, and acts for all.

"There is nothing in the Constitution which excludes *incidental* or *implied* powers, The Articles of Confederation gave nothing to the United States but what was expressly granted; but the new Constitution dropped the word *expressly*, and left the question whether a particular power was granted to depend on a fair construction of the whole instrument. No constitution can contain an accurate detail of all the sub-divisions of its powers, and all the *means* by which they might be carried into execution.

It would render it too prolix. Its nature requires that only the great outlines should be marked and its important objects designated, and all the minor ingredients left to be deduced from the nature of those objects. The sword and the purse, all the external relations, and no inconsiderable portion of the industry of the nation, were entrusted to the General Government; and a Government entrusted with such ample powers, on the due execution of which the happiness and prosperity of the people vitally depended, must also be entrusted with *ample means for their execution.* Unless the words imperiously require it, we ought not to adopt a construction which would impute to the framers of the Constitution, when granting great powers for the public good, the intention of impeding their exercise, by withholding a *choice of means.* The powers given to the Government imply the ordinary means of execution; and the Government, in all sound reason and fair interpretations, must have the choice of the means which it deems the most convenient and appropriate to the execution of the power. The Constitution has not left the right to Congress to employ the necessary means for the execution of its powers to general reasoning. Article I, section 8, of the Constitution, expressly confers on Congress the power 'to make all laws that may be necessary and proper to carry into execution the foregoing powers.' Congress may employ such means and pass such laws as it may deem necessary to carry into execution great powers granted by the Constitution; and *necessary* means, in the sense of the Constitution, does not import an absolute physical necessity, so strong that one thing cannot exist without the other. It stands for any means calculated to produce the end. The word necessary admits of all degrees of comparison. A thing may be necessary, or very necessary, or absolutely, or indispensably necessary. The word is used in various senses; and in its construction, the subject, the context, the intention, are all to be taken into view. The powers of the Government were given for the welfare of the nation. They were intended to endure for ages to come, and to be adapted to the various *crisis* in human affairs. To prescribe the specific means by which Government should in all future time execute its power, and to confine the choice of means to such narrow limits as should not leave it in the power of Congress to adopt any which might be appropriate and conducive to the end, would be most unwise and pernicious, because it would be an attempt to provide, by immutable rules, for exigencies which, if foreseen at all, must have been foreseen dimly, and would deprive the Legislature of the capacity to avail itself of experience, or to exercise its reason, and accommodate its legislation to circumstances. If the end be legitimate, and within the scope of the Constitution, all means which are appropriate, and plainly adapted to this end, and which are not prohibited by the Constitution, are lawful."

It is plainly within the scope of the Constitution that the Government should maintain itself; that the army should be supported; that the navy should be maintained. The ways and means of doing this are left to Congress to provide. Congress may do this entirely by taxation. It may provide by law to levy and collect taxes enough every year to pay the whole expenses of the war during each current year, and so "pay as we go." It may issue six per cent. bonds and sell them on the market for what they will bring—even if they will not sell for over fifty cents on the dollar—to raise money to carry on the war. It may issue Treasury notes payable on demand, and make them a legal tender in payment of debts. Either one or all of these modes of paying the expenses of the Government is left to the discretion of Congress. Either mode is constitutional; and it is left to the *sound discretion* of Congress to decide which mode it will adopt, or whether it will adopt a part of each, as being the best in the present crisis.

My own impression is, that it will be best for us to adopt, in part, all of these modes for providing the means.

1. Raise by taxation the current year, over and above the amount received from duties on imports, the sum of $150,000,000.

2. Issue $100,000,000 of demand Treasury notes in addition to the $50,000,000 authorized in July, making them a legal tender in payment of debts, and exchangeable at any time for 6 per cent. twenty years' bonds; with a further issue of demand notes if Congress shall hereafter deem it necessary.

3. Provide for the issue of all the twenty years' 6 per cent. bonds that may be necessary to fund the demand Treasury notes, and other fundable Treasury notes that may be issued, (say $500,000,000 six per cent. twenty years' coupon bonds,) and pledge $30,000,000 of the annual taxes to pay the interest half-yearly thereon, and pledge $25,600,000 more, as a sinking fund to redeem the principal in twenty years.

1. This tax of $150,000,000 would afford an ample basis on which to rest the credit of the Government for this large issue of Treasury notes and bonds, and would insure the punctual payment of the interest to the capitalists who might hold them.

2. The demand notes put in circulation would meet the present exigencies of the Government, in the discharge of its existing liabilities to the army, navy, and contractors, and for supplies, materials, and munitions of war. These notes would find their way into all the channels of trade among the people; and as they accumulate in the hands of capitalists, they would exchange them for the six per cent. twenty years' bonds.

These circulating notes in the hands of the people would enable them to pay the taxes imposed, and would facilitate all business operations between farmers, mechanics, commercial business men, and banks, and be equally as good as, and in most cases better, than the present irredeemable circulation issued by the banks.

3. The $500,000,000 six per cent. twenty years' bonds in the hands of the Secretary of the Treasury, ready to be issued, would afford ample opportunity for funding the Treasury notes as fast as capitalists might desire to exchange Treasury notes not bearing interest for coupon bonds of the United States bearing six per cent. interest, and amply secured by a tax upon the people and all their property.

In this way the Government will be able to get along with its immediate and pressing necessities without being obliged to force its bonds on the market at ruinous rates of discount; the people, under heavy taxation, will be shielded against high rates of interest; and the capitalists will be afforded a fair compensation for the use of their money during the pending struggle of the country for national existence.

A suspension of specie payment is greatly to be deplored, but it is not a fatal step in an exigency like the present. The British Government and the Bank of England remained under suspension from 1797 to 1821—'2—a period of twenty-five years. During this time England successfully resisted the imperial power of the Emperor Napoleon, and preserved her own imperilled existence. During all this time the people of Great Britain advanced in wealth, population, and resources. Gold is not as valuable as the productions of the farmer and mechanic, for it is not as indispensable as are food and raiment. Our army and navy must have what is far more valuable to them than gold and silver. They must have food, clothing, and the material of war. Treasury notes issued by the Government, on the faith of the whole people, will purchase these indispensable articles, and the war can be prosecuted until we can enforce obedience to the Constitution and laws, and an honorable peace be thereby secured. This being accomplished, I will be among the first to advocate a speedy return to specie payments, and all measures that are calculated to preserve the honor and dignity of the Government in time of peace, and which I regret are not practicable in the prosecution of this war.

I do not despair; on the contrary, I have an abiding faith in the patriotism, firmness, and resources of the people to maintain this Government. I feel that we are in great peril; but when the people and our rulers become sufficiently aroused to fully appreciate the magnitude and probable duration of the rebellion—a rebellion that has grown into most gigantic proportions—then shall we be able to put forth the energy and the means necessary to crush it.

An early and successful advance of our armies is of the utmost importance. We need such an advance to sustain the financial credit of the Government. We need it to prevent foreign intervention; we need it to rouse the flagging energies of the people; and above all, we need it to vindicate the courage and invincibility of our brave soldiers, who are so anxious to be led on to victory.

APPENDIX.

TABLE A.

True Value of Real and Personal Estate, according to the seventh Census, 1850, aud the eighth Census, 1860, respectively.

STATES.	1850. Real and Personal Estate.	1860. Real and Personal Estate.	Increase.	Incr'ase per ct. for 10 years.
Alabama	$ 228,204,332	$ 495,237,078	$267,032,746	117 01
Arkansas	39,841,025	219,256,473	179,415,448	450 32
California *	22,161,872	207,874,613	185,712,741	837 98
Connecticut	155,707,980	444,274,114	288,566,134	185 32
Delaware	21,062,556	46,242,181	25,179,625	119 54
Florida	22,862,270	73,101,500	50,239,230	219 74
Georgia	335,425,714	645,895,237	310,469,523	92 56
Illinois	156,265,006	871,860,282	715,595,276	457 93
Indiana	202,650,264	528,835,371	326,185,107	160 95
Iowa	23,714,638	247,338,265	223,623,627	942 97
Kansas		31,327,895		
Kentucky	301,628,456	666,043,112	364,414,656	120 81
Louisiana	233,998,764	602,118,568	368,119,804	157 30
Maine	122,777,571	190,211,600	67,434,029	54 92
Maryland	219,217,364	376,919,944	157,702,580	71 93
Massachusetts	573,342,286	815,237,433	241,895,147	42 19
Michigan	59,787,255	257,163,983	197,376,728	330 13
Minnesota	not ret'd in full.	52,294,413		
Mississippi	228,951,130	607,324,911	378,373,781	165 26
Missouri	137,247,707	501,214,398	363,966,691	265 18
New Hampshire	103,652,835	156,310,860	52,658,025	50 80
New Jersey†	200,000,000	467,918,324	267,918,324	133 95
New York	1,080,309,216	1,843,338,517	763,029,301	70 63
North Carolina	226,800,472	358,739,399	131,938,927	58 17
Ohio	504,726,120	1,193,898,422	689,172,302	136 54
Oregon	5,063,474	28,930,637	23,867,163	471 35
Pennsylvania	722,486,120	1,416,501,818	694,015,698	96 05
Rhode Island	80,508,794	135,337,588	54,828,794	68 10
South Carolina	288,257,694	548,138,754	259,881,060	90 15
Tennessee	201,246,686	493,903,892	292,657,206	145 42
Texas	52,740,473	365,200,614	312,460,141	592 44
Vermont	92,205,049	122,477,170	30,272,121	32 83
Virginia	430,701,082	793,249,681	362,548,599	84 17
Wisconsin	42,056,595	273,671,668	231,615,073	550 72
D. of Columbia	14,018,874	41,084,945	27,066,071	193 06
Nebraska		9,131,056		
New Mexico	5,174,471	20,813,768	15,639,298	302 24
Utah?	986,083	5,596,118	4,610,035	467 50
Washington		5,601,466		
	7,135,780,228	16,159,616,068	8,925,481,011	126 45

* Only 13 counties in California have been returned.

† In New Jersey, as the real estate was only returned, the above is partly estimated.

TABLE B.

Table showing the Federal Population, and the Assessed Value of Real and Personal Property of the Several States of the Union.—Census 1860.

STATES.	Federal Population.	Value of Real Estate.	Val. of Personal Property.
Alabama	790,243	$155,034,089	$277,164,673
Arkansas	390,985	63,254,740	116,956,590
California	380,016	66,906,631	72,748,036
Connecticut	460,151	191,478,842	149,776,134
Delaware	111,498	26,273,803	13,493,439
Florida	115,737	21,722,810	47,206,875
Georgia	872,436	179,801,441	438,430,946
Illinois	1,711,753	287,219,940	101,987,432
Indiana	1,350,941	291,829,992	119,212,432
Iowa	674,948	149,433,423	55,783,560
Kansas	107,110	16,088,602	6,429,630
Kentucky	1,065,517	277,925,054	250,287,639
Louisiana	576,086	280,704,988	155,082,277
Maine	628,276	86,717,716	67,662,672
Maryland	652,158	65,341,438	231,793,800
Massachusetts	1,231,065	475,413,165	301,744,651
Michigan	749,112	123,605,084	39,927,921
Minnesota	172,022	25,391,771	6,727,002
Mississippi	616,717	157,836,737	351,636,175
Missouri	1,136,331	153,450,577	113,485,274
New Hampshire	326,072	59,638,346	64,171,743
New Jersey	672,031	151,161,942	145,520,550
New York	3,880,727	1,069,658,080	320,806,558
North Carolina	860,234	116,366,573	175,931,029
Ohio	2,339,599	687,518,121	272,348,980
Oregon	52,464	6,279,602	12,745,313
Pennsylvania	2,906,370	561,192,980	158,060,355
Rhode Island	174,621	83,778,204	41,326,101
South Carolina	542,795	129,772,684	359,546,444
Tennessee	999,533	219,991,180	162,504,020
Texas	530,159	112,476,013	156,316,322
Vermont	315,116	65,639,973	19,118,646
Virginia	1,399,731	417,952,228	239,069,108
Wisconsin	775,873	148,238,766	37,706,723
	29,568,427	12,006,756,585	5,081,661,050

At the conclusion of Mr. Spaulding's speech, Mr. VALLANDIGHAM obtained the floor and offered a substitute for the bill, which was read. .(Congressional Globe, p.p. 526.)

MR. STEVENS said :—"I will follow an example set me, and give notice of an amendment which I shall offer to the bill. It is to make the semi-annual interest payable in coin. I shall make it when we reach the proper time and place."

MR. VALLANDIGHAM.—"That is included in the amendment I propose. Mr. Stevens—"Yes! but my amendment is to the original bill." Mr. Vallandigham—"I do not desire to speak upon the bill at this stage of the debate, and therefore I will cheerfully yield to my colleague (Mr. Pendleton), who proposes to discuss the constitutional question of legal tender." Mr. Pendleton obtained the floor.

MR. PENDLETON'S SPEECH.

MR. PENDLETON, on the 29th inst. made an elaborate speech in opposition to the constitutionality as well as the expediency of the legal tender clause. He commenced by saying,

"MR. CHAIRMAN, I was glad to hear the announcement made by the gentleman from Vermont, (Mr. Morrill), a member of the Committee of Ways and Means, by my colleague (Mr. Vallandigham), by the gentleman from New York, (Mr. Roscoe Conkling), and by the gentleman from Pennsylvania, (Mr. Stevens), that they each intended to propose to the House to make changes in this bill, either by way of amendment or substitute."

MR. PENDLETON—"These notes are to be made lawful money and a legal tender in discharge of all'pecuniary obligations, either by the Government or individuals, a character which has never been given to any note of the United States, or any note of the Bank of the United States by any law ever passed. Not only, sir, was such a law never passed, but such a law was never voted on, never proposed, never introduced, never recommended by any department of the Government; the measure was never seriously entertained in debate in either branch of Congress." MR. CONKLING interrupting, enquired "whether the present Secretary is in favor of making paper a legal tender?" MR. SPAULDING—"In reply to the question of my colleague, I will say that the Secretary of the Treasury has been called upon for his opinion in regard to this bill. We were assured that his reply would be sent to us yesterday, but we did not receive it. We expect his answer every hour." MR. CONKLING—"I am not certain that I understand what my colleague said. Does he expect a letter from the Secretary of the Treasury which will contain his views on the financial question, and also on the legal question?" Mr. Spaulding—"Upon the bill specifically." Mr. Conkling—"Containing the legal tender clause?" Mr. Spaulding—"Yes, sir." MR. PENDLETON—"I cannot answer the question so far as the opinions of the present Secretary of the Treasury are concerned. I affirm again the statement I have made, that a proposition of this kind has never been recommended to either House of Congress by any Department of the Government from its organization The report of the Secretary of the Treasury, made at the opening of the Session, contains no such recommendation."

Mr. Pendleton contended that the bill, if passed, would impair the obligation of past as well as of future contracts, and that it would make it illegal to make a contract for dealing in gold or silver coin, for the reason that these legal tender notes might be tendered in payment of coin contracts. He insisted that there was no express power granted in the Constitution to make United States notes lawful money and a legal tender in payment of debts, and that the power "to regulate commerce" gave no such power. He then said:

"The gentleman from New York (Mr. Spaulding), in his argument yesterday, deduced this power from the general powers of the Government. He told us that Congress had power to lay and collect taxes; to raise and support armies, to provide and maintain a navy, and that all power necessary to effectuate these purposes was expressly given by the general grant of the Constitution. If I should admit his statement in the very language in which he has made it, am I not entitled to ask whether he has shown us any legitimate connection between making these notes a legal tender and the power to raise an army? Might I not ask whether the repudiation of the obligations of the Government to pay its interest is a legitimate means for providing and sustaining a navy? Whether impairing the obligations of contracts between private individuals throughout the country, will in any degree assist the Government in its great duty in laying and collecting taxes? We had no demonstration of the necessity or propriety of these means to accomplish those ends.

The gentleman spoke quite at large in reference to the sovereign power of the Government. He told us that this power was not prohibited in the Constitution. He told us that in times of great emergency every thing may be done except that which is prohibited; and he read an argument from the Attorney General which concludes as it began, with the proposition that such a power is not prohibited to Congress. Sir, I repudiate this whole idea. I think it has no solid foundation in the Constitution.

When I come to examine the powers of Congress according to the principles of interpretation to which I adhere, I look to the grants of the Constitution. I find no grant of this power in direct terms, or, as I think, by fair implication. It is not an accidental omission: it is not an omission through inadvertency. It was intentionally left out of the Constitution, because it was designed that the power should not reside in the Federal Government."

MR. PENDLETON continued his argument at great length against the Constitutional power of the government to issue legal tender notes to circulate as money. He quoted from Story, Madison, Hamilton, Calhoun, and made long extracts from Mr. Webster's speeches which were made while the government was on a peace footing, denying the power of the Government to issue currency and make it a legal tender. He insisted that no State, and that even Congress itself could not make anything but gold and silver coin a legal tender in payment of debts. That the language of the Constitution, and the weight of authority, it seemed to him, settled the question that Congress had not the power to do that which it is proposed shall be done by the provisions of this bill. He concluded as follows:

"Let gentlemen heed this lesson of wisdom. Let them, if need be, tax the energies and wealth of the country sufficiently to restore the credit of the Government. Let them borrow whatever money in addition may be necessary—borrow to the full extent that may be necessary—and let us adhere rigidly, firmly, consistently, persistently, and to the end, to the principle of refusing to surrender that currency which the Constitution has given us, and in the maintenance of which this Government, has never, as yet, for one moment wavered."

The letter of Secretary Chase of the 22d inst. was regarded by a majority of the Committee of Ways and Means and many Members of the House, as non-committal on the legal tender clause of the bill, and many believed that when pressed to a decision, he would declare against its constitutionality. In order to obtain the opinion of the Secretary more fully, MR. CORNING offered a resolution in the Committee of Ways and Means, which was adopted, referring the bill (No. 240) to the Secretary, and requesting him to communicate to the Committee at as early a day as possible, his opinion as to the propriety and necessity of its immediate passage by Congress. After considerable delay the Secretary sent to the Committee of Ways and Means the following reply:

EXTRACT FROM A LETTER OF THE SECRETARY OF THE TREASURY TO THE COMMITTEE OF WAYS AND MEANS,

TREASURY DEPARTMENT, Jan. 29, 1862.

SIR: I have the honor to acknowledge the receipt of a resolution of the Committee of Ways and Means, referring to me House bill No. 240, and requesting my opinion as to the propriety and necessity of its immediate passage by Congress.

The condition of the Treasury certainly needs immediate action on the subject of affording provision for the expenditures of the Government, both expedient and necessary. The general provisions of the bill submitted to me, seems to me well adapted to the end proposed. There are, however, some points which may, perhaps, be usefully amended.

The provision making United States notes a legal tender has doubtless been well considered by the committee, and their conclusion needs no support from any observation of mine. I think it my duty, however, to say, that in respect to this provision my reflections have conducted me to the same conclusions they have reached. It is not unknown to them that I have felt, nor do I wish to conceal that I now feel, a great aversion to making anything but coin a legal tender in payment of debts. It has been my anxious wish to avoid the necessity of such legislation. It is, however, at present impossible, in consequence of the large expenditures entailed by the war, and the suspension of the banks, to procure sufficient coin for disbursements; and it has, therefore, become indispensably necessary that we should resort to the issue of United States notes. The making them a legal tender might, however, still be avoided, if the willingness manifested by the people generally, by railroad companies, and by many of the banking institutions, to receive and pay them as money in all transactions, were absolutely or practically universal; but, unfortunately, there are some persons and some institutions which refuse to receive and pay them, and whose action tends not merely to the unnecessary depreciation of the notes, but to establish discriminations in business against those who, in this matter, give a cordial support to the Government, and in favor of those who do not. Such discriminations should, if possible, be prevented; and the provision making the notes a legal tender, in a great measure at least, prevents it, by putting all citizens, in this respect, on the same level, both of rights and duties.

The committee, doubtless, feel the necessity of accompanying this measure by legislation necessary to secure the highest credit as well as the largest currency of these notes. This security can be found, in my judgment, by proper provisions for funding them in interest-bearing bonds; by well-guarded legislation authorizing banking associations with circulation based on the bonds in which the notes are funded; and by a judicious system of adequate taxation, which will not only create a demand for the notes, but—by securing the prompt payment of interest—raise and sustain the credit of the bonds. Such legislation, it may be hoped, will divest the legal tender clause of the bill of injurious tendencies, and secure the earliest possible return to a sound currency of coin and promptly convertible notes.

I beg leave to add, that vigorous military operations and the unsparing retrenchment of all necessary expenses, will also contribute essentially to this desirable end.

*　　*　　*　　*　　*　　*　　*　　*　　*　　*

I have the honor to be, with very great respect, yours truly,

S. P. CHASE.

Hon. THADDEUS STEVENS, Chairman.

LETTER FROM HON. S. P. CHASE, SECRETARY OF THE TREASURY.

TREASURY DEPARTMENT, Jan. 30, 1862.

MY DEAR SIR—It was impossible to get my answer ready before yesterday afternoon, when it was sent to the Chairman of the Committee; the messenger boy instructed to deliver it to Mr. Stevens or yourself. The House having adjourned, he left it, he says, for you at the National Hotel instead of at Mr. Steven's lodgings.

Had I been aware that the part read to you would have been acceptable as an extract, (to insert in your speech,) I would have sent it earlier in advance of completing the answer.

I read your speech carefully last night. It seems to me to need no change. You do not attach, I see, so much importance as I do to the Banking Act as a measure of relief; nor so much as I am confident you will upon reflection. I confess too, that I was a little disappointed in being merely let off without censure when I thought myself entitled to some credit. My two first loans were negotiated considerably above the market rate, and the last at a rate almost equal at the time, and below, while the market almost immediately afterwards fell.

Your friend,

S. P. CHASE.

Hon. E. G. SPAULDING, House of Representatives.

LETTER OF JOHN A. STEVENS, PRESIDENT OF BANK OF COMMERCE.

NEW YORK, Jan. 29, 1862.

MY DEAR SIR—I beg to offer you my thanks for your able exposition of the financial affairs of the Government. It is clear that there are but the alternatives you state to obtain any substantial relief—the one, to flood the market with the long stocks, submit to the very great depression in the price, and abide the consequences; a great augmentation of the public debt, and ruin to many of the warmest supporters of the Government; the other, for the present to issue demand notes, *making them a legal tender in order to enable you to use them.* No other plans have been, or in my opinion can be devised, I have long entertained and freely expressed these views, here and in Washington. Even if an attempt, more or less successful, had been made at the first to sell the long stock, yet, with the profligate expenditure since made to such fearful amounts, "to this complexion had we come at last." It is idle to look back, but had there been economy in the great departments of expenditure from the beginning, inspiring full public confidence in their able and honest management, it may be questioned if the necessary funds could not have been provided without making irredeemable paper money. The war would have been shorter, the patriotism of the whole people fully sustained, and foreign nations shown that this Government could not be divided.

I am, dear sir, respectfully and truly yours,

JOHN A. STEVENS.

Hon. E. G. SPAULDING, Washington.

LETTER FROM HON. GEORGE OPDYKE, MAYOR OF NEW YORK.

MAYOR'S OFFICE, NEW YORK, Feb. 3, 1862,

MY DEAR SIR—Accept my kind thanks for your note of yesterday, and also my apology for not having sooner expressed the gratification I felt on reading your very able and statesmanlike speech on the national finances. That speech has received, as it deserved, the hearty approval of every one who fully appreciates the imminent danger we are in of a collapse of the public credit. If the present financial embarrassments of the Government should be aggravated by military disasters, or threatened foreign intervention, it might precipitate a panic that would so depress the public securities, that it would be difficult to obtain supplies for the army, and thus arrest the further prosecution of the war. The only safe way of avoiding this danger is to promptly pass the bill you have introduced and advocated so ably. I shall not fail to give you whatever aid I can. I have tried in several instances to bring Mr. Bryant and Mr. Greeley over to our faith, but thus far without success.

I remain, dear sir, very truly yours,

GEORGE OPDYKE.

COMMONWEALTH BANK.

PHILADELPHIA, Feb. 14, 1862.

MY DEAR SIR—I have read your speech on the finances of the nation with the liveliest interest. It is at once clear, forcible, argumentative and conclusive, worthy alike of a financier, a statesman, and a patriot.

Very truly yours, R. MORRIS.

Hon. E. G. SPAULDING.

LETTER FROM STEPHEN COLWELL, ESQ.

PHILADELPHIA, Jan. 30, 1862.

Hon. E. G. SPAULDING, House of Representatives, Washington.

DEAR SIR—I have just read your very able and statesmanlike exposition of our public finances and our financial policy during the war, with a satisfaction I cannot refrain from expressing to you by letter.

You have grasped the subject strongly and comprehensively, as well as practically. I can not doubt that your views will prevail. I trust you will now extend the same kind of effort to accomplish some harmonious action between the Associated Banks and the Government. I believe that these, and other leading banks can, by the aid of the Treasury and by concert in emergencies, keep the United States notes or currency at par; that is at par less only the special premium on gold, which will not be greater than now if the Treasury currency is well managed. The regular circulation of paper currency will absorb in no very long period the whole $200,000,000, and keep that amount moving. But as currency in the channels of business necessarily at times gorges in particular places, and depreciates at once if the holders are not relieved, such occasions should not only be watched by the fiscal agents of the Government, but the proper remedy should be applied. It would cost the Treasury no sum worth mentioning, if the banks would enter into the plan heartily, to keep their currency in such credit that it would perform with complete success every function of a sound currency. According to my view, the banks are deeply interested in keeping up the credit of those notes. The continued demand for them created by the loans, by the payment of debts at banks, and the payment of taxes, will create a rapid circulation and an absorbing power, which will enable the Government to re-issue the whole amount several times a year. But there can be no doubt that an average of one hundred millions will remain so prominently in the channels of business as seldom to revisit the Treasury. If the banks will lend their aid effectively to support their circulation it is not likely that any further issue will be needed, if they don't, they must depreciate, and further issue will be inevitable, if the war continues. Even the banks should be willing to acknowledge, that whatever their opinion about the propriety of issuing this currency, the whole financial policy of the war and commercial interests of the country, will depend very much on its management. They should accept the necessity and make the best of it; and they can make a very good thing for themselves by making the best of it. There can be no doubt that the city banks can enlarge their discounts by the use of the United States notes beyond what they could safely do upon their own circulation. But I regard their hearty co-operation in sustaining this issue which you have so well justified, as so important, that I think it would be well worth while for the Treasury to pay them for the sort of services they can render. I contributed an editorial on this subject to the *North American*, which I send you. If your speech is to appear in pamphlet form please send me one. I send you also an article in the *Banking Magazine* for January, 1862, on the subject of banks and the Treasury. Be good enough to present my respects to Mr. Horton, of your committee, who is an old acquaintance of mine.

With great respect, very truly yours,

STEPHEN COLWELL.

EXTRACT FROM A LETTER OF M. S. HAWLEY, ESQ.

BUFFALO, Jan. 21, 1862.

DEAR SIR—I suppose of course a large issue of demand notes for circulation will be authorized, receivable for all dues and made a legal tender; and sufficient taxation to sustain the credit of all such issues and of the Government bonds. I see no other method so economical and effective.

Very respectfully yours,

M. S. HAWLEY.

EXTRACT FROM A LETTER OF J. H. VAN ANTWERP, ESQ., OF THE STATE BANK, ALBANY.

ALBANY, Feb. 8, 1862.

DEAR SIR—Accept my thanks for a copy of your speech on the national finances. The demand notes, in addition to the legal tender, need only to be fortified by a sinking fund yearly of $10,000,000, derived from taxation, to every $100,000,000 of notes issued, to make them pass equal to coin.

Yours truly,

J. H. VAN ANTWERP.

LETTER FROM HON. ROBERT DENNISTON, LATE COMPTROLLER OF NEW YORK.

SALISBURY MILLS, Orange Co., N. Y., Jan. 30, 1862.

HON. E. G. SPAULDING.

DEAR SIR—I have read your financial speech (as reported in the *Tribune*) twice over with great interest. The necessity for such measures is greatly to be regretted, but I do not see with the light I have, how they are to be avoided. In our national exigency, determined boldness, both in civil and military affairs, will be worth a mint of money to us.

Please send me your speech for preservation, when printed in pamphlet form.

With great respect, your obedient servant,

ROBERT DENNISTON.

LETTER OF C. H. RUSSELL, VICE PRESIDENT OF THE BANK OF COMMERCE.

NEW YORK, Jan. 29, 1862.

MY DEAR SIR—I have just read your speech as published to-day in the *Times*, it appears to me a very fair and clear exposition of the present financial condition of the Government, its necessities, its resources, and the emergency which now demands the immediate passage of the bill reported by the Committee of Ways and Means. The exigency of the Government to which I referred recently before that Committee, to justify the legal tender of the notes, I think is now reached, and we have no choice of any other measure as good as you propose. But protect the issue of this currency by limitation of its amount, by large taxation, and be sure to require by amendment that the payment of interest by the Government shall be certainly paid in coin on all its public debts.

In haste, yours truly,

C. H. RUSSELL.

P. S.—In some quarters are suggestions not to receive these notes from customers. This is wrong. Such a proceeding, or to make any exception against them as *lawful money* of the United States, would affix a taint and affect the public confidence in them.

ELEAZER LORD, LATE PRESIDENT OF THE NEW YORK AND ERIE RAILROAD.

PIERMONT, Jan. 29, 1862.

HON. E. G. SPAULDING, M. C.

DEAR SIR—I beg to congratulate you on your lucid, forcible, and comprehensive opening of the debate on the legal tender Treasury note bill. It is unanswerable, and I trust will issue in an early triumph. I only wish the sum proposed was larger, so as to extinguish all hopes of national bonds being forced on the market and sacrificed. I think there will be a struggle in certain quarters to withdraw them from circulation and turn them into bonds on interest. The people would do that gradually without reducing the circulation too much, were there plenty more expected; and with a discretion for a larger sum the inimical parties could do no harm.

Should your speech be printed in pamphlet form, which I hope it will, please favor me with one or more.

Respectfully, &c.,   ELEAZER LORD.

LETTER OF HON. E. S. PROSSER.

BUFFALO, Feb. 7, 1862.

HON. E. G. SPAULDING, Washington, D. C.

DEAR SIR—I thank you for a printed copy of your speech on the finances of the country, received this morning; I had read it in the paper before with great interest and entire approval, but desire this copy for preservation. Whilst all loyal citizens must regret the necessity which compels the Government to suspend specie payments and make its own demand notes a lawful tender instead, I am quite unable, after very considerable thought, to suggest any other measure of relief, which I think would answer the purpose so promptly, or so well; hence, I hope the bill as reported by the committee will speedily become a law, and this is I think quite the general wish here. As the Spring approaches, anxiety increases for a vigorous prosecution of the war to a conclusion; for sometime or other, *not very remote*, necessity will compel at least a large decrease in our land and naval forces; $500,000,000 annually, can and will be paid cheerfully awhile, but I need not say to you that it cannot be very long; so it behooves the Government to act with all practicable energy to end the rebellion by any means in its power, in the very shortest time it can be done. I hope we shall come out of the conflict speedily and triumphantly; and that all the States may be again united under the present Constitution; still most of the slave states, except upon the border, seem almost *hopelessly estranged*, and will not, I fear, ever again, with their present people, yield obedience to the fundamental law of the land and the acts of Congress, unless they *know* the penalty for *treason henceforth* is to be *rigidly* enforced, and that the power of the Government is quite equal to capture the leaders of the rebellion by hundreds and thousands, *and are determined to do it, and to execute them as fast as captured*, unless they throw down their arms and disband, and return to loyalty. Can it be possible the Rebel leaders would long hold out against such a proclamation, after they saw that it was the intention of the Government to fulfil it to the letter, and they were virtually surrounded by a superior force.

Yours truly,   E. S. PROSSER.

LETTER OF GEO. B. BUTLER, OF THE HOUSE OF A. T. STEWART & CO., NEW YORK.

NEW YORK, Jan. 30, 1862.

MY DEAR SIR—I send you the 4th of a series of articles written to show that the bills of the Government should be a legal tender. I belong to the creditor class, but my interest in the Government absorbs all others. In my view the war cannot be conducted except on this plan. I would pay the interest in gold and silver and lay heavy taxes. There should be $100,000,000 of demand notes of $1000, bearing 5 per cent. interest.

Yours, very truly, GEO. B. BUTLER.

LETTER FROM T. W. OLCOTT, ESQ., MECHANICS' AND FARMERS' BANK.

ALBANY, Jan. 31, 1862.

HON. E. G. SPAULDING.

DEAR SIR—I have read your well constructed argument on national finances, and the issue of Treasury notes made a legal tender. I do not suppose that a loan can be made, *and I regard this issue of Treasury notes the only adequate measure for sustaining the credit of the Treasury and the well being if not the very existence of the Government. Money must be had or the war cannot be successfully prosecuted.*

This measure will secure means, no other will except at ruinous sacrifices. It is not a debatable question. The struggle is for life. The knife is at our throat. We must strike with the most available weapon, and leave theory for a more convenient season. Of course you will pass a tax law. The people will hail it, and it will inspire confidence in our public securities. I had hoped that you would authorize funding at 4 or 5 years in an 8 per cent. stock, and 20 years in a 6 or 6½ per cent. stock. The short 8 per cent. stock would tempt to a large amount of funding, and when that short period expires, it is to be hoped that the Government can borrow at 5 per cent,

We want to encourage funding so as to prevent a *redundant currency*, and to prepare the way for possible if not probable further issues.

I have the honor to be, Your Obedient Servant,

THOMAS W. OLCOTT.

OFFICE OF THE COLUMBIAN INSURANCE COMPANY,

NEW YORK, Jan, 31, 1862.

HON. E. G. SPAULDING, Washington, D. C.

DEAR SIR—I have read your able exposition of the condition of the national finances, and the bill which you reported to authorize the issue of $150,000,000 of demand notes, and I beg leave to express the opinion, that there is no other means by which the Government can escape the utter ruin of their credit, than the immediate passage of the bill, and a bill to raise an amount of revenue which shall render the prompt payment of interest on all their loans beyond contingency. Should the passage of this bill be delayed until the banks have paid their last installment to the Government, and the banks should refuse to receive the demand notes, and pay them out, they would of course depreciate to an extent sufficient to damage the credit of the Government essentially. If the experience of a life, not now short, is of any value, I say unhesitatingly, that this is the most critical period in our history within my knowledge. *Those in power must take the responsibility and do the needful instantly,* or the consequences may be, and I think will be terrific. As to paying in gold during the war, it is utterly and totally impracticable, and the idea of doing so should at once be discarded. After the present emergency is provided for, I trust the bill for banking on the Government stock will be passed. The plan will be approved by nearly all the intelligent community when once adopted, and is now by a large majority of the men of wealth and influence, so far as I am informed. With apologies for trespassing upon your valuable time,

I am, your obedient servant,
THOMAS LORD.

POSTPONEMENT OF THE SPECIAL ORDER.

On Thursday, the 30th inst., MR. STEVENS moved to postpone the special order—the Treasury note bill—until to-morrow, for the purpose of going into the Committee of the Whole on the Army bill. The motion was agreed to. And on Friday, the 31st inst., he again moved to postpone the Treasury note bill until Monday, the 3rd of February, which was agreed to by the House.

On Monday, the 3rd of February, Mr. Vallandigham offered a modification of his substitute for the bill, for the purpose of having it printed for examination. This substitute will be found printed at length in the *Congressional Globe*, page 614.

MR. ROSCOE CONKLING—With the permission of the gentleman from Ohio, I desire to submit for the same purpose, the following, which I propose to offer, at the proper time, as a substitute for the whole bill. *Congressional Globe*, page 615.

MR. VALLANDIGHAM'S SPEECH.

MR. VALLANDIGHAM being entitled to the floor, addressed the Committee of the whole House for one hour, in favor of his substitute, and in opposition to the legal tender clause in the original bill. His speech will be found reported at length in the appendix to the *Congressional Globe*, pages 42, 43, 44 and 45.

He commenced by saying:

"It has been my habit, Mr. Chairman, to premeditate, whenever premeditation was possible, whatever I have had to say in this House; for no man has a right, in my judgment, to obtrude his immature thoughts and opinions upon a deliberative assembly. * * * * * * *

"I propose to-day to discuss the subjects involved in this bill to the best of my ability, and with becoming candor and freedom, and I may add earnestness too; for I have the profoundest conviction of their incalculable importance to the interests, present and future, of the United States, and of the people of this whole continent. Nor am I to be deterred from a faithful discharge of my duty by the consciousness that my voice may not be hearkened to here, or in the country, because of the continued, persistent, but most causeless and malignant assaults and misrepresentations, to which for months past, I have been subjected. Sir, I am not here to reply to them to-day. Neither am I to be driven from the line of duty by them. "Strike—but hear." Whatever a silenced or mendacious press, outside of this House may choose to withhold, or to say, no man who is fit to be a member of this House, will allow his speech or his votes, or his public conduct here, to be controlled by his personal hates or prejudices. Sir, I recant nothing, and would expunge nothing from the record of the past, so far as I am concerned, But my path of duty now, as a Representative, is as clear as the sun at broad-noon. THE SHIP OF STATE IS UPON THE ROCKS. I was not the helmsman who drove her there; not had I part or lot in directing her course. But now, when the sole question is, how shall she be rescued? I will not any longer, or at least just now enquire who has done the mischief.

* * * * I do not agree, Mr. Chairman, with the gentleman who has opened this debate, (Mr. Spaulding,) that this bill is a war measure. Certainly, sir, it has been forced upon us by the war, but if peace were restored to-morrow, these $100,000,000 would be just as essential to the "public credit as they are to-day."

Mr. Vallandigham continued his argument at great length. He insisted that the legal tender clause was unconstitutional, that it was *a forced loan*, and that it would be disastrous and unjust. He said no scheme of loan or taxation, or national bank, or currency, or other similar contrivance, could be devised, and put into operation in time to avert ruin and disaster. The Government has no money, no gold and silver coin, which is the only money in the world. He advocated Treasury notes, without any promise to pay money, and without the legal tender clause, which should pass as currency from hand to hand, between the Government and its creditors and debtors, and be supported by a nearly equal amount of taxes—such taxes to be received by the Government in these notes.

He urged that the experiment of forcing a paper currency upon the country, was a dangerous experiment, that it would lead to other enormous issues, gold and silver would be banished from circulation, an immense inflation would take place, "cheap in materials, easy of issue, worked by steam, signed by machinery, there would be no end to the legion of paper devils which shall pour forth from the loins of the Secretary." That inevitably there would follow bloated currency, high prices, extravagant speculation, enormous sudden fortunes, immense factitious wealth, and general insanity.

He objected to their being called "United States notes" instead of "Treasury notes," as they had always heretofore been called, and deprecated the idea that they were likely to be a permanent currency, or at least until the Secretary's grand fiscal machine, "his magnificent *National Paper Mill*, founded upon the very stock provided for in this bill can be put into operation." He insisted that these notes were not money, that they would not circulate as currency, would not be taken as legal tenders, and in discharge of judgments, and contracts, and state debts, or private debts, "though you should send them forth bearing ten times the image and superscription—the fair face and form of ABRAHAM LINCOLN, now president and CÆSAR of the American Republic."

He urged the substitute presented by him as follows:

"The fundamental idea of this substitute is to support and float these $150,000,000, by nearly an equal amount of taxation and revenue, payable of course in these notes. The Government owe the people and the people owe the Government, each $150,000,000, and these notes are primarily to be used as a common medium of payment between them. * * * * I do not propose or pretend that these notes are to be convertible into gold and silver. They are not payable on demand; they are not payable to bearer, nor payable at all. They are not *to be* paid, but to circulate as currency receivable in Government dues, and finally to be funded in twenty year's stocks. They are not promises to pay, and are not therefore paper money. They do not represent gold and silver, of which the Government has none. * * * * * * * * The United States are to cease in part, for a time, to be a specie paying hard money Government, I deplore it profoundly. But imperious necessity demands it. There is no alternative, no matter what evils may follow.

But I utterly deny, sir, the right of the Federal Government to provide a paper currency, intended primarily to circulate as money, and meet the demands of business and commercial transactions, and to the exclusion of all other paper. It is not the intent or object of the substitute to furnish such a currency for the country. * * * * * *

Such, Mr. Chairman, is the substitute which I have submitted. It differs essentially from the bill. The one relies on force, the other upon credit; the one looks to the direct and despotic coercion of law and arms, and the other to the indirect and ordinary coercion of taxes. * * *

To my political friends let me now appeal for support, not only for this substitute, but of the taxation which must follow it, as essential to the maintainance of the good faith and credit of the Government."

At the conclusion of Mr. Vallandigham's speech, Mr. Hooper, of Mass., obtained the floor.

MR. HOOPER'S SPEECH.

MR. HOOPER—"The unusual exigencies of this country require that we should look for other and deeper sources of revenue than any to which we have heretofore been accustomed. We are contending for the maintainance of the Government, for the preservation of the Union, and for the enforcement of the laws, on which depend the existence, as well as the security of property.

To insure our success in this contest, great and unusual exertions have already been made. An enormous army, a powerful navy, with vast stores of artillery and ammunition, have been created. In providing for the sustenance, comfort, and equipment of the Army and Navy, the Government have been obliged to incur expenses far exceeding in magnitude any which have been hitherto known in our history. To continue them in their present state of efficiency, large additional sums must be expended; and it now becomes the duty of Congress to devise methods by which these sums can be obtained with the least hardship to the people, and the least risk to the credit of the Government. In considering the means by which this is to be effected, it must be remembered that it is hardly possible for the Government to raise money for any purpose without occasioning some inconvenience to individuals. To oppose necessary measures, therefore, simply upon the ground that it will injuriously affect this class or that class of the people, is unreasonable. Parties interested may endeavor to show that the same objects can be effected with less hardship than by the methods proposed, or may endeavor to obviate any objectionable features, so far as may be consistent with the attainment of the desired end; but they should always remember that the end aimed at must be attained; that its attainment will require individual sacrifices in some form, and that it is the part of wisdom, of patriotism, and of discretion, to submit to such necessary sacrifices cheerfully when called upon, and not by their opposition attempt to excite popular clamour, and weaken the public confidence in the Government, to which they are indebted for the safety of their persons, and the security of their possessions. Every step which tends to weaken the public credit has the effect of rendering private property more insecure, because it obstructs the Government in procuring its necessary funds in the ordinary way, and may oblige it to resort to the arbitrary modes of forced loans and heavier rates of taxation. At this moment, therefore, when for the time every hope of aid from foreign capital is idle, when the country is compelled to look to her own resources for the means with which to maintain her integrity and subdue the rebellion, not only does every dictate of patriotism, and every enobling sentiment of humanity, call upon the capitalists of the country to rally in defence of the Government, but the meaner instincts of self-preservation admonishes them to submit to slight sacrifices now, that they may secure and preserve their property.

Three measures have been considered in the Committee, which are, to some extent, connected together, and form a comprehensive system by which, it is believed, the Government will be enabled to procure the sums necessary to the successful prosecution of the war; while, at the same time, the burden upon the capital of the country will be light, and the public will be benefited in some important particulars.

The first of these measures is the one now before the House, by which the Secretary of the Treasury is authorized to issue United States notes, not to exceed $150,000,000 in amount (including those authorized by previous laws), of denominations not less than five dollars. They are not to bear interest, but are to be issued and received as money, convertible, at the option of the holder, into six per cent. stock of the United States, the principal and interest being payable either here or abroad, and these notes are to be a legal tender.

The second measure consists of a tax bill, which shall, with the tariff on imports, insure an annual revenue of at least $150,000,000.

The third is a national banking law, which will require the deposit of United States stock as security for the bank notes now circulated as currency.

In order more fully to understand and more easily to meet any objections which may be urged against the first of these measures, being the one now occupying the attention of the House, it will be desirable to notice the other two, which are designed to be more permanent in their character., and upon the expected results of which the present measure is in some degree based."

Mr. HOOPER here explained the various modes of the proposed taxation, by which the credit of the government was to be supported, and also went into a full explanation of the National Currency Bank bill which had been prepared, and the manner in which the government bonds would be absorbed by the banks, as soon as the bill should go into operation. He then proceeded as follows :

"The levying of the contemplated tax, the proper inauguration of the new banking scheme, and the successful negotiation of a new loan, are matters that will require time. In the meanwhile, the Treasury is comparatively empty, and the demands upon the government are numerous and pressing. To enable the government to support itself during this interval of time, and to facilitate the negotiation of their loans, the committee have decided to recommend the issue of government notes.

There is a necessity for money, and the object of the authority to issue $150,000,000 U. S. notes, not bearing interest and made legal tender, is to pay the creditors of the United States, and enable them to discharge their debts.   *   *   *   *   *   * The propositions of committees from Boards of Trade and banks, which recently visited Washington, submitted to the Secretary of the Treasury and declined by him, differed from the theory of this bill so far, as to require that instead of the issue of the United States notes the banks should be relied upon to furnish the amount needed. The effect of this would be that the government bonds must first be disposed of, and the money received for them paid to the contractors; in other words, that the government should go into the money market and negotiate their bonds, without restriction as to the rate or terms, at a time when the government is discredited by the delay and the difficulties that have occurred in paying contractors and others; taking the notes of suspended banks in payment of these bonds, and with these bank notes, thus obtained, pay off the contractors. The obvious effect of such an arrangement would be to put the reins of our national finances in the hands of the banks, leaving to them the direction of our path, with little opportunity for the government to exercise any influence on the subject. Exactly upon what terms the government bonds could be negotiated now, under such circumstances, no one can say; but last Summer, when the banks made their negotiation with the Secretary of the Treasury for $100,000,000, they at first refused to do anything, because the Secretary was restricted by law to taking par for seven per cent. bonds payable in twenty years, and for seven and three-tenths Treasury notes payable in three years. They finally decided, though with great reluctance—influenced by patriotic regard for the public interest as well as wisely consulting their own—to take $100,000,000 of the latter; though at that time, as now, money was not worth for commercial purposes more than five per cent. It is proposed in this bill to limit the Secretary to par for six per cent. bonds, the principal and interest to be payable in specie or its equivalent. It is believed that there can be nothing more secure than these bonds, which thus become, as it were, a standard of value in reference to the currency.

In the war of 1812 the Government paid for its supplies with funds obtained from the banks in the same manner as proposed in the plan recently submitted to the Secretary by those committees. The bonds of the United States were then negotiated in some instances at twenty per cent. less than their par value, and paid for in bank currency of different degrees of depreciation, according to locality, but averaging from twenty to twenty-five per cent. discount, as compared with coin. To render the government financially more independent, it is necessary to make the United States notes a legal tender. It is possible that they would become a practical tender, like bank notes, without providing for them to be a legal tender. If this were a foreign war there would be no doubt of it; but in this present emergency, when those who are openly or secretly disloyal to the government are found everywhere to suggest obstacles that may embarrass the government, nothing should be omitted that will add to their efficiency. I am, therefore, in favor of making the notes a legal tender, believing the Secretary of the Treasury, who alone has the power to issue them, can and will use the power with his well known discretion, and that it will assist him in his endeavor to keep the notes at par with coin. We shall probably be told that England, in her great struggle, while specie payments were suspended, never made paper money a legal tender. But in this respect her example should serve us as a warning rather than a guide, because instead of it she did what was much worse, by suspending the laws to enforce the payment of debts in cases where the paper money had been refused as a tender.

* * * * * * * * * * * * * * *

It is important in this great struggle to show the superiority of the principles of freedom, of education, of the elevation of mankind, upon which society at the North is based, over those of slavery, which doom men to hopeless ignorance in order to insure abject obedience. To do this our resources of every kind are abundant, both in men and in means; and it is only necessary to draw them out in order to be successful.

To fail, would not be because the nation was so poorly endowed as to be without the means of success, but because it refused to make use of them. Such a result, if it were possible, would not weaken the truth of the great principles for which we are contending; but would simply demonstrate that we, of this generation, were faithless in guarding those principles; faithless to ourselves; faithless to our country; faithless to good government throughout the world; and, since such infidelity is a violation of unquestionable duty, faithless to God."

MR. ROSCOE CONKLING obtained the floor.

MR. MORRILL, of Vermont—"I ask the gentleman from New York to yield the floor. Two members of the majority of the Committee of Ways and Means have spoken on this question, and if the gentleman will permit me now *to express the views of the minority of the Committee against the pending bill,* I will be obliged to him."

MR. ROSCOE CONKLING—"I yield to the gentleman from Vermont."

MR. STEVENS—"I feel it my duty to state that the Treasury Department is urgent for the passage of this bill, and I trust, therefore, that the vote on it will not be put off longer than Thursday next."

Mr. SPAULDING—"I desire to call the attention of the House to a letter which I have just received from the Secretary of the Treasury. It is a note to me urging the immediate passage of this bill without further delay. For the purpose of letting the House understand the necessities of the Treasury, I ask the Clerk to read an extract from that letter."

The Clerk read as follows:

"Immediate action is of great importance. The Treasury is nearly empty. I have been obliged to draw for the last installment of the November loan. So soon as it is paid, I fear the banks generally will refuse to receive the United States notes, unless made a legal tender. You will see the necessity of urging the bill through without more delay." * *

Mr. THOMAS, of Massachusetts—"Has the gentleman any further communication that has been received from the Secretary of the Treasury with reference to this bill? If there has been any received I hope he will be kind enough to have it read to the House."

Mr. SPAULDING—"A communication has been addressed by the Secretary of the Treasury to the Committee of Ways and Means, and I have no objection to its being read."

Mr. ROSCOE CONKLING—"I would like to know whether the gentleman intends to have the whole of the communication read, or only extracts?"

Mr. SPAULDING—"I ask the Clerk to read what I send to him. The balance of the communication is in relation merely to formal amendments. What the Clerk will read is all of the communication that refers to the principle of the bill."

Mr. VALLANDIGHAM—"Has the Committee of Ways and Means received the letter it was expecting from the Secretary of the Treasury?"

Mr. SPAULDING—"This is the one."

(The Clerk here read the letter of the Secretary of the Treasury, dated January 29, 1862, as published on page 45.)

Mr. ROSCOE CONKLING—"I now call for the reading of the rest of that letter."

Mr. SPAULDING—"There is not the least objection to its being read. It is, however, in the committee room. I will state what the remainder of the letter is. The Secretary of the Treasury suggests some amendments to the bill. He proposes two new sections to the bill, one relating to counterfeiting and the other in regard to the manner in which the notes shall be executed. He proposes instead of having them signed by clerks that there shall be a seal or die engraved upon them, which will indicate the authority under which they are issued."

Mr. ROSCOE CONKLING—"Are those the only amendments?"

Mr. SPAULDING—"There are two or three smaller amendments not affecting the principle of the bill, however, in any way. We propose in the committee to act on those amendments to-morrow morning. If the letter were here I would not have the slightest objection to its being read."

Mr. LOVEJOY—"I want to ask the gentleman of the Committee of Ways and Means whether they intend to propose to have action on this bill before action is taken on the tax bill?"

Mr. SPAULDING—"*I have been anxious to have the tax bill brought in to be first considered; but the gentleman from Vermont* (Mr. MORRILL), *who is chairman of the sub-committee on the Tariff and Tax bills, informs us that the sub-committee having that matter in charge will not be able to report to the Committee of Ways and Means for several days yet. The necessities of the Treasury, therefore, will compel us to act on this bill, however reluctantly, before the Tax bill can be introduced.*"

Mr. ROSCOE CONKLING—"I hope that the remaining portion of the letter of the Secretary of the Treasury will be printed in the *Globe.*"

Mr. SPAULDING—"I have no objection to that."

Mr. ROSCOE CONKLING—"The gentleman has read the whole letter, and *I ask him to state whether the Secretary is for or against this bill with the legal tender provision in it.*"

Mr. SPAULDING—"He is for it. I have another letter from him in which he states that he is anxious to have it passed in that form."

Mr. ROSCOE CONKLING—"Let us have that read."

Mr. SPAULDING—"It is a letter to myself."

Mr. MAYNARD—"I ask my colleague on the Committee of Ways and Means whether the portion of the Secretary's letter which has been read is not all of it that appertains to the principle of the bill; and whether the balance does not relate merely to matters of detail."

Mr. SPAULDING—"Yes, sir. I will read a paragraph of the letter written by the Secretary to myself this afternoon:

"I came with reluctance to the conclusion that the legal tender clause is a necessity; but I came to it decidedly, and support it earnestly. I do not hesitate since I have made up my mind. * * * * * The conclusion I have arrived at has convinced me that it is important to the success of the measure."

And then, on motion of Mr. Wright, the House (at half-past four o'clock P. M.) adjourned.

The following is a copy of the letter of Secretary Chase referred to in the foregoing proceedings of the House, and from which extracts were read:

LETTER FROM HON. S. P. CHASE.

MONDAY, 3d February, 1862.

MY DEAR SIR:—Mr. Seward said to me on yesterday that you observed to him, that my hesitation in coming up to the legal tender proposition embarrassed you, and I am very sorry to observe it, for my anxious wish is to support you in all respects.

It is true that I came with reluctance to the conclusion that the legal tender clause is a necessity, but I came to it decidedly, and I support it earnestly. I do not hesitate when I have made up my mind, however much regret I may feel over the necessity of the conclusion to which I come.

I have just sent a note to Mr. Stevens, with two sections (penal) instead of one. You will, I think, see the necessity of them. The one I have already sent I fear is not quite strong enough. What has the Committee done about the amendments suggested? I thought them important.

Immediate action is of great importance. The Treasury is nearly empty. I have been obliged to draw for the last installment of the November loan; so soon as it is paid, I fear the banks generally will refuse to receive the United States notes. You will see the necessity of urging the bill through without more delay.   Very sincerely yours,
   Hon. E. G. SPAULDING.   S. P. CHASE.

On the 4th of February, the House gave consent to Mr. Morrill to have printed a substitute having the sanction of *one-half the Committee of Ways and Means,* which he proposed to offer at the proper time in place of the original bill. Mr. Stratton, one of the Committee. changed his mind, and now favors the substitute instead of the bill first reported, leaving the Committee of Ways and Means equally divided.

MR. MORRILL'S SPEECH.

MR. MORRILL, of Vermont—"MR. CHAIRMAN: Engaged as I have been upon other matters of at least equal importance, I have not had the time to prepare an elaborate speech; but the subject of issuing $150,000,000 of paper currency and making it a legal tender by the Government at a single bound—the precursor, as I fear, of a prolific brood of promises, no one of which is to be redeemed in the constitutional standard of the country—could not but arrest my attention, and having strong convictions of the impolicy of the measure, I should feel that I utterly failed to discharge my duty if I did not attempt to find a stronger prop for our country to bear upon than this bill—a measure not blessed by one sound precedent and damned by all.

I know the gentlemen who have had the latter in charge have bestowed upon it much time and perplexing thought, and from their thorough knowledge of the subject and large acquaintance with the monetary circles of the country, their opinions will have great weight in this Committee-deservedly so—and I shall only claim a candid hearing in behalf of the substitute of the minority of the Committee of Ways and Means, well knowing that we are all inflamed by the same zeal for the triumphant success of our arms, the same solicitude for the honor and welfare of the people, who mean to live and die under the flag of our Union, and that we can have but one wish, which is, that the best plan shall be adopted.

* * * * * * * * * * * * * *

We are urged by the gentleman from New York (Mr. Spaulding) to pass this bill as "a war measure"—"a measure of necessity," and to enforce this idea he gives you the figures of our probable requirements, if the war should be prolonged until July 1, 1863. Sir, I have no expectation of being required to support a war for that length of time. The ice that chokes the Mississippi is not more sure to melt and disappear with the approaching vernal season, than are the rebellious armies upon its banks when our western army shall break from its moorings and rush with the current to the Gulf, and baptise as it goes, in blood, the people to a fresher allegiance. At the same time, the men of the East will only ask for an opportunity to cross bayonets with the chivalry—to leave epithets and try what virtue there is in steel! That hour is approaching, and I have no fear of the result.

'Fly swiftly round, ye wheels of time!'

We can close this war by the 30th day of July next as well as in thirty years. Let us second general McClellan for a 'short and sharp' conflict. By so doing we shall economise both blood and Treasury notes.

If this paper money is 'a war measure,' it is not waged against the enemy, but one that may well make him grin with delight. I would as soon provide Chinese wooden guns for the army as paper money alone for the army. * * * * * * * * * * *

If, by the provisions of this bill, we cut ourselves off from all other resources, it is to be considered how much could be realized from this, in my judgment, the weakest resource within our grasp, which is the power of a bank issue, without any capital, and not even specie enough to tender the odd change. It is an experiment to inject, by a governmental force pump, into the arteries of commerce a new currency, when the arteries are already filled. The whole bank circulation of the United States in 1860 was $207,102,477; that of the rebel States was $50,647,028, leaving for the loyal States $156,566,449. But at this time, in consequence of the diminution of all business, except that nourished by the war, the bank circulation is over $20,000,000 less, or about $136,000,000. I admit that we can drive a considerable share of this home upon the banks, and substitute that of the notes of the United States in its place. * * * *

It is thus apparent that $20,000,000 is about all that would be absorbed by this country, or kept afloat in the present condition of monetary affairs without the intervention of Congressional omnipotence in making them a legal tender. If so made, they would, to the extent they are tendered for public dues, be a forced loan; and to the extent of the difference between their current value and that of standard coin, it would be a breach of public faith. It is true that the measure might be hailed with delight by bankrupts; and if the bill passes, my friend from New York (Mr. Conkling) no longer need press his bankrupt law, for they would have no occasion to go into Chancery in order to scale and settle off with their creditors, as "legal tenders" would soon be offered at rates entirely within their means. * * * * * * * * *. The Government can flood the country with 150,000,000 paper dollars, but from that moment you would vastly increase the cost of carrying on the war; prices would go up, and the addition we should pile upon our national debt would prove that it might have been even wiser to have burnt our paper dollars before they were issued. The inflation of the currency would be inevitable. In ordinary times few comprehend the Archimedean leverage of a few millions added to or subtracted from the currency of a nation actively engaged in the affairs of the world. * * * * * *

No one here contemplates but that at *some* future time the banks and the Government shall resume specie payments—the banks depending entirely upon whether the Government does so or not—and if so, I invite them to calculate the cost of the descent from that basis, the cost of the return, the expiratory pains to be suffered, and then determine whether we shall carry on this war on a specie basis, or on a ceaseless flood of paper, bartered at discordant prices in every city, town and hamlet of the country, bearing in mind, however cheaply obtained, every dollar is to be and will be ultimately repaid in gold and silver coin raised by taxation.

That I am not wrong in supposing if we launch this measure that we have nothing else to put afloat, is quite apparent in the able speech of my friend from New York (Mr. Spaulding), who plainly occupied his ground reluctantly; for besides the 150,000,000 of notes he now proposes to authorize, he more than hints at the possibility of "a further issue of demand notes, if Congress shall hereafter deem it necessary." I maintain that the bill, as reported by the Committee of Ways and Means, should not pass, because it will infinitely damage the national credit; because it will cut off all other chance of supplies; because it will reduce our standard of legal tender, already sufficiently debased; because it will inflate the currency and increase manyfold the cost of the war; because it would slide into the place proper for taxation; because, as a resource, it must ultimately fail, and tend to a premature peace; because it is a question of doubtful constitutionality; because it is an *export facto* law, immoral, and a breach of the public faith; because it will at once banish all specie from circulation; because it will dampen the ardor of our men at home, as well as soldiers in the field; because it will degrade us in the estimation of other nations; because it will cripple American labor, and throw at least larger wealth into the hands of the rich; and because there is no necessity calling for such a desperate remedy. I agree with the gentleman from New York (Mr. Spaulding) in one thing most cordially; our finances stand in need of the tonic of decided military success. Without that our stocks will continue to be quoted *flat*. And yet I am no chronic grumbler. Standing at zero, our army rose as if by a magical wand and illumined the whole heavens by its magnificent sweep. Do not let it be said we rose like the rocket and fell like the stick.

Mr. Chairman—It will be seen from the substitute, as proposed on the part of *one-half of the Committee of Ways and Means*, that I do not object to the issue of United States notes to a limited extent, to circulate as currency. It is both convenient and proper. But I wish to have this issue marked by metes and bounds, saying at the outset, 'thus far shalt thou go and no further.' Then, let them be based on as solid a foundation as the everlasting hills *that they shall be the full equivalent of standard coin*. This can be done by fixing the amount ample, but reasonable, that no more than the fixed amount shall at any time be put in circulation, and by providing taxation sufficient at all times to retire them or to maintain their full value. But, with all the earnestness I possess, I do protest against making anything a legal tender but gold and silver, as calculated to undermine all confidence in the Republic, whose reputation should be dearer to statesmen, as well as to soldiers, than life itself.   *   *   *   *

We propose no new issue of Treasury notes, but leave the fifty millions already authorized to be issued and re-issued as may be found necessary or convenient. This will secure us against an inflated currency.

Then it is proposed to issue $100,000,000 in United States notes, bearing interest at the rate of three and sixty-five hundredths per cent., payable at the pleasure of the United States, and allowing them with accumulated interest to be received for all debts and demands (taxes included) due to the United States, except duties on imports, and exchangeable at the will of the holder, whenever presented in sums not less than fifty dollars, for United States seven and three-tenths per cent. coupon or registered stock. They are also to be received at par, with accumulated interest, for any bonds the Government may hereafter issue. These are to be paid out for all salaries, debts and demands due to individuals and corporations, *at their option within the United States*. In substance this is very like English Exchequer notes issued in anticipation of revenue. It is most probable these notes would maintain their credit at or near par; and if there should be any difference between these and gold, it would be an honest difference, visible to all men. As they accumulate they will be funded and retired, or re-issued, as the exigencies of the Government may require. They equip the Treasury as well as any legal tender paper could do, while bearing interest they would not pass into the general volume of the currency, and they afford the only possible channel of obtaining any considerable sums to be consolidated into stocks. They cannot exceed the amount of internal duties that will be levied, which will create a sure and constant demand for these notes, and sustain their credit in every State and Territory in the country.

We do not propose to receive these notes for duties on imports, for the reason that it is desirable to leave the tariff stable amid all fluctuations, and also that we may secure the coin we promise to pay out as interest on the bonds.

It is then proposed, in order to perfect this plan in all its parts, to issue $200,000,000 in coupon or registered bonds, payable in ten years, with interest semi-annually in coin, at the rate of seven and three-tenths per cent. per annum. This is comparatively a high rate of interest, and it may be necessary that it should be so, in order to get the stock taken up by capitalists; but the time the bonds are to run is limited to ten years, because it would be much against the interest of the United States to engage to pay a high rate of interest for a long period of time. We think there can be no doubt that these bonds will all be taken, commencing as soon as the tax bill shall be passed. Unless the credit of the United States shall be utterly shattered, which is not for a moment to be apprehended, these bonds must be considered a most desirable investment, both in large and small sums.

It is proposed to issue $300,000,000 in coupon or registered bonds, payable in twenty-five years, with interest at six per cent., payable semi-annually in coin. Usually, government bonds running for the longest time command the highest price, and for permanent investment are most eagerly sought after, at home and abroad. As we emerge from our present embarrassments, the other forms of debts due by the United States will naturally be funded in such stock.

We promise coin for all interest on bonds, as it is indispensable that all engagements assuming this solemn form should in no instance repudiate the standard of the Constitution.

We strike out all words in relation to any foreign loan, as during this war we expect to fight our own battles, furnish our own means, without any foreign aid or assistance; and if we can be permitted to do that we shall ask no favors.

The substitute avoids all the material, and, we might say, fatal objections to the original bill; is entirely practical and feasible in its character, and will not only relieve the Treasury from its present necessities, but do something toward making provision for the future wants. It is a question that will mark for weal or for woe an important page of our history; and I invoke the courage and judgment of the Committee to meet the question with that cool deliberation its high moment demands."

"MR. CHAIRMAN—The member of the Committee of Ways and Means (Mr. Spaulding), by whom this bill was reported, was well warranted in all he said of its great magnitude, and of the thoughtful, serious, courageous attention due to its consideration. It concerns the life of the nation —the means whereby it lives. The credit of the government, like the credit of an individual, consists of the ability and integrity to pay all debts and perform all promises with scrupulous exactness and punctuality. This ability and integrity, this untarnished public faith and unquestioned pecuniary solvency is that without which no Government can long survive. Public credit alone cannot confer national immortality or national longevity, but the loss of public credit will be inevitably and swiftly followed by national decrepitude and national death. This is true in peace, when wars and rumors of wars are hushed throughout the earth; it is true in uneventful times, in periods barren of action and prolific of repose; but what shall be said of its urgent, warning truth, as applicable to us in this dark hour of trial and of danger? *Immediate and adequate financial facilities constitute, beyond all question, the overtopping, overmastering subjects with which we have the power to deal.*

Gentlemen have longed for victories to re-invigorate the languishing energies of finance. Victory, no doubt, would exert a potent influence; but, sir, the Treasury will control and decide the war, not the war the Treasury. Indeed, the question of money and credit is all there is before us; it is practically the only unsettled question of the war. Armies and navies may perish, and a public credit, well preserved, can replace them; but if the public credit perishes, the army and navy can only increase the disaster and deepen the dishonor. * * * * * * *

I deny that any necessity is upon us to take the case out of settled rules. We need money—large sums of money—and the whole resources and property of the nation are liable to pay tribute to raise it. We owe debts —large debts—and the whole property of the country is holden to pay them. Does anybody suppose that the security is not ample, or the resources not abundant? My colleague from the Erie District (Mr. Spaulding) told us that the taxable property of the nation amounts to sixteen thousand millions of dollars; and he produced a statement from the Census Bureau to prove it. In reality it is vastly more than that, because he gave us a self-fixed valuation—the valuation fixed by proprietors themselves, having an interest in reducing and covering up the amount.

According to my colleague, at the end of this fiscal year our debt will be only $650,000,000. One would think here was margin enough for Wall street, State street, or Chestnut street. Sir, it is margin enough, properly husbanded from first to last, to enable us to raise all the money we want at five per cent., and history proves it.

Now, sir, what does this plea of necessity mean—this plea upon which we are invited to leave the trodden paths of safety, and seek new methods of 'winning false moneys from the crucible called debt?' What is the necessity which prevents adherence to the old and approved methods of raising money? The arguments must be two-fold: First, that the people will be better ready at some other time than the present to pay what, in the end, they must pay, with interest; and second, that necessary and legitimate taxation will be unpopular, and bring denunciation upon those who vote it. Sir, I take issue upon both propositions. I say the country is rich and ready. Money is abundant—very abundant. There is in the loyal States $250,000,000 of gold—the gentleman from Massachusetts (Mr. Alley) said the other day $300,000,000—more than ever before, and if we deserve it, we can have it. The whole country is full of wealth. The enormous expenditures of this home war have been made among ourselves, and the money has remained here and not gone into the channel which foreign war prescribes for currency. The harvest has been abundant; materials and productions, raw and wrought, have been in great demand; and nearly every loyal State teems with the elements of material prosperity. From a very extravagant, we have lately become a very economical people, and thus the percentage, as well as the aggregate of savings of earnings, is unusually great. We are able to pay now, and we never can pay better than now. * * * * * *

There is one thing, however, about the proposed banking scheme, and about the bill before us, intended probably to attract votes, which seems of very questionable policy and very doubtful ethics. I mean hostility to the existing banks of the country. And inasmuch as I own not a farthing in the stock of any bank, and have not the slightest connection with one, perhaps a word in behalf of banks in loyal States will be borne with from me.

The present troubles, or rather their own patriotic action, have broken the banks; for every commercial man in this House knows that the banks were never stronger than when the Secretary of the Treasury appealed to them for loans. *They allowed the Government to carry off their specie, their capital from their vaults*, and if that did not break them, they at all events might have adopted a policy which would have saved them. But they had to suspend, and the design of this bill would seem to be to prevent their resumption of specie payment. At all events, it is obviously the policy in some quarters to preach a crusade against the present banks, and array prejudices and votes on that issue. * * * * * *

I propose to assign my reasons briefly for voting against the attempt by legislation to make paper a legal tender. The proposition is a new one. No precedent can be urged in its favor; no suggestion of the existence of such a power can be found in the legislative history of the country; and I submit to my colleague, as a lawyer, the proposition that this amounts to affirmative authority of the highest kind against it. Had such a power lurked in the Constitution, as construed by those who ordained and administered it, we should find it so recorded. The occasion for resorting to it, or at least referring to it, has, we know, repeatedly arisen; and had such a power existed, it would have been recognized and acted on. It is hardly too much to say, therefore, that the uniform and universal judgment of statesmen, jurists and lawyers has denied the constitutional right of Congress to make paper a legal tender for debts to any extent whatever. But more is claimed here than the right to create a legal tender heretofore unknown. The provision is not confined to transactions in *future*, but is retroactive in its scope. It reaches back and strikes at every existing pecuniary obligation. This was well put by the gentleman from Ohio (Mr. Pendleton), and I concur with him that substituting anything for gold and silver in payment of debts, and still more of precedent debts, is of very doubtful constitutionality. * * * * * * *

But, sir, passing, as I see I must, from the constitutional objections to the bill, it seems to me that its moral imperfections are equally serious. It will, of course, proclaim throughout the country a saturnalia of fraud—a carnival for rogues. Every agent, attorney, treasurer, trustee, guardian, executor, administrator, consignee, commission merchant, and every debtor of a fiduciary character who has received for others money, hard money, worth a hundred cents in the dollar, will forever release himself from liability by buying up for that knavish purpose, at its depreciated value, the spurious currency which we shall have put afloat. Everybody will do it except those who are more honest than the American Congress advises them to be. Think of savings banks entrusted with enormous aggregates of the pittances of the poor, the hungry, and the homeless, the stranger, the needlewoman, the widow and the orphan, and we are arranging for a robbery of ten, if not of fifty, per cent. of the entire amount, and that by a contrivance so new as never to have been discovered under the administration of Monroe Edwards or James Buchanan.

To reverse the picture: after the act shall have gone into effect, honest men undertake transactions based upon the spurious tender at its then value. By and by comes a repeal, and they are driven to ruin in multitudes by the inevitable loss incident to a return to metallic currency.

* * * * * * * * * * * * * *

The whole scheme pre-supposes that the notes to be emitted will be lepers in the commercial world from the hour they are brought into it; that they will be shunned and condemned by the laws of trade and value. If this is not to be their fate, what is the sense, as was said in the Federal Constitutional Convention, in attempting to legislate their value up. Now, sir, I do not believe that you can legislate up the value of a thing any more than you can make generals heroes by legislation.

* * * * * * * * * * * * * *

Mr. Chairman—I believe all the money needed can be provided in season by means of unquestionable legality and safety. The substitute I have offered will, I believe, without essential alteration, effect that result."

Mr. Conkling estimated the national debt up to July 1, 1862, at $806,000,000, and concluded as follows:

"There has been no such occasion presented to a nation, no such demand made upon a nation during the lifetime of the human race. The history of America, the history of free government, the history of constitutional liberty begins or ends now. We have our career and our traditions as a nation; they are safe; but our history is yet to be made. Our destiny is without an ally in the world, with nations banded against us, to hold fast a continent in the midst of the greatest, guiltiest revolution the world has ever seen."

Mr. Bingham, of Ohio, obtained the floor.

Mr. Stevens offered a substitute for the original bill, which he asked to have printed. After Mr. Bingham had concluded his speech, the substitute. thus offered by Mr. Stevens was ordered to be printed.

MR. BINGHAM'S SPEECH.

MR. BINGHAM—"It was far from my purpose, when I came early to the House to-day to attend a meeting of the Committee on the Judiciary, to enter upon any discussion of the important question which now commands the attention of the Representatives of the people; and but for some remarks which have been made to-day by the honorable gentleman from New York (Mr. Roscoe Conkling), I would not feel disposed now to address the Committee. But, sir, as a Representative of the people, I cannot keep silent when I see efforts made upon this side of the House and upon that to lay the power of the American people to control their currency—a power essential to their interests—at the feet of brokers and of city bankers, who have not a title of authority, save by the assent or forbearance of the people, to deal in their paper issued as money.

I am here to-day to assert the rightful authority of the American people, as a nationality, sovereignty, under and by virtue of their Constitution. In saying that the people of this Republic are one people, a sovereignty, I do not feel that I shall be confronted by any of the great names of the illustrious dead who have suddenly found favor with gentlemen upon the other side of the House. Living, there was no epithet in our language too severe in its condemnation, or too much uncharitable in its import, for the fit denunciation by certain parties of the alleged political heresies of the illustrious man, Alexander Hamilton, and that other illustrious man, Daniel Webster, who for strength of intellect stood alone among the living; and now dead, in his honored grave, sleeps alone by the sounding sea. I am not myself of that class of admirers who persecute men while living and heap tuns of granite and pour empty adulation upon their ashes when dead. I prefer to respect them and their authority while they stand among the living men of to-day. These great names have been invoked in this debate. For what purpose? For the purpose of denationalizing the people; for the purpose of stripping the American people of the attributes of sovereignty; for the purpose of laying, as I said before, at the feet and at the mercy of brokers and hawkers on 'Change the power of the people over their monetary interests in this hour of national exigency.

Sir, there is nothing in the records of these illustrious men that justifies any such base use of their utterances, which were made not only for the instruction of the men of their own day, but for the guidance of all that were to come after them. I venture to affirm—without having recently had the opportunity to read much of what he said upon that subject—that Alexander Hamilton, peerless almost among the founders of the Constitution, never intimated in any paper of his that the Government of the United States could not, at its pleasure, issue Treasury notes, either payable upon demand or payable upon time. There was much said by my respected colleague (Mr. Pendleton) with which I entirely and altogether agree; but, sir, when my colleague *seemed* to intimate in his argument that he found any warrant in the elaborate papers of Alexander Hamilton against this authority or power of the Congress of the United States to authorize the issue of Treasury notes, either payable upon time or upon demand, he greatly mistook the spirit of all he has written, and which has been transmitted to us. My colleague was adroit in the handling of the papers of Hamilton, which will live as long as our language lives. He was one of those men upon whom it pleased God to confer those extraordinary gifts which command the homage and admiration of men, whether they agreed with him or not. The passage which my colleague quoted from his work was an argument in which he showed the propriety of establishing a national bank, authorized to issue currency, and he gave certain reasons therefor. My colleague is a most excellent lawyer. He knows well, and so did Hamilton know well when he made that argument, that what the Government does by another it does by itself."

MR. BINGHAM argued at great length that Congress had the power under the Constitution to authorize the issue of Treasury notes, payable on demand or payable on time, redeemable in gold and silver, or other legalized coin, and make them a legal tender; and that the present bill did not contemplate any other issue. He insisted that Congress, by the Constitution, was invested with certain powers, and as to the objects, and within the scope of those powers, *it was sovereign.* That the Constitution contained no words giving to Congress the power to make gold or silver coin, either foreign or domestic, a legal tender. It has the power to coin money, and regulate the value thereof and of foreign coins, but the Constitution does not contain any words declaring that these coins shall be *a legal tender.* The point I make is this: Congress has power by the Constitution to fix the standard value of foreign coin and of domestic coin, and the power to declare a legal tender, and that these powers are distinct. It may *declare what shall be a legal tender,* either foreign coin or domestic coin, or *paper* representing coin. It is done by *act of Congress.* Nothing ever was a legal tender under the Constitution in discharge of debt but by express provision of an act of Congress. That the power "to regulate commerce" confers on Congress the power to declare what should be received in payment of debt. It is not restricted to gold and silver, but the Government may issue Treasury notes, redeemable in gold and silver, and declare them a legal tender in payment of debts. He denied that this bill would "impair the obligation of contracts." There is no such limitation as that imposed by the Constitution upon the power of Congress. It is a limitation upon the *States,* and not upon the United States. It was not by inadvertence that the framers of the Constitution omitted to impose upon Congress this express restriction upon the States against impairing the obligation of contracts. They proclaimed in the absence of such limitations that whoever, within the jurisdiction of the United States, enters into any mere money contract, either public or private, enters into it subject to the sovereign power of the people, to determine at any time, by legislative enactment, what shall discharge it. It is of the essence of the contract.

He did not share in any of the fears entertained or intimated that the people will revolt at this measure. He had an abiding faith in their loyalty, in their love of law, in their settled purpose to suffer and strive, to labor and sacrifice, that they may maintain their Government and transmit it unimpaired to their children."

MR. SHEFFIELD, of Rhode Island, followed Mr. Bingham in a lengthy speech in opposition to the legal tender clause in the bill. He insisted that it was unconstitutional, and an odious feature. The fact that you propose to force these notes upon the public against the will of the people implies that force is necessary, in your judgment, to induce people to take them. He said that if the legal tender clause was stricken out he would vote for the bill, notwithstanding it was objectionable in other respects. (Mr. Sheffield's speech will be found reported in the *Congressional Globe*, page 640–1.)

On Wednesday, February 5th, several speeches were made for and against the bill, all of which are fully reported in the *Congressional Globe*, but the limits of this narrative will not admit of their being published here. Only a brief sketch can be given at this time.

MR. CHRISFIELD, of Maryland, spoke for one hour in opposition to the legal tender clause in the bill.

"He admitted that the accustomed currency was wholly inadequate to meet the exigencies of the war. The Government has for many years used gold and silver, and it is deeply to be regretted that it is obliged to depart from this desirable standard. But we are left no option. The supply of the precious metals is inadequate to our wants. If all the gold and silver in the country was placed at the control of the Government, it would be received and paid out twice in one year. It is, therefore, impossible for the Government to pay in coin. The business of the country and the business of the Government require some substitute for coin. We must therefore create a new or vastly enlarge the existing currency. We must therefore create a public debt, establish a currency, and impose new taxes. This necessity being admitted, the only question is how can these objects be accomplished with the least prejudice to the people, and the greatest convenience to the Government? *This is a grave question—the gravest which these times present. It is the question which lies at the foundation of all other questions; and on its solution depends success in every other enterprise.*"

He argued at great length that the legal tender clause was unconstitutional, and that it would not be just to the creditor class of the community. He moved to strike out this clause in the bill, and also the clause which compelled persons in the employ of the government to receive the notes for "salaries, debts and demands *owing* by the United States," so as to make them only "receivable for all debts and demands *due* the United States.' He urged heavy taxation, and was generally favorable to the bill, if the amendments were made which he proposed, but could not vote for the bill with the legal tender clause retained. (Appendix to *Congressional Globe*, page 47–48.)

MR. PIKE, of Maine, spoke for one hour in favor of the bill.

"He argued that the plan was expedient as well as constitutional. Upon the clause in the bill providing that the notes shall be a legal tender there has been much discussion here and elsewhere. Its importance to the measure cannot be overestimated. *He regarded it as the life of the plan.*

Strike it out and we are but duplicating notes already at a discount. It is really the specie clause, and no hard money man—and he claimed to be one—should vote for the issue of these notes without it. It is well known that Mr. Clay rested his support of the second bank upon the clause granting Congress "the power to make all laws which shall be necessary and proper for carrying into effect the powers," expressly granted by the eighteenth section of the first article. The great patriot of the West, in time of profound peace, was disposed to consider the financial question of such magnitude as to plan a law calling into being a fiscal agent among those which were "necessary and proper." With how much more force can we, situated as it were, among the dying agonies of the republic of our fathers, acting as many wise men believe, as the last Congress which, under the Constitution, shall represent the whole country, claim that all power which, under any circumstances, could be exercised by the Representatives of the people, should be used now."

MR. ALLEY, of Massachusetts, made a well-considered speech of one hour in favor of the bill.

"The measure before the House received the approbation of his judgment. He could see clearly that under its provisions the rights of all will be protected, the prosperity of the whole people promoted, the credit of the Government revived and its power and dignity maintained. Beneficent as this measure is, as one of relief, nothing could induce him to give it his sanction but uncontrolable necessity. While he had always believed it to be the duty of Congress to regulate and control the currency by such legislation as would make it of uniform value throughout the country, he had never regarded it as politic or wise for the Government to make issues of paper at any time, except for temporary emergencies. Disguise it as you may, everybody knows that knows anything of the laws of trade, that to carry this people through this crisis, collect $150,000,000 tax, maintain these vast expenditures, and conduct the legitimate and necessary business of the country, you must increase the volume of the currency to such an amount as to make it impossible, under the present banking system, to give it confidence upon the ground of its immediate convertibility into specie. The question then for Congress to decide, is whether the Government shall share with the banks—and keep them in check—this circulation, or purchase their irredeemable bills at ruinous rates. If you do not adopt this measure you will see the country flooded with irredeemable bank currency, a great deal of which will be found, as after the war of 1812, utterly worthless. At that time Government securities were exchanged at eighty cents on the dollar for worthless bank promises, not worth the paper upon which they were written."

MR. ALLEY concluded his remarks as follows:

"Why, I ask, are government securities worth in the market to-day but ninety cents on the dollar in exchange for irredeemable bank paper? Is it because they have confidence in bank paper, or because it will command specie? Not at all; but because the bank paper will liquidate the obligations of debtors. It is for you to determine whether government obligations shall be as good as irredeemable bank notes; and whether you will allow these irredeemable issues to be preferred and take precedence of a national currency issued by a Government that never repudiated a dollar of its indebtedness; and a nation whose fabulous growth, immense interests and exhaustless resources, have excited the wonder and admiration of an astonished world. I confess that when I reflect upon our condition, and the misery and suffering which such a policy inflicts upon the business interests of the country, I can have no toleration for such suicidal action. Congress has the power to inaugurate to-day a system of financial policy, both for Government and people, which will establish our prosperity upon a firm foundation, and give strength and stability to all our institutions; and I conjure you, by all the memories of the past and every hope in the future, not to disappoint in this moment of peril the just expectations of the American people."

While Mr. ALLEY was making his speech, Mr. Spaulding received from Secretary Chase a private note, urging the importance of having the vote taken on the bill that day. It was known that Mr. Horton, a prominent member of the Committee of Ways and Means, desired to speak in opposition to the bill, and that several other members desired to express their views of the measure before the vote was taken.

The Treasury was nearly empty. Money, or other available means must be had right off. The pressing demands made upon the Treasury could not be put off much longer without ruin to the credit of the Government. The Secretary had authority under the Loan Act, passed at the extra session in July, still remaining, to issue $46,000.000 of Treasury notes bearing 3-65 per cent. interest, or, at his option, to issue 7-30 notes; but was unable to put out either class of this paper without a discount. The 7-30 notes could not be paid out from the Treasury except at a discount of two per cent., and he could not pay out the 3-65 notes at all, because they would not pass as currency, except at a still greater discount—the rate of interest was so low that they were not desirable as an investment, and not being a legal tender they could not be made available at par as a currency.

The following is a copy of the note received from Secretary Chase at this time:

"Such men as Nathaniel Thayer, of Boston; Alexander Duncan, of Duncan, Sherman & Co.; Shepard Knapp and John D. Wolf, and numerous able and leading financial men, have told me within two days that you were perfectly right, and they are deeply anxious that the legal tender clause should stand in the bill. They say the country is lost without it."

TREASURY DEPARTMENT, February 5, 1862.

MY DEAR SIR—I make the above extract from a letter received from the Collector of New York this morning. It is very important the bill should go through to-day, and through the Senate this week. The public exigencies do not admit of delay.

Yours truly,

HON. E. G. SPAULDING.   S. P. CHASE.

After receiving this note from the Secretary, Mr. Spaulding thought it desirable that a time should be fixed for closing the debate on the bill. He thought it desirable that Mr. Horton and Mr. Stevens, members of the Committee of Ways and Means, should speak, and such others as were prepared, and that the vote should be taken the next day.

The following proceedings took place in the House.

MR. WRIGHT obtained the floor.

MR. SPAULDING—"I move that the Committee rise with a view of closing this debate."

MR. CAMPBELL—"I hope this motion will be agreed to, and that this bill will be pressed to a vote to-day."

MR. SPAULDING—"I desire to say, in connection with this motion, that I have within the last two or three hours received a note from the Secretary of the Treasury informing me that it is absolutely necessary that we should press this measure to a vote without further delay. Therefore I move that the Committee rise, with a view of closing debate."

MR. HORTON—"I wish to say that the Committee of Ways and Means do not make this motion, and I hope it will be voted down." ("Good!" "Good!")

THE CHAIRMAN—"The Chair would state that this question is not debatable."

MR. ENGLISH—"I move to lay the motion upon the table."

THE CHAIRMAN—"That motion is not in order in committee."

The question being upon the motion that the Committee rise.

MR. ROSCOE CONKLING demanded tellers.

Tellers were ordered, and Messrs. Blair, of Missouri, and Thomas, of Massachusetts, were appointed.

The Committee divided, and the tellers reported—yeas, 52; nays, 62.

So the motion was not agreed to.

MR. SPAULDING—"With the permission of the gentleman from Pennsylvania, I wish to make one word of explanation in reference to the motion I made. The object of the motion was simply that we should limit this debate, with a view that we might take a vote upon the bill to-morrow, say at one o'clock. I expected to go immediately back into committee to allow the gentleman from Pennsylvania to make his speech, and then to allow Mr. Horton to speak, and then Mr. Stevens to close the debate. After that the vote would be taken."

MR. THOMAS, of Massachusetts—"Then you arrange the manner in which speeches shall be made on this floor."

MR. LOVEJOY—"I would like to know whether the gentleman from New York has any right to farm out the floor?"

MR. SPAULDING—"I make this explanation with a view to show the House that I have no disposition to cut off any member of the Committee or to force a vote unduly. The motion was made under the necessity which, the Secretary of the Treasury assures us, exists for passing this bill. I did not make it with a view to cut off those who are entitled to speak, by courtesy or otherwise. I think this explanation will satisfy the House that there was no effort upon my part to force a vote improperly. I did not expect to have a vote until to-morrow at one or two o'clock. After the debate is closed, we proceed to voting upon amendments which are pending, and which may be offered, and then five-minute speeches will be in order, as upon other bills. Those speeches can be continued until amendments are exhausted."

MR. WRIGHT, of Pennsylvania, spoke for half an hour in opposition to the legal tender clause of the bill.

"He was willing to do almost anything that he considered constitutional to aid in putting down the rebellion, but he did not feel justified in going so far as to vote any such measure as the legal tender bill. He concurred in the views of Mr. Pendleton that it was unconstitutional, that nothing but gold and silver could be made a legal tender in payment of debts. The people have means enough in their possession, and he was willing to go for taxation to the uttermost limit, but the time had not yet arrived when we should resort to such an extreme measure as to make these notes a legal tender." * * * * * * * * *

MR. HORTON, of Ohio, a prominent member of the Committee of Ways and Means, made a lengthy speech in opposition to the legal tender clause in the bill.

"He thought we were taking a dangerous departure from the financial system of the country. If this bill passes, as he hoped it would not, this will be a point from which we shall date a new financial system for the United States. "Old things will have been done away; all things will have become new." He thought the Loan bill and the Tax bill should have been passed through this House side by side. The Committee of Ways and Means were convinced of the importance of this, and were desirous that it should be done. (Mr. Horton was one of the sub-committee on the Tax bill.) It is from no neglect of the Committee of Ways and Means, or of the sub-committee which has had the preparation of the Tax bill in charge, that the Tax bill and Loan bill have not been brought forward side by side. The sub-committee on the Tax bill have worked night and day; and although they do not get much credit for being industrious, still substantial progress had been made.

There were two measures before the House, and he proposed to discuss them. One was the proposition of the gentleman from New York (Mr. Spaulding) and the other that of the gentleman from Vermont (Mr. Morrill). He insisted that the three-sixty-five hundredths per cent. notes, proposed in Mr. Morrill's plan, possessed "all the characteristics for circulation which the Treasury notes of Mr. Spaulding's bill will have (save the legal tender clause), and have the important advantage of earning interest, and being fundable in a more desirable stock for the holder, because bearing a higher rate of interest, and more advantageous to the Government, because having only half the time to run, the Government can redeem them at an earlier day." The Committee of Ways and Means are equally divided in regard to the two bills. He was for the substitute of Mr. Morrill, and decidedly opposed to the legal tender scheme. He thought we had not yet reached the point when the Government, exercising its high prerogatives, as Mr. Spaulding called them, can take for its use the property of the citizen without pay. Necessity for this measure has been asserted, but not proved. The Secretary of the Treasury thinks it is necessary, but he thought he was mistaken."

Mr. Horton argued at great length against the injustice and inexpediency of making the notes a legal tender, and concluded as follows:

"Mr. Chairman—I thank the Committee for listening to me so long. You know that I am unaccustomed to speaking in the House, and my remarks of course have been very desultory. But I wish to impress upon the Committee that these opinions of mine are not merely opinions superinduced by a hopeful temperament. I have, according to the best of my knowledge, examined this whole question in all its bearings, and I am willing to take the responsibility of voting against this legal tender clause of the bill for the reasons that I have given, and for divers and sundry reasons which I have not given. I ask the Committee to pause before they take a step which, once taken, will be irrevocable. When you have once broken a pitcher it never becomes whole again; and this fair fabric of our untarnished faith and unbounded wealth and credit ought not to be destroyed, simply because our leaders—men that we have faith in—have become alarmed, and have told us that there is a necessity for it. When there is danger, Mr. Chairman, then is the time to be cool and look about you, and to see that you take no false step. Now is that time, and if you take this step, it is a step downwards, and you will find that to regain the high eminence from which we shall have descended is a labor very difficult to accomplish."

Mr. Kellogg, of Illinois, obtained the floor.

Mr. Spaulding—"I ask the gentleman to give way to me for a few moments, and then I will move that the Committee rise."

Mr. Kellogg, of Illinois—"I yield for that purpose."

Mr. Spaulding—"I wish to make one statement in reference to the condition of the Treasury, which I presume all will be anxious to know before we adjourn. The Secretary of the Treasury has yet unexpended of the loan of last July $46,000,000. He has a right to issue this sum in three and sixty-five hundredths per cent. notes, or in seven and three-tenths per cent notes; but he is unable to put out either of these classes of paper without a discount. He cannot pay out the seven and three-tenths per cent. notes without a discount of two per cent., and he cannot pay out the three and sixty-five one hundredths per cent notes because they will not be taken as currency. *This bill of Mr. Morrill proposes simply to repeal the authority to issue the same kind of notes, which cannot be issued advantageously by the Secretary of the Treasury at this time.* I move that the Committee do now rise."

The motion was agreed to.   *   *   *   *   *   *

Mr. Spaulding—"I move that all debate on House bill No. 240 be closed in one hour after its consideration shall have been resumed in the Committee of the Whole on the state of the Union."

Mr. THOMAS, of Massachusetts—"I suggest to the gentleman to modify his motion, so as to make it read two hours."

Mr. SPAULDING—"The exigencies of the country are such that I cannot consent to do so unless the House so order it."

Mr. VALLANDIGHAM—"I move to amend the motion by striking out 'one hour' and inserting 'two hours.'"

The amendment was adopted, and the motion as amended was agreed to.

PASSAGE OF THE BILL IN THE HOUSE.

Thursday, February 6, 1862, was an exciting and important day in the House. The final vote on the legal tender note bill was to be taken, and in anticipation of the vote there was a very full house. In pursuance of the order passed last night, general debate was to be closed in two hours after the bill should be taken up in Committee of the Whole. The House on meeting and disposing of a little preliminary business, immediately resolved itself into Committee of the Whole, and resumed the consideration of the bill. The Chairman announced that general debate on the bill would close at ten minutes past two o'clock P. M. While debate was continued, Mr. Frank and Mr. Colfax, who were friendly to the bill, passed around the House with a list, making a canvass of how the different members would vote on the legal tender clause. Upon footing up the list, it was ascertained that there was a large majority in favor of making the notes a legal tender.

Mr. KELLOGG, of Illinois, being entitled to the floor, spoke for over half an hour in favor of the bill, not as a *peace* measure, but as a *war measure*. He said:

"I intend to detain the Committee but a little while. I should not have sought the floor for the purpose of offering any remarks, but for the consideration that, in my judgment, this bill was being considered and discussed as it might with propriety have been discussed and *considered in time of peace*, and when there was no pressing necessity for the action of Congress in placing the Government in possession of all the means and powers that can be safely gathered and exercised under the Constitution. If this question came up in ordinary times, *I am frank to confess, that I might, perhaps, have had some doubt of its constitutionality sufficient to induce me to oppose it. I mean by that only to say that in time of peace, when the integrity of the Government is not threatened, I would be more careful and cautious; and if I doubted the constitutionality of the measure I would not vote for it. But, sir, in this our extremity, while we are struggling to perpetuate our Government, I am willing to go to the very verge of the Constitution.* I will go as far as I feel that the Constitution will permit me, to gather up the power and means to carry on the Government to that great consummation which the fathers contemplated when they established it. But while I might have some doubt in time of peace, when the monetary affairs of the country might safely be left to work out their own level and settlement, of the policy of this measure, I have none now. What may be policy in the one case may be vastly different in the other.

I treat this, Mr. Chairman, *as emphatically and clearly a war measure*. It may appear strange that a money bill should be considered a war measure, and yet it is; for *it is necessary* in order to raise means to carry on the Government in a war direction—a direction in which all our measures are or should be tending. Sir, we should not disguise the fact of our complications. We should not deceive ourselves. The worst deception that men ever practice is that practiced on themselves. We should not allow ourselves to be deluded, now that we have a mighty rebellion—nay, revolution—before us, and that the Powers of the Old World, who have looked with a jealous eye on the mighty progress of the Western Continent, are seeking occasion to cripple our onward and upward career. Talk not of their sympathy for us. Our Government antagonizes theirs. The principles are different. We must gird up our loins; we must take all the power we have; we must throw every energy, all the means of our Government, in the direction of the war power, for the purpose of self-preservation and perpetuation.

Mr. Chairman, we must look this matter in the face, not only of this continent, but in the face of surrounding nations. We must come to the conclusion that although the world shall rise against us, this Republic must and shall be preserved. All the energy of the country, all the blood and treasure of the country, if need be, must be summoned in from every part of the land to accomplish that object. Sir, we must give to this Government arms of iron and muscles of steel. We must think as with fire and strike as with spears. It is necessary, sir, it must be; and if we now meet this emergency as true men should meet it, we shall succeed. *The money of the country must come to its aid, the powers of the Government must come to the aid of the Administration, as well as the strong hands and warm hearts of our people.*

Mr. Chairman, I am pained when I sit in my place in the House and hear members *talk about the sacredness of capital; that the interests of money must not be touched. Yes, sir, they will vote six hundred thousand of the flower of the American youth for the Army, to be sacrificed, without a blush*; but the great interests of capital, of currency, must not be touched. We have summoned the youth; they have come. *I would summon the capital;* and if it does not come voluntarily, before this Republic shall go down, or one star be lost, I would take every cent from the treasury of the States, from the treasury of capitalists, from the treasury of individuals, and press it into the use of the Government.

What is capital worth without a Government? Gentlemen must understand me, when I indulge in this strain and speak in this strain and speak of this talk and quibble about capital, that *I do not charge it upon the real capitalists of the country, for they do not hold back. The true capitalists of the country are patriotic;* they have furnished their means liberally; but there is a class of huckstering capitalists, there is a class of bankers proper, there is a class of brokers, who would make merchandise of the hopes and fears of the Republic. * * * * * * * * *

It is said there is no power to make these notes a legal tender, and that

that is not a legitimate way of expressing their value. If gentlemen are sure upon that subject, they would do well to run back a little further and ascertain whether there is any power under the Constitution vested in Congress to issue the notes at all. And I confess the argument of the gentleman from Ohio (Mr. Pendleton) ran back legitimately to that proposition. At least it carried my mind back to that proposition so fairly and certainly, that if I found no power to issue these notes, I would have voted against this bill. To that my mind has turned with every argument that has been made. I may have been obtuse, but I confess that I have come to the conclusion that we have the constitutional power to issue these notes; and having that constitutional power we have, as an *incident to that power*, the power also to make them of value by making them a legal tender. The gentleman has voted more than once for the issue of Treasury notes to pay debts owing by the Government, which were payable in coin. If we have power to issue Treasury notes, we have the power to fix the value of the issue. It is an incident to the power of issuance. Let them be issued as money, to take the place of money. Let there be no deception; let the creditors of the Government know whether we are to palm off a spurious depreciated currency under the guise of money. If we have the right to issue it, and impress with the denomination of five dollars, why not stamp upon its face that it is five dollars everywhere?"

Mr. THOMAS, of Massachusetts, made a speech against the legal tender clause in the bill.

"He regarded this clause as unconstitutional, unjust, and inexpedient. The question had never been settled by judicial authority, but the weight of reasoning by Webster, Madison, and others, was strongly against the validity of this clause in the bill. He argued that nothing but coined money could be made a legal tender in payments of debts; that a matured debt could not be paid by another *promise*. He regarded this clause in the bill in the nature of a forced loan, in itself a confession of weakness. The friends of this feature of the bill admit the reluctance with which they assent to it. The only ground of defence is its necessity, that no alternative is left to us. He deeply respected their motives, but could not himself see the necessity."

Mr. EDWARDS, of New Hampshire, made a speech in favor of the bill.

"We find ourselves confronted by an exhausted Treasury, and without the means of meeting its existing, or its constantly accruing liabilities. The amount of floating liability now due is $100,000,000. The figures presented in the opening speech of this debate are immense—almost appalling. Funded and floating it is now $400,000,000; on the first of July next it will be $650,000,000, and if the war continues $1,200,000,000 in one year from that time. He was in favor of taxation to pay ordinary expenses and interest, and ultimately a sinking fund, but he was in favor of the issue of Treasury notes for the purpose of meeting immediate expenditures, and all parties seemed to concede that Treasury notes in some form must be issued. The bill reported by the Committee of Ways and Means, and the substitute offered by Mr. Morrill, may be regarded as the only propositions now before the House. It is understood that the other propositions will be withdrawn, and that the dissenters from the bill will concentrate on this substitute. They agree in the main features of the plan, and differ only in details. He thought the notes proposed by Mr. Morrill's plan would not pass current among the people or the banks, but would necessarily depreciate. The army and navy might be compelled to receive them at par, because the Government had nothing else to give them, but they could not afterwards pass them without a large discount, which would be unjust to the men fighting our battles. He thought that would be a lack of faith of the most flagrant description—more objectionable by far than the legal tender clause. He also objected to the high rates of interest proposed for the bonds to be issued in funding the notes.

The substitute provides for a *depreciated currency and a high rate of interest* He thought the currency proposed by the substitute would demoralize the country as much, or more, than the legal tender notes, and would not possess as many advantages to the Government.

The legal tender notes would give *instant means* to the Treasury, so much needed at this time, without looking to intermediate negotiation to furnish them. The original bill was the one in all material respects to be preferred to the substitute, one of which it is distinctly understood will be adopted."

Mr. RIDDLE, of Ohio, made a speech against the propriety and expediency of issuing the legal tender notes.

"He doubted the constitutionality of the measure. He thought there was no real money, except the metals coined in pursuance of law and a fixed standard. Can money be made of paper? Clearly not, by calling it money or by stamping it as money by the Government. It would not stand the commercial test. Paper has no appreciable intrinsic value, and its exchangeable value is of the lowest possible grade. The only high degree of value it can ever attain is that which may be imparted to it by that which is written or printed upon it. It is apparent that the whole quantity of the circulating medium must be materially increased, for obviously that which was only equal to the demands of commerce and the ordinary wants of the Government, is wholly inadequate now to the same demands and the extraordinary wants of the Government. He was opposed to the legal tender clause, and would vote to strike it out; if that fails, I will choose between the bill and its defeat." (He voted for the bill on its final passage.)

Mr. BLAKE, of Ohio, spoke in favor of the bill.

"At no time in the history of our country was the peril to our free institutions greater than now. The bill is brought forward as a war measure, to meet the pressing demands now on the Treasury. He argued that it was constitutional to issue Treasury notes and make them a legal tender. He insisted that it was a necessary and proper means of carrying into effect the war powers—to raise and support armies and to provide and maintain a navy. We are now in the midst of a great National exigency, and one, too, that we must provide for; and one that in the application of the means there must of necessity be great latitude of discretion, and denied that legal tender paper money was prohibited." (He read from the debates on the formation of the Constitution, Vol. 5, page 435.)

Mr. MASON—"He was unwilling *to tie the hands of the Legislature.* He observed that the late war could not have been carried on had such a prohibition existed."

Mr. BUTLER—"That paper was a legal tender in no country in Europe."

Mr. MASON—"Was still averse to tying the hands of the Legislature altogether. If there was no example in Europe, as just remarked, it might be observed, on the other side, that there was none in which the Government was restrained on this head."

Mr. BLAKE continued his argument, insisting "that the Convention which framed the Constitution did not attempt any prohibition, but left it to Congress to make Treasury notes a legal tender whenever the exigency should arise to make it necessary. It was denied in express terms to the *States*, and permitted in implied terms to Congress. It being constitutional, is it necessary to make Treasury notes a legal tender? By these notes we are enabled to pay our soldiers, and it is the only means we have to pay them. Does not every gentleman know that if these notes were paid to our soldiers without making them a legal tender, *they will immediately be sold at a loss to the soldiers of from four to twenty per cent.? This is not conjecture: this very thing was done here only last month; soldiers were shaved by the money-shavers of this District from four to twenty per cent. on the demand Treasury notes they had received from the Government. We are not legislating for the money-shavers, who oppose this bill, but for the people, the soldiers, and laboring classes.*"

Mr. CAMPBELL, of Pennsylvania, spoke in favor of the bill.

"He said, it is proper that each member of this House should, however briefly, express his views on the pending bill—one of the most, if not the most, important bills of this season. To support our armies in the field and navies on the seas is a plain, patriotic and necessary duty; to do this with prudence, economy and foresight, is the highest evidence of statesmanship. That we have vast National resources, all admit; that the public debt has for its security the whole property of the nation, is equally plain. The powers of the Government are ample—they extend to life and property. He would fall short of his duty in this tremendous issue, in which free government is on its final trial, who would not, if necessary, *vote the last man and the last dollar to defend and perpetuate the priceless inheritance of our fathers.*

I humbly conceive my duty to be a plain one. The path I have marked out for myself I will follow, let it lead where it may. Whatever measure is now or hereafter may become *necessary* to adopt in order to maintain the Union and perpetuate free Government, that will I support. Speak not to me of "objections" and "scruples" and "dangers," of "Constitutional objections" and "conservative influences." Sophistry is ever plausible, and opposition to a just and necessary measure generally wears the mask of a "Constitutional objection." The highest duty of every member is to maintain the Union—to sustain the Constitution against this causeless and wicked rebellion; and in doing this, let us bear in mind that the Constitution was made for the people—to secure to them and their posterity the blessings of free government. Therefore, with me the primary inquiry is, is this measure necessary to suppress the rebellion? If it is, here am I ready to sustain it. It will be found the Constitution gives ample power to sustain this view.

The bill now before the Committee is necessary to sustain the credit of the country, and to carry on the war. It is with reluctance that I have come to this conclusion. I do not like the necessity which exists for the legal tender clause; still less do I like to place the issues of the Government in the hands of the brokers and money-lenders of the country. Depreciated now, let the legal tender clause fail, and mark the result to-morrow. The Treasury notes will fall from four per cent. to fifteen and twenty-five below par, and the Government will have to pay that per centage additional for every article they purchase. Your soldiers will be shaved that amount on *their blood-bought wages*, and the country, flooded with a vast amount of depreciated paper, will grow restless and discontented under so fatal a mistake. If we make the Government issues a legal tender, the demand for specie will be so limited that they will maintain their value."

CLOSING THE DEBATE ON THE BILL.

By order of the House general debate was now closed. The standing rules of the House, however, provide that the member introducing the measure shall have the right, after general debate is closed, to speak one hour in reply to adverse speeches, in finally closing the debate. Mr. Spaulding, having introduced the bill, was entitled to the floor to close the debate. Mr. Stevens, who had not yet spoken, was desirous of expressing his views on the measure, and Mr. Spaulding was willing to give him most of the hour to which he was entitled, and intended to yield the floor to him for that purpose.

Mr. Spaulding, in closing, summed up, on his part, as follows:

"I have listened with a great deal of attention to the arguments and propositions which have been submitted by the various gentlemen who have addressed the House, but I shall not now make the concluding speech. I shall leave it to the able Chairman of the Committee of Ways and Means to close the debate. If I may be indulged, however, for a few moments, I desire to say, summing up, first: that all agree that taxation, in various forms, must be imposed to the amount of at least $150,000,000 on which to rest the credit of these notes and bonds, a sum sufficient to pay the ordinary expenses of Government on a peace footing, the interest on all the war debt, and a sinking fund to liquidate annually a portion of the principal. Second: we all agree that hereafter the war must be carried on principally upon the *credit* of the Government, and *that paper in the form of notes and bonds* must be issued to an equally *large amount, whichever plan is adopted*. After deducting the sum raised by internal revenue, by direct taxation, and duties on imports, *the amount of paper to be issued can only be limited by the actual expenses of the Government*. The respective plans of Messrs. Vallandigham, Conkling, and Morrill, require the same amount of paper to be issued as the legal tender bill proposed by the Committee of Ways and Means, and supported by the Secretary of the Treasury. Third: the main difference between the several plans is, that the legal tender bill stamps demand notes as money, with the highest sanction of the Government to circulate as a National currency, the same as bank notes, in all the channels of trade and business among all the people of the United States; whilst all the other plans proposed contemplate the issue of an *inferior* currency that will not, in my opinion, circulate as money either among the banks or the people, but will, on the contrary, be depreciated and sold at a large discount by all officers, soldiers, and others that are compelled to receive it from the Government in payment for services and supplies furnished. For myself, I prefer to issue the demand notes, based on adequate taxation, and with the *highest legal sanction* that can be given to them by the Government, placing the soldiers and capitalists all on the same footing in regard to these notes."

Mr. SPAULDING then yielded the floor to Mr. Stevens.

Mr. LOVEJOY objected to the gentleman yielding the floor.

THE CHAIRMAN—"If objection is made, the gentleman from Pennsylvania cannot occupy the floor. The gentleman from New York cannot yield the floor to him, except by unanimous consent."

Mr. MORRILL—"I trust no objection will be made; only the same time will be consumed."

Mr. LOVEJOY—"Well, I will withdraw the objection."

MR. STEVENS' ADDRESS.

"MR. CHAIRMAN—This bill is a measure of necessity, not of choice. No one would willingly issue paper currency not redeemable on demand, and make it a legal tender. It is never desirable to depart from the circulating medium which, by the common consent of civilized nations, forms the standard value. But it is not a fearful measure, and when rendered necessary by exigencies it ought to produce no alarm.

The late administration left us a debt of about $100,000,000, and bequeathed to us also an expensive and formidable rebellion. This compelled Congress, at the extra session, to authorize a loan of $250,000,000; $100,000,000 of these were taken at 7 3-10 per cent., and $50,000,000 six per cent. bonds at a discount of over $5,000,000; $50,000,000 were used in demand notes, payable in coin, leaving $50,000,000 undisposed of. *Before the Banks had paid much of the last loan they broke down under it and suspended specie payment. They have continued to pay that loan, not in coin, but in demand notes of the Government; that has kept them at par, but this last of the loan was paid yesterday, and on the same day the banks refused to receive them. They must now sink to a depreciated currency.* The remaining $50,000,000 the Secretary of the Treasury has been unable to negotiate. A small portion of it, say $10,000,000, has been issued at 7 3-10 per cent. in payment of debts.

He estimated the present floating debt at $180,000,000; daily expenses, $2,000,000; to carry us to next meeting of Congress, $600,000,000 more. That if sufficient six per cent. bonds were forced on the market to pay our expenses up to December, or $700,000,000, as the money should be wanted, he thought they would sell as low as sixty per cent., as in the last English war; and even then it would be impossible to find payment in coin. A large part of it must be accepted in depreciated notes of suspended banks, for no one expects the resumption of specie payments until the close of the war.

Without the legal tender clause the notes could not be kept at par. Brokers, bankers, and others would depreciate them. The National Bank scheme recommended by the Secretary might, in ordinary times, be very useful, but while the banks are under suspension it was not easy to see how it would relieve the Government. They would have the circulation without interest, and at the same time would draw interest on the bonds, and afford no immediate relief. He thought the Government should have the benefit of the circulation of legal tender notes, and did not see how we could get along in any other way.

He argued in favor of the constitutionality of the legal tender clause, and that it was a necessary and proper measure at this time. In short, whenever any law is *necessary* and proper to carry into execution any delegated power, such law is valid. That necessity need not be absolute, inevitable, and overwhelming—if it be useful, expedient, profitable, the necessity is within the constitutional meaning. Whether such necessity exists is solely for the decision of Congress. Their judgment is absolute and conclusive. If Congress should decide this measure to be necessary to a granted power, no department of the Government can rejudge it. The Supreme Court might think the judgment of Congress erroneous, but they could not review it. Now, it is for Congress to determine whether this bill is necessary "to raise and support armies and navies, to borrow money, and provide for the general welfare." They are all granted powers. It is for those who think that it is not "necessary, useful and proper," to propose some better means, and vote against this; if a majority think otherwise, its constitutionality is established.

If constitutional, is it expedient? It is objected by the gentleman from Ohio, that the legal tender clause would depreciate the notes. All admit the necessity of the issue; but some object to their being made money. It is not easy to perceive how notes issued without being made immediately payable in specie, can be made any worse by making them a legal tender. And yet that is the whole argument, so far as expediency is concerned. Other gentlemen argued that this would impair contracts, by making a debt payable in other money than that which existed at the time of the contract, and would so be unconstitutional. Where do gentlemen find any prohibition on Congress against passing laws impairing contracts? There is none, though it would be unjust to do it. But this impairs no contract. *All contracts are made not only with a view to present laws, but subject to the future legislation of the country. We have more than once changed the value of coin.* Neither our gold nor our silver coin is as valuable as it was fifty years ago. Congress in 1853, I believe, regulated the weight and value of silver. They debased it over seven per cent., and made it a legal tender. Who ever pretended that that was unconstitutional? The gentlemen from Vermont (Mr. Morrill), and Ohio (Mr. Pendleton), think it an *ex post facto* law. It is not wonderful that my distinguished colleague, not being a professional lawyer, should not be aware that the *ex post facto* laws prohibited by the Constitution refer only to crimes and misdemeanors, and not to civil contracts. The gentleman from Ohio no doubt knew, *but forgot it.*

* * * * * * * * * * * *

Gentlemen are clamorous in favor of those who have debts due them, lest the debtor should the more easily pay his debt. I do not much sympathize with such importunate money-lenders. *But widows and orphans are interested and in tears, lest their estates should be badly invested. I pity no one who has his money invested in United States bonds, payable in gold in twenty years, with interest semi-annually.* But while these men have agonized bowels over the rich man's case, they have no pity for the poor widow, the suffering soldier, the wounded martyr to his country's good, who must receive these notes without legal tender or nothing, and who must give half of it to the Shylocks to get the necessaries of life. Sir, I wish no injury to any, nor with our bill could any happen; but if any must lose, let it not be the soldier, the mechanic, the laborer or the farmer.

Let me relate the various projects. *Ours proposes United States notes, secured at the end of twenty years to be paid in coin, and the interest raised by taxation semi-annually; such notes to be money, and of uniform value throughout the Union.* No better investment, in my judgment, can be had; no better currency can be invented. The amendment of the gentleman from Ohio (Mr. Vallandigham) proposes the same issue of notes, but objects to a legal tender; but does not provide for their redemption on demand in coin. He fears our notes would depreciate. Let him who is sharp enough to see it instruct me how notes that every man must take are worth less than the same notes that no man need take, and few would, being irredeemable on demand. But he doubts its constitutionality. *He who admits our power to emit bills of credit, nowhere expressly authorized by the Constitution, is a sharp and unreasonable doubter when he denies the power to make them a legal tender.*

The proposition from the gentleman from New York (Mr. Roscoe Conkling) authorizes the issuing of seven per cent. bonds, payable in thirty-one years, to be sold ($250,000,000 of it) or exchanged for the currency of the banks of Boston, New York and Philadelphia.

Sir, this proposition seems to me to lack every element of wise legislation. Make a loan payable in irredeemable currency, and pay that in its depreciated condition to our contractors, soldiers and creditors generally! The banks would issue unlimited amounts of what would become trash, and buy good hard-money bonds of the nation. Was there ever such a temptation to swindle?

He further proposes to issue $200,000,000 United States notes, redeemable in coin in one year. Does not the gentleman know that such notes must be dishonored, and the plighted faith of the Government broken? No one believes that we could then pay them, and it would run down at once. If we are to use suspended notes to pay our expenses, why not use our own? Are they not as safe as bank notes? During the suspension, the Government would have the benefit of the whole circulation, without interest, until they were funded—that is, the interest of all we could keep out would accrue to the Government. If the $150,000,000 were constantly afloat, it would be a loan to the Government, without interest, to that amount, $9,000,000 a year. But if we used the suspended paper of the banks our bonds would bear interest from the instant we got their notes—a good thing for suspended banks. Besides, the Government would have the benefit of all the lost and destroyed notes—a considerable item.

Last comes the substitute of the minority of the Committee (introduced by Mr. Morrill). I look upon it as a curiosity. It proposes to issue United States notes, not a legal tender, bearing an interest of three and sixty-five hundredths per cent., and fundable into seven and three-tenths per cent. bonds, but not payable on demand, but at the pleasure of the United States. This gives one and three-tenths per cent. higher interest than our loan, and not being redeemable on demand, would share the fate of all non-specie-paying notes not a legal tender. But the ingenious minority have invented a kind of currency never before known—*a circulation bearing interest.* Bonds or notes intended for investments bear interest, but no one expects they will be used as currency; whether in the shape of bonds or notes, they will be used only as investments, or as pledges on which to procure loans. Suppose a tailor, shoemaker, or other mechanic, or laborer, were to take one of these bills, and in a week he should wish to use it in market or store, or elsewhere, he must sit down and calculate the interest on the days he has had it to find its value. This would be rather inconvenient on a frosty day. This currency would make it necessary for every man to carry an arithmetic or interest table with which to guage the value of the circulating medium. Gentlemen must see how ridiculous, if not impracticable, this scheme is.

Here, then, in a few words, lies your choice. Throw bonds at six or seven per cent. on the market between this and December, enough to raise at least $600,000,000—about this sum is already appropriated, $557,-000,000—or issue United States notes, not redeemable in coin, *but fundable in specie-paying bonds at twenty years;* such notes either to be made a legal tender, or to take their chance of circulation by the voluntary act of the people.

I maintain that the highest sum you could sell your bonds at would be seventy-five per cent., payable in currency itself at a discount. That would produce a loss which no nation or individual doing a large business could stand a year.

I contend that I have shown that such issue, without being made money, must immediately depreciate, and would go on from bad to worse. I flatter myself that I have demonstrated, both from reason and undoubted authority, that such notes, made a legal tender and not issued in excess of the demand, will remain at par and pass in all transactions, great and small, at the full value of their face; that we shall have one currency for all sections of the country and for every class of people, the poor as well as the rich.

Some gentlemen are as much frightened as if this were an unwonted apparition, for the first time prowling forth to swallow the rich creditor and smouse the poor debtor. No nation, it is said, has ever tried anything like it.

Let us look at the greatest and wisest commercial nation in the world. In 1797 England was struggling for existence against armed Europe. She needed money, as we do now. She found it impossible to borrow. Gold was likely to leave the country. She passed a law prohibiting the Bank of England from paying coin for her notes until six months after the final ratification of peace. That law remained in force till 1823. It is said she did not make those notes a legal tender. She provided that whoever refused to take them for a debt should have no remedy for its collection; and that a plea of such tender should be a bar to the action. This, I think, is the most stringent legal tender; yet those notes never depreciated to any great extent."

Mr. VALLANDIGHAM—"Did they not depreciate twenty per cent.?"

Mr. STEVENS—"No, sir; at no time after they were made a legal tender did they depreciate twenty per cent."

Mr. VALLANDIGHAM—"I have the authority of Mr. Canning, which I think is quite as good as that of Mr. McCulloch. They were receivable all the time for Government dues."

Mr. STEVENS—"Yes, sir; but they still run down until they were made a legal tender, and after that they never depreciated a single dollar. Had they been made an absolute tender, they would not have depreciated a farthing. But now, in times of peace, *the notes of the Bank of England are a legal tender in all the vast business of that nation, and in every place, except at the counter of the bank.* What else are Bank of England notes than bills of credit of the Government? Her whole capital consists of Government securities, and her issues are based on that alone. Prussia holds the currency in paper issueable by Government alone, and is always at par. What becomes of the fine-spun theories of the opponents of this bill? I think they have distressed themselves very unnecessarily; and yet, gentlemen have shown all the contortions, if not the inspirations, of the Sibyl, lest Government should make these notes a uniform currency, rather than leave them to be regulated by sharks and brokers. *I look upon the immediate passage of the bill as essential to the very existence of the Government.* Reject it, and the financial credit, not only of the Government, but of all the great interests of the country, will be prostrated."

MR. CHAIRMAN—"Let me say in conclusion, that unless this bill is to pass with the legal tender clause in it, it is not desirable to its friends, or to the Administration, that it should pass at all, and those who think as I do will have to vote against it, if it should be thus mutilated and emasculated. If it is to be defeated, I should be glad if we had the power which they have in the British Parliament—to resign our places on the Committee of Ways and Means, and leave it to those who oppose this bill to mature some other measure. So far as I am concerned, I shall be modest enough not to attempt any other scheme. The Committee of Ways and Means have labored in the preparation of this measure anxiously, and to the best of their poor abilities. We are not infallible. We do not come near it. I am but poorly qualified for anything of this kind. But we have given it our most anxious consideration, and have consulted those whom we believed to be the best qualified to advise us. We have sought to harmonize conflicting views in the substitute which the majority of the Committee have prepared, and we hope it will pass. We believe that the credit of the country will be sustained by it, that under it all classes will be paid in money which all classes can use, and that it will confer no advantage on the capitalist over the poor laboring man. If this bill shall pass, I shall hail it as the most auspicious measure of this Congress; if it should fail, the result will be more deplorable than any disaster which could befall us."

At the conclusion of Mr. Stevens' speech the Chair announced that general debate was closed. Amendments were now in order, and under the rules of the House, five-minute speeches could be made in favor of, or in opposition to, each amendment proposed. Under this rule, several short speeches were made by members who had not an opportunity to speak during the general debate.

Mr. F. A. CONKLING, who opposed the legal tender clause in the bill, read an extract from an eminent citizen of New York, as follows:

"The advocates of a paper substitute may find an argument in the necessities of the crisis, but are certainly not guided by the light of experience, if they recur to the fact that in 1814 *a Boston bank note was capable of buying twice its nominal value in Treasury notes* (not a legal tender).

I had some little experience of the working of 'paper vs. gold,' in Denmark, in 1813, when their currency, which was printed on *blue* paper, depreciated to such an extent that the King, to remedy the evil, issued a new currency, printed on *white* paper, accompanied by an edict that one *rix* dollar of the new emission should be regarded in all transactions as worth six of the old, and taken as a legal tender, which required an amount of faith equal to that which was exacted by Lord Peter of Martin and Jack: that they should believe 'a loaf of brown bread to be a shoulder of mutton,' or suffer for their incredulity.

This arbitrary edict led to the ruin of many creditors, especially mortgagees, who were thus compelled to receive 'rags and lampblack' in satisfaction of debts contracted in gold and silver.

At that time I had bargained with the King's painter, in Copenhagen, to take my portrait (a half length, still in my possession), for *three hundred and six dollars*, the frame included. Such was the rapid decline in the paper currency of the Government, that when it was completed I purchased with *nine* Spanish milled dollars the three hundred and six dollars to pay for the portrait and frame; and such was the faith and loyalty of the painter, that he believed, or was bound by law to believe, that the one currency was just as good as the other! Being in London during the same year, I was guilty of the felonious act of selling my gold guineas for twenty-seven shillings in paper, while honest, patriotic and credulous John Bull insisted that in theory their value was the same; and Right Honorable the Chancellor of the Exchequer could cause the transportation to Botany Bay of any man who *practically* proved the contrary."

Mr. HUTCHINGS—"I would like to inquire as to the *occupation of the gentleman who wrote that letter?*"

[Here the hammer fell.]

Mr. CRISFIELD—"In order to accommodate what seems to be the wish of the Committee, or some members of it, I propose to modify my amendment by confining the motion to strike out to the words, "and shall also be lawful money and a legal tender in payment of all debts, public and private, within the United States."

Mr. SHELLABARGER—"Mr. Chairman, I rise to oppose the pending amendment. I did desire to submit to the Committee some views touching this measure when we were in general debate, but omitted to do so in deference to the more matured views which other members of the Committee desired to submit. I propose to occupy the few minutes I have, in making some statements in relation to the charges of bad faith and injustice which have been so persistently, earnestly, and, doubtlessly, sincerely made by the opponents of the bill.

Now, sir, I think it must be plain, beyond all cavil, that if these notes, proposed to be issued under this bill, are made of the value imposed upon them by law, so that they will be to the citizen the true and real representatives of that amount of *the intrinsic wealth of the country, which is stamped by law upon them as their nominal value, then there can be no practical injury, injustice, or bad faith in the law which makes them pay a debt precisely equal to that real value or wealth of the country, which that note, so made a tender, represents.* It is, of course, not my purpose now either to discuss or state those views by which others see in this measure—as distinguished from those they advocate—only disaster, in the shape of 'destruction of all standards of value;' in the 'inflation of the business and the prices of the country;' in disordering the 'operations of trade and commerce;' and in the ultimate 'bankruptcy' of the Government and of the people. I have no doubt this cry is made sincerely by many, and perhaps it is believed by all who make it. I do not discuss the sources and reasonableness of this cry of alarm, but only wish to present a parallel to it, and say that this cry is, to my mind, as unreasonable as that other to which I allude. I find that parallel in the history of the growth of the debt of England; and in the light of that history, I declare that this cry of 'bankruptcy' and national disaster and ruin is utterly unreasonable, and just now most pernicious.

Sir, the history of the growth of that debt, which one of the great Commoners of England calls 'the greatest prodigy that ever perplexed the sagacity and confounded the pride of statesmen and philosophers,' furnishes as conclusive refutations of the theories and predictions of our alarmists of this House, as it did in the past of other Parliaments.

Sir, at the end of the war of England with Louis XIV, in 1713, the debt of England was, in round numbers, $250,000,000. But, sir, at that period, not pot-house politicians merely, but profound thinkers, declared the Government permanently crippled. But while these were engaged in proving the nation ruined, the nation was growing richer and richer. Soon came that war which was ended by the peace of Aix la Chapelle; and the national debt had come to be $400,000,000 in 1748. Now, again, historians, statesmen and economists concurred in declaring that the case of England was certainly now desperate; but now again the nation persisted, although demonstrated by the books to be a bankrupt, in becoming far richer than in any period of her history. Soon the nation became again involved in the continental wars of the reign of George II, and at the end of Chatham's administration, at the period of 1760, the national debt came to be $700,000,000. Then, again, it is declared that both men of theory and of business united in declaring that now, at all events, the fatal day had certainly arrived. Adam Smith, the father of politico-economical science, thought the limit had been reached, and an increase of the debt would be fatal. David Hume, the profoundest man of his age, declared it would have been better that England had been conquered and crushed by Prussia and Austria, than by debts for which all the revenues of the Kingdom north of Trent and west of Reading were mortgaged. He said the madness of England exceeded that of the crusaders. Richard Cœur de Lion and St. Louis had not gone in the face of arithmetic. England had. You could not prove that the road to Paradise was not through the Holy Land; but you could prove that the road to national ruin was through a national debt. But still, in defiance of Hume and Smith, and even Burke, the nation would live and grow richer, and pay the interest on its public debt.

Then came George Grenville's policy to tax the colonies of America to help pay the interest on this debt, and brought on our war of the Revolution. In that England lost the colonies, and found an addition to her public debt of $500,000,000—making the aggregate, at the time of the treaty of peace, $1,200,000,000. Again England was pronounced hopeless; but again she continued to be more prosperous than ever before.

Then came the wars growing out of the French Revolution; and the debt of England ran up to $4,000,000,000. Again the cry of despair and of bankruptcy was louder than ever; but also again the cry was false as ever; and the interest on the debt of England not only continued to be paid to the day at the bank, but such was her prosperity that at the close of these French wars, her people expended for railroads in the island, in a few years, more than $1,200,000,000!

Such is a sketch of the history of the debt of England, and such the refutation furnished by the logic of history to the logic of abstract reasoning, however profound.

A great historian and a great commoner of England declares that all these cries of bankruptcy and ruin were based on a double fallacy. *They who raised these cries imagined that there was an exact analogy between the case of an individual who is in debt to another, and the case of a society which is in debt to itself; and they also forget that other things grew as well as the debt.*

Sir, I do not make this allusion to the debt of England to show that 'a national debt is a national blessing,' nor to indicate that this nation ought permanently to depart from its old and traditional policies of avoiding public debt and direct taxation. I do not think we either ought to or will. But, sir, this parallel between the alarms of this day and this country, and those of the past in another country, is only introduced to indicate the strange infirmities of vision in all these prophets of evil, and to indicate how unjust and cruel it is to weaken, by these refuted cries of ruin and bankruptcy, the faith of the people in the Government, which now, in its day of peril, so preeminently rests upon the faith of her children.

Sir, all these obligations of this Government go out to the people borne up by all the faith and all the property of the people; and they have all the value which that faith untarnished, and that property unestimable, can give them. It is not because they lack intrinsic value that they need the quality of 'lawful tender,' but it is to secure to the Government in their issue their true value, and to retain for them that true value as you pass them—as all agree you must—to your noble soldiery in the field, and to all classes of the people not engaged, *as the most persistent outside opposition to this bill is, in endeavoring to destroy the value of these, so that out of the blood of their sinking country they may be enabled to coin the gains of their infamy.*"

MR. HICKMAN'S SPEECH.

Mr. HICKMAN, of Pennsylvania, spoke in favor of the bill:

"The only question, Mr. Chairman, which I have ever had with reference to this bill, has not been a question as to the powers of Congress, but as to the policy of the enactment. I would, myself, have preferred that this bill had followed the tax bill. I would have preferred that, before the credit of the Government had been tried to that extent, the basis of that credit should have been exhibited to the country. Before I take my neighbor's note, I should require him to show me on what his credit rests; of what his capital consists. I have, therefore, had great doubt as to the propriety of voting for this bill as it stands at this time. But being assured by the Chairman of the Committee of Ways and Means that the Treasury, and, perhaps, the Administration, regard this as a governmental necessity, I am disposed to waive the question of propriety or expediency, and to vote for it as a necessity, having no doubt about the right. That clause of the Constitution which gives to the Government the right to coin money, and to regulate the value thereof, is, to my mind, conclusive of the great question that has been raised in this House, 'To coin money.' It does not indicate of what the material shall consist, which is to be regarded as money. It might be gold, or silver, or copper, or brass, or iron, at the pleasure of the Government. In other words, it is not demanded that the thing itself, which shall be coined as money, shall have any intrinsic value. The coining of money is merely impressing upon that which is designated to be the circulating medium the mark of the sovereign, indicating the will of the sovereign that it shall be received in the exigencies of trade and commerce at the stated value. And that mark of the sovereign, indicating the will of the sovereign, may just as well be impressed upon paper as upon gold or silver. Nothing else can be made out of the Constitution in this regard.

According to the arguments which have been addressed against this bill, the Constitution should have been made to read: 'Congress, or the Government, shall have power to coin gold and silver money according to their intrinsic value.' Why, sir, the Government is not restricted as to the material out of which it may make money; is not restricted as to the metal that shall be adopted as money; it has perfect power to adopt iron as well as any other metalic basis; and if any other metal, why not paper? Why not impress upon paper the mark of the sovereign, indicating the will of the sovereign as to the value at which it shall be received, and make it a circulating medium, there being nothing in the Constitution to restrict us in this necessary exercise of sovereign power, without which no Government can carry on its operations; without which no Government could exist?

I have no doubt, whatever, in regard to the right of Congress to pass this bill, and I am therefore willing to vote for it upon the ground that it is a necessity at this time.

MR. LOVEJOY'S SPEECH.

Mr. LOVEJOY, of Illinois, opposed the bill:

"MR. CHAIRMAN—I have endeavored for a day or two to obtain the floor, for the purpose of expressing my views a little more at length than I can in the five minutes to which I am now limited; but, by an arrangement between the Chair and the Committee of Ways and Means, my purpose has been averted.

I will now simply say in regard to the question of constitutionality, that there has not been a respectable argument advanced in defense of the constitutionality of this bill; and, inasmuch as great talent and eminent ability have been brought to bear upon it, I take it that no respectable argument can be made in vindication of the constitutionality of this bill. I would admit the plea of necessity, if I believed it; and I think it is more manly to confess, as Jefferson did, than it is to attempt to torture the constitution into the support of a measure which everybody must see to be unconstitutional.

Now, Mr. Chairman, in regard to the general idea of the bill, it is a mere fallacy. The whole argument used in favor of the issue of these legal tender notes is based upon precisely the same foundation as the old theological dogma, *crede ut edes, et edes*—believe that you eat the real flesh of Christ in the *wafer*, and you do eat it. Believe that this piece of paper is a five dollar gold piece, and it is a five dollar gold piece; believe it is worth five dollars, and it is worth five dollars.

Now, sir, I am prepared to state that it is not in the power of this Congress, nor in the power of any legislative body, to accomplish an impossibility in making something out of nothing.

The piece of paper you stamp as five dollars is not five dollars, and it never will be unless it is convertible into a five dollar gold piece; and to profess that it is, is simply a delusion and a fallacy. You may say even by legislative enactment that sixty or eighty or even ninety-nine cents are a hundred, but the rigid, inexorable digits will stand fixed and immovable by your legislative legerdemain.

Mr. Chairman, we are urged by the Chairman of the Committee of Ways and Means to pass this bill, because ruin is before the Government if we do not pass it. It reminds me very forcibly of Cowper's Needless Alarm. I cannot undertake to give it in rhyme, but I will give the substance of it. You will remember that, hearing the deep braying of the hounds, and the sound of the hunter's horn, the sheep coursed round and round the field, until the frightened flock came to the brink of a precipice, and to get away from the hounds and huntsman the *pater gregis* advised them thus:

> " I hold it, therefore, wisest and most fit
> That life to save, we leap into the pit."

The matron of the flock, more discreet than the spouse, replies:

> " How? leap into the pit our life to save?
> To save our life, leap all into the grave?"

Sir, there is no precipice, there is no chasm, there is no possible yawning, bottomless gulf before this nation so terrible, so appalling, so ruinous, as this same bill that is before us, and that it is proposed to pass under the pressure of these influences brought to bear upon it.

You issue $100,000,000 of those notes. The gentleman tells us they are already due. We have got to pay the paper out almost before we can make it. It has taken us six months to manufacture $50,000,000, and we cannot manufacture it as fast as we shall spend it at that rate; so that when we have issued $100,000,000 we must issue another $100,000,000, and then another $100,000,000. And thus we plunge from lower depth to still lower, till we are buried in an ocean of inconvertible paper. At every step your paper will depreciate more and more, until the expenses of the war will swell to such an appalling sum that redemption will be impossible, and repudiation inevitable. *Facilis deocensus averni*, etc., which means it is easy to slide down hill, but very hard work to draw the sled back over smooth ice. But the question is pressed: what will you do? What do you propose? I propose this:

First—Adequate taxation, if need be, to the extent of $200,000,000.

Second—*Adopt legislation that shall compel all banking institutions to do business on a specie basis. Every piece of paper that claimed to be money, but was not, I would chase back to the man or corporation that forged it, and visit upon them the penalties of the law.* I would not allow a bank note to circulate that was not constantly, conveniently and certainly convertible into specie.

Third—I would issue interest-paying bonds of the United States, and go into the market and borrow money and pay the obligations of the Government. This would be honest, business-like, and in the end economical. This could be done. Other channels of investment are blocked up, and capital would seek the bonds of investment.

This is, in substance, what I propose. This would bring us through the war poor indeed, for half the nation has to support the other half, but with the health and vigor of the athlete, and not with the bloated flesh of the beer guzzler. Did I not know that the passage of this bill was a foregone conclusion, I would move to re-commit, with instructions to that effect."

SPEECH OF MR. WALTON.

Mr. WALTON, of Maine, advocated the bill.

"Necessity compels us to pay our creditors in treasury notes. Our credit is exhausted; or perhaps it will be more accurate to say that the means of those who are willing to lend to the Government have become exhausted. To lay and collect taxes will require considerable time; besides, it cannot reasonably be expected that revenue enough can ever be derived from taxation to meet all the expenses of the Government while the war lasts. Practically, therefore, our Government is reduced to the necessity of paying not only its other creditors, but our brave soldiers, in its own notes. Thus compelling our creditors (our brave soldiers included) to take their pay in treasury notes; is it not just, is it anything more than common honesty, to allow them to pay their debts in the same way. If these treasury notes are made a legal tender, they will circulate as readily as specie in the payment of debts, and will only cease thus to circulate, if ever, when they have reached the hands of those who have no debts to pay. And if, as the enemies of the legal tender clause predict, they ever fall in value below par, will not the loss fall upon those who have money, and no debts to pay? And can it fall on a class who will feel it less? And as it is this class of persons that constitute our money-lenders, it will be rather a favor than an injury to them; for these notes are convertible into United States bonds, with semi-annual interest coupons attached, and therefore accomplishes for them just what they desire—a safe loan of their money. I say a safe loan, for the issue of these notes is to be followed by vigorous taxation; and in equity the lender will have a lien on the whole property of the United States as security for every dollar of his debt, and a pledge of the public faith that this security shall be made available.

The legal tender clause of the bill, therefore, while it secures to our soldiers and the poorer class of our citizens, who have debts to pay, great advantages, does no real injury to capitalists, and ought to be retained.

The constitutional objections have not been overlooked. I think the Federal Government has the same power to make these notes a legal tender that it has to make anything else a legal tender. *It can make nothing a legal tender by virtue of any express power. It has but an implied power in any case.* And if it is admitted, as it always has been, that the Government possesses the power to declare what shall be a legal tender in any case, it has it without limitation. It can make one thing a legal tender as well as another; and whether these notes shall have that character or not, is a question of expediency only, and not one of power.

It is objected by some that to make these notes a legal tender will impair the obligation of contracts, and is therefore unconstitutional. But this is not true. In every contract payable in money, and no particular kind of money is named, it is implied, and is a part of the contract, that it may be discharged in what shall be the legal currency at the time of payment. A change or enlargement of the legal currency of the country, and a payment in such new currency, is no violation of the new contract, but is in pursuance of one of its implied conditions.

Having the power, and believing, on the whole, that the legal tender clause is a beneficial one, I am in favor of retaining it in the bill."

The question recurred on Mr. Crisfield's amendment, to strike out the legal tender clause in the original bill. The vote was taken in Committee of the Whole by tellers.

On taking the vote the tellers reported—ayes 53, noes 93, so the amendment was rejected.

Several other amendments were made in Committee of the Whole, but inasmuch as they were all cut off, modified or adopted by subsequent proceedings, after the bill was reported to the House, it is not necessary to report them here. The bill, as adopted, is copied at the end of this day's proceedings.

Having gone through the bill in Committee of the Whole, there was a good deal of preliminary skirmishing on the part of different members, who had proposed substitutes and amendments as to the order of taking the vote. Some members feared that they would not be able to get a square vote in the House on their respective propositions. Several members were on the floor at the same time. Motions, objections and counter-motions were made in quick succession, and in various forms, which continued for some time, causing confusion and preventing any action of a practical character, and preventing any vote being taken on either proposition. It finally resulted in an arrangement being made that the bill should be reported to the House, and a square vote be had on the two main propositions pending before the Committee. Mr. Vallandigham and Mr. Conkling withdrew their substitutes, so that all of the opponents of the legal tender clause could concentrate on the substitute agreed to by Mr. Morrill, Mr. Horton, Mr. Corning and Mr. Stratton, one-half of the Committee of Ways and Means; and that the vote should be first taken on that substitute, which was modified to meet the conflicting views of the various gentlemen on that side, in order to make it as acceptable as possible to all the opponents of the original bill. This substitute finally offered by Mr. Horton, will be found (*Cong. Globe, p.* ——,) and is as follows:

The substitute which was read was, to strike out of the bill all after the word "that," in the first section, and insert the following:

"For temporary purposes, the Secretary of the Treasury be, and he is hereby, authorized to issue on the credit of the United States $100,000,000 of Treasury notes, bearing interest at the rate of three and sixty-five hundredths per cent. per annum, payable in two years after date, to bearer, at the Treasury of the United States, or at the office of the Assistant Treasurer, in the city of New York, or at the office of the designated depository in the city of Cincinnati, and of such denominations as he may deem expedient, not less than five dollars each; and such notes shall be receivable for all public dues, except duties on imports, and for all salaries, debts and demands owing by the United States to individuals, corporations and associations, within the United States, at the option of such individuals, corporations and associations; and any holder of said United States notes, depositing any sum not less than fifty dollars, or some multiple of fifty, with the Treasurer of the United States, or either of the Assistant Treasurers, or either of the designated depositories at Cincinnati or Baltimore, shall receive in exchange therefor duplicate certificates of deposit for the amount, with any accumulated interest thereon, one of which may be transmitted to the Secretary of the Treasury, who shall thereupon issue to the holder an equal amount in bonds of the United States, coupon or registered, as may be desired, bearing interest at the rate of seven and three-tenths per cent. per annum, payable semi-annually in coin, and redeemable at the pleasure of the Government after ten years from date; and such Treasury notes shall be received the same as coin, at their par value, with accumulated interest, in payment for any bonds that may be hereafter negotiated by the Secretary of the Treasury; and the Secretary of the Treasury may, from time to time, as the exigencies of the public service may require, issue any amount of such Treasury notes equal to the amount redeemed. There shall be printed on the back of the Treasury notes, which may be issued under the provisions of this act, the following words: 'The within note is receivable in payment of all public dues, except duties on imports, and is exchangeable for bonds of the United States, bearing seven and three-tenths per cent. per annum, payable in coin, semi-annually.'

SEC. 2. *And be it further enacted,* That to enable the Secretary of the Treasury to fund the Treasury notes and floating debt of the United States, he is hereby authorized to issue, on the credit of the United States, coupon bonds, or registered bonds, to an amount not exceeding $500,000,000,— $200,000,000 bearing interest at the rate of seven and three-tenths per cent. per annum, payable semi-annually in coin, and redeemable at the pleasure of the Government, after ten years from date, and $300,000,000, redeemable at the pleasure of the Government, after twenty-four years from date, and bearing interest at the rate of six per cent. per annum, payable semi-annually in coin. And the bonds herein authorized shall be of such denominations, not less than fifty dollars, as may be determined upon by the Secretary of the Treasury; and the Secretary of the Treasury may also exchange, at par, such bonds at any time for lawful money of the United States, or for any of the Treasury notes that have been, or may hereafter be, issued under any former Act of Congress, or that may be issued under the provisions of this Act.

§ 3. *And be it further enacted,* That the Treasury notes and the coupon or registered bonds authorized by this Act, shall be in such form as the Secretary of the Treasury may direct, and shall bear the written or engraved signature of the Treasurer of the United States and the Register of the Treasury; and also, as evidence of lawful issue, the imprint of a copy of the seal of the Treasury Department, which imprint shall be made under the direction of the Secretary, after the said notes or bonds shall be received from the engravers, and before they are issued; or the said notes and bonds shall be signed by the Treasurer of the United States, or for the Treasurer, by such persons as may be specially appointed by the Secretary of the Treasury for that purpose, and shall be countersigned by the Register of the Treasury, or for the Register, by such persons as the Secretary of the Treasury may specially appoint for that purpose; and all the provisions of the Act entitled, 'An Act to authorize the issue of Treasury notes,' approved the 23d day of December, 1857, so far as they can be applied to this act, and not inconsistent therewith, are hereby revived and re-enacted; and the sum of $300,000 is hereby appropriated out of any money in the Treasury not otherwise appropriated, to enable the Secretary of the Treasury to carry this act into effect.

§ 4. *And be it further enacted,* That any person or persons, or any corporation, holding Treasury notes, may, at any time, deposit them, in sums of not less than $500, with any of the Assistant Treasurers or designated depositaries of the United States, authorized by the Secretary of the Treasury to receive them, who shall issue therefor, transferable certificates of deposit, made in such form as the Secretary of the Treasury shall prescribe, and said certificates of deposit shall bear interest after thirty days, at the rate of five and two-fifths of one per cent. per annum; and any Treasury notes so deposited may be withdrawn from deposit at any time, on the return of said certificates, but no interest shall be allowed except after thirty days. And all such deposits shall cease and determine at the pleasure of the Secretary of the Treasury, and after ten days' notice shall have been given to the depositor.

§ 5. *And be it further enacted,* That if any person or persons, shall falsely make, forge, counterfeit or alter, or cause or procure to be falsely made, forged, counterfeited or altered, or shall willingly aid or assist in falsely making, forging, counterfeiting, or altering any note, bond or certificate, issued under the authority of this act, or heretofore issued under acts to authorize the issue of Treasury notes or bonds, or shall pass utter, publish, or sell, or attempt to pass, utter, publish, or sell, or bring into the United States, from any foreign place, with intent to pass, utter, publish or sell, as true, or shall have, or keep in possession, or conceal, with intent to utter, publish or sell, as true, any such false, forged, counterfeited or altered note, bond or certificate, with intent to defraud anybody, corporate or politic, or any other person or persons whatsoever; every person so offending, shall be deemed guilty of felony, and shall, on conviction thereof, be punished by a fine not exceeding $5,000, and by imprisonment and confinement to hard labor, not exceeding fifteen years."

Upon the bill being reported from the Committee of the Whole to the House, the vote was first taken on this substitute.

The yeas and nays were ordered.

The question was taken, and it was decided in the negative—yeas 55, nays 95, as follows:

Yeas—Messrs. Ancona, Baxter, Biddle, George H. Brown, William G. Brown, Cobb, Frederick A. Conkling, Roscoe Conkling, Conway, Corning, Cox, Cravens, Crisfield, Crittenden, Diven, Eliot, English, Goodwin, Grider, Harding, Holman, Horton, Johnson, Law, Lazear, Lovejoy, May, Menzies, Justin S. Morrill, Morris, Nixon, Noble, Norton, Nugen, Odell, Pendleton, Perry, Pomeroy, Porter, Edward H. Rollins, Sedgwick, Sheffield, Shiel, William G. Steele, Stratton, Benjamin F. Thomas, Francis

Thomas, Train, Vallandigham, Wadsworth, E. P. Walton, Ward, Webster, Chilton A. White and Wright—55.

NAYS—Messrs. Aldrich, Alley, Arnold, Ashley, Babbitt, Goldsmith F. Bailey, Joseph Bailey, Baker, Beaman, Bingham, Francis P. Blair, Jacob B. Blair, Samuel S. Blair, Blake, Buffinton, Burnham, Campbell, Chamberlain, Clark, Colfax, Cutler, Davis, Delano, Delaplaine, Duell, Dunlap, Dunn, Edgerton, Edwards, Ely, Fenton, Fessenden, Fisher, Franchott, Frank, Gooch, Granger, Gurley, Haight, Hale, Hanchett, Harrison, Hickman, Hooper, Hutchins, Julian, Kelley, Francis W. Kellogg, William Kellogg, Killinger, Knapp, Lansing, Leary, Loomis, McKean, McKnight, McPherson, Marston, Maynard, Mitchell, Moorhead, Anson P. Morrill, Olin, Patton, Timothy G. Phelps, Pike, Price, Alexander H. Rice, John H. Rice, Richardson, James S. Rollins, Sargent, Shanks, Shellabarger, Sherman, Sloan, Spaulding, John B. Steele, Stevens, Trimble, Trowbridge, Upton, Van Horn, Van Valkenburg, Van Wyck, Verree, Wall, Wallace, Charles W. Walton, Whaley, Albert S. White, Wyckliffe, Wilson, Windom and Worcester—95.

So the substitute was not agreed to.

The question then recurred on the modification of the original bill, offered by Mr. Stevens as a substitute, which was not read, but which Mr. Stevens had just before explained as follows:

Mr. STEVENS—"I wish to state in regard to my amendment, that it is a modification of the original bill. Those who are in favor of the original have agreed upon this in lieu of it. We thought it better to adopt the suggestion contained in the amendment of the gentleman from Ohio of $150,000,000, retiring the $50,000,000 of demand notes (authorized last July), and of making $150,000,000 the maximum to which they shall go. That is about all the change there is, except that we have left out the foreign loan clause, which is in the original; and we have agreed to adopt an amendment by which the holders of these notes may convert them either into a twenty years' bond at six per cent., or five years' bonds at seven per cent., at their option."

This modification of the original bill had the concurrence of the other half of the Committee of Ways and Means—Messrs. Stevens, Spaulding, Hooper and Maynard, and was adopted by the House without a division.

The bill, as amended, was ordered to be engrossed and read a third time. The yeas and nays were ordered on the final passage of the bill. The question was taken, and it was decided in the affirmative—yeas 93, nays 59, as follows:

YEAS—Messrs. Aldrich, Alley, Arnold, Ashley, Babbitt, Goldsmith F. Bailey, Joseph Bailey, Baker, Beaman, Bingham, Francis P. Blair, Jacob Blair, Samuel S. Blair, Blake, Buffinton, Burnham, Campbell, Chamberlain, Clark, Colfax, Cutler, Davis, Delano, Delaplaine, Duell, Dunn, Edgerton, Edwards, Ely, Fenton, Fessenden, Fisher, Franchot, Frank, Gooch, Granger, Gurley, Haight, Hale, Hanchett, Harrison, Hickman, Hooper, Hutchins, Julian, Kelley, Francis W. Kellogg, William Kellogg, Killinger, Lansing, Leary, Loomis, McKean, McKnight, McPherson, Marston, Maynard, Mitchell, Moorhead, Anson P. Morrill, Nugen, Olin, Patton, Timothy G. Phelps, Pike, Price, Alexander H. Rice, John H. Rice, Riddle, James S. Rollins, Sargent, Shanks, Shellabarger, Sherman, Sloan, Spaulding, John B. Steele, Stevens, Trimble, Trowbridge, Upton, Van Horn, Van Valkenburgh, Van Wyck, Verree, Wall, Wallace, Charles W. Walton, Whaley, Albert S. White, Wilson, Windom and Worcester—93.

Nays—Messrs. Ancona, Baxter, Biddle, George H. Brown, Cobb, Frederick A. Conkling, Roscoe Conkling, Conway, Corning, Cox, Cravens, Crisfield, Diven, Dunlap, Eliot, English, Goodwin, Grider, Harding, Holman, Horton, Johnson, Knapp, Law, Lazear, Lovejoy, Mallory, May, Menzies, Justin S. Morrill, Morris, Nixon, Noble, Norton, Odell, Pendleton, Perry, Pomeroy, Porter, Richardson, Robinson, Edward H. Rollins, Sedgwick, Sheffield, Shiel, William G. Steele, Stratton, Benjamin F. Thomas, Francis Thomas, Train, Vallandigham, Voorhees, Wadsworth, E. P. Walton, Ward, Webster, Chilton A. White, Wickliffe and Wright—59.

Thus the legal tender act, after a protracted debate, and a most determined opposition, by prominent and influential Republicans, as well as Democrats, was passed through the House by a large majority.

The following is a copy of the bill as it first passed the House, on the 6th of February, 1862:

"*An Act to authorize the issue of United States notes, and for the redemption or funding thereof, and for funding the floating debt of the United States.*

SECTION 1. *Be it enacted by the Senate and House of Representatives of the United States of America, in Congress assembled:* That to meet the necessities of the Treasury of the United States, and to provide a currency receivable for the public dues, the Secretary of the Treasury is hereby authorized to issue, on the credit of the United States, $150,000,000 of United States notes, not bearing interest, payable to bearer at the Treasury of the United States, at Washington or New York, and of such denominations as he may deem expedient, not less than five dollars each. Provided, however, that $50,000,000 of said notes shall be in lieu of the demand Treasury notes authorized to be issued by the Act of July 17, 1861; which said demand notes shall be taken up as rapidly as practicable, and the notes herein provided for substituted for them: And provided, further, that the amount of the two kinds of notes together, shall, at no time, exceed the sum of $150,000,000. And such notes, herein authorized, shall be receivable in payment of all taxes, duties, imports, excise, debts and demands of every kind due to the United States, and for all salaries, debts and demands owing by the United States to individuals, corporations and associations within the United States, and shall also be lawful money and a legal tender, in payment of all debts, public and private, within the United States. And any holders of said United States notes, depositing any sum not less than $50, or some multiple of $50, with the Treasurer of the United States, or either of the Assistant Treasurers, shall receive in exchange therefor duplicate certificates of deposit, one of which may be transmitted to the Secretary of the Treasury, who shall thereupon issue to the holder an equal amount of bonds of the United States, coupon or registered, as may by said holder be desired, bearing interest at the rate of six per centum per annum, payable semi-annually, at the Treasury or Sub-Treasury of the United States, and redeemable at the pleasure of the United States, after twenty years from the date thereof. Provided, that the Secretary of the Treasury shall, upon presentation of said certificates of deposit, issue to the holder thereof, at his option, and instead of the bonds already described, an equal amount of bonds of the United States, coupon or registered, as may by said holder be desired, bearing interest at the rate of seven per cent. per annum, payable semi-annually, and redeemable at the pleasure of the United States, after five years from the date thereof. And such United States notes shall be received the same as coin, at their par value, in payments for any loans that may be hereafter sold or negotiated by the Secretary of the Treasury, and may be re-issued from time to time, as the exigencies of the public interests shall require. There shall be printed on the back of the United States notes, which may be issued under the provisions of this act, the following words: 'The within is a legal tender in payment of all debts, public and private, and is exchangeable for bonds of the United States, bearing six per centum interest at twenty years, or in seven per cent. bonds at five years.'

§ 2. *And be it further enacted,* That to enable the Secretary of the Treasury to fund the Treasury notes and floating debt of the United States, he is hereby authorized to issue, on the credit of the United States, coupon bonds, or registered bonds, to an amount not exceeding $500,000,000, and redeemable at the pleasure of the Government, after twenty years from date, and bearing interest at the rate of six per centum per annum, payable semi-annually; and the bonds herein authorized shall be of such denominations, not less than fifty dollars, as may be determined upon by the Secretary of the Treasury; and the Secretary of the Treasury may dispose of such bonds at any time for lawful money of the United States, or for any of the Treasury notes that have been, or may hereafter be, issued under any former act of Congress, or for United States notes that may be issued under the provisions of this act; and all stocks, bonds, and other securities of the United States, held by individuals, corporations, or associations, within the United States, shall be exempt from taxation by any State or county.

§ 3. *And be it further enacted,* That the United States notes and the coupon or registered bonds, authorized by this act, shall be in such forms as the Secretary of the Treasury may direct, and shall bear the written or engraved signatures of the Treasurer of the United States, and the Registry of the Treasury, and also as evidence of lawful issue, the imprint of a copy of the seal of the Treasury Department, which imprint shall be made under the direction of the Secretary, after the said notes or bonds shall be received from the engravers, and before they are issued; or the said notes and bonds shall be signed by the Treasurer of the United States, or for the Treasurer by such persons as may be especially appointed by the Secretary of the Treasury for that purpose, and shall be countersigned by the Register of the Treasury, or for the Register by such persons as the Secretary of the Treasury may especially appoint for that purpose; and all the provisions of the act entitled "An act to authorize the issue of Treasury notes," approved the 23d day of December, 1857, so far as they can be applied to this act, and not inconsistent therewith, are hereby revived and re-enacted; and the sum of $300,000 is hereby appropriated, out of any money in the Treasury not otherwise appropriated, to enable the Secretary of the Treasury to carry this act into effect."

Two *penal* sections (§ 4 and § 5) were adopted as part of this bill, to guard against counterfeiting, but it is not important to insert them here, as they do not affect the principles of the bill.

LETTER FROM GEORGE DAWSON, ESQ., TO THE ALBANY EVENING JOURNAL.

"WASHINGTON, February 6, 1862.

"This has been an exciting day in the House. A fierce battle has been waged against the 'legal tender' Treasury notes. But, as I think, the right has prevailed, and by a vote of 95 to 59—a much stronger force than was counted upon, the real argument was reduced to a very small compass. All admitted the necessity of a resort to paper currency; and the question was whether that paper should be made as nearly par value as possible, or subjected to the fluctuations and depreciations of an ordinary irredeemable currency. If made a legal tender, these notes could never sink below the best bank paper. If not so made, they would very soon cease to be available as a circulating medium.

Besides, if Treasury notes were to be used to pay the Government creditors, why should not their creditors be required to take them? Why should the soldier be required to take what the sutler might refuse? To be sure, the now legal tender bill left it optional with the soldier, whether he should take the notes or not; but if he availed himself of the 'option,' what had the Government to give him? Practically, it would be Treasury notes or nothing, as, during a general Bank suspension, it is irredeemable bank bills 'or no pay.'

It was not strange that members of the same political family, differed on a question of really doubtful expediency. And but for the necessities of Government, I doubt whether the 'legal tender' principle would have received a dozen votes in the House. It is a new financial principle, and its workings may result in some, if not all the evils predicted from it. Nevertheless, as Treasury Notes *had* to be resorted to, the common sense of the House, as well as the common sense of the people, determined that they should be made as near the practical value of gold as possible. Mr. Spaulding, of Erie, has had to assume the laboring oar in this financial expedient. He had but a bare majority of his Committee with him at the outset; and, when the Secretary of the Treasury hesitated, as he did for several days, the Committee became equally divided. And yet, the measure carried a large majority of the House with it—a fact as gratifying to Mr. S. as it is complimentary to his financial acumen.

The country breathes freer! The legal tender bill has passed the House, and national bankruptcy is averted. The grateful thanks of all loyal men are due to Mr. Spaulding and the representatives who supported the measure, for this timely effort in behalf of the public credit. The relief comes not a moment too soon. Now let the Senate do its duty promptly, and we shall be clear 'of the breakers.'"

PROCEEDINGS IN THE SENATE ON THE BILL.

The legal tender bill was sent to the Senate on the 7th inst., and was, on motion of Mr. Fessenden, read twice by its title, and referred to the Finance Committee.

The Treasury was nearly empty, and the Secretary was unable to negotiate any more of the loan authorized by the act passed at the extra session in July, at the rates fixed by the law. The act limited him *to par* in disposing of any of the bonds or notes authorized by that act. The six per cent. twenty year bonds were then selling at about 88, and the 7 3-10 notes were below par. In this emergency, Secretary Chase sent to Mr. Fessenden a letter, urging the immediate passage of a bill giving temporary relief, while the legal tender bill was being perfected in the Senate. Mr. Fessenden obtained unanimous consent to consider the subject forthwith. The following proceedings were had:

Mr. FESSENDEN—"I have just received a letter from the Treasury Department, which I will read:

"TREASURY DEPARTMENT, Feb. 7, 1862.

"Sir: The condition of the Treasury requires immediate legislative provision. What you said this morning leads me to think that the bill which passed the House yesterday, will hardly be acted upon by the Senate this week. Until that bill shall receive the final action of Congress, it seems advisable to extend the provisions of the former acts, so as to allow the issue of at least $10,000,000 in United States notes, in addition to the $50,000,000 heretofore authorized. I transmit a bill framed with that object, which will, I trust, meet your approval and that of Congress. Immediate action on it is exceedingly desirable.

Yours, truly, S. P. CHASE."

"Hon. WILLIAM P. FESSENDEN,
    Chairman Committee Finance, Senate."

The bill is a very short one, and I will read it:

"*A Bill to authorize an additional issue of United States Notes.*

Be it enacted, etc., That the Secretary of the Treasury, in addition to the $50,000,000 of notes, payable on demand, of denominations not less than five dollars, heretofore authorized by the acts of July 17, and August 5,

1861, be, and he is hereby, authorized to issue like notes, and for like purposes, to the amount of $10,000,000, which said notes shall be deemed part of the loan of $250,000,000 authorized by said acts."

"I will state that this has just been received by me. It has not been submitted to the Finance Committee, but the emergency is known to all. The bill is simple and easily understood, and I presume there will be no objection to passing it now. At all events, I ask the unanimous consent of the Senate to enable me to introduce the bill without notice, and to have it considered now."

By unanimous consent, leave was granted to introduce the bill, (S. No. 190,) to authorize an additional issue of United States notes; and it was read three times and passed. This bill was sent to the House on the 10th inst., and on being read was immediately passed, without opposition.

On the 10th inst. Mr. Fessenden reported the bill (House Bill No. 240) from the Finance Committee, with amendments. The important amendments thus reported were:

First—That the legal tender notes should be receivable for all claims and demands against the United States of every kind whatsoever, *"except for interest on bonds and notes, which shall be paid in coin."*

Second—That the Secretary might dispose of United States bonds *"at the market value thereof, for coin or Treasury notes."*

Third—A new section, No. 4, authorizing deposits in the sub-Treasuries at five per cent., for not less than thirty days, to the amount of $25,000,000, for which certificates of deposit might be issued.

Fourth—An additional section, No. 5, "that all duties on imported goods and proceeds of the sale of public lands," etc., should be set apart to pay coin interest on the debt of the United States; and one per cent. for a sinking fund, etc.

On the 12th inst. Mr. Fessenden, Chairman of the Finance Committee, opened the debate on the bill in a lengthy speech. (*Cong. Globe, p.* 762.)

SPEECH OF MR. FESSENDEN.

"I propose, Mr. President, before any question is taken on any one of the amendments, to make some remarks upon this bill. They may be very dull and dry, for it is rather a dry subject, but still it becomes my duty, as the organ of the Committee on Finance, to explain the provisions of this bill.

The honorable Secretary of the Treasury, at the beginning of the session, recommended two measures—*taxation* and a *bank*. Both of these subjects require, at this stage of the country, and under existing circumstances, peculiar and long consideration. The opinion of the country has tended towards what is called indirect taxation, taxation upon different American and other products, and different kinds of property. Sir, that requires great time. I have examined it sufficiently to be aware that it is not the labors of a day, or a week, or a month. It is substantially new in this country, and it requires much time, much study, and much information to acquire all the knowledge of the various products which would be likely to produce a revenue, and upon which a tax might, with propriety, be laid. So, too, with reference to the scheme suggested by the honorable Secretary of the Treasury with regard to a bank. And yet, notwithstanding all that, a bill of that description has been reported. With regard to the particular bill now before the Senate, we all know that it was resorted to as a temporary measure, not in the beginning, but in consequence of the necessities of the Treasury, arising from a greater expenditure than the Secretary could have imagined, and arising from the nesessary delay with reference to other measures. Can it be said that a measure like the one now pending before the Senate and the country is a measure of a day or an hour? Why, sir, what does it propose? It proposes something utterly unknown in this Government from its foundation; a resort to a measure of doubtful constitutionality, to say the least of it, which has always been denounced as ruinous to the credit of any Government which has recourse to it; a measure, too, about which opinions in the community are divided as perhaps they never have been divided upon any other subject; a measure which, when it has been tried by other countries, as it often has been, has always proved a disastrous failure. Sir, it would hardly be expected that a measure of this description, brought into the House of Representatives and the Senate for the first time in the history of the country, involving questions of such infinite importance, not only with reference to to-day, but with reference to the future, to all time, because it is setting a precedent which may be followed, should be taken up and passed at once, as we pass appropriation bills. *It needed long, careful and vigorous discussion. It has had it in the other branch of Congress. I have read that discussion from beginning to end. It has been able and clear upon both sides of the question.* The subject deserved that discussion; and the House of Representatives would have been faulty if it had suffered a measure of this kind to be passed without its having undergone a discussion which should not only enlighten the House, but enlighten the country upon all the aspects of it. Shall Congress be considered in fault because they have not before acted, or did not act heartily, upon a measure of that description? I think not, sir. The time has been well spent, and although I regret as much as any man can regret that we have not been able to act more promptly, I see no fault to be imputed anywhere; not in the other House of Congress, and certainly not in this; for it has reached this body as soon as it could possibly reach it, when you consider the nature of the questions that were to be discussed by the Committee to whom it was referred.

I have already said that we have never attempted to resort to such a measure before. We have had a war with England since our Government was formed; and if I am rightly informed, at that day, the stocks of the Government went down to sixty per cent, and pay was taken for them in such currency as could be received, itself depreciated; and yet it did not occur as a serious question to the men of that day to put forth, under the Constitution, irredeemable paper made a legal tender for the payment of debts. To be sure, the country then was poor; it is now rich, comparatively. The country had not then the resources that we have; and perhaps it would have had the more excuse for adopting such a course. I do not urge this as an argument against it at the present time, but only as showing the nature of the measure itself, to which it is now proposed to have recourse, in order to place the Government in a better position;

especially, sir, when you observe that everybody who has spoken on this question, I believe without an exception—there may have been one or two—but all the opinions that I have heard expressed, agree in this: that only with extreme reluctance, only with fear and trembling as to the consequences, can we have recourse to a measure like this, of making our paper a legal tender in the payment of debts.

* * * * * * * * * * * *

The Committee on Finance have reported several very important amendments. The first amendment, which the Senate will notice is made in the first section, is that the interest on the public debt shall be paid in coin. The Senate will observe that without this, under the provisions of the House bill, a creditor of the Government, holding Government paper, notes, or bonds, would be compelled to take his interest in notes or bonds, as the case might be, when the time for the payment of the interest came round. He would have no choice. The tender of a note for the interest that might be due on his bonds, however large or small, would be equivalent in its effect to the tender of coin. According to our amendment, the Government will be obliged to provide itself with coin for the payment of the interest. The object of this provision is not only to do justice in this regard, but also to make it raise and support the credit of the Government obligations; and it will be perceived how very important it is to that end. The Secretary, by the provision which I have referred to, is obliged to provide himself with coin for that purpose, and he is obliged to do it at whatever sacrifice may be necessary, in order to accomplish that purpose. This certainly will have one effect; it proves the good faith of the Government; that it means to do all it can; that it means to spare no effort at whatever cost, to give to those who take the Government paper, what they wish to receive, something besides Government paper, and thus running round in a circle of paper, for the interest upon their debts.

But, sir, it was not enough, perhaps, to show the good faith of the Government in this particular. The Committee have recommended that we go further, and that we provide a specific fund, in order to accomplish that purpose, and set it aside for that object. It was proposed in the Committee—and it struck me favorably at first—to set aside, specifically, the public duties, by providing that the duties on imports should be paid in coin; but on consideration, it was deemed by the Committee that that would be hardly fair. The result would be to make a distinction between different classes of the community, and to impose a very heavy burden upon those who are engaged in trade, and who would be called upon to pay duties. If we provide a paper currency, the natural and inevitable effect of it is, that coin increases in price. The consequence would be, unquestionably, that those obliged to pay duties on imports might be compelled to make a severe sacrifice, in order to raise the coin to pay the duties; and, in the next place, the general effect would be to, in effect, increase the duties provided by our tariff. Necessarily, if coin appreciates, if it becomes worth more than the ordinary currency, and duties are to be paid in coin, the effect of such a provision would be to increase the duties, which are already very high, and in some cases almost prohibitory. The Committee, therefore, thought that, under the circumstances, that would not be wise; although it will be perceived that, not having done so, the converse of the proposition may be true: that the effect, if we inflate the currency by paper, and allow the duties to be paid in paper, is necessarily to diminish the duties on imports, and thus, perhaps, to lead to a greater importation.

Having rejected this, it becomes necessary to make some other provision; and accordingly provision was made, and will be found in the fifth section, by setting aside the amount of duties received, the amount received from the sales of the public lands, and the amount that may be received from the confiscation of the property of the rebels, to form a fund. The Senate will consider whether all these provisions are necessary and wise, to create a fund which shall be devoted, in the first place, to pay the interest upon the coin and on the notes; and, in the second place, to create a sinking fund, which, in the end, might be able to pay the whole debt, and would in a certain course of time.

This, undoubtedly, will be a very sufficient security; but, sir, the Committee have gone further. In order that the Secretary may be sure, and that the public creditors may feel safe with reference to it, *they give to the Secretary the power to sell the bonds of the Government at any time that it may be necessary, at the market price, in order to raise coin.* That can always be done. The sacrifice may be great, or it may not; it depends upon circumstances; but at any rate that will bring coin. These two provisions, taken together, have the effect necessary to create an entire confidence in the minds of the purchasers of the public obligations, that the interest will be surely paid at the time it is due, and paid in coin; and having done that, the result is obvious to the Committee that our securities must necessarily be placed upon a more stable foundation, and be of very much greater value in the market, because what the holder of public securities wants, is to be sure that his interest will be paid, especially if it is on long time. But, sir, the power to sell the obligations of the Government at the market price is not confined to the interest. The Senate will observe that it is made general; that instead of being confined and obliged to sell the obligations of the Government at par, the Secretary of the Treasury is authorized *to sell them at any time at the market price;* and instead of being confined to sell them for coin, merely for the purpose of raising money to pay the interest on the public debt, he is permitted to sell any amount at any time that it may be necessary, for what he can get. This is a bold, strong measure, and it may strike the Senate with some surprise, or, at any rate, it may lead them to deliberate upon the subject.

* * * * * * * * * * * *

But the Committee thought, in giving this enlarged power to the Secretary at this time, that it was bound—if this legal tender was to be resorted to, especially if the bill of the House as it stood should be adopted by the Senate, and should become a law—that an assurance should be given to the country that it was not to be resorted to as *a policy;* that it was what it professed to be, *but a temporary measure.* The opinions of the Secretary of the Treasury are perfectly well known. He has declared that, in his judgment, it is, and ought to be, but a temporary measure, not to be resorted to as a policy, but simply on this single occasion, because the country is driven to the necessity of resorting to it. I have not heard anybody express a contrary opinion, or, at least, any man who has spoken on the subject in Congress. The Chairman of the Committee of Ways and Means, in advocating the measure, declared that it was not contemplated, and he did not believe it would be necessary to issue more than the $150,000,000 of Treasury notes made a legal tender, provided by this bill. All the gentlemen who have written on the subject, except some wild speculators in currency, have declared that as a policy it would be ruinous to any people; *and it has been defended, as I have stated, simply and solely upon the ground that it is to be a single measure, standing by itself, and not to be repeated.*

Section four of the bill, as reported by the Committee, contains a provision to which I will call the attention of the Senate. It provides for certain deposit certificates.

This provision was very much desired by the banks in all the cities. It was thought that it would afford them facilities that would give greater currency to the notes, that it would enable them to deal with them better; and therefore we have offered a provision, that for a period of not less than thirty days, any person or institution may deposit their Treasury notes, in sums of not less than $500, at the Sub-Treasury, and receive an interest of five per cent.

Mr. President, I wish now to say something upon the main question of the bill, which I have avoided touching, except incidentally; and that is *the clause making these notes a legal tender; for, after all, that is the great question now submitted to the Senate.* The Senate will observe that the Committee make no recommendation on that subject, except such as may be inferred from the fact that they report it back, retaining the clause, and so far an inference might be drawn that the Committee were in favor of it. Under the circumstances of the case in the Committee, (of which, perhaps, I may speak with propriety as the Committee as a whole, had no opinion upon the subject, their opinions being so divided,) I deem myself at liberty, as I should, perhaps, be under any circumstances, if need be, and if my opinions lead me that way, to say what I have to say in opposition to that clause. I do not propose to do this except incidentally. I propose rather to state the argument as I understand it, on both sides, in relation to the matter as briefly as I can, without attempting to go into the argument of the subject myself.

The ground upon which this clause making these notes a legal tender is put, I have already stated. It is put upon the ground of *absolute, overwhelming necessity;* that the Government has now arrived at that point when it must have funds, and those funds are not to be obtained from ordinary sources, or from any of the expedients to which we have heretofore had resource, and therefore, this new, anomalous, and remarkable provision must be resorted to in order to enable the Government to pay off the debt that it now owes, and afford circulation which will be available for other purposes. The question then is, does the necessity exist? That is a question which I propose in some degree to discuss, because I admit fully and decidedly that the Government, or the country, rather, is to be sustained in its present undertaking, and that we are bound to obtain the means to effect that object. If the necessity exists, I have no hesitation upon the subject, and shall have none. If there is nothing left for us to do but that, and that will effect the object, I am perfectly willing to do that. The question, however, is whether it is necessary, whether we have arrived at that stage, and whether something can or cannot be done in order to accomplish the object.

Sir, I do not hesitate to say here, that *I would advocate the use of the strong arm of the Government to any extent in order to accomplish the purpose in which we are engaged. I would take the money of any citizen against his will to sustain the Government, if nothing else was left, and bid him wait until the Government could pay him. It is a contribution which every man is bound to make under the circumstances.* We can take all the property of any citizen. That is what is called a forced contribution. Thank God, we have not arrived at that; but I am not certain that it would not be a more manly course to meet the matter straight in the face, and if we are to compel a man to part with his property, to do it without offering him what may appear to be security, and yet I am not certain that that would not be the more manly and praiseworthy course to pursue. Then, sir, as to this question of necessity, I wish to ask the gentlemen to consider upon what public credit is founded? According to my reading and my view of the case, it has but one foundation, and that is, the confidence of the people in the ability and integrity of the Government, and its power and its will to pay. Public credit has no other foundation that I am aware of than that. If that is so, then the question arises, what is the ability and what is the integrity of this Government, and what is its will to pay? Are they such as of themselves, under proper legislation, will enable the Government to raise means in the ordinary way?"

Mr. FESSENDEN went on to show that the country was rich in means, land fertile, people industrious, agricultural and manufactured products in 'great abundance, and that under any circumstances we must be entitled to credit for our ability to pay, and that no person placing himself in the position of a money-lender could hesitate to say that we were entitled to all the credit of a great, productive, strong and healthful people. He said our credit had been somewhat injured by the conduct of the war, and yet he thought unreasonably. He saw no reason for loss of credit by the conduct of the war.

He then proceeded:

"The question, after all, returns: is this measure absolutely indispensable to procure means? If so, as I said before, *necessity knows no law.* What are the objections to it? I will state them as briefly as I can. The first is a negative objection. A measure of this kind certainly cannot increase confidence in the ability or the integrity of the country. It can make us no better than we are to-day, so far as this foundation of all public credit is concerned.

Next, in my judgment, it is a confession of bankruptcy. We begin and go out to the country with the declaration that we are unable to pay or borrow, at the present time, and such a confession is not calculated to increase our credit.

Again, say what you will, nobody can deny that it is bad faith. If it be necessary for the salvation of the Government, all considerations of this kind must yield; but, to make the best of it, it is bad faith, and encourages bad morality, both in public and private. Going to the extent that it does, to say that notes thus issued shall be receivable in payment of all private obligations, however contracted, is in its very essence a wrong, for it compels one man to take from his neighbor, in payment of a debt, that which he would not otherwise receive or be obliged to receive, and what is probably not full payment.

Again, it encourages bad morals, because, if the currency falls, (as it is supposed it must, else why defend it by a legal enactment?) what is the result? It is, that every man who desires to pay off his debts at a discount, no matter what the circumstances are, is able to avail himself of it against the will of his neighbor, who honestly contracted to receive something better.

Again, sir, necessarily as a result, in my judgment, it must inflict a stain upon the national honor. We owe debts abroad yet. Money has been loaned to this country, and to the people of this country, in good faith. Stocks of our private corporations, stocks of our States and of our cities, are held and owned abroad. We declare that for the interest on all this debt, and the principal, if due, these notes, made a legal tender by act of Congress, at whatever discount they shall stand, shall be receivable. Payment must be enforced, if at all, in the courts of this country, and the courts of this country are bound to recognize the law that we pass. That result, then, is inevitable.

Again, sir, it necessarily changes the values of all property. It is very well known that all over the world gold and silver are recognized as money, as currency; they are the measures of value. We change it here. What is the result? Inflation, subsequent depression, all the evils which follow from an inflated currency. They cannot be avoided; they are inevitable; the consequence is admitted. Although the notes, to be sure, pass precisely at par, gold appreciates and property appreciates.

Again, sir, a stronger objection than all that I have to this proposition—I am stating the objections which everybody must entertain, because I suppose these facts are palpable—is, that the loss is to fall most heavily upon the poor, by reason of the inflation."

Mr. Fessenden continued his argument at great length, urging taxation, good faith and economy, as the best means of maintaining the credit of the Government. Said he would not argue the constitutional question, proposing to leave his own mind uninstructed on this question, and if need be, leave that question to be settled by the courts. That this was a great crisis truly, but he believed we would be as well able to meet the difficulties without the legal tender clause as with it. And concluded as follows:

"We always meet, and must always expect to meet, in a Government like ours especially, difficulties such as attend us now—perhaps not so great, but greater or less—in the course of time. No nation ever escaped them, and no nation can hope to escape them. I would not have perfect quiet always, in a republic especially. It would be a bad sign if it were so. It is contrary to the very nature of our Government that it should exist. You never find quiet except under a tyranny. Only in the dead sea of despotism is there a perfect calm. It cannot be looked for in the wide ocean of liberty. Storms arise inevitably, and the waves roll and dash turbulently, but bright skies again cheer us, the agitated waters subside, and their broad bosom is traversed by thousands of tall ships laden richly with hope for the nations of the world."

JUDGE COLLAMER'S SPEECH.

Mr. COLLAMER, of Vermont, made an elaborate speech against the legal tender clause in the bill:

"He argued that it was unconstitutional, and that even if it was a *necessity*, he could not vote for the measure. To him, the oath he had taken to support the Constitution, was recorded in Heaven as well as upon earth, and there is no necessity that, in his estimation, would justify him in the breach of it. He admitted that when the Government borrows money, it must give some evidence of the debt, whether by the name of Treasury note or some other name, is immaterial, but denied the power of Congress to make them a tender in payment of debts. He quoted largely from Story on the Constitution, to show the illegality as well as inexpediency of this measure. He said it would be aiding and assisting men who owed debts, to pay those debts with a depreciated paper, at the cost and expense of the creditor. His honest opinion was that the Constitution never intended to invest Congress with any such power. He referred to the debates in the convention that formed the Constitution, to show that the men of that period always entertained the opinion that the 'United States could have nothing else a tender but coin.' While they lived there never was such a thing thought of as attempting to make the evidences of the debt of the Government a legal tender, let their form be what they might. He argued that there was an express power 'to borrow money on the credit of the United States.'

That where there is an *express* power to do a thing, there can be no *implied* power to do the same thing. There were two modes of replenishing the Treasury. One was by taxation, and the other to borrow money. To borrow money there must be a lender and a borrower, and both should act voluntarily, and not compel the lender to part with his money without an inducement. The operation of this bill was not anything like as honorable or honest as a forced loan. Such paper always depreciates, and generally fails altogether, and is never paid."

He urged taxation, and the issue of Treasury notes receivable for public dues, and closed as follows:

"You have nothing to do but to exercise the powers you possess in commanding the resources that you can command, and you can have money and credit enough. I think some little courage becomes us, too, in performing our duty. I have no doubt that this country is able to sustain itself in this strife, pecuniarily as well as physically. I, for one, desire to do that; but I do not want to do it by saying that now, because the necessity requires money, I will go and steal it, or authorize anybody else to steal it. I will not say to a man: 'Here is my note for so much, and if I do not pay it, you must steal the amount from the first man you come to, and give him this note in payment.' I will do nothing of that kind. I have faith in the Government. I no way despair of the success of this Government. It cannot fail. Its power, its resources, its members are such that it is not possible it should fail. If we are not competent to exercise the proper moral courage to do our duties and come up to what is wanted, I hope we shall give place to men who are."

MR. HOWE'S SPEECH.

Mr. HOWE, of Wisconsin, made a lengthy speech in favor of the bill, which will be found in the Appendix to the *Cong. Globe*, p. 51-2-3.

"Mr. PRESIDENT—Hitherto the effort of the Government has been to borrow the immense sums demanded for the war in coin. It is clear to my mind that this effort should be abandoned. We are excluded from borrowing in foreign markets for the present. It suits both the financial and political purposes of other nations, at this time, to discredit our ability. Not until we have demonstrated that, in the devotion of our own people, the Government has resources equal to its utmost needs, can we command the confidence of the gold-mongers of Europe? To borrow of those communities, in their present temper, would subject us to such discounts now as would neither comport with our interests or our honor, and would subject us hereafter to heavy annual exportations of specie for the payment of interest.

To continue borrowing of our own banks, and *borrowing coin, is impossible. They have not the coin to lend. In their efforts to lend to the Government they have already been forced to suspend the payment of specie upon their own notes.* The entire sum of specie in all the banks in the United States, in May last, was only $99,751,627; of that sum $27,125,000 was in the vaults of banks within the seceded States, and not just now available for the purposes of this Government. Thus the specie capital, which the banks of the loyal States could place at the disposal of the Government, was but *little more than seventy-two millions of dollars. That sum will not defray the expenses of the Government for fifty days.* The Government may be able to borrow of the banks, but the Government cannot borrow specie of the banks. If it borrows anything from them it must borrow, not their money, but their promises to pay money. Nothing is more certain than that, whatever our wishes may be, it is impossible to command the revenues for this war in coin. We must rely *mainly upon a paper circulation;* and there is another thing equally certain, which is, that that paper, whoever issues it, *must be irredeemable.* All paper currencies have been, and ever will be, irredeemable. It is a pleasant fiction to call them redeemable; it is an agreeable fancy to think them so. I would not dispel that fancy, I would not expose that fiction, only that the great emergency which is upon us seems to me to render it more than usually proper that the nation should begin to speak truth to itself; to have done with shams, and to deal with realities.

* * * * * * * * * * * * * * *

To talk of borrowing of your banks the money to support your army and your navy, is as idle as for England to talk of borrowing from her national bank the money to pay her national debt. There is but one fund adequate to supply the national finances, *and that is, the property of the nation. There is but one guarantee upon which the national credit can securely rest, and that is the national faith.* In the discharge of that duty Congress is clothed with unrestricted power to *raise* and *support* armies, to *provide* and *maintain* navies. Congress is also clothed with power 'to make all laws which shall be necessary and proper for carrying into execution the foregoing powers, and all other powers vested by this Constitution in the Government of the United States.'

To preserve for these eleven misguided States a republican form of government, we have raised such armies and provided such navies as this continent never before saw—such as the world has rarely seen. I deem those armies and navies 'necessary and proper' for the occasion. To *support* those armies and *maintain* those navies I deem the measure before the Senate 'necessary and proper.'

Those who deny the constitutional authority to pass this bill must deny its necessity or its propriety. Those who deny its necessity or its propriety ought to show us some plan for avoiding it, some measure adequate to the emergency, and more *proper* than the one proposed by this bill.

Two months have elapsed since the policy of this bill has been discussed, and no one of its opponents has yet produced a substitute. The total neglect to offer a substitute is *prima facie* evidence of the necessity for this. But it is not the only evidence of that necessity. It is evident that no substitute can be provided, except it be taxation or direct loans.

I have already said that taxation is inadequate to the supply demanded for this terrible occasion. No nation of modern times has been able to provide from taxes alone, the immense sums we are called upon to expend. I will presently show that direct loans are quite as impracticable as taxation.

* * * * * * * * * * * * * * *

The Senator from Ohio [Mr. Sherman,] proposes to amend this bill, so as to authorize the Secretary of the Treasury to sell the public stocks for whatever he may be offered for them; to go into the market with the national credit, and to sell it for whatever the crippled capital of the country chooses to offer for it, to fling the financial character of the Republic, as a bone, to be quarreled and growled over by the bulls and bears of the stock market. To that amendment I am opposed. If you notify the capital of the country that you are prepared to pay for money, whatever it is pleased to exact, it will be hoarded to wait the extremity of your distress. No man likes to sell for less than he buys. No man likes to buy for more than his neighbors. And if we advertise to the world that, like any other spendthrift, we are prepared to pay for money according to our necessities for it, no man will purchase our bonds at ninety cents for fear we shall presently sell at seventy-five; and if we offer them at seventy-five per cent., we give the best of assurances that we will soon sell at fifty.

* * * * * * * * * * * * * * *

Sir, if one of your soldiers shrinks from duty, and deserts his country's cause for fear of losing his life, he is called a coward, and he is ignominiously dismissed from his company, or shot in its presence. By what fitting term, then, shall we designate him who deserts his country in its greatest need, for fear of losing his money? By what penalties should he be visited?

Money and men alone do not constitute the wealth of a nation. The genius, the generosity, the courage, the intellect, and the patriotism of the people are all national resources. In an emergency like this, the Government should not draw upon one fund alone, but every fund should respond alike. Surely avarice and cowardice should not alone be exempt from the common burdens."

Mr. FESSENDEN moved to amend the bill so that the six per cent. bonds should be "*redeemable in five years, and payable twenty years from date.*"

MR. CHANDLER'S SPEECH.

Mr. CHANDLER, of Michigan, spoke on the amendmennt to make the bonds *redeemable* in *five* years."

Mr. CHANDLER—"I am in favor of the amendment of the Senator from Maine, for the reason that I believe we need not borrow money at long dates at a high rate of interest. Still, I object to the Senator's hypothesis that this war may last one or two years. There has not been a day since the 1st day of November, when we could not have closed the war in sixty days, with our forces then in the field, and from this day forth we can close the war in sixty days, by an advance of our armies; and I believe that the time has now arrived when we will advance our armies, and when the war will *be brought to a close within sixty days from this date.* I am therefore, in favor of restricting the bonds, and giving the Secretary of the Treasury the right to redeem them within five years, and I would even make the time shorter than that, and say "within three years." The time has arrived when this rebellion is within our grasp. The time has arrived when the order, "forward," will close this rebellion. The obstacles are small. The objects are great. We can remove the only obstacle that stands in our way, and we can close this rebellion before the 1st day of May next, and I believe, I believe solemnly, that we shall do it. We have but one obstacle, and that obstacle is so small that we can remove it to-morrow, if Congress, if the Senate say so. *It is a very small obstacle, yet it has stood in our way for four months.*

I hope that the amendment of the Senator from Maine will prevail; and I would prefer to reduce the time which he has fixed, from five years to three years. I would not pay seven per cent., nor even six per cent., more than three years. Our five per cent. bonds will be worth more than par in three years from this date. I know that the money market is the touchstone of the national credit; but I know, at the same time, that the United States five per cent. would be worth more than par to-day, if the country and Congress knew our present position. *One obstacle stands in our way, and that is a very small one.*

I hope the amendment will prevail, and that we shall reduce the time at least to five years. I should prefer its reduction to three years. This war is nearly ended. A single order, "forward," to-morrow, and we have the man to give the order in the Secretary of War, and the war is ended."

The amendment was agreed to.

On the 13th inst. Mr. Collamer moved to strike out the *legal tender clause* in the bill, and on this motion Mr. Wilson obtained the floor.

MR. WILSON'S SPEECH.

Mr. WILSON, of Massachusetts, spoke as follows:

"Mr. PRESIDENT—This proposition is a very simple and plain one, and certainly very easy of comprehension; but, it seems to me, the fate of the measure itself is involved in the decision. If the amendment proposed by the Senator from Vermont is accepted, I shall vote against the whole bill under any and all circumstances, for I conceive that it would be unjust to issue a currency of $150,00,000 of Government paper, and impose it upon all persons in the employ of the Government, upon our soldiers in the field, and upon those who have made contracts to supply the armies of the Republic, and to do nothing to protect the credit of that currency when in their hands, imposed upon them by our necessities. I should consider such a measure as that unjust, wickedly unjust; and I could not, and I would not, under any circumstances, be guilty of giving a vote of that character. If that amendment should be adopted, I hope every Senator in favor of the legal tender clause will vote against the bill and defeat it if possible. I think we owe it to the character of the Senate, and the character of the country.

Passing by the question of constitutional powers, and coming to it simply as a practical question, it is a contest between brokers, and jobbers, and money-changers on the one side, and the people of the United States on the other. I venture to express the opinion that ninety-nine of every hundred of the loyal people of the United States are for this legal tender clause. I do not believe that there are one thousand persons in the State I represent who are not in favor of it. The entire business community, with hardly a solitary exception, men who have trusted out of the country in commercial transactions their tens and hundreds of millions, are for the bill with this legal tender clause. Yes, sir, the people in sentiment approach unanimity upon the question. What is true of Massachusetts is, in my judgment, true to a considerable extent of New England, and true to some extent of the Central States and the West. I believe that no measure that can be passed by the Congress of the United States, unless it be a bill to raise revenue to support the credit of the Government, will be received with so much joy as the passage of this bill with the legal tender clause. On that question I entertain no shadow of doubt. If you pass this bill with the legal tender, the legal tender cannot injuriously affect the credit of this currency you propose to circulate. No harm can certainly come of it. It seems to me, sir, the argument made by the Senator from Vermont, and the Senator from Maine, is an argument against issuing these notes as a currency at all. The legitimate inferences from their arguments are against this proposition for $150,000,000 of demand Treasury notes. I have received several letters from my own State in favor of the bill—persons representing millions, in favor of the legal tender clause. The intelligence I obtain from all portions of the country is to the same effect. I shall, therefore, vote against striking out that clause. If it is retained, I shall vote for the bill; if it is stricken out, I shall give my vote against putting upon the people, upon the soldiers of the country, $150,000,000 of demand notes, and doing nothing to protect those upon whom we impose this Government paper."

MR. SHERMAN'S SPEECH.

Mr. SHERMAN, of Ohio, made an elaborate speech in favor of the bill, and in opposition to the motion of Mr. Collamer to strike out the legal tender clause.

"The motion of the Senator from Vermont now for the first time presents to the Senate the only question upon which the members of the Committee of Finance had any material difference of opinion, and that is, whether the notes provided for in this bill shall be made a legal tender in payment of public and private debts? Upon this point I will commence the argument where the Senator from Maine left it.

In the first place, I will say, every organ of financial opinion—if that is a correct expression—in this country agrees that there is such a necessity, in case we authorize the issue of demand notes. You commence with the Secretary of the Treasury, who has given this subject the most ample consideration. He declares not only in his official communications here, but in his private intercourses with the members of the Committee, that this clause is indispensably necessary to the security and negotiability of these demand notes. We all know from his antecedents, from his peculiar opinions, that he would be probably the last man among the leading politicians of our country to yield to the necessity of substituting paper money for coin. He has examined this question in all its length and breadth. He is in a position where he feels the necessity. He is a statesman of admitted ability, and distinguished in his high position. He informs us that without this clause, to attempt to circulate as money the proposed amount of demand notes of the United States, will prove a fatal experiment.

In addition to his opinion, we have the concurring opinion of the Chamber of Commerce of the city of New York. With almost entire unanimity they have passed a resolution on the subject, after full debate and consideration. That resolution has been read by your Secretary. You have also the opinion of the Committee of Public Safety of the city of New York, composed of distinguished gentlemen, nearly all of whom are good financiers, who agree fully in the same opinion. I may say the same in regard to the Chambers of Commerce of the city of Boston, of the city of Philadelphia, and of almost every recognized organ of financial opinion in this country. They have said to us in the most solemn form, that this measure was indispensably necessary to maintain the credit of the Government, and to keep these notes anywhere near par. In addition, we have the deliberate judgment and vote of the House of Representatives. After a full debate, in which the constitutionality, expediency and necessity of this measure were discussed, in which all the objections that have been made here, and many more, were urged, the House of Representatives, by a large vote, declared that it was necessary to issue demand notes, and that this clause was indispensable to their negotiation and credit."

He continued his argument at length:

"A hard necessity presses the Government. $100,000,000 is now due the army, and $250,000,000 more up to July first. The Banks of New York, Boston and Philadelphia, have exhausted their capitals in making loans to the Government. They have already tied up their capital in your bonds. Among others, the cashier of the Bank of Commerce, (Mr. Vail,) the largest bank corporation in the United States, and one that has done much to sustain the Government, appeared before the Finance Committee, and stated explicitly, that the Bank of Commerce, as well as other banks of New York, could no further aid the Government, unless your proposed currency was stamped by, and invested with the attributes of lawful money, which they could pay to others as well as receive themselves.

Bonds cannot be sold except at a great sacrifice, because there is no money to buy them. As soon as the banks suspended, gold and silver ceased to circulate as money. *You cannot sell your bonds for gold and silver, which is the only money that can now be received under the Sub-Treasury law.* This currency made a legal tender was necessary to aid in making further loans. He argued that the bill was constitutional. The Senator from Vermont has read extracts from the debates in the national convention, and from Story's Commentaries, tending to show that Congress cannot authorize the issue of bills of credit. But I submit to him that this question has been settled by the practice of the Government. We issued such bills during the war of 1812, during the war with Mexico, and at the recent session of Congress. We receive them now for our services; we pay them to our soldiers and our creditors. These notes are payable to bearer; they pass from hand to hand as currency; they bear no interest. If the argument of that Senator is true, then all these notes are unauthorized. The Senator admits that when we owe a debt and cannot pay it, we can issue a note. But where does he find the power to issue a note in the Constitution? Where does he find the power to prescribe the terms of the note, to make it transferable, receivable for public dues? He draws all these powers as incidents to the power to borrow money. According to his argument, when we pay a soldier a ten dollar demand bill, we borrow ten dollars from the soldier; when I apply to the Secretary of the Senate for a month's pay, I loan the United States $250. This certainly is not the view we take of it when we receive the money. On the other hand, we recognize the fact that the Government cannot pay us in gold. We receive notes as money. The Government ought to give, and has the power to give, to that money, all the sanction, authority, value, necessary and proper, to enable it to borrow money. The power to fix the standard of money, to regulate the medium of exchanges, must necessarily go with, and be incident to, the power to regulate commerce, to borrow money, to coin money, to maintain armies and navies. All these high powers are expressly prohibited to the States, and also the incidental power to emit bills of credit, and to make anything but gold and silver a legal tender. *But Congress is expressly invested with all these high powers, and to remove all doubt, is expressly authorized to use all necessary and proper means to carry these powers into effect.*

If you strike out the tender clause you do so with a knowledge that these notes will fall dead upon the money market of the world. When you issue demand notes, and announce to the world your purpose not to pay any more gold and silver, you then tender to those who have furnished you provisions and services this paper money. What can they do? They cannot pay their debts with it; they cannot support their families with it, without a depreciation. The whole then depends on the promise of the Government to pay at some time not fixed on the note. Justice to our creditors demands that it should be a legal tender; it will then circulate all over this country, it will be the life blood of the whole business of the country, and it will enable capitalists to buy your bonds. The only objection to the measure is that too much may be issued. He did not believe the issue of $150,000,000 would do any harm. It is only a mere temporary expedient, and ought not to be repeated."

He closed as follows:

"I have thus, Mr. President, endeavored to reply to the constitutional argument of the Senator from Vermont. Our arguments must be submitted finally to the arbitration of the courts of the United States. When I feel so strongly the necessity of this measure, I am constrained to assume the power, and refer our authority to exercise it to the courts. I have shown, in reply to the argument of the Senator from Maine, that we must no longer hesitate as to the necessity of this measure. That necessity does exist, and now presses upon us. I rest my vote upon the proposition that this is a necessary and proper measure to furnish a currency—a medium of exchange—to enable the Government to borrow money, to maintain an army and support a navy. Believing this, I find ample authority to authorize my vote. We have been taught by recent fearful experience that delay and doubt in this time of revolutionary activity are stagnation and death. I have sworn to raise and support your armies; to provide for and maintain your navy; to borrow money; to uphold your Government against all enemies, at home and abroad. That oath is sacred. As a member of this body, I am armed with high powers for a holy purpose, and I am authorized—nay, required—to vote for all laws necessary and proper for executing these high powers, and to accomplish that purpose. This is not the time when I would limit these powers. Rather than yield to revolutionary force, I would use revolutionary force. Here it is not necessary, for the framers of the Constitution did not assume to foresee all the means that might be necessary to maintain the delegated powers of the national Government. Regarding this great measure as a necessary and proper one, and within our power to enact, I see plain before me the path of duty, and one that is easy to tread."

MR. COWAN'S SPEECH.

Mr. COWAN, of Pennsylvania, made a lengthy speech in favor of the amendment to strike out the legal tender clause in the bill, on the ground that Congress had no power to make anything but gold and silver a tender in payment of private debts.

"He argued at length that Congress had no power to 'emit bills of credit, make anything but gold and silver coin a tender in payment of debts, or pass any law impairing the obligation of contracts.' They are powers which belong neither to the United States nor to the States, *and they ought to belong to no Government anywhere.* He had supposed that this question could never enter the American Senate; that the day had gone by when it was open to discussion, if it ever was open since the Constitution was formed. Surely, if anything in the world is settled—settled by the fathers, by cotemporary history, painful experience, and the total absence of all precedent for the exercise of these powers—it is that they were not delegated, nor intended to be delegated. The exercise of such a power would be subversive of all our notions of Government, and the ends for which it is established, which are, the protection and preservation of society. The life and soul of society is the faith man has in his fellow-man; that he will speak truth, deal justly, and perform his engagements and maintain his credit. Will it strengthen this credit? It proposes that in all money contracts *notes* shall be taken as *money*, the same as gold and silver; all men who have money due them will be obliged to receive these notes as money at par; they are made a legal tender on all debts. The power claimed for the Government subverts the Government itself, and makes it destroy that which it was intended to protect and preserve. It is abhorrent of reason, justice and all notions of right. He thought that the legal tender clause would not give the notes credit, but would be injurious to them. It would disturb the relations between debtor and creditor, and impair all the contracts of the people, more or less, all over the country."

He concluded as follows:

"I am willing to yield to the better judgment of the administration in all matters of policy or expediency, but I am still my own conscience keeper, and in all questions of *power* under the Constitution I must judge for myself, and act accordingly. That Constitution is the charter of our liberties, and the covenant for the Union which we are all so anxious to preserve and defend. I will stand upon it to the last, despite every necessity, however imperious; and if the time comes when we must all go down together, I say let it come; but let us go down as honest men, with our faith unviolated; and in that spirit, I hope the amendment to the bill may prevail."

MR. DOOLITTLE'S SPEECH.

Mr. DOOLITTLE, of Wisconsin, regretted that this bill must be acted upon before the tax bill was matured.

"If we had a sufficient tax law to sustain the credit of the Government, he would vote to strike out the legal tender clause. He was assured that this bill must pass immediately, or the Government could not go on. As an original proposition, he did not believe in paper money, but it had become engrafted on our system. He thought the framers of the Constitution intended nothing but hard money, coined gold and silver. Had their intentions been carried out; had we always held fast to the Constitutional currency; had not paper money, under both State and Federal authority, become the actual currency of our people; had we to-day no other currency but gold and silver, I would not tolerate the idea of passing this bill for a single moment. But, such is not our condition; we are in the midst of a gigantic war; we can not go back; we must go forward; we must go through; we must start from where we are, and not from where we would be; we must behold the real necessities of our position as it is, and not as we would have it, and look those necessities squarely in the face.

The truth is, while in theory the only money of our people is gold and silver, the fact is otherwise. It is almost exclusively of paper. Aye, sir, at this moment it is the irredeemable paper of suspended bank corporations. Most unfortunately, paper money does now exist, and has existed so many years in this country, issued under the sanction of State authorities in violation, as I admit, of the spirit and intentions of those who framed the Constitution, that a man must be blind, indeed, who would not now, in time of war, in a measure of practical legislation, recognize the stubborn fact that these banking corporations, created by the States, so long acquiesced in by this Government, have become great and powerful institutions, and have practically displaced the currency of the Constitution, by substituting in its stead their own paper money. At all times it is much the greater part of our circulating medium, and when, in times of panic and disaster, comes suspension of specie payments, it becomes our only currency. Such is our condition now. What shall we do now? We must have deeds, not words; facts, not theories. We cannot sell our bonds abroad. The paper money issued by banking corporations is all, or nearly all, the money our own people have. Shall we sell our bonds for the paper money of suspended banks? No, sir; no man will advocate that.

The only alternative is to issue these Treasury notes, which will go into the circulation of the country as a part of its currency. If, as I have said, the question now were whether we should begin to build up a paper currency in this country, or hold fast to the currency of the Constitution, I would oppose this measure. But we cut our moorings from the solid ground long, long ago. We have been embarked upon a sea of paper money for years. We have suffered periodically financial crashes and revulsions, tossed upon its uncertain waves, blown up and down by the breath of speculation. We are still at sea, and in the beginning of a terrific financial storm, and the question is whether we shall seize the rudder and direct the ship, or suffer it to go without direction, to founder and make shipwreck of all public and private securities and values, to become the prey and spoils of wreckers along the shore. The simple question which presses upon us in this extremity is, whether we shall rule this currency, created by these corporations, in violation, in my opinion, of the original intention of the Constitution of the United States, or whether they shall rule us.

For their good, for the security of all, as well as for its own safety, this Government must assert its Constitutional authority over the currency of the country, in some practicable way, and it seems to me that the mode proposed in this bill is the simplest and most direct in the present exigencies, as a temporary measure, until the great measure of finance, the tax bill, can be perfected and set in operation."

MR. SIMMONS' SPEECH.

Mr. SIMMONS, of Rhode Island, opposed the legal tender clause in this bill.

"He did not see its necessity, nor the Constitutional power for passing it. He thought the Constitutional objection about as difficult a matter to get over as anything could well be. He thought that if the legal tender clause was stricken out, the notes would not be bills of credit, but mere evidences of debt. In contemplation of the Constitution, the old fashioned bills of credit were promises to pay, with a State law enforcing their passage against the will of those who were to take them. These were the national bills of credit, which were made a tender by State laws under the old Confederation. He thought it better to make our securities desirable by increasing the rate of interest, as high even as eight per cent. He intended to move an amendment at the proper time, to increase the interest to eight per cent. on notes and bonds payable in two years."

MR. BAYARD'S SPEECH.

Mr. BAYARD, of Delaware, opposed the legal tender clause, because it is unconstitutional, impolitic and inexpedient.

"He concurred in the argument of the Senator from Vermont, who has moved to strike out the legal tender clause in the bill. The first article of the Constitution, in its first section, provides that 'all legislative powers herein granted shall be vested in a Congress of the United States'—not an indefinite delegation of all powers of legislation, as is the case in our State Constitutions, where the legislative power of the community is vested in a Senate and House of Representatives; but here in this Constitution of specially delegated powers, 'all legislative powers herein granted shall be vested in a Congress,' and none other. When you come to the other clause, which specifies these powers, you find but a solitary provision which has any relation to the power to make money. The power to borrow is a distinct thing; but the power to make money, is 'to coin money, regulate the value thereof, and of foreign coin, and fix the standard of weights and measures.' I have supposed that the power being designated in that form, and Congress having a right to exercise only the power granted, under no species of interpretation could you hold that a power to coin money implied, or could be extended to a power, to make your own paper, your promise to pay money, for the purpose of discharging debts between individuals, or as against yourself.

In my judgment, therefore, apart from the constitutional objection, which alone would be sufficient to control my vote, upon the ground that you have no power to insert this clause in any law, I cannot vote for a bill which embodies it. It is impolitic and inexpedient, as well as unconstitutional. It is a mere temporary expedient. It may give present inflation and present relief for the hour, and a very brief hour indeed, but it will be followed by a weakening of the resources of the Government, a depreciation of its credit, and it will produce nothing but disaster and ruin to the country."

SPEECH OF MR. WILLEY.

Mr. WILLEY, of Virginia, spoke as follows:

"I do not rise, Mr. President, certainly not at the present time, for the purpose of making a speech, but I wish to place upon record the reason why I shall give the vote which I feel compelled to give on the present occasion. If this were a question merely of expediency, I would most readily defer my judgment to that of other gentlemen better capable of forming a correct estimate. But, sir, consulting my own opinion, I should say that the legal tender clause of this bill will have the contrary effect upon the currency and credit of the Treasury notes from that which some gentlemen seem to suppose. I believe it will depreciate their credit, and I fear it will depreciate the character of our Government and our country in the estimation of all honest and well-meaning nations abroad. But, sir, believing, as I sincerely do, that this clause is unconstitutional, I can not vote to retain it in the bill. I have felt the appeal of my honorable friend from Ohio—the plea of necessity. Sir, that is a dangerous plea, and it found its origin in a dangerous quarter. It is said that the plea of necessity is the plea of tyrants. I nevertheless recognize the fact that there are occasions in the history of a nation when the old maxim *salus populi suprema lex*, may apply; but it is my opinion that the exigencies of the country do not, at this time, warrant the application of that maxim; and I should be sorry if, in prosecuting this holy war to put down an infamous rebellion, to restore and maintain the Constitution, we are ourselves, in the very act of doing so, guilty of a most palpable violation of that instrument."

SPEECH OF MR. HOWARD.

Mr. HOWARD, of Michigan, said:

"I do not rise, Mr. President, at this late period of the discussion, to detain the Senate longer than a minute or two. When this measure was first proposed, and after I had given it merely a perusal, I came, or thought I came, to the same conclusion at which the gentleman from Virginia seems to have arrived, and was rather disposed to think that there was no authority in the Constitution to warrant such an enactment as this, which constitutes the Treasury notes a legal tender in the payment of private debts. The thing was so anomalous, so unusual to me, that I could scarcely entertain the idea, and I confess that my mind struggled strongly against it. But after a little reflection, and giving the question of constitutional power such examination as I have been able to give it, I have arrived at the conclusion that Congress has the constitutional power, particularly under the clause authorizing them to borrow money, to declare this species of paper a legal tender in the payment of debts between individuals.

It is undoubtedly a hard necessity to which we are driven; but the necessity of the case I submit, has nothing to do with the naked question of authority, under the Constitution. If I were convinced that we had no authority, under the Constitution, to enact such a clause as this, I should not feel at liberty to vote in favor of it, and should certainly vote to strike it out; but such is not my conviction. I believe that we have the authority; and still, while I say this, I must say at the same time, that I think several gentlemen who are friends of this bill, have placed too high an estimate upon this particular clause in the bill. I doubt very much whether it will add greatly to the currency and credit of the paper itself. They think it will, and I am certainly disposed to give it a trial.

We have, under the Constitution, the power to borrow money. This no one disputes. If we have the power to borrow money, we have the right; and it is our duty to place in the hand of the lender, an evidence of the fact that we have so borrowed it, and further, that we intend to pay what we have borrowed. These two things are manifestly, in their very nature, inseparable; and the only real question, it seems to me, which addresses itself to the Senate is this: whether we have any power, after having issued this description of paper to the public creditors, in payment of their debts, to protect the credit of the United States, expressed upon the face of the paper, while it is in the hands of innocent and honest holders? I think we have. I think this is one of the most obvious means of extending protection to the public credit thus expressed upon the paper. If we have it not; if we cannot subject, so to speak, the entire property of the nation, to something like an assistance to the public credit, then this power to borrow money at once ceases to be a power of any value, and it is a mere mockery upon the face of the Constitution. If we cannot declare that this paper shall, in commercial transactions, be of equal validity to transactions based upon gold and silver, then I say that the power to borrow money ceases, in and of itself, to be of any benefit to the Government or to the nation; and it is because I believe that we have this power, thus to protect the public credit, expressed and pledged on the face of a Treasury note, that I shall vote to retain this clause in the bill. I think we have the constitutional power, and I am willing to use it on this occasion."

MR. McDOUGALL'S SPEECH.

Mr. McDOUGALL, of California, advocated the bill as a lawful and proper measure to be adopted at this time.

"He thought this a just and reasonable war measure. Necessity, it is said, is above all law; it is better said, 'necessity makes its own laws.' Our Treasury is now exhausted. Money is the first necessity of war—vigorous successful war. Delay is not to be contemplated—not to be permitted. Prompt present action is a necessity. To give efficiency, the legal tender clause should be retained—the bill ought not to be amended by striking it out. He argued that the bill was constitutional; that we had the right to issue these notes as money, to be used as a currency for the country in the present exigency. He was not able to maintain against it any good constitutional objection, and did not see in it any special injustice. We are at war; this is a war measure; we must take war responsibilities. This measure can ruin no one, destroy no one, and we are advised upon the highest authority that it is needed for the maintainance of the Republic. I believe the law constitutional, just and necessary. I hope to see it passed, and when passed, I shall hope on."

MR. SUMNER'S SPEECH.

Mr. SUMNER, of Massachusetts, made a lengthy speech in favor of the constitutionality and expediency of the legal tender clause, and said he would confine his remarks to this feature of the present bill.

"In the present exigency, money must be had; and we are told that the credit of the Government can be saved only by an act that seems like a forfeiture of credit. Paper promises to pay are to be made a legal tender like gold and silver, and this provision is to be ingrafted on the present bill authorizing the issue of Treasury notes to the amount of $150,000,000. It seemed to him that the power of Congress to make Treasury notes a legal tender was settled as long ago as when it was settled that Congress might authorize the issue of Treasury notes; for from time immemorial the two have gone together; one is the incident to the other, and, unless expressly severed, they naturally go together.

It is true, that in the Constitution there are no words expressly giving to Congress the power to make Treasury notes a legal tender; but there are no words expressly giving to Congress the power to issue Treasury notes. If we consult the text of the Constitution, we shall find it as silent with regard to one as with regard to the other. But, on the other hand, the States are expressly prohibited to 'emit bills of credit, to make anything but gold and silver coin a tender in payment of debts. Treasury notes are 'bills of credit,' and this prohibition is imperative on the States. But the inference is just that this prohibition, expressly addressed to the States, was not intended to embrace Congress indirectly, as it obviously does not embrace it directly. The presence of the prohibition, however, shows that the subject was in the minds of the framers of the Constitution. If they failed to extend it still further, it is reasonable to conclude that they left the whole subject in all its bearings to the sound discretion of Congress, under the ample powers intrusted to it.

The stress that is so constantly put upon the prohibitions addressed to the States will justify me in introducing the opinion of Mr. Justice Story in his Commentaries: 'It is manifest that all these prohibitory clauses as to coining money, emitting bills of credit, and tendering anything but gold and silver in payment of debts, are founded upon the same general considerations. *The policy is to provide a fixed and uniform rule throughout the United States,* by which commercial and other dealings of the citizens, as well as the moneyed transactions of the Government, might be adjusted."—(2 *Story's Com.,* Sec. 1372.)

If this view be correct, then no inference adverse to the powers of the national Government can be drawn from these prohibitory clauses; for whatever may be the policy of the national Government, it will be a fixed and uniform rule throughout the United States.

From the proceedings of the Federal Convention it appears that a proposition empowering Congress 'to emit bills of credit' was negatived, after discussion, in which Mr. Madison said: 'Will it not be sufficient to prohibit the making them a tender? This will remove the temptation to emit them with unjust views.' And in a note to the debate, this same great authority says that he 'became satisfied that the striking out the words would not disable the Government from the use of public notes, as far as they could be safe and proper, and would only cut off the pretense for a *paper currency*, and particularly for making bills a *tender*, either for public or private debts.' Then it appears that the suggestion was made to prohibit the making of bills a tender; but this suggestion was not acted on, and no such prohibition was ever moved. It is evident that the Convention was not prepared for a measure so positive. Less still was it prepared for the prohibition to emit bills. Such is the record. While all words expressly authorizing bills were struck out, nothing was introduced in restraint of the powers of Congress on this subject. Indeed, Mr. Madison declares his own personal belief, that the striking out of the power 'to emit bills of credit,' would not disable the Government from the issue of public notes, so far as they could be safe and proper, but would *only cut off the pretext* for a paper currency. It would seem from this language, in so careful a writer, that he imagined the whole subject was left substantially to the sound discretion of Congress. Indeed, the inference from his report and comment, is identical with the inference from the text of the Constitution itself. (*See Madison's Papers, vol.* 3, *p.* 1343.)

But in conceding that Congress might issue 'public notes, as far as they could be proper,' in other words, 'bills of credit,' the whole question was practically settled; and the usage of the Government has been in harmony with this settlement. Treasury notes were issued during the war of 1812, also during the war with Mexico, and constantly since, so that the power to issue them cannot be drawn into doubt. If there was any doubt originally, an unquestioned practice, sanctioned by successive Congresses, has completely removed it. I do not stop to consider whether the power is derived primarily from the power 'to borrow money,' or the power 'to regulate commerce,' or from the unenumerated powers. It is sufficient that the power exists. But it is difficult to escape the conclusion, that if Congress is empowered to issue Treasury notes, it may affix to these notes such character as shall seem just and proper, declaring the conditions of their circulation and the dues for which they shall be received. Grant the first power and the rest must follow. Careful you will be in the exercise of this power, but if you choose to take the responsibility, I do not see what check can be found in the Constitution.

It appears that the phrase 'bills of credit,' was familiarly used for bank notes as early as 1683, in England, and also as early as 1714, in New England. But the first issue in America was in 1690, by the Colony of Massachusetts, and the occasion, identical with the present, was to pay soldiers returning unexpectedly from an unsuccessful expedition against Canada.

Mr. Sumner went into a brief history of the issue of bills of credit—paper money—in the States of Massachusetts, Rhode Island, Connecticut, Virginia and North Carolina, which led to the passage of an act by the Imperial Parliament, (24 *George II, Sec.* 2, *Chap.* 53,) 1751, which expressly forbade the issue of any paper bills, or bills of credit, except for certain specific purposes, or upon certain specified emergencies; and declaring that such paper money should not be a legal tender for private debts. Continental paper money was issued during the Revolutionary war, not made a legal tender by Congress, although the States were recommended to make them such. He argued at great length the power of Congress to issue Treasury notes and make them a legal tender; and that it was purposely left by the framers of the Constitution to the sound discretion of Congress, in great emergencies, to decide whether it was necessary to exercise the power or not."

He closed as follows:

"But, while recognizing the existence of the discretion, in the last resort, under the law of necessity, the question still remains if this necessity now exists? And now, as I close, I shall not cease to be frank. Is it necessary to incur all the unquestionable evils of inconvertible paper, forced into circulation by act of Congress—to suffer the stain upon our national faith—to bear the stigma of a seeming repudiation—to lose for the present that credit which, in itself, is a treasury—and to teach debtors everywhere that contracts may be varied at the will of the stronger? Surely, there is much in these inquiries which may make us pause. If our country were poor or feeble, without population and without resources; if it were already drained by a long war; if the enemy had succeeded in depriving us of the means of livelihood, then we should not even pause. But our country is rich and powerful, with a numerous population, busy, honest, and determined, and with unparalleled resources of all kinds, agricultural, mineral, industrial and commercial; it is yet undrained by the war in which we are engaged; nor has the enemy succeeded in depriving us of any of the means of livelihood. It is hard—very hard—to think that such a country, so powerful, so rich, and so beloved, should be compelled to adopt a policy of even questionable propriety. If I mention these things—if I make these inquiries—it is because of the unfeigned solicitude which I feel with regard to this measure, and not with the view of arguing against the exercise of a constitutional power, when, in the opinion of the Government, in which I place trust, the necessity for its exercise has arrived. Surely, we must all be against paper money—we must all insist upon maintaining the integrity of the Government—*and we must all set our faces against any proposition like the present, except as a temporary expedient, rendered imperative by the exigency of the hour.* If I vote for this proposition it will be only because I am unwilling to refuse to the Government, especially charged with this responsibility, that confidence which is hardly less important to the public interests than the money itself. Others may doubt if the exigency is sufficiently imperative; but the Secretary of the Treasury, whose duty it is to understand the occasion, does not doubt. In his opinion the war requires this sacrifice. Uncontrolable passions have been let loose to overturn tranquil conditions of peace. Meanwhile your soldiers in the field must be paid and fed. Here, then, can be no failure or postponement. A remedy which, at another moment you would reject, is now proposed. Whatever may be the national resources, they are not now within reach, except by summary process. Reluctantly, painfully, I consent that the process should issue. And yet I cannot give such a vote without warning the Government against the dangers from such an experiment. The medicine of the Constitution must not become its daily bread. Nor can I disguise the conviction that better than any legal tender will be vigorous, earnest efforts for the suppression of the rebellion, and for the establishment of the Constitution in its true principles over the territory which the rebellion has usurped."

The question was then taken by yeas and nays on the motion of Mr. Collamer to strike out the legal tender clause in the bill, and resulted as follows:

Yeas—Messrs. Anthony, Bayard, Collamer, Cowan, Fessenden, Foot, Foster, Kennedy, King, Latham, Nesmith, Pearce, Powell, Salisbury, Simmons, Thompson and Willey—17.

Nays—Messrs. Chandler, Clark, Davis, Dixon, Doolittle, Harlan, Harris, Henderson, Howard, Howe, Lane (of Indiana), McDougall, Morrill, Pomeroy, Rice, Sherman, Sumner, Ten Eyck, Wade, Wilkinson, Wilson (of Mass.) and Wilson (of Mo.)—22.

So the motion to strike out the legal tender clause was not agreed to.

On Mr. Simmons' motion to pay eight per cent. interest on two years' notes or bonds, the amendment was agreed to—ayes 20, noes 16.

The other amendments proposed by the Finance Committee were agreed to substantially as reported by the Committee.

Mr. DOOLITTLE moved to limit the legal tender clause to debts *hereafter* contracted, but the amendment was not adopted.

MR. KING'S SPEECH.

Mr. KING, of New York, spoke as follows:

"My opinion is so decided against this measure, which, it is evident, has the favor of a large majority of the Senate, that I must vote against it; but I deem it due to myself to offer a substitute for the first section. I propose to strike out the first section of the bill, which relates to Treasury notes and the tender, and to insert what I send to the chair in three sections. The second and subsequent sections of the bill, providing for bonds and making other provisions, I do not propose to interfere with.

* * * * * * * * * * * * * * *

The change which this amendment proposes, is to strike out the tender clause, to make the demand notes, which are issued without interest, five year notes, bearing an interest of seven and three-tenths per cent. per annum, receivable for all Government dues, or exchangeable for long bonds at six per cent., interest payable semi-annually, at the option of the holder, and providing by tax a sufficient sum, which is pledged to the redemption of these notes, and ultimately to pay them, principal and interest; which I think is a provision that ought to accompany any measure providing for borrowing money, either by notes or bonds."

The amendment was not agreed to.

MR. PEARCE'S SPEECH.

Mr. PEARCE, of Maryland, opposed the legal tender clause in the bill.

"Ours is a Government of limited and granted powers. We can exercise no authority which Congress has not, by reason of the grant of some express power, or some power necessarily implied from that which is granted. If there be a power necessary and proper to carry into execution any of the granted powers, we possess it under the general clause of the Constitution in reference to that subject. The power to make a legal tender is not granted expressly in the Constitution, nor, as I think, by any implication from any of the granted powers. It is true there is a qualified power of making a legal tender to be found in the clause which authorizes us to coin money, and to regulate the value thereof, because there can be no purpose in regulating the value of the money we are authorized to coin, except to make it a legal tender. When we establish the value of gold and silver coin, which we have the express authority to do, we of course have the implied authority to declare that its value thus fixed by law, shall be the measure of value in all contracts, and to make it a legal tender. There is no other purpose for giving us the authority to regulate the value of the money which we are authorized to coin; and, accordingly, Congress has declared silver coins to be a legal tender. I do not know whether that provision is in the law regulating the value of the gold coins. I suppose, however, that it must be so. I know that when we passed the act by which we apportioned the silver and the alloy in our silver coins, we did declare that coinage to be a legal tender for sums under five dollars. Even, however, if that were not so, it would follow necessarily, it being provided in the Constitution expressly that gold and silver may be coined by authority of Congress, and their value regulated by law, that they must necessarily be a legal tender. It is so according to the custom of all civilized nations, and so the convention that framed the Constitution assumed it to be. But I can see no power from which we can infer authority in this Government to make paper money a legal tender. It clearly cannot be inferred from the power to coin money, which is to be made of metal. I do not see how it is to be inferred, as I think one Senator derived it, from the power to borrow money, since, to make paper money cannot be necessary to the execution of the power to borrow money. As well could we infer a general authority to lend money or to deal in brokerage.

Mr. President, the exigencies of the country are very great; I admit my obligation to co-operate with gentlemen here in furnishing the Government with the means of carrying on all its operations; but when a constitutional objection is presented to me, the very allegiance which I owe to the Constitution, and therefore to the Union, compels me not to violate any one of its provisions, as I think I shall do if I vote for this bill. I must, therefore, cast my vote against it."

Mr. SAULSBURY, of Delaware—"It was my desire and intention to vote for this bill, provided the provision making these notes a legal tender had been stricken out. That provision has been retained in the bill. It is so clearly unconstitutional, in my opinion, that I cannot conscientiously vote for it. I cannot attempt at this late hour to assign the reasons for my opinion. The speech of the Senator of Vermont has not been answered, and it is not in the power of man to answer it."

Mr. POWELL, of Kentucky—"It is not my purpose to make a speech. It would afford me pleasure to vote for any measure I thought constitutional to relieve the country from its present embarrassment; but believing that this bill is unconstitutional, I cannot vote for it. I had intended, if time permitted—but the hour is too late now—to give briefly, my reasons for the vote I shall give; but after the very exhaustive speech made by the Senator from Vermont yesterday, it would be unnecessary, particularly after the excellent speech made by the Senator from Pennsylvania to-day, and the brief but very pointed speech of the Senator from Maryland, who has just taken his seat.

In my judgment this bill is plainly and palpably violative of the Constitution of the United States, and I do not believe that issues of paper money, unless they are convertible into coin at the pleasure of the holder, ever did, or ever will, relieve any country permanently from any embarrassment. I think all such issues of irredeemable paper lead the country into further and greater embarrassments, instead of relieving it; and I very much fear that those who expect great benefits to the country from this bill will be greatly disappointed. I shall not detain the Senate by speaking."

PASSAGE OF THE BILL.

THE PRESIDING OFFICER—"The question is on the passage of the bill."

Mr. HOWARD—"I call for the yeas and nays."

The yeas and nays were ordered.

Mr. LATHAM, of California—"I merely desire to say, in order that I may appear right upon the record, that I have entertained very grave doubts during this discussion as to the constitutionality of the legal tender issue, and entertaining those doubts, I cast my vote against that clause when it was under consideration. The majority of this body having now, however, indicated their desire that it should be in the bill, I cannot, consistently with my sense of duty, withhold my vote from the bill. I shall therefore vote for it."

Mr. ANTHONY, of Rhode Island—"I voted against the vital clause of this bill making the paper issued by the Government a legal tender, but having no project of my own to present to the Senate, I shall not take the responsibility of voting against the only measure which is proposed by the Government, and which has passed the House of Representatives, and received the sanction of a majority of this body."

The question being taken by yeas and nays, resulted—yeas 30, nays 7; as follows:

Yeas—Messrs. Anthony, Chandler, Clark, Davis, Dixon, Doolittle, Fessenden, Foot, Foster, Grimes, Hale, Harlan, Harris, Henderson, Howard, Howe, Lane (of Indiana), Latham, McDougall, Morrill, Pomeroy, Rice, Sherman, Sumner, Ten Eyck, Trumbull, Wade, Wilkinson, Wilson (of Massachusetts) and Wilson (of Missouri)—30.

Nays—Messrs. Collamer, Cowan, Kennedy, King, Pearce, Powell and Saulsbury—7.

So the bill was passed.

AUTHORSHIP OF THE LEGAL TENDER BILL.

Letter of JAMES W. SIMONTON to *N. Y. Times.*

"WASHINGTON, D. C., Feb. 13, 1862.

"The passage, by the Senate, of the Treasury Note bill, including the legal tender clause, is a subject of very general congratulation among the friends of the Administration. Among the opponents of the legal tender provision were some of the ablest and firmest friends of the Administration, whose sincere desire for the most effective support of the Government cannot for a moment be justly questioned. They honestly believed the policy injudicious, and made strenuous fight in support of their theory.

But the overwhelming necessity existing for the measure is a stronger argument than anything offered against the bill, and received the decisive vote of 30 to 7. Having made their record, the opposition yielded with excellent grace, and the Democratic opponents in both Houses confess to a sense of relief when the bill, legal tender and all, had passed. There are few members who would care to assume the responsibility which would have rested upon them in the event of the defeat of the measure, and the risk of the consequences to themselves of the financial panic that would speedily follow the admitted bankruptcy of the Government.

Now that the bill has passed, it is but just that due credit should be awarded to the author of the legal tender scheme, the Hon. E. G. Spaulding, Member of Congress from the Buffalo (N. Y.) District. It was Mr. Spaulding who originated the proposition to force a fixed paper currency upon the country by making Treasury notes a legal tender. His practical knowledge and experience as a banker and financier, early disclosed to his own mind the fact, which since then has become so patent to overwhelming majorities in each House of Congress and the country, to wit: that no other scheme could possibly provide for the wants of the Government *in time* to save it from absolute financial ruin. He gave the subject unremitting study and attention, devoting to it the entire holiday season, and maturing, finally, a measure which has received the endorsement of the Administration and of Congress, and withstood the combined assaults of selfish and honest opponents alike. He has reason to be proud of the triumph he has achieved, and the country will not soon forget his services."

OBJECTION TO SENATE AMENDMENTS.

The main principles of the bill seemed to be well settled by the preceding full and able discussion, and its passage by large majorities through both Houses; and the Secretary of the Treasury in administering the Finances during the war, would find it easy to execute the two simple provisions of the bill, viz:

1. Issue these Treasury notes fitted for circulation as money, and by the legal tender provision made a forced loan from the people to the Government, without interest, which could only be justified by the imperative necessities of the Treasury, and by the fair and equitable provision,

2. That these notes might at any time, at the option of the holder, be funded in six per cent. twenty year bonds, interest payable semi-annually.

The Secretary could issue notes and pay them out for supplies and material of war, and to the Army and Navy, making money plenty, and filling all the channels of circulation, which would, as soon as it became redundant, enable him to float the six per cent. bonds, and funding would take place, thereby preventing too great an excess of this circulating medium. The Senate amendments seemed in some measure to complicate these simple provisions. Several of the amendments of the Senate were very important in regard to details and special provisions of the bill, but the most of them were verbal and unimportant. The four amendments of the Senate, to which a large number of the members of the House made the most objection, were in substance as follows:

1. Requiring payment of 'interest semi-annually in *coin* on bonds and 7-30 notes.'
2. Conferring on the Secretary power to sell six per cent. bonds, 'at the *market value* thereof for coin,' which would reduce the price.
3. And the provision making the bonds '*redeemable* in five years, and payable in twenty years from date,' at the option of the Government, making them less valuable.
4. Temporary deposits in the Sub-Treasury at 6 per cent., which would retard funding in long bonds.

All former loan laws passed by Congress, from the organization of the Government to this time, contained only a provision to pay 'dollars.' The word *dollars* had a well known legal meaning under our coinage and legal tender laws, and it was difficult to see any good reason for changing the phraseology, and thereby make a departure from established usages at this time, especially if six per cent. bonds (which were then selling at about 88,) should, as a necessary consequence of such provision, be sold at the *market price* to raise the coin to pay this interest. *At this stage of the bill there was no provision in it, or in the Senate amendments, to collect the duties on foreign imports in coin, so that as the bill then stood, there was no other mode of obtaining the coin except by a forced sale of bonds.* This coin provision was deemed by many members to be an unnecessary discrimination in favor of the bond-holders over other creditors of the Government equally meritorious. It was difficult to see the propriety of paying coin interest to the bond-holders while the soldiers and others were paid in notes; and besides, the terms used made the coin payment of interest applicable to the 7-30 Treasury notes and bonds issued to the banks during the previous summer.

BILL RETURNED TO THE HOUSE.

The bill and Senate's Amendments were returned to the House on the 14th inst, and on motion of Mr. Stevens, were referred to the Committee of Ways and Means. This Committee had a long discussion upon the Senate's Amendments, and were about equally divided on the most material and important of them. Some were disagreed to, others were concurred in, and some unimportant amendments to the Senate amendments were recommended. On the 18th, Mr. Stevens, from the Committee of Ways and Means, reported back the bill and amendments to the House and said:

"I have no purpose of considering the bill at this time. I desire that it shall be referred to the Committee of the Whole, and be made the special order for to-morrow at one o'clock. I hope gentlemen of the House will read the amendments. *They are very important, and, in my judgment, very pernicious*, but I hope the House will examine them."

The motion was agreeed to.

On Wednesday, the 19th inst., the amendments of the Senate to the bill being the special order, Mr. Spaulding opened the debate in opposition to some of them, as follows:

MR. SPAULDING'S SPEECH.

Mr. CHAIRMAN—I desire especially to oppose the amendments of the Senate which require the interest on bonds and notes to be paid *in coin* semi-annually, and which authorizes the Secretary of the Treasury to sell six per cent. bonds at the market price for coin to pay the interest.

The Treasury note bill, as reported first from the Committee of Ways and Means as a necessary war measure, was simple and perspicuous in its terms, and easily understood. It was so plain that everybody could understand that it authorized the issue of $150,000,000 of legal tender demand notes, to circulate as a national currency among the people in all parts of the United States, and that they might, at any time, be funded in six per cent. twenty years' bonds. The passage of this measure in this House was hailed with satisfaction by the great mass of people all over the country. It received the hearty indorsement of such bodies as the Chambers of Commerce of New York, Cincinnati, St. Louis, Chicago, Buffalo, Milwaukee, and other places. I have never known any measure receive a more hearty approval from the people.

Nearly every amendment to the bill since it was matured has rendered it more complex and difficult of execution. I regret to say that some of the amendments of the Senate render the bill incongruous, and tend to defeat its great object, namely: to prevent all forcing of the Government to sell its bonds in the market to the highest bidder for coin. It might be very pleasant for the holders of the seven and three-tenths Treasury notes and six per cent. bonds, to receive their interest *in coin* semi-annually, but very disastrous to the Government to be compelled to sell its bonds, at ruinous rates of discount, every six months to pay them gold and silver, while it would pay only Treasury notes to the soldier, sailor, and all other creditors of the Government.

I am opposed to all those amendments of the Senate which make unjust discriminations between the creditors of the Government. A soldier or sailor who performs service in the army or navy is a creditor of the Government. The man who sells food, clothing, and the material of war, for the use of the army and navy is a creditor of the Government. The capitalist who holds your seven and three-tenths Treasury notes, or your six per cent. coupon bonds is a creditor of the Government. All are creditors of the Government on an equal footing, *and all are equally entitled to their pay in gold and silver.*

I am opposed to all those amendments of the Senate which discriminate in favor of the holders of bonds and notes by compelling the Government to go into the streets every six months to sell bonds at the 'market price,' to purchase gold and silver in order to pay the interest 'in coin' to the capitalists who now hold United States stocks and Treasury notes heretofore issued, or that may hold bonds and notes hereafter to be issued; while all other persons in the United States (including the Army and Navy and all who supply them food and clothing,) are compelled to receive legal tender Treasury notes in payment of demands due them from the Government.

Why make this discrimination? Who asks to have one class of creditors placed on a better footing than another class? Do the people of New England, the Middle States, or the people of the West and Northwest, or anywhere else in the rural districts, ask to have any such discrimination made in their favor? Does the soldier, the farmer, the mechanic, or the merchant ask to have any such discrimination made in his favor? No, sir; no such unjust preference is asked for by this class of men. They ask for the legal tender note bill pure and simple. They ask for a national currency which shall be of equal value in all parts of the country. They want a currency that shall pass from hand to hand among all the people in every State, county, city, town and village in the United States. They want a currency secured by adequate taxation upon the whole property of the country, which will pay the soldier, the farmer, the mechanic, and the banker alike for all debt due. They ask that the Government shall stand upon its own responsibility, its own rights, and exert its vast powers, preserve its own credit, and carry us safely through this gigantic rebellion, in the shortest time, and with the least possible sacrifice. *They intend to foot all the bills, and ultimately pay the whole amount, principal and interest, in gold and silver.*

Who, then, are they that ask to have a preference given to them over other creditors of the Government? Sir, it is a very respectable class of gentlemen, but a class of men who are very sharp in all money transactions. They are not generally among the producing classes—not among those who, by their labor and skill, make the wealth of the country; but a class of men that have *accumulated* wealth—men who are willing to lend money to the Government if you will make the security beyond all question, give them a high rate of interest, and make it payable *in coin*. Yes, sir, the men who are asking these extravagant terms, who want to be preferred creditors, are perfectly willing to lend money to the Government in her present embarrassment, if you will only make them perfectly secure, give them extra interest, and put your bonds on the market at the 'market price,' to purchase gold and silver to pay them interest every six months. Yes, sir, entirely willing to loan money on these terms! Safe, no hazard, secure, and the interest payable 'in coin!' Who would not be willing to loan money on such terms? Sir, the legal tender Treasury note bill was intended to avoid all such financiering and protect the Government and people, who pay the taxes, from all such hard bargains. It was intended as a shield in the hands of the patriotic people of the country against all forced sales of bonds, and all extravagant rates of interest.

The legal tender note bill is a great measure of equality. It proposes a currency for the people which is based upon the good faith of the people and all their taxable property. All are obliged to receive and pass it as money, *and all are obliged to submit to heavy taxation to provide for its ultimate redemption in gold or silver.* Every attempt on the part of any class of citizens to create distinctions and secure a legal preference, mars the simplicity and success of the whole plan. The very discrimination proposed carries on its face notice to everybody that although the notes are declared to be 'lawful money and a legal tender in payment of debts,' yet that there is something of higher value, that must be sought after at a sacrifice to the Government, to pay a peculiar class of creditors to whom it owes money—a kind of absurdity and self-stultification which does not appear well on the face of the bill. It is an unjust discrimination which does not appear well now, and will not look well in history. *You will, if the Senate's amendment is adopted, depreciate, by your own acts, your own bonds and notes, and effectually destroy the symmetry and harmonious working of the whole plan.*

I am in favor of having the Government pay in coin, if it can do so without too great a sacrifice; but I am unable to see any good reason for departing, in this case, from the usual practice of the Government in expressing the mode of paying the interest. All bonds and Treasury notes heretofore issued are payable generally without specifying that either the principal or the interest shall be paid in coin, and yet the legal effect is the same. I do not see why we should now, in the present embarrassed condition of the Goverment, give any preference to one creditor over another, or change the form of our bonds and Treasury notes by inserting the words 'payable in coin.' The capitalist who holds your bonds or seven and three-tenths Treasury notes is not entitled to any preference over the soldier or the man who furnishes supplies to your Army. We should pay both in specie, if possible; but I am unwilling to tie up the hands of the Government by compelling it to pay 'in coin,' the interest on all the bonds and notes heretofore issued, or that may hereafter be issued. The bonds and notes heretofore issued contain no such express provision; it is not 'so nominated in the bond;' and I am unwilling to have it inserted at this time, either as to those now outstanding or as to those that are hereafter to be issued. Besides, if you commence in this way, by stipulating expressly to pay in coin on the bonds to be issued, it becomes a contract which cannot, without a breach of faith, be changed by a repeal of the law. You unnecessarily commit the Government to a stipulation which may be very inconvenient, if not impossible, to fulfill, if the public debt runs up to $2,000,000.000, the interest upon which, at six per cent. per annum, would be $120,000,000 annually, requiring $60,000,000 of coin every six months to pay interest on your funded debt. I think we should pause before committing ourselves to any such proposition, for no man here is wise enough to tell how long this war will continue, or how many complications with foreign nations will grow out of it, or how great will be the war debt. *By all means let us pay the interest in gold to those who desire it, if it is practicable to do so;* but let us keep the power in the Government itself, and exercise it wisely for the best interest of the whole people.

The people in the country who hold seven and three-tenths Treasury notes are patriotic enough, while the war lasts, to receive their interest in any money that will pass currently at the banks and among the people. Money with them is only valuable for its uses. Legal tender Treasury notes can be used for all business purposes, without compelling the Government to sell its bonds at fifteen or twenty per cent. discount to procure coin when it is entirely unnecessary. * * * * * * *

At the extra session in July we passed two very important bills—one to borrow $250,000,000, for which bonds and notes were to be issued, and the other to call into the service five hundred thousand volunteers, and pay the soldiers thirteen dollars per month, and the officers a higher rate of fixed compensation, Both bills were war measures, both were necessary, and action has been had under both. Under the first bill the associated banks of New York, Boston and Philadelphia took the sum of $100,000,000 of seven and three-tenths three years Treasury notes at par, and $50,000,000 twenty years six per cent. bonds at a discount of ten and two thirds per cent. from their face—say net $44,661,230.97, being a loss of $5,338,769.03 on this transaction. This is a higher rate of interest than our Government, with all its immense power and resources, ought to pay; but the loan has been made, and I only refer to it now for the purpose of showing what has been done under these two acts of Congress.

Under the army bill, five hundred thousand volunteers have been called into the service, and are now in the field. Under both of these bills a debt has been created against the Government. The associated banks of New York, Boston and Philadelphia are creditors of the Government to the extent of $150,000,000. The five hundred thousand volunteer army are also creditors of the Government to a large amount. We owe them both, and both are creditors under laws passed by us at the extra session. Are not both classes of these creditors on the same footing? Are the bankers entitled to any preference over the volunteer army? Is the banker's money any more sacred than the services of the soldier in battle, on guard, or in the tented field? I cannot see that the banker or the holder of Treasury notes is entitled to any preference over the soldier, under these two laws of Congress, and yet, if you concur in these *hard-money* amendments of the Senate, you will compel the soldier to take legal tender Treasury notes in payment for his thirteen dollars per month which you agreed to pay him, while you pay the banker his high rate of interest, semi-annually, in gold and silver coin. Is this right? Will this be meting out just and equal laws to the loyal citizens of this Government? What will your army say to an arrangement of this kind? Sir, I can consent to no such discrimination, no such amendment, no such injustice. * * * * * * * * * * *

It is to be hoped that this will be a short war. It is very desirable that it should be pressed on with the utmost vigor, and be brought to a speedy and successful termination. God grant that this may be the issue. I have no expectation, however, that the authority of the United States Government will be respected and enforced in all the Southern States for many years. I think the rebels are desperate and determined, and will never submit to the Constitution and laws until compelled to do so by armed force. They may be beaten and compelled to fall back, but until Union governments are successfully established in all the Southern States the laws of the United States will not be respected, and can only be enforced by the army and navy in actual occupation of the rebellious States. This will require a large and expensive army for many years, the total expenses of which cannot now be estimated. It will require Federal troops in every rebellious State to collect your direct taxes and internal duties; and until you can peaceably collect taxes in all the rebellious States the rebellion is not ended. * * * * * * *

In every aspect in which you view this hard-money provision, its practical workings will be disastrous. It would be all very well if the amount was small and applied to carrying on the Government on a peace footing, when you know what amount will be required; but in carrying on the Government at this time, when the magnitude of the expenditures are so overwhelming, all *theories* applicable to peace must give way to the inexorable necessities that are forced upon us in the prosecution of this war. Look at your long line of offensive operations, extending from Kansas to this capital, and thence to Fortress Monroe, Hatteras, Beaufort, Key West, Pensacola, and Ship Island—a distance of more than four thousand miles. This very long line of military operations cannot be maintained except at an enormous expense for transportation, supplies, and material of war. One million six hundred thousand dollars does not cover the daily expenditures. Peace theories of finance must give way to what is practicable to be done in the present exigency. The Government is at this moment in the situation of a merchant who has overtraded, who owes more than he has the present means of paying. He may be compelled to stop payment in specie, when he has ample assets to cover all his liabilities. A mere suspension of specie payments does not imply bankruptcy or insolvency.

* * * * * * x * * x * * * x

Our country and Government at all hazards must be preserved. To accomplish this, our plan of finance must be simple and practical. As has been shown, we have various descriptions of property in abundance. We have not the money to meet the sudden demands that are thrown upon us. Is it not better to pledge our honor, our lands, houses, personal estate, incomes, and wealth of all kinds to create this money, on the faith of the nation, than to run the risk of utter ruin to all interests for the sake of holding on to theories which may be excellent in time of peace, but which are wholly impracticable in the prosecution of this war. x * +

It is very clear that in the prosecution of this war to maintain this Union, the ways and means of carrying it on can only be limited by the actual expenditures.

We must, while the war lasts, incur all the debt necessary to crush out the rebellion, and maintain the authority of the United States Government over all the thirty-four States. We cannot, therefore, now limit the amount of the debt to be incurred, nor can it be accurately estimated. Notes and bonds must be issued in some form for all the debt incurred, excepting what we may realize annually from taxes, excises, and duties on imports. In issuing these notes and bonds I think it will be much better for the Government, and for the people, to have one uniform system. It would be better for all concerned to have a fixed policy, not to be changed, so that all business men may conform to it at once. That policy should, in my judgement, be the issue of legal tender demand Treasury notes not bearing interest, to be paid out for what is necessary to support the army and navy, and fundable at any time in twenty years bonds, bearing interest at six per cent., payable semi-annually. This is as high a rate of interest as the Government ought to pay, especially as our people are to be heavily burdened by taxation to pay, ultimately, the interest and principle in gold and silver of all this debt. Let our policy be distinctly fixed and settled, and we shall hear no further importunities for higher rates of interest, or for any preference of one class of creditors over any other class equally meritorious.

I regret that my sense of duty compels me to differ so widely from the Senate. I have great respect for that body, and would gladly yield to their views, if I did not regard it so fatal to the public interest. So soon as our funded debt reaches $700,000,000, which will be in a very few months, I believe it will be impossible to procure the coin to pay the interest semi-annually without the most serious consequences to our credit. The amount of discount on our bonds to procure specie would be very large. In every view, the Senate amendment seems to me unnecessary, injurious, partial and unjust. I trust the House will non-concur in the amendments."

At the time the above remarks were made by Mr. Spaulding, *the duties on imports* were, as the bill then stood, payable in legal tender notes, but this was afterwards changed in the Committee of Conference, making those duties payable *in coin,* so that the interest might be paid in coin, without being obliged to force the bonds on the market to obtain coin for that purpose. This was probably the best compromise that could be made, as will more fully appear in finally adjusting the disagreeing votes between the Senate and House.

SPEECH OF MR. POMEROY.

Mr. POMEROY, of New York, spoke one hour in favor of paying the *interest in coin* on bonds and Treasury notes. He said:

"The action already had upon the bill has, so far as the sense of Congress is concerned, settled, if not the constitutionality and expediency of issuing, to a limited amount, Treasury notes, made a legal tender in payment of debts, at least the existence of a necessity, under which such constitutional power will be assumed and its exercise declared expedient. I do not propose, therefore, to enter at all upon the discussion of those questions, nor would it be pertinent to the only amendment I propose to discuss, to wit: that providing for payment of interest on the national debt in coin. They were fully discussed when the bill was first before the committee, to the neglect, as I then thought and now think, of the point presented by the pending amendment, upon which alone I desire to submit a few remarks.

The question is not now whether $150,000,000 of Treasury notes shall be issued and made a legal tender in payment of public and private indebtedness. That proposition has been decided in the affirmative; but if my faith in the necessity and expediency of such issue was stronger even than that of the able and distinguished Representative, [Mr. Spaulding,] who has originated this measure, and carried it triumphantly over the Administration and through Congress, still, deeming this amendment, as proposed by the Senate and now under consideration, vital to the success of the scheme, and the only regulation by which financial explosion under it can be prevented, I could not, as an original proposition, and cannot now, without such amendment, support this bill. My opinion may be unfounded and erroneous. I hope it is, if this amendment is to fail. I have no pride of opinion upon this matter, but I have convictions, clear, decided and conscientious, which I cannot trample upon without violating my own sense of self-respect and of public duty. The opposition which this amendment meets from the framers of the bill sufficiently demonstrates to us and to the country that it is not merely formal in its character, but is of primary importance and entitled to the highest consideration. I shall be very brief, and will endeavor to be plain in my views respecting it.

It is conceded by the friends of the House bill, that the policy of issuing Treasury notes under it with the characteristics of money is to be temporary, and that it is a divergence from the correct principles of political economy, to be justified only by necessity, and yet the primary and principal fault I find with it is, that instead of being a temporary measure, it really, by its failure to make adequate provision to raise money by loan, inaugurates and necessitates the perpetuation of a reliance upon a forced paper currency alone to meet the demands of the war, the amount of the issue of which, if sufficient for that purpose, must depreciate it to a mere nominal value, and result in ultimate repudiation. *It may be expedient as a remedy for an existing political disorder, but it is death if relied upon for permanent existence.*

The credit of the Government has been recently brought to the test of practical experiment in a much more favorable time than the present, when the banks were plethoric with gold beyond all former experience and promptly meeting all engagements in coin, when suspension had not been thought of, and the patriotism of the people was fully aroused in the enlistment of those armies that are to-day more than meeting our proudest anticipations; and yet, under those most favorable auspices, the rate of interest, as established, was seven and three-tenths per cent. for three year coupon bonds, and seven per cent. for those running twenty years, each payable semi-annually in coin, and with the added advantage to the banks, who were the purchasers, of holding the proceeds on deposit without interest until drawn out in the usual course of expenditure; and $50,000,000 of the long bonds, authorized at the extra session, have not been, and could not be, sold even at the rate above named. *   *   *

The science of Government is one purely experimental. A code of laws designed for men as they ought to be, would be a terrible code applied to men as they are. We experience no difficuly in recognizing in legislation the natural laws of matter, and we should have no more in recognizing the natural laws of mind, association, trade, commerce and business.

If we are to borrow money, we must recognize these laws; and I may well call them higher laws, for while legislation cannot change them, they are continually changing legislation. One of these is that the precious metals are the representative of value. *The gold dollar of our currency is the unit of value. Conversion into this representative is the only criterion of value.* Those who invest money or loan will make it a condition precedent that the interest shall be in money, *and not in promises to pay money.* Legislation has not changed, and cannot change, paper currency into coin or its equivalent, except through convertibility. Without this requisite it is a mere naked promise. We cannot make Treasury notes money until we can change by act of Congress a promise into a performance, and Almighty power alone can do that. We propose to compel the Government and citizens to receive this paper as money in payment for debt; but we do not propose to attempt to compel anybody to take it by way of loan, nor to compel anybody to loan it, not even to Government. Then people must be induced to loan it; and how can you expect them to do it at rates less favorable than you have already established in more prosperous times, to wit: a rate of seven and three-tenths per cent., payable in coin.

Now, this paper is or is not equal to gold. My colleague may take whichever horn of the dilemma he pleases. If it is not, it is folly to suppose that people are voluntarily going to place themselves in a position where, for a term of years, they compel themselves to receive it as interest, and assume all the risk of depreciation. If it is equal, then there can be no unjust discrimination in paying interest in gold. I prefer to look at the question just as it is, and admit the fact that it is not and cannot be made equal, because it lacks the essential quality of *convertibility.* To the extent to which it is not equal, we work a hardship in forcing it into circulation; but we have already decided that a necessity exists which compels us to accept this hardship rather than to inflict upon the people or submit the Government to a greater. And we believe farther, that the evils thus produced will, in the aggregate, if not in each individual case, be more than compensated by the relief they will afford from financial stringency, and as a medium of exchanges, especially with the Government itself.

While, however, we exercise the power to compel the people to receive it as gold in payment of debts, we, unfortunately, have not the power to compel them to loan it back to us on time, and receive more of the same kind as interest. There is just the practical point where our new political physiology fails. As 'Artemus Ward' would say, 'its *forte* is not in borrowing, but in paying,' and we have got to make it work both ways. It is all nonsense to say that while we pay out Treasury notes from necessity in some cases, we will forbear to borrow money, without which our credit must go down entirely, because it will necessitate the payment of interest in coin, and thus conflict with our theory; that because we pay ourselves and our soldiers and everybody else with whom we are under contract, in paper, we will stop paying even them rather than to continue the ability to do so by borrowing money and stipulating in advance to pay the interest in a different commodity. The inconsistency consists in not considering that we must first get the principal before we put on airs about the manner in which we will pay the interest, in which transaction the lender as well as the borrower is usually consulted. The Committee of Ways and Means are talking about paying, whereas the problem is how to borrow.

Nor does the agreement to pay interest in coin tend in the least to depreciate the value of the notes. The very necessity for this agreement arises from the fact of the pre-existing differences in value between coin and paper. It does not create the inequality. It recognizes an existing fact, and applying legislation practically to that fact, enhances the value of the paper, by allowing its conversion into a permanent loan, the principal and interest of which are to be paid in money; and instead of depreciating the paper, checks depreciation by reason of this very convertibility, and presents the only possible mode, that I can conceive of, by which serious depreciation can be prevented and the funding process kept in operation. In fact, this very difference between the intrinsic values of notes and coin, thus recognized and embodied in our legislation, tends to produce the very object desired—the funding of the public debt. If capital will seek Treasury notes at par, for the purpose of investment in bonds, with the interest payable in notes, how much more readily will it seek these same notes, at a slight depreciation, for the purpose of such investment, with the interest to be paid in gold; and the very demand for this purpose, while it prevents serious depreciation, is induced by the very depreciation inherent in the character of the paper which it continually checks. It produces a self-adjusting funding access, based upon things as they exist in the commercial world, by which the disparity between the value of the two currencies ceases to be an element of discord, and becomes, during the temporary period in which the funding process is going on, an element of good. In this manner, and through the happy instrumentality which may in this way be exerted by these notes, imperceptibly, and through the ordinary channels of financial operations, the whole process of funding the public debt will be accomplished. * * * * * * * * * * *

One thing further is evident. If the debt can be funded under the provisions of the House bill, it certainly can under the Senate amendments. The Treasury has prided itself on its ability to obtain money at the rate proposed by the latter in more prosperous times. If it was satisfactory then, it should be still more satisfactory now. In this work we cannot afford to fail. The part of wisdom is, then, to accept the greater safety. When paper shall have taken the place of coin, and the latter, true to its instincts, shall have taken wings and flown away—it cannot be whistled back. It is idle to argue that two representatives of value of equal nominal amount, but intrinsically unequal, will stay together and consent to become convertible. The more valuable always abandons the field.

One fact more must not be overlooked in considering this matter—that the security remains the same in all cases, namely: the faith of the Government. No inducement is offered by the House to fund these notes in the nature of the new security. *The credit of the Government is alike bound for the payment of both classes of indebtedness ultimately in gold. Each derives its entire value from that.* The only advantage that can be then offered in funding is the mere convenience in the form of the security, and the payment of interest in a commodity similar to that which the principal represents. * * * * * * * * * *

Now, I do not know by what class of soldiers my colleague [Mr. Spaulding,] may be represented in the field, but I do know the character of the two thousand soldiers from my own county, and of the four thousand soldiers in the field from my congressional district, and I know that their present condition as soldiers is purely ephemeral. Their normal condition is that of citizens, and as such I represent them here; and they will appreciate at what it is worth the appeal of my colleague in their behalf as a class, as soldiers, in distinction from their character as American citizens. * * * * * * * * *

I believe I have never failed to sustain, whether it be to my credit or otherwise, any recommendation backed by a majority of the Committee of Ways and Means of this House. As amended by the Senate in this respect, I will cheerfully support this bill. In its original form I could not, though it has been unpleasant to diverge from so large a proportion of my political associates. It were easier to have followed in the wake of inclination, and covered myself from criticism with the mantle of necessity. I have preferred to walk the plank of duty, trusting to time and practical results for the vindication of its policy."

SPEECH OF MR. CALVERT.

Mr. CALVERT, of Maryland, advocated the payment of interest in coin. He said:

"Let me tell the gentleman from New York, [Mr. Spaulding,] that it is useless to talk about the injustice of paying brokers in one currency and other people another. When you want to borrow money you must go to the brokers to borrow it. Farmers and others may be induced by the brokers to invest their money in your bonds; but they will not do it without the advice of the brokers or agents with whom they are in the habit of counseling, and therefore it is the broker at last who holds in his hands your credit, and it is useless for gentlemen of this House to talk about a proposition to put down the brokers who are constantly dealing in these notes. He contended that the amendment of the Senate would benefit the credit of the Government more than anything else that could be done. People would not loan money to be payable in paper, because, although you make paper a legal tender by legislation, it will not be so in fact—the question has yet to be tried before the State Court, as well as before the United States Court. The only way in which you can possibly have any notes funded is by paying the interest in coin. Then if the notes fall below par they will be immediately funded."

SPEECH OF MR. MORRILL.

Mr. MORRILL, of Vermont—"Our whole difficulty in this matter, it appears to me, arises from our departure from sound principles in the first place. It appears that the House and the Senate have both decided that they will issue paper and make it a legal tender. I deeply deplore the fact as a blot on our national history that cannot be effaced; but as I do not now see it probable that any other result will be reached, my only purpose and desire is to perfect and pass the best possible bill to be obtained.

I believe the Senate amendments are, on the whole, a great improvement upon the bill as it passed the House. I could wish that we might, even at this hour, slaughter both the original bill and the Senate's amendments, and then mature such financial measures as would preserve a sound specie-paying basis; but having no hope of that now, I trust we may adopt the Senate amendments, which will, in some degree at least, mitigate the evils to be apprehended from the bill as it left this House.

Now, the gentleman from New York (Mr. Spaulding) talks as though it would be an abandonment of the honor and good faith of the Government to pay the soldiers in any different species of money from that which we pay our public creditors. I recollect to have read that Frederick the Great, upon a certain occasion, directed his minister, when he was about to seize upon some province of one of his neighbors, to draw up a proclamation justifying the measure to the world; and his minister drew it up, commencing, 'In the name of God.' Said Frederick, 'strike out all about God, and say that I did it.' Now, I recommend to the gentleman from New York, when he is talking about this subject of compelling the public and private creditors to take paper money for all debts *heretofore* or hereafter contracted, to omit all mention of 'honor and good faith.'

But what is the fact in reference to this matter of paying off the soldiers in any different money? Why, the fact is that we are going to pay them in paper, according to this bill. Now, if these soldiers were debtors, and owed a grocer at home or here, and could make a tender of this paper, it might then indeed be of some service; but how are you to compel the grocer, or any man who has anything to sell upon which these soldiers or their families subsist, to take this paper at anything more than its market value? Of course, if coin is worth more than paper, they have to pay to that extent more than they would pay if they had coin; and I am in favor of keeping our promises equal to coin. In my judgment, if we pay the interest on the public debt in specie, it will have a tendency to keep up the credit of the country, and there will be less depreciation upon these notes than there otherwise would be.

But, Mr. Chairman, the great object is to fund some portion of the public debt. Now, it is perfectly apparent, not only from the statement of the gentleman from New York (Mr. Spaulding), but from the knowledge all have of the subject, that our wants are large, and that we will be compelled to issue our bonds or notes, or paper of some kind, to a large amount hereafter. Now it is proposed to issue twice, thrice or quadruple the amount of this legal tender paper before this session of Congress closes? Within sixty days we must have at least twice the amount of notes which is proposed now; and unless they can be funded into debts due at some future time, from *necessity*, as we shall again be told, we shall have to repeat the dose we are now offering to the public. Anybody may see that while it might be possible for this country to endure $150,000,000 of additional currency, even if it did unhinge all commercial transactions, that it would be utterly impossible that we could absorb twice or thrice that amount without a vast expansion of the whole monetary system of the country—turning even sober and industrious citizens into the wildest of speculators. * * * * * * * * * * * *

But, Mr. Chairman, I believe that if we could stand up here in the vigor of a nation not yet taxed a single dollar for the cost of this war, and mature a proper policy by which we can negotiate a loan standing on the credit of the country, standing on the proposed taxation of the country, standing on our hitherto untarnished honor, that there could be no need whatever of a resort to such a desperate scheme as the one now under consideration. I hope, therefore, that we shall adopt the amendment of the Senate. I wish that we might go much further, but that at least is better than a measure whose symmetry is only measured by its exclusively paper character."

SPEECH OF MR. DUNN.

Mr. DUNN, of Indiana, spoke as follows:

"Mr. Chairman—when this bill was under consideration in the House, (in Committee of the Whole,) a direct vote was taken upon the proposition to pay the interest on the bonds in coin, and the Committee sustained that proposition by a very decided vote. I do not quite understand by what legerdemain the bill went to the Senate in a different form. I voted then that the interest should be paid in coin, and I shall vote so now, notwithstanding the arguments employed here to induce us to vote differently.

The principal argument urged against the Senate amendment is that it provides for paying our creditors in different ways, and an appeal is made to the patriotism of the House to know if we are willing to pay different kinds of money for our interest from that with which we pay our soldiers. Now, I shall vote for this proposition with the direct view and object of making the paper we offer to the soldier as good as possible. I believe that it is impossible to pay them in coin, or I would vote for that. It is necessary to make our notes as good as possible, and if there is any equivalent for coin, let us approach that point as nearly as possible. If we cannot remove the cloud of debt, let us, at least, give it a golden lining. One mode of sustaining the credit of the notes is to have them converted into bonds; and in order to make those bonds acceptable to those who have money to lend, we must make the interest payable in coin. We must try to induce capitalists to lend us money; for we have no mode of compelling them to do so. The gentleman from Vermont, [Mr. Morrill,] who has just taken his seat, said that the West expected some advantages from making Treasury notes a legal tender. The members from the West, generally, who voted for making the notes a legal tender, did so because we believed it to be a governmental necessity. We wanted a bridge to carry us over the morass. We make it of trestle-work, a temporary work, to serve only until the ground hardens. *We do not believe this war is to be of long continuance. We do not believe the necessity of the legal tender clause will long exist.* I think that those who were despondent ten days ago have now great reason to rejoice. The rapid succession of Union victories has filled every loyal heart with joy, and I do not doubt but that we shall soon be relieved from our pecuniary difficulties."

MR. ENGLISH'S SPEECH.

Mr. ENGLISH, of Connecticut, spoke in favor of paying the interest in coin.

He concurred with Mr. Pendleton on the constitutional question, and considered it settled by his argument that it was not constitutional to make these notes a legal tender. He also argued at considerable length that the measure was not *necessary* at this time. He was in favor of ample taxation, and that the States should be allowed to collect the taxes and pay over the money to the United States. He wanted no Government tax collectors.

On the pending amendments he said:

"In order to make these bonds valuable to those who have money to invest, we must adopt the amendment of the Senate providing that the interest shall be paid in gold and silver. When it is ascertained that the interest is to be paid in gold and silver, then the bonds will be sought for investment. If you issue Treasury notes, and if these Treasury notes go into the market and depreciate—as I think they will not—what will be the effect? The effect will be that, just in proportion as the Treasury notes depreciate, in the same proportion will the interest payable on bonds be diminished. These Treasury notes answer very well as a means of circulation, provided the amount of the issue shall not exceed that provided for in this bill. My opinion is that these Treasury notes may answer a very good purpose; but the moment their volume is swollen beyond that, so soon will they depreciate.

I trust that the amendment of the Senate will be concurred in by this House. In my judgment, it is the very best thing that we can do under the circumstances. I voted for the issuing of these Treasury notes, but against the 'legal tender' clause. Otherwise, I was in favor of the measure; but the judgment of the House was against me on that point. I think that now the best thing the House can do is to concur in the Senate amendment; and I trust that it will be concurred in."

SPEECH OF MR. PIKE.

Mr. PIKE, of Maine, spoke as follows:

"Mr. Chairman—with all due deference to gentlemen who differ with me on this subject, it does seem to me that this matter of paying interest in coin is a controversy about goat's wool. The interest will be paid in coin in any event. The recent victories of our armies have changed the whole matter. (Just heard of the capture of Fort Donelson and the movement on Nashville.) We have now to return to a normal condition of currency. * * * * * * * * * * *

"I not only assent most cheerfully to the proposition to pay the interest in coin, but I also assent to the cognate proposition to sell these bonds at the highest price we can get for them. We are returning now to a solid basis. I hail the cause of the return as well as the return itself. Let us sell our bonds to pay the creditors whom we are under contract to pay. We never can have a better time for doing so than now, when an effervescence of delight is felt all over the country, because of the victories achieved by our armies. It is felt everywhere now that we not only have a Government, but a country on which to base this issue. Therefore, I say, let us now sell these bonds. Let us realize as much money from them as we can. Let us provide to pay the interest in coin, and let us pay the public creditors."

SPEECH OF MR. DIVEN.

Mr. DIVEN, of New York, spoke as follows:

"It strikes me, Mr. Chairman, that the fallacy of all the arguments in favor of this amendment consists in the fact that the amendment fails to meet the evil. It is not proposed to go back and remedy the great national wrong, national dishonor, and inconsistency of the step that has been taken by declaring that these notes shall be a legal tender. If this House is determined to adhere to that, if—as the gentleman from Vermont has said—the child is dead, if the national credit is gone, if we are ready to assume the humiliating attitude that national credit and honor are dead, then the argument of the gentleman from New York (Mr. Spaulding) is sound.

The same plea of necessity which is resorted to in support of the legal tender clause, will require us *to resort to every effort to do away with all distinction between this paper money and coin. The requiring the payment of interest in coin will have a tendency to make such distinction.* It will have that effect, and all that we can do will not help it. Let me make one appeal to members. It is not yet too late to retrieve the error. We have not yet declared that we will compel men to take those promises to pay, and to treat them as substance. The way to recede from that dangerous proposition is before us.

The times are auspicious. One good reason urged in favor of that policy was that the people were discouraged from the want of success in our army. We have now the encouragement of success. Only let the moneyed men of the country believe that the Government is to succeed in putting down this rebellion, and we will not have to plead for credit. It is not gold and silver that we want. It is not things that are to be taken for gold and silver that we want. It is credit; it is confidence on the part of men who have money to lend, and who can lend it to the Government with the assurance that it will be returned to them. That is all that is wanted. And now, in view of the brilliant prospect before us of a speedy termination of the rebellion, and in view of the immense resources of the Government, in Heaven's name, let us leave no national dishonor, to forever remain a stain upon the country. We will do that, if we do this great wrong. I appeal to the House, in the name of honor and justice, to retrace the step it has taken, and to save the Union from the loss that will afflict it by the passage of this law."

Mr. WINDOM, of Minnesota, objected to the *proceeds of the public bonds* being pledged to pay interest or principal on the bonds, as proposed by the Senate, for the reason that it would tend to defeat the Homestead Law. This provision was afterwards struck out in the Conference Committee.

On the 6th amendment of the Senate, providing that these Treasury notes should be received for all claims and demands against the United States of every kind whatsoever, '*except for interest on bonds and notes, which shall be paid in coin*,' Mr. Pendleton moved an amendment to the effect 'that the officers, soldiers, seamen and mariners engaged in the military service of the United States,' should also be paid in coin. Being opposed to the whole legal tender principle, he offered it to meet the objection of the gentleman from New York, [Mr. Spaulding,] in reference to our unjust discrimination against soldiers and others. He said:

"I am not in favor of that discrimination, but am in favor of paying the officers and soldiers in the military and naval service of the Government in the legal coin of the country."

The amendment was not agreed to.

The amendments of the Senate having been acted upon in Committee of the Whole, Mr. Stevens moved that the Committee rise and report the bill and amendments to the House, which was agreed to. The bill and amendments were accordingly reported to the House.

On the 20th, the House resumed the consideration of the Senate amendments.

Mr. STEVENS was entitled to one hour in closing the debate. He gave a part of this time to Mr. Hooper, of Massachusetts.

MR. HOOPER'S SPEECH.

Mr. HOOPER, of Massachusetts, spoke as follows:

"Mr. SPEAKER—with the present large expenditures of the Government, and while the banks throughout the country are acting under a suspension of specie payments, it is an absurdity to insist on the strict enforcement of the existing laws, which require all Government receipts and payments to be made in coin. It is absurd, in my opinion, because it is impossible; and it is also absurd because it is useless. What private corporations or individuals in this country receive and pay coin in the conduct of their business? There are none. Nearly all the ordinary receipts and payments throughout the country are made in bank notes, bank checks, or credit in some other form; and coin is only required occasionally for a very small per cent. of those receipts and payments, which in amount, extend, in the course of a single year, to thousands of millions of dollars.

The object of this Treasury note bill is to furnish a substantial and uniform currency that will aid the Government, and enable it to receive its dues and make its payments, like all others, with credits. This bill declares that, for all dues to the Government and for all payments by the Government, these notes shall be received 'the same as coin.' One way to make them 'the same as coin' would be to make them at all times convertible into coin. Another is to use them, so far as possible, for all the purposes for which coin is used; and in this latter mode their value will be the same as coin, unless the amount that is issued exceeds the amount needed for such uses.

At the end of twelve months from this time the receipts of the Government and the payments by the Government, amounting to many hundred millions of dollars, will be found to be nearly equal; that is, the Government during that time will have received about the same amount that it will have paid; and if these 'Government notes' are, in part, paid out by the Government, as it is proposed they shall be, in anticipation of the receipts for taxes and loans, they must all come back again in the course of the year, when those taxes and loans are paid for. The people may find a portion of these notes more convenient for other uses, and may, therefore, prefer to make their payments to the Government partly in coin. Unless, therefore, the Government is to be broken down, by the refusal to furnish the means in the form of taxes and loans to carry it on, these notes cannot depreciate to any extent, because they will be needed, and probably a large amount of coin in addition, to pay into the Treasury for the loans and taxes; they will be received by the Government the same as coin, and therefore must be for this purpose, and all others, the equivalent of coin, unless they are imprudently issued in excess of the requirements for such purposes.

I am opposed to this amendment of the Senate which requires the interest on Government notes and bonds to be absolutely paid in coin, *because its effect will be to depreciate these notes as compared with coin, by declaring them in advance to be so depreciated.* It creates a necessity for the Government to obtain a large amount of coin by purchase, if it is not received in payment of taxes and loans, which hold out an inducement to speculate on the necessity of the Government, by collecting and hoarding the coin against the time that will be required by the Government to pay its interest; and because it is an unnecessary inconvenience to require the whole amount of the interest to be paid in coin, when only the small amount is necessary that is to be remitted to foreign holders of bonds, which could easily be obtained at small cost, if the effect of the issue of the Government notes should be what the friends of this bill expect. * * *

If the opponents of this bill have proved anything, they have proved too much in reference to the question now before the House, which is to make a distinction in favor of the holders of Government securities, and pay what may be due to them in coined money, while all other creditors of the Government shall be paid in what they have denounced to the country from the high places they occupy here, as the meanest paper trash.''

CLOSING DEBATE—MR. STEVENS' SPEECH.

Mr. STEVENS, of Pennsylvania, spoke as follows:

"Mr. SPEAKER—I have a very few words to say. I approach the subject with more depression of spirits than I ever before approached any question. No personal motive or feeling influences me. I hope not, at least. I have a melancholy foreboding that we are about to consummate a cunningly devised scheme, which will carry great injury and great loss to all classes of the people throughout this Union, except one. With my colleague, I believe that no act of legislation of this Government was ever hailed with as much delight throughout the whole length and breadth of this Union, by every class of people, without any exception, as the bill which we passed and sent to the Senate. Congratulations from all classes —merchants, traders, manufacturers, mechanics and laborers—poured in upon us from all quarters. The Boards of Trade from Boston, New York, Philadelphia, Cincinnati, Louisville, St. Louis, Chicago and Milwaukee, approved its provisions, and urged its passage as it was.

I have a dispatch from the Chamber of Commerce of Cincinnati, sent to the Secretary of the Treasury, and by him to me, urging the speedy passage of the bill as it passed the House. It is true *there was a doleful sound came up from the caverns of bullion brokers, and from the saloons of the associated banks.* Their cashiers and agents were soon on the ground, and persuaded the Senate, with but little deliberation, to mangle and destroy what it had cost the House months to digest, consider and pass. They fell upon the bill in hot haste, and so disfigured and deformed it, that its very father would not know it. [Laughter.] Instead of being a beneficent and invigorating measure; it is now positively mischievous. It has all the bad qualities which its enemies charged on the original bill, and none of its benefits. *It now creates money, and by its very terms declares it a depreciated currency. It makes two classes of money—one for the banks and brokers, and another for the people.* It discriminates between the rights of different classes of creditors, allowing the rich capitalist to demand gold, and compelling the ordinary lender of money on individual security to receive notes which the Government had purposely discredited.

Let us examine the principal amendments separately, and see their effect. The first important one (being the fifth,) makes the notes issued under the laws of July 17, a legal tender, equally with those authorized by this bill. There can be but little wisdom in putting these two classes on an equality. The notes of July bear seven and three-tenths per cent. interest, and are payable in three years. This gives them a sufficient advantage over notes bearing no interest and payable virtually in twenty years bonds, with six per cent. interest. Why give them this additional advantage? Simply because the $100,000,000 issued are all held by the associated banks, and this is their amended bill. They would displace $100,000,000 of this money in the circulation, and render it impossible to use any considerable amount of these United States notes as a currency. These notes have served their purpose. Why allow them to block up the market against further relief to the Government?

The banks took $50,000,000 of six per cent. bonds, and shaved the Government $5,500,000 on them, and now ask to shave the Government fifteen or twenty per cent. half yearly, to pay themselves the interest on these very bonds. They paid for the $50,000,000 in demand notes, not specie, and now demand the specie for them. Yet gentlemen talk about our making other loans in these times. They are crazy or sleeping, one or the other, I do not know which.

When this question was discussed before, the distinguished gentleman from Kentucky (Mr. Crittenden) asked me whether it was the intention or expectation of the House to go on and issue more than one hundred and fifty millions of dollars of legal tender notes—a pertinent question, which I saw the whole force of at the time. I told him that it was my expectation that no more would be issued by the Government; that they would be received and funded in the twenty year bonds."

Mr. LOVEJOY—"I ask the gentleman from Pennsylvania whether $150,000,000 of gold could not be put into circulation as well as $150,000,000 of Treasury notes?"

Mr. STEVENS—"If this $150,000,000 would come out of the banker's and miser's hoards; but they have suspended specie payment, and would not give out a dollar. They say pay us a discount, and then when these notes are made a legal tender we will be again in the clutches of these harpies. I do not want to use hard names. I suppose these men act from instinct. If I were now to answer the question of the gentleman from Kentucky, I would not give that answer. I do not expect one dollar of the $150,000,000 of legal tender notes ever to be invested in the twenty years bonds. I infer from the amendment that before we adjourn $150,000,000 will be asked for, which will never be funded in those bonds, and so on, as they are needed, *as no bonds will be funded until our circulation will become frightfully inflated.* * * * * * * * * * * *

But now comes the main clause. All classes of people *shall* take these legal tender notes at par for every article of trade or contract, unless they have money enough to buy United States bonds, and then they shall be paid in gold. Who is that favored class? The banks and brokers, and nobody else. They have already $250,000,000 of State debt, and their commissioners would soon take all the rest that might be issued.

But how is this gold to be raised? The duties and public lands are to be paid for in United States notes, and they or bonds are to be put up at auction to get coin for these very brokers, who would furnish the coin to pay themselves, by getting twenty per cent. discount on the notes thus bought. * * * *

I have proposed an amendment to the Senate amendment upon the principle of legitimate parliamentary rules, that you may make as palatable as you can an amendment which you do not like, before the vote is taken upon it. My amendment is offered for the purpose of curing a little the evils and hardships of the original amendment of the Senate. And though it may be adopted, I shall vote against the whole as amended. My amendment is to except from the operation of the legal tender clause *the officers and soldiers of the army and navy, and those who supply them with provisions,* and thus put them upon the same footing with the Government creditors who hold their bonds. I hope they will not be thought less meritorious than the money-changers. I trust it will be adopted as an amendment to the Senate amendment, so that if this pernicious system is to be adopted, if the beauty of the original bill is to be entirely impaired, those who are fighting our battles, and the widows and children of those who are lying in their graves in every part of the country, killed in defense of the Government, may be placed upon no worse footing than those who hold the bonds of the Government and the coin of the country."

At the conclusion of Mr. Stevens' speech the House proceeded to vote on the Senate amendments, some of which were concurred in, and others were disagreed to.

The first important division of the House was on the sixth amendment of the Senate, as follows:

"Immediately after the clause last quoted, strike out the words 'and for all salaries, debts and demands owing by the United States to individuals, corporations and associations within the United States,' and insert, 'and of claims and demands against the United States, of any kind whatsoever, *except for interest upon bonds and notes, which shall be paid in coin.*'"

To this amendment Mr. Stevens moved an amendment to insert after the word "notes," the following:

"*And payments to be made to officers, soldiers and sailors in the army and navy of the United States, and for all supplies purchased for the said Government.*"

Mr. WHITE, of Indiana—"I appeal to the gentleman from Pennsylvania to withdraw that amendment. It was only intended to illustrate an absurdity, and I hope he will withdraw it."

Mr. STEVENS—"No sir; I cannot withdraw it."

Mr. BINGHAM—"I demand the yeas and nays on the amendment to the amendment."

The yeas and nays were ordered.

Mr. BAKER—"I should like to ask the Chairman of the Committee of Ways and Means a question."

THE SPEAKER—"No debate is in order at this time."

The question was taken, and it was decided in the negative—yeas 67, nays 72; as follows:

Yeas—Messrs. Aldrich, Ancona, Babbitt, Joseph Bailey, Baker, Biddle, Bingham, Francis P. Blair, Jacob B. Blair, Samuel S. Blair, George H. Browne, Buffinton, Campbell, Chamberlin, Clark, Cobb, Davis, Diven, Edwards, Ely, Fenton, Fessenden, Fisher, Franchot, Frank, Gooch, Granger, Hale, Hanchett, Harrison, Holman, Hooper, Johnson, Julian, William Kellogg, Killinger, Lehman, McPherson, Marston, Maynard, Mitchell, Anson P. Morrill, Noell, Odell, Olin, Perry, John H. Rice, James S. Rollins, Shanks. Sherman, Shiel, Sloan, Spaulding, William G. Steele, Stevens, Van Horn, Van Valkenburg, Verree, Voorhees, Wall, Wallace, Ward, Albert S. White, Wilson, Windom, Woodruff and Worcester—67.

Nays—Messrs. Alley, Arnold, Ashley, Baxter, Blake, William G. Brown, Burnham, Calvert, Clements, Frederick A. Conkling, Roscoe Conkling, Conway, Cox, Cravens, Crittenden, Dawes, Duell, Dunlap, Dunn, Eliot, English, Goodwin, Grider, Gurley, Haight, Hall, Harding, Hickman, Horton, Kelley, Knapp, Law, Leary, Loomis, Lovejoy, McKnight, Mallory, May, Menzies, Moorhead, Justin S. Morrill, Nixon, Noble, Norton, Nugen, Patton, Timothy G. Phelps, Pike, Pomeroy, Alexander H. Rice, Riddle, Robinson, Sargent, Sedgwick, Sheffield, Smith, John B.

Steele, Stratton, Benjamin F. Thomas, Francis Thomas, Train, Trimble, Trowbridge, Vallandigham, Charles W. Walton, E. P. Walton, Washburne, Webster, Wheeler, Wickliffe and Wright—72.

So the amendment of Mr. Stevens to pay the army and navy in specie, the same as the bondholders interest in coin, was not agreed to.

The question being upon agreeing to the sixth amendment of the Senate, to pay interest in coin on bonds and notes, in which the Committee of the Whole on the state of the Union recommended concurrence.

Mr. Roscoe Conkling demanded the yeas and nays.

The yeas and nays were ordered.

The question was taken; and it was decided in the affirmative—yeas 88, nays 56; as follows:

Yeas—Messrs. Ancona, Arnold, Ashley, Baxter, Beaman, Biddle, Jacob B. Blair, George H. Browne, William G. Brown, Burnham, Calvert, Clements, Cobb, Frederick A. Conkling, Roscoe Conkling, Corning, Covode, Cox, Cravens, Crittenden, Diven, Dunlap, Dunn, Eliot, English, Goodwin, Grider, Gurley, Haight, Hall, Harding, Holman, Horton, Johnson, Kelley, Knapp, Law, Leary, Lehman, Loomis, Lovejoy, McKnight, Mallory, May, Menzies, Justin S. Morrill, Nixon, Noble, Norton, Nugen, Odell, Patton, Pendleton, Perry, Timothy G. Phelps, Pike, Pomeroy, Price, Alexander H. Rice, Riddle, Robinson, Edward H. Rollins, James S. Rollins, Sargent, Sedgwick, Sheffield, Sherman, Shiel, Smith, John B. Steele, William G. Steele, Stratton, Benjamin F. Thomas, Francis Thomas, Train, Trimble, Vallandigham, Vibbard, Voorhees, Charles W. Walton, E. P. Walton, Ward, Washburn, Webster, Wheeler, Wickliffe, Woodruff and Wright—88.

Nays—Messrs. Aldrich, Alley, Babbitt, Joseph Bailey, Baker, Bingham, Francis P. Blair, Samuel S. Blair, Blake, Buffinton, Campbell, Chamberlin, Clark, Davis, Dawes, Duell, Edwards, Ely, Fenton, Fessenden, Fisher, Franchot, Frank, Granger, Hale, Hanchett, Harrison, Hickman, Hooper, Julian, William Kellogg, Killinger, Lansing, McPherson, Marston, Maynard, Moorhead, Anson P. Morrill, Noell, Olin, John H. Rice, Shanks, Sloan, Spaulding, Stevens, Trowbridge, Van Horn, Van Valkenburgh, Verree, Wall, Wallace, Whaley, Albert S. White, Wilson, Windom and Worcester—56.

So the amendment of the Senate *to pay the interest on bonds and notes in coin was adopted.*

Fifteenth amendment.

In line thirteen, second section, after the word 'time,' insert, 'at the market value thereof;' so that the clause will read:

"And the Secretary of the Treasury may dispose of such bonds at any time, at the *market value thereof.*"

The Committee of the Whole on the state of the Union recommended non-concurrence.

Mr. Horton asked for a division.

Mr. Washburne demanded tellers.

Tellers were appointed.

Mr. Chamberlin called for the yeas and nays.

The yeas and nays were ordered.

The question was taken; and it was decided in the affirmative— yeas 72, nays 66; as follows:

Yeas—Messrs. Ancona, Goldsmith F. Bailey, Baxter, Beaman, Biddle, George H. Browne, William G. Brown, Calvert, Clark, Cobb, Frederick A. Conkling, Roscoe Conkling, Conway, Covode, Cravens, Crittenden, Cutler, Dunlap, Dunn, Eliot, English, Goodwin, Grider, Hall, Harding, Holman, Horton, Johnson, Kelley, Knapp, Law, Leary, Lovejoy, McKnight, Menzies, Justin S. Morrill, Nixon, Noble, Norton, Nugen, Odell, Patton, Pendleton, Perry, Pike, Pomeroy, Porter, Alexander H. Rice, Riddle, Robinson, Edward H. Rollins, James S. Rollins, Sargent, Sedgwick, Sheffield, Shiel, Smith, William G. Steele, Stratton, Benjamin F. Thomas, Francis Thomas, Train, Trimble, Verree, Vibbard, Voorhees, Charles W. Walton, E. P. Walton, Washburne, Wheeler, Woodruff and Wright—72.

Nays—Messrs. Aldrich, Alley, Ashley, Babbitt, Joseph Bailey, Baker, Bingham, Francis P. Blair, Jacob B. Blair, Samuel S. Blair, Blake, Buffinton, Campbell, Chamberlin, Clements, Cox, Davis, Dawes, Diven, Edgarton, Edwards, Ely, Fenton, Fessenden, Fisher, Franchot, Frank, Granger, Haight, Hale, Hanchett, Harrison, Hickman, Hooper, Hutchins, Julian, Killinger, Lansing, Lehman, Loomis, McPherson, Marston, Maynard, Moorhead, Anson P. Morrill, Noell, Olin, Potter, John H. Rice, Shanks, Sherman, Sloan, Spaulding, John B. Steele, Stevens, Trowbridge, Vallandigham, Van Horn, Van Valkenburgh, Wall, Wallace, Albert S. White, Wickliffe, Wilson, Windom and Worcester—66.

So the amendment was concurred in.

Mr. HOOPER—"I consider the adoption of the fifteenth amendment of the Senate, which authorizes the Treasurer to sell the bonds at the *market price*, as an invitation to the public to depreciate their value, and so entirely contrary to the principle of the bill, that I move to lay the bill, with the amendments, on the table."

Mr. WASHBURNE—"The bill is not before the House."

The SPEAKER—"A motion to lay a single amendment on the table carries the bill with it."

Mr. HOOPER—"I move to lay this amendment on the table; and demand the yeas and nays on that motion."

The yeas and nays were ordered.

The question was taken; and it was decided in the negative—yeas 21, nays 110; as follows:

Yeas—Messrs. Baker, Samuel S. Blair, Diven, Eliot, Fisher, Granger, Hickman, Hooper, Anson P. Morrill, Justin S. Morrill, Norton, Olin, Pendleton, Sedgwick, Sheffield, Shiel, Sloan, Stevens, Benjamin F. Thomas, Train and Vallandigham—21.

Nays—Messrs. Aldrich, Alley, Ancona, Ashley, Babbitt, Goldsmith F. Bailey, Joseph Bailey, Baxter, Beaman, Bingham, Jacob B. Blair, Blake, William G. Brown, Buffinton, Calvert, Campbell, Chamberlin, Clark, Clements, Cobb, Frederick A. Conkling, Roscoe Conkling, Conway, Cox, Cravens, Cutler, Davis, Dawes, Dunlap, Dunn, Edwards, Ely, English, Fenton, Fessenden, Franchot, Frank, Goodwin, Grider, Gurley, Haight, Hale, Hanchett, Harding, Harrison, Holman, Hutchins, Johnson, Julian, Kelley, Killinger, Knapp, Law, Leary, Lehman, Loomis, Lovejoy, McKnight, McPherson, Mallory, Marston, Maynard, Menzies, Moorhead, Nixon, Noble, Noell, Nugen, Patton, Perry, Pike, Pomeroy, Porter, Potter, Price, John H. Rice, Richardson, Riddle, Sargent, Shanks, Shellabarger, Sherman, Smith, Spaulding, John B. Steele, William G. Steele, Stratton, Francis Thomas, Trimble, Trowbridge, Van Horn, Van Valkenburgh, Verre, Vibbard, Voorhees, Wallace, Charles W. Walton, E. P. Walton, Ward, Washburne, Webster, Wheeler, Whaley, Albert S. White, Wickliffe, Wilson, Windom, Woodruff, Worcester and Wright—110.

So the House refused to lay the amendment on the table.

The amendment providing for a sinking fund, being the fifth Section of the Senate amendments, was now concurred in—yeas 51, nays 52. The remainder of the amendments being merely verbal, were read, voted on in gross, and all concurred in.

On the same day, 20th inst., the amendments were returned to the Senate with a concurrence of the House in a part of the amendments, a non-concurrence in others, and with some amendments to the Senate's amendments.

Mr. FESSENDEN moved that immediate action be had on the amendments. The motion was agreed to, and after some preliminary remarks by Mr. King and Mr. Sherman, and without any separate action on the several amendments, Mr. Fessenden said:

"I will move, as I understand the House has adjourned until to-morrow, that the Senate insist on its amendments, disagreed to by the House, and disagree to the amendments of the House to the amendments of the Senate, and ask for a Committee of Conference on the disagreeing votes of the two Houses."

The motion was agreed to, and the Chair appointed Mr. Fessenden, Mr. Sherman and Mr. Carlisle, as such Committee.

On the 21st., the action of the Senate was reported to the House, and on motion of Mr. Stevens, a Committee of Conference was appointed on the part of the House, as requested by the Senate, consisting of Mr. Stevens, Mr. Horton and Mr. Sedgwick.

The Conference Committee had long consultation, extending through two or three days. They finally compromised some of the most material of the disagreeing votes between the two Houses.

The most material change made was to require the *duties on imports to be paid in coin*, and held as a fund to pay the *interest in coin* on the funded debt, thereby doing away with the necessity of forcing the bonds on the market to procure coin for that purpose. Several other alterations and amendments were agreed to in the Committee of Conference.

On the 24th, Mr. Stevens reported to the House the action of the Conference Committee, which was agreed to—yeas 97; nays 22.

On the 25th, Mr. Fessenden made the same report in the Senate which was agreed to by the Senate without a division; and on the same day President Lincoln approved the bill, and thus the Legal Tender act, after a most able and determined opposition, became a law.

It is not deemed important to set forth in detail the several amendments and compromises made in the Committee of Conference. A copy of the bill as it passed the House on the 6th inst., will be found on page 96, and the following is a copy of the bill as it finally passed both Houses, and became a law. By comparing them, the amendments made after the bill first passed the House will fully appear:

"An Act to authorize the issue of United States notes, and for the redemption or funding thereof, and for funding the floating debt of the United States."

Be it enacted by the Senate and House of Representatives of the United States in Congress assembled, That the Secretary of the Treasury is hereby authorized to issue on the credit of the United States one hundred and fifty millions of dollars of United States notes, not bearing interest, payable to bearer, at the Treasury of the United States, and of such denominations as he may deem expedient, not less than five dollars each.

Provided, however, that fifty millions of said notes shall be in lieu of the demand Treasury notes authorized to be issued by the act of July 17th, 1861, which said demand notes shall be taken up as rapidly as practicable, and the notes herein provided for substituted for them; and

Provided further, That the amount of the two kinds of notes together shall at no time exceed the sum of one hundred and fifty millions of dollars; and such notes herein authorized shall be receivable in payment ot all taxes, internal duties, excises, debts and demands of every kind due to the United States, except duties on imports, and of all claims and demands against the United States of every kind whatsoever, except for interest upon bonds and notes, which shall be paid in coin; and shall also be lawful money and a legal tender in payment of all debts, public and private, within the United States, except duties on imports and interest as aforesaid; and any holder of said United States notes depositing any sum not less than fifty dollars, or some multiple of fifty dollars, with the Treasurer of the United States, or either of the Assistant Treasurers, shall receive in exchange therefor duplicate certificates of deposit, one of which may be transmitted to the Secretary of the Treasury, who shall thereupon issue to the holder an equal amount of bonds of the United States, coupon or registered, as may by said holder be desired, bearing interest at the rate of six per centum per annum, payable semi-annually, and redeemable at the pleasure of the United States after five years, and payable twenty years from the date thereof; and such United States notes shall be received the same as coin, at their par value, in payment for any loans that may be hereafter sold or negotiated by the Secretary of the Treasury, and may be re-issued from time to time as the exigencies of the public interests shall require.

§ 2. *And be it further enacted*, That to enable the Secretary of the Treasury to fund the Treasury notes and floating debt of the United States, he is hereby authorized to issue on the credit of the United States coupon bonds or registered bonds, to an amount not exceeding five hundred million dollars, and redeemable at the pleasure of the United States after five years, and payable twenty years from date, and bearing interest at the rate of six per centum per annum, payable semi-annually; and the bonds herein authorized shall be of such denomination, not less than fifty dollars, as may be determined upon by the Secretary of the Treasury; and the Secretary of the Treasury may dispose of such bonds at any time at the market value thereof, for lawful money, the coin of the United States, or for any of the Treasury notes that have been, or may hereafter be, issued under any former act of Congress, or for the United States notes that may be issued under the provisions of this act; and all stocks, bonds, and other securities of the United States held by individuals, corporations or associations within the United States, shall be exempt from taxation by or under State authority.

§ 3. *And be it further enacted,* That the United States notes and the coupon or registered bonds authorized by this act shall be in such form as the Secretary of the Treasury may direct, and shall bear the written or engraved signatures of the Treasurer of the United States and the Register of the Treasury, and also, as evidence of lawful issue, the imprint of a copy of the seal of the Treasury Department, which imprint shall be made under the direction of the Secretary, after the said notes or bonds shall be received from the engravers, and before they are issued; or the said notes and bonds shall be signed by the Treasurer of the United States, or for the Treasurer, by such persons as may be specially appointed by the Secretary of the Treasury for that purpose, and shall be countersigned by the Register of the Treasury, or for the Register, by such persons as the Secretary of the Treasury may appoint for that purpose; and all the provisions of the act entitled 'An act to authorize the issue of Treasury notes,' approved the twenty-third day of December, eighteen hundred and fifty-seven, so far as they can be applied to this act, and not inconsistent therewith, are hereby revived and re-enacted; and the sum of three hundred thousand dollars is hereby appropriated, out of any money in the Treasury not otherwise appropriated, to enable the Secretary of the Treasury to carry this act into effect.

§ 4. *And be it further enacted,* That the Secretary of the Treasury may receive from any person or persons, or any corporation, United States notes on deposit for not less than thirty days, in sums of not less than one hundred dollars, with any of the assistant treasurers or designated depositaries of the United States authorized by the Secretary of the Treasury to receive them, who shall issue therefor certificates of deposit, made in such form as the Secretary of the Treasury shall prescribe, and said certificates of deposit shall bear interest at the rate of five per centum per annum; and any amount of United States notes so deposited may be withdrawn from deposit at any time after ten days' notice on the return of said certificates; *Provided,* that the interest on all such deposits shall cease and determine at the pleasure of the Secretary of the Treasury; and *Provided further,* that the aggregate of such deposits shall at no time exceed the amount of twenty-five million dollars.

§ 5. *And be it further enacted,* That all duties on imported goods which shall be paid in coin, or in notes payable on demand, heretofore authorized, to be received and by law receivable in payment of public dues, and the coin so paid shall be set apart as a special fund, and applied as follows:—

First—To the payment in coin of the interest on the bonds and notes of the United States.

Second—To the purchase or payment of one per centum of the entire debt of the United States, to be made within each fiscal year after the first day of July, 1862; which is to be set apart as a sinking fund; and the interest of which shall in like manner be applied to the purchase or payment of the public debt, as the Secretary of the Treasury shall from time to time direct.

Third—The residue thereof to be paid into the Treasury of the United States.

§ 6. *And be it further enacted,* That if any person or persons shall falsely make, forge, counterfeit, or alter or cause or procure to be falsely made, forged, counterfeited or altered, or shall willingly aid or assist in falsely making, forging, counterfeiting or altering any note, bond, coupon, or other security issued under the authority of this act, or heretofore issued under acts to authorize the issue of Treasury notes or bonds; or shall pass, utter, publish or sell, or attempt to pass, utter, publish or sell, or bring into the United States from any foreign place, with the intent to pass, utter, publish or sell, or shall have or keep in possession, or conceal, with intent to utter, publish or sell, any such false, forged, counterfeited, or altered note, bond, coupon, or other security, with intent to defraud any body, corporate or politic, or any other person or persons whatsoever, every person so offending shall be deemed guilty of felony, and shall, on conviction thereof, be punished by fine not exceeding $5,000, and by imprisonment and confinement to hard labor not exceeding 15 years, according to the aggravation of the offence.

§ 7. *And be it further enacted,* That if any person, having the custody of any plate or plates, from which any notes, bonds, coupons, or other securities mentioned in this act, or any part thereof, shall have been printed, or which shall have been prepared for the purpose of printing any such notes, bonds, coupons, or other securities, or any part thereof, shall use such plate or plates, or knowingly permit the same to be used for the purpose of printing any notes, bonds, coupons, or other securities, or any part thereof, except such as shall be printed for the use of the United States, by order of the proper officer thereof; or if any person shall engrave, or cause or procure to be engraved, or shall aid in engraving any plate or plates in the likeness or similitude of any plate or plates designed for the printing of such notes, bonds, coupons, or other securities, or any part thereof; or shall vend or sell any such plate or plates, or shall bring into the United States, from any foreign place, any such plate or plates, with any other intent, or for any purpose, in either case, than that such plate or plates shall be used for printing of such notes, bonds, coupons, or other securities, or some part or parts thereof, for the use of the United States; or shall have in his custody or possession any metallic plate, engraved after the similitude of any plate from which any such notes, bonds, coupons, or other securities, or any part or parts thereof, shall have been printed, with intent to use such plate or plates, or cause or suffer the same to be used, in forging or counterfeiting any such notes, bonds, coupons, or other securities, or any part or parts thereof, issued as aforesaid; or shall have in his custody or possession, any blank note or notes, bond or bonds, coupon or coupons, or other security or securities, engraved and printed after the similitude of any notes, bonds, coupons, or other securities, issued as aforesaid, with intent to sell or otherwise use the same; or if any person shall print, photograph, or in any other manner execute or cause to be printed, photographed, or in any manner executed, or shall aid in printing, photographing or executing any engraving, photograph or other print, or impression, in the likeness or similitude of any such notes, bonds, coupons, or other securities, or any part or parts thereof, except for the use of the United States and by order of the proper officer thereof, or shall vend or sell any such engraving, photograph, print, or other impression, except to the United States, or shall bring into the United States from any foreign place any such engraving, photograph, print, or other impression for the purpose of vending or selling the same, except by the direction of some proper officer of the United States; or shall have in his custody or possession any paper adapted to the making of such notes, bonds, coupons, or other securities, and similar to the paper upon which any such notes, bonds, coupons, or other securities shall have been used, with intent to use such paper, or cause or suffer the same to be used in forging or counterfeiting any of the notes, bonds, coupons, or other securities, issued as aforesaid, every such person so offending shall be deemed guilty of a felony, and shall, on conviction thereof, be punished by fine not exceeding five thousand dollars, and by imprisonment and confinement to hard labor not exceeding fifteen years, according to the aggravation of the offence.

Approved February 25, 1862. A. LINCOLN."

Passage of the Treasury note bill.

SAMUEL WILKESON TO THE N. Y. TRIBUNE.

WASHINGTON, Tuesday, Feb. 25, 1862.

The Conference Committee of the Treasury note bill having concurred, and Mr. Washburne having defeated another endeavor to adjourn the House yesterday as early as two o'clock, the prospect of an invigoration of the war by a supply of money, and the payment of soldiers and contractors, was good. The bill as agreed upon by the conferees authorizes the issue of $150,000,000 of Treasury notes, uniform in similitude, and a legal tender in the payment of all debts, public and private. It withdraws the fifty millions of the July issue as soon as it conveniently can be done, makes the new notes fundable at any time in six per cent. twenty years bonds, redeemable at the pleasure of the United States after five years; makes the interest on the bonds and notes payable in coin, and (a new feature) makes the duties on imports also payable in coin, and devotes them to the payment of the interest on the notes and bonds, and the creation of a sinking fund by setting apart one per cent. of the amount. The provisions insisted on by the Senate authorizing the Secretary of the Treasury to sell six per cent. bonds for what they will fetch, in order to raise coin for interest, is retained in the bill. All the funded debt is exempted from taxation. Authority is given to temporarily deposit demand notes to the extent of twenty-five millions, on an interest of six per cent. after thirty days. The bill has gone through both Houses, and, it is supposed, will receive the President's signature to-night. An influence from New York sent the bill back again to the Senate this morning, for an amendment that should permit sixty millions of Treasury notes to be used for the payment of custom duties, the fifty millions authorized in July, and the temporary relief ten millions authorized this month. This was adopted and accepted by the House, and it is to be hoped that the President will now have a chance to sign the bill, and the abused public creditors get their pay.

It is but just to say, that to the patient labor of the Hon. E. G. Spaulding the country is greatly indebted for the early maturity of this finance measure, and for what vigor has been displayed in its passage through Congress."

TEMPORARY DEPOSITS IN SUB-TREASURY.

It will be noticed that by the 4th section of the Legal Tender act the Secretary of the Treasury was authorized to receive deposits in the sub-Treasury to the amount of $25,000,000, in sums of not less than $100, at five per cent. interest, with the privilege to the depositors of drawing it out again at any time, on ten days notice, after thirty days. This was but another form of borrowing money by the Government at a low rate of interest. Its operation at the sub-Treasury was somewhat like that of a Saving's Bank, and the privilege was largely availed of by banks, insurance companies and individuals. It became a very popular mode of temporary investment for corporations and individuals, and although it operated against funding in the 5-20 bonds, yet it became an advantageous mode for the Government to borrow large sums of money. It became so popular that on the 17th of March, 1862, the authority to receive these deposits was increased to $50,000,000.

On the 11th of July following the power was enlarged to $100,000,000; and by the act of January 30, 1864, the authority was still further enlarged to $150,000,000, and the Secretary was authorized to pay as high as six per cent. on these deposits. Certificates were issued to the persons making the deposits, which were circulated to some extent at the Clearing Houses, and among individuals, which was one mode of increasing the credit circulation of the country, and thereby aiding the general inflation which commenced with the passage of the legal tender act. These deposits reached at one time the sum of $120,176,196.

CERTIFICATES OF INDEBTEDNESS.

The issue of CERTIFICATES OF INDEBTEDNESS at one year, was another expedient resorted to for borrowing money, and was another mode of increasing the credit circulation of the Government. By the act of March 1, 1862, the Secretary of the Treasury was authorized to issue to creditors, who were willing to receive them, 'in satisfaction of audited and settled demands against the United States,' certificates of indebtedness (in effect promissory notes,) in sums of not less than $1,000 each, payable in one year at six per cent. interest. And by the act of the 17th of March, 1862, this power was enlarged, so as to embrace checks drawn in favor of creditors by 'disbursing officers upon sums placed to their credit on the books of the Treasurer.' The power thus conferred on the Secretary to issue certificates of indebtedness for these purposes was broad and unlimited. The certificates issued under these two acts were in the similitude of bank notes fitted for circulation as money, and did circulate to a considerable extent as currency until there was such an accumulation of interest upon them as to make it an object for capitalists to hold them as an investment. The Secretary commenced issuing these certificates simultaneously with the issue of Legal Tender (greenback) notes, and continued to issue them in large amounts during the progress of the war, which was advantageous to the Government, but at the same time was another fruitful source of inflation, and operated directly against any considerable funding in the long 5-20 bonds. The amount of indebtedness in this form on the first of November, 1864, was $238,593,000, being an amount greater than the market would bear; they were consequently depreciated and considerably below par.

MORE LEGAL TENDER AUTHORIZED.

In less than a month after the passage of the first legal tender act another act was passed at the request of Secretary Chase, approved March 17, 1862, by which the demand notes authorized by the act passed at the extra session in July, 1861, and the supplementary act of February 12, 1862, amounting to $60,000,000, were declared to be lawful money and a legal tender, in like manner, and for the same purposes, and to the same extent as the notes authorized by the first legal tender act. These notes, when first issued, were receivable by the Government for duties on imports, but that was not enough to prevent them from depreciating, and some of the banks in the principal cities refused to receive them from their customers as money. The object to make them a legal tender was to make them pass currently as money at the Clearing Houses, and in all business transactions, without loss to the holders.

SECRETARY CHASE ASKS FOR $150,000,000 MORE LEGAL TENDER NOTES.

Secretary Chase sent to the Committee of Ways and Means on the 7th of June, 1862, an official communication, accompanied by a bill proposed by him, asking, among other things, for an additional issue of $150,000,000 of legal tender notes; and that of this sum $35,000,000 should be of a denomination *less than five dollars*. This communication is published as Miscellaneous Document, No. 81, and sets forth at length the reasons why, in the opinion of the Secretary, this additional issue should be authorized by Congress. He states that the daily receipts from customs were about $230,000, and that the average daily conversions of legal tender notes into 5-20 bonds did not exceed $150,000, while the daily expenditures could not be estimated at less than $1,000,000, and would probably exceed that sum; and that he had already exhausted the issue of legal tender notes authorized by the act of February 25th, 1862.

"He proposed that authority be given to the Secretary of the Treasury to issue $150,000,000 in United States notes, in addition to the issue already authorized; and that these be made a legal tender for debts, except interest on loans, and receivable in payment of all loans to the United States, and for all Government dues, except duties on imports and interest.

* * * * * * * * * * * * * *

If Congress shall see fit to authorize the additional emission proposed, it seems highly expedient that such part as the public convenience shall require be issued in denominations *less than five dollars*. *I am aware of the general objections to the issue of notes under five dollars, and concede their cogency.* Indeed, under ordinary circumstances they are unanswerable. But in the existing circumstances of the country, they lose most, if not all, their force.

The country is involved in the expenditures of a contest for national existence, and it is highly desirable that the burdens of the people be made as tolerable as possible. If the restriction on the issue of small denominations be removed, the wants of the country will absorb a circulation of $25,000,000, and perhaps more. The interest on this circulation, say $1,500,000 a year, will be saved to the tax payers.

Payments to public creditors, and especially to soldiers, now require large amounts of coin to satisfy fractional demands less than five dollars. Great inconveniences in payment of the troops are thus occasioned. With every effort on the part of the Treasury to provide the necessary amount of coin, it is found impracticable always to satisfy the demand. When the amount required is furnished, the temptation to disbursing officers to exchange it for any small bank notes that the soldiers or the public creditors will take, is too great to be always resisted. *And even when the coin reaches the creditors it is seldom held, but passes, in general, immediately into the hands of sutlers and others, and disappears at once from circulation.* The inconveniencies, therefore, to the Government and creditors, from the absence of United States notes of small denominations, are not compensated by benefits to anybody.

It may properly be further observed that since the United States notes are made *a legal tender, and maintained nearly at the par of gold,* by the provision for their conversion into bonds bearing six per cent. interest, payable in coin, it is not easy to see why small notes may not be issued as wisely as large ones. The notes made a legal tender circulate as money; and the Government may authenticate, by device and imprint, small notes as well as small coins. The limit is to be found only in public convenience, which indicates denominations in gold, leaving the smaller circulation of silver (less valuable than gold,) as before.

Another consideration which deserves to be taken into the account is this: that resumption of payments in specie can be more certainly and easily effected, and with far less of inconvenience and loss to the community, if the currency, small as well as large, is of United States notes, than if the channels of circulation are left to be filled up by the emissions of non-specie paying corporations, solvent and insolvent.

These considerations of economy, of public advantage, and of private convenience, seem to me to justify fully the removal of the restriction upon the issue of small notes.

I propose, further, to make arrangements for the necessary *engraving and other work for the printing and preparation for issue of these notes in the Treasury Department at Washington.* I am led to believe that a very considerable reduction of expense can be thus effected. The prospect, in my judgment, certainly warrants the trial.

With these objects I have prepared a bill, which I herewith submit to the consideration of the committee. *The condition of the Treasury renders prompt action highly desirable;* and I trust it is not necessary to assure the Committee or Congress that, should the powers asked for be granted, they will be exercised only with the most careful reference to the requirements of the public interests. Whatever the authority granted may be, no issue of notes will be made except to replace notes withdrawn and canceled, and to meet the current expenditures authorized by Congress, which cannot be met from the receipts of revenue, from the increase of deposits, and from the proceeds of the conversion into five-twenties.

With great respect,   S. P. CHASE,
Secretary of the Treasury."

"Hon. THADDEUS STEVENS,
   Chairman Committee of Ways and Means."

The bill thus recommended by Secretary Chase was taken up in the Committee of Ways and Means and duly considered. After considerable discussion Mr. Stevens was authorized to report it to the House, but without the power to issue notes less than five dollars. On the 11th of June, Mr. Stevens reported the bill and the foregoing letter of the Secretary to the House. They were referred to the Committee of the Whole and ordered to be printed. On the 13th inst., the bill was made the special order for Tuesday, the 17th., and to continue the special order until disposed of.

MR. SPAULDING'S SPEECH.

On the 17th of June, the second bill for an additional issue of $150,000,000 legal tender notes, Mr. Spaulding opened the debate in a lengthy speech. The House being in Committee of the Whole (Mr. Phelps, of Missouri, in the chair) on the bill recommended by the Secretary of the Treasury, for authority to issue the additional sum of United States notes, Mr. Spaulding said:

"Mr. CHAIRMAN—This is an important measure, and I desire to submit a few remarks in the opening of the debate upon the subject.

The requirements of the Treasury will probably not be less than $250,000,000 to meet the current expenses to the 1st of January next. How is this large sum to be obtained? I believe it can only be obtained in the mode which has been successfully adopted during the last six months. The financial plan initiated six months ago as a necessary war measure has worked well. It has exceeded the most sanguine expectations of its strongest advocates. The Secretary of the Treasury recommends a continuance of the plan which has so successfully carried the country through the perils of the past six months. I shall cordially co-operate with the Secretary, hoping that it may be equally successful in the future. It is our duty now to provide all the means which shall be necessary to pay all the current expenses to the 1st day of January. The bill now under consideration is deemed necessary for that purpose, and the Secretary assures us that the condition of the Treasury renders prompt action highly desirable.

During the pending war, neither the President, the Secretary of the Treasury, nor Congress, can fix a limit to the expenditures of the Government, and cannot, therefore, fix a limit to the obligations to be issued on its credit. All that the Secretary can say, all that Congress can declare, is, that the President, as Commander-in-Chief, by his subordinate officers, must contract all the debts which shall be necessary to maintain the army and navy, and all other expenses incident to a vigorous prosecution of the war. The largest latitude is given to the President, Secretary of War, and Secretary of the Navy, in carrying on the war. They have full discretionary power to contract all the debts which they may deem necessary to amply supply the army and navy. All parties loyal to the Government are united in urging a vigorous prosecution of the war; all parties, therefore, ought to be willing to furnish all the means necessary for this purpose. We must, at any rate, pay all the debts contracted by the Executive in the progress of the war. If we knew how much this would amount to we could easily figure up the amount of the bonds and notes which Congress must authorize the Secretary to issue. No man, not even the President, the Secretary of War, the Secretary of the Navy, the Secretary of the Treasury, or the Chairman of the Committee of Ways and Means, or all of them together, can give even an approximate estimate as to the whole cost of this war, because they do not know the number of years it will continue, nor what will be the final solution of the grave questions involved. We are working out a great problem, the result of which no man can know. Slavery was the cause of this war; and until the solution of the slavery question is arrived at, and the cause of the rebellion removed, we have no hope of permanent peace and tranquility. This will take a long time; but how long no man is wise enough to determine. The war debt we all know is already large, and that it is growing fearfully larger every day. Many capitalists and bankers have already invested all their surplus means in United States stocks.

During the debate on the Treasury note bill in January and February last, I submitted, with some degree of diffidence as to its accuracy, an estimate of what I thought the whole debt (floating as well as funded debt) of the United States would be on the 1st of July next, and also what the funded and floating debt would be on the 1st of July, 1863, if the war should be prosecuted to that time on the same scale that it is now carried on. I have not seen since, and do not now see, any reason to change the estimates I then made. I then said it was impossible to estimate, definitely, what the war would cost, and therefore it was impossible to fix any limit to the amount of paper (obligations of the Government either in the form of notes, bonds or certificates of deposit) that must be issued during its prosecution. The experience of the last few months has demonstrated the truth of these remarks. We must first apply all the money we can collect from duties on imports, excises, internal duties, direct taxes, and confiscations of the property of rebels, which may amount, during the current year, (of money actually realized) to $125,000,000, perhaps more, and possibly less. All the expenses of the war, over and above the amount realized from these sources, must be provided for by borrowing in some form upon the credit of the Government. Paper credit in some form must be issued during the next fiscal year to a very large amount. However much we may depreciate it, this will be an imperative necessity which we cannot avoid. However much this may be a departure from sound business and financial principles applicable to times of peace, we cannot, we must not, shrink from the responsibility which is forced upon us in the prosecution of this war. We must boldly meet every exigency in financial as well as in military and naval operations. Notes and bonds must be authorized by Congress, and must be negotiated by the Secretary of the Treasury, amply sufficient to sustain the army and navy, or the war must stop. If we have not the money, we have what is equally or more important: the country is full of provisions, clothing, and the material of war. Treasury notes and bonds, issued on the credit of the Government, will procure all these supplies to maintain your army and navy. The war, therefore, can go on, and will go on vigorously if we carry out the views submitted to us by the Secretary of the Treasury.

In what form or mode has the credit of the Government been thus far used in the prosecution of this war? Five different forms of credit have been resorted to. Loans to the Government, for which obligations have been issued, are as follows:

1. United States notes, without interest, made a legal tender, and circulated as money among the people in all parts of the United States. This is the people's loan to the Government, and the most popular mode of borrowing ever adopted by any Government. It has given the country a sound national currency, in which the people have had entire confidence. Every man, woman and child having a five dollar legal tender greenback note in possession, has directly or indirectly loaned to the Government that amount, and becoming thereby interested in the perpetuity of the Government, is a strong advocate for a vigorous prosecution of the war. A fair test of the loyalty of all such holders of notes may be seen in their manifestation of confidence that they are perfectly good. The soldiers and sailors give their services, risk their lives, and endure all the hardships, sickness, and privations of the campaign, and cheerfully take these notes in payment. Supplies, subsistence, and material of war of every kind is eagerly furnished, and these greenbacks taken in exchange for the same. This kind of loan is so popular with the people, and being without interest, is so advantageous to the Government, it is desirable that it should be extended as far as it can be done safely, and without unduly stimulating speculations to such an extent as to cause an unfavorable reaction to the legitimate business of the country. *But when bonds can be negotiated at par, I think it will be safer to have bonds negotiated than to issue legal tender notes.*

2. The second kind of loan has been the issue of bonds running from five to twenty years at six per cent. interest per annum, which is an advantageous mode for the Government to borrow money, because the debt is then funded; and it is also favorable to commerce, because it causes no disturbance in the money market or business of the country, provided the money is not taken from the capital of men engaged in active business, but is obtained from capitalists who desire permanent investments, and who only want to use the interest half-yearly. This mode of borrowing must necessarily be limited to the amount of accumulated capital in the country, held by those who are willing to invest it in this way. It is a permanent and safe investment in the hands of those persons who want to use only the interest on their accumulated capital.

3. A third kind of loan which has thus far worked very well in practice, are *deposits* in the Treasury of the United States, for which certificates

are issued, bearing four and five per cent. interest, and which deposits may be withdrawn from the Treasury on giving ten days' notice after thirty days. The Government has borrowed over fifty million dollars at this low rate of interest, and the bill now before us proposes to give the Secretary power to extend the amount to $100,000,000. To guard against any sudden call that may be made for these deposits, the Secretary proposes to keep on hand, in Treasury notes, ready to be issued, one-third of the amount of the current deposits which may at any time be in the Treasury. With this safeguard, this kind of loan will be very advantageous to the Government as well as to the depositors.

4. Certificates of indebtedness at one year,'.bearing six per cent. interest per annum, given in payment of supplies, transportation, and material furnished in the prosecution of the war. This is an advantageous form of credit given to the Government, because it is for a definite time and at the customary rate of six per cent. interest. This form of indebtedness has already reached about fifty million dollars, and may be still further increased under the law already in existence.

5. Treasury notes at three years, bearing seven and three-tenths per cent. interest per annum, payable half-yearly, and convertible into twenty-years six per cent. bonds. This is the most objectionable form of borrowing of any that has been adopted, for the reason that the rate of interest is too high—a much higher rate than this great Government, with all its immense power and resources, ought to pay. I think this form of borrowing money should only be resorted to when we cannot obtain the money to carry on the war in any other way.

The *liquidated* and *funded* debt of the United States, as reported by the Secretary of the Treasury to Congress, May 29, 1862, was as follows:

	Rate of Interest.	Amount.
Loan, 1842	6	$2,883,364
Loan, 1847	6	9,415,250
Loan, 1848	6	8,908,342
Loan, 1858	5	20,000,000
Loan, 1860	5	7,022,000
Loan, 1850	5	3,461,000
Loan, 1861—February 8	6	18,415,000
Loan, 1861—July 17	6	50,000,000
Loan, 1861—July 17	7.3	120,523,450
Loan, 1861—Oregon	6	878,650
Loan, 1862	6	2,699,400
Treasury Certificates	6	47,199,000
Treasury notes, ordered	6	3,382,162
United States notes	0	145,880,000
Temporary deposits	5	44,865,524
Temporary deposits	4	5,913,042
Total, (average interest 4.35)		$491,446,184

Reducing the above total to the round sum, in English money, of £100,000,000 sterling, we have this contrast of the magnitude of the public debts respectively of Great Britain and the United States, and the annual cost of their support; public debt of Great Britain, £800,000,000, at an annual charge of £28,262,000; public debt of the United States, £100,000,000, at an annual charge of £4,350,000.

There is still another kind of indebtedness—the *floating debt* created in various forms every day by officers of the Government. This accrued indebtedness, existing in different forms, must, with our extended line of military and naval operations, be very large. It exists in the shape of accounts, services, transportation, bounties, and all other modes in which debts are made against the Government in enlisting, calling out the militia, aud in supplying the army and navy with the necessary material of war. On this kind of indebtedness the Government gets a credit of from one to four months. The whole accrued indebtedness of the United States, funded and unfunded, on the 1st day of July next, it is believed, will not exceed $650,000,000.

I never have been, and I trust I never shall be, unnecessarily an advocate for the creation of an unsound or an inflated currency; but, sir, I have long ago resolved, since this savage war has been forced upon us, to do whatever was necessary, and which I might lawfully do, to crush out the traitors and annihilate their armies. This cannot be done without the 'sinews of war.' Your army and navy must be supplied with all the terrible armament necessary to crush the enemy. Your sick, wounded and famishing soldiers must be supplied with hospitals, medical attendance, and all necessaries and conveniences to make them comfortable. This is a plain duty which we cannot any of us fail to perform. If, in the performance of this duty, it becomes necessary to authorize a further issue of United States notes, I shall not hesitate to give my vote for it. *I am not in favor of increasing the issue of them beyond the imperative necessities of the Government to sustain the army and navy. I much prefer to have our six per cent. bonds issued on permanent loans. I would like to see the Secretary of the Treasury borrow at par all the money he can on the six per cent. bonds heretofore authorized to be issued.*

When money can be obtained at par on six per cent. bonds, I would prefer to have that done to the issuing a very large amount of legal tender notes. Too large an issue of demand notes, to circulate as money, will no doubt lead to an expansion which will inflate prices, stimulate undue speculation, aud ultimately produce a reaction that will derange the whole business of the country. This is to be avoided if possible. I cannot, therefore, advocate any greater issue of demand notes than the absolute necessities of the Government require to carry on the war with vigor. I am disposed to give the Secretary power to issue the additional $150,000,000 United States notes asked for by him; but, at the same time, *I feel the importance of having this power exercised discreetly, and I trust that he will not issue, or pay them out at all, when money can be obtained at par on our six per cent. bonds.* I do not understand that the Secretary intends to have them all issued and put into circulation at any one time; on the contrary, I believe he has no such intention. He wants the power to issue and use them if necessary, but not otherwise. When he can obtain a sufficient amount of money at par, on six per cent. bonds, or by temporary deposits in the Treasury, there will be no necessity for their issue, *and the Secretary assures us in his letter that no further issue of notes will be made when that can be done;* and, besides, the bill provides for his retaining in his own hands legal tender notes equal to one-third of the temporary deposits that may be in the Treasury. Our army and navy and all debts of the Government should be punctually paid. No sacrifice on our part should be too great to raise all the means necessary for this purpose. The Secretary should, therefore, be clothed with ample power to meet any exigency that may arise.

The money for the large liabilities of the Government that have actually been met and canceled since the passage of the first legal tender note bill, could not have been raised by a forced sale of six per cent. bonds without a heavy sacrifice. *When that bill passed this House our six per cent. twenty-years bonds were ten per cent. below par. Now they are from one to two per cent. above the price of gold.* If, at the time of the passage of the first note bill, large amounts of bonds had been forced upon the market, as would have been necessary but for the passage of that bill, it would have depressed the six per cent. bonds still lower. There was not then money enough in the country seeking permanent investment, to absorb all the bonds required by the Government to meet the immediate and pressing demands upon the Treasury. This state of things may again occur. I hope not. I trust that there will be no necessity for any considerable issue of new notes; but to guard against possible contingencies, I am willing to confer large powers upon the Secretary, believing that he will exercise the power wisely, patriotically, and for the best interests of the country. I shall not, therefore, hesitate to clothe him with this great power, and shall, under the exigencies of the crisis, vote for this additional issue of legal tender notes.

As to the propriety of authorizing the Secretary to issue a portion of this amount in sums less than five dollars, I should, under ordinary circumstances, oppose giving such authority. As a general rule, the issue of small notes should not be adopted for a national currency; but I am disposed, in the present exigency, to vote for this provision, in accordance with the suggestions of the Secretary of the Treasury, and for the reasons urged by him in his communication, sent to us on the 7th inst.

I have thus briefly stated the condition and wants of the Treasury. Two hundred and fifty million dollars will be required, as I stated before, to carry us to the 1st of January next. That is more than the coin in all the banks of the United States, and nearly equal to all the coin of the United States in the hands of individuals and banks; the whole amount of gold and silver held by the banks and individuals being only about $265,000,000. The ground upon which the Secretary of the Treasury, and upon which the Committee of Ways and Means rest this issue of notes, is the necessity of the case. The Secretary urges immediate action in view of the condition of the Treasury. I therefore trust the House will take up this bill in the regular way, debate it to the extent which may seem desirable and necessary, and pass it at as early a day as possible."

MR. COLFAX'S SPEECH.

Mr. COLFAX suggested that the bonds, into which the notes are convertible, ought to be *absolutely twenty years bonds*, instead of allowing the Government the right to redeem them after five years. The bonds of '81 having absolutely twenty years to run, were selling yesterday in New York at six per cent. above par for greenbacks, while the 5-20 bonds would not bring such a premium. If they would command any such premium, these notes, convertible into such bonds, would be brought in for conversion with great rapidity, and there would not be a margin of six per cent. between gold and legal tender notes. He thought it best to legislate in such a manner as to approximate these notes to gold.

Mr. STEVENS—"I agree perfectly with the remarks made by the gentleman from Indiana. I opposed the substitution of five years bonds for twenty years bonds when the question was before the House, but the House differed with me. The Senate amended the bill, and when it came back from the Senate, the House agreed with the Senate after discussion here. He said that a majority of the Committee of Ways and Means were not in favor of the recommendation of the Secretary to issue notes less than five dollars, but he understood that some member of the Committee would offer an amendment in accordance with the recommendation of the Secretary of the Treasury."

Mr. SPAULDING afterwards offered an amendment that no part of these legal tender notes should be "for fractional parts of a dollar, and that not more than $50,000,000 should be of a less denomination than five dollars," which was adopted.

The bill continued to be discussed by different members of the House from day to day until the 24th of June, when it passed the House in substantially the same form as recommended by the Secretary of the Treasury, by yeas 76, nays 47, as follows:

Yeas—Messrs. Aldrich, Alley, Arnold, Babbitt, Bailey, Beaman, Bingham, Francis P. Blair, Jacob B. Blair, Samuel S. Blair, Blake, William G. Brown, Campbell, Casey, Chamberlin, Clark, Colfax, Cutler, Davis, Delaplaine, Duell, Dunn, Edgerton, Edwards, Ely, Fenton, Fessenden, Franchot, Granger, Gurley, Haight, Hale, Hall, Hanchett, Harrison, Hooper, Hutchins, Kelley, Francis W. Kellogg, Lansing, Loomis, Lovejoy, Law, McKnight, Maynard, Mitchell, Moorhead, Nixon, Noell, Nugen, Olin, Timothy G. Phelps, Pomeroy, Potter, Price, John H. Rice, Riddle, Sargent, Shanks, Shellabarger, Sherman, Sloan, Spaulding, Stevens, Trimble, Trowbridge, Van Horn, Van Valkenburgh, Verree, Wall, Wallace, Washburne, Wheeler, Whaley, Wilson, Windom and Worcester—76.

Nays—Messrs. William J. Allen, Baker, Biddle, George H. Browne, Buffinton, Calvert, Clements, Cobb, Roscoe Conkling, Corning, Cravens, Crisfield, Dawes, Delano, Dunlap, Eliot, English, Fouke, Goodwin, Grider, Harding, Johnson, Law, Menzies, Justin S. Morrill, Norton, Pendleton, Perry, John S. Phelps, Porter, Alexander H. Rice, Richardson, Sheffield, Shiel, Stiles, Benjamin F. Thomas, Francis Thomas, Vallandigham, Vibbard, Wadsworth, Walton, Ward, Webster, Chilton A. White, Wickliffe, Wood and Woodruff—47.

So the bill was passed.

BILL IN THE SENATE.

On the 25th of June the bill was received in the Senate and referred to the Finance Committee. On the 28th this Committee reported the bill with amendments. On the 2d of July it was fully discussed, and after being amended, passed the Senate by yeas, 22, nays 13, as follows:

Yeas—Messrs. Anthony, Browning, Chandler, Clark, Dixon, Foot, Hale, Harris, Henderson, Howard, Howe, Lane (of Indiana), Lane (of Kansas), Morrill, Pomeroy, Simmons, Sumner, Ten Eyck, Wade, Wilkinson, Willey and Wilson (of Missouri)—22.

Nays—Messrs. Carlisle, Collamer, Cowan, Davis, Foster, Harlan, King, Powell, Saulsbury, Sherman, Stark, Trumbull and Wright—13.

The amendments of the Senate were not agreed to by the House, and the disagreeing votes between the two Houses, were finally settled by a Conference Committee, consisting of Mr. Fessenden, Mr. Sherman and Mr. Wright on the part of the Senate, and Mr. Stevens, Mr. Spaulding and Mr. Phelps on the part of the House. The report of the Conference Committee was finally agreed to on the 8th of July, and on the 11th President Lincoln approved the bill, which is as follows:

CHAPTER CXLII.

"*An Act to authorize an additional issue of United States Notes, and for other purposes.*

Be it enacted by the Senate and House of Representatives of the United States of America, in Congress assembled, That the Secretary of the Treasury is hereby authorized to issue, in addition to the amounts heretofore authorized, on the credit of the United States, one hundred and fifty millions of dollars of United States notes, not bearing interest, payable to bearer at the Treasury of the United States, and of such denominations as he may deem expedient; *Provided*, That no note shall be issued for the fractional part of a dollar, and not more than thirty-five millions shall be of lower denominations than five dollars; and such notes shall be receivable in payment of all loans made to the United States, and of all taxes, internal duties, excises, debts and demands of every kind due to the United States, except duties on imports and interest, and of all claims and demands against the United States, except for interest upon bonds, notes, and certificates of debt or deposit; and shall also be lawful money and a legal tender in payment of all debts, public and private, within the United States, except duties on imports and interest, as aforesaid; and any holder of said United States notes, depositing any sum not less than fifty dollars, or some multiple of fifty dollars, with the Treasurer of the United States, or either of the assistant treasurers, shall receive in exchange therefor, duplicate certificates of deposit, one of which may be transmitted to the Secretary of the Treasury, who shall thereupon issue to the holder an equal amount of the bonds of the United States, coupon or registered, as may by said holder be desired, bearing interest at the rate of six per cent. per annum, payable semi-annually, and redeemable at the pleasure of the United States after five years, and payable twenty years from the date thereof; *Provided, however,* That any notes issued under this act may be paid in coin, instead of being received in exchange for certificates of deposit as above specified, at the discretion of the Secretary of the Treasury. And the Secretary of the Treasury may exchange for such notes, on such terms as he shall think most beneficial to the public interest, any bonds of the United States bearing six per centum interest, and redeemable after five, and payable in twenty years, which have been or may be lawfully issued under the provisions of any existing act; may re-issue the notes so received in exchange; may receive and cancel any notes heretofore lawfully issued under any act of Congress, and in lieu thereof issue an equal amount in notes such as are authorized by this act; and may purchase, at rates not exceeding that of the current market, and cost of purchase not exceeding one-eighth of one per centum, any bonds or certificates of debt of the United States as he may deem advisable.

SECTION 2. *And be it further enacted,* That the Secretary of the Treasury be, and is hereby, authorized, in case he shall think it expedient to procure said notes, or any part thereof, to be engraved and printed by contract, to cause the said notes, or any part thereof, to be engraved, printed and executed, in such form as he shall prescribe, at the Treasury Department in Washington, and under his direction; and he is hereby empowered to purchase and provide all the machinery and materials, and to employ such persons and appoint such officers as may be necessary for this purpose.

§ 3. *And be it further enacted,* That the limitation upon temporary deposits of United States notes with any assistant treasurer, or designated depositary authorized by the Secretary of the Treasury to receive such deposits, to fifty millions of dollars be, and is hereby repealed; and the Secretary of the Treasury is authorized to receive such deposits, under such regulations as he may prescribe, to such amount as he may deem expedient, not exceeding one hundred millions of dollars, for not less than thirty days, in sums not less than one hundred dollars, at a rate of interest not exceeding five per centum per annum; and any amount so deposited may be withdrawn from deposit, at any time after ten days notice, on the return of the certificate of deposit. And of the amount of United States notes authorized by this act, not less than fifty millions of dollars shall be reserved for the purpose of securing prompt payment of such deposits when demanded, and shall be issued and used only when, in the judgment of the Secretary of the Treasury, the same, or any part thereof may be needed for that purpose. And certificates of deposit and of indebtedness issued under this or former acts, may be received on the same terms as United States notes, in payment for bonds redeemable after five, and payable in twenty years.

§ 4. *And be it further enacted,* That the Secretary of the Treasury may at any time, until otherwise ordered by Congress, and under the restrictions imposed by the 'Act to authorize a national loan, and for other purposes,' borrow on the credit of the United States, such part of the sum of two hundred and fifty millions mentioned in said act as may not have been borrowed, under the provisions of the same, within twelve months from the passage thereof.

§ 5. *And be it further enacted,* That any part of the appropriation of ten thousand dollars for the detection and bringing to trial of persons engaged in counterfeiting the coin of the United States, made by the act entitled 'An Act making appropriations for the legislative, executive and judicial expenses of the Government, for the year ending the thirteenth of June, eighteen hundred and sixty-one,' approved June twenty-three, eighteen hundred and sixty, may be applied in detecting and bringing to trial and punishment, persons engaged in counterfeiting Treasury notes, bonds, or other securites of the United States, as well as the coin of the United States. And to carry into effect the preceding sections of this act the sum of three hundred thousand dollars is hereby appropriated, out of any money in the Treasury not otherwise appropriated.

§ 6. *And be it further enacted,* That all the provisions of the act entitled 'An Act to authorize the issue of United States notes, and for the redemption or funding thereof, and for funding the floating debt of the United States,' approved February twenty-five, eighteen hundred and sixty-two, so far as the same can or may be applied to the provisions of this act, and not inconsistent therewith, shall apply to the notes hereby authorized to be issued.

Approved, July 11, 1862. A. LINCOLN."

POSTAGE STAMPS AND FRACTIONAL CURRENCY.

Another expedient resorted to for providing means to carry on the war, was the issue of postage stamps and fractional currency. After the suspension of specie payments by the banks and the passage of the first legal tender act, gold and silver were in a great measure banished from circulation. There was a great scarcity of small change in ordinary business transactions. Corporations, individuals and firms commenced issuing *shinplasters* to supply the deficiency. It soon became apparent that unless some action was taken to prevent it, the country would be flooded with a heterogeneous fractional currency of very little value, and very vexatious in business transactions.

To remedy these evils, and in order that the Government might avail itself of the advantages of this circulation, Congress, at the request of Secretary Chase, passed the following bill:

CHAPTER CXCVI.

"*An Act to authorize payment in Stamps, and to prohibit circulation of notes of less denomination than one dollar.*

SECTION 1. *Be it enacted by the Senate and House of Representatives of the United States of America in Congress assembled,* That the Secretary of the Treasury be, and he is hereby directed to furnish to the Assistant Treasurers, and such designated depositaries of the United States as may be by him selected, in such sums as he may deem expedient, the postage and other stamps of the United States, to be exchanged by them, on application for United States notes: and from and after the first day of August next such stamps shall be receivable in payment of all dues to the United States less than five dollars, and shall be received in exchange for United States notes when presented to any Assistant Treasurer or any designated depositary, selected as aforesaid, in sums not less than five dollars.

§ 2. *And be it further enacted,* That from and after the first day of August, eighteen hundred and sixty-two, no private corporation, banking association, firm or individual, shall make, issue, circulate, or pay any note, check, memorandum, token, or other obligation for any less sum than one dollar, intended to circulate as money or to be received or used in lieu of lawful money of the United States; and every person so offending shall, on conviction thereof in any district or circuit court of the United States, be punished by fine not exceeding five hundred dollars, or by imprisonment not exceeding six months, or by both, at the option of the Court.

Approved July 17, 1862."

The use of *stamps* for small change did not work well in practice, and Secretary Chase recommended that *fractional currency* should be authorized in the place of postage and revenue stamps. This recommendation was carried into effect by the 4th section of the act of March 3d, 1863, by which the Secretary was authorized to issue fractional currency to any amount not exceeding $50,000,000, redeemable in United States notes in sums not less than three dollars, and receivable for postage and revenue stamps, and also in payment of any dues to the United States less than five dollars, except duties on imports. This fractional currency was not made a legal tender for private debts, but upon the whole it has served a useful purpose; and the second section of the act of July 17, 1862, prohibiting all other shinplasters, has kept the country free from a flood of small "paper trash," which at one time was very annoying to the business community. The Government has had the benefit of an average circulation of this form of credit to the amount of about $30,000,000, which is still outstanding, and which should at an early day be replaced by the silver coins which were in common use before the war. Would it not be well to destroy this currency as fast as it becomes mutilated and is returned to the Treasury Department? If no more should be printed or issued it would not be long before the present issue would wear out and be replaced by small coins.

SECOND ANNUAL REPORT OF SECRETARY CHASE, DEC. 4, 1862.

Secretary Chase again earnestly recommended the National Currency Bank Bill, and urged its passage by additional arguments, which he presented more in detail than in his first report.

"He still adhered to the opinion expressed in his last report that a circulation furnished by the Government, but issued by banking associations organized under a general act of Congress, is to be preferred to either United States legal tender notes or notes of State Banking Corporations. Such a circulation, uniform in general characteristics, and amply secured as to prompt convertibility by national bonds deposited in the Treasury by the associations receiving it, would unite, in his judgment, more elements of soundness and utility than can be combined in any other.

* * * * * * * * * * * * * *

Little direct aid is, however, to be expected from this plan during the present, nor very much, perhaps, during the next year. He briefly argued the *constitutionality* of this plan as an auxiliary to the power to borrow money; as an agency of the power to collect and disburse taxes; and as an exercise of the power to regulate commerce, and of the power to regulate the value of coin."

He recommended a further limited issue of legal tender notes as a wise expedient for the present time, and as an occasional expedient in future times, and the immediate passage of the bank bill for raising the additional means to carry on the war.

$900,000,000 LOAN ACT.

We now come to the consideration of the $900,000,000 Loan Act, which, in connection with loan acts already passed, conferred more *discretionary power* on the Secretary of the Treasury than was ever granted by law to any other Finance Minister in the world; and which ultimately led to a dangerous expansion of credit circulation in various forms, and in connection with the bank bill, which passed about the same time, to an enormous inflation of prices, caused by the over-issuing of paper money which came very near proving fatal to the finances of the Government and the legitimate business of the country.

The bill having been carefully considered in the Committee of Ways and Means, was, on the 8th of January, 1863, reported from the Committee to the House by Mr. Stevens. It was entitled, "A bill to provide Ways and Means for the support of the Government;" which was read twice, ordered to be printed, referred to the Committee of the Whole, and made the special order for Monday, the 12th inst. (House bill No. 659.) The bill as reported did not contain some provisions which Secretary Chase was very anxious to have passed—one was to repeal the provision restricting him in the sale of bonds to the 'market value'— another was to abrogate that most equitable and just provision contained in the original legal tender act, allowing the holders of legal tender notes to convert them at any time into 5-20 six per cent. bonds, interest payable semi-annually in coin. The Committee did not deem it just to abrogate this provision, while Secretary Chase believed its repeal would enable him to make better terms in selling bonds.

MR. SPAULDING'S OPENING SPEECH ON THE BILL.

On the 12th, the bill being the special order, was taken up in Committee of the Whole, and, an amendment having been offered by Mr. Stevens, Mr. Spaulding opened the debate upon it in the following speech:

"Mr. CHAIRMAN—This subject is a very dry one, but it is intensely interesting at the present time. I propose to discuss the bill reported by the Committee of Ways and Means, with the amendment of the gentleman from Pennsylvania, so far as I shall be able during the hour allotted to me under the rules of the House.

The immediate requirements of the Treasury are not less than $100,000,000. Before you can pass this bill through both Houses, have it approved by the President, and get bonds and notes engraved, printed and issued, at least $50,000,000 more will be required. *The pressing demands upon the Treasury between this and the first of next month, for the pay of soldiers and other creditors, may be put down at* $150,000,000. The gold and silver in the banks in New York, Boston and Philadelphia, on the first of this month, probably did not exceed $49,000,000; to which you may add the gold and silver in all other banks in all the loyal States, as will appear in official reports to the first ot January, 1863, and the whole sum will not exceed $87,000,000. All this coin is necessary for the banks to take care of their own liabilities; but even if the Secretary could, on the credit of the Government, by a sale of bonds at any sacrifice, or by the aid of the military power, visit every bank in the country, and by force compel all this coin to be paid into the Treasury, it would not pay fifty cents on the dollar on the demands due from the Government, and which ought to be paid in the next twenty days. It is therefore perfectly plain that even the *small* sum of $150,000,000, now due, cannot be paid in gold. It would be a gratification to me, and, I doubt not, to every other loyal citizen, if it were otherwise. *It is no fault of the Secretary or of Congress that gold cannot now be paid to the soldiers and other creditors. It is simply an impossibility, by any plan, to get enough for that purpose.* There was never a more pertinent application of the old maxim than when applied to our present condition, 'when we cannot do as we would, we must do as we can.'

I have had a strong desire to provide money upon a specie basis, for the support of the army and navy, during the pending struggle to preserve the Constitution and the National Union. I would much prefer to pay gold and silver to all the creditors of the Government. During the first six months of the war, I was in hopes that our expenditures might be kept within limits that would admit of such a financial policy. I believe that this was the earnest wish of the Secretary of the Treasury, and of every member of the Committee of Ways and Means. But with an army in the field of from seven hundred thousand to one million of men, to be fed, clothed and paid, and all the material of war provided to make them efficient for active duty, it was very soon ascertained that the coin in the country, amounting only to about $250,000,000, if every dollar held by the banks and the people could have been availed of, was far too small to meet these large expenditures. We could not shut our eyes to the vastness of the volume of debt that was open before us. It was very soon made apparent that our national debt would, at an early day, reach $2,000,000,000, equal to half the debt of Great Britain; and that it would be utterly impossible to make loans on a specie basis fast enough to meet such enormous expenditures.

At the last session, and after there had been a general suspension of specie payments by the banks and the Government, Congress authorized the issue of $150,000,000 of legal tender notes; and by another law, passed a few months later in the session, an additional issue of $150,000,000 was also authorized, but the Secretary was required to hold in reserve $50,000,000 to meet any calls that might be made for temporary deposits in the sub-Treasury. We all hoped that this would be all the legal tender notes that would be necessary. Congress also authorized the Secretary to borrow $500,000,000, payable in twenty years, and redeemable at the pleasure of the Government after five years, bearing interest at the rate of six per centum per annum. payable half-yearly in coin, *and gave him authority to sell them at any time 'at the market price,' to raise money to carry on the war ; and further authorized the holder of any legal tender notes to convert them at any time, at par, into these six per cent. bonds.*

The Secretary has paid out nearly $250,000,000 legal tender notes, being all that he was authorized to issue; *and notwithstanding he has had authority for the last ten months to sell $500,000,000 of five-twenty six per cent. bonds, at the market price, he has only disposed of about $25,000,000, and has still authority to sell $475,000,000 at the market price, and take his pay for them in legal tender notes.*

One of the reasons why more of these bonds have not been disposed of is, that there has been no redundancy of currency, and it has been difficult for the Secretary to get legal tender notes on a sale of the bonds and seven-three-tenths notes that he has already negotiated.

The War and Navy Departments have almost unlimited power to contract debts for the supply of the army and navy. The volume of supplies and supply trains for your army are enormously large; and extending over such a widely extended field of military operations as that in which our several army corps are engaged, no one can fail to see that it is next to impossible to estimate accurately the amount to be appropriated for a year in advance. But it is painfully certain, that with the present army in the field, there is no way of limiting the amount of expenditures when they are actively operating to put down so gigantic and desperate a rebellion.

We know that the liquidated and funded debt is already large, and that there is a large accrued indebtedness, which ought to be paid at an early day, but without any adequate means in the Treasury to pay it. *There is a large amount due to the soldiers that must be paid at the earliest moment possible. The soldiers now on the field of battle, or encamped in front of the enemy, enduring all the perils and hardships of war, many of whom have not received their pay for months, ought not to be put off any longer.* They can hardly be expected to perform their duties with alacrity, unless they are promptly paid, especially when they know, as many of them do, that their families at home are suffering for the want of the means of life. *It is an imperative necessity that the means for paying the army and navy should not be delayed any longer.* If the Secretary cannot raise the money to pay the creditors of the Government by a loan on five-twenty six per cent. bonds at the market price, other authority must be given him to raise the money, and Congress ought to confer that authority upon him as soon as possible.

The time has arrived when our finances must engage the earnest and united attention of all loyal Representatives. We were in great peril last year, but our dangers are now two-fold what they were then. It was very difficult last year to provide the money to meet the large appropriations made for the support of the army and navy. It will be still more difficult to meet the enlarged requirements of the current and the next fiscal year. The army bill alone appropriates over $731,000,000, which, added to the estimates of all the other expenditures for the fiscal year ending June 30, 1864, amount to the enormous sum of $1,095,431,183.56, to which must be added the amount still required for appropriations and deficiency for the year ending June 30, 1863, and which, according to the report of the Secretary of the Treasury, amounted on the 1st of December last to the sum of $551,221,131.59, making the whole aggregate required to meet appropriations during the next eighteen months $1,646,634,315.15.

NATIONAL DEBT.

Particulars of the public debt outstanding January 2, 1864:

Loan of 1842 in course of payment	$ 2,883,364 11
" 1847	9,415,250 00
" 1848	8,908,341 80
" 1858	20,000,000 00
" 1860	7,022,000 00
" 1861, act of February 8, 1860	18,415,000 00
" 1861, act of July 18, 1861	50,002,000 00
" 1862, five-twenty six per cent	25,050,850 00
Texas indemnity	3,461,000 00
Oregon war debt	1,026,600 00
Texas debt	112,092 69
Old funded and unfunded debt	114,115 48
Treasury notes under acts prior to 1857	104,561 64
" " subsequent	2,750,350 00
Treasury notes seven-thirty per cent. interest	139,998,000 00
Temporary deposits at four per cent	38,458,008 50
" " five per cent	41,777,628 16
United States notes, legal tender and receivable for customs	14,913,315 25
United States notes, legal tender	223,108,000 00
Postal currency less than one dollar	6,844,936 00
Certificates of indebtedness, six per cent	110,321,241 65
Requisitions on the Treasury for soldiers' pay and other creditors, due but not paid	59,117,597 46
Total funded and unfunded debt to January 2, 1863, according to the books in the Treasury Department	783,804,252 64
To which may be added the estimates of appropriations made and asked for to July 1, 1864, (including $100,000,000 that may be undrawn at the end of the year, and which will be due though not paid), amounting to, say	1,216,197,745 35
Public debt estimated to July 1, 1864, if the war continues on the same scale to that time	$2,000,000,000 00

How is this large sum to be obtained?

The Secretary of the Treasury, in his annual report, indicates two modes of obtaining it, as follows:

1. A national bank bill.
2. By loans in some of the forms heretofore authorized.

I propose to examine these modes of obtaining the money in the order above stated.

1. A national bank law. It is proposed by this bill to authorize the formation of banking corporations in all parts of the country, with the

usual powers of State banks. They are to have the power to issue bank notes to circulate as money, and to be secured by United States stocks, deposited in the Treasury Department as security for the redemption of the currency thus issued. This bill in all its essential features is like the free banking law of the State of New York. It proposes to nationalize all the bank currency of the country by the adoption of such a coercive policy toward existing banks as will compel them to throw up their present State charters, and organize anew under this bill. A tax of two per cent. per annum is proposed on all State bank circulation, in addition to the State, county and city taxes which State banks are compelled to pay under State laws, and in addition to the internal revenue tax of three per cent. on their profits, making an aggregate tax upon State banks of about five per cent. By this hostile policy toward existing banks, it is proposed to compel them to surrender their present chartered rights, to make a market for United States stocks, to be deposited in the Treasury Department as a basis for national bank circulation under this new system, to the amount of $250,000,000.

It is anticipated that in the course of a few years, and certainly as soon as the system goes fully into operation, United States bonds will be deposited to this amount. There is no provision requiring new banks, organized under this bill, to redeem their circulating notes in coin. They are to remain under suspension of specie payments, the same as existing banks, until there is a general resumption on the part of the Government and the banks, long after the close of the war. The central idea of the measure, as stated in the Secretary's report, 'is the establishment of one sound uniform currency, of equal value throughout the country, upon the foundation of national credit, combined with private capital,' and making this the settled financial policy of the country. This is the scheme proposed. The first question presented is: will this materially aid the Government in the present exigency? I think it will not, and the Secretary frankly admits that 'little direct aid is to be expected from this plan during the present, and not very much, perhaps, during the next year.' We have already issued, and put into circulation, legal tender notes direct from the Treasury, and without the machinery or expense of a national bank, to about the sum of $250,000,000. These Treasury notes are based, for their security and ultimate redemption, upon the good faith of the people and all their property. For what currency we need in the pending struggle for national existence, will it be wise to attack the State banks? Will it be wise to raise up powerful enemies in the States to oppose any of the measures of the Government? The State bank system is older than the Constitution. It has become deeply rooted. Immense interests are involved in the banks organized all over the country under the protection and guarantee of State sovereignty. Individuals have, in good faith, paid in their money to establish these banks. Vast interests are involved in various ways. They are intimately interwoven with the commerce and business of the country. In the State of New York alone over $19,000,000 of stocks and bonds, many of which have been purchased from the State at a large premium, constitute the security for the redemption of their circulating notes. The State of New York has now the best banking system in the world. These banks are under much more careful supervision, of a superintendent in their midst, than they would be under an officer residing as far off as Washington. The State banks have been liberal in making loans to the Government in this hour of the nation's greatest need, and their stockholders, directors, and managers are mostly loyal and patriotic. Still further aid will be solicited and expected from the existing banks. Will it be wise to make demands upon them that are not made upon all other property? Any invidious discrimination against them, in the way of taxation, it seems to me, would be unjust. *   *

I am not opposed to a national bank, nor am I disposed to interfere with State banks. Both systems of banking may be legitimate within their sphere of action. I am willing that the country should have both. I am willing that they should go on *pari passu* and in competition with each other; but I am unwilling to make war at this time on the State banks, because I do not believe that the benefits to be derived from such a course will sufficiently compensate for the evils that will follow any attempt to destroy the present State bank system.

I now propose to examine the constitutionality of these two systems of banking. If it can be shown that a national bank is constitutional, it can be more clearly established that State banks are also constitutional. Jackson, Jefferson, and other statesmen always insisted that the Constitution did not empower Congress to charter a national bank; and the former was especially favorable to State banks. (For Mr. Jefferson's opinions see his letter to Hon. John W. Eppes, chairman of the Finance Committee, bearing date November 6, 1813, wherein he opposes the charter of a United States bank.)

CONSTITUTIONALITY OF A NATIONAL BANK.

I have no doubt that the general principle of the national bank bill proposed by the Secretary of the Treasury is constitutional. It is true that there is no express grant of power in the Constitution to incorporate a United States bank. The power to create a bank is incidental to the powers expressly granted. The national bank proposed may be considered an appropriate means to carry into effect many of the enumerated powers of the Government. By its provisions it has a direct relation to the national debt, to the power of collecting taxes, internal duties and excises; to that of borrowing money, to that of regulating commerce between the States, and to that of raising money to maintain the army and navy. It would, no doubt, be a useful instrument in administering the fiscal and financial operations of the Government, and it would moreover, in time, be a useful support to the credit of the Government, by providing a market for a considerable amount of the bonds issued in the prosecution of the war. (See Hamilton's celebrated argument submitted to President Washington, in favor of the constitutionality of the United States Bank, in 1791; McCullock *vs.* The State of Maryland, 4 Wheat. R. 422-3, Chief Justice Marshall's opinion.)

STATE BANKS ARE ALSO CONSTITUTIONAL.

In the case of Briscoe *vs.* The Bank of the Commonwealth of Kentucky, (11 Peter's R., 317,) Judge McLean laid down the doctrine that a State cannot emit bills of credit, or, in other words, it cannot issue that description of paper, to answer the purposes of money, which was denominated before the adoption of the Constitution, "bills of credit." But a State may grant acts of incorporation for the attainment of those objects which are essential to the interests of society. This power is incident to sovereignty; and there is no limitation in the Federal Constitution on its exercise by the States in respect to the incorporation of banks.

At the time the Constitution was adopted, the Bank of North America and the Massachusetts bank and some others were in operation. It cannot, therefore, be supposed that the notes of these banks were intended to be inhibited by the Constitution, or that they were considered bills of credit, within the meaning of that instrument. In fact, in many of their most distinguishing characteristics, they were essentially different from bills of credit, in any of the various forms in which they were issued.

If, then, the powers not delegated to the Federal Government nor reserved to the States are retained by the States or the people, and, by a fair construction of the term bills of credit, as used in the Constitution, they do not include ordinary bank notes, does it not follow that the power to incorporate banks to issue these notes may be exercised by a State?

A uniform course of action, involving the right to the exercise of an important power by the State government for three-fourths of a century, and this almost without question, is no unsatisfactory evidence that the power is rightfully exercised to charter banks to issue bank notes to circulate as money. The Supreme Court of the United States decided in this case that the act incorporating the Bank of the Commonwealth of Kentucky was a constitutional exercise of power by the State of Kentucky; and the notes issued by the bank were not bills of credit, within the meaning of the Constitution of the United States, but were ordinary bank bills, issued and circulated as currency.

It was argued in this case that if the Bank of the Commonwealth of Kentucky should be declared unconstitutional by the court, all State banks founded on private capital would be unconstitutional. Justice Story, who gave a dissenting opinion in that case, denied this position, and declared that the States may create banks as well as other corporations upon private capital, and, so far as the prohibition in the Federal Constitution is concerned, may rightfully authorize them to issue bank bills or notes as currency. The Constitution does not prohibit the emission of all bills of credit, but only the emission of bills of credit *by a State;* and when I say by a State, I mean by or in behalf of a State in whatever form issued. It does not prohibit private persons, or private partnerships, or private corporations, (strictly so called,) from issuing bills of credit.

In the case of Darrington *vs.* The State Bank of Alabama, (13 Howard Reports, 12,) the Supreme Court of the United States decided that the bills of a banking corporation, which has corporate property, are not bills of credit within the meaning of the Constitution, although the State which created the bank is the only stockholder, and pledges its faith for the ultimate redemption of the bills.

It must not be understood from anything I have said, that I am in favor of an expansion of the circulation of existing banks. On the contrary, I am opposed to it. The existing banks should be kept under close supervision; and for all increase in their circulation, since they suspended specie payments, I am entirely willing that some policy should be adopted by the States or General Government to prevent them from inflating the currency. I am willing that a tax of two per cent. should be levied on all their increase of circulation since the first of January, 1862. This would be a tax on their abuse of chartered privileges, and not a blow aimed at the total destruction of all banks alike, good and bad. What I oppose is an attempt on the part of Congress to destroy the vested rights of citizens, which they hold under the guarantee of State sovereignty, and which are to be protected as sacredly as any other chartered rights or property held under State laws. Let all property be taxed as nearly equal as possible, leaving no just cause for complaint from any class of citizens.

Having shown that the proposed national bank bill is not only unjust in some of its provisions, but that it will not yield any considerable amount of money to meet the appropriations for the current and next fiscal year, the other question to be considered is:

2. Can the money be obtained by loans? It will be recollected that the amount to be provided for, over and above the sums to be realized from duties on imports and internal revenue, exceeds the sum of $1,000,-000,000. This is a large sum to be borrowed in the ensuing eighteen months. As I have before stated, over $2,500,000 will be required every day, Sundays included, between this and the first day of July next. The receipts from postal currency, customs and taxes during that time will not probably exceed the sum of $600,000 per day, leaving $1,900,000 to be obtained daily in some form by loan. Congress, by its legislation at the last session, has, to a considerable extent, changed the standard of value for all business operations within the United States.

The *standard of value* fixed by Congress is legal tender Treasury notes, convertible at any time into United States specie-paying bonds, bearing interest at the rate of six per centum per annum, payable half-yearly in coin, based upon adequate taxation upon the entire property of the country. Legal tender notes constitute the national currency now established by law. All exchanges of property, all contracts, and all loans, are based upon the value of legal tender notes and United States six per cent. bonds. The law of Congress declares that these notes shall be *lawful money*, and a legal tender in payment of all debts, public and private.

The Secretary states in his Annual Report that previous to the first of November, 1862, 'the coin had been practically demonetized and withdrawn from use as currency, or as a basis for currency.' * * * *
'That on the suspension of specie payments, and the substitution for coin of United States notes, convertible into six per cent. specie-paying bonds, as the legal standard of value, gold became an article of merchandise, subject to the ordinary fluctuations of supply and demand, and to the extraordinary fluctuations of mere speculation.'

Gold does not circulate at all as currency, and there is no probability that it will circulate as money for several years to come—certainly not during the progress of this gigantic war to put down the rebellion. This is to be regretted, but it cannot be avoided. We have the monster rebellion by the ears, like the backwoodsman who held the ferocious wolf—if we let go, he will destroy us; we must therefore hold on till we subdue him. No compromise can be made. The rebels will not negotiate on any basis except that of separation and an acknowledgment of their independence. The war, therefore, must go on. While the war lasts the magnitude of the expenses will be so great that there is not coin enough in the country to carry it on with gold and silver. It cannot be obtained. We must try to mitigate, as far as we can, the evils growing out of the necessity of making legal tender notes the standard of value.

You cannot dispose of your twenty years six per cent. bonds for gold without submitting to a loss of over thirty cents on every dollar; in other words, for every dollar of bonds issued you can only get seventy cents in gold. Even if you should be willing to submit to this sacrifice, it is not at all probable that you could negotiate $25,000,000 of bonds for gold before you would be obliged to submit to a sacrifice of fifty cents on every dollar sold. Not because your bonds are not good, dollar for dollar, as gold, but because the whole amount of gold in the country that could be had for circulation does not probably exceed $250,-000,000. Not a sufficient sum to carry on the immense operations of the people and the Government at this time, even if it could all be brought out and put into circulation—a thing wholly impracticable at this time. No one at all acquainted with monetary affairs believes that we can make sale of any considerable amount of our six per cent. bonds at over fifty cents on the dollar for gold—a sacrifice too great for this House to seriously consider, if any other mode can be devised which is practicable. It is believed to be practically impossible to negotiate your bonds for gold without too great a sacrifice. If you cannot negotiate loans for gold, will it be wise to change the independent Treasury law so as to allow loans to be negotiated for notes of suspended banks? There was a general suspension of specie payments by the banks and the Government on the 31st of December, 1861. In February following, Congress passed the law for the issue of legal tender notes, and authorized the Secretary to make loans, and receive these notes in payment; but the Government has not deemed it best to take suspended bank notes in payment for loans or any other dues to the Government. I do not think it wise to adopt that policy at this time. The question then arises, can you sell bonds enough every day and get your pay for them in legal tender notes already issued? It is perfectly apparent to all who are acquainted with the money market that this cannot be done. Currency has been scarce all the time for the last eight months, an is now very difficult to be obtained in sufficient quantity to meet the business wants of the country. In many places through the interior of the States, bankers and business men have been obliged to pay as high as one-quarter and one-half per cent. premium to get currency (bank bills and greenbacks) to carry on ordinary business operations.

It is well known that all the New England and New York country banks redeem their bills now at the Suffolk Bank, Boston, and the Metropolitan Bank, New York, precisely as they did before the suspension of specie payments. This system checks any tendency to over issue, and is a touchstone by which to test the demand for bank bills. If they are not needed for legitimate business, they flow in rapidly to the redeeming banks, but if they are wanted they stay out. This test is unerring. The daily redemptions, for months past, have not been half what they were when the volume of bank circulation was less by a third than it is at this time. What causes this scarcity of currency? In the first place, as before stated, gold and silver no longer circulate as currency within the United States. Gold is only required to settle foreign balances, pay custom duties and interest on the public debt. It is bought and sold for these purposes as a commodity, but it does not circulate as money in ordinary business operations. Its place is supplied by bank bills and legal tender notes. *In the next place, the large increase of business suddenly created by such a gigantic war as we are now prosecuting, has largely increased the demand for a larger volume of currency than was ever required before.*

There has been a large demand for currency in the western States to purchase and bring forward the immense crops that have been produced during the last two years. The winding up of a large number of badly organized and badly managed banks in those States left a large vacuum to be filled by bills of solvent banks and legal tender notes. The Government has been buying largely, in all parts of the country, food, clothing, and all munitions of war, beside the large sums required for pay and bounty money of the volunteer soldiers that have gone forth from all the States. No doubt considerable amounts of this money still remain in the hands of the soldiers themselves and their families, practically withdrawn from circulation for the time being. Fifty, one hundred, and as high, even, as two hundred dollars, were paid for volunteers to fill up the two last calls made by the President. Fifty dollars paid to each soldier, to the number of six hundred thousand, would require $30,000,000 to say nothing of the amounts required for the army previously sent into the field. It is perfectly plain where the currency has gone during the past six months. *The operations of the army and navy alone have required in all forms, not less than $200,000,000 in bank bills and legal tender notes. It is no wonder that currency has been scarce in all the ordinary channels of trade and business.* It is still very scarce and difficult to be obtained for ordinary business purposes in New York and all the western States. I am assured by bankers and the best financiers in New York, that if the Secretary should put on the market a proposal for a loan of $50,000,000 it could not be taken, for the reason that the legal tender notes could not be obtained in sufficient quantity to pay for a loan of that amount. It is doubtful whether a loan of $15,000,000 could be taken at this time for the want of currency to pay for it.

It is also very difficult for the collectors of internal revenue to make collections on account of the scarcity of legal tender notes. Legal tender notes are not plenty among the people who are required to pay your taxes; they are continually asking for more. Why, then, should we be alarmed at a further issue of legal tender notes? So long as they are wanted by the business of the country, demanded by the soldiers for their pay, begged for by all the needy creditors of the Government, surely Congress ought not to hesitate in an exigency like the present.

It is no time now to depress business operations, or hold back the pay due to honest creditors of the Government. It is much better to stimulate, make money plenty, make it easy for people to pay their taxes, and easy for Government to make loans. This is the only way in which we can go on in the present imperiled condition of the country.

During the last war with Great Britain, Jefferson, in letters written during that period, repeatedly urged upon the Government the propriety of issuing Treasury notes of convenient denominations to circulate as money. In his letters to John W. Eppes, chairman of the Finance Committee, under dates of June 24 and September 11, 1813, he urged upon Congress the importance of issuing Treasury notes whenever loans could not be made upon satisfactory terms. In one of his letters, bearing date October 15, 1814, he says: 'I never did believe you could have gone beyond a first and second loan—not from want of confidence in the public faith, which is perfectly sound, but from a want of disposable funds in individuals. The circulating fund is the only one we can command with certainty. It is sufficient for all our wants; and the impossibility of defending the country without its aid as a borrowing fund renders it indispensable that the nation should take and keep it in their own hands.' He admitted that the issue of Treasury notes would banish gold and silver from circulation, and in another letter adds: 'In such a nation there is one and only one resource for loans, sufficient to carry them through the expenses of a war; and that will always be sufficient, and in the power of an honest Government, punctual in the preservation of its faith. The fund I mean is the *mass of circulating coin*. Every one knows that, although not literally, it is true that every paper dollar emitted banishes a silver one from circulation. A nation, therefore, making its purchases and payments with bills fitted for circulation, thrusts an equal sum of coin out of circulation. This is equivalent to borrowing that sum; and yet, the vendor receiving payment in a medium as effectual as coin for his purchases or payments, has no claim to interest. And so the nation may continue to issue its bills as far as its wants require, and the limits of the circulation will admit.'

So it will be seen that Jefferson, so far from regarding it as an evil that coin should be banished from circulation during war, regarded it as a great advantage; because the Government would then be able to circulate its own notes, without interest, in place of the coin of individuals. Treasury notes issued by the Government, he regarded as a loan from the people, without interest, and the only available resource in time of war.

He urged ample taxation as a basis for Government paper issue, and adds: 'That during the interval between war and war, all the outstanding paper should be called in, coin be permitted to flow in again, and hold the field of circulation until another war should require its yielding place again to the national medium.' An essential feature of the financial plan adopted last year was the passage of the tariff and internal revenue laws. It was of great consequence that our public debt should rest upon a solid foundation. The property of the country, liable to taxation, amounted in 1860 to over $16,000,000,000, and Congress having ample power to tax it to the full amount necessary to pay all Government debts, it was agreed by all parties that it was necessary to impose taxes upon this property, and the profits of business based thereon, in various forms, for an amount sufficient to pay the ordinary expenses of the Government on a peace footing, and all the interest on the extraordinary war debt. The ordinary expenses of the Government in time of peace do not exceed $75,000,000, and the interest on the war debt will not probably exceed during the next year the sum of $45,000,000, while it is believed that the revenues derived from the tariff and internal revenue will not be less than $200,000,000, leaving $80,000,000 as a sinking fund to keep down the war debt. It is believed that the revenue realized on the present tariff and tax law will pay ordinary current expenses of the Government, and interest on the war debt when it reaches $2,000,000,000, which is only half the present debt of Great Britain. * * * * * * * * * * * *

Upon a full examination of the whole subject, and with a deep solicitude for the success of the measures that may be finally adopted by Congress, I see no way in which the ways and means can be obtained to carry on the Government for the next eighteen months, except by a continuance of the measures adopted at the last session, and which have so successfully carried us through the perils of the last year, with such additions and modifications as experience has shown to be necessary.

An additional section has been proposed to the financial plan adopted last year. There is a large amount of available means in the country, which, if it can be drawn into the national Treasury, will be of most essential service at this time. It has been the subject of much consideration as to the best form in which it could be offered to the people to induce them to let the Government have the money for which they have no present use, and be allowed a fair compensation for its use during the time it is borrowed by the Government. Interest bearing Treasury notes are believed to be the best form in which it can be offered to the public.

INTEREST-BEARING TREASURY NOTES

Under the operation of this new section, these interest-bearing Treasury notes and the legal tender notes would be convertible and reconvertible into each other at the will of the holder; and as both can be paid out to the creditors of the Government, they will soon find their way into all the channels of business in all parts of the country. The interest-bearing notes will be laid aside, out of circulation, better than gold as an investment, because yielding a fair rate of interest; while the legal tender notes will continue to circulate as money. The object of this section is to reach the money invested in temporary loans, in all the cities, villages and towns throughout the country, and apply it to sustain the Government at this time. A large amount of money is now held by individuals and corporations, bearing a small rate of interest, or no interest at all, which is on deposit in banks or in private safes and drawers, waiting a good opportunity for permanent investment in the purchase of stocks, mortgages, or other property. Forehanded farmers, mechanics, manufacturers, merchants, and even retired capitalists would like some convenient mode of investing their surplus means at fair rates of interest, and with a certainty that when a good opportunity is presented to make some business transaction they can have legal tender notes returned to them to use as money. Notes issued at six per cent. interest, and in denominations of $20, $50, $100, $200, $500, $1,000, $2,000 and $5,000 would be in a convenient form for all classes; and at this rate of interest there is no doubt that large amounts would be drawn into the Treasury. Savings banks, trust companies, and other places of deposit, now overburdened with money, would, no doubt, have drawn from them considerable amounts for investment in these interest-bearing notes. Guardians, executors, and trustees would largely invest their money in these Government securities. Insurance companies might invest in them, get six per cent. interest, and be sure, in cases of loss, to get legal tender notes with which to pay their outstanding policies. Even savings banks and trust companies might invest a part of their funds in these notes, and be able to respond when their depositors should call for their money. The operations under this section would be like deposits in banks, and it is very probable that $300,000,000 might be reached in a reasonable time. It would be, in fact, a national savings bank, so arranged that its benefits can be extended to all, while, at the same time, the Government would be able to realize a large amount of money to aid in the prosecution of the war. Some would draw out their funds from time to time, as occasions should arise for business operations, while others again would invest in new notes issued under the authority to re-issue them; and the average amount in the Treasury would be about the same from week to week. The average deposits in the banks in the city of New York are about the same. Their weekly published statements show that there is no great variation in the amount for weeks and months. * * * *

I was in favor of giving to them the highest legal sanction and the most desirable character possible, within the power of the Government, not above six per cent. interest, in order to prevent their depreciation. It would have cost so little to have given them this most desirable character of immediate convertibility, that I strongly urged its adoption, and upon the same principle that I urged the legal tender clause last year. The more desirable the notes are as an investment, the longer they would stay out, and the higher would be their price in the market. I trust, however, that, in their present shape, they will be sought after, and be a valuable aid to the people in the payment of internal revenue, and materially assist the Secretary in the arduous duties of furnishing the means for a vigorous prosecution of the war.

In nearly all the plans that have been submitted to the committee for providing means to carry on the Government for the next eighteen months, it has been proposed to issue more legal tender notes, if the exigencies of the service shall render a further issue necessary. The Secretary of the Treasury, in submitting the bill proposed by him for a loan of $900,000,000, says: 'The committee will observe that the provision in respect to loans is very general. Under it the Secretary will have the power to borrow money in any of the ordinary forms, or, if exigencies require, to make additional issues of United States notes.' I have an aversion to any considerable further issue of legal tender notes, and can only consent to it as an imperative necessity. I think too large an issue will tend to inflate prices; but I do not see how it can be avoided. I do not see how the soldiers are to be paid, or how the Government can be carried on, in any other way. I shall therefore vote for this provision, in connection with the other provisions of the bill, as a necessary measure to enable the Government to prosecute the war.

OUR ONLY HOPE OF RESTORING THE UNION IS IN MILITARY SUCCESS.

Sir, since the first gun was fired on Fort Sumter, my conviction has been deep and abiding that this was to be a long, expensive, bloody, and desperate conflict; and that it would be very difficult to determine in advance what results would flow from such a deadly encounter. I have never for a moment doubted that the leading conspirators meant to establish and maintain a separate government, and a total separation from the free States. This has been their deliberate purpose from the beginning. Nearly two years of concerted action, embittered by the most deadly conflict with the armed power of this Government, has consolidated their strength. They have organized a form of civil government, under a constitution, with Jefferson Davis as President for six years, who is surrounded by a cabinet, congress, judiciary, and all other officers necessary to keep it in full operation. This rebel government has organized and maintained a powerful army, which has been able thus far to successfully repulse every attempt that has been made on our part to take their capitol, distant only one hundred and twenty-five miles from the Hall in which we are now sitting.

Sir, I never believed, and do not now believe, that the cabal at Richmond, the only responsible power to which overtures of peace can be made, will listen to any offers of compromise, however liberal, which will induce them to throw up their present *de facto* government, come back into the Union, and submit to the constitutional Government over which Abraham Lincoln presides, or any other President that can be elected by the loyal people of the United States. Jefferson Davis and all the high officers about him are men of high political aspirations. Inordinate ambition, and a desire to rule, were the chief motives that prompted them to rebel against the Constitution and Government they had sworn to support. Those who suppose that Mr. Davis and his co-conspirators will voluntarily negotiate to surrender the power they now hold, have but little appreciation of the motives that stimulate them to so desperate and determined action. These desperate men are in *earnest*, and will fight to the death. They are men of ability, fighting for power, for empire, and will neither compromise nor surrender unless they are compelled to do so at the point of the bayonet, pressed forward by an overwhelming and crushing force. They must be whipped, badly whipped, before they will compromise or surrender. Any expectation to the contrary is not only fallacious, but mischievous in its consequences, because it divides and weakens the people in the loyal States, and prolongs the war.

Sir, I have no expectation that this rebellion will be crushed in many years unless there is a more united and a more determined effort on the part of the people in the northern States. The great fact to be ascertained by all doubting men is will Jefferson Davis compromise on any terms short of a separation? Will he voluntarily surrender the power he now holds? Will he receive any proposal for peace except on the terms of dividing the old Union, and a recognition of his government over the southern half. For myself, I have no desire to compromise, and no proposals to make to Mr. Davis or any of his cabinet; but those who do wish to make peace with the rebel government ought to submit their propositions at once, so that all compromisers may know what to do. If no compromise can be made with the rebel government, short of dissolving the Union, it should be known at the earliest moment possible, so that all doubters and cavilers may decide immediately what they will do. The daily expenses of the war are enormous. The public debt is running up at a fearful rate. This war ought not to be procrastinated a day longer by divisions at home. This state of things cannot be continued for any considerable length of time, without entailing a public debt so large that it will burden present and future generations. The best blood of the nation flows freely. Large numbers are killed in battle, but more die from exposure and disease than in any other way.

Sir, all this blood and treasure is given freely to crush the rebellion and maintain the Union. Why have we not been more successful? It is because we need more earnestness, greater determination manifested, better discipline in the army, and a closer unity of action. Unless these essential requisites can be had, and that speedily, I have very little hope of crushing the rebellion. The way to secure a permanent peace is, first of all, to annihilate the rebel forces. The army between Washington and Richmond must be beaten. The power of the rebel government is in their army. If they can maintain their military strength, their government will be perpetuated. If we cannot achieve decisive victories over the rebel forces, the Union is lost. The Union is priceless; it ought to be maintained, and it will be maintained if all citizens rise above party and perform their whole duty to the country. The people, our commanding generals, Congress, and the Executive, ought all, without regard to party distinctions, to rouse up to the magnitude and perils of the crisis, and by unity of action put forth an *earnest* and *determined* effort to crush the rebel armies. No compromise can be made or ought to be made. Our only hope is in military success. This is the only way in which we can maintain our finances, and restore the national Union.

$100,000,000 LEGAL TENDER NOTES REQUIRED TO PAY THE ARMY AND NAVY.

There was a large amount due to the army and navy, and complaints were being made in consequence of the delay in making payments. The subject was discussed by the Military Committees of the Senate and House. A resolution passed the House as follows:

"WHEREAS, Grevious delays happen in the payment of money due soldiers; therefore, in order to ascertain if any, and what, legislation may be necessary to remedy such delays,

Resolved, That the Secretary of the Treasury be requested to furnish to this House the reasons why requisitions of paymasters in the army are not promptly filled."

The Secretary made answer as follows:

"No one can feel a deeper regret than the Secretary that a single American soldier lacks a single dollar of his pay, and no effort of his has been wanting to prevent such a condition. It is not in his power, however, to arrest the accumulation of demands upon the Treasury beyond the possibility of provision for them *under existing legislation.*" * * * *

"The Secretary, solicitous to regulate his action by the spirit as well as the letter of the legislation of Congress, did not consider himself at liberty to make sales of the 5-20 bonds below the market value; and sales except below were impracticable."

SPEECH OF MR. GURLEY.

Mr. GURLEY, of Ohio, spoke of the great importance of our financial measures.

"The Government which can raise the largest amount of money must, in the end, triumph; that a large army was essential to success, but the most essential thing was money or money means. He did not agree with the Secretary in several things contained in his reports; the banking scheme, *which the Secretary admits would not afford any immediate relief,* should be rejected; we need a sensible, practicable plan that will furnish immediate means to pay the army and navy. He insisted that Congress, by the act of February 25, 1862, authorized the Secretary to sell $500,000,-000 six per cent. 5-20 bonds at 'the market value thereof,' *which he had not done, as intended by Congress,* and the consequence was that the soldiers and sailors were not paid, as they ought to have been before this time. Of course we do not call in question the motives of the Secretary, or deny his good intentions, but when the Secretary says, in his reply to the resolution of the House, that he had no authority, he was evidently *mistaken* in his construction of the law. The words 'market value' do not mean par value, nor at any specified time or sum. The market value was the *price they would bring when offered in the market.* There has been no business day or week since the law was passed, when any of the many agents of the Secretary in New York could not have placed one million, or several millions, in the market, and sold them somewhere near par, to raise money to pay the army and navy."

A joint resolution was proposed that provision ought to be made immediately by the Treasury Department to pay the sums due the soldiers and sailors, and that a preference should be given to this class of creditors. Secretary Chase was consulted on the subject, and in a letter dated January 7, 1863, addressed to the Finance Committee, he stated that the amount then due to the army and navy was about $60,000,000, and that provision ought to be made for immediate payment. He thought the temporary measure proposed might answer for present purposes, and concluded his letter as follows:

"It should be regarded, however, only as an *expedient* for an emergency. *No measure, in my judgment, will meet the necessities of the occasion, and prove adequate to the provision of the great sums required for the suppression of the rebellion, which does not include a firm support to public credit through the establishment of a uniform national circulation, secured by bonds of the United States.* The joint resolution and amendment are herewith returned.

With great respect, yours, etc.,

S. P. CHASE,
Secretary of the Treasury.

Hon. WILLIAM P. FESSENDEN,
Chairman Com. on Finance, U. S. Senate."

After some disagreement between the Finance Committee of the Senate and the Committee of Ways and Means of the House as to the right of the Senate to initiate a bill of this kind, a joint resolution was passed by the House and concurred in by the Senate, by yeas 38, nays 2; as follows:

Yeas—Messrs. Anthony, Arnold, Browning, Chandler, Clark, Collamer, Davis, Dixon, Doolittle, Fessenden, Foot, Foster, Hale, Harding, Harlan, Harris, Henderson, Howard, Howe, King, Lane (of Indiana), Lane (of Kansas), Latham, McDougall, Morrill, Nesmith, Rice, Sherman, Sumner, Ten Eyck, Trumbull, Wade, Wilkinson, Willey, Wilmot, Wilson (of Massachusetts), Wilson (of Missouri) and Wright—38.

Nays—Messrs. Powell and Saulsbury—2.

So the joint resolution was passed, and is as follows:

[PUBLIC RESOLUTION—NO. 4.]

"*Joint Resolution to provide for the immediate payment of the army and navy of the United States.*

WHEREAS, It is deemed expedient to make immediate provision for the payment of the army and navy; therefore

Be it resolved by the Senate and House of Representatives of the United States of America, in Congress assembled, That the Secretary of the Treasury be, and he is hereby authorized, if required by the exigencies of the public service, to issue on the credit of the United States the sum of one hundred millions of dollars of United States notes, in such form as he may deem expedient, not bearing interest, payable to bearer on demand, and of such denominations, not less than one dollar, as he may prescribe, which notes so issued shall be lawful money and a legal tender, like the similar notes heretofore authorized, in payment of all debts, public and private, within the United States, except for duties on imports and interest on the public debt; and the notes so issued shall be part of the amount provided for in any bill now pending for the issue of Treasury notes, or that may be passed hereafter by this Congress.

Approved January 17, 1863."

MESSAGE OF PRESIDENT LINCOLN.

The Speaker laid before the House the following message, in writing, from the President of the United States:

"*To the Senate and House of Representatives:*

I have signed the joint resolution to provide for the immediate payment of the army and navy of the United States, passed by the House of Representatives on the 14th, and by the Senate on the 15th inst.

The joint resolution is a simple authority, amounting, however, under existing circumstances, to a direction to the Secretary of the Treasury to make an additional issue of $100,000,000 in United States notes, if so much money is needed, for the payment of the army and navy.

My approval is given in order that every possible facility may be afforded for the prompt discharge of all arrears of pay due to our soldiers and our sailors.

While giving this approval, however, I think it my duty to express my sincere regret that it has been found necessary to authorize so large an additional issue of United States notes, when this circulation and that of the suspended banks together have become already so redundant as to increase prices beyond real values, thereby augmenting the cost of living to the injury of labor, and the cost of supplies to the injury of the whole country.

It seems very plain that continued issues of United States notes, without any check to the issues of suspended banks, and without adequate provision for the raising of money by loans, and for funding the issues so as to keep them within due limits, must soon produce disastrous consequences. And this matter appears to me so important that I feel bound to avail myself of this occasion to ask the special attention of Congress to it.

That Congress has power to regulate the currency of the country can hardly admit of a doubt; and that a judicious measure to prevent the deterioration of this currency by a reasonable taxation of bank circulation, or otherwise, is needed, seems equally clear. Independently of this general consideration, it would be unjust to the people at large to exempt banks, enjoying the special privilege of circulation, from their just proportion of the public burdens.

In order to raise money by loans most easily and cheaply, it is clearly necessary to give every possible support to the public credit. To that end a uniform currency, in which taxes, subscriptions and loans, and all other ordinary public dues, as well as all private dues may be paid, is almost, if not quite, indispensable. Such a currency can be furnished by banking associations, organized under a general act of Congress, as suggested in my message at the beginning of the present session. The security of this circulation, by the pledge of United States bonds, as therein suggested, would still further facilitate loans by increasing the present and causing a future demand for such bonds.

In view of the actual financial embarrassments of the Government, and of the greater embarrassments sure to come, if the necessary means of relief be not afforded, I feel that I should not perform my duty by a simple announcement of my approval of the joint resolution, which proposes relief only by increasing circulation, without expressing my earnest desire that measures, such in substance as those I have just referred to, may receive the early sanction of Congress. By such measures, in my opinion, will payment be most certainly secured, not only to the army and navy, but to all honest creditors of the Government, and satisfactory provision made for future demands on the Treasury.

January 17, 1863. ABRAHAM LINCOLN."

SPEECH OF MR. MORRILL.

"Mr. MORRILL, of Vermont, said we had often been called upon during this Congress to furnish means to carry on the war. The figures now are larger than ever before, being $900,000,000, and if the war should be prolonged to July 1, 1864, it is believed not to be too much. He was constrained now to give his vote for this measure, although such as in the outset he did not support, and never should have countenanced as an original proposition, because he knew of no other so efficient for immediate relief to the Treasury, and so safe to adopt. He should hold his opposition to legal tender in abeyance, so far as to allow money for the army and navy to be raised in this way, if it could be raised in no other. He was willing to restrain excessive issues of State Bank circulation by a proper tax, but did not think it best at this time to engage in a struggle for its extinction.

He was opposed to the *national bank bill* which he said was urged with great zeal and ability by the Secretary of the Treasury, and gave his reasons at length why, in his opinion, it ought not to pass. The new plan, fully executed, would obtain very little if any more aid from the banks than is already secured, and the Treasury at last, would find itself in actual possession of no more than a new dollar for an old one. *The Secretary admits in his annual report that 'little direct aid is, however, to be expected from this plan during the present, nor very much, perhaps, during the next year.'* "

MR. WARD'S SPEECH.

Mr. WARD, of New York, made an elaborate speech on the Finances and the currency.

"The condition of our financial affairs and the regulation of the circulating medium are regarded with much anxiety by the people of this country, from motives of their own personal interest, and yet more from patriotic devotion to the cause of unity in our great struggle for national existence. He was desirous of supporting the Government of his country in a vigorous prosecution of the war, but was opposed to the legal tender principle and voted against it. My earnest desire is, and always has been, to furnish the Government with every resource and power necessary to the suppression of the rebellion. From my solicitude for the re-establishment of the Republic, I desire to avert any increase of such paper money, as is now in use, knowing how injuriously it affects public confidence, enlarges expenditures by raising prices, lulls the public mind into false security, and lessens the vigilance which prevents frauds. He expressed himself in favor of a commission composed of the most wise and distinguished bankers and commercial men in co-operation with the Secretary to inquire into the best method of arranging our financial affairs."

SPEECH OF MR. WALKER.

Mr. AMASA WALKER, of Massachusetts, made a well considered speech in favor of the general provisions of the bill.

"He maintained that the vast expenditures involved in the prosecution of the war could not be raised except upon the credit of the Government. No ordinary means of raising revenue were sufficient to meet a great emergency like the present. The bill before us proposes measures of finance, currency and taxation. 1. An issue of bonds. 2. An issue of interest-bearing circulating notes, receivable for all Government dues, except customs. 3. An issue of legal tender notes, known in common parlance as greenbacks. 4. The issue of fractional parts of a dollar, to take the place of postal currency now in use. 5. Provides for deposits of bullion in the public Treasury *ad libitum*. 6. To tax the banks of circulation. 7. A proposition that the public funds may be deposited in these same banks, at the discretion of the Secretary of the Treasury.

He did not approve of paying interest in coin on the bonds, it has already exerted a pernicious influence on the public funds. He was in favor of the greenback circulation, and in favor of a six per cent. tax on State bank circulation, in order to drive it out, so as to give place to the national circulation. He urged adequate taxation to sustain the public credit, and thought that these measures had become a stern military necessity, and indispensable to a successful prosecution of the war.

On the 16th inst. Mr. Hooper offered a substitute for the bill, which was ordered to be printed. This substitute will be found printed at length in the *Cong. Globe*, p. 382.

After a long discussion, in which different members of the House participated, a vote was taken on the 23d inst. by tellers, in Committee of the Whole, on Mr. Hooper's substitute—ayes 62, noes 67; so the substitute was lost. Several minor amendments were however made to the original bill, and on the 26th inst. a vote was taken in the House on the substitute offered by Mr. Stevens, and it was decided in the negative—yeas 37, nays 91. The bill as amended was then passed without a division, and sent to the Senate for concurrence.

On the 13th of February the bill, after being amended, passed the Senate by the following vote:

Yeas—Messrs. Anthony, Arnold, Chandler, Clark, Collamer, Cowan, Davis, Dixon, Doolittle, Fessenden, Foot, Foster, Grimes, Harlan, Harris, Henderson, Hicks, Howard, Howe, King, Lane (of Indiana), Lane (of Kansas), Morrill, Nesmith, Pomeroy, Rice, Sherman, Sumner, Ten Eyck, Wade, Wilkinson and Wilson (of Massachusetts)—32.

Nays—Messrs. Carlisle, Powell, Richardson and Wall—4.

So the bill was passed.

Three several Conference Committees were appointed on the disagreeing votes between the two Houses. A compromise was finally made on the section taxing State bank circulation. All the amendments were finally agreed to, and the bill passed.

SYNOPSIS OF $900,000,000 LOAN ACT.

"The act to provide Ways and Means for the support of the Government. Approved March 3, 1863."

1. The first section authorized a loan of $300,000,000 for the then current year, and $600,000,000 for the then next fiscal year, and to issue bonds therefor at not less than ten nor more than forty years, at not exceeding six per cent. interest, in coin, not exceeding in all $900,000,000.

2. By section second of the same act the Secretary, in lieu of an equal amount of said bonds, was authorized to issue $400,000,000 of Treasury notes, bearing interest not exceeding six per cent., payable in lawful money, which notes, payable at periods expressed on their face, *might be made a legal tender at their face value.*

3. By the third section $150,000,000 in amount of United States notes, made a legal tender, might be issued. The restriction in the sale of bonds to '*market value*' was repealed. '*And the holders of United States notes issued under former acts, shall present the same for the purpose of exchanging them for bonds as therein provided, on or before the first of July, 1863, and thereafter the right to exchange the same shall cease and determine.*'

7. This section imposed a tax of one per cent. each half year, on a graduated scale of *State bank circulation*, according to the capital stock of each bank.

BANK BILL PASSED.

On the 2d February, 1863, the National Currency Bank bill, as prepared by Mr. Spaulding, in December, 1861, after being altered and amended in several important particulars, was reported from the Finance Committee to the Senate by John Sherman of Ohio. The debate upon it was opened on the 9th, and continued from day to day until the 12th, when it was passed by the following vote—yeas 23, nays 21, as follows:

Yeas—Messrs. Anthony, Arnold, Chandler, Clark, Doolittle, Fessenden, Foster, Harding, Harlan, Harris, Howard, Howe, Lane (of Kansas), Morrill, Nesmith, Pomeroy, Sherman, Sumner, Ten Eyck, Wade, Wilkinson, Wilmot, and Wilson (of Massachusetts)—23.

Nays—Messrs. Carlisle, Collamer, Cowan, Davis, Dixon, Foot, Grimes, Henderson, Hicks, Kennedy, King, Latham, McDougal,

Powell, Rice, Richardson, Saulsbury, Trumbull, Turpie, Wall and Wilson (of Missouri)—21.

So the bill was passed.

The bill as it passed the Senate was sent to the House on the 13th. On motion of Mr. Hooper it was ordered to be printed, but was not referred to the Committee of Ways and Means. It remained on the Speaker's table until the 19th, when it was taken up for consideration in the House. A motion to refer it to the Committee of the Whole having been defeated, Mr. Spaulding opened the debate in a lengthy speech in favor of the bill, which will be found in the Appendix. The debate continued until the 20th, when the bill was passed without amendment by the following vote—yeas 78, nays 64, as follows:

Yeas—Messrs. Aldrich, Alley, Ashley, Babbitt, Beaman, Bingham, Jacob B. Blair, Blake, Buffinton, Calvert, Campbell, Casey, Chamberlain, Clements, Colfax, Conway, Covode, Cutler, Davis, Delano, Dunn, Edgerton, Eliot, Ely, Fenton, Samuel C. Fessenden, Thomas A. D. Fessenden, Fisher, Frank, Goodwin, Granger, Hahn, Haight, Hickman, Hooper, Hutchins, Julian, Kelley, Francis W. Kellogg, William Kellogg, Lansing, Leary, Lovejoy, Law, McIndoe, McKean, McPherson, Marston, Maynard, Moorhead, Anson P. Morrill, Noell, Olin, Patton, Timothy G. Phelps, Potter, Alexander H. Rice, John H. Rice, Sargent, Sedgwick, Segar, Shanks, Shellabarger, Sherman, Sloan, Spaulding, Stevens, Trimble, Trowbridge, Van Horn, Van Wyck, Verree, Wall, Wallace, Washburne, Albert S. White, Windom and Worcester—78.

Nays—Messrs. William Allen, Ancona, Baily, Baker, Baxter, Biddle, Cobb, Frederick A. Conkling, Roscoe Conkling, Cox, Cravens, Crittenden, Dawes, Edwards, English, Gooch, Grider, Gurley, Hall, Harding, Harrison, Holman, Horton, Johnson, Kerrigan, Knapp, Law, Lazear, Loomis, Mallory, May, Menzies, Justin S. Morrill, Morris, Nixon, Noble, Norton, Nugen, Odell, Pendleton, Perry, Pike, Pomeroy, Porter, Price, Robinson, James S. Rollins, Sheffield, Shiel, John B. Steele, William G. Steele, Stiles, Stratton, Benjamin F. Thomas, Francis Thomas, Vallandigham, Wadsworth, Wheeler, Whaley, Chilton A. White, Wickliffe, Wilson, Woodruff and Wright—64.

So the bill was passed and approved by President Lincoln, March 25, 1863.

No National Bank currency was issued until about the first of January, 1864. After that time it was gradually issued. On the first of July, 1864, the sum of $25,825,695 had been issued; and on the 22d of April, 1865, shortly after the surrender of General Lee, the whole amount of National Bank circulation issued to that time, was only $146,927,975. It will therefore be seen that comparatively little direct aid was realized from this currency until *after* the close of the war. *All the channels of circulation were well filled up with the greenback notes, compound interest notes, and certificates of indebtedness, to the amount of over $700,000,000, before the National Bank act got fairly into operation.* This Bank issue was in fact an additional inflation of the currency.

THE RIGHT TO CONVERT NOTES INTO BONDS ABROGATED.

The first legal tender notes were issued bearing date March 10, 1862, and on the back of them was printed these words:

"This note is a legal tender for all debts, public and private, except duties on imports and interest on the public debt, *and is exchangeable for U. S. six per cent. bonds, redeemable at the pleasure of the United States after five years.*"

The right to exchange these notes at par for *six* per cent. bonds was distinctly authorized by the second section of the legal tender act, *and was in the nature of a contract* made by the Government with the holders of the notes. It was inserted as a just and equitable provision for the benefit of those persons who should be compelled, by the legal tender clause, to take the notes, by giving them, at any time, the privilege of converting them into a six per cent. bond. It was, in effect, a forced loan, but the right of immediately returning them to the Government for gold bonds, divested the forced character of the transaction of any material hardship. It also had a tendency to prevent any great inflation, for the reason that as soon as this currency became redundant in the hands of the people, and not bearing interest, they would invest it in the six per cent. bonds to prevent any loss of interest.

This right to exchange the notes for bonds was, at the request of Secretary Chase, taken away by the third section of the above act after July 1, 1863. It is true that the Secretary had still the *discretionary* power to receive the notes at par for bonds, but it never seemed to be quite right to change the law while any of the legal tender notes were outstanding with the above endorsement upon them.

After passing the $900,000,000 loan act and the national currency bank bill, authorizing $300,000,000 of national currency,

Congress adjourned on the 4th of March, 1863, leaving the Secretary of the Treasury clothed with most extraordinary discretionary power to carry on the financial affairs of the Government,

In April and May it became apparent that the paper currency was sufficiently expanded to enable the Secretary to float the 5-20 bonds authorized, to the amount of $500,000,000, by the first legal tender act, which, up to that time, had been taken only to a very limited amount.

JAY COOKE, an enterprising banker at Philadelphia, was employed as General Agent by Secretary Chase to negotiate these bonds. He advertised very extensively, and employed sub-agents in all the principal cities and towns in all the loyal States. The editors of newspapers and others were enlisted to bring the advantages and importance of this loan before the *people*, in order to make it a great popular loan, to be taken by them in large and small sums in all the loyal States. Mr. Cooke succeeded admirably in this undertaking. The loan became very popular, and was taken extensively by farmers, mechanics and laboring people in all the towns, villages and cities all over the country. By the first of July, 1863, the amount of $168,880,250 of these bonds were taken; and by the first of October following $278,511,500 had been taken up; and by the 21st of January following the whole sum of $500,000,000 had been taken at par, and the rush was so great near the closing out of the loan, that nearly $11,000,000 extra had been subscribed and paid for before notice could be given to sub-agents that the amount authorized by that act had been taken up. Congress, however, soon after authorized this extra sum to be issued.

This successful funding of 5-20 six per cent. bonds showed conclusively that it was not necessary to *inflate the currency* any further in order to raise the means to successfully prosecute the war. The *six* per cent. bonds would furnish sufficient inducement for people to take them at the rate of from $1,500,000 to $2,000,000 a day, which was about the amount required to pay the daily expenses of the Government. It looked as if the limit of paper money expansion had been reached; that the greenback currency would not further depreciate below the standard of gold: and that the price of commodities would not continue to advance.

MISTAKE OF THE TREASURY DEPARTMENT.

The policy of funding into *six* per cent. bonds, which had been successful during the last eight months, was changed to *five* per cent. 10-40 bonds, which proved unsuccessful, and funding to any considerable extent was arrested for several months. The people were not satisfied with this change made by the Secretary in the rate of interest. The loan became unpopular, and only $73,337,750 was taken between the 21st of January, 1864, and the 1st of July following, more than five months, and this sum was taken mostly by bankers, because the five per cent. bonds could be used in the organization of national banks. The Secretary had the *discretionary* power, under the $900,000,000 loan act, to continue the funding at *six* per cent., but he desired to lower the rate of interest, and believed that he could successfully negotiate the five per cent. bonds, which proved to be a mistake.

Congress passed an act supplementary to the $900,000,000 loan act, giving still further *discretionary* power to the Secretary. This act was approved March 3, 1864, and is the law under which the 10-40 five per cent. bonds above mentioned were issued. It authorized the Secretary to issue bonds not exceeding $200,000,000, bearing date March 1, 1864, or any subsequent date, redeemable at the pleasure of the Government after any period not less than five years, and payable at any period not more than forty years from date in coin, bearing interest *not exceeding six per cent.* per annum, payable on bonds not over $100, annually, and on all other bonds semi-annually, in coin.

IMPOLICY AT THIS TIME OF THE 10-40 BONDS—TWO LETTERS BY E. G. SPAULDING ON THIS SUBJECT.

"BUFFALO, March 19, 1864.

To Morris Ketchum, Esq., Banker, New York:

Dear Sir—When I met you in New York in December last, you expressed the apprehension that the rate of interest on government securities would be reduced to five per cent.; that there would be a further inflation of the currency; and, consequently, that gold would advance, and the price of labor and commodities would be greatly increased. The apprehensions which you then expressed are now being realized, and the government and people are alike feeling its evil effects. By reducing the rate of interest from six to five per cent. on bonds and notes issued to redeem greenback currency printed and paid out by the government, one per cent. interest is apparently saved to the government on its notes and bonds, but all the flour, beef, pork, and other supplies for the army and navy have advanced ten to fifteen per cent., thereby making it necessary for the government to pay ten to fifteen per cent. more for all supplies purchased, while it saves only one per cent. on its notes and bonds.

Five per cent. bonds, running from five to twenty years, can, no doubt, be floated on the market nominally at par, if the currency is sufficiently diluted and the volume increased large enough for that purpose; and so may four per cent. bonds be carried on the surface, if the currency is printed and paid out in such a large volume as to still further dilute the government paper already afloat. But if this should be successfully carried out, and four per cent. bonds be negotiated at par in consequence of a further expansion of the currency, gold would advance to 90 or 100 per cent., and all commodities for the army and navy would advance in the same proportion. What would be saved in the rate of interest would be lost fourfold on the enhanced price of all supplies purchased to carry on the war.

Five per cent. interest, payable in currency, which has been the rate since the twenty-first of January last, for redeeming legal tender notes, is a most exhilarating atmosphere to be reveled in by speculators and jobbers, but very unsatisfactory to men of steady purposes, who are engaged in manufactures, commerce, and other legitimate pursuits. With such a money market, all articles consumed by laborers advance in price, rents increase, skilled laborers and common laborers combine and strike for higher wages, in order to be able to pay for the enhanced prices of living caused by the excess of paper issue.

In order to illustrate what I desire to say further on this subject, you will, I trust, allow me to make a brief review of the laws of Congress bearing upon the increased price of labor and commodities, and the advance in the price of gold. Gold and silver, as you well know, are the standard of value in conducting the commerce of all the civilized nations of the world. The commerce of the United States is still carried on with all foreign nations with gold as the standard or measure of value.

The laws of Congress, passed in 1792, fixed the gold standard in the United States, for the ten dollar eagle, at two hundred and forty-seven grains and four-eighths of a grain of pure gold, or two hundred and seventy-five grains of standard gold, and half that quantity for the half eagle. The law of Congress, passed in 1837, changed the gold standard established in 1792, by providing that the standard of both gold and silver should be such, that of one thousand parts by weight, nine hundred parts should be pure metal and one hundred of alloy; that the alloy of silver coins should be of copper, and the alloy of gold coins should be of copper and silver. That the weight of the gold eagle should be two hundred and fifty-eight grains, that of the half eagle one hundred and twenty-nine grains, and that the eagle should be a legal tender for ten dollars, and the half eagle for five dollars. This was the *standard value* up to the time when the legal tender note bill was passed.

The last loan of $50,000,000, made by the government before the suspension of specie payments, was on the issue of six per cent. twenty year bonds at 89¼, being a *discount* of 10¾ per cent., and a loss to the Treasury of about $5,338,769. The agreement for this loan was made with the associated banks of New York, Boston and Philadelphia, in the fall of 1861. It was made on a specie basis, and in the efforts made by the banks to pay the gold on this loan into the Sub-Treasury, it brought on such a stringency in the money market as to cause a general suspension of specie payments on the 31st of December, 1861, which made it exceedingly difficult for the banks to pay the last instalments to complete the loan. No further loans could be negotiated except at a still greater discount; indeed, it was deemed nearly or quite impossible to make any further loans on a specie basis, unless at the most ruinous rates of discount. There was then due to the army and navy, and for supplies, not less than $100,000,000, and at least $200,000,000 more would be required within six months. The *necessity* for immediate action was most pressing and urgent. We were grappling with a most gigantic rebellion. We were in a most extraordinary crisis, and extraordinary measures had to be resorted to, in order to save the government and preserve our nationality. In this great emergency the original legal tender note bill, introduced by me as a necessary war measure, and which, after being amended and passed, was approved by the President February 25th, 1862, changed the standard of value, not with the world at large, but within the United States, by authorizing the Secretary of the Treasury to issue $150,000,000 of United States notes to circulate as currency, making them lawful money and a legal tender for all debts, public and private, and providing for their redemption at all times at the Treasury Department in five-twenty six per cent. bonds, interest payable semi-annually in coin; and further authorizing the issue of $500,000,000 of these bonds for that purpose. This was not the issue of an irredeemable paper currency. There was a fixed standard and measure of value for the redemption of all these legal tender notes as they should be issued and re-issued from time to time. That standard was five-twenty six per cent. bonds, principal and interest payable in gold, whatever might be their value. Every person who should receive these notes voluntarily, or by compulsion, knew exactly what he could do with them. He knew that the laws of Congress provided that he should have gold bearing bonds for all the notes taken by him. The redemption in this case was not gold *on demand* as formerly, but six per cent. *interest* in gold every six months, and the principal payable in gold within twenty years. This was the standard of value fixed by the legal tender note bill. It was in effect a *forced loan* from the people to the government, but at a fair rate of interest for both the lender and the borrower.

This was a radical change in the standard or measure of value within the United States, but it was a *fixed standard established by law*, and every business man could act upon it, and shape all his contracts and business transactions accordingly.

The act of July 11th, 1862, authorized a further issue of $150,000,000 of legal tender notes, and requiring their redemption by the government at all times, on demand, in the 5.20 six per cent. bonds; still leaving the standard of value of legal tender notes by providing for their conversion at any time into six per cent. United States bonds, principal and interest payable in gold. Although this was in effect a forced loan from the people, it was so fair and equitable in its terms, the peril of the country so great, and the object to be attained in crushing the rebellion so important, that no loyal citizen could object to it. There was no very great danger that the currency would become excessively inflated so long as every person holding greenbacks, not bearing interest, could exchange them at his own will into gold-bearing bonds at six per cent. interest per annum.

In the remarks which I made in the House on the 17th of June, 1862, in favor of this additional issue of legal tender notes, I said that 'I never have been, and I trust I never shall be, unnecessarily an advocate for the creation of an unsound or an inflated currency; but, sir, I have long ago resolved, since this savage war has been forced upon us, to do whatever was necessary, and which I might lawfully do, to crush out the traitors and annihilate their armies. This cannot be done without the 'sinews of war.' Your army and navy must be supplied with all the terrible armament necessary to crush the enemy. Your sick, wounded and famishing soldiers must all be supplied with hospitals, medical attendance, and all necessaries and conveniences to make them comfortable. This is a plain duty which we cannot any of us fail to perform. If, in the performance of this duty, it becomes necessary to authorize a further issue of United States notes, I shall not hesitate to give my vote for it. I am not in favor of increasing the issue of them beyond the imperative necessities of the government to sustain the army and navy. I much prefer to have our six per cent. bonds issued on permanent loans. I would like to see the Secretary of the Treasury borrow at par all the money he can on the six per cent. bonds heretofore authorized to be issued.

When money can be obtained at par on six per cent. bonds, I would prefer to have that done to the issuing a very large amount of legal tender notes. Too large an issue of demand notes, to circulate as money, will no doubt lead to an expansion which will inflate prices, stimulate undue speculations, and ultimately produce a reaction that will derange the whole business of the country. This is to be avoided if possible. I cannot therefore, advocate any greater issue of demand notes than the absolute necessities of the government requires to carry on the war with vigor. I am disposed to give the Secretary power to issue the additional $150,000,000 United States notes asked for by him; but, at the same time, I feel the importance of having this power exercised discreetly, and I trust that he will not issue, or pay them out at all, when money can be obtained at par on our six per cent. bonds. I do not understand that the Secretary intends to have them all issued and put into circulation at any one time; on the contrary, I believe he has no such intention. He wants the power to issue and use them if necessary, but not otherwise. When he can obtain a sufficient amount of money at par, on six per cent. bonds, or by temporary deposits in the Treasury, there will be no necessity for their issue, and the Secretary assures us in his letter that no further issues of notes will be made when that can be done; and, besides, the bill provides for this retaining in his own hands legal tender notes equal to one-third of the temporary deposits that may be in the Treasury.'

The government was carried on smoothly and the war prosecuted vigorously under this system up to January 21, 1864, when the 5-20 six per cent. bonds authorized by the act of 25th of February, 1862, were exhausted. In the mean time, the standard of value for the redemption of greenbacks had been changed, *which is the principal cause of the present advance in the price of gold and other commodities and services, as I will now proceed to show.*

The act of the 3d of March, 1863, to provide ways and means for the support of the government, commonly called the $900,000,000 loan bill, so modified the legal tender note bill as to leave it in the discretion of the Secretary of the Treasury to fix the time and manner of issuing the bonds or notes, and the rate of interest they should bear under the act. It gives him the power to issue them at six per cent., five per cent., or even at a lower rate of interest if he deems advisable; but under the modification of the act, *there is no longer any standard of value fixed by law.* It rests with the Secretary to say, from time to time, what the rate of interest shall be. He also has the power to issue and re-issue legal tender notes on demand and on time in sufficient volume to float five per cent., and even four per cent. bonds and notes, if he shall deem it advisable to do so. No man can regulate his contracts or business affairs with any certainty. No person, when he takes legal tender greenback currency, can fix in his own mind what is its real value. It is no longer convertible at the will of the holder into United States six per cent. bonds, nor is there any provision in the law which compels the government to redeem them in any kind of bonds, or in any other way—except for dues to the government. It has, however, been the practice of the Treasury Department during the past two months to redeem legal tender greenbacks, not bearing interest, by exchanging for them one and two years Treasury notes bearing five per cent. interest, both principal and interest payable *in currency*.

I did not, at the last session of Congress, think it wise to change the standard of value fixed in the legal tender note bill. I thought it better to issue and pay out to the army and navy, and other creditors of the Government, an amount of greenbacks sufficient to float, easily, the five-twenty six per cent. bonds, but no more. I believed seven and 3-10 per cent. interest too high a rate; but I deemed it fair and just that on forced loans of this kind that the Government should pay six per cent., and that the war should be prosecuted until the rebellion should be crushed, on the basis of six per cent. interest on all the funded debt to accomplish that result. I thought it better for the Government and the people that there should be that stability attached to business transactions which can only be fully realized by a public law establishing the measure of value. In the remarks which I made in the House on the 12th of January, 1863, I said, 'that Congress, by its legislation at the last session, has, to a considerable extent, changed the standard of value for all business operations with the United States. The standard of value fixed by Congress is legal tender Treasury notes, *convertible at any time* into United States specie-paying bonds, bearing interest at the rate of six per centum per annum, payable half-yearly in coin, based upon adequate taxation upon the entire property of the country. Legal tender notes constitute the national currency now established by law. *All exchanges of property, all contracts, and all loans, are based upon the value of legal tender notes and United States six per cent. bonds.*'

At a later period in the session the $900,000,000 act was passed. I was not in favor of the change made by that act in the standard of value, or rather I was not in favor of the discretionary power given to the Secretary of the Treasury to change it, as provided in the act; not because I had not full confidence in the Secretary, but because I thought it better that so important a matter, relating as it does to the stability of the whole business operations of the country, should be fixed in the law itself, so that all men could shape their business accordingly. This would have relieved the Secretary from a vast responsibility, and the inflations, fluctuations and changes now so apparent would have been less likely to have happened. I reluctantly assented to the change. It was against my better judgment, and I am now satisfied that it was a mistake.

The daily conversions, during the past year, of legal tender notes into the 5-20 six per cent. bonds, at the rate of from one to two millions a day, furnished the means for paying the daily expenditures of the Government; the conversions went on so smoothly, so steadily and so satisfactorily to all parties, without causing any great inflation of the currency, or increase in the price of labor or commodities, that I was in hopes it would be continued by the Secretary, under the discretionary power given him to continue it, under the $900,000,000 loan bill. This would have kept things steady, kept down the price of gold, and would probably have prevented any necessity for paying out the *reserve* $50,000,0000 of greenbacks which have been issued since the meeting of Congress, and over

$150,000,000 five per cent. one and two years legal tender notes, also issued and circulated to a considerable extent as currency, making about $200,-000,000 that have been printed and paid out since the meeting of Congress in December last, which, added to the $400,000,000 of greenbacks previously issued, amounts altogether to $600,000,000 of greenbacks and legal tender Treasury notes, and which is probably a volume of currency large enough to float the proposed new issue of five per cent. ten-forty bonds; but it is not my wish or desire to say a word that will in any way retard or embarrass the operations of the government in a vigorous prosecution of the war to put down this gigantic and wicked rebellion, and effectually remove the cause that brought on such a bloody war. The last man and the last dollar are pledged for this purpose, and, *if necessary*, to inflate the currency to such an extent that 10-40 five per cent. bonds may be floated at par, I am ready to yield my assent to such a measure, and will lend my feeble efforts to sustain the administration in carrying it out. The rebellion must be crushed at all hazards, and at every sacrifice.

The principal object I have in writing to you at this time, is to solicit the co-operation of our friends in New York in submitting to Congress the propriety of *establishing, by law*, the standard value of legal tender notes, by fixing the rate of interest at which they may at any time be converted into the funded debt of the United States, principal and interest payable in gold. If it is to be five per cent. bonds, gold and prices will be considerably higher than they will be if such notes are convertible into six per cent. bonds. I think it will be cheaper in the end, and specie payments can be resumed at an earlier day, for the Government to continue the conversion of legal tender notes into six per cent. bonds, because gold will be lower and prices less; but whatever the rate of interest is to be, I trust it will be fixed in the law itself, so that all business men may be able to shape their contracts and business in accordance with the public law establishing such standard of value.

I intended to say a few words on one or two other points, but this letter is already longer than I intended, and I must defer to some other more convenient time what more I may desire to say on the national finances.

I remain yours, very truly,

E. G. SPAULDING.

NEW YORK, March 21.

My Dear Sir—I am in receipt of your favor of the 19th inst., upon the subject of national finances.

It expresses fully and clearly my own views—so admirably, in fact, that I beg your permission to publish it, as I think it of great importance that the attention of business men should be drawn to the subject—than which nothing is of greater or *more immediate* consequence to their interests. Truly yours,

MORRIS KETCHUM.

Hon. E. G. SPAULDING.

BUFFALO, April 11, 1864.

Morris Ketchum, Esq., Banker, N. Y.:

Dear Sir—Referring to my letter to you of the 19th of March last, I desire to make some additional remarks on the National Finances. It is a subject upon which I feel a deep interest, for you well know that if we fail here there is danger that we may not succeed in accomplishing what is the most ardent wish of all patriotic citizens—that of crushing the rebellion, and a restoration of the national unity. The national debt will increase at a fearful rate, under any policy that can be devised, and prudent, patriotic citizens are looking anxiously at the result of measures that are adopted. Desiring, as I do, the crushing of the rebellion in the shortest time, and with the least possible expenditure of blood and treasure, I venture to make a few suggestions further on the future policy of executing the $900,000,000 loan act.

It seems to me that the policy of the Treasury Department for the last three months has been that of *inflation, and over-issues of a paper circulating medium*. It has, by such a policy, unintentionally stimulated and encouraged speculations in gold, stocks and other things, rather than to encourage industry, the production of commodities, and other legitimate business. Under this policy, gold has advanced 20 per cent., and the price of labor and commodities continues to increase to such an extent as to render it very embarrassing for business men to carry on their ordinary pursuits. I know very well that these evils cannot be fully guarded against during the prosecution of such a gigantic war, and the large amount of paper necessarily issued by the Government; but it is the duty of the Government that these evils should be mitigated and rendered as light as possible.

The Department has partially executed the $900,000,000 loan act; the first section of which authorized the Secretary to borrow the *whole amount* of nine hundred millions of dollars on the ten-forty bonds, bearing six per cent. (or, in his discretion, five or four per cent.) interest payable semi-annually in coin; or, by other sections of the bill, he had the discretionary power to print and pay out to creditors of the Government an additional amount of $150,000,000 of greenbacks, and $400,000,000 legal tender Treasury notes, which, in the form issued by him, circulate to a considerable extent as currency; and a further contingent authority to issue a still further sum of $150,000,000 of greenbacks; but the whole aggregate of all kinds of bonds and notes to be issued under the bill was not to exceed $900,000,000.

In administering and carrying into effect the provisions of this act, it is plain that, by borrowing on the issue of ten-forty six per cent. bonds under the first section of the act, the tendency would be to repress and keep down inflation, prevent speculation in stocks, gold and other commodities, and, at the same time, by holding a steady money market, encourage all kinds of productive industry and other legitimate pursuits.

On the other hand, by resorting to the other sections of the bill and issuing greenbacks and legal tender treasury notes in large volume, the currency is still further expanded and cheapened to such an extent that all legitimate business is greatly embarrassed by the increase in the price of labor, the cost of living, transportation, and the cost of the raw materials used in building, manufacturing, and other industrial operations.

In the partial execution of this law, the Treasury Department has printed and paid out $150,000,000 greenbacks as currency, and over $175,000,000 of one and two years legal tender Treasury notes, which also circulate to a considerable extent as currency, making $325,000,000 of *inflating* paper issued under this act, thus far; while the department has only borrowed on a *permanent loan*, under the first section of the bill and the supplementary act, less than $15,000,000 on *five* instead of six per cent. ten-forty bonds. The whole policy thus far under this law has been one of *inflation* on temporary loans, rather than *funding* on long government bonds at a fair rate of interest.

It has been supposed that by this policy of inflation a five per cent. ten-forty bond might be floated nominally at par. Funding the present excessive floating debt at five per cent. interest is better than not to be funded at all, and I hope that the bonds now offered at five per cent. may be taken up rapidly, and that the evils of the present inflation may be removed; but I fear the conversions will not be rapid enough at this rate of interest. The bonds do not seem to be readily taken, as yet, by the people. It required the printing and paying out of $400,000,000 of greenbacks before the five-twenty *six* per cent. bonds could be floated easily at par, and it will probably require the circulating paper issues of the Government, now amounting to about $625,000,000, to be increased to $650,000,000 or $700,000,000, before the people will be induced to take five per cent. bonds in order to get rid of the surplus circulation that may accumulate in their hands, that cannot be more profitably invested in other modes.

I agree with all that has been said by the Press and in Congress in favor of annual taxation to the amount of $300,000,000. At the extra session of Congress in July, 1861, I advocated immediate taxation to the extent of paying the annual expenses of the government on a peace footing, and the interest on all the war debt, and I have advocated that policy ever since. I hope Congress will not adjourn without providing for raising at least the sum of $300,000,000 each year by taxation. Assuming that Congress will provide for raising that sum by taxation for the next fiscal year, still the whole expenses of the year will not be less than $1,000,000,000, which will leave the additional sum of $700,000,000 to be borrowed in some form to pay the expenses of the army and navy. This brings us to the *practical question:* How is this large sum to be obtained? Shall it be on temporary issues of paper calculated to still further inflate the currency already afloat, thereby adding to the embarrassments already bad enough; or shall it be on a permanent loan, based on the issue of long bonds, principal and interest payable in gold, and at such a fair rate of interest that the bonds will be readily taken, in such large amounts as not only to make any further temporary issues under the $900,000,000 act unnecessary, but also materially diminish the present excess of paper currency? This would check speculation, and bring down the price of gold and all other commodities to a more safe and stable standard.

It is of great consequence for all business men to know what is to be the *future policy* of the Treasury Department. Whether it will still further *inflate* the currency by temporary expedients, or whether it will *contract* the floating debt by funding in long bonds. Shall it be inflation and high prices, or contraction and lower prices? This question is of vital interest, affecting the large purchases of the Government in the prosecution of the war, as well as the legitimate business of the people.

If the Treasury Department will print and put at the disposal of the people ten-forty bonds, paying six per cent. interest semi-annually in coin, for the balance of the $900,000,000 loan, it will be so rapidly taken, judging from the manner in which conversions were made into the 5-20 bonds, that all its other printing presses employed in printing temporary circulating paper may be safely stopped until this loan is exhausted, and with the most beneficial results to the Government and the people.

I remain, yours, truly,

E. G. SPAULDING.

SECRETARY CHASE RESIGNS, AND WM. P. FESSENDEN APPOINTED SECRETARY OF THE TREASURY.

The attempt of the Secretary of the Treasury to float five per cent. 10-40 bonds made it necessary, in order to pay the current expenses of the Government, to issue and keep out large amounts of currency in the form of greenbacks, legal tender notes, interest-bearing Treasury notes, certificates of indebtedness, postal and fractional currency, and national bank notes, besides the currency issued by State banks. Gold and commodities continued to advance in price. On the 15th of January, '64, gold was 1.55, on the 15th of April 1.78, on the 15th of June 1.97, and on the 29th of June 2.35 to 2.50, which showed that the legal tender notes were worth only forty cents on a dollar in gold.

On the 30th of June, 1864, Secretary Chase resigned the office of Secretary of the Treasury. President Lincoln announced the fact to the Senate by nominating David Todd, of Ohio, to fill the vacancy, which was the first announcement of the resignation of Gov. Chase. Gov. Todd declined the appointment. Mr. George Harrington, Assistant Secretary, was appointed Secretary of the Treasury *ad interim*. William P. Fessenden, U. S. Senator from Maine, with some reluctance, finally consented to take the place.

He was nominated and confirmed, and entered upon the duties of the office on the 5th of July.

He subsequently published a statement of the audited public debt as it existed on the books of the Treasury Department on the 30th day of June, which was the close of the fiscal year, and the day that Secretary Chase resigned, showing the total amount of debt to be $1,740,690,489.49. The 10-40 five per cent. bonds amounted only to $73,337,750.

This statement showed that the currency items and others operating to inflate prices were as follows:

U. S. notes, greenbacks	$431,178,670 84
Postal, fractional currency	22,894,877 25
Interest-bearing legal tender Treasury notes	168,571,450 00
Certificates of indebtedness	160,720,000 00
National bank notes	25,825,695 00
Add State bank circulation, not less than	135,000,000 00
	$944,190,693 09
Seven-thirty Treasury notes $109,356,150 00	
Temporary deposits for which certificates were issued $ 72,330,191 44	—$181,686,341 44
June 30, 1864, total inflating paper issued	$1,125,877,034 53

This great inflation, with the military situation doubtful and unsatisfactory, caused gold to advance until July 11, 1864, when it reached its highest quotation, 2.85½, or, more accurately speaking, the United States notes continued to decline until they were only worth in gold 35 cents on the dollar at the Board of Brokers in the city of New York.

It was thought at the time that the *gold bill* passed by Congress, and approved June 17, 1864, prohibiting time contracts for the sale of gold and foreign exchange, operated to *advance the price* of gold, instead of depressing it. It was intended by Congress, in passing the act, to prevent the gold speculators from operating for an *advance*, but it had the contrary effect, and only aggravated the difficulty. The price of gold would advance in spite of the legal enactments, and the act only continued in force fifteen days, (the 2d of July) when it was repealed.

Secretary Fessenden says "that on assuming the office on the 5th of July he found his condition peculiarly embarrassing. The cash balance in the Treasury was, on the first of July, $18,842,558.71, and the unpaid requisitions, chiefly for the army, were $71,814,000, and the daily expenditures $2,250,000." The loan of $33,000,000, advertised by Secretary Chase on the 25th of June, was withdrawn on the 2d of July. Secretary Fessenden raised the means to carry on the Government to March 4, 1865, by the issue of greenbacks, 7-30 Treasury notes, interest-bearing Treasury notes, certificates of indebtedness, loans of money obtained on six per cent. 5-20 bonds, and the receipts from taxes. In his Annual Report he says:

"The experience of the past few months cannot have failed to convince the most careless observer that, whatever may be the effect of a redundant circulation upon the price of coin, other causes have exercised a greater and more deleterious influence. In the course of a few days the price of this article rose from $1.50 to $2.85 in paper for $1.00 in specie, and subsequently fell, in as short a period, to $1.87, and then again rose, as rapidly, to $2.50; and all without any assignable cause, traceable to an increase or decrease in the circulation of paper money, or an expansion or contraction of credit, or other similar influence on the market, tending to occasion a fluctuation so violent. It is quite apparent that the solution of the problem may be found in the unpatriotic and criminal efforts of speculators, and probably of secret enemies, to raise the price of coin, regardless of the injury inflicted upon the country—or, desiring to inflict it."

UNITED STATES NOTES LIMITED TO $400,000,000.

By the second section of the act of June 30, 1864, it was provided that "the total amount of United States notes *issued, or to be issued, shall not exceed* $400,000,000, and such additional sum not exceeding $50,000,000, as may be temporarily required for the redemption of temporary loans."

This act contained a further provision that "all bonds, Treasury notes, and *other obligations* of the United States, shall be exempt from taxation, by or under State or municipal authority;" and the last section of this act declares that "the words '*obligation* or other security of the United States,' used in this act, shall be held to include and mean all bonds, coupons, national currency, United States notes, Treasury notes, fractional notes, checks for money of authenticated officers of the United States, certificates of indebtedness, certificates of deposits, stamps, and other representatives of value of whatever denomination, which have been or may be issued under any act of Congress."

This act also authorized the issue of $200,000,000 of interest-bearing *Treasury notes*, payable at any time not exceeding three years from date, and made a legal tender at their *face value* to the same extent as United States notes, except in redemption of notes issued by banks. And the power to issue interest-bearing Treasury notes, *of this character*, was still further enlarged by the act of January 28, 1865. *This was the last act of Congress giving power to the Secretary of the Treasury to issue any kind of legal tender notes.*

HOW SECRETARY McCULLOCH PAID THE ARMY AT THE CLOSE OF THE WAR.

Upon the inauguration of President Lincoln for a second term, Hugh McCulloch was appointed Secretary of the Treasury in place of Mr. Fessenden, who wished to be relieved from the duties of the office, and who returned again to the Senate. Secretary McCulloch did not increase the issue of United States notes, but continued the issue of bonds, 7-30 Treasury notes, and compound interest-bearing Treasury notes made a legal tender at their face value. After the surrender of the rebel armies to General Grant and General Sherman, the volunteer army was mustered out of the service, and had to be paid in full. Secretary McCulloch obtained the means to pay them chiefly by the issue of 7-30 Treasury notes, which were negotiated under the general agency of Jay Cooke, at par. The amount required for this purpose was very large, and the amount of 7-30 Treasury notes outstanding in October, 1865, after paying the army was $830,000,000, which were convertible in three years into 5-20 six per cent. bonds. The public debt during that month run up to about the highest figures it ever reached. The following is a statement of the debt, without deducting funds in the Treasury, as it stood on the books of the Treasury Department on the 31st of October, 1865.

STATEMENT OF THE PUBLIC DEBT.

Bonds, 10-40's, five per cent., due in 1904		$172,770,100 00
Bonds, Pacific Railroad, 6 per cent., due in 1895		1,258,000 00
Bonds, 5-20's, 6 per cent., due in 1882, 1884 and 1885		659,259,600 00
Bonds, 6 per cent., due in 1881		265,347,400 00
Bonds, 5 per cent., due in 1880		18,415,000 00
Bonds, 5 per cent., due in 1874		20,000,000 00
Bonds, 5 per cent., due in 1871		7,022,000 00
		$1,144,072,100 00
Bonds, 6 per cent., due in 1868	$ 8,908,341 80	
Bonds, 6 per cent., due in 1867	9,415,250 00	
Compound interest notes, due in 1867-'68	173,012,141 00	
7-30 Treasury notes, due in 1867 and 1868	830,000,000 00—	1,021,335,732 80
Bonds, Texas indemnity, part due	760,000 00	
Bonds, Treasury notes, etc., part due	613,920 09—	1,373,920 09
Temporary loans, ten days' notice	99,107,745 46	
Certificates of indebtedness, due in 1866	55,905,000 00	
Treasury notes, 5 per cent., Dec. 1, 1865	32,536,901 00—	187,549,646 46
United States notes	428,160,569 00	
Fractional currency	26,057,469 20—	454,218,038 20
Total debt October 31, 1865		$2,808,549,437 55
National bank notes issued		$185,000,000 00
State bank notes issued		65,000,000 00
Total bank circulation		$250,000,000 00

TARIFF AND INTERNAL REVENUE LAWS.

The act of July 1, 1862, called the INTERNAL REVENUE LAW, was passed, providing for a levy of duties on various domestic manufactures, upon trades and occupations, and also providing a system of stamp, license, income, and other duties. And the act of July 14th, of the same year, largely increased the duties on imports. These laws were from time to time amended and enlarged, until large sums were realized from this mode of taxation, and formed a very substantial basis on which to rest the credit of the Government for the large issue of notes, bonds and other obligations. Enough money was realized from these sources to pay the ordinary expenses of the Government, all the interest on the war debt, and liquidate a considerable portion of the principal. The total debt, October 31, 1865, was over $2,800,000,000, and it does not at the present time much exceed $2,500,000,000, exclusive of Pacific Railroad bonds.

CONTRACTION OF THE CURRENCY.

Secretary McCulloch, in his first annual report, 4th of December, 1865, expressed the opinion "that the legal tender acts were war measures, passed in a great emergency; that they should be regarded only as temporary; that they ought not to remain in force a day longer than would be necessary to enable the people to prepare for a return to the gold standard; and that the work of retiring the notes which have been issued, should be commenced without delay, and carefully and persistently continued until all are retired." The House of Representatives on the 18th December, 1865, concurred in these views, expressed in the annual report of Mr. McCulloch, by the adoption of the following resolution offered by Mr. Alley, of Massachusetts:

Resolved, That this House cordially concurs in the views of the Secretary of the Treasury in relation to the necessity of a contraction of the currency, with a view to as early a resumption of specie payments as the business interests of the country will permit; and we hereby pledge co-operative action to this end as speedily as possible.

The above resolution was passed by the following vote—yeas 144, nays 6, as follows:

Messrs. Alley, Allison, Ames, Ancona, Anderson, James M. Ashley, Baldwin, Banks, Barker, Baxter, Beaman, Bergen, Bidwell, Bingham, Blow, Boutwell, Boyer, Brandegee, Brooks, Broomall, Bundy, Reader W. Clarke, Sidney Clarke, Conkling, Cook, Cullom, Darling, Dawes, Dawson, Defrees, Delano, Deming, Dennison, Dixon, Driggs, Eldridge, Eliot, Farquhar, Ferry, Finck, Garfield, Grider, Griswold, Hale, Aaron Harding, Abner C. Harding, Hart, Hayes, Henderson, Higby, Hill, Hogan, Holmes, Hooper, Hotchkiss, Asahel W. Hubbard, Chester D. Hubbard, Demas Hubbard, John H. Hubbard, Edwin N. Hubbell, James R. Hubbell, Hulbard, James Humphrey, Ingersoll, Jencks, Johnson, Julian, Kasson, Kelley, Kelso, Kerr, Ketcham, Kuykendall, Laflin, Latham, George V. Lawrence, William Lawrence, Longyear, Marshall, Marston, Marvin, McClurg, McIndoe, McKee, McRuer, Mercur, Miller, Moorhead, Morrill, Moulton, Myers, Niblack, Nicholson, Noell, O'Neill, Orth, Paine, Patterson, Perham, Phelps, Pike, Plants, Price, Radford, Samuel J. Randall, William H. Randall, Raymond, Alexander H. Rice, John H. Rice, Ritter, Rollins, Ross, Rousseau, Sawyer, Scofield, Shanklin, Shellabarger, Sitgreaves, Sloan, Spaulding, Starr, Stillwell, Strouse, Taber, Taylor, Thornton, Trimble, Trowbridge, Upson, Van Aernam, Burt Van Horn, Robert T. Van Horn, Voorhees,

Ward, Warner, Elihu B. Washburn, William B. Washburn, Welker, Wentworth, Whaley, Williams, James F. Wilson, Stephen F. Wilson and Wright—144.

Nays—Messrs. Baker, Cobb, Eckley, Harris, Smith, and Thayer—6.

In order to carry into effect the above resolution, Congress, by the act of March 12, 1866, authorized the Secretary of the Treasury to exchange bonds for notes, but "that of United States notes not more than $10,000,000 should be retired and canceled within six months from the passage of the act, and thereafter not more than $4,000,000 should be retired in any one month."

Under the provisions of this act the Secretary commenced retiring and canceling legal tender notes, but *contraction* very soon began to affect speculators and the debtor class of the community, who raised a cry against the course pursued by the Secretary. As contraction gradually went on, money became more in demand, and it soon became unpopular with a large class of the community. Members of Congress very soon changed their opinions on the subject, and in January, 1868, a law was passed, declaring "that from and after its passage, the authority of the Secretary of the Treasury to make any reduction of the currency by retiring or canceling United States notes, shall be and is hereby suspended."

Before this law was passed Secretary McCulloch had reduced the circulation of United States notes down to about $356,000,000, which at this time (April, 1869), is the amount outstanding, and for which the Government is still liable, besides fractional currency amounting to over $36,000,000.

THE PUBLIC FAITH.

Since the close of the war there has been considerable discussion in regard to the meaning of the words used in the legal tender act.

It has been insisted by a large class of citizens that the 5-20 bonds might, after five years, be redeemed in legal tender notes, instead of gold and silver. Others insisted that the bonds are payable in "dollars," which means gold and silver coin, and that an attempt to pay in legal tender notes would not be payment but merely changing the *form* of the debt. That a matured debt cannot be discharged by another promise; that it is contrary to reason that a bond should be paid in an inferior obligation; and that it would be unjust to force inconvertible paper, without interest, in payment of an interest-bearing obligation, especially as the right was given in the original act to fund legal tender notes at any time in the bonds which were authorized by the same act. Taking up bonds not due with greenback notes, would simply be to *unfund* a debt already funded, which would be contrary to the whole spirit and intent of the legal tender act.

To remove all doubt upon the subject, and with a view to improve the public credit, Mr. Shenck, Chairman of the Committee of Ways and Means, reported a bill, which, after a lengthy discussion, was amended, and finally passed both Houses of Congress.

The following is the vote by which it passed the House. Yeas 97, nays 47.

Yeas—Messrs. Allison, Ambler, Ames, Armstrong, Arnell, Asper, Axtell, Bailey, Banks, Beaman, Benjamin, Bennett, Bingham, Blair, Boles, Boyd, Buffinton, Burdett, Cessna, Churchill, Cobb, Cook, Conger, Cowles, Cullom, Dawes, Donley, Duval, Dyer, Farnsworth, Ferriss, Ferry, Finckelnburg, Fisher, Fitch, Gilfallan, Hale, Hawley, Heaton, Hoar, Hooper, Hotchkiss, Jenckes, Jones (N. C.), Judd, Julian, Kelsey, Ketcham, Knapp, Laflin, Lash, Lawrence (Ohio), Lynch, Maynard, McCrary, McGrew, Mercur, Moore (Ill.), Moore (N. J.), Morrill (Me.), Negley, O'Neill, Packard, Paine, Palmer, Phelps, Poland, Pomeroy, Prosser, Roots, Sanford, Sergeant, Sawyer, Schenck, Scofield, Sheldon, Smith (Ohio), Smith (Vt.), Smythe (Iowa), Stokes, Stoughton, Strickland, Tanner, Tillman, Twichell, Upson, Van Horn, Ward, Washburn (Wis.), Washburn (Mass.), Welker, Wheeler, Whittemore, Wilkinson, Willard, Williams, Winans—97.

Nays—Archer, Beatty, Beck, Briggs, Bird, Burr, Butler (Mass.), Butler (Tenn.), Cobb, Coburn, Crebs, Dewees, Dickinson, Eldridge, Getz, Golladay, Hawkins, Holman, Hopkins, Johnson, Jones (Ky.), Kerr, Knott, Marshall, Mayhem, McCormick, McNeely, Moffett, Mungen, Niblack, Orth, Reading, Reeves, Rice, Shanks, Smith (Oregon), Stevenson, Stiles, Stone, Strader, Sweeney, Taffe, Trimble, Tyner, Van Trump, Wilson (Ohio), Winchester, Woodward—48.

The bill was approved by President Grant on the 18th of March, 1869, and was the first act approved by him after his inauguration, and is as follows:

"*An Act to strengthen the public credit of the United States.*

Be it enacted, *etc*., That in order to remove any doubt as to the purpose of the Government to discharge all its obligations to the public creditors, and to settle conflicting questions and interpretations of the law, by virtue of which such obligations have been contracted, it is hereby provided and declared that the faith of the United States is solemnly pledged to the payment in coin, or its equivalent, of all the obligations of the United States not bearing interest, known as United States notes, and of all the interest-bearing obligations, except in cases where the law authorizing the issue of any such obligations has expressly provided that the same may be paid in lawful money, or in other currency than gold and silver; but none of the said interest-bearing obligations, not already due, shall be redeemed or paid before maturity, unless at such times as United States notes shall be convertible into coin at the option of the holder, or unless at such time bonds of the United States, bearing a lower rate of interest than the bonds to be redeemed, can be sold at *par* in coin. *And the United States also solemnly pledges its faith to make provision at the earliest practicable period for the redemption of the United States notes in coin.*

Approved March 18, 1869. U. S. GRANT."

DECISIONS OF THE COURTS ON THE CONSTITUTIONALITY OF THE ACT.

In most of the States where the constitutionality of the legal tender act has been raised, the State Courts have decided that the law was constitutional and valid. The decisions in such cases were generally made upon the ground that the United States had express power to wage war, to raise and support armies and navies; to borrow money on the credit of the United States; and pass all laws necessary and proper to carry into execution these great powers. In borrowing money to carry on the war, it was necessary and proper for the Government to give its notes for the amount borrowed; that Congress had the right to affix to such notes the attributes, and prescribe the terms which would give most value and the greatest facility to their negotiation, in order to obtain the necessary means of sustaining the army and navy in the prosecution of the war; that it was a form of credit justified by the exigency of the crisis, and necessary to the execution of the war powers expressly granted in the Constitution. And that upon the authority of Chief-Justice Marshall, "Congress must possess the choice of means, and must be empowered to use *any means* which are in fact conducive to the exercise of the powers granted by the Constitution."

The Court of Appeals, the highest Court in the State of New York, decided in the case of Myer vs. Rosevelt, 27 N. Y. Rep., 400, "that the power to borrow money on the credit of the United States, carries with it the power to attach the quality of a legal tender to the notes issued, when, in the judgment of Congress, it is necessary to make them effectual for the purpose of borrowing."

Judge Davies, in his opinion, says:

"We take notice of the fact, that to maintain armies and provide a navy for the prosecution of the war, more money is needed annually than all the specie within the United States, and that a resort by the Government to the *use of its own credit*, was not only a matter of necessity, but the result has demonstrated that it was a measure of prudence and wisdom."

The issue of Treasury notes under the Constitution commenced during the last war with Great Britain. On the 30th of June, 1812, the first act was passed. Further issues were authorized by the acts of Congress of February 25, 1813; March 4, and December 26, 1814; October 12, 1837; January 31, and August 31, 1842; July 22, 1846, and January 28, 1857. In Thorndike vs. The United States, (2 Mason, 1, 18,) Judge Story said:

"By the statutes of the United States, under which the Treasury notes have been from time to time issued, it is enacted that such notes shall be receivable in payment to the United States, for duties, taxes and sales of public lands, to the full amount of the principal and interest accruing due on such notes. It follows, of course, that they are a legal tender in payment of debts of this nature due to the United States, and by the very tenure of the acts, public officers are bound to receive them."

The legality of the issue of Treasury notes has been sanctioned by all the departments of the Government since 1812, but the United States Supreme Court has not yet decided that Treasury notes can be made "lawful money and a legal tender in payment of all debts public and private," but on the contrary it has decided that contracts expressly payable in coin, must be paid in coin.

COIN CONTRACTS DECLARED VALID.

The Court of Appeals in the State of New York, in the case of Bronson vs. Rhodes, went so far as to decide that a contract made *before* the passage of the legal tender act, payable expressly "in gold and silver coin, lawful money of the United States," might be paid and satisfied by a tender of United States notes, issued under the act of February 25, 1862.

But the U. S. Supreme Court at Washington reversed this decision. Chief Justice Chase announced the opinion of the Court on the 15th of February, 1869, as follows:

"This is an appeal from a judgment of the Court of Appeals of the State of New York, holding that a tender of Treasury notes for the satisfaction of a mortgage made in 1851, by its terms to be satisfied in gold and silver coin, was sufficient. The tender was made in January, 1865, when a dollar in coin was equal to two dollars and twenty-five cents in legal tender notes, and, the tender being refused, action was commenced to compel the cancellation of the mortgage. The Supreme Court of the State subsequently adjudged the mortgage paid, and required it to be satisfied of record, holding the tender to have been sufficient. The Court of

Appeals affirm that judgment, and the affirmance is here for review. The Chief Justice delivered the opinion of the Court, holding that it is the duty of courts of justice to enforce contracts according to the intent of the parties to them; and in this case it is held that it is clear that the intent of the parties was that payment should be made in coin. There were two descriptions of money in use at the time the tender in this case was made, both authorized by law, and both made legal tender. The general denomination of both descriptions was dollars, but they were essentially unlike in nature. The coined dollar was a piece of gold or silver of a certain degree of purity and weight. The note dollar was a promise to pay a coined dollar, but not on demand, nor at any fixed time, nor was it convertible into a coined dollar. It was impossible, in the nature of things, that these two dollars should be equivalents of each other, nor did the currency act purport to make them so. There were then two descriptions of money issued by the same Government, and contracts to pay either were equally sanctioned by law. No question can be made as to this fact; doubt concerning it can only spring from that confusion of ideas which always attends the introduction of varying and uncertain measures of value into circulation as money. In the absence of any specific control for the payment of coin, legal tender notes may be a sufficient tender, but it is clear to the Court that express contracts for the payment of coined dollars can only be satisfied by the payment of coined dollars. They are not debts which may be satisfied by the tender of Treasury notes. As to the judgments to be entered on contracts for the payment of coin, it is said the difficulty arises in the supposition that damages can be assessed in only one description of money; but where there are two kinds of currency provided by law, it is necessary, in order to avoid ambiguity and prevent a failure of justice, to render judgment for coined money where the contract provides for payment in coined money. Where no specified description of money is made, judgments may be entered generally without such specification. Judgment below reversed.

Mr. Justice Miller dissented, holding that, although it was the intention of the parties that gold should be paid, it was only so because gold was then the currency of the Government, the lawful money of the United States, mentioned in the contract. There was nothing in the contract to make it differ from any other ordinary contract payable in dollars. When Treasury notes became lawful money of the United States, their tender was sufficient to discharge the contract, and within its terms and within the understanding and intention of the parties. This decision in no way affects the legal tender cases argued by Mr. Potter and the Attorney General at the present term of the Court, although argued at the time of the argument of those cases."

The constitutional question has been argued and is still pending before the Supreme Court of the United States: "was Congress authorized, under the extraordinary exigencies of the war, to make United States notes fitted for circulation as currency, 'lawful money and a legal tender in payment of all debts, public and private?'" The business men of the country are anxiously waiting for the highest tribunal under the Government to answer this question.

CONCLUSION.

Having completed the Historical narrative of the origin, progress and development of the system of Finance adopted during the rebellion, and which furnished the means of prosecuting to a successful issue the greatest civil war known in the history of the human race, some reflections on the subject may not be uninteresting.

At the breaking out of hostilities, the financial affairs of the banks and people were in a remarkably good condition, except, perhaps, in some of the Northwestern States, where the banks were badly organized.

In the Atlantic cities the banks were never in a better condition. The balances were settled through the Clearing House, in New York and other cities, with great regularity. There was paper currency and gold and silver enough to do the legitimate business of the country. Bank notes were regularly convertible at the will of the holder into specie, and to a large extent these notes were redeemed in New York, Boston and other Atlantic cities. The financial machinery and credit institutions of the country were in a prosperous condition, and there was no lack of means for legitimate wants.

It was not long after the war began before it became apparent to the best financial men of the country, that a financial system adequate to the wants of the nation in time of peace, was wholly inadequate to meet the requirements of a great war; that the war was a new and great business of itself, demanding new and additional facilities, greater even than existed before the war. That the facilities for carrying on the business of the country as they existed before the war, were still necessary to carry on that business, and could not safely be withdrawn from it; and that a new currency, national in character, and to some extent a new financial system, must be *created* to meet the new and enlarged demands of the war which had been forced upon the country. This was an exigency not foreseen, and the Government was obliged to exercise all the power it possessed in passing the *war measures* detailed in the foregoing narrative.

The plan of Finance adopted in 1861-2 was successful, and proved adequate to these enlarged requirements. The Government was maintained and the Union preserved. By this plan all the men and material of war necessary to crush the rebellion were obtained without difficulty. Many mistakes were made in the conduct of the war, but the financial plan, including taxation, was an ample resource sufficient at all times to meet the vast requirements of the War and Navy Departments. The credit of the Government was brought into immediate action in the most available form. Some mistakes were also made by the Secretary of the Treasury in administering the Loan acts, and too large an inflation occurred in 1864, which might have been prevented by continued funding in 5-20 six per cent. bonds, yet in the main the financial management during the war was a decided success, because it carried the country through the terrible ordeal, and brought the ship of state safely into port. It is true that this plan was not at all in accordance with peace notions of finance, but by it all officers, soldiers, sailors and marines were paid in full, and all demands for supplies and material of war were promptly discharged. It was a complete success as a means of carrying into effect the war powers of the Government. These facts abundantly prove the efficiency and wisdom of the plan adopted in bringing the war to a successful termination. Although successful it was a heavy drain upon the resources of the country, and at times very embarrassing to business men, and they had to submit to many sacrifices. The withdrawal of such a large number of youthful laboring men into a vast army of unproductive labor, and the mistake made in the over-issue of paper currency, so inflated prices as to materially increase the expenses of the war. It also embarrassed the people engaged in legitimate pursuits; laborers struck for higher wages, and the price of commodities greatly increased, causing considerable difficulty in keeping up the productive energies of the country, especially in establishments where large gangs of men are employed.

Nor can it be denied that the management of the fiscal affairs of the Government, both legislative and executive, during the war, was a material departure from sound political economy, applicable to ordinary times of peace. The demand for money means forced upon the country by such a gigantic rebellion, was wholly unprecedented—nothing ever recorded in history equaled this demand—and reached to such overwhelming amounts, so vastly beyond any former financial requirements, that the careful observer cannot but look back with wonder and amazement that the Government was at all able to pass successfully through such an extraordinary crisis. The authorization of a loan of $900,000,000, in one act, and an increase of the public debt in one year of over $940,000,000, over and above custom duties and internal taxes, are matters of history. The amount of the issue of paper currency and temporary obligations in various forms was almost appalling. Considerably over one million of men were at one period of the war withdrawn from productive labor. The strain upon the credit of the Government, with eleven States practically out of the Union, was very great. It would seem that no other country could have borne up under such a sudden expansion of the credit circulation, and the changing of so many men from producers to destroyers of life and property. This great inflation of the paper medium had, however, some compensating advantages. It stimulated into wonderful activity all the productive energies of common labor, skilled labor, and machinery of all kinds. War material was produced with amazing rapidity, and in abundant quantity, for equipping, supporting and moving all the great armies in the field and navies afloat. The people never flagged, hesitated, or faltered in producing and furnishing all these vast war materials, and receiving in exchange for it the promises issued to them by the Government. They *seemed* to be getting rich by the operation, and although it was to some extent unreal, yet this stimulus, aided by patriotic determination to maintain the Union, was great enough to induce the people to furnish every thing necessary to supply the army and navy to crush the rebellion, at the mouth of the cannon and point of the bayonet. No compromise was made. Superior force, backed by powerful and abundant resources, accomplished this great achievement. The army and navy were powerful and victorious, because they were sustained by all the vast resources of the country, brought to their aid voluntarily, and by the superior power of the Government which commanded these resources. These bold and decisive financial measures gave power and dignity to the Government, and although it operated upon the unwilling as a forced loan, the crisis demanded it; it was the price of the national Union; the national faith is pledged, and every dollar of this debt must be paid, principal and interest, in gold and silver.

The value of the Union and the Government preserved in full vigor under the Constitution, cannot be estimated in dollars and cents. It is above all price. A vast continent, embracing territory and people, is now held under the control of a mighty central and consolidated Government, based upon the will of an enterprising, intelligent and powerful people. The mind of man is incapable of estimating the future progress and destiny of the American people under such a Government wisely administered. But in a financial and economical aspect, these vast sums expended present an entirely different view. Viewed simply as an economical question, the immense war debt represents only *lives and property consumed.* All the unproductive labor, vast material of war, provisions and supplies of all kinds are used up, wasted and blotted out of existence. This immense debt rolled up during four years of bloody war, stands out in bold demand upon the nation for liquidation from the future earnings and income of the people. Future labor and economy must furnish the means for its payment. This debt is the price of the Union and Constitutional Government, but their value cannot be estimated in dollars. The Government value is intangible and not present as a means of payment, but the war debt is already tangible; the bills are footed up, and the total amount is over $2,500,000,000.

This sum must be paid, principal and interest, not by the issue of new promises to pay it, but by the *production of actual value*, measured by gold and silver, the world's commercial standard, as well as the standard regulated by law.

To illustrate more fully. When individuals in commercial transactions give their notes, bonds or other promises to pay money, they usually receive in exchange either real or personal property, or labor, which is made valuable in some form to pay the obligation given for it. Not so with the war debt; the property received and services performed for the United States notes and obligations, outstanding, has not, in a financial sense, been employed in such a useful way as to furnish present value to pay them with, but on the contrary it was consumed by the war. Hence the difference between a debt created for commercial purposes and a war debt. The one is generally for property or labor made useful and productive, while the other is for unproductive labor or property consumed, wasted or destroyed not for any pecuniarily useful purpose.

Immediately after the war began we commenced our departure from the gold standard, for the reason that every dollar expended for the waste of war was expended for a pecuniarily unproductive purpose. Every dollar expended took out of existence a dollar of value for which the Government gave its promise to pay. Every dollar of property thus destroyed led us farther and farther away from the specie standard, and has to be produced again by labor before the value is restored. In one year, from July 1, 1864, to July 1, 1865,

The Expenditures of the War Department were	$1,031,323,360 79
For Navy Department	122,567,776 12
Total waste of War in one year	$1,153,891,136 91

The history of the human race shows no such consumption and waste in any war during a single year. *One billion, one hundred and fifty-three million, eight hundred and ninety-one thousand, one hundred and thirty-six dollars and ninety-one cents* expended in one year! At the close of this year, July 1, 1865, and the close of active hostilities, one dollar in gold was worth, in greenbacks, 1.41, at the Broker's Board in New York. All the bonds and greenback promises to pay dollars, now outstanding, do not represent tangible property or means owned by the Government, but property in the possession of the people under its jurisdiction, and from which all this waste must be reproduced again, and the value restored, in order to bring us to the specie standard and enable us to pay the debt. In short, the debt must be paid from the earnings and income of the people, in some form of taxation to be enforced by the Government.

It was fortunate that the debt, during the war and since, was distributed to a large extent among all classes of people. In fact, this was the only way in which the resources necessary to sustain the war could be obtained. The legal tender notes were paid out and distributed to the army and navy and for supplies and material of war. Certificates of indebtedness and interest-bearing Treasury notes, were also paid out to contractors and others. The loans were negotiated by direct appeals to the people to subscribe in large and small amounts. The great body of the people in the loyal states took up the loans, and became directly interested in sustaining the Government, and the great diffusion of the notes, bonds and certificates all over the country, was the only way in which the enormous debt so suddenly created could be carried through to the close of the war. The greenback notes were very popular among the people. It was a currency in daily use, uniform in value, and passed freely in every state. It was the people's loan to the Government, without interest, and was at the same time advantageous to them, because it was money in all business transactions. It immediately became the people's war. All became pecuniarily intrusted in its success, and they furnished the means to carry it on. The crushing of the rebellion was the people's triumph; and the people will in due time pay the debt, and thereby preserve the honor and good faith of the nation.

Notwithstanding the great destruction of values consequent upon the prosecution of the war, the nation was, at its close, still possessed of great power and resources, and the material interests of the Northern and Western States were still advancing. They continue to advance; and now that peace and order are restored, and the whole country North and South have a common interest and a common destiny, will continue to advance. There is a rapid increase of population; new fields of enterprise are continually opening, adding new strength and ability to the people to work back to the specie standard, and ultimately pay, without embarrassment, every dollar of the debt incurred in maintaining the national Union.

To make this more plain the following estimate of the increase of the population of the United States is submitted.

According to the rate of increase in past years, our population will advance in the following proportion:

In 1870	42,000,000,	In 1880	56,500,000,
In 1890	76,500,000,	In 1900	103,600,000,
	In 1910	138,900,000.	

The vast means for prosecuting the war to a successful issue were furnished by a population not over 20,000,000. The population subject to the jurisdiction of the national Government and giving it support in 1870, will be double what it was in 1862. The resources of the country will increase with as great rapidity as its population. New and improved systems of communication are expanding in all directions; the Atlantic and Pacific slopes will very soon be bound together by iron bands "across the continent;" the mechanic arts, improved machinery, with agricultural, mineral and commercial facilities fully developed, will carry the nation so rapidly forward in power and resources, that nothing need prevent the Government, if wisely and economically administered, from retiring the legal tender notes within a reasonable time, and as early as the year 1900, pay the last dollar of the debt incurred in crushing the greatest rebellion known in the world's history, and without retarding the growth and prosperity of the great Republic.

APPENDIX.

MR. SPAULDING'S SPEECH ON THE NATIONAL CURRENCY BANK BILL, FEBRUARY 19, 1863.

"Mr. SPEAKER—This is a very important bill, and I may be indulged in a few remarks upon its scopes and objects. I have already stated in the debate on the finance bill that I had no doubt of the constitutionality of the national bank bill proposed by the Secretary of the Treasury, nor had I any doubt that State banks were also constitutional; that both systems of banking might be useful within their sphere of action, and that I was willing that the country should have both kinds of banking; that inasmuch as the National-Government had hitherto failed to establish a permanent system of national banking, State banks had, as a necessary means of commerce and the operations of State governments, become firmly established, and that the Supreme Court of the United States, by repeated decisions, held that they were constitutional and legitimate State institutions.

The coercive features in the pending bill against State banks having been stricken out, I intend to give it my vote; not because I think it will afford any considerable relief to the Treasury in the next two or three years, or that it will in any manner lessen the issue of paper money, but because I regard it as the commencement of a permanent system for providing a national currency that will, if wisely administered, be of great benefit to the people, and a reliable support to the Government in the future.

The President, in his annual message, and the Secretary of the Treasury, in his annual report, recommend the passage of a free banking law, authorizing the issue of a national currency which shall be of uniform value in all parts of the country, and to be secured by a pledge of United States stocks, deposited in the Treasury of the United States. The bill, in all its essential features, is like the free banking law of the State of New York, which has been in successful operation in that State since 1838. Legal tender notes issued direct from the Treasury, without the agency of a bank, constitute a national currency uniform in value, in all parts of the United States, and bearing no interest, is an advantageous loan to the Government by the people who receive and circulate this kind of currency. These legal tender notes are based solely on the faith of the Government and all the taxable property under the jurisdiction of the United States. If Congress performs its duty by imposing taxes on this property, and the Executive enforces the collection thereof, all these notes will be ultimately redeemed and retired from circulation.

These notes are declared by law to be money, and they circulate as money in all parts of the United States. The free banking law is proposed by the Executive for the purpose of combining private capital with the credit of the Government in the issue of bank bills, similar in all respects to legal tender notes. The only difference between them will be that the legal tender notes have only the United States Government to provide for their redemption, while the bank bills, when issued, will have, in addition to the liability of the Government, the direct promise of the banking associations issuing them that they will redeem them on presentation at the bank, not in specie, certainly, during the suspension of specie payments, but in legal tender notes, and after a general resumption of specie payments by the banks and the Government, then to be redeemed in coin. Legal tender notes issued direct from the Treasury constitute a loan to the Government without interest. Bank notes, under this bill, would be loaned to the Government and the people at six and seven per cent. interest. We give to the banking associations the interest on the national currency issued by them, as an inducement to them to form these associations and become liable for its redemption. Instead of the Government issuing this national currency direct to the soldiers and other creditors without interest, it sells its own six per cent. bonds to the banking associations, and takes its pay in legal tender notes; the banking associations take the six per cent. bonds from the Secretary of the Treasury and deposit them with the Treasurer, and thereupon the Comptroller of the Currency furnishes to such banking associations the national currency, the Treasurer holding the bonds as security for their redemption.

This national circulation is, then, money owned by such associations, like any other bank bills. They may be loaned to the people or the Government, like any other money belonging to a bank; and when loaned, the banking associations get six or seven per cent. interest for its use. The associations also draw the interest on the bonds previously hypothecated with the Treasurer. By this operation the associations gain, first, six per cent. interest on its loans; and second, six per cent. interest on the bonds hypothecated with the Treasurer. In this way the banking associations get ten or twelve per cent. gross interest per annum, and the Government pays six of it on the bonds sold to the associations, and which are hypothecated with the Treasurer. The Government gives this bonus and the privileges of banking to capitalists, to induce them to combine their credit with the credit of the Government in issuing this national currency, and providing for its redemption, during suspension, in legal tender notes, and after resumption of specie payments, in coin. The Secretary of the Treasury, in his annual report, recommends 'the organization of banking associations to supply circulation secured by national bonds, and convertible always into United States notes, and after resumption of specie payments into coin.'

The additional advantages held out by the bill to induce rich men, men of accumulated capital, to join the Government in maintaining this national currency, are:

1. The national character given to the bills to circulate at par in all parts of the United States.

2. It is made receivable at par for all internal taxes and all other dues to the Government, except customs, and payable to the army and navy, and all other creditors of the Government.

3. The banking associations are to be exempt from all State and United

States taxation, and only pay two per cent. per annum for engraving, paper, and printing their circulating notes, and which is to include all the other expenses of the Currency Bureau at Washington.

On a full review of this proposed plan of a national currency, it will be seen that it is based on public and private faith; that it proposes to combine the interest of the nation with the rich individuals belonging to it. Men of surplus capital only can profitably engage in the business of banking. If speculators and adventurers, without positive capital, attempt to bank under this bill they will fail. Money-lenders, and not money-borrowers, can successively organize and manage banking associations under the provisions of this act.

How far it will be found practicable to extend the organization of associations on the credit of the public and of individuals, can only be ascertained by the experiment. A banking association of $100,000,000 capital, all paid in by wealthy individuals, and firmly established in the city of New York, and acting as the fiscal agent of the Treasury Department, would be a most valuable support to the credit of the Government. It might be made the depository for all the public moneys in that city. It might receive the public moneys derived from loans, from customs and internal taxes, and disburse all these moneys to the creditors of the Government. This would give the moneyed men who are stockholders of the bank an immediate pecuniary interest in upholding the credit of the Government. Similar organizations in Boston, Philadelphia, New Orleans, and other principal cities of the Union might be made with less amount of capital, and, in like manner, become fiscal agents of the Government in those cities. The Bank of England is a striking example of the combined power of public authority and private influence in sustaining the credit of the Government. We may safely profit by this example. This bank has been the chief agent in sustaining the British Government in the long and exhausting wars in which she has been engaged. The Bank of England is the fiscal agent of the British Government, and notwithstanding it is a bank of discount, deposit and circulation, it has thus far received and disbursed the public moneys without the loss of a dollar of the money entrusted to it.

It is also well known that our Government never lost any of the money deposited in the first or second Bank of the United States. They were both fiscal agents of the Government. All the public money was received and disbursed by them with fidelity and usefulness to both parties. Sound and well-managed banks tend to increase public and private credit, and extend as well as to facilitate commerce with States and individuals. They stimulate industry, commodities are multiplied, agriculture, mining, and manufactures flourish; these constitute the true wealth, greatness, and prosperity of the country.

I have no doubt that the framers of the Constitution contemplated a national currency adequate to the wants of the general Government, and that for all national purposes it has the power to control and regulate the currency. In all Government transactions it has the right not only to provide by law for issuing the kind of currency that shall be received for taxes, custom duties, and all other dues to the United States, but also the kind of money that shall be paid to the army and navy, and all other creditors of the Government. If there had been established years ago a sound national bank of $200,000,000 capital, which had been in full operation as the fiscal and financial agent of the Government at the time of the breaking out of the present rebellion, what a mighty support it would have been in sustaining the Government at the present time! The independent Treasury law unnecessarily isolated the Government from all the capitalists and the accumulated capital of the country.

At the very outset of this rebellion there was no money in the Sub-Treasury, and, notwithstanding the hostility heretofore and now manifested toward State banks, the Government was obliged to resort at once to the State banks in New York, Boston and Philadelphia, for money to prosecute the war. The States had fostered and built up strong State institutions, while the general Government had been vacillating and weakened by conflicting views and opinions as to the constitutionality and policy of a national bank. It is now most apparent that the policy advocated by Alexander Hamilton, of a strong central Government, was the true policy. A strong consolidated Government would most likely have been able to avert this rebellion; but if not able to prevent it entirely, it would have been much better prepared to have met and put down the traitorous advocates of secession and State rights, who have forced upon us this unnatural and bloody war. A sound national bank, upheld and supported by the combined credit of the Government and rich men residing in all the States of the Union, would have been a strong bond of Union before the rebellion broke out, and a still stronger support to the Government in maintaining the army and navy to put it down.

Sir, the United States Government has thus far established no permanent system of national currency except that of gold and silver. Ever since the adoption of the Constitution there has been a conflict of opinion among the ablest statesmen of the country upon the question of a national currency. Jefferson opposed the creation of all banks, both State and national. Alexander Hamilton proposed a national bank during the struggle for American independence in 1780, but his suggestions were not then adopted. During Washington's administration, in 1791, the first Bank of the United States was incorporated, mainly under the influence of Mr. Hamilton, which continued in operation until 1811, when its charter expired. No national bank was in existence during the second war with Great Britain. That war was carried on by loans and by the issue of Treasury notes. In 1816, the second Bank of the United States was chartered, and continued in existence until 1836, when its charter again expired. All will remember the decided opposition of General Jackson to its re-charter, and the fierce struggle that ensued between the friends and opponents of a United States bank. The friends of the bank were finally beaten when Jackson was re-elected President in the fall of 1832. The friends of a United States bank again rallied in 1840-41, but were again defeated by the veto of John Tyler. In 1846 the independent Treasury law was finally adopted, by which it was established that the operations of the Government should thereafter be carried on wholly in gold and silver coin, and that this money of the Government should be kept separate from all banks and banking transactions. Thus the law continued up to the session of the present Congress.

No settled policy has as yet been established by which the Government has assumed permanent control over the national currency. State banks still go on issuing circulating notes, selling exchange, discounting promissory notes and bills, and receiving deposits, and the Sub-Treasury law is still unrepealed. A national currency, adequate to the operations of the Government in *peace* and *war*, has yet to be established. It seems that the present is a propitious time to enact this great measure as a permanent system, and that the duty of the Government in providing a national currency shall no longer be neglected.

Sir, the Government of the United States ought not to depend on State institutions for the execution of its great powers. In the administration of the high prerogatives conferred by the Constitution, this Government need not depend at all upon State officers, State institutions, or State laws. Its own powers and its own means, if brought into active exercise, are fully adequate to the ends for which the Government was established. In the long interval of peace many of the powers granted in the Constitution have not been fully exercised, nor was it necessary during peace to put them fully into execution. But now, when engaged in a gigantic war, when the very existence of the Government is in such imminent peril, it is of the highest importance that it should exert all those great powers to maintain itself, preserve its own dignity, and enforce its own prerogatives. Congress and the Executive cannot fail now to do all in their power to save the Government and restore the national Union.

Sir, this Government has power to issue a national currency entirely independent of State authority; power to support armies independent of Governors of States or State laws; power to provide and maintain a navy in like manner; and power to regulate commerce with foreign nations, among the several States, and with the Indian tribes. These great powers may, by means of proper legislation, be made to operate directly upon the people independently of State boundaries or State sovereignty. Under the power 'to raise and support armies' we may provide for calling the able-bodied men of the nation directly into the army of the United States, and without the aid of Governors of States; and in like manner the navy may be increased. As a necessary means for 'supporting' such an army and 'maintaining' such a navy, we may provide for the issue of a national currency, through the agency of banks, or by the issue of legal tender notes direct from the Treasury. Either mode will require about the same amount of currency to be issued to pay the army and navy; either mode will be constitutional; and it is in the sound discretion of Congress to decide which is the best mode of providing the means for carrying on the Government in the present exigency.

Sir, all the powers conferred on the general Government are self-acting, self-sustaining, and wholly independent of State authority; and when enforced by men of will, strong nerves, enlightened self-reliance, energy, and ability sufficient to put them into active exercise, are fully adequate to the putting down of this gigantic rebellion and maintaining the Constitution and laws over all the thirty-four States and the Territories included in the national Union. The duty of putting these constitutional powers into active exercise devolves upon Congress and the Executive. Congress cannot fail to perform every duty devolved upon it in the present great emergency.

In the absence of a national bank the State banks have been liberal in making loans to the Government since the war begun. It has been ascertained from reliable data that on the 19th day of January, 1863, the banks in the State of New York alone held United States securities to the amount of $153,637,174; being $45,000,000 more than the entire capital of all the banks in the State, their capitals being only $108,606,062. This shows the ability and willingness of the banks in New York to support the Government in her present peril. There is in the present imperiled condition of the Union more distrust of the stability of the general Government than there is of the State Governments. Some doubt exists, owing to divisions at the North, as to our final success in crushing the rebellion. Could you make it certain that the Union will be preserved, and the national jurisdiction maintained over all the thirty-four States and the $16,000,000,000 of taxable property therein, which is liable for our public debt, excluding therefrom the debt of the rebel government, said to be $900,000,000, the six per cent. bonds of the United States would not be five per cent. below par, while the six per cent. bonds of the State of New York are worth a premium of twenty-eight per cent. Capitalists are naturally timid, and will hesitate about entering into new projects until they can see the way clear. They desire to know that the Union is to be maintained and the Government perpetuated. Being fully assured of this, your bonds will be immediately above par, and there will be less difficulty in organizing banking associations and carrying this act into effect.

Sir, banking is eminently a practical business. To be successful, it must be based on accumulated capital, and conducted by practical men, who are intimately acquainted with the commerce and business of the country. Finance and financial questions must all be finally brought to a practical standard. However fine spun the theories of visionary men may be, they cannot now be relied on to provide money in the present exigency to pay the army and navy and other needy creditors of the Government. Our plan of finance must be simple, efficient and practical. It consists of two parts, debts and taxation, namely:

1. Contracting debts for the supply of the army and navy, issuing legal tender notes, and borrowing money in some form on the faith of the Government.

2. Taxation on the entire property, commerce, and business of the country, amply sufficient to pay the principal and interest of all the debts which have been or may be contracted on the faith of the Government.

Sir, no theories can be imagined, nor shifts made that will be allowed to evade the tariff on imports and internal taxes on property and business adequate to the payment of the entire debt contracted, both principal and interest. The property and business of the country are amply sufficient for this purpose; but it will require a strong, stable Government, wisely administered, to adjust and enforce the collection of so large an amount of taxes as will be required to pay the extraordinary war debt that must be contracted to crush the rebellion and restore peace and tranquility over the whole Union. I have no doubt that the patience and energies of the people are to be taxed to the utmost before the Union is restored and we be assured of future loyalty in all the southern States. You are not yet able to collect taxes in the disloyal States without the aid of a powerful army. Before you can be assured of loyalty in the rebellious States, Union State Governments must be established and maintained in each of them. To do this will require a large army for many years. Until you can collect your taxes in all the rebel States without the aid of military force the rebellion is not subdued.

Many of our friends express sanguine expectations of immediate relief from the passage of this national bank bill, and I should be much gratified to know hereafter that their expectations have been fully realized. But, sir, in my judgment, the Secretary of the Treasury must not place too much reliance upon this plan. It will not give much relief to the Treasury for one, two, or three years. It will not to any considerable extent, supersede the necessity for the issue of Treasury notes. It will go into operation slowly. The Government having heretofore failed to provide a national currency, the State banks in the older States have been organized, become deeply rooted, and firmly established. It will take a long time to supplant these banks. Every coercive or violent attempt to do so will do more harm than good. This new system will come in competition not only with existing institutions, but will encounter the prejudices of a large class of people who are hostile to banks, and especially hostile to a United States bank. It will be towards the close of the war, when the Government is firmly established and its authority respected in all the States, that it will be most valuable in providing a way for funding the public debt and establishing a permanent system of national currency. It is chiefly on this ground that I am induced to support the bill at this time. It is more for the benefits to be realized in the future than during the pending war that I am induced to give it my support.

Debt and taxation are the inevitable necessities of war. Hence the importance of a reunion of all parties in a vigorous prosecution of the war, in order to crush the rebellion in the shortest time and with the least possible expenditure of blood and treasure. This is the only way to stop the burdens and calamities of the present war. Fight vigorously and in earnest while the war lasts. Every consideration of duty and patriotism require all the loyal people to come at their country's call, to fight the rebels forthwith, by all the means within the range of civilized warfare, to save us from a protracted war, save the further effusion of blood, and stop the vast expenditures which must, unless speedily terminated, burden present and future generations.

We need more economy in the management of the war. It is manifest there is not that close supervision and scrutiny over the expenditures that are necessary. Every man in the service should be required to perform with fidelity the duties devolved upon him. All supernumerary officers and men should be dispensed with. All disbursing officers should be held to a rigid economy and strict accountability. As we approach the termination of this war the expenses must be greatly reduced, and preparation made for a resumption of specie payments. Our public debt will then appear in all its vast proportions, for it must all be paid ultimately in gold and silver. This makes it necessary for us to cut off all unnecessary expenses of every kind.

Every day that the war is prolonged the debt is largely increased. The daily increasing debt of $2,500,000 must all be raised by taxation in some form, or the debt will not be paid. The Government is spending at a fearful rate the accumulations of former years of prosperity. Every dollar of debt contracted becomes a first mortgage upon the entire property and productive industry of the country. It affects the farmer, laborer, mechanic, manufacturer, merchant, banker, commission merchant, professional man, and retired capitalist. Every pound of tea, coffee and sugar used is taxed to pay the expenses of the war, and the persons using these articles of daily consumption pay the tax in the increased price. Every person that uses wine, brandy, whisky, beer, cigars, or tobacco, pays a portion of the war tax. All necessary articles of dress, such as shoes, boots, hats, and wearing apparel, are taxed in like manner, and all superfluous and unnecessary articles, such as silks, laces, diamonds and jewelry, are heavily taxed, and I would be glad to see the tax still further increased on them, in order to prevent, if possible, their use at this time.

Every person that rides upon the railroads, reads a newspaper, draws a check, or sends a telegraphic message, is taxed for war purposes. But I need not further enumerate the different modes in which every body is taxed every day to pay the expenses of the war.

Sir, this war debt is a mortgage alike on all the productive industry and property of Republicans, Democrats, old line Whigs, conservatives, and abolitionists. All these classes of persons are taxed alike to pay the war debt. Every Democrat or Republican who chews tobacco, drinks beer or bad whiskey in the sixth ward of New York pays his proportion of the war debt, the same as the conservative who drinks his choice wine on the Fifth Avenue. This war tax is already beginning to be noticed by the people; but as the war is procrastinated, and the debt increased, the burden will be more deeply felt. While we are running along at forty miles an hour, under the pressure of irredeemable paper, necessarily issued and circulated to prosecute the war, the present taxation is easily paid, and there is a seeming prosperity; but I can assure gentlemen that a reckoning day will surely come. Look at the immense army in the field, their commissariat, supply vessels, supply trains, ambulance corps, sutlers, teamsters, hangers-on, idlers and assistants of all kinds, extending over a line of military operations of more than four thousand miles, and you will be impressed with two important facts:

1. The enormous expenditures necessary to their present support, and the future bounties and pensions that must be paid.

2. The number of men that are withdrawn from industrial pursuits, and the consequent loss of productive industry which ought to be added to the wealth of the country.

All this immense army add nothing by their labor to the wealth of the country, and the expense of supporting such an army devolves upon those who do labor and those who have already acquired property. What a mighty drain this war is upon the productive energies and resources of the country. It is, indeed, an exhausting as well as bloody war. Whether it be successful or unsuccessful, vast consequences are involved. If terminated successfully within three years, the Union maintained and the Government perpetuated under the Constitution, the results to flow from such a triumph would amply compensate for all this expenditure of blood and treasure. If it terminates unsuccessfully, the Union divided and the rebel government maintained, the war debt must still be paid; but no man here is wise enough to predict what results will follow such a calamity.

I am asked almost daily, will the Union be maintained and the national Government perpetuated all over the States and Territories? I cannot doubt that it will. No efforts of mine certainly shall be wanting to accomplish so desirable a result. I cannot, however, shut my eyes to the formidable character of the rebellion, nor to the difficulties in the way of accomplishing such a result. The inherent difficulties of conquering and subduing so large and intelligent a people, extending over such a wide extent of territory as is contained in the revolted States, are very great. It is very difficult to move and supply large armies. An advance in the enemy's country for any considerable distance always involves the difficulties of keeping the rear line open to the base of supplies. This has been demonstrated in the advances that have been made in attempting to take Richmond. Even the armed occupation of a part of any one of the revolted States does not make the people in the State loyal to the General

Government. The hatred of the people in the rebellious States is deep-seated and abiding. They have a separate *de facto* confederate government, and separate State governments. As States they revolted from the United States Government, and with their State governments remaining intact and in full force. They still maintain their separate State organizations, with power to enforce their State laws. This insurrection was commenced very differently from most other insurrections. It was not commenced by disorganized bodies of the people, but by the constituted authority of States in their capacity of independent sovereignties. These State authorities had power to suppress immediately the Union sentiments of the people within their jurisdiction, and to enact as well as to enforce any new laws that might be necessary to accomplish their wicked purposes. Hence the formidable character of the rebellion at the outset. It will take a long time to supplant the present State organizations in the revolted States, and to institute new Union State governments in their stead. It can only be accomplished by armed force. It will require a large standing loyal army in the actual occupation of each State. Until Union State governments are organized and permanently maintained in all the Southern States, you cannot hope for a lasting peace.

Sir, it is proper for us to look these difficulties square in the face. All the people in the Northern States ought to look at the formidable character of this rebellion, and act up to the demands of the hour. It will require the active energies of a *united North* to maintain the integrity of the Union. It is unwise, ay, criminal for us, while incurring a debt of $2,500,000 every day, to deceive ourselves as to the real situation. The business men, at a distance, are going on making money, speculating, buying and selling, almost unconscious of the dangers that surround us. Party organizations are maintained, party platforms set up, and a partisan struggle constantly made for power, wholly inconsistent with the mighty issues involved in the present war. This applies to all parties and all party organizations. The people in the loyal States, without regard to party distinctions, have a common interest and a common destiny; all are intensely interested in the deadly conflict, all become liable for the debts contracted in the prosecution of the war, and all must be taxed to pay both principal and interest.

But, sir, the higher inspirations of duty and patriotism impel us to sustain the President in a vigorous prosecution of the war—a war that has been forced upon us by ambitious men, whose chief object is power. Considerations infinitely above mere party or pecuniary gains or losses should compel us to united action. Your country, my country, is in danger of being divided and destroyed. Oaths have been broken, the Constitution defied, and the laws trampled under feet of rebels. 'United we stand, divided we fall.' I appeal to gentlemen of all parties to uphold and sustain the constituted authorities in vindicating the majesty of the Constitution and laws over all the States and Territories, from the great lakes to the Gulf of Mexico, and from the Atlantic to the Pacific oceans. This is our country. Let it have one national Government—one destiny."

REDEMPTION OF NATIONAL CURRENCY—ASSORTING HOUSE.

"BUFFALO, September 30th, 1865.

Dear Sir—I am in receipt of your favor of the 28th inst., asking me to communicate my views of the plan proposed by the New York banks for the redemption of national currency.

In reply, I would say that I am clearly of the opinion that a prompt redemption of the national currency is necessary to insure success and permanency to the system. No system of banking is safe that does not enforce rigidly the obligation of each bank to redeem its circulating notes on demand. During the suspension of specie payments they are required to be redeemed in legal tender demand notes, and on the resumption of specie payments they must be redeemed in coin. This is one of the requirements of the National Banking Law, which should be strictly enforced, and every sound and well managed bank will no doubt be able and willing to conform to this law, and every weak and badly managed bank should be compelled to live up to its requirements. But in stating these general propositions, which no sound banker will controvert, it does not follow that a combination called an Assorting House is the best mode of compelling them to fulfill its obligation to redeem.

An Assorting House would require large rooms, a great number of clerks; they would handle a large amount of currency, the expenses would be heavy, and in these times of knavery and fraud, the risk would be very great. And to what end would this assorting process be carried on? Simply to separate the money of each bank into packages to be sealed up and sent home by an express company for redemption. Is this necessary? Is it necessary to incur all this expense and risk to secure a prompt redemption of the national currency. Let us consider the subject a little more in detail, and see if a prompt redemption of it cannot be attained under the law as it now stands, or by a proper amendment of it if found defective.

In the first place, it is not necessary to assort and send home this currency for redemption so long as it is required by the people to carry on the business operations of the country. Every time a hundred dollar bill passes from one person to another it is a practical redemption of it by the person who takes it. Every time a merchant at Chicago pays to a farmer $500 in national currency for a car load of wheat, the farmer by the operation redeems such national currency, not in greenbacks, nor in gold, but in a commodity better than either, namely wheat, a staple article useful to all. So every merchant in New York that sells a bale of cotton goods and receives his pay for it in currency, redeems such currency, not in the way that banks redeem it, but in cotton goods, which is far better because it performs the true functions of money by facilitating the legitimate sale of commodities. So every time that a merchant or manufacturer pays his internal revenue tax to the United States Collector in national currency, the Government redeems such currency by receiving and discharging such tax. So every mechanic or laborer that receives national currency for his services, redeems such currency by the labor performed. So it will be seen that just so long as the national currency is practically redeemed every day in its passage from hand to hand in the payment of commodities and services and in the ramified operations of trade and business both with the Government and the people whose operations it greatly facilitates, there is not the slightest necessity for resorting to the expensive and risky operation of assorting and sending it home for redemption.

With a proper amendment to the National Bank law, I am clearly of the opinion that it would be unwise to establish an Assorting House, and even without such amendment, I do not think it good policy to establish it. In the first place the Assorting House will be as I have stated, attended with great risk and expense. And in the next place it is opposed to sound policy and will have a mischievous effect upon the legitimate circulation of the national currency. The leading object of the national bank law was to furnish a currency of uniform value and similitude to be used by the Government and people as an instrument to facilitate the exchange of commodities and services, and the collection of internal taxes, in all parts of the United States. It is amply secured by gold bearing bonds deposited with the Treasurer of the United States at Washington. Only ninety per cent. of currency is issued on the amount of bonds hypothecated, thus leaving a margin of ten per cent. for depreciation. The Government stamps it with the imprint of the Treasury and guarantees the ultimate payment of every dollar put in circulation by any bank, whether such bank is solvent or insolvent. It is made a legal tender for all taxes and other debts due to the Government except customs, and for all debts due from the Government except interest on the funded debt. All national banks are obliged by law to receive it for all debts due them, and each national bank depositary is further obliged to receive it on all Government deposits made in the bank by any public officer. These provisions in the bank law give great advantages and credit to the national circulation over that of State banks. These provisions of the law provide to a considerable extent for a *practical redemption* of this currency in the every day operations of the Government and people, not only in New York, Boston and Philadelphia, but also in Charleston, New Orleans, St. Louis, Cincinnati, Chicago and Buffalo, and in every other city and village throughout the length and breadth of the whole country. With the facility thus given to the national currency to circulate *at par* in every part of the United States, and the guarantee of the Government that every dollar of it shall be paid, it passes freely among all classes of people and corporations without any one stopping to enquire whether a particular bank is badly managed or not. The national currency with the pledged security and guarantee of the Government, is good in any event, and is not likely to become a dead weight in any of the banks in the principal cities. If a weak or badly managed bank (like the First National Bank of Attica, for instance) should fail, its creditors may be large losers by the failure, but every dollar of the circulation will be paid, and the notes continue to circulate equally as well after as before its failure. No one ever stopped taking the circulating notes of the First National Bank of Attica, notwithstanding its failure more than six months ago. It is not the bill holder that will lose by the failure of a national bank, but its depositors and other creditors, hence the security of national currency over all other currency. Thus far the national banking system in respect to its circulation has gone on smoothly. All this currency in miscellaneous packages consisting of the issues of banks in Maine, Minnesota and Tennessee, pass equally well without being assorted, in all parts of the United States. This system of furnishing a circulating medium thus far works as well, or better than was anticipated by its most sanguine advocates. It is fulfilling admirably the great desideratum of a true national currency, so long needed to carry on successfully the business of the enterprising people of this great country.

I should regret very much to see a combination of bankers in any of the principle cities organize an Assorting House to disorganize the harmonious working of this system by assorting this currency, sealing it up in separate packages, and sending it home to each bank issuing it for redemption, unless there should be an imperative necessity for so doing. The tendency of such an operation would be to materially disturb the financial operations of the country. Once begin the operation of assorting currency by a large organized Assorting House in the city of New York, with a large number of clerks under good salaries, and you begin a system that will ultimately draw into its support every bank in the whole country. What will be the operation of such a combination? In the first place it may not be illegal, but is not specially authorized by the national law. In the next place it begins by the city banks sending all national currency received by them to the assorting house, whether necessary or not, to be assorted, sealed up in packages, and sent home to each bank, either through its redeeming agency or directly by express to the bank that issued them. Each bank, on receiving this currency so sent home, is obliged to provide for it either in legal tender greenbacks, which are no safer than national currency, or by drafts which are at par in New York, but generally by providing a fund in advance at a bank in one of the principal cities. As the currency continues to be assorted and sent home, it *creates* the necessity for each bank out of New York to provide more par funds to be placed to their credit ready for redeeming their notes as they shall be again assorted and sent home for that purpose. These banks not being able to make exchange or par funds in other modes, will very soon begin to gather up the circulating notes of other banks, and especially notes issued by other banks in their own locality, and send them to New York for their own credit. These notes, on reaching New York, will again go immediately to the assorting house, and be again counted, sealed up, and sent back by express to the country. As this process of sending money packages to and from New York goes on through the machinery of the assorting house, the volume will continue to increase until every bank in the country will be obliged to contribute directly or indirectly to the support of a combination unknown to the law. It seems to me that the good to be attained by any such combinations will be greatly overbalanced by the mischiefs it will create to the present harmonious working of the system. It would no doubt be a profitable business for the express companies to carry these money packages to New York and back again to the country, but I am greatly puzzled to know how it will be any advantage to the people, the Government, or the banks, either in New York or elsewhere, to carry such a scheme into practical operation. If this combination is adopted, the national currency issued by the banks in New York city which now circulate freely everywhere, will be unnecessarily returned upon them for redemption under the operations of their own assorting house. This will be one of the legitimate results of the system of assorting which cannot be avoided.

I watched with considerable care the working of the system instituted by the Suffolk Bank of Boston and the Metropolitan Bank of New York, compelling the old State banks to redeem their circulating notes by a similar process. This was no doubt a check against the excessive issues of banks at that time, especially to banks in New England, which were not very strongly restricted by law as to the amount of these issues, but I very much doubt whether even this plan to coerce the redemption of even an inferior currency did not do more hurt in deranging the free and legitimate circulation thereof than it did good in preventing excessive issues. It certainly afforded a fine business for the express companies in carrying money packages to and from New York; and it is certain also that the activity with which these packages were hurried back and forth, greatly accelerated the panic that occurred in August, September, and the first half of October, 1857; until finally the banks in New York, by common consent, ceased sending it home, and took this *secured* currency of the State of New York and made it a basis for Clearing House Certificates, which had an important influence in stopping the panic and restoring confidence.

Upon a full examination of the subject, I arrive at the conclusion that so long as the national currency is required for legitimate business purposes, it will not largely accumulate in the banks of either of the three cities of New York, Boston or Philadelphia, nor will it be sent home for redemption. Thus far it does not appear that there has been a plethora or glut of national currency in either of those cities. But suppose that in the course of a few months there should accumulate a few millions dollars of national currency in those banks more than could be readily disposed of in the operations of the Government and the people, in what manner should it be disposed of?

In such a contingency, when it does occur, I think the issuing banks should be called upon to redeem their circulating notes, and it seems to me to be right that each bank should be required by law to redeem in the principal city where such surplus currency accumulates, as well as at their own counter.

New York city is the great commercial emporium, and is clearly indicated by the course of business, foreign and domestic, as the proper place for each bank located out of that city, to have an agent for the redemption of its circulating notes.

An amendment to the national banking law can probably be made at the next session of Congress, which shall require all the banks to have an agent for the redemption of their circulating notes in the city of New York, instead of being allowed to select as they now do, any one of the seventeen cities named in the present law. This being accomplished, any bank or individual in New York, or elsewhere, in any city or town in the United States, could send the circulating notes of any bank to the agency selected by it for redemption without the expense and risk of an assorting house, which I think is the true mode of providing for the redemption of the national currency. This would be in accordance with the law, and would, I think, give better satisfaction and better promote the welfare of all concerned.

This is my answer to your request.

Yours truly, E. G SPAULDING.

J. U. ORVIS, Esq.,
Pres't 9th National Bank, New York."

MR. RANDALL'S BILL TO DESTROY NATIONAL BANKS.

BUFFALO, January 22, 1867.

Hon. H. R. Hulburd, Comptroller of Currency, Washington;

Dear Sir—I am much obliged for the information contained in your letter, and I trust you will pardon me for the remarks I am about to make.

I have watched with a good deal of interest the various plans brought forward in Congress, in relation to the National Finances and Amendments to the National Banking Law. Every man in the country is on the lookout to see what is to come next. Every one engaged in legitimate pursuits wants a fixed policy and steadiness in financial affairs, and yet all are under constant apprehensions, fearing that some scheme will be hastily passed by Congress which will derange monetary affairs, and upset all their business calculations. Many enterprises are postponed. The building of railroads, ships, warehouses, elevators, furnaces, and other manufacturing establishments, are held in abeyance until it can be more clearly seen what is to be done with these schemes, and what is to be the future in regard to financial affairs.

It is obvious that this suspense and apprehension operates very unfavorably upon individuals, as well as upon the revenues of the Government. Congress in its official capacity has thus far acted wisely. It has not passed any of the individual schemes that have been brought forward. It has been content to 'let well enough alone.' It has refused to increase the national currency above $300,000,000. It has not passed Mr. Randall's grand scheme of repudiating the faith of the Government with the National Banks, and turning the Treasury Department, in time of peace, into a permanent machine, for the issue of an irredeemable paper currency when there is not the least necessity for it, and when all history proves it to be unwise, as tending to retard the resumption of specie payments, and resulting in general financial disaster, bankruptcy and ruin, both to the Government and people. It has refused to pass the twenty pages of pending amendments to the National Bank act, (House Bill No. 771,) which, if passed, would make the law worse instead of better. In short, the Senate and House, as legislative bodies, have submitted to the introduction of these injudicious measures to be talked about, but as yet they have not been unwise enough to let any of them be passed into laws to further disturb existing arrangements under laws already passed, and which, up to the time of the meeting of Congress, were operating very favorably, under a moderate contraction of the currency, in preserving a good degree of steadiness and uniformity in the money market, keeping business steady and prosperous, and enabling the Secretary of the Treasury to establish more certainly the public credit at home and abroad, and make a most favorable exhibit of the national debt. These are matters of great consequence to the welfare of the nation, and I sincerely hope that no hasty or indiscreet measures will be allowed to pass. The people of the country need rest, and in order to secure it I trust that Congress will hold a steady purpose, and not pass laws at one session to be repealed in the next. We are cursed with too much legislation, and I am gratified to see the present Congress holding back on all impracticable schemes.

The act of Congress passed on the 12th of April last, it seems to me is a wise and judicious measure. It authorizes the Secretary of the Treasury to dispose of 5-20 gold bonds, and with the proceeds to retire six per cent. compound interest notes, and the plain legal tender greenback currency and other indebtedness of the Government, but not to retire more than $4,000,000 of greenbacks a month, or $48,000,000 a year, but without restriction as to the amount of compound sixes that may be retired during any week or month. This law is discretionary with the Secretary of the Treasury. Power is given him to contract the currency, but he will no doubt use his discretionary power prudently, and not retire either greenbacks or compounds, any faster than it can be done without materially disturbing the legitimate business of the country. His object will be in the future, as it has been during the past year, to keep a steady and uniform money market. This will be a necessity on his part to enable him to successfully carry on the fiscal affairs of the Government. Under a very stringent and paniky money market, the 5-20 bonds would fall below par, thereby stopping conversion of 7-30 into the 5-20 bonds, and this, in view of $650,000,000 of 7-30s falling due between this and July 15, 1858, would embarrass and derange all the operations of the Treasury Department. The Secretary of the Treasury must therefore, of necessity, be moderate and discreet in contracting the currency under the law of the 12th of April.

The Secretary will no doubt, by a moderate and prudent course of contraction, endeavor to keep the business and industry of the nation in a prosperous condition, in some degree check wild speculation, gradually reduce prices, and bring greenbacks and national currency nearer the specie standard. On this point the Secretary, in his last annual report, makes the following judicious remarks: 'How rapidly the United States notes may be retired must depend upon the effect which contraction may have upon business and industry, and can be better determined as the work progresses. No determinate scale of reduction would, in the present condition of affairs, be advisable. The *policy* of contracting the circulation of Government notes should be definitely and unchangeably established, and the process should go on just as rapidly as possible without producing a financial crisis, or seriously embarrassing those branches of industry and trade, upon which our revenues are dependent.' As the volume of currency is reduced, it will increase in value, and as soon as the specie standard is reached, the national banks will be obliged to redeem their circulating notes in specie. The Government can retire whenever it seems best, from the field, as an issuer of paper currency, and consequently will not be under the necessity of providing gold and silver to redeem it. The burthen of redeeming the national currency in gold and silver will then be thrown exclusively upon the banks that issue it, and they will be required to keep the necessary reserves of coin for that purpose.

It seems to me that the act of the 12th of April contains all the power for contracting the currency which is necessary to bring the business of the country back to the specie standard, as it was before the rebellion. It may take three years, five years, or even ten years, to accomplish that result. When the old uniform standard of gold and silver is reached, and prices and the business of the country are again based thereon, national banks will take the place of State banks in the issue, circulation and redemption of the currency necessary to carry on the fiscal affairs of the Government and people. The Treasury Department will be relieved from a duty that was forced upon it as an imperative necessity during the war, and the Government left to perform its legitimate functions under the Constitution, the currency being thereafter regulated by the wants of trade and industrial pursuits.

It was never intended by the originators of the legal tender acts that the issue of an irredeemable paper currency should ever become the permanent policy of the Government. In the opening speech I made in the House on the 28th of January, 1862, on the bill introduced by me, I said that 'the bill before us is a war measure; a measure of *necessity* and not of choice, presented by the Committee of Ways and Means, to meet the most pressing demands upon the Treasury, to sustain the army and navy, until they can make a vigorous advance upon the traitors and crush out the rebellion. These are extraordinary times, and extraordinary measures must be resorted to, in order to save our Government and preserve our nationality.'

The credit of the Government, by the legal tender act, was brought into immediate requisition, and in the most available form to provide ways and means for sustaining the army and navy to crush the rebellion. It was in effect a forced loan from the people to the Government, in a most perilous period in our history, and was justified mainly on the ground of imperative necessity. It was a temporary measure passed in a most pressing exigency, and should not be continued any longer after peace is restored than seems to be necessary to conduct us safely back to that standard of value, which is recognized by all the nations of the world.

In the speech to which I have above referred, I further said, 'a suspension of specie payments is greatly to be deplored, but it is not a fatal step in an exigency like the present.'

'The British Government and the bank of England remained under suspension of specie payments from 1797 to 1821-2, a period of twenty-five years;—gold is not as valuable as are the productions of the farmer and mechanic, for it is not as indispensable as are food and raiment. Our army and navy must have what is more valuable to them than gold or silver, they must have food, clothing and the material of war. Treasury notes issued by the Government on the faith of the whole people, will purchase these indispensable articles, and the war can be prosecuted until we can enforce obedience to the Constitution and laws and an honorable peace be thereby secured. This being accomplished, I will be among the first to advocate a speedy return to specie payments, and all measures that are calculated to preserve the honor and dignity of the Government in time of peace, and which I regret are not practicable in the prosecution of this war.'

The national banking law, passed to continue for twenty years, was intended as a permanent system. It was intended that it should take the place of the State banks, in furnishing a solvent national currency of uniform similitude and value for the whole country. The arguments put forth in the last annual reports of yourself and the Secretary of the Treasury in favor of sustaining the national bank currency seem to me to be cogent and conclusive. I advocated the national bank law, not for any immediate relief it would give to the Treasury, but as a permanent system of currency and banking. In the remarks which I made in the House on the day of the passage of the bill, I said 'that I should vote for it, not that I think it will afford any considerable relief to the Treasury in the next two or three years, but because I regard it as the commencement of a permanent system for providing a national currency that will, if wisely administered, be of great benefit to the people, and a reliable support to the Government in the future.'

All the advocates of the legal tender act while it was pending in Congress, based their arguments upon the necessity of its passage as a temporary relief to the Treasury during the war, and not as a permanent policy of the Government. On the contrary, the national banking law was advocated as a permanent system of national currency and banking for the whole country. The State banks in this and other States, especially the banks in the State of New York, gave up their State organizations with great reluctance. But in consequence of the law which taxed State circulation out of existence, the State banks were obliged to come under the national banking law for self-preservation, a law which on its face was to continue for twenty years.

It has taken something over three years to put in successful operation about 1,650 national banks under one system, and which are directly under the control and regulation of the officers of the Government at Washington. A few of the banks have but recently perfected their organizations and obtained from the Department their circulating notes. Before the ink is fairly dry on the last issue of national currency we are startled with a bill reported from the bank committee in the House to emasculate and destroy this system of national banking. I say destroy it, for no man at all conversant with the advantages of private banking and its freedom from taxation and other restrictions, would consider it any inducement to remain under the inquisitorial supervision imposed by the national banking law, if the right to issue circulating notes is taken away from them. These banks have been organized in good faith by the stockholders under the national law, because in the first place State bank circulation was killed by United States taxation, and in the next place great inducements were held out to them for a national circulation to continue twenty years. What a breach of faith on the part of the Government in holding out inducements to organize under this law, killing off the State banks first, and then turning a short corner to kill off the national banks, children of its own creation. Are all the rights which the stockholders of the banks have acquired under this law to be thus summarily disposed of? How many banks would have organized under this law if the stockholders had supposed that their rights to issue circulating notes would be taken away from them as soon as they were organized? Not one in a hundred, for the simple reason that there would be no inducement to come under the restraints of the national law without circulation.

It is said that these banks can continue to do business on their capital and deposits, this is no doubt true, but it could be much better carried on by the stockholders as private bankers without the onerous taxation and restrictions imposed by the national law. The organization of State and private banks would be much better, larger latitude being given to operate, and much freer from inquisitorial examinations.

If this bill now pending in the House is passed and becomes a law, it will pretty effectually use up the national banking system. It has taken about four years to build it up, and within three years it will be so far destroyed as to make it no object for stockholders that can organize into private banking companies to remain in the emasculated and restricted condition in which they will be placed.

What security can men have for investing their money and basing their business calculations under a national law? The insecurity and scandal that will attach to such hasty and inconsiderate legislation will deter all prudent men from placing too much reliance upon a law of Congress, passed at one session, organizing a great system of national policy, to be emasculated or repealed before it gets fairly into operation. It looks too much like confiscating the property of individuals under the pretence of creating a sinking fund to pay off the national debt.

I hope the Senate and House will carefully consider this measure in all its bearings before they pass a law involving such important consequences in regard to its breach of faith in destroying the acquired rights of the stockholders in these banks, and the disastrous consequences likely to follow the issue of Government paper money as a permanent policy.

Yours very truly,

E. G. SPAULDING.

MR. SPAULDING TO SECRETARY McCULLOCH.

FARMER'S AND MECHANICS' NATIONAL BANK,
No. 3 Spaulding's Exchange,
BUFFALO, December 4, 1866.

Dear Sir—You will do me a favor by sending to me by mail a pamphlet copy of your report and accompanying documents. I have only seen a synopsis of it, but it seems to me that you understand the situation, and have stated it with force and ability. I congratulate you on the favorable exhibit of the public debt, which is in a great measure due to your discreet and prudent management of the national finances. You have no doubt now, to a large extent, control of the finances of the country, and I think that you will, of necessity, contract moderately, so as to preserve a tolerably easy money market, in order to be able to fund the compound 6's and the 7-30's into long gold-bearing bonds, between this and the 15th of July, 1868. There may be occasional spasms and tightness for money with the *speculators*, but generally I shall look for plenty of money for legitimate business for at least a year to come. If the speculators should get some check it would be a good thing for the country, and all men engaged in industrial pursuits would not complain.

I hope you will be able to reach the specie standard with at least $250,000,000 of plain legal tender United States notes still outstanding. The amount of gold and silver coin now available in this country is so small that it constitutes a very adequate basis on which to rest the largely increasing volume of business to be transacted, and unless we can have legal tender in some form, other than gold or silver coin, I think we will hereafter be very much subjected to panics and revulsions, to the injury of legitimate business, and, consequently, diminished revenues. If we can maintain $250,000,000 of the paper tender at the specie standard, in addition to the supply of gold and silver, I think the business of the country would, in the future, be more steady and uniform.

Yours truly,
E. G. SPAULDING.

Hon. HUGH McCULLOCH,
Secretary of the Treasury.

SECRETARY McCULLOCH'S REPLY.

TREASURY DEPARTMENT,
WASHINGTON, December 7, 1866.

Dear Sir—Your favor of the 4th inst. is received. You will receive a copy of my report through the Comptroller of the Currency. It was very hastily written, but is, I think, sound in doctrine.

What we need is an increase of labor. If we could have the productive industry of the country in full exercise, we could return to specie payments without any very large curtailment of United States notes. My object has been to keep the market steady, and to work back to specie payments without a financial collapse. I shall act in the future as I have in the past, with great caution, and attempt no impracticable thing.

I am very truly yours,
H. McCULLOCH.

Hon. E. G. SPAULDING,
Farmer's and Mechanics' Bank, Buffalo, N. Y.

NATIONAL DEBT—NO REPUDIATION.

Will the public debt of the United States ever be repudiated? The answer to this question depends upon the efficiency and fidelity of the national Government. The Government has ample power under the Constitution and ample means at its disposal to pay every dollar of the public debt. Believing that the Government will continue faithful and efficient, I answer no! the public debt will not be repudiated. A large majority of the people also say no, but nevertheless there is a small minority that have answered this question in the affirmative, and continue to repeat the assertion that the public debt will never be paid. This reckless assertion has some influence in depressing the national securities and keeping up the price of gold. This grumbling class of people say that the "old Continental money" issued during the war for independence, became worthless and was never paid. This is no doubt true—the Continental money did greatly depreciate and was never fully paid, but it was issued under the feeble authority of the old Continental Congress, when there was no adequate executive authority to enforce the collection of taxes for the payment of the public debt. This depreciated currency was issued both before and after the adoption of the articles of Confederation of the old thirteen states, and before the formation of the present efficient Government under the new Constitution.

Under the articles which composed the old compact, there was no power vested in the Continental Congress to collect taxes. The power to enforce the collection of taxes was left to the legislatures of the several States. Upon a quota furnished and a requisition made by Congress, the several States were required to levy and collect taxes to support the Federal Compact. This plan was a fallacious system of quotas and requisitions, inconsistent with every idea of vigor or efficiency which pertains to every well organized Constitution of civil Government. It is not at all surprising that the Continental money which depended upon thirteen other Governments to levy and collect taxes to raise money for its payment, should depreciate and become of little or no value. The power contained in the old Continental Compact was nominal, without a president or other executive to enforce its requisitions. It was ineffectual to raise money by taxation, and consequently the old Continental money fell into disrepute and was never fully paid.

Under the present Constitution all is changed. Instead of the old feeble compact existing at the close of the seven years war for independence, we have now a strong, well organized civil Government, under a Constitution with ample executive legislation and judicial powers, fully adequate to the objects for which it was formed. This Government is now invested with power to protect and defend the Constitution, enforce the laws and preserve its own existence; power to provide for the common defence and promote the general welfare; and for these purposes has power to raise and support armies, to provide and maintain a navy, and provide for calling forth the militia to execute the laws of the Union, suppress insurrections and repel invasions. To raise the money for these purposes, the Government is invested with further power to borrow money on the credit of the United States, and to repay the money thus borrowed, to levy and collect uniform taxes, duties, imports, and excises throughout the United States. These are some of the great powers intrusted to the general Government for the preservation of its own existence.

When this most wicked and gigantic rebellion broke out, in an open and avowed determination to break up the Union, it became necessary to bring into active exercise all these high powers of the Government. Armies and navies had to be raised and supported. All the material of war necessary for their efficiency had to be provided. Money had to be borrowed, and in vast amounts. The old Continental money possessed none of the elements of vitality and credit that is imparted to the legal tender demand notes and bonds issued under the present Constitution, with this great power vested in the President to enforce the laws.

The debt thus incurred in the prosecution of the war to put down the rebellion and restore the national authority over all the States, will be about $3,000,000,000. This large sum has been borrowed on the credit of the United States, to maintain the Government and perpetuate the Union, and the beneficial results flowing from the triumph of the national cause are amply sufficient to compensate for all the money expended in accomplishing this great achievement. The securities issued as evidence of this large indebtedness, consist of bonds, notes and certificates, which are widely distributed among all classes of people.

All the forms of law have been complied with to bind the Government and give validity to these different forms of indebtedness. The good faith of the nation is pledged in the most solemn manner to the payment of every dollar of this debt, both principal and interest.

The Government of the United States is not now dependent at all on the State Governments for the execution of its great powers. All the powers conferred on the General Government by the present Constitution are self-acting, self-sustaining, and wholly independent of State authority. The Constitution and laws of the United States operate directly upon the people, without any regard to State boundaries. We have now a Congress to pass all the tariff and tax laws necessary to raise all the money required to pay the current annual expenses of the Government, pay the interest on the public debt, and raise a surplus sufficient to retire annually a portion of the principal.

The grand results of the last four years have most abundantly shown the power and efficiency of the present National Government under the existing Constitution.

It is clearly demonstrated that we have a strong, stable and efficient Government, fully competent to levy and enforce the collection of custom duties and internal revenue adequate to support the Government.

The true value of the property, real and personal, within the United States, according to the census of 1860, was $10,000,000,000, and it has, notwithstanding the exhausting nature of the war, greatly increased since that time. All this property is liable to be taxed to the full extent necessary, to support the Government and pay every dollar of the debt incurred in the prosecution of the war. The Government has a claim under the Constitution, a mortgage in fact, which is the first lien on all this real and personal property to that extent. All the debts of States, counties, cities, corporations and individuals are second and subordinate to this first claim of the National Government.

Our credit rests on this property and the good faith and fidelity of the Government to collect these taxes.

Since the creation and distribution of this large debt among all classes of people, and a large part of it made the basis for the organization of over sixteen hundred banks, the whole fabric of credit, public and private, must, to a great extent, rest on the efficiency and determination with which these taxes are to be levied and collected. Public and private credit are so interwoven with all the commercial transactions of the country, that if the public credit fails, individual credit must also fail. The value of legal tender notes, national currency, five-twenty bonds, ten-forties and seven-thirties, all depend upon the revenues derived from custom duties and internal taxes. Our own people and the people of Europe must be fully assured, not only of the ability, but of the willingness and determination of the Government to pay promptly every one of the obligations of the Government as they become due, and that the financial credit of the Government will be maintained on the stable and sure basis of ample taxation. There is no other sure basis for it to rest upon.

There can be no doubt that the suggestions of the Secretary of the Treasury to gradually retire a portion of the currency, are wise and judicious. If it cannot be done by funding without bringing down the price of five-twenty six per cent. bonds below par, so as thereby to embarass the operations of the Treasury in providing for the large temporary debt as it becomes due, then I think it should be accomplished by Congress providing for an increase of revenue. The credit of the Government can be maintained, and it ought to be maintained at all hazards, and prices should be reduced. All who have read the late admirable reports of the Secretary of the Treasury, the Comptroller of the Currency, and the nearly unanimous resolution of the House of Representatives, must be satisfied that the Government is united and strong in its determination to enforce the full power it possesses to carry us safely through all our financial difficulties, and bring the business of the country back to a more safe and secure standard. So long as Congress and the Executive departments of the Government continue, as they now do, to discharge their duties with efficiency and fidelity, the repudiation of the public debt will be an impossibility.

I have lately seen and read in the public newspapers much that is of a fault-finding character, and much theorizing on the subject of our national finances, but after all that has been said or written on the subject, it comes down to a plain matter-of-fact business, which seems to be well understood by the Secretary of the Treasury, viz:

1. That frugality and economy should be practiced in all the departments of the public service.

2. Find out all the taxable property and business of the country, and the best modes of collecting revenue therefrom.

3. Levy and collect a tax upon it amply sufficient to raise a sum that will pay the yearly expenses of the Government, pay the interest on all the public debt, and leave a surplus of at least $50,000,000 annually towards retiring a part of the public debt, and the credit of the Government will be firmly maintained. No repudiation of the public debt will ever take place so long as this policy is pursued with vigor on the part of the national Government.

The great mass of the people are honest and patriotic, and believe that the public debt was incurred for just and patriotic purposes. They will stand by their rulers in maintaining the public faith. They will pay the taxes freely, and will never consent that the fair fame of their free Government shall ever be tarnished by a repudiation of one dollar of the debt incurred in such a righteous and noble cause.

E. G. SPAULDING.

NO STATE TAXATION OF UNITED STATES BONDS.

The Supreme Court of the United States, at Washington, has decided that United States Government Bonds and Treasury Notes cannot be taxed by States, Counties or Cities. The power to borrow money by the Government of the United States is supreme, and cannot be interfered with by any State law. All the Government securities have been issued under a positive law, which makes it a part of the contract that they should not be taxed for local purposes, and the contract cannot be changed. The first section of the act of Congress, passed June 30, 1864, provides that 'all bonds, Treasury notes and other obligations of the United States shall be exempt from taxation by or under State or Municipal authority.'

The Constitution of the United States provides that 'This Constitution and the Laws of the United States, which shall be made in pursuance thereof, *shall be the supreme law of the land*, and the judges in every State shall be bound thereby; anything in the Constitution or laws of any State to the contrary, notwithstanding.'

The Supreme Court of the United States has decided that all the State laws passed to tax United States securities are unconstitutional and void.

These loans are the best security in the market. No searches of title are necessary. The Constitution of the United States and the act of Congress make the public debt the first lien on the real and personal property of the country. The Government bonds and notes are the first claim to be paid, city bonds, railroad bonds and bonds and mortgages, are only a second lien, to be paid after the Government securities are paid.

E. G. SPAULDING.

PUBLIC DEBT—GOOD FAITH—HON. E. G. SPAULDING'S LETTER TO SENATOR MORGAN—SENATOR SHERMAN'S FUNDING BILL.

BUFFALO, Dec. 24, 1867.

Hon. E. D. Morgan, U. S. Senator, Washington.

Dear Sir—I am in receipt of the recent report of the Finance Committee brought in by Senator Sherman, and Senate Bill No. 207, 'for funding the national debt, and for the conversion of the notes of the United States,' accompanied by your letter of the 19th instant, asking my opinion on the proposed measure, or any of its parts, and desiring me to communicate my suggestions at an early day.

I am deeply impressed with the importance of a return to the specie standard at the earliest moment consistent with the operations of the Government and people. I concur fully in that part of the report of your committee which seeks 'to secure to the holders of United States notes, as soon as possible, their value in gold.' This, in my opinion, should engage the earnest efforts of Congress and the Executive; and I am much gratified to see your committee so earnest and decided in urging a return to the specie standard at the earliest practicable moment. A resumption of specie payments by the Government, the banks and people, is the first great thing to be accomplished. This would dispose of nearly all the complicated and disturbing issues that have been raised by politicians and others, as to the time when, and the kind of money in which, the public debt shall be paid. It would demonstrate more clearly than any thing else, our resources and ability to pay the public debt, and our determination to preserve unimpaired the good faith of the nation, and establish all business operations on a firm and enduring basis.

I notice that Senator Sherman, in his report, (pages 6 and 7,) giving countenance to the idea that the 5-20 bonds, under the act of 25th February, 1862, may be paid in the depreciated greenback currency, is laboring under a material misapprehension of the facts in regard to the representations made by the agents of the Government when the loan was negotiated, and especially as to the time when those representations were made. Mr. Sherman says: 'It is said that the distinguished Secretary of the Treasury who negotiated the 5-20 loan, gave a construction to this act at the time the loan was offered; that this was announced to the people, and upon the faith of this the loan was taken. Your committee can find no official declaration made by the Secretary on this subject, until after the loan was negotiated,' and then refers to a letter written by Secretary Chase, May 18, 1864, as being the first official declaration on the subject that has come to his knowledge. The Senator seems to concede that if the Secretary made official declarations, at the time the loan was negotiated, giving a construction to the act, to the effect that the principal, as well as the interest, was payable in coin, and that if both parties understood that to be the construction of the law, such declarations would form a part of the contract, and that the Government would be bound to make these declarations good, and to give effect to the contract as understood by both parties when it was made. Now, the proofs are at hand that such official representations were made by the distinguished Secretary of the Treasury, before and at the time the loan was being negotiated, as I will now proceed to show.

Secretary Chase, who negotiated that loan, decided as early as December, 1862, that a fair construction of all the loan acts under which the funded debt was contracted, required us to pay actual money—gold and silver—on all the funded debt of the Government; that a pretended payment in another promise of the United States was no payment, but merely changing the form of the debt. In other words, that a payment of the bonds in greenbacks, would be merely substituting the debt of the Government in the form of legal tender notes bearing no interest, for bonds bearing six per cent. interest,—which would be manifestly unjust. This question came up on the kind of money that should be provided for paying that part of the funded debt, created prior to the rebellion, which fell due January 1st, 1863, and this decision was then made and published. The Committee of Ways and Means, in December, 1862, a short time before its maturity, desired to know whether any further legislation would be necessary to ensure the payment of coin on that part of the funded debt falling due within a few days. In order to ascertain in a formal manner what construction the Secretary of the Treasury would put upon the law, a Sub-Committee from the Committee of Ways and Means was appointed, consisting of Mr. Hooper, Mr. Morrill and myself, to confer with the Secretary on the subject. This Sub-Committee called upon the Secretary at the Treasury Department, and after a full and free conference, the Secretary decided that a fair construction of the law, as well as good faith, required him to pay all the funded debt in coin, and that he did not deem it necessary to have any further law passed to enable him to do so.

Under these circumstances, the Committee of Ways and Means did not deem it necessary to report a bill authorizing or requiring the funded debt to be paid in coin, and consequently no further law was passed; and on the first of January, 1863, the funded debt falling due at that time was paid in coin. From the time this decision was made by Secretary Chase, down to the present time, the same language has been held by each Secretary of the Treasury, namely, that the funded debt of the Government was payable in coin, both principal and interest, and that the Government would not seek to avail itself of the five years option to redeem the 5-20 bonds until it was prepared to pay coin for the principal as well as the interest. But this is not the only proof.

Messrs. FISK & HATCH, bankers in New York city, were prominent sub-agents of the Government in negotiating the 5-20 bonds under the act of February 25, 1862. Many persons who were desirous of subscribing to this loan, wanted to know authoritatively, whether the principal of the bonds was payable in coin as well as the interest. In order to have the proof in hand to satisfy people on this point, Fisk & Hatch, at the very time they were negotiating large amounts of this loan, addressed a letter to the Secretary of the Treasury on the 3d of August, 1863, and received from him an official reply, signed by the Assistant Secretary of the Treasury, which was immediately published in the *New York Times*, as follows:

THE POPULAR LOAN.

To the Editor of the New York Times:—We are receiving numerous inquiries as to whether the United States 5-20 bonds are redeemable in gold. We have received a letter from the Treasury Department most satisfactorily answering this question, (as it was once before answered by Mr. Chase,) a copy of which we hand you herewith. The popular character of this loan, and its wide distribution among the people, renders the subject one of universal public interest and importance, and we presume the publication of this letter will be acceptable to your readers.

(Signed,) FISK & HATCH, Bankers.

TREASURY DEPARTMENT, WASHINGTON, D. C.,
August 5th, 1863.

Gentlemen—Your letter of the 3d instant, relative to the redemption of 6 per cent. 5-20 bonds of the loan of February 25, 1862, has been received. The following is the decision of the Secretary of the Treasury in regard to the redemption of the public debt: 'All coupon and registered bonds forming a part of the permanent loan of the United States, *will be redeemed in gold.* The 5-20 sixes, being redeemable at any time within twenty years after the lapse of five years, belong to the permanent loan, and so also do the twenty years sixes of July 17, 1861, into which the three years 7-30s are convertible. All obligations and notes forming a part of the temporary loan will be paid at maturity in United States notes, unless before such maturity payment in specie shall have been generally resumed. The 7-30 three year bonds or notes form part of the temporary loan, with the privilege of conversion into 20 years sixes, in sums not less than $500. They will therefore be paid, if the holders prefer payment to conversion, in United States notes.

GEORGE HARRINGTON,
Acting Secretary of the Treasury.

To Messrs. FISK & HATCH, Bankers, New York.

This official letter from the Treasury Department, in addition to its being published in all the newspapers, was published in hand-bill form, (one of the original hand-bills being now in my possession,) and sent broadcast among the people, to induce them to come forward and take up these bonds—which were then on the market under the direction of the

Secretary of the Treasury, and offered by him at par. I was at this time actively engaged in negotiating this loan. I advertised and circulated this letter extensively myself, and gave copies of it to subscribers at the time of making their subscription to this loan. I regarded these representations, made by authority of the Treasury Department, and upon the faith of which people were induced to subscribe for the loan, as forming a part of the contract, and that the Government is now bound to make these representations good; and that, whenever they seek to redeem these bonds, the principal as well as the interest should be paid in coin. I should regard it as a gross breach of faith on the part of the Government to attempt to evade these declarations, or equivocate in fulfilling this contract, or any part of it.

But aside from these representations made by the Secretary, I would suggest that the plain meaning of the act of '62, when read in connection with its title, leads to the same conclusion, and that Secretary Chase, in giving the construction to the law which he did in negotiating the loan, gave a correct, practical, common sense decision. The argument of the present Secretary, in his last annual report, (pages 24, 25 and 26,) is able and conclusive on this point. The interpretation given to the act by both these distinguished Secretaries is in exact accordance with my intention at the time I drew and introduced the bill in the House, in January, 1862, and as I believe it was fully understood by Congress when it passed. The title of the act is expressive of the intention and purpose for which it was passed, namely, 'an act to authorize the issue of United States notes, and for the redemption or funding thereof, and for funding the floating debt of the United States.'

It was intended by this measure, in the imminent peril in which we were then placed by rebellion, to make a forced loan from capitalists, by compelling them to take legal tender United States notes, which should be paid out to the army and navy, and for supplies and material of war, but at the same time give them a fair rate of interest for the use of their money, by allowing them to fund these legal tender notes as they should accumulate in their hands and not bearing interest, into a twenty years bond bearing six per cent. interest. In the opening speech which I made in the House on the 28th of January, 1862, I said: 'The demand notes put in circulation would meet the present exigencies of the Government in the discharge of its existing liabilities to the army and navy, and contractors for supplies, materials and munitions of war. These notes would find their way into all the channels of trade among the people, and as they accumulate in the hands of capitalists, they would exchange them for six per cent. 20 years bonds. These circulating notes in the hands of the people, would enable them to pay taxes imposed, and would facilitate all business operations between farmers, mechanics, commercial business men and banks, and be equally as good as, and in most cases better than, the present irredeemable currency issued by the State banks. The $500,000,000 six per cent. twenty years bonds in the hands of the Secretary of the Treasury, ready to be issued, would afford ample opportunity for funding the Treasury notes as fast as capitalists might desire to exchange notes not bearing interest for coupon bonds of the United States bearing six per cent. interest, and amply secured by a tax on the people and all their property. In this way the Government will be able to get along with its immediate and pressing necessities, without being obliged to force its bonds on the market at ruinous rates of discount; the people under heavy taxation will be shielded against high rates of interest, and the capitalists will be afforded a fair compensation for the use of their money during the pending struggle of the country for national existence.

'A suspension of specie payments is greatly to be deplored, but it is not a fatal step in an exigency like the present. The British Government and the Bank of England remained under suspension of specie payments from 1797 to 1821-2, a period of twenty-five years. Gold is not as valuable as are the productions of the farmer and mechanic, for it is not as indispensable as food and raiment. Our army and navy must have what is more valuable to them than gold or silver—they must have food, clothing and the material of war. Treasury notes, issued by the Government on the faith of the whole people, will purchase these indispensable articles, and the war can be prosecuted until we can enforce obedience to the Constitution and laws, and an honorable peace be thereby secured. This being accomplished, I will be among the first to advocate a speedy return to specie payments, and all measures that are calculated to preserve the honor and dignity of the Government in time of peace, and which I regret are not practicable in the prosecution of this war.'

These are, in part, the remarks I made in the House on the loan bill introduced by me, and which became a law February 25th, 1862. The operation of the bill, in the issue of the legal tender notes, the paying them out to the army and navy, their final funding into a twenty years six per cent. bonds, have been substantially what I stated would be its operation at the time I introduced it into the House. The object of the bill was to provide the means by which the floating and temporary debt, then bearing heavily upon the Treasury, might, by the operation of the act, be funded into a long bond without a heavy sacrifice in making the negotiation. Some gentlemen are now trying to reverse the obvious intent of the act, and *unfund* all this bonded debt, by again putting it into a *floating* and temporary form. I regard all these late shifts and quibbles to unsettle what is already honorably fixed and determined by the Treasury Department under and in pursuance of law, as unworthy of this great nation, unstatesmanlike in those who advocate it, and, if persisted in, will, I think, inevitably destroy the credit of the Government, and postpone indefinitely a resumption of specie payments.

Why take the back track under these funding loan bills? Why open the question at all at this time? The *floating* debt and temporary loans are *already funded*, or so nearly funded that there cannot be any reasonable doubt that, by the 15th of July next, when the last series of 7-30 notes fall due, the whole will be funded into bonds, none of which are payable until 1882, being fifteen years yet before they become due. The Government is not legally or morally bound to pay one dollar of the principal of these bonds until they become due. Then why trouble ourselves about funding that which is already funded, especially when it has to be done by repudiating the acts and declarations of the Secretary of the Treasury in the discharge of his official duties? Why raise the question now as to the kind of money with which we are to pay bonds already outstanding, and which are not becoming due until 1882?

The $830,000,000 of three years 7-30 notes were all negotiated under representations made by the Treasury Department, similar to those made in respect to the 5-20 loan of '62, with an express stipulation that the holders of these notes should have the privilege of converting them at maturity into 5-20 bonds. The bonds of '62, as well as the bonds issued in redemption of the three series of 7-30 notes, all stand upon the same footing, and the Government is no doubt bound to pay the principal as well as interest in coin, whenever it seeks to retire these bonds under the five years option, reserved in the face of the bonds. That such is the view taken by the present Secretary of the Treasury, fully appears by his letter to L. P. Morton & Co., bankers in New York, in which he says:

TREASURY DEPARTMENT, Nov. 15, 1866.

Gentlemen—Your favor of the 13th instant is received. I regard, as did also my predecessors, all bonds of the United States *as payable in coin.* The bonds that have matured since the suspension of specie payments have been so paid, and I have no doubt that the same will be true of all others. This being, as I understand it to be, the established policy of the Government, the 5-20 bonds of 1862 will either be called in at the expiration of five years from their date, *and paid in coin,* or be permitted to run until the Government is prepared to *pay them in coin.*

I am, very truly yours,

HUGH McCULLOCH,
Secretary.

Messrs. L. P. MORTON & Co., New York.

Under the influence of this official declaration, most of the bonds have been taken on the exchange of the 7-30 notes, in pursuance of the stipulation on the back of the notes, and long before these bonds become due, specie payments will no doubt be resumed, and we shall then have but one standard of value, and only one kind of money, namely, coin, or its equivalent, in which to pay these bonds. Our population and resources will be nearly double then to what they are now. We shall be abundantly able to pay at that time in that currency which is recognized by all civilized nations as the true standard and measure of value, and thereby the honor and good faith of the nation will be fully maintained.

I would suggest that it is not wise to prematurely agitate the question, and am not able as yet to see any good reason for doing so. On the contrary, I think all agitation now, on this branch of the financial question, is mischievous, and calculated unnecessarily to impair our credit at home and abroad.

I would suggest further, that the provision in the bill which limits the legal tender currency to $400,000,000, is a good one, provided there is any sane man in Congress who proposes, in a time of peace, to dilute and still further depreciate the currency, by increasing it above that sum; but I think the maximum of the greenback currency must not exceed $250,000,000 or $300,000,000 when we reach the specie standard, if we would successfully maintain specie payments. And it seems to me that it would greatly facilitate a resumption of specie payments if the national banks were required to hold a part of their reserves in coin, and that some safe plan should be devised by which the sub-treasuries in the principal cities, especially in New York, could make daily settlements with the banks through the clearing-house, and requiring only balances to be paid, substantially in the same manner as the banks in the principal cities make their daily settlements with each other. In this way no large movement in coin to or from the sub-Treasury would be necessary, and the daily payments could be made with comparative ease. But this letter is already too long, much longer than I intended when I commenced it, and I will not enlarge further on this subject at this time. I may desire to make some further suggestions, and if so, will write you again.

I remain, very truly, your friend,

E. G. SPAULDING.

FROM HON. F. E. SPINNER.

WASHINGTON, Nov. 9.

Hon. E. G. Spaulding, Buffalo, N. Y.:

My Dear Sir—Your note of the 6th inst. has been received. If some one who believes in high-toned swindling will write in favor of open repudiation, I will agree to give the subject the consideration of a careful reading, but I have not the patience to read anything advocating the sneaking expedient of paying the national debt in depreciated currency.

The Secretary of the Treasury is sound on this subject; and in his forthcoming Annual Report will address an argument to the Congress and the country, that I am sure will please you and those who are neither knaves nor fools.

The finance question is to become the leading one in the organization of parties, and I had hoped that such men as Butler and Stevens would have remained with the great body of their friends. Having an abiding faith in the honesty of the people, I believe the question will be settled honestly, and that honest Americans will be spared the shame of having their nation stigmatized as a band of cheats and swindlers.

Very truly, your friend,

F. E. SPINNER.

NATIONAL CURRENCY—LEGAL TENDER.

The avowed policy of the Government is to retire the legal tender greenback currency, issued during the war, and bring the business of the country back to a gold standard, and a resumption of specie payments. This policy is avowed by the President in his annual message, and by the Secretary of the Treasury in his Fort Wayne speech, and in his annual report. As this policy will sooner or later be carried out, it is important we should look ahead and be prepared for the change. It will take time to accomplish so great a result, and it must be done with great prudence and discretion, or it will produce a shock to the legitimate business of the country, which will paralyze our business operations and thereby diminish the revenues that will be so much needed to maintain the public credit. Whatever measures will aid in promoting the healthy and legitimate business of the country during the process of contraction will be of essential service both to the Government and the people.

It is not so very important just at this time, that there should be any material change made in the functions of the national currency, but as the Government legal tender notes are withdrawn from circulation, and the contraction policy fairly begun, I think it will be of great importance to the country, in giving stability to its financial operations, that the national currency should be, like the Bank of England notes, made a legal tender, except for debts owing by the banks. I feel confident that it would lessen the liability to a panic, as contraction goes on, and be useful and beneficial to the Government and people, in maintaining the financial credit and business of the country.

The national currency is limited to a proper amount, so that there will be no chance for an over issue, and as the banks issuing it are required on the resumption of specie payments, to redeem it in coin, I can see no harm that would arise from making it a legal tender, but on the contrary, much good to follow the enactment of such a law. Let us consider this subject a little more in detail.

What the Government and people want and must have in this great and enterprising country, is a currency of universal credit and uniform value. Such a currency is a vital necessity to the well being of the business of the country. It should possess all the attributes of money, adequate in amount, and receivable alike in all payments, public and private. Men engaged in large commercial transactions have no especial worship for gold and silver, either as money or for ornament; but I would not discard those metals in fixing the standard of value of paper money, and the relative value of commodities and services. In devising and regulating a system of national currency, I would have coin and paper money as nearly on an equality as it is possible by having the paper convertible into coin on demand.

I know it is insisted by some persons that the only money is coined metal, and that paper money as its substitute, is only credit. This may be true in a certain sense, but at the same time both coined money and paper money are the creation of law, and it is equally true that credit underlies the whole financial operations of the Government and people, and if that credit is broken down, the Government and people will become bankrupt, business paralyzed and revenues largely diminished. Coined money like paper money is made in pursuance of statute law, and has impressed upon it the Government stamp, indicating its weight and purity. This stamp does not, however, give the metal its value, the value is in the metal independent of the stamp, but gold of individuals so coined into eagles under the laws of the United States, does determine the rate in arithmetical terms at which the metal thus coined shall be a legal tender, and the standard of value in all exchanges and payments, and this makes it by law money. Paper money is made by a somewhat different process, but when both are stamped with the functions of money they are both the creation of law. It is true that gold and silver are esteemed a valuable commodity without being coined, and are within a small fraction, rated as high in the form of bullion, as in the form of coin. The coined money rests on its own inherent or estimated value, while the paper money is based upon a well-founded credit. A payment in coin or bullion closes the transaction, because the bargained for equivalent is rendered at once, leaving no credit to be upheld or promise to be performed in the future. United States demand Treasury notes, are also by law made lawful money and a legal tender as a substitute for coin, and their value is based upon the credit of the Government, and all the taxable property under its jurisdiction. If they were not issued in excess they would not be below the gold standard, and would constitute as good, and even a better currency than coin, because less expensive and more convenient, and because they are based on a well founded credit, no less than an adequate tax on all the real and personal property of the country. The principal difference between coin and paper money may be stated thus: the exchange and delivery of one hundred bushels of wheat for one hundred dollars, in value of gold bars or coined gold, the transaction is closed on the spot, by each party delivering to the other, what is regarded by them as an equivalent; according to the estimation of both parties, it is an exchange of equivalent values. In such a transaction, no credit is given on either side; but if instead of gold, the purchaser of the wheat should deliver to the seller in exchange for it, one hundred dollars in paper money, the equivalent for the wheat, although perfectly secured, would not be rendered on the spot, but a credit would intervene in taking the paper money, which contained only a promise to deliver one hundred dollars in gold at another time. In one sense it is true that the seller of the wheat takes even gold on a credit, trusting that it will continue at all times as valuable as it now is, notwithstanding it possesses very few useful qualities, and is not intrinsically as valuable as iron. Franklin says, 'that the value of gold and silver rests chiefly in the estimation they happen to be in, among the generality of nations, and the credit given to the opinion that that estimation will continue; otherwise a pound of gold would not be a real equivalent for a bushel of wheat.' It is the universal estimation in which gold and silver are held, that gives them their present value, and not the labor expended upon them, or any particularly useful qualities contained in the metal itself. Any other well founded credit is as much an equivalent as gold and silver, and in some cases more so, or it would not be preferred by commercial people in different countries. For this reason a well secured convertible paper money, in a normal state of the business of the country, is fully equal to gold and silver, because less expensive, and more convenient. But where commercial transactions are small, and among barbarous nations where credit is unsafe, gold and silver, on account of their comparatively steady value, and the universal estimation in which they are held by all mankind, no doubt constitute the best money. These precious metals, so called, being limited in amount, and used extensively in the arts and luxuries of life, are desired the world over, not only by civilized, but by barbarous nations, and having great estimated value in small bulk, are easily transported from continent to continent. This universal estimation gives them pretty steady value as money, and an equally steady value in the arts, and for ornament. They therefore constitute at present, the best standard by which to measure the relative value of all other commodities. They are, therefore, the standard of value in all countries, and it will be very difficult, if not impossible, for the nations of the world to agree upon any other standard of value. They have not become so by reason of a congress of nations, nor by any concert of action among them, but by the quiet action of commerce among the people for many centuries, and in all countries and climes. Gold and silver therefore, are the universal standard of value, made so by the acquiescence of all mankind, and consequently all foreign balances are settled in gold and silver. But owing to the scarcity of the precious metals, and the great expense attending their use as money, and the risk of transporting them from place to place, credit has been resorted to in some form by all civilized countries, under well established Governments, as a substitute for gold and silver, and especially for domestic purposes; for instance, the Bank of England notes, for the British Empire.

Bills of exchange, promissory notes, credits on bank ledgers, checks, bank bills, and clearing house certificates are among the forms of credit chiefly used in commerce at the present time. In consequence of this scarcity of gold and silver money adequate to the wants of commerce, these forms of credit have been extensively used by the people of all commercial countries, because business in this form could be done more cheaply, with much greater facility, and in vastly greater amounts, than it could be done by contracting it to the actual use of gold and silver in each transaction; and although there is no actual use of coin in the exchange of commodities and services, nevertheless all these credit transactions have a relation to gold and silver, as the standard or measure of value, and ought to have an equally close relation to the amount of commodities and services to be exchanged; and to be safe, should never exceed the wants of legitimate business. It is generally conceded that these different forms of credit, when not carried to excess, are of the greatest usefulness to every well regulated society. So apparent are their advantages, that they are deemed indispensable, and that without them, the present large volume of commercial transactions could not be carried on. Most of these forms of credit have grown into use by the necessities of commerce for centuries past, and are governed by universal commercial law, modified in some particulars by local statutes, but generally the law merchant regulates and governs all of them, except in the case of bank bills and Government paper money, which are wholly the creation of local laws, and are regulated and governed by the statute laws under which they are created. This brings me to the consideration of a paper currency authorized and regulated by statute laws.

NATIONAL CURRENCY—LEGAL TENDER.

In discussing the subject of a national currency, and the functions that should be imparted to it by law, I assume that Congress deems it necessary and proper to have a paper national currency, not only to carry on the fiscal operations of the Government, but also to facilitate the business operations of the people; and that such a currency is created because it is the duty of the general Government to provide a domestic circulating medium of uniform value, to be used and circulated as money in all parts of the United States. Now, if it is desirable and proper to have a national paper currency at all, as I think it is, it seems to me to be obvious that it should be the best that the Government is capable of making. If it is necessary to create a paper currency, as a substitute for, or as a representative of, gold and silver, why not give it all the attributes of money, so far forth as it can be made so by law? Why should not Congress confer upon it in all respects, the highest qualities possible to make it suitable, useful and acceptable in all the ramified operations of the Government and people over the whole country? This currency is a creation of the Government. Its object is to make money for circulation; to make it of uniform value all over the United States in effecting exchanges and payments, and as nearly equal to gold and silver as it is possible to make it.

This great nation surely ought not to create a currency inferior to the best paper money in the world. It should have all the attributes of money to pay debts and facilitate exchanges. It should be backed by the whole power of the Government to make it what it purports to be, a national currency, and the representative of gold and silver, and convertible into gold coin on demand. Nothing should be withheld by Congress which would in any degree add to the stability or usefulness of such a currency. It is created as an instrument of usefulness to benefit the Government and people, and if made at all, it should be, like a locomotive, or any other instrument, the best that can be made. I took this ground on the passage of the legal tender act introduced by me in 1862. I then said that if we issued a Government paper money at all, it ought to have imparted to it the highest legal sanction that could be given to it by the Government, to make it fulfill the purpose for which it was made. There are very few business men who now question the wisdom of that enactment. Though in the administration of the laws authorizing it, more was unnecessarily issued, and less funded, than was intended by the originators of the measure.

The British Government is the great pioneer in providing a paper national currency. The Bank of England, a creation of that Government, has existed one hundred and seventy-two years. She has had great experience in the issue, circulation and redemption of the circulating notes of that bank; and the British Empire has increased in material wealth and power with astonishing rapidity since the bank was established. Previous to 1834, the circulating notes of the Bank of England were not made a legal tender, but after an experience of over 140 years, she passed an act making them a legal tender for all debts, except those owing by the bank itself; and for the avowed reason that it would not remove any of the guards against over-issues, and that it would increase the stability of the bank, guard against panics, and consequently improve the whole monetary system of that empire. Since that act of Parliament was passed, she requires the notes of the bank to be perfectly secured by gold and Government stocks; requires the bank to redeem in coin on demand at its own counter, and then makes them a general legal tender except at the bank.

The Bank of England notes admirably perform the functions of money. They are current money in all parts of the empire. They are probably the most perfect paper currency in the world, because they are not only perfectly secured and redeemable in gold on demand at the bank, but they have imparted to them by law the functions of money in the payment of debts and effecting exchanges, in the cities and villages remote from London, as well as in the metropolis itself. They are backed by the whole power of the British Government, and circulate with as much vitality at the circumference as at the centre of the empire. The bank and its circulating notes are as stable and secure as the Government itself.

Why should we not profit by the experience and example of the British Government in respect to its national currency? We have provided by Congressional enactment for the organization of a system of national banks, and the issue of a national currency. This was deemed a necessary measure for the support of the Government in providing a circulating medium to facilitate the easy exchange of commodities, thereby stimulating enterprise, industry and production; adding to the ability of the people to pay revenue, and furnishing a currency in which the internal taxes may be paid. The leading idea was to combine the capital of individuals with the credit of the Government, to provide a national currency, and throw the burthens of redeeming such currency upon the banks that issue it, the Government only guaranteeing its ultimate payment.

The national currency act is generally right as far as it goes. It limits the amount to $300,000,000; requires the circulating notes to be well secured by gold-bearing Government bonds, deposited with the Treasurer of the United States; requires each bank to redeem its circulating notes in lawful money on demand, and to keep an adequate reserve for that purpose; makes them a legal tender for all taxes and other debts due to the Government, except customs, and for all debts owing *by* the Government, except principal and interest of the funded debt; it also makes them receivable by each national bank for all ordinary debts due to them, and each bank, designated as a depository, is also required to receive it on deposit from all public officers. These are important provisions in the law for *nationalizing* this currency, and it consequently obtains a wide circulation. I would not change or alter any one of these provisions for *de-centralizing* the currency, but I think it does not go quite far enough in that direction. It will be perceived that all persons in the employ of the Government are compelled to receive it in payment for salaries and for materials and other services performed for the Government. It is now in effect made a legal tender from the Government to all this class of persons, including the salary of the President, Cabinet, Members of Congress and the army and navy. If the President and other officers of the Government are obliged to receive it in payment for their salaries, why should not everybody else be required to take it from them for all ordinary debts they may incur? I can see no valid reason why they should be a legal tender to persons employed by the Government, unless such persons can also compel other parties to receive it from them. I think that sound policy requires the act to be still further extended. I would go one step further and make the national currency, like the Bank of England notes, a general legal tender, so long as the bank issuing it, redeem in lawful money, except that the currency issued by any bank separately should not be a legal tender for any debts such bank might itself owe.

I would not relax any of the duties or obligations now imposed on the banks. I would compel them to redeem their circulation in legal tender United States notes on demand, until the resumptions of specie payments, and after that in specie, and oblige them to keep a sufficient reserve for that purpose. The reason for such additional legislation would not be so much for the benefit of the banks, as it would be to benefit the public, by providing a domestic currency, made legal tender the same as gold belonging to individuals is made a tender, and which could be used to the greatest common advantage among all classes of people in all parts of the country. I would make it a legal tender because it would lessen the demand for coin, and have a tendency to prevent unnecessary runs on the banks to obtain it. It is argued by many persons, with much plausibility, that a well secured paper currency would be better in many respects, if not made redeemable in coin, for the reason that coin is scarce as compared with the volume of business to be done; that it is easily exported, and that when brought to the test of requiring the paper money issued to be redeemed in coin it has always failed, and always will fail, because there is never available coin enough for that purpose. I admit that the frequent suspension of specie payments, whenever there is a panic or revulsion, furnishes an argument in favor of those who present this view of the subject, but as no proper standard can be had at present, without making paper currency equal to coin, I think it must be convertible into coin on demand. Every attribute, however, that can be given to improve its quality will lessen the necessity for its redemption in coin, and consequently the more steady and uniform will be the business of the country.

With this object in view, I can see no valid reason why the highest legal sanction should not be imparted to this currency by the Government, which holds the pledged security and guarantees its payments, not only to give it stability, and guard against panics and suspensions of specie payments, but to make it useful to the people as money, in the remote districts as well as at the centre of business, and make it fulfil in the highest possible degree the object for which it was created, *a national currency.*

E. G. SPAULDING.

February 28, 1866.

LEGAL TENDER IN TIME OF PEACE.

BUFFALO, December 9, 1868.

Hon. Hugh McCulloch, Secretary of the Treasury:

Dear Sir—Will you be kind enough to send me a pamphlet copy of your Annual Report; I have seen a synopsis of it in the newspapers, and desire to study it in a more readable form. I have always read your able and well-matured reports with pleasure and profit. I judge, from the extracts of the report which I have seen, that you continue firm in the opinion that we should get rid of the evils of a depreciated currency by returning to the specie standard at the earliest practicable moment; this is the first great and important duty of the Government, and I sincerely hope that efficient measures will be adopted to that end at the present session of Congress.

You justly observe that the legal tender act was adopted as a war measure—a measure of necessity to sustain the army and navy while crushing the rebellion. In the summer and fall of 1861, all the great powers expressly granted in the Constitution had been brought into active exercise in bringing into the field an army of half a million of men, which had to be fed, clothed and provided with all the material of war necessary to make them effective, requiring an average daily expenditure of $2,000,000. This required very large amounts of money, and we had to have it right off—delay would have been fatal. The banks in New York, Boston and Philadelphia had exhausted themselves in loaning to the Government $150,000,000 in gold during the summer and fall of 1861. A large part of the available gold in the country had thus been paid over to the Government, and expended during that time, and so scattered that it was not available as a reserve for the banks, or in a situation to be re-loaned to the Government. The Government and banks suspended specie payments on the last of December, 1861. No more gold could be loaned because it was not to be had, except in small and wholly inadequate amounts. State bank bills could be obtained, but the banks having suspended specie payments this currency was depreciated, and was only local in character and credit.

In this great emergency, with this large army to be supported and the navy to be maintained, and which were organized under the unlimited war powers expressly granted in the Constitution, there arose an overwhelming necessity for resorting to the incidental and implied powers, and especially to that provision in the Constitution which empowers Congress 'to make all laws which shall be necessary and proper for carrying into execution the foreign powers and all other powers vested by this Constitution in the Government of the United States, or any department or officer thereof.' In the imminent peril in which we were then placed by a gigantic rebellion, Congress decided that the legal tender act was a measure necessary and proper to carry into effect those powers expressly granted in the Constitution, to maintain the army and support the navy. Secretary Chase relied at this time mainly upon the passage of the national currency act to furnish the means, but it appeared to me that it would be wholly inadequate, and besides it could not be made available quick enough. I therefore introduced the legal tender bill early in January, 1862, immediately after the suspension of specie payments. In this great crisis I advocated the bill as a war measure, a measure of temporary relief to the Treasury, and on the ground that it was an imperative necessity to preserve the life of the nation. I conceded that it was a forced loan, and could only be justified on grounds of necessity.

As a war measure passed during war, continuing during the war, and as long as the exigency lasted, I believe it was necessary and proper to successfully carry on the war, and was therefore constitutional. I am equally clear, that as a peace measure it is unconstitutional. No one would now think of passing a legal tender act making the promises of the Government, (a mere form of credit,) a legal tender in payment of 'all debts, public and private.' Such a law, passed while the Government is on a peace footing, could not be sustained for one moment.

I think now that it is unfortunate that we did not have incorporated into the original legal tender act, at the time of its passage, a provision that the legal tender clause should cease to be operative in one year after the close of the war. In that case all parties would have shaped their business accordingly, and the law would have served its purpose as a war measure, and would not have been continued (as I think unnecessarily,) so long after the close of the war.

I see that the constitutionality of the law has finally come up for decision before the Supreme Court of the United States, at Washington. If the Court had been called upon to decide the question during the war, or at its close, they would most likely have decided that the law was valid, inasmuch as Congress had decided that it was a necessary and proper means to be used in crushing the rebellion; but the law has been continued in force so long after the close of the war without any real necessity for it, that I should not be much surprised if the Court should now declare it unconstitutional.

Three great measures were adopted by the Government, which, in my judgment, were necessary to crush the rebellion and maintain the national unity, viz.:

1. The *legal tender act*, by which the credit of the Government was brought into immediate action in the most available form.

2. *Emancipation*, by which 4,000,000 slaves became intensely interested in the Union cause.

3. The *draft*, by which the army was speedily re-inforced at the turning point of the rebellion.

These three measures, backed by the people, and enforced by the army and navy, finally gave us a national triumph.

If Congress will not act promptly in devising some plan for bringing the legal tender greenback currency on a par with gold, rather than continue the demoralization incident to a postponement of specie payments, it will perhaps be as well for the country in a long run, if the Court, on due deliberation, should decide the legal tender clause to be unconstitutional. This would involve serious consequences for a while, and business arrangements would be materially affected, but we would very soon accommodate ourselves to the situation, and we would then emerge from the evils of an irredeemable currency, and all business operations would be established on a firm and enduring basis.

This letter is much longer than I intended when I sat down to write, and I trust you will pardon me for writing so much.

I remain, yours truly,

E. G. SPAULDING.

PRESIDENT LINCOLN'S VETO.

President's Message in favor of a National Currency, but vetoing irredeemable bank notes in the District of Columbia, June 23, 1862.

To the Senate of the United States:

The bill which has passed the House of Representatives and the Senate, entitled, 'An act to repeal that part of an act of Congress which prohibits the circulation of bank notes of a less denomination than five dollars in the District of Columbia,' has received my attentive consideration, and I now return it to the Senate, in which it originated, with the following objections:

1. The bill proposes to repeal the existing legislation prohibiting the circulation of bank notes of a less denomination than five dollars within the District of Columbia, without permitting the issuing of such bills by banks not now legally authorized to issue them. In my judgment it will be found impracticable, in the present condition of the currency, to make such a discrimination. The banks have generally suspended specie payments, and a legal sanction given to the circulation of the irredeemable notes of one class of them will almost certainly be so extended in practical operation as to include those of all classes, whether authorized or unauthorized. If this view be correct, the currency of the District, should this act become a law, will certainly and greatly deteriorate, to the serious injury of honest trade and honest labor.

2. This bill seems to contemplate no end which cannot be otherwise more certainly and beneficially attained. During the existing war, it is peculiarly the duty of the national Government to secure to the people a sound circulating medium. This duty has been, under existing circumstances, satisfactorily performed, in part at least, by authorizing the issue of United States notes receivable for all Government dues except customs, and made a legal tender for all debts, public and private, except interest on the public debt. The object of the bill submitted to me, namely, that of providing a small note currency during the present suspension, can be fully accomplished by authorizing the issue, as part of any new emission of United States notes, made necessary by the circumstances of the country, of notes of a similar character, but of less denomination than five dollars. Such an issue would answer all the beneficial purposes of the bill; would save a considerable amount to the Treasury in interest; would greatly facilitate payments to soldiers and other creditors of small sums, and would furnish to the people a currency as safe as their own Government.

Entertaining these objections to the bill, I feel myself constrained to withhold from it my approval, and return it for the further consideration and action of Congress.

ABRAHAM LINCOLN.

SPEECH OF HON. E. G. SPAULDING, OF NEW YORK,

DELIVERED IN THE HOUSE OF REPRESENTATIVES,

Friday, May 3d, 1862.

The House having under consideration the bills to confiscate the property and free from servitude the slaves of rebels, Mr. Spaulding said:

Mr. SPEAKER—It seems to be right and proper, while we are taxing our own loyal people to pay the enormous expenses of this war, that we should endeavor to make the ring-leaders of the rebellion, who have fomented and brought on this terrible state of things, pay as large a portion of these expenses as is possible. To this end it is fit and proper that Congress should exert all the power it possesses in confiscating the property of rebels, and having it sold under an order of the court, and the proceeds thereof, paid into the Treasury of the United States; and also that such rebels should be deprived of the labor and services of their slaves, from which they derive their chief support. These propositions are now pending in this House, and we shall be called to vote upon them on Monday next. These are important measures, and I desire to say a few words before giving my vote. After the able arguments that have been made in the Senate and House by those who have been especially charged with the subject of confiscating the property of rebels and the emancipation of their slaves, I do not deem it necessary for me to make any extended remarks.

Sir, the time has come when we must meet the actual condition of things, and dispose of these and other momentous questions presented for our consideration in a practical way, and with a firm determination to suppress this rebellion and establish law and order in every part of the United States. Success, regardless of the cost, is the all-important thing to be attained. This rebellion must be crushed out, and all the means which God has given us must, sooner or later, be brought into requisition to accomplish that result. The sooner we earnestly put forth every effort, and apply all the means at our command, the sooner will the rebellion be suppressed, and the less of life and treasure will be expended.

What is the actual condition of things? All the horrors of war are upon us. War on a gigantic scale—savage, unrelenting war is waged against us by the rebels. Not only do they kill our brave sons and brothers on the field of battle, but they murder them stealthily, stab and scalp them when wounded, and disfigure and mangle them after they are dead. The rebels in arms against us are enemies *de facto*, possessed of all the bitterness and determination of the most unrelenting foreign enemies. We are obliged to accept this condition of things. It has been forced upon us by their own acts. The life of the nation is attacked, and a most determined effort made to overthrow the Government of the

United States in all of the confederate States. They *are* our enemies. I am disposed, while they are so in rebellion, to treat them as enemies, and to give them only the rights of war, and apply to them all the disabilities and penalties of war.

As alien enemies, throwing off all allegiance to the Government, trampling the Constitution and laws of the United States under their feet, how can they claim any protection from us? As enemies *de facto*, they can claim no rights except the rights of war. Any gentleman on this floor holding up the Constitution as a shield to protect these rebels it seems to me has not duly considered the subject. Is it possible that men who utterly repudiate the Constitution, confederate together, declare war, issue letters of marque and reprisal, and are in open war against us, can claim any rights under the Constitution? The laws of war are against it. Common sense and common justice would revolt at any such claim, even if the public law was not so emphatically against it.

If we were to proceed and indict the traitors in arms against the Government for treason, (as we have an undoubted right to do,) under the provisions of the Constitution, then they might, in such case, claim to have their criminality decided by the court, under the strict rules of the common law and the Constitution and statute laws of the United States. In such a case, the argument of the gentleman from Massachusetts [Mr. Thomas,] might have some application. But when the traitors are engaged in actual war, then you apply to them the laws of war. Having themselves repudiated the Constitution, and having expelled the United States courts from all the rebel States, so that you cannot indict and try them under the ordinary forms of judicial proceedings, they cannot complain if you apply to them the laws which are clearly applicable to the position which they have voluntarily, but most criminally, chosen for themselves. Having declared war against the United States, they must submit to all the rules of civilized warfare, and if their property is confiscated and their slaves emancipated, they have no right to complain.

What is the war power conferred on the President and Congress? By the Constitution, the President is made 'Commander-in-Chief of the army and navy of the United States, and of the militia of the several States when called into the actual service of the United States.' The Constitution confers on Congress the power, first, 'to raise and support armies;' second, 'to provide and maintain a navy;' third, 'to make rules for the government of the land and naval forces;' fourth, 'to provide for calling forth the militia to execute the laws of the Union, suppress insurrections, and repel invasions;' fifth, 'to grant letters of marque and reprisal;' sixth, 'to make rules concerning captures on land and water;' seventh, 'to declare war;' eighth, 'to make all laws which shall be necessary and proper for carrying into execution the foregoing powers.' In pursuance of these war powers conferred on Congress by the Constitution, laws have been passed to carry them into execution. The public laws of nations declare the rights and penalties of war. More than one hundred articles of war have been adopted by Congress for the government of our army. At the extra session in July last, Congress passed various laws which were then deemed 'necessary' to crush out the rebellion. Congress passed those laws, and the President executes them, in accordance with the rights of war.

Among the rights of war is the power to confiscate the enemy's property and liberate their slaves. One of the express powers conferred on Congress by the Constitution, is to call out the militia 'to suppress insurrections,' which means that you have unlimited power to effectually suppress the present or any other insurrection. All the means necessary may be employed to suppress it. Nothing within the range of civilized warfare is withheld from you in this crisis. Congress may, in the language of the Constitution, pass 'all laws which may be necessary and proper' to suppress the 'insurrection.' If the laws now on the statute-book are not sufficient, it is our duty to pass other and more stringent laws, confer more power on the President, give him ample power to make our success complete and certain. Let the rebellion be terminated in the shortest time, and with the least possible sacrifice of life and treasure. The continuance of the war is extremely hard and exhausting to our volunteer soldiers, and the enormous expenses will impose heavy burdens upon the people. Every consideration of patriotism and duty requires us to put into active exercise at once all the means within our reach to bring the war to a speedy and successful termination.

What are the rights of war, and what are the ordinary means which may be brought against these rebels to weaken their power and crush out the rebellion? As enemies *de facto* it is conceded you may blockade their ports, preventing all exports and all imports or supplies from abroad; you may cut off all internal supplies by depriving them of the use of railroads, canals, lakes, rivers, and all other means of transportation; you may cut off all communication by mail, telegraph, express, or otherwise; you may capture their vessels, their supply trains, sink their ships, destroy their military stores, and meet them face to face in battle, and kill, capture and disperse their hostile forces. All these ordinary means have been tried during the last year, and still the ring-leaders who fomented this rebellion are more desperate than ever. War, gigantic, unrelenting war, still goes on. The rebels are more determinedly our enemies than ever before, and a call is made by the President for more troops to fight them. In this state of things what is to be done? Are there no other means that can be used to strengthen ourselves and weaken the power of the rebels, and thereby insure their defeat? This is the great question we are now considering. All the authorities sustain the doctrine that you may, under the war power, confiscate the property of enemies, and may liberate their slaves.

On the power of liberating slaves, John Quincy Adams lays down the doctrine that, in time of war, civil or foreign, 'not only the President of the United States, but the commander of an army, has the power to order the universal emancipation of the slaves.' It is evident, however, that he regarded it as a power subject to the action of Congress. With a call to suppress insurrection, he says, 'comes full and plenary power to the Senate and House over the whole subject. It is a war power.'

The extreme measures of confiscating the private property of rebels, and the liberation of their slaves, have not yet been tried to any considerable extent during the war. Is it a war measure necessary to success at this time? If it is necessary, will Congress and the President have the courage and the firmness to exercise this power boldly? Will this Government strike these rebels where it will do them the most harm? Will you take from them their property and liberate their slaves? Will you deprive them of the most effective means of carrying on the war? Take away their individual property, and deprive them of the labor and services of their slaves, and you strike a blow at the heart of the rebellion. You would then strike directly at the root of the evil. Give a death-blow to slavery, and you would soon be able to terminate the war.

We have already taken some positive steps in advance on the slavery question during the present session. Slavery has been abolished in the District of Columbia. The capital of the nation is forever freed from the taint of involuntary servitude. We have passed a new article of war, which prohibits commanders of divisions from returning slaves that voluntarily come within their lines. We have extended the ordinance of 1787, prohibiting slavery in all the Territories of the United States. And we have passed a resolution offering pecuniary aid to States that shall enter upon a gradual emancipation of the slaves within their limits. These enactments are in accordance with public sentiment and the progressive spirit of the age. Shall we advance still further in the work of emancipation? This depends somewhat upon the necessity of such a measure and the probable duration of the war. How long is the war to continue? No man here is wise enough to determine how long it will continue, nor how much blood and treasure will be expended in its prosecution. The Richmond *Enquirer* (official organ of the confederate administration) uses the following language, evidently by authority:

'But we are gratified to say that the time has come when, for the future at least, we all shall be agreed. All voluntary falling back has ended, and the fighting has commenced. What the enemy gains henceforth he gains by the bayonet. What we can win from him we will have. We will break his columns, and pursue him into his own country, if God shall prosper our arms. Strike! strike often, strike hard, strike at every opportunity—is henceforth the rule. Vigilance, activity, enterprise, daring, are, we trust, to be its interpreter.'

The longer the war continues, the more desperate will it become, and the more certain will it be that slavery is doomed. The advice of the Richmond *Enquirer* to the rebels, to "strike! strike often, strike hard, strike at every opportunity," shows the desperate character of their cause.

Are we to be struck often, and struck hard at every opportunity, without giving hard blows in return? I trust not. War means to strike often and strike hard on both sides. "An eye for an eye, and a tooth for a tooth." War teaches us to use all the means within our power to strengthen ourselves and to weaken our enemy. Let us weaken him in every possible way within the rules of civilized warfare. We should strike him personally, strip him of his property, and strike the shackles from every slave that by his labor and services gives him support. These are the rights of war, and I am prepared to see them fully enforced.

We have been forced by rebels into this unnatural and unnecessary war. We have already expended over six hundred millions of dollars in its prosecution; besides, what is of far greater consequence, many thousands of our brave soldiers have been slain on the field of battle, and have died by disease brought on by the perils and hardships of the campaign. Is all this blood and treasure to be expended without accomplishing anything beneficial to the nation, to civilization, and the rights of man? I trust not. We now want and must have a final settlement of this whole difficulty. Slavery was the cause of this gigantic and wicked rebellion. Slavery should receive its doom, thereby removing the cause of future difficulty. Rebels have fomented and brought on the war, and their property should pay a large share of the expenses incurred. These questions must now be met. They cannot be postponed. The laws of God and man require us to vote on the side of justice and humanity. I shall, under the circumstances, vote to confiscate the property of leading rebels, and to liberate their slaves.

APPENDIX TO SECOND EDITION.

WAR LEGAL-TENDER VINDICATED.

SPAULDING'S EXCHANGE, BUFFALO, April 20, 1870.

Mr. Henry Brooks Adams,

DEAR SIR,—I have just finished reading your article in the April number of the *North American Review*, in which you review somewhat at length the history of the Legal-Tender Act recently prepared by me, criticising the measure very freely and the course pursued by those who took a prominent part in its passage through Congress. The measure has always been open to public scrutiny, and I have no complaint to make of any fair criticism which you or any other gentleman see fit to make. It was passed in a great emergency as a "war measure," and not with a view to have it continued indefinitely as a permanent policy of the Government in time of peace. As a war measure it proved a success, and has therefore vindicated itself.

Seeing, however, that you criticise individual action, I desire to correct one mistake which you have fallen into, and when corrected it will leave your criticism without much force and certainly less pointed in regard to myself. In your article you assert that I claim to have carried the measure "over the administration and through Congress," and this assertion is quoted and repeated by you several times in the course of your article; whereas the words quoted are not taken from any remarks of mine, but are contained in the speech of Hon. Theodore M. Pomeroy, one of my colleagues from New York, delivered in the House of Representatives, February 19, 1862, while the amendments of the Senate were under consideration. On looking at page 132 of the history of the measure, you will find Mr. Pomeroy's remarks, in which *he* asserts that I originated this measure and carried it triumphantly "over the administration and through the Congress," but nowhere can you find any such words of mine. On the contrary, I only gave a narrative of the *facts* in chronological order, and on page 6 of the book you will find that I expressly state that " I do not claim any particular *merit* or *demerit* for what I did in preparing and aiding to secure the passage of the bill. I was placed in a position where, if I performed my duty, I must act, and act with vigor and promptitude. The perilous condition of the country did not admit of hesitancy or delay. I endeavored, in the peculiar and responsible position in which I was placed, to do what I conceived to be my duty, and that is all that I claim to have done. My associates performed their duty with equal fidelity and usefulness." These were the words I used instead of the words which you quoted from Mr. Pomeroy's speech and attribute to me. In giving the history of the measure it was my aim to state *facts*, leaving it for others to decide upon the merits and demerits of those who aided in the passage of the act, as well as those who opposed it, without any unkind or harsh expressions on my part, and without attributing the action of the parties of either side of the question to stupidity or ignorance, which seems to be the drift of your article, assuming on your part, superior knowledge and wisdom.

I am glad to notice among the disparaging epithets you use against true men like Thadeus Stevens, John A. Bingham, John Sherman, Henry Wilson, and other zealous patriots in the union cause, that you speak kindly of my late friend, Wm. Pitt Fessenden, who as chairman of the Finance Committee, reported it to the Senate, and in his opening speech upon the great importance of the measure said, "it needed long, careful and vigorous discussion. It has had it in the other branch of Congress. I have read that discussion from beginning to end;" and, notwithstanding you think the debate was weak and full of absurdities, Mr. Fessenden further says: "It has been able and clear on both sides of the question." He voted to strike out the Legal Tender clause in the bill, and failing in that, he, on the final passage of the bill, voted for it, including that clause.

I am pleased, also, that in your article you speak so favorably of the "superior discernment" of the late Judge Collamer, for moving to strike out the legal tender clause on the ground that it was unconstitutional.

In his speech on that occasion he said in substance, "That the oath he had taken to support the constitution was recorded in heaven as well as on earth, and that even if it was a *necessity* he could not vote for the bill." Preston King took the same ground, and yet both of these gentlemen in less than a year voted for $100,000,000 legal tender notes in addition to the $300,000,000 which had been previously issued. They were true men; and when the exigency arose for paying three or four months back pay of the soldiers who were periling their lives in the field in a gigantic struggle with the rebel armies during the cold month of January, 1863, both these senators recorded their votes for the additional issue of $100,000,000 to enable the Secretary to redeem the promises of the government to the union army, so that the men could send money home to their half starved families, while they were fighting rebellion in front. (See history of legal tender, page 182.) Mr. Fessenden, Judge Collamer and Preston King, three patriots now dead, thus recorded their votes, holding their constitutional scruples in abeyance.

The vote on this additional issue of greenbacks stood as follows :

Yeas—Messrs. Anthony, Arnold, Browning, Chandler, Clark, *Collamer*, Davis, Dixon, Doolittle, Fessenden, Foot, Foster, Hale, Harding, Harlan, Harris, Henderson, Howard, Howe, *King*, Lane, (of Indiana;) Lane, (of Kansas,) Latham, McDougall, Morrill, Nesmith, Rice, Sherman, Sumner, Ten Eyck, Turnbull, Wade, Wilkinson, Willey, Wilmot, Wilson, (of Mass.,) Wilson, (of Missouri,) and Wright—38 in the affirmative.

Nays—Messrs. Powell and Salisbury.—2 in the negative.

Approved January 17, 1863.

When Mr. Lincoln signed the bill to authorize this issue, he expressed his reluctance thus :

"While giving this approval, however, I think it my duty to express my sincere regret that it has been found necessary to authorize so large an additional issue of United States notes, when this circulation and that of the suspended banks together, have become so redundant as to increase prices beyond real values, thereby augmenting the cost of living, to the injury of labor and the cost of supplies, to the injury of the whole country."

This patriotic record on earth, in a desperate struggle for liberty and union will, I trust, on the day of final account stand justified in the sight of God, as it is now by all true men, and that "a tear from the recording angel in heaven's chancery" will blot out all their other conflicting records. In a crisis presented like the dark hour of January, 1863, I shall ever honor all those noble men of both Houses of Congress for the votes thus given in favor of paying the soldiers and their starving families. This record has passed into history, and will ever remain an enduring memorial of their fidelity to the national cause.

You claim in your flippant article, that the legal tender act was not necessary, even as a war measure, and that it was passed under a "fraudulent" misrepresentation of the facts. In the view thus taken by you, I think you are mistaken. I am gratified, however, to notice you say "it is but just to add that Mr. Spaulding did strongly and invariably insist upon the difference between legal tender notes which were fundable, and the latter issue which were not so." I regard this as a vital part of the measure, and still think that the right of funding into 6 per cent. bonds ought to never have been abrogated. It was necessary to prevent redundancy, and consequently to prevent depreciation of the notes.

I have no desire to multiply words on this subject at this time. My main object in this letter is to correct your erroneous statement in regard to myself, and at the same time speak kindly of my associates who sustained the union cause in its hour of extreme peril. Notwithstanding your individual criticism of those who spoke in favor of the legal tender even to the construction and rhetoric of some of the speeches, it is probable they will not deem it necessary, as I do not, to make any defense. Deeds, not words, are their best defense.

If you find that you are in error in your statements in regard to myself I would like to have you make the correction, and advise me.

   Very respectfully,
    Your obedient servant,
       E. G. SPAULDING.

HISTORY OF OUR WAR FINANCES.

Letter from the Hon. E. G. Spaulding.

BUFFALO, May 16, 1870.

To the Editor of the Cincinnati Gazette:

I have just finished reading your articles in the *Gazette* of the 12th and 13th inst., on the "first material mistake" made by the Secretary of the Treasury, in the first six months of the war. You show very clearly and forcibly the antagonism of the sub-treasury to modern commercial transactions, and the utter impossibility of carrying on a war upon a specie basis, while it is in operation, discarding, as it does, the bank check and the system of settling large transactions by offset through the Clearing Houses now in operation in all the great centres of commerce, and which forced the banks to prematurely suspend specie payments the last of December, 1861.

I agree with you that the time has come for gathering up into convenient form, the facts in respect to the financial management during the war, in order to improve the lessons drawn from the past nine years of experience.

Another material mistake in the management of the finances followed the first, but it was not in the adoption of the legal tender act, nor in the issue of fundable greenbacks, but in the unnecessary large *overissue* of *un*fundable greenbacks and five and six per cent. interest bearing treasury notes.

The whole scope and object of the first legal tender act was to quickly create a national currency then imperatively necessary for disbursement to the army and navy (because there was then no national currency in existence that could be had), and at the same time provide for funding it, as soon as it became excessive, into 6 per cent. gold bonds in order to prevent any great inflation of currency or prices; and I am free to say that I never advocated the issue of any greenbacks that were not so fundable. Not one dollar of greenbacks ought to have been issued beyond the amount necessary to float the six-per cent. five-twenty bonds. The funding in these bonds was a practical redemption of them, and there was no great excess while they were so redeemed. It was not a redemption equal to being redeemed in gold, but its redemption in six per cent. gold bonds was a good practical redemption, the best in that great crisis the Government could offer, and it formed a pretty good standard of value on which to rest all the internal transactions of the business during the war; and certainly no one could be very materially injured by being compelled to receive greenbacks in payment of debts, so long as they could be immediately returned to the Government in exchange for gold bonds. Gold became demonetized, and the standard of value fixed by that act was greenback currency convertible at the will of the holder into six per cent. gold bonds. No large amount of funding took place until May, 1863, because there was no excess of greenbacks. At that time the greenbacks had filled up the channels of circulation, became somewhat redundant, and funding, which had been tardy, now became more active. This returning of greenbacks to the Treasury for bonds, furnished the means for carrying on the war, and the further issue of greenbacks became unnecessary. Jay Cooke, during the nine months following April, 1863, successfully funded the balance of the first $500,000,000 5-20 bonds, which proved conclusively that it was not necessary to inflate the currency another dollar, either by the issue of greenbacks, interest bearing treasury notes, or any other form of inflating paper, in order to provide sufficient means for carrying on the war. The greenbacks were printed and paid out for government disbursements, and when funded were returned to the Treasury ready to be reissued and again funded, and so on from week to week and month to month. The act as at first adopted was self regulating. When there was an excess of greenbacks, not bearing interest, they would naturally flow into the six per cent. bonds in order to save interest. It was a great blunder to abrogate this healthy redemption of the greenbacks. It unsettled the vital principle of the act, and destroyed the standard of value fixed by it. Serious mischief followed. A very large increase of greenbacks and interest-bearing Treasury notes were issued by the Secretary. Inflation of prices, wild speculation, uncertainty and demoralization was the consequence throughout the remainder of the war, and which still continues, so that even up to the present time there is no standard of value for the greenback, and no provision made for redeeming it either in bonds or gold, and specie payments seem to be indefinitely postponed. The present Secretary prints new plates and *reissues* this currency without any fixed standard of value, thereby perpetuating the uncertainty which attaches to all legitimate business. If the right of funding the greenbacks in accordance with the original legal tender act had not been abrogated, the standard of value would never have been so reduced, the demoralization would have been very much less, people would have shaped their business in accordance with the law, and very likely specie payments would have been restored after the war, and certainly, at no time would the value of greenbacks have been below the price of the six per cent 5-20 bonds.

The right given to the holders of greenbacks to fund into six per cent. bonds was by the original legal tender act in the nature of a contract; its abrogation was unjust to the holders of the notes, and I always regarded it as the second and most material mistake in the management of the finances during the war. The facts necessary to a full understanding of this question you will find stated in the history of the legal tender act, from page 167 to 201, and I hope you will ellucidate the subject as clearly as you have the first material mistake above mentioned.

1. The first material mistake on the part of the Secretary of the Treasury was in compelling the associated banks of New York, Boston and Philadelphia to pay the gold loan of $150,000,000 into the sub-treasury, instead of checking directly on the banks for it, thereby forcing the banks into a premature suspension of specie payments in December, 1861.

2. The second great mistake, and the one that will be the longest felt, was in abrogating the provision in the first legal tender act, which gave the right to the holders of the greenbacks to fund them at any time into six per cent. 5-20 gold bonds. It will take a long time yet to recover from the evil effects of this mistake.

I am, very truly yours,

E. G. SPAULDING.

(From the *American Bond Detector*.)

THE OLD UNITED STATES BANK AND NATIONAL BANKS.

By the Hon. E. G. SPAULDING, of Buffalo, N. Y.

"Among the other beneficial results left us by the Great Rebellion, was the system of national currency and banking—a very important governmental and commercial agent, as well as bond of national union; but which, in consequence of a conflict of opinion among the ablest statesmen of the country, was not attainable in time of peace.

"The first United States Bank was established in 1791, under the influence of that peerless statesman, Alexander Hamilton. It was approved by Washington, performed important service to the country, and continued in existence until 1811, the year previous to the last war with Great Britain, when its charter expired, and consequently great embarrassments were experienced in prosecuting that war, because the government was left without any adequate national currency to carry it on.

"The second United States Bank was chartered in 1816, and continued with like beneficial results as the first until 1836, when its charter expired. Both these banks were fiscal agents of the Government. They received and disbursed all the public money entrusted to them without expense, and without the loss to the Government of a single dollar. These banks were likewise of great advantage to the business community. Some of the ablest efforts of Webster and Clay were in favor of its continuance, and notwithstanding the decision of the Supreme Court, headed by Chief Justice Marshall, in favor of its constitutionality, President Jackson, by reason of his official position, effectually resisted a re-charter, removed the Government deposits to certain State Banks, which proved very disastrous, heavy losses were sustained by the Government, overtrading ensued, and there was a general suspension of specie payments in 1837.

"The friends of a United States Bank again passed a bill through Congress for another bank in 1841, which was defeated by the veto of John Tyler. The sub-treasury system was finally adopted in 1864, which isolated the Government from all banks and paper money, leaving it without any monied institution, like the bank of England, or other national agency to resort to for aid in case of war. Consequently at the breaking out of the Rebellion there was no system of currency adequate to the requirements of a great war.

"The sub-treasury and state banks were tried, and very soon found to be wholly inadequate. Secretary Chase recommended the present national banking system, which he urged upon Congress in his first and second annual reports, as well as in special communications. The first draft of this bank bill was prepared by Mr. Spaulding, chairman of the Sub-Committee of Ways and Means, having this subject in charge, in December, 1861, but it did not pass and become a law until February 25, 1863, and although some national bank currency was issued in 1864, the system did not get fully into operation until 1865. It was of considerable benefit in supporting the public credit towards the close of the war, and all the banks over the country rendered essential service in negotiating the loans, but the Government issue of the legal tender notes with, and without interest, was the vital measure and main support of the Army and Navy, during the war for the union.

"The experience of the last eighty years under our present form of government, has clearly shown that the power to coin money from the precious metals, and regulate its value, and the power to issue bank notes should be exercised by the same authority and be equally under governmental supervision. The power to coin money is, by the constitution, vested in the

United States Government, and forbidden to the separate states. In regulating the value of coined money, it is essential that the government should also regulate and control the paper money issued by banks, because a convertible paper money is only an extension of coined money, and when both kinds of money circulate in the same jurisdiction, they constitute the measure of value for all business operations. It is plain, therefore, that both kinds of money should be under the same authority and control in order to regulate the value of both. State bank issues are local in character and credit, and possess none of the attributes of a national currency.

"The function of regulating the currency of a great nation possessed of large internal as well as foreign commerce, and subject to the calamities of war, can only be successfully performed by the general Government. The extention of railroads, water ways, and internal commerce all over the country without regard to state boundaries, and the vast requirements of the late war, have more clearly demonstrated than ever before, the necessity of a convertible paper currency, co-extensive with the boundaries of the United States.

"The important resulting benefits growing out of the great rebellion are many and various, but none of them will be of more lasting benefit to the government and people, than the inauguration of the System of National Currency and Banking, now in full operation, and which, with proper amendments, will be adequate to the wants of the nation in time of *peace* as well as in the time of *war*. Banking is a business requiring accumulated capital and loanable funds. The issue of circulating notes is another important feature, the leading idea of which is the establishment of one sound uniform currency of like similitude and value, co-extensive with the boundaries of the United States, based upon national credit combined with private accumulated capital, and under the general control and supervision of the Treasury Department at Washington.

"By the National Currency act the Government guarantees the currency and limits the amount to $300,000,000, (since 1874 there is no limit); requires it to be secured by gold bearing bonds deposited with the Treasurer of the United States with a margin of ten per cent.; requires each bank to redeem its own notes in lawful money on demand, and to keep an adequate reserve for that purpose; makes them a legal tender for all taxes and other dues to the government except customs, and for all salaries and other dues owing by the government within the United States, except the principal and interest of the funded debt. It also makes them receivable by each National Bank for all ordinary debts due them, and each bank designated as a depository, is also required to receive it on deposit from all public officers. These provisions in the law operate to nationalize and de centralize this currency; the United States Government tax of ten per cent. on all State Bank bills effectually kills the issues of all State institutions, and consequently the national currency with all these advantages has a wide circulation all over the United States, and connected as it is with the greenback legal tender notes, they together are the measure of value in carrying on the *internal* commerce of the country, notwithstanding their depreciation. Their present depreciation is a fault which can only be remedied by a general resumption of specie payments, in which the government must take the lead by placing the greenback currency on a par with gold.

"Two things remain to be done in order to make it the best banking system ever devised :

"1. Redemption of this currency on demand in gold and silver; at the same time divest the law of every feature of monopoly by making it free and open to all.

"2. Organize one or more banks at commercial centres, with large capitals but limited circulation, under the supervision and control of the Treasury Department, to receive and disburse the public money, without expense, somewhat like the Bank of England, and a repeal of the Sub-Treasury act, which in its operation is antagonistic to legitimate business, does more harm to the finances than it does good, and which may be discontinued without detriment to the public service, and thereby save the expense of keeping it in operation.

"This would make the National Banking System adequate to the wants of the nation in *peace* and *war*, and combine a large share of the capital of the country in support of the government, and thereby become a strong bond of national union."

HON. HUGH M^cCULLOCH,
Late Secretary of the Treasury.

PRINCE GEORGE'S CO., MD, }
October 23, 1869.

MY DEAR SIR:—I have been absent from home for some weeks past, on a visit to Minnesota. This will explain to you how it has happened that the receipt of your favor of the 15th ult. has remained so long unacknowledged. I have read the "Financial History of the War," which you were kind enough to send me, and am greatly pleased with it. Such a work was much needed, and it has been prepared by you with care and ability. No one had more to do with the financial legislation of the United States in the trying years of 1861 and 1862 than yourself, and no one was more familiar with the views of those members of Congress who approved of the issue of the legal tender notes. Had you and the other distinguished gentlemen who co-operated with you in the preparation of "financial measures for the support of the Government" in the years referred to, supposed that the notes, the issue of which you so vigorously and successfully advocated, would be used as a circulating medium after the exigency which, in you judgment, justified their issue had ceased to exist, I hazard nothing in saying that other measures would have been resorted to to raise the means for the prosecution of the war. Nothing shows how far the country has departed from cardinal principles in finance and morals more clearly than the fact that the measure which was advocated by its friends *solely as a war measure* under the pressure of a great necessity, is now sustained by Congress and the people as a financial policy. You know as well, if not better, than other men, under what circumstances and for what purposes the legal tender notes were issued, and it is in the highest degree creditable to you that as you had the nerve to advocate their issue when the measure was unpopular, you also have now the nerve to advise that they be retired, in opposition to a decided and overwhelming public sentiment in favor of their being continued in circulation as a part of the financial policy of the Government. Very truly yours,

HUGH McCULLOCH.

Hon. E. G. SPAULDING, Buffalo, N. Y.

HON. CHARLES FRANCIS ADAMS,

Late Minister to England,—On Legal Tender.

QUINCY, October 13, 1869.

E. G. Spaulding, Buffalo, N. Y.

MY DEAR SIR:—It is now some weeks since I received your note and the book which you were so kind as to send me. In the midst of interruptions of one kind and another, I have been able to make only slow progress in reading it.

I think I can very fully appreciate the difficulties in which you were placed in regard to the course to be taken, and I have no disposition to censure any one who acted on a firm and honest conviction that he was doing his best to save the country. I have no doubt that you did so, and I do not pretend to affirm that you may not have been right, in your judgment, of the nature of the crisis.

The whole article in favor of Legal Tender seems to me to resolve itself into the single word *necessity*. The same argument that justified the Russians for setting fire to their own homes in Moscow to drive out Napoleon. If it be notoriously the tyrant's plea it may not the less sometimes be a justification in the cause of liberty and right.

Unfortunately for myself I am slow to be convinced that the cause was so desperate as absolutely to need a desperate remedy. The great objection which I have to the enactment of Legal Tender, is that the country through it has for the first time taught a lesson of *fraud*. Much noise has been made about paying the debt of the country in greenbacks. I do not see wherein it is more than an application of the same rule—to wit: that a government can by mere force of its strength, make a creditor take less than the amount honestly due to him.

The worst of it is that the moral sense of a people is permanently blunted by the resort to such an expedient. I do not see when or how we shall return to sound ideas; for all the great army of debtors created since the war, by allowing seventy cents to count for a dollar, are not likely to be very soon ready to pay a dollar and thirty cents or its equivalent in property in satisfaction of the creditors. Charles XII. of Sweden, in his day of "necessity," issued a set of copper coins on which was stamped the word "dollar," and paid his army just as if it really was what it professed to be. Was not this a cheat? Yet where is the difference except in the degree between the two proceedings? The Government will not even consent to take this paper, which it forces upon its creditors, in payment for a part of its own claims on debtors, and yet it pretends to claim character for equal and honest dealing in money transactions. I do not hesitate to say that if a private banker or merchant were to think of introducing such an expedient, supposing it to be possible, he would instantly lose all his reputation of an honorable man.

What is distinctly perceptible in the transactions between man and man, does not change its nature when applied to great bodies, merely because they are too strong to be resisted. So long as a legal tender note remains in circulation at less than its professed value, it is a solemn lie. The public, to be sure, accommodates itself to the fraud by raising the price of its commodities and selling for a dollar what is really worth seventy cents. But everybody cannot do this. Myriads of those with fixed incomes based upon the old standard fall a sacrifice, in their privations suffered every day of the year. Who is there then can make the loss good to them?

If I saw any symptom of return to sound morals within any reasonable time I should qualify my language. But the experience of the past teaches us that this road once taken terminates only in utter disregard of the whole obligation. If that be the end in our case, it would have been cheaper to have tried to go on without it.

Yours truly, etc.,

C. F. ADAMS.

HON. J. T. HEADLEY, THE HISTORIAN.

NEWBURGH, Sept. 15, 1869.

DEAR SIR:—Your kind favor came to my address while I was buried in the Adirondack Mountains, whither I had gone on account of my son's health, else I should have acknowledged it sooner. I have read your book with much interest. It is just what we needed to fill a hiatus in the history of the civil war, and you were the proper person to write it. I watched your course in Congress on the financial question with much interest. Your views always seemed to me more practical than those of most others. You seemed to act as if it was not the time to discuss theories, but do the best we could under the circumstances. In short, as we were situated, the only course was a choice between two evils.

I value your work highly as a book of reference, which I sadly needed. With many thanks for it, I remain, Very sincerely yours,

J. T. HEADLEY.

(From the New York *Times*).

SPECIE PAYMENTS.

WHY THE BANKS SUSPENDED IN 1861—EFFECT ON THE SUB-TREASURY LAW—LETTER FROM HON. E. G. SPAULDING.

The following important letter on the suspension of specie payments in 1861, and what led to it, was recently written by Hon. E. G. Spaulding, President of the Association of National Banks, and author of the History of the Legal Tender act, to J. S. Gibbons, Esq., of this city, who recently produced a work on the New York banks:

BUFFALO, March 29, 1870.

J. S. Gibbons, Esq.,

DEAR SIR:—Yours of the 24th inst. has been received, and in reply to your inquiry, I would inform you that the sixth section of the loan act of August 5, 1861, partially suspending the independent treasury law of 1846, was at first drafted by me, but was considerably modified and limited in its operation by amendments suggested by Secretary Chase before it passed the two Houses, and became a law. I was in favor of making the suspension of the sub-treasury act general in regard to all loans, so that the Treasurer might draw checks directly on the banks for the amount loaned, in order that the usual bank expedients might be resorted to in liquidating such checks without disturbing the gold reserves held by the banks, then in a remarkably strong and healthy condition.

This subject was discussed in the Committee of Ways and Means at that time. I expressed the opinion that the loan of $250,000,000, which was authorized at the extra session in July and August, 1861, could not be made, and the gold actually paid over into the sub-treasury, without so weakening the banks that they would be obliged to suspend specie payments. William Appleton, then a member of the committee, and a practical banker, from Boston, concurred with me fully in that opinion. Mr. Corning, of Albany, another member of the committee, also a banker and practical business man, predicted that if the gold reserves of the banks were drawn upon for such large loans, there would be a general suspension of specie payments in less than six months, and his prediction was verified. There were, however, conflicting opinions in the Committee on the subject, and Secretary Chase seemed to be very desirous of carrying on the war by the actual disbursement of gold and silver, or treasury notes convertible into gold on demand, and without suspending the sub-treasury law. Finally, Mr. Appleton and myself were appointed a sub-committee to prepare a section suspending the sub-treasury law in respect to all moneys obtained on loans, and to confer with Mr. Fessenden, Chairman of the Finance Committee in the Senate, as to the probability of its passage in that body. Upon a full and free consultation with Mr. Fessenden, he consented to support a section of that kind, and thought it would pass the Senate. Mr. Appleton was in feeble health, and the duty of preparing the section devolved upon me. I prepared a section in which he concurred, and which, in general terms, suspended the sub-treasury law in regard to all moneys realized upon loans, allowing it to be deposited in solvent specie-paying banks (state banks, of course, because there were then no national banks), and authorizing the Treasurer to check, from time to time, directly on the banks for the amount. From a careful reading of the books you have published, I am impressed with the belief that you know the clearing-house, locomotive and telegraph are among the most useful of modern inventions, and that the sub-treasury law is better adapted to the sixteenth than the nineteenth century. You are familiar with the New York Clearing-house, and know that seventy-five millions of dollars of checks and drafts may be daily liquidated and fully cancelled by paying in gold a resulting balance of not exceeding from two millions to three millions of dollars, and that the whole operation could be concluded in three or four hours, and that a similar balance at the London Clearing-house would be paid mainly by the other banks and bankers giving their checks on the Bank of England, and without using any gold at all. This, you are aware, economizes time as well as the volume of currency necessary to do this large business, and that it could as easily be applied to government operations as to private business. In this way I believe that the great bulk of the supplies and material of war for the army and navy could be paid for by the usual bank expedients, and by offset through the Clearing-house of New York and other cities, without materially disturbing the gold reserves of the banks, except in the payment of balances.

The sub-treasury law at that time seemed to be popular with the Secretary of the Treasury, and with some members of the Committee of Ways and Means, as well as the Finance Committee of the Senate; and the section finally passed in the modified form in which it now appears in the law of the 5th of August, 1861, and is as follows:

§ 6. And be it further enacted, That the provisions of an act entitled "An act to provide for the better organization of the Treasury, and for the collection, safe-keeping, transfer and disbursements of the public revenue," passed August 6, 1846, be and the same are hereby suspended, so far as to allow the Secretary of the Treasury to deposit any of the moneys obtained on any of the loans now authorized by law to the credit of the Treasurer of the United States, in such solvent specie-paying banks as he may select, and the said moneys so deposited may be withdrawn from such deposit for deposit with the regular authorized depositaries or for the payment of public dues, or paid in redemption of the notes authorized to be issued under this act, or the act to which this is supplementary, payable on demand as may seem expedient to or be directed by the Secretary of the Treasury.

No question can be raised as to the good intentions of Secretary Chase in administering the loan laws, but it is obvious now that he did not at that time fully comprehend the labor-saving, money-saving and general utility which results in the settlement of checks and drafts through the banks, and the admirable system of offset through the clearing-house. The wonderful facility then in operation in New York, Boston and Philadelphia, for transferring and liquidating debts without disturbing the gold reserves held by the banks, was wholly ignored by the Secretary. This operated almost as unfavorably as if the Secretary of War had rejected the locomotive in transporting the army. The rejection of the bank check and clearing-house made it necessary to increase the volume of currency in various forms in about the same proportion as the rejection of the locomotive would have made it necessary to increase the number of horses to supply and transport the army.

The banks in the three cities above named most patriotically agreed to loan to the Government about $150,000,000, which could have been easily passed to the credit of the Treasurer on their books. The Secretary had the power, under the above section, to have directed the Treasurer of the United States to check directly upon the banks for this large sum, and the largest amount of the checks so drawn would have been settled by offset through the clearing-house without requiring but a small balance to be paid in gold. Instead of doing so, the Secretary required the money to be counted and paid over into the sub-treasury on all these loans. This very soon disturbed the gold reserves of the banks, and it became painfully certain to the managers of the banks in New York and other cities, as early as December, 1861, that the policy which the Secretary adhered to must inevitably lead to a general suspension of specie payments.

A meeting of bank officers was held at the American Exchange Bank in the city of New York, December 28, 1861. One of the bank presidents, in a well-considered speech delivered on that occasion, criticising the course of Secretary Chase in regard to these loans, said that

"He (Secretary Chase) was urged to draw directly on the banks. Coin being the basis of credits, it was only in that way the increased financial operations of the Government could be conducted, for it was impossible to maintain the superstructure of credit when the basis is withdrawn, for in destroying the basis the superstructure is also swept away. He refused to draw directly upon the banks for the proceeds of the loan taken by each. We are informed that the act of Congress was passed expressly for the purpose of authorizing him to do so, but he gave it a different interpretation, which may be the correct one, although I do not think so."

The failure of the Secretary to recognize the suspension of the sub-treasury law, and his rejection of the bank-check and clearing-house, was the first material mistake made in the management of the finances during the war. The Secretary was intent upon having the gold for disbursement, without fully comprehending the effect this large drain would have upon the banks and the general finances of the country.

The banks immediately thereafter suspended specie payments, and there is but one opinion among practical bankers, that such suspension was hastened by the injudicious action of the Secretary of the Treasury.

The attempt of the Secretary to carry on the finances during the war upon a specie basis, without the aid of the bank-check and clearing-house, having broken down, I immediately introduced in the House the first legal tender act, which, after an able and full discussion in both Houses of Congress, finally became a law on the twenty-fifth of February, 1862. I sent you yesterday a book recently prepared by me, containing a history of this most important measure.

This is my answer to your inquiry:

I desire to add that I have reflected much during the last nine years upon the sub-treasury law and its effect upon Government loans, as well as upon the general business of the people. It is my deliberate conclusion that a great war can never be successfully carried on without a suspension of specie payments while the sub-treasury law is in operation. I believe further that the financial affairs of the Government, as well as the general business of the whole people, could be much better conducted without the sub-treasury law and with much less expense.

A system of finances for this great country which will be adequate to the wants of the Government and people, in peace and war, has yet to be organized. Very truly yours, E. G. SPAULDING.

REPLY OF J. S. GIBBONS, ESQ.

NEW YORK, April 6, 1470.

Hon. E. G. Spaulding,

DEAR SIR:—I have to thank you most cordially for your note of March 28th and the book therein ordered, and for your interesting letter at length of the 29th in answer to my enquiry concerning the legal tender act. With all your views I fully concur. If Mr. Chase had ever been a banker or a merchant, he might have joined theory and practice and had the aid of both, but as it was he only had the former; and that was a theory of his own brain, which through his inordinate self-conceit has cost the country, in all probability, a thousand millions of debt, beyond what would have been contracted on lower prices. I do not believe a more ignorant man, of practical business affairs can be found in public life. If he had only been *a general reader* of history, to say nothing of political economy, he would not have blundered so dreadfully, nor at last, have failed so utterly as a Financial Minister. There were people to praise him at the outset, but they were ignorant like himself, of all fiscal history ; and even they have now generally joined in with the popular condemnation of his management.

I find the data of the Independent Treasury history so mixed and voluminous, and greatly in very small type, that I am much discouraged in my attempt to reduce it to an intelligent narrative. But I shall persevere. It is a patent absurdity that the hoarding of the most valuable part of our currency, is a strength to the currency! What you say is perfectly true—that an abstraction of coin from use, necessitates a corresponding enlargement of the other media of exchange.

I am heretical enough not to believe in the National Bank Scheme. It is an insidious plan of currency that is never practically redeemed, and never will be. But we have learned from it, and tested the advantages of a "national circulation," and that is a good deal. It will serve its day and go by the board.

Then, we may adopt the scientific idea of a National Bank, of which the Bank of England is the most conspicuous example. Our finances must be *Federalized*, as our states have been, and we should then soon govern the exchanges of the world. The present system is a national bank with all its capacity of mischief, and little of its good. Again thanking you for your letters and the book.

Very truly,

J. S. GIBBONS.

The following letter, addressed to Mr. Spaulding by J. E. Williams, Esq., President of the Metropolitan Bank, New York, is one that ought to command attention. Mr. Williams has no superior among the bankers of the country in financial ability and experience. His views, with respect to the financial situation of affairs, coinciding with those made public by Mr. Spaulding, are expressed with great clearness and force :

METROPOLITAN BANK,
NEW YORK, April 6, 1864.

Hon. E. G. Spaulding,

MY DEAR SIR:—Many thanks for your letter, which I have read in the Buffalo *Express*. It is quite time, I think, that the friends of the administration, who care more for that, and for our general government, than for the crude notions of finance prevailing at Washington, should speak out, and fearlessly criticise the measures they disapprove.

The five per cent. loan is a failure—at least so regarded here, by every business man I have heard speak of it—and ought to be withdrawn at once from the market. That which has been taken should be exchanged for six per cent. bonds at the option of the owners, and a loan bearing six per cent. interest, payable in gold, offered to the public without delay.

I understand that between seventy and eighty millions of demands on the Treasury have accumulated in Washington, and now await payment. This ought not to be. The money market is easy—the loan at six per cent. would now readily be taken, and this favorable state of financial affairs should be seized on to secure money for the Government.

And why not pay six instead of five per cent. interest?

Do not the people pay the taxes from which this interest is paid? Is not money in this country worth fully six per cent? Can the Government reasonably expect to carry on an expensive war and hire money by the hundreds of millions at less than six per cent.? Is it fair to tax the people to their utmost capacity to pay and then expect them to furnish funds at less than the market price? Is not such a course an unjust tax on the good sense and patriotism of the people of this country?

This constant increase in the volume of the paper currency is having a very discouraging effect on all the prudent, thinking people. Prices have felt the last addition of one or two hundred millions much more than the previous four hundred millions; for the reason, that the first issue was needed for the business of the country, while it would seem, from the effect produced on the market values, that the last issues were not required by any business demand whatever, but are merely a make-shift of Mr. Chase to meet present demands on the Treasury. Yours truly,

J. E. WILLIAMS.

JOHN P. ELTON, ESQ.

President of the Waterbury Bank, Connecticut, an experienced financier and business man.

WATERBURY, April 1, 1864.

Hon. E. G. Spaulding,

DEAR SIR:—I have just received the Buffalo *Morning Express* of the 26th March, in which is your admirable letter to Morris Ketchum, Esq., of New York, on the finances of the country. I had previously seen extracts from it in the *Tribune*, and its remarks upon it. On reading the letter in full I discover the same standard views ever expressed by you, and to which I have always given my hearty assent. As I have before stated to you, it has ever appeared to me perfectly plain and simple, this matter of our finances. When it was fully settled that we could not carry on this war on a gold basis, and that some form of paper money must be substituted, while the war was continued, it has seemed to me that there was but one proper course for the Government to pursue, and that to issue legal tender notes and pay every claim against the Government as fast as presented, and to create (or issue) a government bond bearing six per cent. interest in gold, in which these legal tenders could at all times, at the pleasure of the holder, be converted. In my opinion there should not have been but one kind of bonds issued, and that a 20-year bond, at least until one thousand million had been issued; after that point had been reached, I would not have particularly objected to the issue of 5-20 6 per cent. bonds, redeemable after five years, but as you state in your letter to Mr. Ketchum, there should never have been but one standard of interest for government bonds.

(Temporary loans such as 2-year 5 per cents. or any other temporary loan, would have no effect on the general principle). 6 per cent. is a fair standard for the Government and the people, and to that all standard values should bear a proper relation.

In my opinion the country could never be flooded with a depreciated currency so long as the door was open to convert surplus money into 6 per cent. gold bearing bonds. I have a simple metaphor which I sometimes apply to this matter. I compare it to a flowing stream, on which a dam is built, and when the water rises to its height it easily and gracefully flows over and nothing more is seen of it. Now when the country has more floating paper money than it wanted, it will surely flow into a place of rest, (*or bonds*). It will be impossible to keep afloat an amount great enough to materially inflate prices.

Since it has been given out that we were to have a bond bearing 5 per cent. put upon the market, I have discovered more uneasiness as to the future of our financial affairs than ever before since the war commenced. It is so apparent that it is to be forced upon the people against their will, that it produces distrust. If it could be done without diluting or watering the currency, it might be a debatable policy. But as it cannot it does not even admit of that. What Mr. Chase can mean by his present policy I cannot *divine*. If this loan has to be negotiated abroad it might not effect us here, but no great amount of it can be, nor do I deem it advisable it should be.

We can absorb all the Government needs at home, and without the least inconvenience, if they will keep within easy reach of the people a 6 per cent. gold bearing bond, and I should prefer that not one dollar should go abroad.

Let heavy taxation follow a free issue of legal tender, and a wide door open for conversion into 6 per cent. gold bearing bonds, the Government may without fear ride out the financial storm in perfect composure.

Truly your friend,

JOHN P. ELTON.

HON. H. H. VAN DYCK.

ALBANY, April 4, 1864.

E. G. Spaulding,

DEAR SIR:—Accept my thanks for the several papers forwarded. Your letter "hits the nail on the head" beyond a doubt, and I agree fully in your expressed views, as to the evil consequences of Mr. Chase's action in unsettling the rate of interest on conversions The whole country will see ere many months, that your opinion, and congressional action, was most sound throughout. The Committee of Ways and Means, now entirely under the control of Mr. Hooper, on financial subjects. * * * * * *

It looks as if the 10-20 loan was to be a failure. Had Chase kept right on with the 6's he would have absorbed all the spare capital, (or rather credit,) of the country, and been in a *sleek* condition, instead of coming out "spring poor," as a barnyard horse. Yours truly,

H. H. VAN DYCK.

HENRY F. VAIL.

National Bank of Commerce in New York.

February 24, 1869.

E. G. Spaulding, Esq., Buffalo,

DEAR SIR:—I duly received your favor of 16th inst., with the advanced sheets as stated, of your intended publication on the Legal Tender act, which will, I think, prove a work of interest to financial men.

You are doubtless aware that the officers, and a majority if not all of the Directors of the Bank of Commerce, did not coincide with the views of Mr. Gallatin and associates, who visited Washington in January, 1862. We had no hand in appointing them as delegates on behalf of the banks, but on the contrary, Messrs. Chas. H. Russell and Deming Duer, directors of the bank, and myself as its cashier, were in Washington early in January, 1862, as a committee from the Bank of Commerce on the subject of the national finances, when several gentlemen, delegates from certain banks in New York, Boston and Philadelphia, appeared in Washington in opposition to the financial measures then proposed and under consideration by Congress.

The Committee of the Bank of Commerce not concurring in the views of these gentlemen, did not unite in the meeting called on Saturday, January 11, 1862, at the office of the Secretary of the Treasury, to confer with the Committee of Ways and Means and the Finance Committee of the Senate. Mr. Russell, (and I think one or two other directors of the bank then in Washington), did, however, by invitation of the Secretary of the Treasury, attend the meeting, but totally dissenting from the propositions then made, took no part in the proceedings of the gentlemen present. Mr. Russell was before the Committee of Ways and Means, and frequently with the members of that Committee and of the Senate Committee, who were considering the matter of issuing legal tenders, and stated fully his own and the views of the Committee of the Bank of Commerce on that subject, which were adverse to such issues if other means could be realized by the Government, and to be adopted only in the exigency of failure otherwise, as appears to have been stated to you by Mr. Russell's letter of January 29, and in the views he then expressed I believe the president and all, or nearly all of the directors as well as the committee, concurred.

By the way, Mr. Russell was a director, but not the Vice-President of the Bank of Commerce—which please correct in your publication.

I was, as you state, in Washington while the bill was pending in the Senate, and at the request of Mr. Secretary Chase, I appeared before the Senate Finance Committee with him and fully explained to them the workings of the bank settlements through the Clearing House, and the impossibility of forcing a circulating medium of the demand notes issued by the Treasury, unless they were made a legal tender. and in answer to the enquiries expressed my thorough conviction that the emergency had arisen requiring the issue of legal tenders.

You are correct in your supposition regarding my instrumentality in procuring the interest on bonds, &c., being made payable in coin.

I have shown your letter and the pages to Mr. Russell and to Mr. Kennedy, and will show them to the other gentlemen named.

Yours very truly,
HENRY F. VAIL.

LATE SAMUEL NELSON.
United States Supreme Court.

COOPERSTOWN, August 14, 1869.

MY DEAR SIR:—I received this morning your History of the Legal Tender act, and as far as I had time to look into it, found what I knew could not be otherwise, to be very accurate.

We shall dispose of this question, I presume, in due course of our coming session of the court, which begins 1st of October. I have always regretted that the greenbacks were made a Legal Tender, and I think the Chief Justice now is of opinion that the *omission* would not have had much effect one way or the other, in its operation upon the bills. Not at least as much as he thought at the time the bill was passed. That the necessities of the government and business interests of the country would have given them all the credit, important or material.

I am very much obliged to you for this authentic record of one of the most important measures growing out of the war, and difficult to deal with since.

Very truly yours,
S. NELSON.

Hon. E. G. SPAULDING.

LATE JUDGE GRIER.

PHILADELPHIA, August 26, 1869.

DEAR SIR:—On my return home I am pleased to find a copy of your history of the "Legal Tender Paper Money." It is a valuable historical document, and I am thankful for your kindness to me—in remembering me in the distribution of it, and concur with you fully in the views you take on the subject.

Why our court has for two years *postponed* their consideration of the question, is unknown to me, and I don't feel any responsibility for its postponement. Excuse my pencil. I write with difficulty.

Very respectfully and truly, yours &c.,

R. C. GRIER.

Hon. E. G. SPAULDING.

HON. SAMUEL F. MILLER,
United States Supreme Court.

KEOKUK, August 17, 1869.

Hon. E. G. Spaulding,

DEAR SIR:—I received both your letter and the "Financial History of the War," for which I am very much obliged to you.

I read the book with much interest, because it gives the first clear view, as a whole, of the financial measures of the Government during the war, that I have had; but mainly because it gives an accurate and full account of the relation of the Chief Justice, while he was Secretary of the Treasury, to those measures; and especially to the legal tender clause, about which there was some uncertainty and much curiosity.

A careful examination of all that is to be found in your book on that subject, leaves the impression on my mind that he had never had any doubt as to the constitutionality of that measure, but doubted its policy or expediency. This doubt seems to have been entirely removed, and his conviction of the necessity of that provision to enable him to carry on the department of the government under his charge, made him at last an advocate of it.

If judicial propriety admitted of it, I could not give you any reliable opinion of the probable action of the Supreme Court. Of course I know the views of some of its members, but there are enough whose views I do not know (some of them are propably undetermined in their own minds), to make the matter as uncertain to me as to you. I have a very strong impression that the opinion of the majority of the court, if rendered while constituted as it now is, will be such as the Chief Justice shall think it ought to be, when delivered. But with all my intimacy with him, and some knowledge of his character and habits of thought, I have no idea what that will be. * *

I am, very truly, your friend,

SAMUEL F. MILLER.

JUDGE BRADLEY,
United States Supreme Court.

WASHINGTON, April 19, 1870.

DEAR SIR:—Hon. D. S. Bennett has handed me your book on the "Financial History of the War." Accept my thanks for the same. It subserves a very great convenience in bringing into a small and accessible compass matter that would require days of search in the *Congressional Globe* and public journals to find. Yours very truly,

JOS. P. BRADLEY.

Hon. E. G. SPAULDING.

JUDGE NOAH DAVIS.

114 Broadway,
New York, Nov. 13, 1869.

Hon. E. G. Spaulding,

My Dear Sir:—If I have neglected to acknowledge your kindness in sending me a copy of your excellent book, it has been that I might write after a careful perusal should enable me to speak understandingly of its value. I have given it an attentive perusal, and while I thank you heartily for your courtesy in sending it, I thank you still more cordially for your labor in collecting and publishing it. To those who take an interest in the subject of the currency, the book is invaluable. I am glad also to see that, while you put forth no claims to personal credit, yet you have established by the force of documentary evidence, in the most irrefragible form, your own just claims to the merit of standing foremost amongst the statesmen who carried on their shoulders the soldiers who won the victories over the rebellion.

Much is due to the army and to the heroes who led it; but nothing less is due to the heroic statesmen whose sagacity and genius gave to the war "the sinews, without which the army would have striven in vain."

I am truly respectfully yours,

NOAH DAVIS.

JUDGE F. J. FITHIAN.

110 Broadway,
New York, Dec. 7, 1869.

Hon. E. G. Spaulding,

Dear Sir:—I have received your kind note, together with your (too brief) little volume on the "Financial History of the War." I have read it with much interest. It is a valuable contribution to the legislative history of the country at a most important and critical period. The idea of issuing U. S. treasury notes for currency, and making them legal tenders in payment of debts, was in my opinion the result of wise and sagacious statesmanship and a thorough knowledge of the *character* and resources of the American people. The latter was undoubtedly the keystone of the financial arch, and without it the whole structure must have crumbled in pieces before the close of the war. Here was a people who from their earliest history had been taught to look upon a public debt as public calamity, scarcely surpassed by any other. In times before they had been restive under a debt of a hundred millions; and now the necessity was upon them of going, no doubt, not only by the hundred, but by the *thousand* millions. And unless some scheme could be devised whereby gold and silver could be dispensed with as a measure of value or a circulating medium for cancelling of indebtedness, and something else substituted in its place capable of being enlarged to a magnitude equal to any emergency, the finances must have failed. This substitute the legal tender notes gave us. They it was that stimulated and encouraged the business interests of the country, kept up prices, and afforded ample facilities for the prosecution of all the best industries consequent upon a state of war. Yet it was a bold measure from which, as you well know, many of the wisest and best of your associates shrank. Secretary Chase never gave his adhesion until he was compelled by the clamor of hungry soldiers to devise some way to get money. Especially was this the case with the leading men in the Republican party of Democratic antecedents—men whose political opinions had been formed in the school of Jackson, Van Buren, Wright and Benton. To these men the support of a measure making government paper a legal tender, seemed like giving the lie to the whole political record. I remember very well that while you were preparing the bill I had several conversations with you on the subject. You feared for the fate of the measure in the Senate. Believing the measure to be of pressing necessity, I desired to use whatever influence I might possess (if any) in its favor, and accordingly I sought an interview with the late Preston King, senator from this state, on the subject. I found him, as I expected, opposed to the bill; but also (what I did not expect) very earnestly and bitterly opposed to it. It seemed to him utterly at war with all his pronounced opinions on financial subjects. And although as pure and devoted a patriot as ever existed, he seemed to be apparently doubting whether the Union was worth saving by such money. He would listen to no argument about it, and such as I ventured to try made no impression. He declared he would not consent to it as long as any other conceivable means remained untried, and if I recollect right, he did oppose the bill to the last. However, the measure was successful, and it is no more than simple justice to say what I personally know to be true, that for its origin, maturing and becoming a law, the country is indebted to you more than any one man. Your persistent and unwearied labors, your complete and thorough mastery of the subject, the respect and defference with which you were regarded by your fellow members, securing to you at all times a friendly and attentive hearing. All these it was that turned the scale in favor of the bill.

I have never had any doubt as to the constitutionality of the bill. Ample authority is found for it, not only in the grant of all necessary means to carry into effect the express powers, but in three at least of the expressly enumerated powers of Congress. I should be sorry to see any compromise decision of the court, to the effect that such a measure was constitutional in war and not in peace. If the power is there for any purpose or time, then Congress must be the exclusive judge as to the necessity or propriety of its excuse. But this letter is extending beyond due limits. Permit me to say in conclusion that I am of the opinion that your speech on the presentation of the bill was one among the very ablest forensic efforts ever delivered in that house. I thought so then, and now, on a careful re-perusal of it, after what was then prophesy has become history, I am confirmed in that opinion. The great events and measures of that Congress, in which you bore so prominent a part, are sufficient of themselves to secure you a position in history which few of your countrymen have the good fortune to attain.

Thanking you for your kind expressions towards me personally, and with best regards to yourself and family,

I am, very truly your friend,

F. J. FITHIAN.

JUDGE HENRY E. DAVIES.

NEW YORK, Sept. 17, 1869.

MY DEAR SIR:—I thank you for your courtesy in sending me a copy of your "Financial History" and your kind remembrance of me. I have only thus far been able to read your opening speech, and which, in view of the events which have transpired since its delivery, was wonderfully prophetic and eminently sound and able. I think you have demonstrated beyond all cavil that the only resource available to the Government at that time, to enable it to support its armies and maintain its navy, was the issue of treasury notes. I think you have also shown what was always clear to my mind, that these notes would have failed utterly to have accomplished the desired purpose if they had not been made a legal tender. This brings us to the constitutional power to declare what shall be a legal tender. It is the conceded attribute of every government to declare what shall be legal tender—in other words, what shall be the money. This power was exercised by the colonies and the states prior to the adoption of the constitution of 1789. If the states could not declare what they pleased as legal tenders, then what sense in the prohibition upon them, that they should not make anything but gold and silver a legal tender. So also the prohibition upon the states not to emit bills of credit. It has never been but that Congress could do this, it follows logically that it could also declare what should be a legal tender. This view is amplified in my opinion in 27 New York, and very neatly and succinctly stated by Attorney-General Bates, in his letter to you, which I first saw in your book. I have no doubt of the constitutional power of Congress to pass the legal tender act, and I think the United States Supreme Court will so hold when the question is presented to them. The expediency or necessity of such a law is quite another question. I have only looked at it as a question of power, and your speech and subsequent events have fully satisfied me of the necessity and wisdom of your action. It saved our Union, and we must now see how we can the most speedily get back to a specie basis. After I have looked through your most interesting and valuable book, I will write you again, at the peril of being too prolix. Judge Davis would like a copy, and is there any place here where I could procure two or three more.

Very cordially yours,

HENRY E. DAVIES.

PRESIDENT WOOLSEY,
Yale College.

NEW HAVEN, November 29, 1869.

Hon. E. G. Spaulding,

DEAR SIR:—I received your "History of the Legal Tender Paper Money issued during the great Rebellion," in due course of mail, and beg you to accept my thanks for the gift. As a teacher of political economy I shall find it particularly valuable, and although I have had no time to do more than look at the arrangement of topics, I can see that it would have saved me a good deal of labor if I had had it in my hands before.

It would be an idle thing for me to make any observations on the subject. I do not see how the Government could have stood under its burdens if it had taken a course materially different from that which was taken. And in regard to the return to specie payments, I do not see how a decision of the Supreme Court against the constitutionality of the act in private bargains can of itself bring about such a return.

Very respectfully yours,

THEODORE WOOLSEY.

PROF. PERRY.

WILLIAMS COLLEGE, August 27, 1869.

Hon. E. G. Spaulding,

MY DEAR SIR:—I am very much obliged to you for a copy of your book. It will be of essential service to me, and to all others who, like me, wish to learn from an authentic source the exact financial lessons which our war is fitted to teach. I have begun to read the book in course, am pleased with it as far as I have read, but thought I would not delay acknowledging it till I had finished. When I am through with it, I will perhaps communicate with you again. I may be in Buffalo in the course of the autumn, and if so I shall do myself the pleasure of calling on you.

With great respect, yours,

A. L. PERRY.

PROF. JAMES P. WHITE, M. D.

BUFFALO, March 10, 1870.

Hon. E .G. Spaulding,

DEAR SIR:—Accept my thanks for a copy of the "Financial History of the War." The college term having closed, I availed myself of the first leisure moments since its reception, and have perused it with care and interest. It is a very valuable contribution to the history of the war. This little volume furnishes a connected account of the financial difficulties encountered in subduing the rebellion, and the manner in which they were overcome. Always aware of the importance of the measures originated and carried to completion mainly by your unremitted exertions, I am more than ever convinced that without the "Legal Tender" our armies could not have been maintained in the field, and all our efforts to preserve the union by force must have resulted in discomfiture. How helpless would have been our patriotic President and resolute Lieut.-General and his brave soldiers, without the necessary "sinews of war." History will, I am sure, place those services which preserved the credit of the government during its peril in the same exalted rank with the more brilliant achievements in the field which command our admiration and gratitude.

Again thanking you for the volume which you have been kind enough to compile, and which was certainly a great desideratum.

I remain ever truly, your obedient friend and servant,

JAMES P. WHITE.

JOHN T. HEARD, ESQ.

BOSTON, October 2, 1869.

DEAR SIR:—Your kind letter of the 18th ult., I had the pleasure to receive in New York on the 21st. On that day also came to hand your valuable work, the "History of the Legal Tender Act," for which please accept my thanks. I have examined it with great interest, and regard it as an authorative statement of the financial legislation during the war. Owing to your intimate and prominent connection with that legislation, no one, it seems to me, was better qualified to treat fully and justly the subject, as the book incontestably proves.

The late gold speculation will have a good result if it quicken the public mind to the importance of an early return to specie payments. Had not Congress interfered with the policy of contraction of the late Secretary, we should have by this time been well on our way to a gold standard. Had the new administration kept its gold and not sold any of it, would not such policy have reduced the premium? Would not such a course have brought us easily and naturally, (in the line of trade) even now, far on the road to specie payments?

With kind regards to Mrs. Spaulding and yourself,

I am respectfully yours,

JOHN T. HEARD.

Hon. E. G. SPAULDING, Buffalo.

C. L. VALLANDIGHAM.

DAYTON, Ohio, July 17, 1869.

Hon. E. G. Spaulding, Buffalo, N. Y.,

MY DEAR SIR:—Accept my thanks for the copy kindly sent me, of your "Financial History of the War." It is an important and valuable work for the historian and the student, of the wonderful times to which it relates—discussing, as it does, the problem of furnishing "the sinews" for the greatest civil war of modern days. How much military glory think you, in any war, would be acquired on land or sea, by gentlemen of the army and navy at the front, if the "ways and means" were not first *invented* by statesmen in the rear? Here, in part at least, *cedant arma togae.*

I still think it was neither constitutional, necessary nor wise to declare the notes a "legal tender." But of this I am content that courts and history shall judge now.

Yours truly, etc.,

C. L. VALLANDIGHAM.

GEO. H. PENDLETON.

CINCINNATI, Ohio, July 15, 1869.

Hon. E. G. Spaulding, Buffalo,

MY DEAR SIR:—I have the honor to acknowledge the receipt of your letter of the 12th inst., and of the volume entitled "Financial History of the War."

For both I beg to return my thanks. I have not yet been able to read the volume, but I have no doubt it will fill a vacuum which every student of our late history, and even many actors in it, has most sensibly felt. Your position at the time gave you special facilities for knowing all which lay beneath the surface of the pages of the *Globe* or the newspapers.

Very truly and respectfully,
GEO. H. PENDLETON.

HON. MR. CRAWFORD.

COLUMBUS, Ga., Sept. 16, 1869.

MY DEAR SIR:—Allow me to thank you for the "Financial History of the War," as well as for your kind letter accompanying the same, which I have this day received. Pressing professional engagements will prevent me from examining the book at present; but it is a most capital idea to have in such concise form the history of the financial legislation of Congress during the war. Otherwise, volumes upon volumes, and report upon report, would have to be searched to find what you have here in 300 pages.

I sincerely hope, however, that "the sinews of war" may not be needed again very soon, and that we may be permitted to repair the waste places in our impoverished land. Hoping that we may at some time meet again and renew our kind personal relations, I beg to remain,

Very truly yours,
MARTIN J. CRAWFORD.

Hon. E. G. SPAULDING.

PRESIDENT GRANT'S VETO OF THE INFLATION BILL.

EXECUTIVE MANSION,
WASHINGTON, April 22, 1874.

To the Senate of the United States:

Herewith I return Senate bill No. 617, entitled "An act to fix the amount of United States notes and the circulation of national bank notes, and for other purposes," without my approval. In doing so I must express my regret at not being able to give my assent to the measure which has received the sanction of a majority of the legislators chosen by the people to make laws for their guidance, and I have studiously sought to find sufficient arguments to justify such an assent, but unsuccessfully. Practically, it is a question whether the measure under discussion would give an additional dollar to the irredeemable paper currency of the country or not; and whether, by acquiring three-fourths of the reserves to be retained by the banks, and prohibiting interest to be received on the balance, it might not prove a contraction. But the fact cannot be concealed that theoretically the bill increases the paper circulation one hundred million of dollars, less only the amount of the reserves restrained from circulation by the provisions of the second section.

The measure has been supported on the theory that it would give an increased circulation. It is a fair inference, therefore, that if in practice the measure should fail to create the abundance of circulation expected, the friends of the measure, particularly those out of Congress, would clamor for such inflation as would give the expected relief. The theory, in my belief, is a departure from the true principles of finance, the national interest, national obligation to creditors, congressional promises, party pledges on the part of both political parties, and of the personal views and promises made by me in every annual message sent to Congress, and in each inaugural address.

In my annual message to Congress in December, 1869, the following passage appears:

"Among the evils growing out of the rebellion and not yet referred to, is that of an irredeemable currency. It is an evil which I hope will receive your most earnest attention. It is the duty, and one the highest duties of the government, to secure to its citizens a medium of exchange of a fixed, unvarying value. This implies a return to a specie basis, and no substitute for it can be devised. It should be commenced now and reached at the earliest practicable moment consistent with a fair regard to the interest of the debtor class. Immediate resumption, if practicable, would not be desirable. It would compel the debtor class to pay beyond their contracts the premium on gold at the date of their purchase, and would bring bankruptcy and ruin to thousands. The fluctuations, however, in the paper value of the measure of all values—gold—is detrimental to the interest of trade. It makes the man of business an involuntary gambler, for in all sales where future payment is to be made both parties speculate as to what will be the value of the currency to be paid and received. I earnestly recommend to you, then, such legislation as will insure the gradual return to specie payments, and put an immediate stop to the fluctuations in the value of the currency."

I still adhere to the views then expressed. As early as December 4, 1865, the House of Representatives passed resolutions, by a vote of 144 yeas to 6 nays, concurring in the views of the Secretary of the Treasury in relation to the necessity of contracting the currency with a view to as early a resumption of specie payments as the business interests of the country will permit, and pledging co-operative action to this end as speedily as possible.

The first act passed by the Forty-first Congress, on the eighteenth day of March, 1869, was as follows:

"*An act to strengthen the public credit of the United States:*

"Be it enacted, etc., That in order to remove any doubt as to the purpose of the government to discharge all its obligations to public creditors, and to settle conflicting questions and interpretations of law, by virtue of which such obligations have been contracted, it is hereby provided and declared that the faith of the United States is solemnly pledged to the payment in coin, or its equivalent, of all obligations of the United States, and of all interest-bearing obligations, except in cases where the law authorizing the issue of any such obligations has expressly provided that the same may be paid in lawful money, or in other currency than gold or silver; but none of said interest-bearing obligations not already due shall be redeemed or paid before maturity, unless at such times as the United States notes shall be convertible into coin at the option of the holder, or unless at such time the bonds of the United States bearing a lower rate of interest than the bonds to be redeemed can be sold at par in coin. The United States also solemnly pledges its faith to make provision, at the earliest practicable period, for the redemption of United States notes in coin.

This act still remains as a continuing pledge of the faith of the United States to make provision, at the earliest practicable moment, for the redemption of United States in coin. The declaration contained in the act of June 20, 1864, created an obligation that the total amount of United States notes issued or to be issued should never exceed four hundred millions of dollars. The amount of actual circulation was actually reduced to three hundred and fifty-six millions of dollars, at which point Congress passed the act of February 4, 1868, suspending the further reduction of the currency. Forty-four millions have even been regarded as a reserve, to be used only in case of an emergency such as has occurred on several occasions, and must occur when from any cause the revenues suddenly fall below the expenditures, and such reserve is necessary, because fractional currency amounting to fifty millions is redeemable in legal tender on call. It may be said that such a return of fractional currency is impossible, but let steps be taken for a return to a specie basis and it will be found that silver will take the place of fractional currency as rapidly as it can be supplied.

When the premium on gold reaches a sufficiently low point, with the amount of United States notes to be issued permanently within proper limits, and the treasury is so strengthened as to be able to redeem them in coin on demand, it will then be safe to inaugurate a system of free banking, with such provisions as to make the compulsory redemption of the circulating notes of banks in coin, or United States notes themselves redeemable and made equivalent to coin, as a measure preparatory to free banking, or for placing the government in a position to redeem its notes in coin at the earliest practicable moment. The revenues of the country should be increased so as to pay the current expenses, provide for a sinking fund required by law, and also a surplus to be retained in the treasury in gold.

I am not a believer in any artificial method of making paper money equal to coin, when coin is not owned or held ready to redeem the promises to pay, for paper money is nothing more than promises to pay, and is valuable exactly in proportion to the amount of coin it can be converted into. When coin is not used as the circulating medium, or the currency of the country is not convertible into it at par, it becomes an article of commerce as much as any other produce. The surplus will seek a foreign market, as will any other surplus. The balance of trade has nothing to do with the question. The duties on imports being required in gold, and about enough to satisfy that demand remains in the country. To increase this supply I see no way open but by the government hoarding, through the means above given, and possibly by requiring national banks to aid.

It is claimed, by the advocates of the measure herewith returned, that there is an unequal distribution of the banking capital of the country. I was disposed to give great weight to this view of the question at first, but on reflection it will be remembered that there still remains $4,000,000 of authorized bank-note circulation assigned the states having less than quota not yet taken. In addition to this the states having less than their quota of bank circulation have the option of $25,000,000 more to be taken from those states having more than their proportion. When this is all taken up, or when specie payments are fully restored or are in rapid process of restoration, it will be time to consider the question of more currency.

U. S. GRANT.

HON. T. O. HOWE.

GREEN BAY, Sept. 13, 1869.

MY DEAR SIR:—I give you many thanks for sending me a copy of your "Financial History of the War." But I give you more thanks for publishing the work itself.

Last winter I became painfully aware of the want of such a work. I attempted to prepare a speech upon our financial condition. Upon looking around I could find no account of the financial measures resorted to during the war save in the statutes and the *Globe*.

Mining in those mountains was so tedious that my speech was not prepared until all debate to which it was pertinent had been closed.

The book came to hand this morning. Of course I have only looked to see its contents, and have not read those contents. That I shall do hereafter, and I am sure I shall read not only with interest but with gratitude.

I remember the leading ideas argued in my speech upon the legal tender act, to which you refer in terms of compliment. If I were to make the speech under like circumstances, but with the light of all the experience we have since had, I do not know wherein I should wish to change it.

I thought we should resort to a paper circulation because we could not command coin—that the Government should make the paper because it could make safer paper than the banks—that it should make the capitalist take them because we made the soldier take them—that this circulation should be in the form of promises to pay, because within the usual form, but not to pay on demand because we know we could not pay on demand—that we never should make a dollar of paper when we could borrow a dollar at a fair rate of interest—we should stand ready to take in exchange for notes that did draw interest. The great mistake of our time, I think, was when we refused to make our notes convertible into bonds.

Very truly yours,

T. O. HOWE.

Hon. E. G. SPAULDING.

HON. O. P. MORTON.

INDIANAPOLIS, Aug. 28, 1869.

Hon. E. G. Spaulding,

DEAR SIR:—I received your letter containing your speech and accompanied by your book, for which please accept my thanks. I regard them as very valuable, and your book will be very useful in enabling politicians to make an accurate study of the financial question. The ultimate redemption or proposal to redeem the greenbacks is the true way to resumption, and for that purpose a larger revenue of gold is necessary. This was the burden of my speech and of my bill last winter.

While I regard Schenk's "bill to strengthen the public credit," as a misfortune, yet the clause which pledges the faith of the Government to make provision at the earliest practicable period for the redemption of the greenbacks in coin, was an amendment which I proposed in the Conference Committee on the bill which Johnson pocketed. The bill finally passed was a copy of that. Preparation to resume specie payment is in my opinion the first great duty of the Government.

I dissent from you reluctantly on one point—reference to the repeal of the clause authorizing the conversion of greenbacks into Five-Twenties. That repeal was indispensible to the sale of the bonds. Capitalists would not buy bonds at par, which could not by any possibility get above par. As long as the people could take their greenbacks and convert them into bonds at par, the bonds would not get above par in the market. The two things were of unequal value inherently, and could not both be kept afloat at the same time if convertible.

If the bonds appreciated, the greenbacks would be converted and pass out of circulation, and as a circulation was necessary more would have to be issued, and the effect would be to drag down the bonds, because these in turn would be convertible, and so on. The provision of convertibility I always regarded as impracticable. If the conversion was not made it was because the bonds were depreciated and would not sell at par. If they were converted the purpose of a circulation was defeated unless they were constantly renewed.

I would write more at length if I had time.

I am very truly yours,

O. P. MORTON.

HON. R. E. FENTON.

COMMITTEE OF FINANCE, U. S. SENATE,
WASHINGTON, May 7, 1870.

MY DEAR SIR:—I owe you an apology for my delay in acknowledging the receipt of your "Financial History of the War." The truth is, I have been so much occupied that I have not until the last few days, examined it. My official connections with the Congress during the time embraced in your work, enables me to speak of its accuracy and value. *And as relating to extraordinary and necessary legislation to sustain the Government during the years of its great trial*, it will be hereafter, as well as now, a convenient and well received authority. Very truly yours,

R. E. FENTON.

Hon. E. G. SPAULDING.

HON. CARL SCHURZ,
Late Senator.

ST. LOUIS, Mo., Sept, 25, 1869.

DEAR SIR:—I have received the copy of the "Financial History of the War," which you had the kindness to forward to me. The work is a very meritorious one, and you have obliged me very much by sending it to me.

Very truly yours,

C. SCHURZ.

Hon. E. G. SPAULDING.

POINTS MADE BY SENATOR SCHURZ, IN HIS SPEECH IN JANUARY, 1874.

"1. The government of the United States is in law and honor bound to pay the debt incurred by the issue of its promises to pay, as soon as by its own action it can render itself able to pay.

"2. When, under circumstances like ours, an irredeemable paper currency is constantly depreciated, at a discount as to coin, that depreciation proves that its volume is in excess of the real wants of the general business of the country. This being the case with our paper currency, the present crisis cannot have been caused by any insufficiency of that currency as to the real requirements of business.

"3. While a sudden fright or panic, showing itself in runs upon banks, &c., may under certain circumstances be momentarily checked by an additional issue of currency—a stage of affairs which lies several months behind us—a crisis caused by the unproductive consumption of capital and overspeculation, cannot be remedied by an addition to an already redundant paper currency.

"4. The proposition that the Government may, without the most pressing necessities, springing from extreme public danger, issue any additional amounts of irredeemable paper currency at its arbitrary discretion, merely to exercise a certain influence upon the business of the country, tends to create a system which will place all the private fortunes of the city at the mercy of the Government.

"5. A currency, which to the vice of inconvertibility adds the vice of redundancy, has always had, and must naturally have, the effect of stimulating over-speculation, and gambling; of diverting the energies of the people from honest, productive labor; of leading to the unproductive consumption of capital and the creation of fictitious values ; of naturally expanding the system of credit ; of demoralizing business as well as social life ; and thus of seriously aggravating the causes which produce the general break-down at once.

"6. The further expansion of such a currency, during or after a crisis, can only revive and stimulate anew the influences which have already demoralized business and brought forth crops of disaster.

"7. An addition to such currency does not only not add to the wealth of the country, but does not increase the efficiency of the currency itself as a means of exchange, for the reason that it drives up prices, and by stimulating speculation causes its being drawn away from the legitimate business of the country to the centres of speculation. It will not make, permanently, money easy, but rather raise than reduce the current rates of interest.

"8. For the same reason every addition to such currency will not satisfy, but excite the demand for more and more, and thus push the country forward on the road to bankruptcy and repudiation.

"9. No legitimate economic interest of the country will, therefore, be permanently benefitted by such expansion, but all will be injured.

"10. Least of all is the agricultural interest benefitted by our irredeemable and redundant currency. It is, on the contrary, most grievously injured by it, because the farmer must pay extravagant prices for all he has to buy, while the prices of the principal products he has to sell are regulated by a foreign market untouched by our home inflation, and controlled by the competition of the world.

"11. These evils will be increased by every further expansion and consequent depreciation of the currency, and the idea that the agricultural interest and those sections of the country—the west and the south—whose prosperity depends on a profitable cultivation of the soil, can be readily benefitted by further expansion, is therefore fallacious in the highest degree.

"12. On the other hand, the agricultural interest will be vastly benefitted by an early return to specie payments, because resumption will greatly reduce the price of the commodities the farmer has to buy, while it will not in a proportion, reduce the price of the principal products he has to sell, thus adding greatly to the purchasing power of his income.

"13. The idea that the return to specie payments can be facilitated by that sort of prosperity which would be brought forth by further inflation involves a mischievous fallacy. Further inflation would only revive and stimulate all the evil influences of a redundant irredeemable currency upon all economic movements, again excite over-speculation, promote excessive importations, thus turning and keeping trade balance against us; again expand the credit system to the bursting point, and lead to new and more disastrous revulsions.

"14. Such expansion would render impossible the fulfilment of the conditions which must precede the resumption of specie payments ; retrenchment and economy in public and private affairs, contraction of the credit system and of private indebtedness, prudent management of business, &c.

"15. The idea that the return to specie payments can in the safest way be brought about by doing nothing and waiting until the development of the resources of the country and the growth of business have brought our paper money and gold to a par in commercial value is equally fallacious, for the reason that the period of relief thus vaguely pointed out lies in an undefined and undefinable future; that in the meantime all the demoralizing and dangerous influences of our irredeemable and redundant currency remain at work with undiminished vigor and activity; that there will be continued danger of further inflation being forced upon us by agencies beyond our control, as the government at the present moment is already expanding the currency; that thus the day of promise is put off further and further, and that the very difficulties and disasters which the advocates of the do-nothing policy fear will spring from legislative action in the direction of specie payments will naturally occur, and have in fact occurred, under the do-nothing policy itself, as recent events have clearly demonstrated.

"16. The resumption of specie payments cannot surely be brought on but by legislative action ; and no more propitious moment can be found for the inauguration of a resumption policy than the present, for the reason that much of the work of preparation which must precede resumption has already been done by the crisis. Private indebtedness has been greatly reduced; credit in business transactions has been largely contracted; the prices of com-mo.lities have already declined to a low point; business men have generally but light stocks on hand, and for months have been circumspect in their operations. The possibility of loss through the appreciation of the current money or the decline of prices will therefore be now as little as we ever can expect it to be."

HON. E. W. LEAVENWORTH

SYRACUSE, Oct. 31, 1869.

Hon. E. G. Spaulding,

MY DEAR SIR:—On my return from New York, last evening, I found your letter of the 26th, and also your work on our finances as affected by our legislation in the early years of the rebellion. I have, of course, as yet only given it a very hasty examination, but it is sufficient to perceive that you have made a most valuable contribution to the history of the country during that most eventful period. And what greatly enhances its value is the fact that, while its importance cannot be overlooked or gravely over-estimated, it has been almost ignored by all the various historians of the great rebellion. Your position in Congress, and the part you took in the great financial questions of the day, your familiarity with the whole subject, and your tastes, all peculiarly fitted you for this important work, and you seem to have exhausted the subject. I hope, in justice to yourself and also for the general good, that you will see that a copy of the work is put in most of the important libraries of the country, for the future benefit of the historians of that period. There are great lessons to be learned from our experience, and the "almighty dollar" is the great power, without which campaigns are never successful. Thanking you for your kind remembrance, I remain,

Most truly yours,

E. W. LEAVENWORTH.

HON. D. A. WELLS.

TREASURY DEPARTMENT, }
WASHINGTON, Sept. 25, 1869. }

Hon. E. G. Spaulding,

MY DEAR SIR:—When in Boston last week I saw for the first time a copy of your "Financial History of the War," and was intending to order it immediately on my return home, when your letter and the book in question arrived. I have not had time to more than glance at its contents; I know, however, that it supplies an important element of our recent history, and that the work has been well done. Please receive my thanks for your kind remembrance. I have thus far read everything that you have published that I have seen, and agree with you fully upon all matters, with a single exception, and that is this:

I do not believe that with the present volume of currency, and the consequent maintenance of abnormal prices, that resumption of specie payments is practicable by any method. I do not believe that any legal enactment compelling the Treasury or the banks to retain and accumulate gold will produce a sufficient sum to meet redemption, or that gold could be kept here for any length of time after redemption had been commenced, on any basis of accumulation. If you, in conjunction with your ideas of accumulating gold, will advocate a measure of contraction, I am with you, heart and hand.

Have you read a recent work by Bonamy Price, professor of political economy at Oxford, Eng., entitled " Principles of Currency ? " If not, allow me to recommend it to you as worthy of perusal, although I do not fully agree with all the propositions contained in it.

I do not know how valuable a report I can get up for this year. I sometimes feel almost discouraged, as the results of investigation are so paradoxical and unsatisfactory. It sometimes seems to me that the more I investigate and discuss these matters the less I know; but, at the same time, I have an abiding confidence that we shall in the end manage to struggle through all our difficulties, but perhaps at the cost of a sad experience. Trusting that I may have, at no distant day, the pleasure of a personal interview, I remain, yours very truly,

DAVID A. WELLS.

HON. AMASA WALKER.

NORTH BROOKFIELD, Sept. 1, 1869.

Hon. E. G. Spaulding,

DEAR SIR :—Yours of the 26th is just at hand, and I have also the pleasure to acknowledge the receipt of your " History of the Legal Tender Paper Money issued during the great Rebellion." I have glanced at it sufficiently to see that it is a valuable contribution to our financial literature—a work that will be found very convenient and useful for reference in the future. I am much obliged to you for it, and shall peruse it at my leisure. I arrived at home, from my summer's tour to the Gulf of St. Lawrence, last evening, so that at present I am much occupied.

I am glad you took so strong ground in your letter to Mr. McCulloch in favor of restoring the currency to par with gold. It is, by far, the most serious matter now before the nation. What the action of Congress, at its next session, will be, no one can predict. There will be a strong effort to further inflate, and if that cannot be done, then to hold on to the present amount of currency. I think, with you, that the intervention of the Supreme Court may be the only way in which the country can be relieved; and, undesirable as that mode of relief is, it will be far better than to float on under our depreciated monetary system.

I shall ever be ready to afford any assistance in my power toward securing a gradual but efficient contraction of the circulating medium. I don't know whether you saw my plan, proposed last winter, of withdrawing the greenbacks by issuing compound interest notes instead; if so, I should like to know how it strikes you. I am, yours truly,

AMASA WALKER.

HON. ALEXANDER H. RICE.

BOSTON, Oct. 27, 1869

Hon. E. G. Spaulding, Buffalo, N. Y.

MY DEAR SIR:—I am very glad to possess the volume received from you this morning, and thank you for sending it to me. I have not yet had time to more than glance at its contents, but I know that no one is more competent than you are to treat the subject intelligently and exhaustively.

I am, dear sir, yours very truly,

ALEX. H. RICE.

MAJOR-GENERAL SHERMAN.

WAR DEPARTMENT,
WASHINGTON, Oct. 12, 1869.

DEAR SIR:—With many thanks for your kindness in sending it, I beg to acknowledge the receipt of a copy of your lately-issued "History of the Legal Tenders." I have not been able to more than glance through it here, but have sent it down to my house, where I can read it more leisurely.

In answer to your request for my views upon the work, I can only say now, that the magnitude of the subject, and its importance to the future, certainly warranted, if it did not actually demand, its publication; and it is equally certain, from your known connection with the measure from its inception to its final adoption, that you were the one to collect, prepare and send forth its history. Very truly yours,

W. T. SHERMAN,
Gen'l and Sec'y of War.

Hon. E. G. SPAULDING, Buffalo, N. Y.

GENERAL BUTLER.

BAY VIEW, near
GLOUCESTER, Aug, 17, 1869.

DEAR SIR:—I have the honor to acknowledge the receipt of your "Financial History of the War," which I intend to examine with the care its merits require. I think it will fill a need in the financial history of the country. There can be no more abstruse problem than our present financial relations, and anything which shall show the origin of our present system, so as to elucidate the principles upon which it operates, will be a benefit to the country. With many thanks for your courtesy,

I am, yours truly,

BENJ. F. BUTLER.

Hon. E. G. SPAULDING, Buffalo, N. Y.

HON. JAMES A. GARFIELD.

WASHINGTON, D. C., June 5th, 1869.

Hon. E. G. Spaulding, Buffalo, N. Y.

DEAR SIR:—Yours of the first, together with your "Financial History of the War," came duly to hand. Please accept my thanks for your kind consideration. I know of no man so well fitted as yourself to write that history, and I am delighted that you have performed what I am sure, with your sound views on the subject, will prove a service to the whole country in the work you have accomplished.

      Very truly yours,
         J. A. GARFIELD.

HON. EDWARD HAIGHT,

The only Democrat in the House who voted for the Legal Tender Act.

      BANK OF THE COMMONWEALTH, }
       NEW YORK, Oct. 29, 1859. }

Hon. E. G. Spaulding, Buffalo, N. Y.

DEAR SIR:—Some time has elapsed, and more than I intended there should, between the receipt of your book and its acknowledgment; allow me first to thank you for it, and then to say that having examined it carefully, I regard it as a most valuable manual of the financial events of the War—events that have culminated in a gladdening peace, and that are yet to exert an influence upon the monetary affairs of our own country—and perchance of the world—most useful and salutary or most mischievous and pernicious, according as wisdom or folly may most prevail in our councils.

Highly as those of us who participated in the financial events of the war, must regard your book to the future historian, who will be called to weave them into a narrative of the deepest interest to future generations; it will be more than doubly valuable. Sincerely congratulating you therefore, and renewedly thanking you for my copy, I remain with the highest respect,

    Yours very truly,
       EDWARD HAIGHT.

HON. J. O. PUTNAM.

       BUFFALO, June 26, 1869.

MY DEAR SIR:—I thank you for your volume vindicating the "Truth of History." It is not a new idea to me, that to you is attributable, in a very large measure, the adoption of the "Legal Tender System" of our War Finance. You have rendered a valuable service, and your book will always be an authority on the subject of which its treats, and which it seems to me to exhaust.

It is a rare distinction to be so identified as are you with that policy, without which the late struggle of the government had been a failure.

I most heartily congratulate you. With renewed thanks for your courtesy,

  I am, as ever, very truly, your old friend,
       JAMES O. PUTNAM.

Hon. E. G. SPAULDING.

HON. A. M. CLAPP,
Public Printer Washington.

OFFICE OF THE CONGRESSIONAL PRINTER,
WASHINGTON, Oct. 18, 1869.

MY DEAR SIR:—I am in receipt of a copy of your "History of the Legal Tender paper money issued during the Great Rebellion," for which please accept my sincere acknowledgments.

The great financial achievement which this work so clearly and ably presents to the public mind, is the most wonderful known to the history of nations, and I but do you simple justice when I say, that, to your financial wisdom and skill the country is in a large degree indebted for its accomplishment. It detracts nothing from the honor due to the brave officers and soldiers who rallied in defence of the Union and Constitution when in peril, and through whose courage and patriotism our national salvation was perfected. to say that like credit is due to the Statesmen who grappled with the great financial problem on the floor of Congress, and solved it in law, so successfully that the Ways and Means for prosecuting the war, subduing the rebellion, restoring peace, and extending the blessings of freedom to all the people of this nation, were obtained without recourse to other agencies than the national faith.

Your able exposition of this question in the work before me—a question upon which hung the national life—entitles you to the gratitude of the American people.

I am, sir, with much respect,
Your ob't servant,

Hon. E. G. SPAULDING.   A. M. CLAPP.

J. D. F. LANIER,
Banker.

NEW YORK, May 6, 1873.

E. G. Spaulding, Esq.

DEAR SIR:—Yours of the 24th April is received, as also the book for Mr. Harmon, for which please accept my thanks. The Book shall have my careful attention.

The fact is I do not see how we could have got through with the late war, but for the Legal Tender Law.

We had no money, no credit at home or abroad. The Tender Law was absolutely necessary to our continued existence. No one has suffered by it, but all have gained. The Treasury note law would have been a dead letter but for the legal tender act.

Yours, truly,
J. F. D. LANIER.

HON. H. L. DAWES,
Senator from Massachusetts.

PITTSFIELD, Mass., Nov. 6, 1869.

Hon. E. G. Spaulding,

MY DEAR SIR:—I am very much gratified that you should remember me with a copy of your book, "The Financial History of the War." It does, indeed, supply a very important omission in all other histories of the war, and will become at once a book of reference. It is also a monument to your own statesmanship in the darkest hour of our trial, of which you may well be proud, and to which you have a right to call the attention of your countrymen. I am, truly yours,

H. L. DAWES.

GOOD MANAGEMENT OF FRENCH FINANCES.

The following facts relating to the currency of France are compiled from documents accessible to all the world:

1. The aggregate circulation of notes of the Bank of France, including "notes payable to order," was on

September 11, 1873. .... 2,890,244,276 francs.
September 9, 1875...... ....2,361,819,283 francs.

Decrease....... .... 528,424,993 francs.

2. Counting five francs as equal to one dollar, this is a contraction of $105,684,999 in twenty-four months.

3. The notes of the Bank of France are the only paper money which circulates in France. They are a legal tender, are paid and received as the equivalent of specie, and for a year or more have been as good as gold.

4. The maximum note circulation of the Bank of France was reached on October 31, 1873, when it was 3,071,000,000 francs, or $614,200,000. The total on September 9, 1875, as above given, is equal $472,400,000, being a contraction of $141,800,000 in less than two years.

5. This contraction is not accidental, like the trifling reduction which has taken place during the current year in our legal tender and bank note issues. In the language of the inflationists, it is "forced."

6. During the war and the payment of the indemnity, the French Government borrowed of the bank an immense sum in notes, for which it paid only one per cent. per annum interest, that rate being barely a sufficient compensation to the bank for manufacturing and handling the notes.

7. For the past two years the French Government has been steadily paying its debt to the bank, preferring to fund its one per cent. loan into five per cent *rentes* rather than encounter the risks of an inflated paper circulation.

8. The total amount of this one per cent. war debt due from the government to the bank was, on

September 11, 1873.... ....1,374,052,500 francs.
September 9, 1875...................... 649,620,000 francs.

Reduction...................... .... 724,432,500 francs.
Equal to........................ . $144,886,500

9. By a recent treaty with the bank, the government engages to pay off the entire amount of this war debt by the end of the year 1879.

10. The bank is pledged to resume the full payment of all its liabilities in coin on Jan. 1, 1878, by which time the government engages to reduce its war debt to $60,000,000.

11. In the interval the policy of the bank is not "to make the volume of the currency equal to the wants of trade," but on the contrary, it has steadily contracted its advances to the mercantile community by maintaining a higher rate of discount than that ruling in the open market. As a consequence of this policy the discounts of the bank have diminished as follows. They were on

September 11, 1873.......................948,569,253 francs.
September 9, 1875 ....505,834,586 francs.

Decrease..... ....442,734,667 francs.
Equal to............... ....$88,546,933

12. At the present time the rate of discount at the Bank of France is four per cent., while that at the Bank of England is only two, and the current rates in Paris outside of the bank are from 2½ to 3⅜.

13. In consequence of this double operation, i. e., the repayments of the government and of the private debtors, the circulation has diminished, as we have shown above, and the specie in possession of the bank has increased as follows: It was on

September 11, 1873....................... 708,869,992 francs.
September 9, 1875.....................1,618,943,228 francs.

Increase........................... 910,073,236 francs.
Equal to........ ....$ 182,014,647

The above summary embraces, we believe, all the important facts in relation to the changes which have been made in the paper circulation of France. Bold and energetic as the action of the bank has been, no injurious effects on trade are visible. General business for two years past appears, in fact, to have been much better in France than it has been in either England, Germany, or the United States. No candid man can extract from the conduct of the French Government and bank a particle of countenance for any of the quack money schemes which have been broached among us. They have fixed a day for resumption, as we have done, but not without making provision for decreasing their paper and increasing their specie. They have not aimed at a cheap currency, with the maximum of paper and the minimum of coin. They have not confounded gold and government bonds together, and deluded themselves with the idea that there is no essential difference between the two. The end to which the Bank of France is aiming is to make its notes at all times and under all circumstances convertible into specie, and to accomplish that object they know that they cannot safely issue all the notes that the business community will absorb in times of confidence, nor do they trust to any other resources in time of difficulty than an ample stock of the precious metals in their vaults. This, as we understand the matter, is the lesson taught by English, German, Dutch and French banking—always to have on hand a full supply of the exportable precious metals in order to maintain the credit of the non-exportable promises to pay those metals.

HON. DAVID WILDER,
State Treasurer of Massachusetts.

STATE HOUSE,
BOSTON, Sept. 16, 1864.

Hon. E. G. Spaulding, President F. & M. Nat. Bank, Buffalo, N. Y.

DEAR SIR:—Your note of the 11th inst. was duly received, and the interesting volume prepared by you has since come to hand and been looked over, so far as I have been able to command the necessary time. I hardly need say that I am greatly obliged for both, though I think I am in duty bound to assure you that, to those of us who care to watch the financial machinery of the country, nothing could be more opportune or interesting than your account of the steps by which we are able to make the industry of our people available, and carry on the war so much better than could be done by our foes, who lacked the sinews which you and your associates supplied. Your book should have a wide circulation, and, after being read, many persons will realize, as now they do not, how much you had to contend with, and how fatal to our national life would less energy on your part have proved.

I have been more or less intimate with the finances of Massachusetts since 1840, as clerk in the Treasury and State Auditor, to which office I was appointed when it was created in 1849, and I can understand the work you did for us. I should have been glad if our idolatrous worship of gold as a currency (not as money) had been less, and that it could have been seen that all we had to do was to create a debt or lay a tax, and that the most direct and, under the circumstances, perhaps the most equitable course, was to make the debt.

Free banking, with prompt, par, central convertibility of notes and checks, is what the country needs of all things ; having first, of course, an immediate return to the specie standard, or change from the debased or seventy-five cent dollar to one worth one hundred, providing that all contracts now existing and payable in the degraded currency shall be paid in that when due, or in an equivalent of the other, so that there shall be no real change in the relation between parties, as there was when we abandoned specie and substituted paper, with the idea that legislation could affix or determine its value.

If interest had been provided for on the legal tenders, and the notes taken and paid as currency *for all purposes*, and convertible always into long bonds with gold interest, there would have been no real harm done. At any rate, legislation could not have swindled the then creditors by depriving them in many cases of one-half the real value of their claims. Legal tenders without interest were bad, while with interest they would have been doubly good.

Truly and respectfully yours,
DAVID WILDER.

GEORGE S. COE, ESQ.

AMERICAN EXCHANGE NAT'L BANK, }
NEW YORK, Sept. 28, 1875. }

E. G. Spaulding, Esq.,

DEAR SIR:—Your favor of the 25th inst. is at hand, with pamphlet enclosed, which I have only time at the moment hastily to read. I will give it a more careful perusal, and send you, as desired, such comment upon the subject as my familiarity with the early financial events of the war may suggest. I fully agree with you that the two great errors of Secretary Chase were, first, his refusal to use the instruments and expedients that the experience of commercial nations has made necessary for banks in distributing the money which our associated banks loaned the government. Second, that he assented to the suggestion of the brokers, whom he afterwards employed to sell the government bonds, by divorcing the *currency* debt from the *funded* debt, so that the former could no longer be converted into the latter, and was therefore left to indefinite deterioration. This was a clever device to facilitate the sale of bonds, but a fatal one to the currency. I do not believe it possible to restore specie payments otherwise than by re-enacting this funding power and cancelling every note thus exchanged. But the public feeling of obligation has become so weakened that a rate of interest will be insisted upon too low to accomplish the object. Yours truly,

GEO. S. COE.

H. BOWLBY WILLSON, ESQ.

90 DREXEL BUILDING, }
NEW YORK, Oct. 1, 1875. }

Hon. E. G. Spaulding, Buffalo, N. Y.

DEAR SIR:—I am in receipt of advanced sheets containing the introduction to the second edition of your valuable work on "The Financial History of the War," for which attention please accept my best thanks. The second edition, and especially the introduction to it, appears before the public very appropriately at this time, when the currency question is rapidly assuming national importance.

I have read the introduction twice over, and have to say "it is all gold and no dross." It makes entirely clear who was responsible for the financial policy of the government which led to an over issue of irredeemable paper money, which produced the fathomless abyss in which the country is now floundering. In 1869, I pointed out in the columns of the New York *Herald* this erroneous policy; but I was then, and so remained, until I received your new introduction, quite in the dark as to the originators of that policy and the exact *modus operandi* by which it was worked out to its fatal results on our whole financial and commercial system. This introduction, I repeat, comes most acceptably at this time, and adds materially to the interest of your "Financial History."

On the principles of paper money or currency proper, we entirely agree, as indeed all students of political economy must—those principles being established by scientific and analytical reasoning. If there is any room for difference, it may possibly be found in devising the safest and best method for the issue and regulation of such money. It now more than ever seems to me to be desirable that we should adopt the English and French systems of withdrawing the power from the banking corporations to issue currency notes, and lodge the same in the hands of a department of the government, so constituted that, like the supreme bench, the whole monetary system of the country may be, so far as possible, removed from the vortex of party politics. Professor Price, in his Oxford lectures, characterizes the issue department of the Bank of England as "a government department carried on on the premises of the bank." I would not place any bank in that responsible position.

The question, in my judgment, should now be permanently settled by a constitutional amendment, leaving no option to Congress but to pass laws in conformity with its provisions ; and one should be, that no more paper money shall at any time be issued than can be maintained at par with gold. There is no other method, as yet known, whereby the amount of such money necessary to meet the requirements of business can be determined. It is the simple natural law of supply and demand, the indications of which are always clear and easily understood by those issuing circulating notes. Under such a system the legal tender character of government notes may be dispensed with, and our national paper, like our gold, will pass everywhere on a par with each other. Excuse this digression, and believe me to remain,

   Very truly yours,
        H. BOWLBY WILLSON.

HON. ISAAC SHERMAN,
  Political Economist.

       18 WEST 20TH STREET,
       NEW YORK, Oct. 10, 1875.

Hon. E. G. Spaulding :

I have received and read with great pleasure the preface to your new edition of "The History of the Legal Tender Act." Your work will not only do good at present, but it will remain as an historical authority on the subject, and cannot fail to be an important contribution to the reliable records of our recent war. It will also put in a compact and accessible form the most forcible arguments for a return to specie payments. I doubt if you know how much good and effective results your work is doing, and I hope that you will continue to make new editions—at least until we shall have a resumption of specie payments.

I wish to call your attention to a fact that it is possible may not have been brought to your notice. In the case of Rosvelt vs. Meyer, 1 Wallace, 512, involving the constitutionality of the legal tender, a motion to dismiss was granted; and in the case of Trefilcock vs. Wilson, 12 Wallace, 687, involving the same question. The case of Rosevelt vs. Meyer was fairly and squarely submitted. Now, have you ever reflected what would have been the decision in the case of Rosevelt vs. Meyer, in the winter of 1864, if the case had not been dismissed? If you will examine the list of judges, you will see that seven members of the court would have voted against the constitutionality of the law. I suppose the case was undoubtedly dismissed for political reasons, and not on law grounds. Mr. Chase was still Secretary of the Treasury, and the war progressing, and an adverse decision would have entailed great financial disturbance while we were confronting the enemy. Mr. Roelker, the counsel of Mr. Meyer, has told me that Mr. Chase was very anxious that the case should not be decided on its merits, and that it should be dismissed. It is probable, considering the later overruling of the dismissal, that the dismissal was a *judicial dodge*. The court quite probably, therefore, has been once manipulated and once packed on the legal tender question. It seems to me that in some of your future editions of your work it would be well to insert in full the conflicting decisions of Rosevelt vs. Meyer and of Trefilcock vs. Wilson. These decisions are very instructive, and will show to those who hereafter come upon the political stage not only what Congress will do in great national emergencies, but also what the highest court will do in such emergencies. I do not mean by this language to condemn either Congress or the judiciary, because I have always said that if it was absolutely necessary to save the country to violate the constitution, I would not hesitate to violate the constitution. The constitution was made for the country, and not the country for the constitution; and the absolute safety of the country must therefore be paramount to the constitution. Still, I think it best to give posterity all the facts, and I think you can with propriety say that your only hope is that future generations, in a like great emergency, will only act as wisely, discreetly, magnanimously and patriotically as the people in your generation have acted against the great slave rebellion. Yours very respectfully,

ISAAC SHERMAN.

Hon. JOHN J. KNOX.

TREASURY DEPARTMENT,
OFFICE OF COMPTROLLER OF THE CURRENCY.
WASHINGTON, Oct. 29, 1869.

MY DEAR SIR:—I have received your note of the 25th inst., and also the volume you were so kind as to send me. "Truth is stronger than fiction," and the "History of the Legal Tender Paper Money used during the Great Rebellion," and the results are more interesting and wonderful than any work of fiction.

You have done yourself great honor by your services as a financial general during the rebellion, and in the preparation of this little volume you have furnished a most convenient record of the sayings and acts of those servants of the people whose duty it was to supply the means with which to protect and finally save the country. Please accept my thanks for the volume, and believe me, Very truly yours,

JNO. JAY KNOX.

Hon. E. G. SPAULDING, Buffalo, N. Y.

HON. W. P. FESSENDEN.

PORTLAND, Aug. 7, 1869.
Hon. E. G. Spaulding,

MY DEAR SIR:—On my return from a short visit to the eastern portion of our state, I found your letter of the 21st of July, and the book referred to therein. I have not yet had time to examine the history, but, from your close connection with the financial events of the war, I have no doubt of its correctness and value. As a participator in those events, I am able to testify to the want of comprehension of all previous writers upon the subject. You were entirely able to fill the void, and I have no doubt you have done so. Please accept my thanks, and believe me,

Truly yours,
W. P. FESSENDEN.

HON. JOHN COBURN,
Member of Congress from Indiana.

HOUSE OF REPRESENTATIVES,
WASHINGTON, D. C., April 12, 1870.

Hon. E. G. Spaulding,

DEAR SIR:—Your letter, with "Financial History of the War," came duly to hand. Please accept my thanks for the work. It is really an invaluable portion of the great history of the great struggle for national life. Your opportunities for knowledge of the subject being of the finest character, posterity, as well as the present age, must owe you a debt of gratitude for this timely service in fixing in permanent form a clear and concise statement of all the facts The conduct of our finances and the struggle in the field are equally creditable and memorable, and must be forever linked inseparably together as exhibitions of the energy and genius of our race.

Yours truly,
JOHN COBURN.

A. R. ENO.

NEW YORK, March 29, 1864.
Hon. E. G. Spaulding,

DEAR SIR:—If the truths in your letter could have been placed before the public at an earlier day, in the clear and forcible manner in which you have stated them, I think they would have so influenced public sentiment that we should have been spared a portion of the mischief resulting from present inflation. Mr. Chase has done well. I hope his great success will not render him indifferent to wise counsel. I thank you for sending me the letter, and am, Very truly, your obedient servant,

A. R. ENO.

F. A. CONKLING.

NEW YORK, Oct. 17, 1875.
Hon. E. G. Spaulding,

DEAR SIR:—Accept my hearty thanks for the advanced sheets of the "Introduction" to a further publication of your "Financial History of the

War of the Rebellion." I am glad that you contemplate the issuing of a new edition of a work, for the prepartion of which you are fitted above all other men. Your position as Chairman of the Sub-committee of Ways and Means of the House of Representatives, at the time the legal tender act was passed, placed you in possession of facts which, from the nature of the case, others could not know.

The Thirty-seventh Congress was one of the most statesmanlike and patriotic bodies which ever assembled in this or any other country. It promptly apprehended the magnitude of the questions before it, and to the utmost of its ability met them in the most efficient manner. It was, perhaps, the greatest calamity of the war that the financial policy established by that Congress was not cordially seconded and continued by successors and by the head of the Treasury Department.

Mr. Chase was pressed for that position because of the regard of the people for his high personal reputation. He had been an original free-soiler, and had won the favor of the men of advanced views upon that subject. He had been originally chosen to the United States Senate by Democratic votes on the supposition that his views on financial and analagous questions were acceptable to the Democratic party as it was then constituted. He was a conspicuous candidate for the presidential nomination in 1860, and, in the estimation of many, presented the ideal of an American statesman.

Upon the election of Mr. Lincoln, it was the demand of Mr. Chase's friends that he should occupy a leading position in the cabinet. The President-elect was himself disposed to comply with this desire. At the request of Mr. Horace Greeley, I accompanied him on a visit to Mr. Lincoln, to urge that Mr. Chase should receive the portfolio of the Treasury. We had been led to believe that another choice had been made for this all-important position. We represented to Mr. Lincoln that a struggle was imminent which would be decided in favor of the party whose resources held out the longest, and accordingly that a minister of finance was required who would command, in the highest degree, the public confidence. Mr. Chase, as we believed, possessed that confidence as no other man did whose name was under consideration.

The day following this interview I received a note from Greeley, informing me that Mr. Chase had declined the offer of the Treasury Department. I lost no time in calling upon him at his hotel. Mr. Chase pleaded that his education and habits had not fitted him for the duties of the place ; and, he added with his accustomed courtesy, that if he had had an education like my own, he would feel less distrust of his qualifications for the office. His appropriate sphere he believed to be the Senate, to which he had just been chosen for the full term of six years. In response, I assured him that his friends regarded it as his duty to accept the Secretaryship of the Treasury; and furthermore, that he could at all times count upon the support of every patriotic man whose services he might desire to command. Mr. Chase finally said, substantially, that he would be guided by the convictions of his friends.

A few days subsequently on my return to New York, I took the liberty to suggest to him the advisability of inviting proposals for what remained of the twenty-five million loan which had been authorized in the closing days of Mr. Buchanan's administration. At his invitation I visited Washington, but I found him disinclined to offer the loan except upon terms which I felt confident could not then be obtained. It was apparent that he had thus early become a convert to the so-called paper policy. Finding it of no use to argue the point, I made no further attempt to influence his views. It was an acute disappointment that the man whom we had regarded as the strongest supporter of a stable financial system, had so utterly abandoned that idea. If he had depended on loans properly secured by taxation, and had placed his reliance upon the patriotism of the country, it is my belief that the credit of the nation would have been maintained upon a permanent foundation, and the depreciation of our currency would have been, in a great measure, obviated. The machinery of our banks was at his disposal, and never had a more generous disposition been shown by the monied interest of any country to support the measures of a financial minister.

The two loan acts passed at the extra session of the Thirty-seventh Congress provided for the modification of the sub-treasury law, for the express purpose of enabling the Secretary to avail himself of these facilities. But he refused to accept them, and persisted in demanding that the banks should pay *in coin* the amount of the loans for which they had subscribed. The effect was most disastrous. He thus destroyed, almost at a blow, the basis of bank credits, and forced a suspension of specie payments. The gold which had constituted the basis of banking transactions was absorbed by the Treasury, to be paid out to contractors, and immediately to be hoarded where it could no longer be useful in business or for the public exigencies. Mr. Chase might have avoided this, but he saw fit to precipitate the disaster. To do this in a period of national calamity, I shall always regard, as an act of most extraordinary infatuation.

Immediately after the failure of the banks, the bill was introduced by yourself authorizing the issue of United States notes to circulate as currency, and providing for the funding of them in six per cent. bonds. Your plea was that of necessity. I did not share your views. Accordingly, I opposed in debate the proposition to issue a legal tender paper currency which the framers of the constitution had wisely intended to inhibit. At the same time, I am free to admit, that the accompanying provision to fund these paper promises promptly in the bonds of the United States was a measure of redemption which could not, under the circumstances, be too highly commended. At this moment it presents the only means possible for an early and safe return to specie payments. Had it been consistently adhered to, it would have brought the country to that point before the present administration came into power.

But unhappily, a Congress succeeded to the thirty-seventh which was not controlled by the high moral considerations, and which did not possess the capacity of its predecessor. Loose views of financial integrity were entertained. The Secretary of the Treasury found the majority were pliable to his purposes. At his demand legislation was had abrogating the provision for the conversion of the legal tender notes into bonds and also empowering him to issue other evidences of debt at his discretion. A power so tremendous has seldom, if ever before, been lodged in the hands of a minister. I am constrained to say that it was exercised almost wantonly. The credit of the nation was depreciated to the verge of bankruptcy. A five per cent. loan was placed on the market; compound interest notes and other ephemeral devices were resorted to in order to shove up the stupendous financial fabric which seemed to be tottering to its fall. I counted the different varieties of paper which were emitted until, if my memory serves me right, the number reached *thirty-three*, when I gave up in despair.

The instinct of the people was wiser than the subtlety of the men who assumed to guide it. Mr. Lincoln was placed a second time in the field for President, while Mr. Chase was compelled to yield to the storm which he had created and retire from the Treasury. To the errors of his three years of office the country is indebted for the needless augumentation of the public debt by the sum of at least one thousand million dollars. But perhaps a still greater evil was the repudiation, by an obsequious majority in Congress, of the national faith which had been pledged to the holders of the legal tender notes. By section I of the act approved February 25, 1872, it is provided that " any holder of said United States notes, depositing any sum not less than fifty dollars, or some multiple of fifty dollars, with the Treasurer of the United States, or either of the Assistant Treasurers, shall receive in exchange therefor duplicate certificates of deposit, one of which may be transmitted to the Secretary of the Treasury, who shall thereupon issue to the holder an equal amount of the bonds of the United States, " etc. This provision, which was endorsed upon every note issued, was repealed in a manner which I must characterize as *clandestine*. Henceforth the notes were irredeemable, and in that form they sunk from one depth of degradation to another, until they were worth but one-third of their face value. The moral sense of the community was also debased until it became as low as that of the government.

Under the ensuing administration an ability and integrity of purpose was displayed by the Secretary of the Treasury, the Hon. Hugh McCulloch, which, had he been properly seconded by Congress, might still have retrieved the national faith. But a career of jobbery had now been entered upon. Partisanship superseded the dictates of national honor. This chapter of our history will be perused by Americans in the future only with emotions of shame.

The appointment of Mr. Boutwell to the Treasury Department was a concession to the spirit of the times. Under his administration of the public finances, the currency, which had been legalized only as a war measure outside and beyond the constitution, was still further expanded, although peace had been restored and its original purpose had been accomplished.

It is an encouraging omen that the public mind has at length become aroused to the importance of restoring the constitutional currency. Wherever elections have been held, the people, in disregard of partisan considerations, have voted against any further inflation of the currency. I devoutly trust that the good work will go on until the great wrong which has been inflicted upon the industry of the nation shall be righted. You will, I trust, pardon me for saying in conclusion that the first requisite for the accomplishment of this desirable end is a radical change in the administration of the government. Faithfully yours,

F. A. CONKLING.

Hon. S. S. Cox having made a good speech in the House in opposition to inflation and repudiation, Mr. Spaulding addressed him a letter on the subject. The following is an extract from Mr. Cox's letter in reply:

"You see I have refreshed myself at your fountain. I am happy that the opportunity occurred to hit repudiation between the eyes. We are all on our side so entirely powerless we cannot but challenge the Republicans *to do something* in the coin line. I will never cease to remind them of your pledges and the plighted faith of Congress. As if a debt in the people's pockets was not as honorable an obligation, and more so, than any other! * * *

Yours truly,

December 24, 1869. S. S. COX.

A. A. LOW, ESQ.

NEW YORK, Sept. 24, 1869.

Hon. E. G. Spaulding, Buffalo,

DEAR SIR:—Your valued favor of the 17th instant was duly received, together with the volume on the "Financial History of the War," for which I am much obliged. It is an interesting and valuable work. I can say this without having progressed very far in the reading of it. I shall take it up and finish it at my leisure.

I was, from the first, in favor of the "legal tender" act, of which you were so largely the author, believing it to be a necessity. I have not seen any reason to change my mind with the progress of events. But the war being over, I confess to a good deal of disappointment to find how great and how general is the unwillingness of the people at large to return to a sound currency. The patriotism that carried the North through the war seems to be exhausted, and demoralization to have taken its place. Some few there are in favor of returning to specie payments, professedly, but if any plan is suggested looking to contraction as a means to this end, it will be found to have no friends.

If we cannot have existing evils remedied in any other way, I hope the Supreme Court of the United States will find that while the law making United States notes a "legal tender" was "necessary and proper" during the war, it is neither constitutional or right, now that the war and the necessity have passed away. Certainly this view should apply to any further issue. Unless we get relief in this way, I despair of any that does not come by the severe discipline that follows wrong doing. * * * I remain, dear sir,

Most respectfully yours,

A. A. LOW.

GEN. J. D. COX.

DEPARTMENT OF THE INTERIOR, }
WASHINGTON, Nov. 10, 1869. }

MY DEAR SIR:—I thank you very heartily for the copy of the "Financial History," which I recognize as a valuable contribution toward the elucidation and final solution of our great financial problem. I have so often heard your views referred to by my brother and his partner, Mr. Robinson, that I am eager to have the opportunity of personal conference with you on what I regard as the crucial question this administration has to meet, viz., the return to specie payments, and a currency with a real and fixed value.

To turn our faces at once, and like a flint, in the *direction* of resumption, I hold to be our cardinal duty. The *rapidity* of the movement is of less consequence, the danger being rather that we should go too fast when once started.

I am rejoiced that the country is to continue to have the benefit of your experienced counsels, and trust it may not be long till I shall have the opportunity of discussing these matters with you in person.

Very respectfully and truly, your obedient servant,

Hon. E. G. SPAULDING. J. D. COX.

HON. JUSTIN S. MORRILL,
A member of the Senate Finance Committee.

STAFFORD, Vt., Oct. 9, 1875.

Hon. E. G. Spaulding, Buffalo, N. Y.,

MY DEAR SIR:—I have received and read with interest your "Introduction" to the second edition of your "Financial History of the War." It is able, impartial and timely, and, like the original work, reflects great credit upon the author. I hope it is destined to exert all the influence in the settlement of the grave questions pending that its merits so well deserve. If you differed from me at the inception of some of these financial measures, we do not differ now, and I am glad you find leisure and feel it to be your duty to still render services to your country.

Very sincerely yours, JUSTIN S. MORRILL.

HON. JOHN J. CISCO,
Asst. Treasurer in New York while Mr. Chase was Sec'y of the Treasury.

59 WALL STREET, }
NEW YORK, Oct. 25, 1875. }

MY DEAR SIR:—With your letter I duly received the advance sheets of your "Introduction" to a further edition of the "History of the Legal Tender Act," for which please accept thanks.

I have carefully read your statement of facts, and they fully accord with my memory regarding them. Your volume will be an exceedingly valuable acquisition to the financial histories of the world. Since the close of the rebellion there has been no well defined financial policy leading us in the direction of specie payments, and to this failure on the part of the government we may attribute the downfall in the panic of 1873 of the "paper structure" we had reared, and the subsequent paralysis of the mercantile and industrial interests of the nation. There can be no permanent prosperity to our country until we are restored to a sound basis for our transactions. With kind regards, Yours very truly, JOHN J. CISCO.

Hon. E. G. SPAULDING, Buffalo, N. Y.

GEORGE S. COE, ESQ.,
On our early Financial War Measures and the First and Second Mistakes of Secretary Chase—War Currency—Specie Payments, Sub-Treasury, etc.

AMERICAN EXCHANGE NATIONAL BANK, }
NEW YORK, Oct. 8, 1875. }

Hon. E. G. Spaulding, Buffalo, N. Y.,

DEAR SIR:—Your favor of the 25th ult. came duly to hand, in which you ask me to give my personal recollection in full of the circumstances connected with the early part of the financial history of the war.

After the accession of Mr. Lincoln to the Presidency, the securities of the government became difficult of sale, and they declined to such an extent that for the week ending June 24, 1861, the following quotations were published:

U. S. Bonds, 1881 (coupon), 6 per cent............... 83¾   83¾
"   Treasury notes, 12 per cent. int................ 101¾ 102
"   "   "   11   " 101   101¼
"   "   "   10¾   " 100¼

Zealous exertions had been made by carefully-organized committees of the New York Chamber of Commerce, the month before, to obtain subscriptions to government loans by sending circulars throughout the Northern States, in which citizens, public officers, banks, and other institutions, were solicited to act as voluntary agents. But the aggregate secured was inconsiderable, and utterly failed of the amount required for pressing necessity. The great conflict was rising daily into more appalling magnitude. Moneyed capital, with instinctive timidity, buttoned tightly its pockets, and shrank from the danger.

Fortunately, the commercial conditions of the Northern States were altogether favorable. The panic of 1857 had been followed by three or four years of great productiveness and economy, which had so turned international exchanges in favor of this country that larger balances in coin than ever before had, during 1860 and 1861, been imported from Europe. The banks in New York alone holding the unpredecented amount of fifty millions, equal in August, 1861, to about fifty per cent. of their liabilities, while the apprehension of war had produced a general curtailment of credit throughout the Northern States.

After the disastrous battle of Bull Run, and when Washington was closely beleaguered, and the avenue thence to New York through Baltimore was intercepted by the enemy, Mr. Chase, then Secretary of the Treasury, came to this city via Annapolis, and immediately invited all persons in this community who were supposed to possess or to control capital to meet him on the evening of August 9th, at the house of John J. Cisco, Esq., then Assistant Treasurer of the United States in New York. This invitation drew together a large unmber of gentlemen of various occupations and circumstances. During the discussion which ensued, I suggested the practicability of uniting the banks of the North by some organization that would combine them into an efficient and inseparable body, for the purpose of advancing the capital of the country upon government bonds in large amounts, and through their clearing-house facilities and other well-known expedients, to distribute them in smaller sums among the people in a manner that would secure active co-operation among the members in this special work, while in all other respects each bank could pursue its independent business. This suggestion met the hearty approbation of the assembled company, and arrested the earnest attention of the Secretary. At his request it was presented to the consideration of the banks at a meeting called for that purpose at the American Exchange Bank on the following day, and was so far entertained as to secure the appointment of a committee of ten bank officers, to give it form and coherence. The committee convened at the Bank of Commerce, whose officers zealously united in the effort, and a plan was reported unanimously. It may be found, with the names of the committee, in the *Bankers' Magazine* of September, 1861. Their report was cordially accepted and adopted by the banks in New York, those in Boston and Philadelphia being represented at the meeting and as zealously and cordially united in the organization. It was greatly desired to include also the banks of the West, but it was found impracticable to secure the co-operation of the state banks of Ohio and Indiana, and the state banks of Missouri, the only other organization under a compacted system, were surrounded by combatants.

It was at once unanimously agreed that the associated banks of the three cities would take fifty millions of 7 3-10 notes at par, with the privilege of an additional fifty millions in sixty days, and a further amount of fifty millions in sixty days more, making one hundred and fifty millions in all, and offer them for sale to the people of the country at the same price, without change. In this great undertaking the banks of New York assumed more than their relative proportion. To ensure full co-operation and success, the expedient of issuing clearing-house certificates, and of appropriating and averaging all the coin in the various banks as a common fund, which had been invented but the year before, was applied to this special object with good effect.

So vast a responsibility, involving figures of such magnitude, had never before been attempted in this country, and the assumption of it with such promptitude was without precedent in history.

The capitals of the banks thus associated made an aggregate of one hundred and twenty millions, an amount greater than the Bank of England and the Bank of France combined, each of which institutions had been found sufficient for the gigantic struggles of those great nations, from time to time, in conflict with all Europe. And this combination, made up of distinct and independent corporations, while it possessed all needed capacity for government work, was free from the objections made to one great financial institution. The following figures also show that its financial condition was one of great strength:

	LIABILITIES		ASSETS IN
	Deposits.	Circulation.	COIN.
Banks in New York	$ 92,046,308	$ 8,521,426	$49,733,990
" Boston	18,235,061	6,366,466	6,665,929
" Philadelphia	15,335,838	2,076,857	6,765,120
	$125,617,207	$ 16,964,749	
		125,617,207	

Total.....................$142,581,956 against $63,165,039 coin on hand, equal to 45 per cent. of all liabilities. Surley, such conditions as these, with judicious administration, were adequate to the work which the country required. A great merit of this bank combination at that critical moment, when the life of the nation hung in the balance, consisted in the fact that it fully committed the hitherto hesitating moneyed capital of the North and East to the support of the government. The bank officers and directors who thus counselled and consented were deeply sensible of the momentous responsibility which they assumed, but all doubt and hesitation were instantly removed, and perfect unanimity was secured by the question, "*What if we do not unite!*" And, acting as guardians of a great trust exposed to imminent danger, they fearlessly elected the alternative best calculated to protect it.

The problem to be practically resolved by the Banks was this. How can the available capital be best drawn from the people, and devoted to the support of Government, with the least disturbance to the country? and by what means can arms, clothing and subsistence for the army be best secured in exchange for Government credit? These were simply questions of domestic exchange, and most naturally suggested the use of the ordinary methods of Bank checks, deposits and transfers, that the experience of all civilized nations had found most efficient for the purpose, and that this should be accomplished by the Associated Banks, in a manner best calculated to prolong their useful agency, and to preserve the specie standard, it was indispensible that their coin reserves remain with the least possible change. Accordingly it was at once proposed to the Secretary that he should suspend the operations of the Sub-Treasury Act in respect to these transactions, and following the course of commercial business, that he should draw checks upon some one Bank in each city representing the Association, in small sums as required, in disbursing the money thus advanced. By this means his checks would serve the purpose of a circulating medium, continually redeemed, and the exchanges of capital and industry would be best promoted. This was the more important in a period of public agitation when the disbursement of these large sums exclusively in coin, rendered the reserves of the Banks all the more liable to be wasted by hoarding. To the astonishment of the committee, Mr. Chase refused. Notwithstanding the act of Congress of August 5th, which it seemed to us was passed for the very object then presented, but which he declared upon his authority as finance minister, and from his personal knowledge of its purpose, had no such meaning or intent. This issue was discussed from time to time with much zeal, but always with the same result. It was seen by the most experienced Bank officers to be vital to the success of their undertaking. To draw from the Banks in coin the large sums involved in these loans, and to transfer them to the Treasury, thence to be widely scatter over the country at a moment when war had excited fear and distrust, was to be pulling out continually the foundations upon which the whole structure rested. And inasmuch as this money was loaned to the Government, and was in no sense a trust reposed in the Banks, there appeared to them no reason why it should not be drawn by checks in favor of Government contractors and creditors, who would require to exchange them for other values in commerce and trade, through the processes of the clearing-house. And this consideration was greatly strengthened by the fact that these advances were made and the money publicly disbursed, a long time before the Treasury Notes were ready for delivery to the Banks which had paid for them. In the light which has since been shed upon the act of Congress referred to, it is evident that undue weight was given to the views of the Secretary, and that the Banks would have conferred an incalculable benefit upon the country, had they adhered inflexibly to their own opinions. But the pressure of startling events required prompt decision, and the well known intelligence and patriotism of the Secretary, gave to his judgment overwhelming power. It soon became manifest that in consenting to have their hands tied, and their most efficient powers restricted, while engaged in these great operations, and in allowing their coin reserves to be wasted, by pouring them out upon the community in a manner so unnecessary and exceptional, the Banks deprived themselves and the Government of the ability of long continuing, as they otherwise could have done, to negotiate the national loans upon a specie standard.

This first great error, if it did not create a necessity for the legal tender notes, it certainly precipitated the adoption of that most unhappy expedient, and thereby committed the nation at an earlier day, to the most expensive of all methods of financiering.

One other subject of discussion between the Secretary and the Associated Banks at the same time arose, which led in the same direction. Congress by its act of 17th July, had authorized loans to the amount of two hundred and fifty millions. This could be issued either in Bonds running twenty years at not over seven per cent. interest—7-30 notes running three years, or fifty millions of the amount could, at the discretion of the Secretary, be made in currency notes payable on demand without interest. As the undertaking of the Associated Banks covered one hundred and fifty millions of this sum, and it was desired that they continue the work thus auspiciously begun, a question of the expediency of putting out the circulating notes was immediately raised by one of its members. A very small amount had been emitted. The Treasury was empty of coin to redeem them, and could only be replenished by the proceeds of the Bank loans. It was evident to the Bank officers that they could not sustain coin payments, if the transfers from their vaults to that of the Treasury, were subject to be intercepted and absorbed by these notes of Government. Nor could the Banks receive them upon deposit from the public as money, while they were responding to the Government and to their own dealers in coin. It was an inflation of the currency in the form most embarrassing to the enterprise they had commenced. Accordingly the Secretary was urgently solicited to refrain from exercising the discretionary powers given him of creating the Treasury currency, until all other means were exhausted. In response to a resolution to that effect, the Secretary assured the Bank officers of his acquiescence in their suggestion, but at the same time insisted that it was improper for a public officer to openly pledge himself *not* to exercise a power conferred by the law. With this understanding the Banks began their work, paying into the Treasury in coin one hundred and fifty millions in sums at the rate of about five millions at intervals of six days. Even with all these unfavorable circumstances surrounding them, it was an encouraging fact observed by those who were anxiously watching the practical operation of this great and novel experiment, that while the circulating notes in the country were restricted, the disbursements of the Government for the war, were so rapid, and the consequent internal trade movement was so intense, that the coin paid out upon each instalment of the loan, came back to the Banks through the community, in about one week. The natural effect of this general commercial activity upon the circulating medium, being simply to quicken its flow.

After taking the third amount of fifty millions by the Associated Banks, those in New York who had at that time paid in of their proportion over eighty millions in all, found themselves in this position.

Their aggregate coin, which on the 17th August, before the
first payment into the Treasury, was.................. $49,733,990
Was in December 7th................................. 42,318,610

A reduction of only $7,415,380

and the other two cities in like proportion.

In the meantime the 7-30 notes taken by the banks had been purchased by the people to the extent of some fifty millions, notwithstanding a prolonged and vexatious delay in issuing them by the Treasury Department. The popular feeling was all that could have been desired for continuing that method of distribution. It may be confidently affirmed that had the banks been permitted to exercise their own methods of exchanging the bonds for the varied products of industry required by the Government, they could have continued their advances in sums of fifty millions for an indefinite period, and until the available resources of the people had been all gathered in. It is to be borne in mind that these resources were all existing at home, and that the increased industry which the war excited, was daily creating new means for investment. It may be presumptuous to affirm that the legal tender notes could have been dispensed with altogether. But it is safe to say that the causes which seemed to justify that act would have been long deferred to the saving of hundreds of millions to the country.

But at this time the demand notes were paid out freely by the Treasury, and began to appear as a cause of embarrassment among the banks who were pressed to receive them upon deposit, and while they could not decline them without diminishing public confidence in the Government credit, they could not give them currency without impairing their own specie strength. In fact the notes became at once a substitute for coin withdrawn from circulation, and their emission expressed a purpose of resorting to Government paper issues to carry on the war. So soon as these notes thus appeared the reflux of coin to the banks at once sensibly diminished. During three weeks from the 7th December, the reserves of the banks in New York fell to $29,857,712; a loss of thirteen millions within that short period, and on the 28th December, after conference with the Secretary, in which he still adhered to the views before expressed, it was decided as expedient for the banks to suspend specie payments.

At that moment the associated banks yet held over forty millions in coin, and it was still possible for them to continue their advances to the Government but for the two obstacles thus interposed. Before entering into this last conference with the associated banks, some of the members expressed to the Secretary the importance of continuing his relation to an organization which combined so much of experience, capital and financial resource, and which was yet capable of rendering the Government invaluable service. And that if an irredeemable paper currency was the inevitable resort, it would be more expedient and economical for the Government not to become involved in its dangers, but to impose the duty and responsibility of issuing the notes upon the banks, who would naturally be compelled to keep the day of redemption continually in view. Thus, as a suspension of coin payment was about to be declared, it was practicable to preserve from distribution and set aside the forty millions of coin then owned by the banks, together with one hundred and fifty or sixty millions of Government bonds, which could be taken by them as a special security for two hundred millions of notes, which could then be immediately issued by the associated banks from their own plates, and be verified and made national by the stamp and signature of a government officer. And that such an issue, so supported by coin and bonds, at once simple and expeditious, would serve the temporary purpose required, with little, if any, deterioration below coin value, and that it would be then practicable for the banks to continue without further agitation their advances. But the Secretary declined to entertain this suggestion, preferring the system of national banks, which he had already conceived.

Looking back over events that have since transpired, it must be admitted that this suggestion possessed true merit. It would have preserved a coin basis for the currency, prevented the destructive expansion, relieved the Government from its almost inextricable entanglement with the circulating notes, and compelled an early restoration of coin payments. And with a proper use of the expedients and machinery of banks, by utilizing their power of effecting exchanges, which was subsequently applied by the Secretary in the national banking system without reserve, this amount would have been found sufficient. When we review the excessive cost of the war, the vast increase of the national debt, and the public and private evils which a profuse currency have entailed upon the country, it must appear evident that in failing early to use and to exhaust all those means and appliances of commerce and banking that the experience of other civilized nations have proved most effective, a great and irreparable mistake was made.

One more good service the banks in New York were yet enabled to perform, which, although not great in amount, was most important in its effect upon the credit of the government.

On the first day of January, 1863, $8,000,000 of the national debt, issued in 1842, became due. It was the first loan that matured after the passage of the legal tender act, and upon its prompt payment in coin, in which the debt was incurred, depended the reputation and credit of the United States at home and abroad, and its ability to make future loans upon favorable terms. It was a momentous question whether the government would apply the new law to its own obligations, and thus establish a precedent for the future. There was not sufficient money in the Treasury to pay the debt, and up to the latest hour the question was anxiously discussed in the departments at Washington, and almost decided, to plead inability and to fall back upon the legal enactment. At this juncture Mr. Cisco, Assistant Treasurer in New York, to whose patriotic service and wisdom the nation is greatly indebted, zealously interposed his influence. Upon his application to the banks there, they promptly furnished the requisite amount in gold, receiving his personal assurance that it should be repaid out of the revenue when received at his office, and thus the country was again saved from an irretrievable financial disaster.

The legal tender act was regarded by very many men of influence, from the beginning, as a foregone conclusion, and as a measure of inevitable necessity in war. Great doubt was continually expressed whether this people would submit to the necessary taxation for war purposes, and whether the country would bear the strain of so gigantic a struggle if conducted upon principles of sound commercial economy. However we may now honestly differ upon that subject, as we did then, it is certain that had the real temper of the nation been earlier felt by the government, it would have greatly modified and retarded the financial legislation of Congress, and the practical administration of the Treasury. The people proved themselves to be thoroughly in earnest. They needed no patronage to awaken the most heroic devotion, and to draw out the noblest sacrifices as well in private life as in the army.

It is more immediately practical to enquire what was the nature and effect of that important act?

It was, in simple fact, an arbitrary and absolute decree of the government, that with an empty treasury, and in need of all things, its notes payable whenever able and without interest, should be accepted by the people as money. The primary object was to secure material of war without present payment, and in order to effect this exchange it was necessary, secondly, that the edict should empower those who first received the notes to enforce them as money in like manner upon others, and so to distribute the burthen throughout the community.

This forcible entry of the government into the private affairs of the people, so utterly at variance with the fundamental principles of our system, so great an abridgment of personal liberty, and operating as a tax so unequal in its effects, was a rigorous measure of war, and as such was vindicated only as a temporary act of dire necessity. In enforcing this unequal burthen, Congress did not leave the holders of the notes without some measure of relief, but it gave to all the option of converting them at pleasure into a six per cent. gold-interest-bearing bond, payable in twenty years. By this means, the notes became equal in value to the bonds for which they were made exchangable, and while during the war the payments of gold interest continually operated to produce a curtailment of the volume of the notes in circulation, the return of peace opened a market abroad for the bonds, which would have ensured the early and entire absorption of the war currency, and thus cleared the way for specie payments.

But, in an evil hour for the country, other counsel obtained possession of the good judgment of the Secretary, and yielding to it, he consented and urged Congress to withdraw this privilege of converting the notes, so that thenceforth all issues were made without it. All notes emitted consequently became an unmitigated burthen upon commerce of indefinite duration, from which there was no escape. A new currency was created utterly at variance with all economic laws, and in conflict with all recognized rules of commerce and exchange. It did not, like all sound currency, naturally spring out of industry, production and trade, but it was an enforced result of exhaustion and necessity. It did not come and go, following the beneficent courses of commerce, expanding and contracting with the times and seasons that required it. But it remained an unyielding, inflexible mass, subject only to the chances and vicissitudes of war. As the war progressed and the country became poorer, this currency increased, giving new instruments and facilities to expend just in proportion as the means of payment were consumed. With a compulsory currency thus made, the measure of prices and daily deteriorating yet still increasing, is it strange that all other property was eagerly sought for in preference to this, and that prodigal expenditure became the law of the land?

In depriving the currency of its convertible privilege, it has been made perpetual. Ten years of peace have elapsed and it yet remains. Commerce did not originate and cannot absorb it. There is no natural relation between the two, but they continue in their original antagonism.

I believe that the only practicable relief to the country must come from restoring this privilege. Not of conversion into *six* per cent. bonds, but in those bearing such rate of interest—say five per cent.—as will induce holders to exchange them. This simple measure, coupled with the repeal of the legal tender act for all future operations, will, in my judgment, open the way for the gradual and easy disposition of this unnatural currency—will restore commerce to the operations of natural laws, give a new and healthy stimulus to industry and trade, and with a country as rich and productive as ours, we shall speedily return to general prosperity. This is the last struggle of the war, and I believe that the whole country earnestly desire to meet and to finish it. Very truly yours,

GEO. S. COE.

HON. JOHN E. WILLIAMS.
Historical and Prophetic Letter to Secretary Chase.

METROPOLITAN NATIONAL BANK, }
New York, Oct. 21, 1875. }

Hon. E. G. Spaulding,

MY DEAR SIR:—Since I read your greenback history and introduction to the second edition, I have looked over copies of some of my letters of the war period. I found one dated Oct. 4, 1861, to Secretary Chase which so

coincides with your views that I have copied it and send it to you enclosed.
Do with it what you please, * * *
Yours very truly,
J. E. WILLIAMS.

METROPOLITAN BANK,
New York, Oct. 4th, 1861.

Hon. Salmon P. Chase, Secretary, etc., Washington City:

MY DEAR SIR:—Many thanks for the kindly words to me, personally, in your letter of the 1st instant. I only wish they were better deserved.

Will you permit me to add a few more plain words—as you like frankness—on this all engrossing subject? In the hope, not only that I may make myself more intelligible, but with the hope, also, (I confess,) of modifying your views.

A complete understanding of this subject is of quite as much importance to the Government as to the banks. Indeed, as you substantially suggested, our interests in this matter are identical. Whatever strengthens the banks' vaults, increases public confidence in them, and in their ability to carry the Government through. While an increase in the Sub-Treasury's coin weakens us and the Government too. For the public, the people understand that you rely on us. Herein is a mutual interest, then, which I propose to speak of plainly, directly and respectfully.

You give as a reason for not drawing your checks on the "Loan Banks," that, "however, harmless or beneficial it might be, if confined to the New York banks, it would inevitably result in a general payment and receipt for public dues of bank notes, which in turn would lead to expansion, which in turn would terminate in suspension and vast injuries to the sound banks."

1st. I confess this dark array of disastrous consequences has a black face on it. But as neither of us is afraid to look *into* faces of that color, let us try and see what lies beneath.

The law authorizes you to *select* specie paying banks. Suppose you designate, as such, only banks in New York, Philadelphia and Boston, as "Loan Banks" to draw upon. You are thus relieved from any necessity of looking at what might be the consequences if you were to draw on other or less responsible banks. This narrows the question down to those three cities in which the banks have made common cause with you, and they guarantee each other for the fulfilment of their contract with you. The banks in all these cities are as sound as the banks in either city.

2d. What you seem to regard as a dangerous element, the bank officers look upon as essential to their safety. What you think would guard against suspension of specie payments, they think most likely to precipitate that demoralizing calamity. What you claim for the Sub-Treasury, they ask for the banks—the disbursement of all United States funds! While you regard the payment of public dues in bank notes, convertible at the pleasure of the holder into coin, as an evil to be avoided, they hold it to be as convenient and safe a mode of discharging public obligations as it is private debts. While you speculate as to what is best for sound banks, they think, with their practical experience, they *know* what is best for their institutions. And inasmuch as the law was made to give the banks this advantage, they feel they have a right to demand it.

3d. Their general reasons for these conclusions are that Congress *meant something*, (it is but fair to suppose) when they passed the act of August 5th, 1861, suspending so far the Sub-Treasury Act as to *allow* you to do what we ask, namely, draw on the loan banks. You will remember you agreed, so far as it was in your power, to conform your operations in this regard to our wishes. That was the result of our understanding with you as taken down after you left us on Saturday, from the lips of each of the bank officers composing the committee, who heard all you said and noticed your earnest manner. For myself, I was *instructed* not to agree to take our share of the second fifty millions *unless* the Government would so far agree to *help us* as to draw on the banks that furnished the money. This feeling arose, not so much from a desire to derive any petty gain of time or interest by this mode, as it did from a wish to adopt a method which would enable the banks to *carry through*, without ruin to themselves, this unprecedented loan to the Government. In point of magnitude without a precedent, I believe, in any country.

4th. You can now, perhaps, better than before, enter into our feelings and understand our surprise that you should not take our judgment in this matter, but rather argue on the supposition that we do not understand the legitimate operations of our own business so well as you do. This happens, too, under circumstances very peculiar. *But for the banks* the Government could *not pay* at all! It would have been bankrupt six weeks ago. Surely, my dear sir, this is no time for splitting hairs, or for you to tell bank officers—(impliedly, it is true,) that they don't understand what dangers they propose to encounter. Nor is it a time for you to refuse what they ask merely on an abstract theory of yours as to what might happen. If, on the other hand, you should persist in the course you indicate, is there not danger that you will *create* the very evil we all desire to avoid, namely, a suspension of specie payments?

5th. As to the two-years' treasury notes, I am more and more of the opinion that you have no legal right to take them of the people at large, whether our treasury note committee requests you to take them or not to take them, it is all the same, in my opinion, as to your duty. The associated banks paid you a *consideration* for taking these notes out of their vaults, and you contracted to do so. They pay you in another loan of fifty millions. If the public or a foreign country had loaned you fifty millions on similar terms, you would have been justified, no doubt, by Congress in making a law unto yourself predicated on public necessity. But no such loan has been made, either by the public or by Europe.

Already the brokers are telling us that they shall pass in the two-years' notes, which they have bought at a discount, take out the 7-30 notes and sell them on the street at a discount, which they can, and make a profit—thus commanding the market. This is the first disastrous demonstration, but, I fear, by no means the last.

The case plainly stated looks unsightly. You hire money at 7-30 to pay obligations bearing only 6 per cent. interest not due for a year and a half, when you need that very money to maintain your existence, and when, as I sincerely believe, you are under no moral or legal obligation to pay a dollar, but on the contrary, are bound *not* to pay without the sanction of Congress.

One word and I have done. You will remember that you said to us in the committee, "I am so desirous of meeting your views that I would almost place myself in the hands of this Treasury Note Committee, to do as they should say, confident they would not ask of me anything illegal or improper." This, sir, induced me to move the taking of the second fifty millions.

I am, most respectfully and very truly yours,

J. E. WILLIAMS.

HON. GEORGE WILLIAM CURTISS.

WEST NEW BRIGHTON,
STATEN ISLAND, Oct. 11, 1875.

MY DEAR SIR:—I thank you for your introductory pamphlet, which comes at a most opportune moment, and will be of great assistance in enlightening the public mind and in forming a sound opinion.

With great regard, very truly yours,

GEORGE WILLIAM CURTISS.

Hon. E. G. SPAULDING.

HON. E. H. STOUGHTON.

NEW YORK, Nov. 25, 1869.

DEAR SIR:—Accept my thanks for the copy you were kind enough to send me of your instructive and interesting "History of the Legal Tender Paper Money Issued During the Great Rebellion." I there find, within a narrow compass, admirably arranged, all that need be studied on the subject; and in connnection with what is purely historical, may also be found thoughts and suggestions on questions of finance worthy of deep attention. The extent to which the book may be circulated will be the measure of its usefulness.

Very truly yours,

E. H. STOUGHTON.

Hon. E. G. SPAULDING.

HON. MONTGOMERY BLAIR.

456 LOUISIANA AVENUE,
WASHINGTON, D. C., Oct. 19, 1875.

DEAR SIR:—I thank you for the "Introduction" to the new edition of your "Financial History of the War." The work will always form an interesting chapter in the history of our great struggle, and it ought now especially to attract attention when the effort is being made to perpetuate the error of abolishing money, which, in effect, abolishes property, and which your book shows was only consented to amid the excitement of war, and in the belief that it was necessary to maintain the Union.

I did not concur in the measure even then, and still think it only aggravated the evils it was intended to meet, and added, as General Dix estimates, at least $1,000,000,000 to our debt. Is there anything more susprising than that now, more than ten years after the war, after the man who, as Secretary of the Treasury, recommended the measure, has, as Chief Justice, pronounced it not only unconstitutional, but a blunder, and as having impaired instead of aiding our credit; and when the great body of those who then supported it to aid the government have abandoned it, that a portion of those who then opposed the war, and opposed this and all other measures adopted to carry it on, and denounced it as unconstitutional, should now seek to make permanent this disastrous policy? The fact that the Supreme Court *validates only the legal tenders issued during the war*, to which you call attention, shows, however, that there need be no fear of that, and that the court will soon put down the fraud even if the people would tolerate it, of which I have no fear.

Yours truly,

MONTGOMERY BLAIR.

Hon. E. G. Spaulding, Buffalo, N. Y.

SENATOR CHRISTIANCY.

Gold and Paper—Their Actual Value.

Senator Isaac P. Christiancy, of Michigan, in his letter to the Hard-money Convention, in Detroit, said: "Now, I am so old fogy in my notions and opinions as to hold that, when an individual or nation is deeply in debt, the true and only honest way of getting rid of that burden is the plain, old-fashioned way of paying the debt in money where it was agreed to be paid in money, or in something of equal value and convertible into money; and if we cannot pay the whole at once, or when due, then to pay the interest in the meantime, and the debt as fast as we can. If we have not the money to pay with, then the better plan is to go to work in any and every form of productive industries, producing values which will command the money, rather than to adopt the plan substantially followed by a large proportion of our people of speculating out of each other in purely fictitious values, like two boys who shut themselves up in the same room for a week, and both got rich, or fancied they had got rich, by trading and retrading jackets with certain offers of boot money each way, which neither ever intended to pay.

GOV. E. D. MORGAN.

NEWPORT, R. I., Sept. 13, 1869.

Hon. E. G. Spaulding, Buffalo,

My Dear Sir:—I have read just enough of the "Financial History of the War," this morning, which you have very kindly sent to me, to be much interested therein. As a history it is invaluable, showing as it does, in the clearest possible manner, how the means were obtained for prosecuting the war which finally saved the Union. I feel under great obligations to you for preparing this valuable and concise narrative. I am, dear sir,

Very truly yours,

E. D. MORGAN.

(From the Washington Daily Chronicle, Oct. 4, 1869.)
HISTORY OF THE GREENBACK.

Hon. E. G. Spaulding, of Buffalo, who was a member of the Committee of Ways and Means of the House of Representatives at the time of the passage of the legal tender act, as well as of the sub-committee which had especial charge of that subject, has written a "History of the Legal Tender Paper Money Issued During the Great Rebellion." This has just been published in the form of a neat octavo volume of two hundred and thirteen pages, and constitutes one of the most valuable contributions to the history of the late struggle for the preservation of the Union. It presents copious extracts from the speeches of members of both Houses of Congress for and against the bill, and is a complete compendium of the views which then prevailed on both sides of the question, as well as a faithful record of the circumstances under which the measure was resorted to. The moment when the nation was engaged in a struggle which taxed its utmost energies and resources, was certainly not the time for that elaborate consideration necessary to the development of the most desirable system of finance. Action, prompt, decisive, and practical, was what the crisis demanded; and while it cannot be denied that the issue of a legal tender paper money unsettled values, and thus occasioned more or less injustice among the people in their settlements with each other, besides increasing the expenses of the war through the general rise in prices of all commodities, it is equally undeniable that it was a most efficient instrument in the hands of the government in enabling it to meet the exigencies of the time, and in bringing the war to a successful termination. It is not as an advocate of a particular plan of finance, however, but as its historian, that Mr. Spaulding appears before the public, and in this light his book is of incalculable value. Its strict accuracy is endorsed by the most prominent of the members of both houses of Congress who aided or opposed the measure whose history he relates, and participated in the discussions by which it was preceded. The experience of that time contains invaluable instruction for our future guidance, and even the mistakes committed may be converted into benefits by turning to profitable account the lessons which they afford. This instruction, and these lessons, Mr. Spaulding has placed before us in the most compendious form possible, and no statesman, business man, or student of finance—indeed, we might almost say no citizen—can afford to be without his book.

HON. ALMON M. CLAPP,
Public Printer.

WASHINGTON, Oct. 15, 1875.

MY DEAR SIR:—I am indebted to your polite attention for an advance sheet of your "Introduction" to the second edition of that more than excellent "Financial History of the War," which emanated from your pen some years since. I read that effort, soon after it made its appearance, with more than ordinary pleasure and profit, and now have just completed the perusal of your introductory to the forthcoming edition.

It is but the part of candor that I should here express the opinion that your criticisms relating to the management of our national finances during the period that has intervened since the commencement of the war to crush rebellion occurred, are but merited and just. That war found the nation with an empty treasury, and an imperious necessity for the ways and means to enlist, equip, pay and sustain an army of sufficient force to maintain the National Union from overthrow. That was a trying and fearful crisis, but the ingenuity of statesmanship proved adequate to the emergency. The nation had neither gold nor silver nor paper currency with which to meet the wants of that important and critical period, and hence the national faith was pledged in bonds and paper money to an extent that met the demands of a protracted and expensive struggle. That achievement was without parallel in the history of nations, and reflected great credit upon the wisdom of our statesmanship and the patriotism of our people.

To you, sir, as much as to any other statesman of that period, is the nation indebted for a financial policy that bore it through the war successfully. I apprehend that the second edition of your " Financial History of the War" is superinduced by an effort now being made to inflate our paper currency and postpone the day of its redemption in gold and silver. This movement may be regarded as of serious import. It seems, indeed, incredible that any considerable number of citizens should make an assault upon the national faith and credit by placing our currency beyond the hope of immediate or remote redemption, but such is the lamentable fact. The call for an unlimited volume of paper money issue, when every effort should be made in the direction of early resumption, is indeed alarming. A more reprehensible policy at this period of our history cannot well be imagined, and it demands all the wisdom available to avert the impending evil. The government is pledged to resumption at the earliest day practicable. To postpone that important period indefinitely, as the advocates of inflation propose, would bring discredit upon the national faith and honor, and cover our government with inevitable disgrace. And, beyond this, it would involve the industrial and commercial interests of the country in a common ruin.

Our currency is irredeemable now, and yet it is proposed that the government shall issue untold millions more, and thus plunge the nation into ultimate repudiation. This policy is a delusion, and would, if it should obtain, border upon crime. It is a fraud in its intent, and its consummation would stamp the nation with infamy. Its advocates contend that the issue of five or six hundred millions, more or less, of government promises-to-pay will give an impulse to the business energies of the country and bring early prosperity, when its effect would be to depreciate every paper dollar to a standard of value below fifty cents. Now a paper dollar is worth but eighty-five or eighty-six cents, with a downward tendency. It would not take long under inflation to bring us to a point where it would require two dollars of paper currency to purchase one dollar of gold or silver. Such a prospect is to be deeply deplored, and the danger that it foreshadows should be promptly met and turned aside.

If the nation should yield to the demands of the inflationists, and set its printing presses and paper mills at work to pour forth a flood of new-made paper money, that would afford no adequate relief to the business interests of the country. There is more currency now than can be reached for general business purposes, inasmuch as there are but two ways of calling it forth from the vaults of the Treasury and the banks. One is to purchase with currency property or labor, and the other is to obtain it by stealth. Hence to make millions more would not afford the promised relief, for the simple reason that the people do not seem to possess the means of purchase, and the chances for theft are not very favorable.

The ills complained of, and which seem to prompt to inflation, arise from the fact that we have in this country at the present time too many consumers and too few industrious producers. There is a numerous class who have undertaken to live by their wits and upon the efforts of the more industrious. This condition of affairs brings business want and distress where there should be abundance, and those who have thus brought themselves to such estate by idleness, extravagance, or mismanagement, are now loudest in their demands for inflation. It is upon such that the engineers of this pernicious measure rely for its success, and yet that class would suffer the deepest disappointment when it should fully be consummated.

It occurs to me that your views of finance are peculiarly adapted to the work of bringing this nation back to the paths of resumption, prosperity and happiness, and that it will be a fortunate day for the country when they are fully accepted and adopted as the policy of the government.

In 1861 we were called upon to make sacrifices to preserve the national unity and integrity. In 1875 the duty is none the less imperious to rally in behalf of honest money, and that we may preserve the national faith and honor. I am, sir, with much respect,

Your obedient servant,

A. M. CLAPP.

Hon. E. G. SPAULDING.

GEN. J. R. HAWLEY.

THE POSITION FOR SANE MEN TO TAKE.

GENTLEMEN, I repeat, there is no road to resumption through expansion, except the road that goes through repudiation. If I am not altogether wild in this matter—I have with me the boards of trade, the chambers of commerce, the great merchants and bankers and financiers—if I am not altogether wild in this matter, this is the decisive, the turning-point in the national finances, and what is of infinitely less importance, a turning-point in the history of political parties. Many men who long for political reorganization have looked eagerly for the action which was to bring it about. Sir, parties are not called into existence by a proclamation. Parties create themselves. They grow out of some profound belief, some great moral purpose. You are furnishing that belief and that purpose to-day, by making it necessary for men to rally, without regard to party lines, for the defense of sound economical principles and the preservation of the honor of the nation. There is no man so good that I will vote for him for any office, from president down to constable, if he is unsound upon this financial question. There is no man so dear to me that I will not fight him from the word "go" until the election closes, if he is unsound on this question. And I know very many men who agree with me on this point. But I do not care whether there be five, or fifty, or five hundred; I am planted as firmly on this ground as in the days when I was a radical abolitionist, though I could not see the possibility of triumph within a hundred years. I believe, I know what is right upon this matter, and I have no doubt that what is right will come uppermost in this country, that the people will sustain.—*Speech of Gen. J. R. Hawley, of Hartford, in the House of Representatives, April* 1, 1874.

ADDRESS

OF THE

Hon. Elbridge Gerry Spaulding,

AT THE

BANK OFFICERS AND BANKERS' BUILDING,

CENTENNIAL GROUNDS, FAIRMOUNT PARK,
PHILADELPHIA,

ON THE

OCCASION OF THE FORMAL OPENING, MAY 30, 1876.

American Bank Note Co. Phila.
THE SIGNING OF THE DECLARATION OF INDEPENDENCE, JULY 4, 1776.

CENTENNIAL.

OFFICE CENTENNIAL COMMITTEE.
14 Pine Street, New York, June 5th, 1876.

To the Subscribers to the Bank Officers' and Bankers' Building, Centennial Grounds, Fairmount Park, Philadelphia:

THE undersigned committee appointed to take into consideration the comfort and conveniences of Bank Officers, Bankers and their families during their attendance at the Centennial International Exhibition, to be held in Fairmount Park, Philadelphia, in 1876, in commemoration of the one hundredth anniversary of our nation's independence, in the discharge of the duties of their appointment, addressed circular letters to all Bank Officers and Bankers of the United States, asking their co-operation, and a small contribution in money from each, to be applied to the erection and maintenance of a suitable building on the grounds of the Centennial Commission. The Committee have the pleasure to acknowledge a prompt and generous response from all sections of the country to their appeal. The Centennial authorities kindly furnished an eligible site, east of Memorial Hall. The supervision of the erection of the building was confided to a committee, consisting of Messrs. George Philler, President of the First National Bank of Philadelphia, and B. B. Comegys, Vice-President of the Philadelphia National Bank. The building being completed and furnished, was formally dedicated to the purpose of its erection on the 30th of May last, in the presence of a large assembly of Bank Officers and Bankers.

E. C. Knight, Esq., President of the Guarantee Trust and Safe Deposit Company of Philadelphia, Chairman of the Reception Committee, called the meeting to order, and made a few remarks in reference to the object and purpose of the building. After prayer by the Rev. J. Walker Jackson, D. D., the meeting adjourned to the Judges' Pavilion, where, on motion, Joseph Patterson, Esq., President of the Western National Bank of Philadelphia, and President of the Clearing House Association, was called upon to preside. On taking the chair, Mr. Patterson in a few appropriate and eloquent remarks, introduced the Hon. Elbridge Gerry Spaulding, President of the Farmers and Mechanics' National Bank of the City of Buffalo, New York, who responded in an interesting historic review of banking in the United States during the past one hundred years.

The undersigned, for themselves, the Bank Officers and Bankers of the United States, desire to express their grateful thanks to Col. J. E. Peyton, of Haddonfield, New Jersey, for his kindly and courteous assistance in the accomplishment of the work, to the use and purpose for which it is intended, and to the Building Committee for the valuable services, good judgment and taste displayed by them.

Thanks are also due to the American Bank Note Company, Philadelphia, for the compliment of their beautifully engraved card of admission to members.

Your committee recognize in banking an identity of interest in common with all the great industries of the country; and in conclusion, feel that they cannot too strongly recommend the Exhibition as illustrating the progress in the arts and industries of the world. As an educational instrumentality, its benefits can only be attained through personal inspection. It is eminently worthy of the event it so appropriately commemorates.

Committee of the Associated Banks of the City of New York.

BENJ. B. SHERMAN, *Chairman*,
    President Mechanic's National Bank.
GEO. S. COE, *Treasurer*,
    President American Exchange National Bank.
CHARLES BARD,
    Continental National Bank.
W. A. HALL,
    President Oriental National Bank.
C. N. JORDAN,
    Cashier 3d National Bank.
GEORGE F. BAKER,
    Cashier 1st National Bank.

COMMITTEE OF RECEPTION.

E. C. KNIGHT, Pres't Guarantee, Trust and Safe Deposit Co., Philadelphia.
JNO. A. STEWART, Pres't United States Trust Co., New York.
DANIEL E. DODD, Pres't Newark Savings Co., Newark, N. J.
ARCH'D STERLING, Pres't Savings Bank, Baltimore, Balt., Md.
WM. R. VERMILYE, ESQ., Vermilye & Co., Bankers, New York.

A. J. DREXEL, ESQ., Drexel & Co., Bankers, Philadelphia.
W. A. TOWER, ESQ., Tower, Giddings & Co., Bankers, Boston.
G. H. LOKER, Loker & Bro., Bankers, St. Louis.
MERRIL LADD, M. Ladd & Co., Bankers, Chicago.
JOS. F. LARKIN, Larkin, Wright & Co., Bankers, Cincinnati.
HENRY G. GOWEN, President Philadelphia Stock Exchange.
G. W. MCLEAN, President New York Stock Exchange.

COMMITTEE ON COINS AND CURRENCY

Invite your attention to the Exhibit by the American Bank Note Company of the City of New York. In their card they present specimens of bank notes in the greatest perfection of the art attained through progressive civilization to the date of the exhibition, and in all the written languages of the world.

The card should receive the attention of all who visit the building. It forms a subject for study and gives assurance that the art has attained its greatest perfection in this country,

HON. JAMES POLLOCK, Superintendent U. S. Mint, Chairman, Philadelphia, Pa.
ALBERT G. GOODALL, American Bank Note Co., 142 Broadway, New York.
W. S. APPLETON, Boston, Mass.
CHAS. J. HOADLEY, State Librarian, Hartford, Conn.
R. C. DAVIS, Philadelphia.

COMMITTEE ON BUILDING.

GEO. PHILLER, Pres't 1st National Bank, Philadelphia.
B. B. COMEGYS, Vice-Pres't Philadelphia National Bank, Phila.

NATIONAL CENTENNIAL COMMITTEE TO REPRESENT THE STATES AND TERRITORIES.

New York—Chas. M. Fry, President Bank of New York, Chairman.
Alabama—Charles Hopkins, President National Commercial Bank, Mobile.
Arizona—L. M. Jacobs, Tuscon.
Arkansas—Logan H. Roots, President Merchants' National Bank, Little Rock.
California—George F. Hooper, President First National Gold Bank, San Francisco.
Colorado—Hon. Jerome P. Chaffee, President First National Bank, Denver.
Connecticut—James Bolter, President Hartford National Bank, Hartford.
Dakota—J. C. McVay, President First National Bank, Yankton.
Delaware—Edward Betts, President First National Bank, Wilmington.
District of Columbia—Fitzhugh Coyle, President National Bank of the Republic, Washington.
Florida—J. W. C. Moore, President First National Bank of Florida, Jacksonville.
Georgia—Henry Brigham, President Merchants' National Bank, Savannah.
Idaho—B. F. Channel, President First National Bank of Idaho, Boise City.
Illinois—L. J. Gage, Cashier First National Bank, Chicago.
Indiana—Hon. Wm. H. English, President First National Bank, Indianapolis.

Iowa—Lyman Cook, President First National Bank, Burlington.
Kansas—Lucien Scott, President First National Bank, Leavenworth.
Kentucky—H. C. Caruth, President Merchants' Bank, Louisville.
Louisiana—S. H. Kennedy, President State National Bank, New Orleans.
Maryland—J. S. Norris, President First National Bank, Baltimore.
Maine—H. J. Libby, President First National Bank, Portland.
Massachusetts—Franklin Haven, President Merchants' National Bank, Boston.
Michigan—Alex. H. Dey, President American National Bank, Detroit.
Minnesota—Horace Thompson, President First National Bank, St. Paul.
Mississippi—John A. Klein, President Mississippi Valley Bank, Vicksburg.
Missouri—J. H. Britton, President National Bank of the State of Missouri, St. Louis.
Montana—S. T. Hauser, President First National Bank, Helena.
Nebraska—Ezra Millard, President Omaha National Bank, Omaha.
Nevada—George Tufly, President Carson City Savings Bank, Carson.
New Hampshire—W. H. Y. Hackett, President First National Bank, Portsmouth.
New Jersey—O. L. Baldwin, Cashier Mechanics' National Bank, Newark.
New Mexico—Hon. S. B. Elkins, President First National Bank, Santa Fe.
North Carolina—Isaac B. Grainger, President Bank of New Hanover, Wilmington.
Ohio—D. J. Fallis, President Merchants' National Bank, Cincinnati.
Oregon—Henry Failing, President First National Bank, Portland.
Pennsylvania—James W. Weir, Cashier Harrisburg National Bank, Harrisburg.
Rhode Island—Col. Wm. Goddard, President Providence National Bank, Providence.
South Carolina—C. O. Witte, President People's National Bank, Charleston.
Tennessee—James Whitworth, President Fourth National Bank, Nashville.
Texas—J. M. Brown, President First National Bank, Galveston.
Utah—Hon. Wm. H. Hooper, President Deseret National Bank, Salt Lake City.
Vermont—Hon. John B. Page, President National Bank, Rutland.
Virginia—Geo. M. Bain, Jr., Cashier Exchange National Bank, Norfolk.
West Virginia—J. N. Camden, President First National Bank, Parkersburg.
Wisconsin—C. S. Bradley, President Milwaukee National Bank, Milwaukee.
Wyoming—A. R. Converse, President First National Bank, Cheyenne.

    E. G. SPAULDING, President of Farmers' and Mechanics' National Bank, Buffalo, President of the Association.

    GEORGE PHILLER, President of First National Bank, Philadelphia, Vice-President of the Association.

    GEO. S. COE, Esq., President of the American Exchange National Bank, Broadway, N. Y., Treasurer.

BENJ. B. SHERMAN,
CHARLES BARD,
W. A. HALL,   } *Committee.*
C. N. JORDAN,
GEORGE F. BAKER,

At a meeting of Bank Officers and Bankers of the United States, held on May 30, 1876, at 10½ A. M. in the Banker's Building on the Centennial Grounds, E. C. Knight, Esq., Chairman of the Committee of Reception, called the meeting to order by the following remarks:

GENTLEMEN:—As Chairman of the Committee of Reception, I take pleasure in extending to you a hearty welcome. The Building which we now dedicate has been erected and furnished out of the funds contributed by the Banks, Bankers and Trust Companies of the United States, under the supervision of a Building Committee, consisting of Mr. George Philler, President of the First National Bank of Philadelphia, and Mr. B. B. Comegys, Vice-President of the Philadelphia National Bank. For the good services rendered by these gentlemen we are greatly indebted. The object is that the subscribers and their families may have a suitable and convenient place to use during their visits to the Centennial.

The Judges' Pavilion has been tendered for our use this morning, to which, after prayer by the Rev. J. Walker Jackson, whom I now have the pleasure of introducing, we will adjourn to complete the exercises of the day.

PRAYER.

REV. JNO. WALKER JACKSON, D. D.

O Almighty God and most merciful Father, who day after day dost minister to sinful men infinite occasions of praising Thee, accept of our unfeigned thanks for all the blessings we have and every day receive, from Thy good providence.

Thou hast given us being in a land blessed with abundance of temporal blessings, a land rich with the bounties of Thy providence, favored with all the conditions necessary to material and intellectual progress and prosperity. Thou hast blessed us with civil and religious liberty; and by Thine own right hand hast led us, through all the dangers that have encompassed us in the past, up to this glad year of our joy and rejoicing, in the divine goodness that made and preserved us a Nation. We bless Thee for the republican form Thou hast given to our government; for the success Thou hast given to the great experiment of self-government, in the assured liberty to worship God according to the dictates of conscience; in the wide provision for the education of the people by our common schools and colleges and other institutions of learning; in the prosperity of our free churches; in the liberty of the press. We thank Thee, O God, that we celebrate this hundredth year of our National life at peace with each other and with all mankind. O Lord, mollify all exasperated minds, take away all animosities and prejudices, contempt and heart-burnings, and by uniting the hearts of the people, prepare for the reconciling all opinions, for the furtherance of Thy glory in the continued preservation of our national being and well-being.

We thank Thee, O God, for the success Thou hast given to the efforts of Thy people, appropriately to celebrate this year in peaceful rivalry with all nations, in the exhibition of their and our relative progress in all the arts and industries that adorn and add comfort to the homes of men. There is a spirit in man, and the inspiration of the Almighty giveth him understanding. Inspire us, O God, to glorify Thee in the meditations of our hearts, in the words of our mouth, in the products of our hands, guided by the intelligence with which Thou hast endowed us.

O, that the prosperity with which Thou hast so abundantly blessed us may not lead to dissoluteness of life; but may we be established in true holiness, putting away all sin, and clothing ourselves in all righteousness of endeavor.

Bless Thou those who have met here to-day to dedicate this building. Thou hast given them the heart to honor Thee in prayer and praise and thanksgiving. May their lives and health be precious in Thy sight. Let Thy blessing rest upon the entire commercial interests of this land, that all buying and selling and getting gain may be done in the fear of God.

Give to all rulers, both in national and State governments, wise and understanding hearts. Bless all the nations of the earth; sanctify their intercourse with each other in the interests of human brotherhood, to the abolition of war, and for the universal dissemination of the knowledge of the glory of the Lord. Forgive us, O God, our sins, accept our praises and answer our prayers as they are in accordance with Thy will; we humbly beseech Thee, O our God and Father, through the infinite riches of Thy goodness and mercy in Christ Jesus, our Lord. Amen.

The Bankers' Building not being of sufficient capacity to accommodate all who were present there the meeting was adjourned to the *Judges' Pavilion* in which seats had been provided, when on motion Joseph Patterson, Esq., President of the Western National Bank of Philadelphia, and President of the Philadelphia Clearing House Association, was made president of the meeting, who on taking the chair made the following introductory remarks:

GENTLEMEN:—In obedience to your request, I have assumed the Chairmanship, and direction of this meeting, and I thank you for the honor you have conferred on me. The duties of the Chair will not be difficult to discharge, being only to present to you the distinguished gentleman from the State of New York, who will address you on topics appropriate to the character of this meeting of Bankers from all parts of our country; and afterward, to share with you the pleasure of hearing one, who, from his large experience as a Banker, and the positions he has filled in public life, is well qualified to interest and instruct you; and I will not invade his province by reference to or discussion of subjects relating to Banking, but will confine myself to expressing to you a cordial welcome to this birth-place of the nation, and to the patriotic commemoration of the one hundredth anniversary of that great event.

Did I speak of Mr. Spaulding as from the State of New York? I recall that expression. On other occasions, and in any other place than this, we may regard our local habitations and State separations as worthy of advertisement; not so here, and to-day, surrounded as we are by so many hallowed memories of the first years of our national life, associated with this locality; standing on ground almost sanctified by Revolutionary dust, for just across this river a few miles is the scene of the battle of Germantown; up this same river, a few miles distant, is Valley Forge, where Washington and his exhausted army endured the rigors of the severe winter of 1777 and '78.

Here, almost within your sight in this beautiful Park, is the old Belmont mansion, where Washington, Robert Morris, and other Revolutionary worthies were honored guests, and their feet have often trod the turf pressed by yours to-day.

In this city was the home of Robert Morris, the Financier of the Revolution, whose name should be an honored one by this assembly, who devoted his personal services, property, and credit to his country in the hour of its greatest need, and of whom it may be said, as truly as it was of Hamilton, that "He smote the rock of the national resources, and streams of revenue came forth; he touched the dead body of the public credit, and restored it to life."

In that historical building in the city, the Hall of Independence, there is now deposited the original paper on which is inscribed that memorable declaration which, one hundred years ago, in that room, the conscript Fathers made, and there you may now see the venerable bell which, in the language of its prophetic inscription, "Proclaimed Liberty throughout the land, and to all the inhabitants thereof," and standing here, at the close of the first century of the nation's life, with all these clustering associations, and grateful and solemn memories, it is right that we meet here, not as citizens of New York, or Pennsylvania, or any other State or territory in our land, and hence it is, gentlemen, that I bid you welcome as citizens of the United States, all regarding with pride that flag which, wherever it meets the eye of a true American, is to him the symbol and declaration of the authority, not of any State, but of the government of the people of the United States.

You have come here, not only to assist in a great national commemoration, but to witness an International Exhibition of the World's Industry and Art; comparing the progress made in our country with that of others, in all that affects and promotes the welfare of man; and to this the governments and people of the world are invited, and are represented here; and there is no nation on earth which at present is attracting so much inquiry and observation as is this young Republic.

Thoughtful men abroad are looking at the working of our political system with interested attention, and good men everywhere desire the success of this experiment of republican liberty, for they know that the Democratic Idea is extending in European society, that it is gathering strength with the passing years, and they hope that when the time will come for its expression as a force, it may be directed by our successful example, and result in peaceable modifications of existing forms of government, and not in violence, bloodshed, and anarchy.

More than a century ago, it was said, "Westward the star of Empire takes its way." That which, when first uttered, was received only as the rhapsody of the Poet, is now accepted as the prophetic judgment of a Philosopher, applying the lessons of History. Let us hope that it will move on its destined course a brilliant and benignant orb, to the enlightenment and benefit of mankind; and now, with revolution achieved, popular liberty secured, and the authority of government established, in the coming century, we may seek no victories except those which follow in the train of Peace; that in our country, the Arts will find a peaceful asylum, that here may be the chosen seat of Science and the home of Learning, that toward this western world all men may look for opportunities of rational life, and examples of wise and beneficent government, and gratefully and freely acknowledge, that "Time's noblest offspring is its last."

One hundred years. How brief a time in the history of a nation, when compared with that of some of the nations of the Old World. The great Napoleon on his expedition to Egypt, when his wearied army was in sight of the gigantic Pyramids, which for more than four thousand years have reared their vast bulk over the sands of the desert, to stimulate the flagging energies of his fainting soldiers, said to them, "From the summit of these Pyramids, forty centuries are looking down upon you." Although we regard the period of our National life as only one century, the first causes of it lie much farther back up the stream of Time; and although this is only the first century of American Independence, it is the nineteenth of Christian Civilization.

In the progress we have made as a nation, in the last century,

there is cause of pride, and much rejoicing; and there should be thanksgiving that so much has been done for the welfare of man on this continent. Let us thank God, and take courage for the future, remembering that in the Divine economy, beside every right, privilege and enjoyment, there is corresponding duty, let us resolve, that as our fathers gave us this pleasant land, and this free government, we will preserve and transmit it to those who will succeed us, a government of controlled and regulated liberty.

Gentlemen, I will no longer detain you from the pleasure and instruction now awaiting you. We rejoice to meet you here to-day, surrounded by so much that reminds us of the founders of our government who did their work so nobly. Let us cherish and honor their memories, and try to emulate their patriotism; and may the citizens of this Republic, now living, so discharge their duty to their country that the unborn millions who a century hence, will be here, when we shall all have passed away, may speak gratefully of the men of this generation, as we now do of the Fathers of the Republic.

Gentlemen, I have now the pleasure of presenting to you the Hon. Mr. Spaulding, at other times, and elsewhere, of the Senate of New York, but to-day, and here, citizen of the United States.

ADDRESS OF HON. ELBRIDGE GERRY SPAULDING.

GENTLEMEN:

Invoking the continued guidance of the Supreme Ruler of the Universe, who has shaped the destiny of this great country for the last hundred years, I appear here to-day with my fellow Bankers to express our grateful thanks to the governments and people participating in this great International Exposition, for uniting with us to commemorate the patriotic deeds of the departed heroes of the American Revolution. We assemble here with reverence and gratitude to join this vast assembly in paying proper tribute to the heroic men who achieved American Independence. This great Centennial gathering has two objects in view; the first inspires patriotic and grateful feeling for the great work accomplished by the founders of our Republican form of government; the second arouses the pride which we all feel in exhibiting, in common with all other countries, the industry and skill developed in a hundred years of progress.

I revere and honor the patriotic fathers of 1776, for organizing the thirteen English Colonies into an independent Union for self-defence, resulting in successful resistance to the civil and military oppressions of King George the Third. On this hallowed ground, in this historic city, they declared their independence of the British Crown. After long years of hardships, privations and blood, this Union was finally made perpetual by the formation of a Constitutional Government, which went into operation in the City of New York in 1789.

The illustrious Washington was there inaugurated its first President by the unanimous voice of the American people. Under this constitution we became a nation, having mutual interests and a common destiny; under it we have greatly prospered. The partial development of this Empire of Freedom has thus far brought forth astonishing results. The grand and imposing display of industry and skill we here witness on these beautiful grounds has no parallel in history. The various departments before and around us, exhibit the marvelous progress which has been made in our own country during the last hundred years. Enlarging our view, and taking in the whole of this International Exposition of art, science, agriculture, manufacturing, mining, commerce, including all the various occupations, business and industries of the human race, we behold a greater collection of products which contribute to the well being and social intercourse of mankind, than was ever before known to be exhibited in the history of the world. I feel that I cannot command language adequate to describe the grand Exposition here presented to our admiring view. Each of the departments will have its own speaker to narrate its discoveries and achievements, and record its history. I will, therefore, without further preliminary remarks, proceed at once to speak of the wonderful progress made in the business of banking, which is the part assigned to me on this memorable occasion.

"ONE HUNDRED YEARS OF PROGRESS."

These are significant words when applied to the business of banking within the United States. Marvelous progress has indeed been made. At the time of the Declaration of Independence, there was no organized bank in the thirteen colonies to furnish any aid or support to the Revolutionary Army. Previous to that time merchants assisted in a qualified way in carrying on a limited commerce, and the foreign exchanges were principally furnished by those engaged in shipping to foreign countries. The exchange of commodities was largely carried on in all parts of the colonies by what was called *barter*, namely, exchanging one commodity for another; and the sturdy yeomanry manufactured their own wearing apparel in their own homes. Gold and silver were, however, the basis of the limited foreign commerce then carried on. Now, there are within the United States 907 chartered State banks, 2,118 National banks, 666 saving banks, and 2,375 private bankers; making a total of 6,066 banks and bankers. [See table in the Appendix, which has been furnished to me by Mr. B. Homans, Editor of the *Bankers' Magazine*, New York]. I am not here to present a treatise on banking, but I may, perhaps, with propriety make some general statements respecting its origin, and the general principles which govern the business. In collecting historical facts I have frequently adopted the verbatim statements of those who have previously written upon the subject. The Bank of Venice, the first establishment of the kind in Europe, was established in 1171, and owed its existence to the Crusades, and the necessity of the government obtaining means for conducting these wars. It was originally a bank of deposit, and in the earlier days of the institution these deposits were not subject to draft, as is generally the case with banks of this kind. These deposits could, however, at the pleasure of the owner, be transferred on the books of the bank. This system was at a later period discontinued, and the deposits became subject to draft. This bank continued in existence without interruption until it was overthrown by the revolutionary army of France in 1797.

The Bank of Genoa was projected in the year 1345, but did not go into full operation till 1407. It was for centuries an important institution in that commercial city, but in 1800 it shared the same fate as the Bank of Venice, by being pillaged by the French army under Massena.

The Bank of Amsterdam was founded in 1609, Holland being then possessed of a large foreign trade. This bank was only a bank of deposit, and the money in its possession was transferred on the books of the institution at the pleasure of its owner or owners. The primary object in the establishment of the bank was to give a standard or certain value to bills which might be drawn upon Amsterdam—rendered necessary by the depreciation of the coin owing to its having been worn or clipped. Here these coins were received on deposit, and had their value established by weight or fineness. It was not the design on founding the institution that the funds should at any time be lent out, but should remain in its vaults. However, the directors having lent to the governments of Holland and Friesland a large sum of money, the fact became known on the invasion of the French army, and produced the ruin of the institution. The Bank of Hamburg was established in the year 1619. This institution is a bank of deposit and circulation, which circulation was based upon fine silver in bars.

BANK OF ENGLAND.

The Bank of England was established in 1694—William and Mary then being on the throne. To the war with France, and the extreme difficulty experienced by the Government in raising funds for that war, is the institution of the monopoly due. Like the earliest of these institutions, the Bank of Venice, it owes its existence to the wants of the government which gave it life. The idea first originated with Mr. William Patterson, a merchant of London, who readily saw that the Government, which had been paying interest at the rate of from 20 to 40 per cent. per annum, would, without much hesitation, grant exclusive and almost unlimited privileges to such parties as would in turn furnish it with a fixed and permanent loan at a reasonable rate of interest. The plan being brought to the attention of the King, was submitted to the Privy Council, where the details were completed, and it was laid before Parliament. There, however, it met the violent opposition of a formidable party. Nevertheless, the bill was carried by the Government, and on April 25, 1694, became a law. It was provided that the capital, £1,200,000, should be permanently lent to the Government at 8 per cent. per annum; and that in addition to the interest, an allowance of £4,000 per annum should be made by the Government for the management of the debt.

The capital has, at various periods, been as follows: 1694, £1,200,000; 1697, £2,201,171; 1708, £4,402,343; 1709, £5,058,547; 1710, £5,559,996; 1722, £8,959,996; 1742, £9,800,000; 1746, £10,780,000; 1782, £11,642,400; 1816, £14,553,000.

Since first this institution was founded, its capital and the loan to the Government have been nearly identical in amount. The following are the dates of the several renewals of the charter, with the amount of Government debt at each period, to wit: 1694,

£1,200,000; 1697, £1,200,000; 1708, £3,375,027; 1713, £3,375,027; 1742, £10,700,000; 1764, £11,686,800; 1781, £11,686,800; 1833, £11,015,100; 1844, £11,015,100.

The management of the entire public debt of Great Britain is placed in the hands of the Bank of England, for which service it has received compensation which has from time to time varied in amount, according to circumstances. During the year 1845 this compensation was £94,111, 19s. 10d.

The Bank of England is a striking example of the combined power of public authority and private influence in sustaining the Government of England, as well as the agricultural, manufacturing and commercial business of that empire. The bank has been the chief agent in sustaining the British Government in the long and exhausting wars in which she has been engaged. It has also been an important aid to the industry and commercial prosperity of its people, and the business of the country has greatly prospered.

The Bank of England is the fiscal agent of the Government. It receives and disburses all the public months; and notwithstanding it is a bank of discount, deposit and circulation, it has thus far conducted the business in a very satisfactory manner, and without the loss of any of the money entrusted to it. It has been in operation 182 years, and the United States Government may safely profit by this example.

There was neither a regularly organized Treasury Department, nor an organized bank, during the first years of the War for Independence, and consequently great embarrassments were experienced in raising the means to prosecute the war. Hon. Robert Morris, an able, experienced financier and true patriot, was very efficient in managing the fiscal affairs of the country. On his own responsibility he frequently borrowed large sums of money for the use of the Government, which, on account of its known embarrassed condition, could not be procured in any other way. In June, 1780, Mr. Morris, in conjunction with other patriotic citizens of Philadelphia, effected a temporary organization by means of which 3,000,000 rations of provisions and 300 hogsheads of rum were forwarded to the army. On February 20, 1781, he was unanimously elected Superintendent of Finance, and by subsequent resolutions of the Continental Congress, was invested with almost the entire control of the financial affairs of the Government. At this time the Treasury was more than $2,500,000 in debt for current expenses, the army destitute, and the credit of the country exhausted.

During the financial administration of Mr. Morris, he several times pledged his private credit for public supplies. In the beginning of 1781, he furnished the suffering army with several thousand barrels of flour; and in the campaign of that year, he supplied nearly everything required for the advance upon the British army under Cornwallis. For this purpose, and as a part of the means used, he issued his own notes to the amount of $1,400,000, which were finally paid.

Our acknowledgments are also due to the French Government and people, for the timely and efficient aid rendered the United States Government, which resulted in compelling Lord Cornwallis to surrender the British forces at Yorktown to the American army under the command of General Washington, in October, 1781.

BANK OF NORTH AMERICA.

The first bank organized in the United States was the Bank of North America, at Philadelphia, in 1781. This institution was established under the auspices of Mr. Morris, Superintendent of Finance, and a delegate to the Continental Congress from the State of Pennsylvania.

During the year preceding its incorporation, the finances and credit, both of the States and of the Continental Congress, were, as before stated, almost entirely exhausted. In order to procure supplies for the support of the army, Congress and several of the State Governments had been obliged to have recourse to the issuing of bills of credit, which was the principal circulating medium.

On May 10, 1775, soon after the battle of Lexington, Congress made provision to issue Continental paper to circulate as money— $2,000,000 of which were put in circulation, commencing five days after the memorable battle of Bunker Hill.

From month to month these issues, which in the aggregate reached $350,000,000, depreciated until eventually they became entirely valueless, notwithstanding the laws making them a legal tender for private debts. Until the issues exceeded $9,000,000 Continental currency, according to the concurrent testimony of Mr. Jefferson and Mr. Paine, passed at its nominal value. The depreciation was afterwards very great. In May, 1781, this currency ceased to circulate as money, but was afterwards bought on speculation at various prices, from 400 to one, up to 1,000 to one. On May 17, 1781, a plan for a National Bank having been submitted to the Continental Congress, the principal provisions of which were as follows: The capital to be $400,000, in shares of $400 each; that there be twelve directors chosen from those entitled to vote, who at their first meeting shall choose one as president; that the directors meet quarterly; that the board be empowered, from time to time, to open new subscriptions for the purpose of increasing the capital of the bank; statements to be made to the Superintendent of the Finances of America; that the bank notes payable on demand shall by law be made receivable in the duties and taxes of every State, and from the respective States by the Treasury of the United States; that the Superintendent of the Finances of America shall have a right at all times to examine into the affairs of the bank. On May 26, Congress passed the following: "*Resolved*, That Congress do approve of the plan for the establishment of a National Bank in these United States, submitted for their consideration by Mr. R. Morris, May 17, 1781, and that they will promote and support the same by such ways and means, from time to time, as may appear necessary for the institution and consistent with the public good; that the subscribers to the said bank shall be incorporated agreeably to the principles and terms of the plan under the name of 'The President, Directors and Company of the Bank of North America.' So soon as the subscription shall be filled, the president and directors chosen, an application for that purpose was made to Congress by the president and directors elected." On December 31, following, Congress passed "an ordinance to incorporate the subscribers to the Bank of North America." The first president was Thomas Willing, and the bank formed a most important auxiliary in aid of the finances of the Government to the final conclusion of the war. This institution was incorporated by the State of Pennsylvania on April 18, 1782. The bank commenced business in January, 1782, with a capital of $400,000, of which $250,000 was subscribed by the Government. In the year 1785, when an ill feeling had arisen between the Government of the State of Pennsylvania and the bank, the former repealed the charter which it had granted in 1782. The bank, however, continued its operations under the charter granted by the General Government until in 1787, when it was re-chartered by the State of Pennsylvania. It has, from to time, been re-chartered, and in 1865 it organized under the National Bank law, and now has a capital of $1,000,000, and a surplus of the same amount.

Previous to the time when this bank went into operation, the

Continental army became very much reduced; the necessary articles of clothing and provisions could not easily be procured, the soldiers became dissatisfied, and fears were entertained that the campaign must terminate unfavorably, or in a relinquishment of everything for which the American people were then contending. Owing, however, to the timely aid of Mr. Morris, and other patriotic citizens, and the support given to the financial department of the Government by the establishment of this bank, confidence was in a great measure restored to the army, provisions and supplies were obtained, fresh vigor was infused among the troops, and to it and the efforts of Mr. Morris may be ascribed the expulsion of the British from the Southern States, and the termination of the conflict that secured American Independence by a treaty of peace in 1782-3. Some further details in regard to the Bank of North America will be found in the Appendix.

BANK OF NEW YORK—1784.

This was the first organized bank in New York. Its business was commenced as an association without charter on 9th of June, 1784, under the name of "The President, Directors and Company of the Bank of New York," in the Walton House, Franklin Square, then known as 159 Queen street.

The first president was General Alexander McDougall; cashier, William Seton.

In 1786, Isaac Roosevelt, President; William Maxwell, Vice-President; Directors—Samuel Franklin, Nicholas Low, Daniel McCormick, Robert Brown, Thomas Houghton, Joshua Waddington, Comfort Sands, Thomas Randall, Gen. ALEXANDER HAMILTON, John Vanderbilt, James Buchanan.

The bank removed to Hanover Square and continued business as an association until 1781, when on the 21st of March of that year a charter was granted by the Legislature of New York for a period of twenty years, with a capital of $900,000, divided into 1,800 shares of $500 each, with the addition of a subscription on the part of the State of 100 shares of the same amount—total, $950,000. Business under the charter began May 3, 1791.

On the 18th of May, 1852, the Bank of New York was reorganized as an association under the general banking law of the State of New York, with the name and title of "The Bank of New York," and the capital increased to $2,000,000. On the 17th of

April, 1857, the capital was increased to $3,000,000, and on July 6, 1865, it was organized under the National Bank act under the name of "Bank of New York National Banking Association." The accompanying Appendix contains further details in regard to this bank.

THE BANK OF THE MANHATTAN COMPANY,

in the City of New York, was organized under an act of the Legislature of the State of New York, passed April 2, 1799, with a capital of $2,000,000. The chief object of the act appearing on its face, was to supply water to the City of New York, but there was a section in the act which, it was claimed, conferred perpetual banking powers. The words in the act were that the corporation might employ its surplus capital "in the purchasing of public or other "stock, or in any other moneyed transactions or operations not "inconsistent with the Constitution and laws of this State or of the "United States." The first directors were Daniel Ludlow, John Watts, John B. Church, Brockholst Livingston, William Edgar, William Laight, Pascal A. Smith, Samuel Osgood, John Stevens, John Broome, John B. Coles, AARON BURR.

On the 25th March, 1808, it was authorized to increase the capital stock $50,000, and it is now carrying on business with a capital of $2,050,000.

The Bank of the Manhattan Company is the fiscal agent of the State of New York in the City of New York. It keeps a registry of the State stocks, pays the interest, and also makes the transfers on the books, under the general supervision of the State Comptroller and Treasurer.

THE MERCHANTS' BANK

is the third of the old banks organized in the City of New York. Like the Bank of New York, it was first organized as a "Company or Limited Partnership" in 1803, with a capital of $1,250,000. On the 26th of March, 1805, an act was passed "to incorporate the stockholders of the Merchants' Bank." On the 2d of February, 1831, the charter was renewed (subject to the provisions of the Safety Fund Act of New York, which was passed April 2, 1829), with authority to continue its business until January 1, 1857. It subsequently organized under the General Banking Law of New York, and in June, 1865, it organized under the National Bank Act, and its present capital is $3,000,000. (See Appendix for further detail.)

BANK OF MASSACHUSETTS.

The Bank of Massachusetts at Boston, was the first bank organized in the New England States.

During the latter portion of the year 1783, a movement was made in the town of Boston, Mass., to obtain subscriptions for the Capital Stock of a Bank, under the following preamble:

"Taught by the experience of many nations, that well regulated Banks are highly useful to society, as they promote punctuality in the performance of contracts, increase the medium of trade—facilitate the payment of taxes,—prevent the exportation of and furnish a safe deposit for cash; and in the way of discount, render easy and expeditious the anticipation of funds at the expense only of common interest; whilst by the same means, they advance the interest of the proprietors: We the subscribers, desirous of promoting such an institution, do hereby engage to take the number of shares set against our respective names, in a bank to be established in the town of Boston."

Under the foregoing preamble, the requisite number of subscribers were readily obtained, and at the Session of the Legislature of Massachusetts, which opened on the first Wednesday in January, 1784, a petition was presented for a Bank Charter, by a committee of the subscribers for stock, consisting of William Phillips, Isaac Smith, Jonathan Mason, Thomas Russell, John Lowell and Stephen Higginson, Esquires.

Upon their application, and after due deliberation, a bill was enacted under the name of the President and Directors of the Massachusetts Bank, with a capital not to exceed Five Hundred Thousand pounds, which bill was passed on the 7th day of February, 1784, signed by

TRISTRAM DALTON,
Speaker of the House of Rep's.

SAMUEL ADAMS,
President of the Senate.

Approved,
JOHN HANCOCK,
Gov'r of ye Commonwealth.

This bank commenced business July 5th, 1784, with a capital of $300,000, at which time it opened an account with the Bank of North America, Philadelphia, and the Bank of New York, and these are continued with the Massachusetts Bank to the present time. In 1865 this bank was organized under the National Bank Act, and its present capital is $800,000. For further details in regard to it, and also for a list of all the early State Banks, with the dates of their organization and the amount of capital stock of each, will be found in the Appendix. William A. Clark, President of the National Bank of Rhode Island at Newport, is probably the oldest active bank officer in the country. In a recent letter he says: "I have continued in this institution in different capacities fifty-eight years, having entered it as a clerk in A. D., 1818. Mr. Mygatt, the United States Bank Examiner, says, that I am probably the oldest bank officer in the country. I have outlived every man on the books doing business with the bank at that time, and also every stockholder and director."

Under the old confederation, formed in 1777, the evils arising from the want of a uniform currency, redeemable in gold on demand, under some general control, were severely felt, and was one of the causes that led to the adoption of the federal constitution, which became operative in 1789.

Upon the organization of our present government, the currency of the country, and the establishment of the public credit, were among the first subjects of legislation that engaged the attention of Congress; accordingly, by a resolution of that body of the 9th of August, 1790, that peerless statesman, Alexander Hamilton, Secretary of the Treasury, was required to prepare and report to them such further provision as might, in his opinion, be necessary for establishing the public credit. Pursuant to this resolution, the Secretary of the Treasury, on the 13th of December following, made a report upon the subject referred to him, in which he recommended the establishment of a National Bank.

The following extracts from the report of Mr. Hamilton upon the subject, will show the principal reasons urged by him in favor of

THE FIRST UNITED STATES BANK.

"That from a conviction that a National Bank is an institution of primary importance to the prosperous administration of the finances, and would be of the greatest utility in the operations connected with the support of the public credit, his attention has been drawn to devising the plan of such an institution, upon a scale which will entitle it to the confidence, and be likely to render it equal to the exigencies of the public. *   *   *   *   *

"It is a fact well understood, that public banks have found admission and patronage among the principal and most enlightened commercial nations. They have successfully obtained in Italy, Germany, Holland, England, and France, as well as in the United States, and it is a circumstance which cannot but have considerable weight, in a candid estimate of their tendency, that, after an experience of centuries, there exists not a question about their utility, in the countries in which they have been so long established. Theorists and men of business unite in the acknowledgment of it.

"Trade and industry, wherever they have been tried, have been indebted to them for important aid, and Government has been repeatedly under the greatest obligations to them in dangerous and distressing emergencies. That of the United States, as well as in some of the most critical conjunctures of the late war, as since the peace, has received assistance from those established among us, with which it could not have dispensed.

"With this two-fold evidence before us, it might be expected that there would be a perfect union of opinions in their favor. Yet doubts have been entertained; jealousies and prejudices have circulated; and, though the experiment is every day dissipating them, within the spheres in which the effects are best known, yet there are still persons by whom they have not been entirely renounced. To give a full and accurate view of the subject, would be to make a treatise of a report; but there are certain aspects in which it may be cursorily exhibited, which may perhaps conduce to a just impression of its merits. These will involve a comparison of the advantages with the disadvantages, real or supposed, of such institutions.

"The following are among the principal advantages of a bank:

"First, the augmentation of productive capital of a country. Gold and silver, when they are employed merely as the instruments of exchange, alienation, have been not improperly denominated dead stock; but when deposited in banks, to become the basis of a paper circulation, which takes their character and place, as the signs or representatives of value, they then acquire life, or, in other words, an active and productive quality.

"Deposits are of immense consequence in the operations of a Bank. Though liable to be drawn at any moment, experience proves that the money so much oftener changes proprietors than place, and that what is drawn out is generally so speedily replaced, as to authorize the counting upon the sums deposited as an effective fund, which concurring with the stock of the bank, enables it to extend its loans, and to answer all the demands for coin, whether in consequence of these loans or arising from the occasional return of its notes. These different circumstances explain the manner in which the ability of a bank to circulate a greater sum than its actual capital in coin is acquired. This, however, must be gradual, and must be preceded by the firm establishment of confidence—a confidence which may be bestowed on the most rational grounds, since the excess in question will always be bottomed on good security of one kind or another. This, every well-conducted bank carefully requires before it will consent to advance either its money or its credit—and where there is an auxiliary capital (as will be the case in the plan hereafter submitted), which, together with the capital in coin, define the boundary that shall not be exceeded by the engagements of the bank. The security may, consistently with all the maxims of a reasonable circumspection, be regarded as complete. The same circumstances illustrate the truth of the position, that it is one of the properties of banks to increase the active capital of a country. This, in other words, is the sum of them: The money of one individual, while he is waiting for an opportunity to employ it, by being either deposited in the bank for safe keeping, or invested in its stocks, is in a condition to administer to the wants of others without being put out of his own reach when occasion presents. This yields an extra profit, arising from what is paid for the use of his money by others, when he could not himself make use of it, and keeps the money itself in a state of incessant activity.

"Purchases and undertakings, in general, can be carried on by any given sum of bank paper or credit as effectually as by an equal sum of gold and silver. And thus, by contributing to enlarge the mass of industrious and commercial enterprises, banks become nurseries of national wealth,—a consequence as satisfactorily verified by experience as it is clearly deducible in theory.

"Secondly, greater facilities to the Government in obtaining pecuniary aids, especially in sudden emergencies. This is another and an undisputed advantage of public banks—one which, as already remarked, has been realized in signal instances among ourselves. The reason is obvious: the capitals of a great number of individuals are, by this operation, collected in a point and placed under one direction. The mass formed by this union is, in a certain sense, magnified by the credit attached to it; and while this mass is always ready, and can at once be put in motion in aid of the Government, the interest of the bank to afford that aid, independent of regard to the public safety and welfare, is a sure pledge for its disposition to go as far in its compliance as can in prudence be desired. There is in the nature of things, as will be more particularly noticed in another place, an intimate connection of interest between the Government and the bank of a nation.

"Thirdly, the facilitating of the payment of taxes. This advantage is produced in two ways. Those who are in a situation to have access to the bank, can have the assistance of loans to answer, with punctuality, the public calls upon them. This accommodation has been sensibly felt in the payment of the duties heretofore laid by those who reside where establishments of this nature exist."

* * * * * * * *

On the reception in the Senate of the report, from which are made the foregoing extracts, the same was referred to a committee consisting of Messrs. Strong, of Massachusetts; Morris, of Pennsylvania; Schuyler, of New York; Butler, of South Carolina, and Ellsworth, of Connecticut. On the 3d of January, 1791, Mr. Strong, chairman of the committee, reported a bill "to incorporate the subscribers to the Bank of the United States."

The history of this bill, on its passage through the Senate, is to be learned only from the Journals of that body. Its debates and proceedings were not then, as now, open to the public. Such extracts from the Journal as appear to be most essential, are herewith given:

A motion was made to subjoin to a certain clause, the following words:

"Provided, nevertheless, that nothing herein contained shall be construed to exclude the right to amend the same (the bank charter), on giving twelve months' notice, from and after the first of January, 1800." It passed in the negative. (Yeas and nays not given.)

On the nineteenth of January, a motion being made to expunge the twelfth section, to wit:

"And be it further enacted, That no other bank shall be established, by any future law of the United States, during the continuance of the corporation hereby created, for which the faith of the United States is hereby pledged." Passed in the negative. (Yeas and nays not given.)

Twentieth January, 1791. On motion to reconsider the term of incorporation and limit it to the year 1801 instead of 1811, the vote stood as follows:

Yeas.—Messrs. Butler, Few, Gunn, Hawkins, Izard and Monroe —6.

Nays.—Messrs. Bassett, Dalton, Dickinson, Ellsworth, Elmer, Foster, Johnson, King, Langdon, Maclay, Morris, Read, Schuyler, Stanton, Strong and Wright—16.

Whereupon, Resolved, that this bill do pass. (The yeas and nays are not given. It is, however, supposed that the vote was unanimous.)

The bill was then sent to the House for concurrence.

On the twenty-first of January, 1791, the bill (in the House of Representatives), was read a first and second time, and committed to a committee of the whole House.

On the twenty-first of January, the House resolved itself into a committee of the whole (Mr. Boudinot in the chair), and the bill was read by paragraphs, and no amendments being offered, the chairman reported it to the House, which voted that it should be read a third time the next day.

Chief Justice Marshall, in his Life of Washington, says (vol. 5, pages 294 to 298):

"On the final question, a great, and it would seem, an unexplained opposition was made to its passage. Mr. Madison, Mr. Giles, Mr. Jackson and Mr. Stone spoke against it. The general utility of banking systems was not admitted, and the particular bill before the House was censured on its merits; but the great strength of the argument was directed against the constitutional authority of Congress to pass an act for incorporating a national Bank.

"The Government of the United States, it was said, was limited; and the powers which it might legitimately exercise were enumerated in the constitution itself.

"The clause which enables Congress to pass all laws necessary and proper to execute the specified powers, must, according to the natural and obvious force of the terms and the context, be limited to the means necessary to the end, and incident to the nature of the specified powers. The clause, it was said, was in fact merely declaratory of what would have resulted by unavoidable implication as the appropriate, and as it were technical means of executing those powers. Some gentlemen observed that 'the true exposition of a necessary mean, without which the end could not be produced.' The bill was supported by Mr. Ames, Mr. Sedgwick, Mr. Smith, of South Carolina, Mr. Lawrence, Mr. Boudinot, Mr. Gerry and Mr. Vining.

"The utility of banking institutions was said to be demonstrated by their effects. In all commercial countries they had been resorted to as instruments of great efficacy in mercantile transactions; and even in the United States, their public and private advantages had been felt and acknowledged.

"Respecting the policy of the measure, no well-founded doubt could be entertained; but the objections to the constitutional authority of Congress deserved to be seriously considered.

"That the Government was limited by the terms of its creation was not controverted, and that it could exercise only those powers which were conferred on it by the constitution was admitted. If, on examination, that instrument should be found to forbid the passage of the bill, it must be regretted, though it would be with deep regret that its friends would suffer such an opportunity of serving their country to escape for the want of a constitutional power to improve it.

"In asserting the authority of the Legislature to pass the bill, gentlemen contended, that incidental as well as express powers must necessarily belong to every Government; and that, when a power is delegated to effect particular objects, all the known and usual means of effecting them must pass as incidental to it. To remove all doubt on this subject, the Constitution of the United States had recognized the principle by enabling Congress to make ' all laws which may be necessary and proper for carrying into execution the powers vested in the Government.' They maintained the sound construction of an authority in the National Legislature, to employ all the known and usual means for executing the powers vested in the Government. They then took a comprehensive view of those powers, and contended that a bank was a known and usual instrument by which several of them were exercised. (See opinion of Chief Justice Marshall in the case of McCulloch vs. State of Maryland, 4 Wheat. R., 422.)

"After a debate of great length, which was supported on both sides with ability, and with ardor which was naturally excited by the importance attached by each party to the principle in contest, the question was put, and the bill was carried in the affirmative by a majority of twelve voices."

The following were the ayes and nays on the final question,— " Shall the bill pass?":

Ayes—39. Messrs. Fisher Ames, Mass.; Egbert Benson, N.Y.; Elias Boudinot, N. J.; Benjamin Boorn, R. I.; Lambert Cadwallader, N. J.; George Clymer, Pa.; Thomas Fitzsimmons, Pa.; William Floyd, N.Y.; Abiel Foster, N. H.; Elbridge Gerry, Mass.; Nicholas Gilman, N. H.; Benjamin Goodhue, Mass.; Thomas Hartley, Pa.; John Hathorn, N.Y.; Daniel Heister, Pa.; Benjamin Huntington, Conn.; John Lawrence, N. Y.; George Leonard, Mass.; Samuel Livermore, N. H.; Peter Muhlenberg, Pa.; George Partridge, Mass.; Jerem. Van Rensselaer, N. Y.; James Shureman, N. J.; Thomas Scott, Pa.; Theodore Sedgwick, Mass.; Joshua Seney, Md.; John Sevier, N. C.; Roger Sherman, Conn.; Thomas Sinnickson, N. Y.; Peter Sylvester, N. Y.; William Smith, Md.; William Smith, S. C.; John Steele, N. C.; Jonathan Sturgess, Conn.; George Thatcher, Mass.; Jonathan Trumbull, Conn.; John Vining, Del.; Jeremiah Wadsworth, Conn.; Henry Wyncoop, Pa.

Nays—19. Messrs. John Baptiste Ashe, N. C.; Abraham Baldwin, Ga.; Timothy Bloodgood, N. C.; John Brown, Va.; Edanus Burke, S. C.; Daniel Carrol, Md.; Benjamin Contee, Md.; Jonathan Grout, Mass.; William B. Giles, Va.; James Jackson, Ga.; Richard Bland Lee, Va.; James Madison, Jr., Va.; George Mathews, Ga.; Andrew Moore, Va.; Josiah Parker, Va; Michael Jenifer Stone, Md.; Thomas Tudor Tucker, S. C.; Alexander White, Va.; Hugh Williamson, N. C.

The following abstract of the first five clauses of the charter will give an idea of the act: 1. The capital shall be $10,000,000, to be divided into 25,000 shares of $400 each.

2. Any person, co-partnership, or body politic, may subscribe for such number of shares as he, she, or they may think proper, not exceeding 1,000, except as regards the subscription of the United States. The subscriptions, except those of the United States, shall be payable one-quarter in gold and silver, and the remaining three-quarters in certain 6 per cent. stocks of the United States. 3. The subscribers are incorporated under the name and style of "The President, Directors and Company of the Bank of the United States," and to continue until March 4, 1811. The bank is authorized to hold property of all kinds, inclusive of its capital, to the amount of $15,000,000. 4. Twenty-five directors are to be elected, by a plurality of votes cast on the first Monday in January of each and every year, for one year only, and the directors are empowered to choose one of their number for President. 5. As soon as the sum of $400,000 is received on account of the subscriptions, in gold and silver, on proper notice being given, the bank may be organized.

The point which had been agitated with so much zeal in the House of Representatives, was examined no less deliberately by President Washington. Thomas Jefferson, Secretary of State, and Edmund Randolph, Attorney-General, concurred in opinion that Congress had transcended their constitutional powers in passing the bill; while Alexander Hamilton, Secretary of the Treasury, with equal clearness, maintained the opposite opinion, in which General Knox, Secretary of War, concurred. The advice of each minister, with his reasons in support of it, was required in writing.

A perusal of the arguments used on the occasion by the heads of departments would afford much gratification to the curious, but the limits prescribed for this historical sketch will not permit the introduction of such voluminous papers. (For an examination of them at full length, the reader is referred to the "Legislative and Documentary History of the Bank of the United States," published at Washington by Gales & Seaton, 1832; p. 82 to 112.)

An outline, however, of that train of reasoning with which each opinion was supported, and on which the judgment of the executive was most probably formed, will be briefly stated.

Opinion of Thomas Jefferson, Secretary of State:

"To prove that the measure was not sanctioned by the Constitution, the general principle was asserted that the foundation of that instrument was laid on the ground, 'that all powers not delegated to the United States by the Constitution, nor prohibited to it by the State, are reserved to the States or to the people.' To take a single step beyond the powers thus specially drawn around the powers of Congress, is to take possession of a boundless field of power no longer susceptible of definition.

"The power in question was said not to be among those which were specially enumerated, nor to be included within either of the general phrases which are to be found in the Constitution. The article which contains this enumeration was reviewed; each specified power was analyzed, and the creation of a corporate body was declared to be distinct from either of them."

The general phrases are:

"First, to lay taxes to provide for the general welfare of the United States. The power here conveyed, it was observed, was 'to levy taxes.'

"The purpose was, 'the general welfare.' Congress could not lay taxes *ad libitum*, but could only lay them for 'the general welfare;' nor did this clause authorize that body to provide for 'the general welfare' otherwise than by laying taxes for that porpose.' Secondly, 'To make all laws which shall be necessary and proper for carrying into execution the enumerated powers. But they can all be carried into execution without a bank. A bank, therefore, is not necessary, and consequently unauthorized by this phrase.

"It had been much urged that a bank would give great facility and convenience in the collection of taxes. Suppose this were true; yet the Constitution allows only the means which are necessary, not those which are convenient. If such a latitude of construction be allowed this phrase, as to give any non-enumerated power, it will go to every one; for there is no one which ingenuity may not torture into convenience, in some way or other, to some one of so long a list of enumerated powers. It would swallow all the list of enumerated powers and reduce the whole to one phrase. Therefore, it was that the Constitution restrained them to necessary means—that is to say, to those means without which the grant of power would be nugatory.

"The existing State Banks would, without doubt, enter into arrangements for lending their agency. This expedient alone suffices to prevent the existence of that necessity when it may justify the assumption of a non-enumerated power as a means of carrying into effect an enumerated one. It may be said that a bank whose bills would have a currency all over the States, would be more convenient than one whose currency is limited to a single State. So it would be still more convenient that there should be a bank whose bills should have a currency all over the world; but it does not follow from this superior conveniency, that there exists anywhere a power to establish such a bank, or that the world may not go on very well without it.

"For a shade or two of convenience, more or less, it cannot be imagined that the Constitution intended to invest Congress with a power so important as that of creating a corporation."

Substance of the opinion of Mr. Hamilton, Secretary of the Treasury, in support of the bill.

In supporting the constitutionality of the act, it was laid down as a general proposition

"That every power vested in a government is, in its nature, sovereign, and includes by force of the term a right to employ all the means requisite and fairly applicable to the attainment of the ends of such power; and where it is not precluded by restrictions and exceptions specified in the Constitution and not immoral, are not contrary to the essential ends of political society. This principle, in its application to government in general, would be admitted as an axiom; and it would be incumbent on those who might refuse to acknowledge its influence in American affairs to prove a distinction; and to show that a rule which, in the general system of things, is essential to the preservation of the social order, is inapplicable to the United States. The circumstance that the powers of sovereignty are divided between the National and State Governments does not afford the distinction required.

"If it could be necessary to bring proof of a proposition so clear as that which affirms the powers of the Federal Government, as to its objects, were sovereign, there is a clause in the Constitution which is decisive. It is that which declares the Constitution of the United States, the laws made in pursuance of it, and the treaties made under its authority to be the supreme law of the land, the power which can create the supreme law in any case, is doubtless sovereign as to such case.

"That the Government of the United States can exercise only those powers which are delegated by the Constitution, is a proposition not to be controverted; neither is it to be denied, on the other hand, that these are implied as well as express powers, and that the former are as effectually delegated as the latter. For the sake of accuracy, it may be observed, that there are also resulting powers. It would not be doubted that if the United States should make a conquest of any of the territories of its neighbors, they would possess sovereign jurisdiction over the conquered territory. This would rather be a result of the whole mass of the powers of the Government, and from the nature of political society, than a consequence of either of the powers especially enumerated. This is an extensive case in which the power of creating corporations is either implied in, or would result from some or all of the powers vested in the National Government.

"A corporation may be created in relation to the collection of taxes, or to the trade with foreign countries, or between the States or with the Indian tribes, because it is in the province of the Federal Government to regulate those objects, and because it is incident to a general sovereign or legislative power to regulate a thing, to employ all the means which relate to its regulation, to the best and greatest advantage.

"A strange fallacy seems to have crept into the manner of thinking and reasoning upon this subject. The imagination has presented an incorporation as some great, independent, substantive thing:—as a political end of peculiar magnitude and moment; whereas it is truly to be considered as a quality, capacity, or mean to an end. Thus a mercantile company is formed with a certain capital for the purpose of carrying on a particular branch of business. The business to be prosecuted is the end. The Association, in order to form the requisite capital is the primary means.

"It is certain that neither the grammatical nor popular sense of the term necessary requires that construction. According to both, necessary means no more than needful, requisite, useful, or conducive to. It is a common mode of expression to say that it is necessary for a Government or person to do this or that thing, where nothing more is intended or understood than that the interests of the Government or person require, or will be promoted by doing this or that thing.

"This is the true sense in which the word is used in the Constitution. The whole tenor of the clause containing it indicates an intent to give it a liberal latitude to the exercise of specified powers. The expressions have peculiar comprehensiveness. They are 'to make all laws necessary and proper for carrying into execution the foregoing powers, and all other powers vested by the Constitution in the Government of the United States, or in any department or office thereof.' To give the word 'necessary,' the restrictive operation contended for, would not only depart from its obvious and popular sense, but would give it the same force as if the word absolutely or indispensably had been prefixed to it.

"The degree in which a measure is necessary, can never be a test of the legal rights to adopt it. The relation between the measure and the end; between the nature of the means employed towards the execution of a power, and the object of that power, must be the criterion of constitutionality, not the more or less necessity or utility.

"While, on the one hand, the restrictive interpretation of the word necessary is deemed inadmissible, it will not be contended, on the other, that the clause in question gives any new and independent power. But it gives an explicit sanction to the doctrine of implied powers, and is equal to an admission of the proposition that the Government, as to its specified powers and objects, has plenary and sovereign authority. It is true that the power to create corporations is not granted in terms. Neither is the power to pass any particular law, nor to employ any of the means by which the ends of the Government are to be obtained.

"The power of the Government then to create corporations in certain cases being shown, it remained to inquire into the right to incorporate a banking company in order to enable the more effectually to accomplish ends which were in themselves lawful.

"To establish such a right it would be necessary to show the relation of such an institution to one or more of the specified powers of Government.

"It was then affirmed to have a relation more or less direct to the power of collecting taxes, to that of borrowing money, to that of regulating trade between the States, to those of raising, supporting, and maintaining fleets and armies; and in the last place to that which authorizes the making of all needful rules and regulations concerning the property of the United States, as the same had been practised upon by the Government."

The Secretary of the Treasury next proceeded, by a great variety of arguments and illustrations, to prove the position that the measure in question was a proper mean for the execution of the several powers which were enumerated, and also contended that the right to employ it resulted from the whole of them taken together. To detail those arguments would occupy too much space, and is the less necessary because their correctness obviously depends on the correctness of the principles which have been already stated.

The opinion of each Minister was considered by President Washington with all that attention which the magnitude of the question and the interest taken in it by the opposing parties, so eminently required. This deliberate investigation of the subject terminated in a conviction, that the Constitution of the United States authorized the measure, and the sanction of the Executive was given to the act by George Washington, July 25, 1791. (Substance of Marshall's Life of Washington, vol. 5, p. 297.)

About the time the bank went into operation, the French revolution broke out. This event produced an increased demand, and an increased price for our agricultural productions. Owing to the facilities afforded by the bank to the trading community, added to the judicious provisions of the act of Congress, of July 20, 1790, imposing a duty of fifty cents a ton upon all foreign vessels entering any port of the United States, while a duty of only six cents a ton was laid on American built vessels, and owned wholly by a citizen or citizens of the United States, the products of our soil, which before had been in a languishing condition, met with a brisk and profitable sale; and our commerce, about one-half of which had been before engrossed by foreigners, was almost exclusively secured to our own citizens. The system seemed to operate like magic in favor of the ship-owners of the United States.

Great advantages, and beneficial results, in consequence of the establishment of a National Bank, were generally experienced by the Government, and by every class of community, during the continuance of its charter,—the public funds were kept in a safe depositary,—the credit of the nation was established upon a firm and solid basis,—the demands of public creditors were promptly paid, at places convenient to them, and in a currency equal to gold or silver, in all parts of the United States. The Government realized a profit of $671,860 on the sale of two millions of its stock. A salutary restraint was exercised upon State Banks, as to the amount of their issues, and as to a failure in promptly redeeming their bills in specie,—a reasonable amount of circulating medium was afforded to the community, whereby the industry of the country was brought into profitable and successful operation, and a steady, uniform, and safe currency was afforded to every one.

During the period covered by the charter of the first United States Bank, the population increased from 3,929,827 in 1790, to 7,239,814, and 89 new banks were created under State charters with an aggregate capital of $40,601,601. This was no more than was demanded by the increased volume of business. The country flourished in all the essential elements of wealth and power. " Public and private credit was raised from its prostrate condition at the close of the war, to a very elevated condition, and the finances of the nation were placed upon the most solid foundation." There was reasonable ground to hope that an institution which had proved so beneficial to the country, would be preserved and cherished as the continuing base on which might be permanently established the industrial and commercial policy of the Government.

SECOND UNITED STATES BANK—1816.

The charter of the First United States Bank expired March 4, 1811. On the 20th of April, 1808, a memorial of the stockholders of the Bank petitioning for a renewal of their charter, was presented to the Senate of the United States, who ordered "that the same be referred to the Secretary of the Treasury, to consider and report thereon at the next session of Congress." On the 2d of March, 1809, Mr. Gallatin, then Secretary of the Treasury, made a report upon the subject, and in favor of renewing the charter. After giving a detailed statement of the general operations of the bank, he says: "It sufficiently appears from that general view, that the affairs of the Bank of the United States, considered as a moneyed institution, have been wisely and skillfully managed;" but no definite action was had at that session of Congress.

On the 18th of December, 1810, the subject was referred in the Senate to a select committee consisting of Messrs. Crawford (Ga.), Lieb (Pa.), Lloyd (Mass.), Pope (Ky.), and Anderson (Tenn.). On the 29th of January, 1811, the committee addressed a note to the Secretary of the Treasury, requesting him, among other things, "to furnish the committee with the facts and reasoning upon which his opinion has been formed, together with other information upon the subject as might be in his possession."

On the 30th of January, 1811, the Secretary of the Treasury addressed a letter to the committee, giving some additional views in favor of a re-charter of the bank, and closed his communication by saying, "The continuation of a bank of the United States has not, in the view which I have been able to take of the subject, appeared to me unconstitutional."

On the 5th of February, 1811, Mr. Crawford reported a bill to amend and continue in force, an act entitled "An Act to incorporate the subscribers to the Bank of the United States;" also a copy of the letter (aforementioned) of the Secretary of the Treasury, of the 30th of January, 1811.

The provisions of the bill are said to have been, in a great measure, conformable to the views of the Secretary of the Treasury, contained in his able report. The question on the passage of the bill was debated with warmth and animation for several days. The principal speakers in its favor were Crawford (late Secretary of the Treasury), Lloyd (Mass.), (Pope (Ky.), Pickering (Mass.), and Taylor (S. C.). Those in opposition were Anderson (Tenn.), Leib (Pa.), Smith (Md.), Giles (Va.), and Clay (Ky.).

For a perusal of the speeches delivered on the occasion, the reader is referred to "Legislative and Documentary History of the Bank of the United States," by Gales & Seaton, p. 302 to 446.

Those opposed to a re-charter, urged that the creation of corporations was not authorized by the Constitution, and that the bank was unconstitutional; that the article in the Constitution giving

Congress authority "to make all laws which shall be necessary and proper for carrying into execution" the delegated powers, did not warrant the establishment of a bank; that a bank was not "necessary," in the sense of the Constitution, to carry into effect the collection of the revenues; that State banks could be employed as a public depositary; that the bank was an aristocratic institution, and calculated to acquire an influence inimical to our republican institutions; that foreigners held a large amount of the stock, and in case of war, the stockholders might exercise an influence dangerous to the Government; that State banks could supply all the wants of the Government on any emergency, and that the resources of the country, added to the patriotism of the people, were a sufficient guaranty against sudden embarrassments.

Those in favor of a re-charter urged, that the right of the National Government to charter a bank as a fiscal agent to the Government, was clearly one of the incidental powers of Congress—that Mr. Jefferson, who was at first strenuously opposed to it upon constitutional grounds, had virtually assented to its constitutionality, by signing a bill establishing a branch at New Orleans. That the bank was indispensably necessary to the successful operations of the Treasury—that as Congress had no control over the State banks, the Government would be subject to such regulations as they might prescribe, and moreover, that the public funds might not always be safe in such institutions. That inasmuch as the general Government would have a reasonable control over a bank of their own creation, it would exercise a salutary influence over State banks, in restraining them from an excessive issue, and from failing to promptly redeem their bills in specie—that the idea of a bank being an aristocratic institution, was wholly fallacious, inasmuch as the stock was owned by any one who might wish to purchase it; and that self-interest alone, on the part of the bank, would restrain it from entering into any combination, unfriendly to the interests and liberties of the people, and that of itself was a sufficient guaranty to the people on that head—that it was impossible for foreign stockholders to exercise any direct or indirect influence, inasmuch' as they could not even vote for directors, and that in case of war, foreigners would furnish us with the necessary weapons to fight them with—that wisdom and prudence dictated the policy of fostering as far as possible, all our moneyed resources, preparatory to a war in which we might be engaged, and with which we were then threatened, by the great contending powers of

Europe—that in the event of a war, and without a National Bank, the United States would be destitute of the necessary means to carry it on—that no reliance could be placed upon State Banks, and that the Government would be completely at the mercy of speculators.

On the 20th of February, 1811, the question, on a motion of Mr. Anderson, to strike out the enacting clause, was decided as follows:

Those who voted in the affirmative were, Messrs. Anderson, Campbell, Clay, Cutts, Franklin, Gaillard, German, Giles, Whiteside, Gregg, Lambert, Leib, Mathewson, Reed, Robinson, Smith (of Maryland), Worthington—17.

Those who voted in the negative were, Messrs. Bayard, Bradley, Brent, Champlin, Condict, Crawford, Dana, Gilman, Goodrich, Horsey, Lloyd, Pickering, Pope, Smith (of New York), Tait, Turner, and Taylor—17.

The Senate being equally divided, the President of the Senate, George Clinton, determined the question in the affirmative, first submitting to the Senate the following prefatory remarks:

"Gentlemen: As the subject on which I am called upon to decide has excited great sensibility, I must solicit the indulgence of the Senate whilst I briefly state the reasons which influence my judgment. Permit me to observe, that the question to be decided does not depend simply on the right of Congress to establish, under any modification, a bank, but upon their power to establish a National bank, as contemplated by this bill. In other words, can they create a body politic and corporate, not constituting a part of the Government, but by forfeiture of charter, and bestow on its members privileges, immunities and exemptions not recognized by the laws of the State, nor enjoyed by the citizens generally?

"It cannot be doubted that Congress may pass all necessary and proper laws for carrying into execution the powers specifically granted to the Government, or to any department or officer thereof; but, in doing so, the means must be suited and subordinate to the end. The power to create corporations is not expressly granted; it is a high attribute of sovereignty, and in its nature not accessorial or derivative by implication, but primary and independent.

"I cannot see that this interpretation of the Constitution will, in any degree, defeat the purpose for which it was formed; on the contrary, it does appear to me that the opposite exposition has an inevitable tendency to consolidation, and affords just and serious cause for alarm.

"In the course of a long life, I have found that government is not to be strengthened by an assumption of doubtful powers, but by a wise and energetic execution of those which are incontestable;

the former never fails to produce suspicion and distrust, whilst the latter inspires respect and confidence.

"If, however, after a fair experiment, the powers vested in the Government shall be found incompetent to the attainment of the objects for which it was instituted, the Constitution happily furnishes the means for remedying the evil by amendment, and I have no doubt that, in such event, on the appeal to the patriotism and good sense of the community, it will be wisely applied.

"I will not trespass upon the patience of the Senate any longer than to say, from the best examination I have been able to give the subject, I am constrained, by a sense of duty, to decide in the affirmative; that is, that the first section of the bill be stricken out."

Thus, the bill to renew the charter of the first United States bank was defeated in the Senate, by the casting vote of the Vice-President.

In the House, a bill to renew the charter of the bank, the vote stood 73 to 74; so the bill was lost in the House by a majority of one vote.

The charter of the First United States Bank expired on the 4th of March, 1811. In the month of June, 1812, the General Government declared war against Great Britain, and in a short time, more than all the disasters to the country predicted by the supporters of the bank in consequence of its dissolution were verified. We soon learned, from sad experience, that although pretended wise legislators could form new plans of finance on paper, which to some would appear quite plausible, still, on trial the most essential thing was wanting—the State bank machinery would not work for national purposes in a great war. The country was soon flooded with from forty to fifty millions of new State bank currency, with scarcely even a nominal basis of coin for its support. The inevitable consequence was little delayed. In September, 1814, all the banks outside of New England suspended specie payments. The Secretary of the Treasury informed Congress that he had been under the necessity of selecting ninety-four different State banks, from Maine to Louisiana, as depositaries of the United States Government.

The various kinds of paper money in circulation made it necessary to keep four separate ledger accounts in each; and thus, instead of a single account, which was all that the Treasury required when the Bank of the United States was its fiscal agent, the Government finances were represented by 276 different bank accounts, scattered from one end of the country to the other. But what was still more serious, it was found impossible to maintain that continuous supervision of the revenues, and to exact those periodic settlements which constitute the only effectual safeguard against error, demoralization and fraud. The banks were ready enough to receive the dues of the Government, but, specie being no longer a part of the currency, the Treasury was forced into a corner. It could not receive irredeemable State bank currency, and all its efforts to obtain settlement were futile. Thus the Treasury funds, amounting to near nine million dollars, were locked up in the suspended banks. As a consequence, the Government fell in default on the interest of its funded debt. Its Treasury notes were dishonored, the business of daily life was prostrated, and universal distrust prevailed. "The multiplication of State banks has so increased the quantity of paper currency," said Secretary Dallas, in his report to Congress, "that it would be difficult to calculate its amount, and still more difficult to ascertain its value."

The last year of the war presented the singular and melancholy spectacle of a nation abounding in self-devoting patriotism, and a Government reduced to the very brink of avowed bankruptcy, solely for the want of a national institution which, at the same time that it would have facilitated the Government loans and other Treasury operations, would have furnished a circulating medium of general credit in every part of the Union.

The Government borrowed, during a short period of the war, eighty millions of dollars, at an average discount of fifteen per cent., giving certificates of stock, amounting to eighty millions of dollars, in exchange for sixty-eight millions of dollars, in such bank paper as could be obtained. In this statement, Treasury notes are considered as stock, at twenty per cent. discount. Upon the very face of the transaction, therefore, there was a loss of twelve millions of dollars, which would, in all probability, have been saved if the Treasury had been aided by such an institution as the Bank of the United States. But the sum of sixty-eight millions of dollars received by the Government was in a depreciated currency, not more than half as valuable as that in which the stock given in exchange for it has been redeemed. Here, then, was another loss of thirty-four millions, resulting, incontestably and exclusively, from the depreciation of the currency, and making, with the sum lost by the discount, forty-six millions of dollars.

The finances of the Government continued in a demoralized condition, when in October 6, 1814, Alexander J. Dallas was called to the head of the Treasury Department. Never before had there been greater need of a master mind in that important office. Within less than a fortnight the new Secretary communicated to Congress a report of extraordinary ability, in which he strongly recommended the establishment of a National Bank, as the remedy required to bring the finances into order. Various plans for a bank were brought forward in Congress, which resulted in nothing until, in January 20, 1815, a bill was passed. Many of the prominent members of both Houses, who had but five years before defeated a renewal of the former bank, now voted for this bill. It was, however, vetoed by President Madison, on the ground that it would not accomplish the objects rendered necessary by the state of the revenue and the condition of the country. On April 3, 1816, however, another bill for a Bank of the United States, which had previously passed the House of Representatives, was adopted by the Senate. The corporate title of this institution was "The President, Directors and Company of the Bank of the United States." Its capital was to be $35,000,000, composed of 350,000 shares of $100 each. $7,000,000 of this stock was to be subscribed by the United States, and the remaining $28,000,000 by individuals, companies, or corporations. The charter was to extend to March 3, 1836, and the Bank was authorized to organize and commence business as soon as $8,400,000, exclusive of the subscription of the United States, had been paid in. It was prohibited from lending on account of the United States more than $500,000, or to any State more than $50,000, or to any foreign prince or power any sum whatever, without the sanction of law previously being obtained.

The Bank was also obliged, by its charter, to give the Government the necessary facilities for transferring the public funds from place to place within the United States without charging commissions, or claiming any allowance on account of the difference of exchange, and to transact all business of commissioners of loans when required so to do. The Bank was prohibited from issuing bills under the denomination of $5.

This bill was approved by the President, James Madison, on the 10th of April, 1816, and the Bank went into operation on the 7th of January, 1817.

In the latter end of the same month, a meeting of delegates from the banks of New York, Philadelphia, Baltimore, and Virginia, took place at Philadelphia, with a view to a general and simultaneous resumption of specie payments. In consequence of a compact between them and the Bank of the United States, sanctioned by the Secretary of the Treasury, cash payments were resumed. To facilitate this object, the Bank of the United States imported from abroad seven millions of dollars in specie, and agreed to afford reasonable assistance to such of the State Banks as might require it. The resumption of cash payments was now general throughout the Union.

The year 1819 was one of great commercial difficulty in America. This distress was attributed to those measures which it had found necessary to adopt in order to effect a return to specie payments. To accomplish this object, the State Banks had been compelled to restrict their issues by limiting their discounts.

Many of those Banks which were formed at the dissolution of the first Bank of the United States, which had in the first instance made very liberal advances to the Western States, were obliged to resort to measures for compelling the repayment of their loans. Those too who had contracted debts either to the Banks or to private parties in the depreciated currency, sustained considerable loss when required to discharge their obligations in a currency convertible into gold.

SOUND CONDITION OF THE U. S. BANK.

Specie payment having been firmly established after the organization of the Second Bank of the United States, the finances of the Government were in a good condition down to 1833-34. A uniform currency upon a specie basis was furnished to the people in all parts of the United States. From 1820 to 1832 the business of the country was in a prosperous condition, and the Government accumulated a large surplus.

Mr. Dallas was succeeded in the Treasury by William H. Crawford, of Georgia. On the 12th of February, 1820, he made an able report on the currency which was very favorable to the bank for so conducting its operations as to establish and maintain a specie basis for all business transactions.

Hon. Richard Rush, of Pennsylvania, succeeded Mr. Crawford in the Treasury, who gives the following picture of the state of commerce subsequent to that date:

"No term of eight years since the establishment of the Government, was so exempt from the influence of external events that disturb the regular operations of National industry and commerce as the term ending with 1828." In the Secretary's report of December 6th, of that year, will be found a general view of the state of the currency, before and after the establishment of the Bank of the United States, sustaining the views already presented by Mr. Crawford concerning the healthful influences of the institution over the general affairs of trade. "It received the paper of the State banks paid on public account, and, by placing it to the credit of the United States as cash, rendered it available wherever the public service required" This was in effect to guarantee the State Bank currency on the footing of par in gold and silver. This gave steadiness and prosperity to the legitimate business of the country, and was a salutary check upon too great an expansion of credit, either in the form of currency or bank loans.

The Bank of the United States located in Philadelphia, established a branch or office in each State. At each branch deposits were received, bills and notes of hand discounted, and letters of credit granted, payable on demand upon all other branches. Their notes were legally payable at the respective branches where they were issued, but were often paid as a matter of courtesy at the other branches. The *five dollar notes*, the lowest issued by any branch, were made legally payable at every branch.

Average Amount for the years 1819–1829, of the principal items of the situation of the Bank of the United States.

	Discounts	Domestic Bills.	Funded Debt.	Total on Interest.	Real Estate.	Specie.	Deposits.	Gross am't of Notes.*
1819	32,211,674	336,760	7,236,153	39,784,587		2,743,834	5,734,682	5,056,829
1820	28,808,267	1,526,600	8,258,701	38,593,568		5,214,773	6,581,628	4,410,332
1821	27,099,050	1,598,473	11,859,296	40,556,619	245,846	6,469,224	6,990,073	5,609,220
1822	28,574,893	2,394,688	13,116,004	44,085,785	579,152	3,711,145	6,365,570	3,562,335
1823	30,584,919	2,588,245	10,911,700	44,084,864	736,370	4,899,686	10,401,786	4,671,271
1824	29,478,255	2,563,672	13,373,095	45,415,022	1,393,193	5,909,351	12,918,108	5,935,496
1825	29,327,219	3,270,699	19,807,665	52,405,583	1,566,728	4,686,557	12,885,829	8,836,646
1826	29,592,103	3,592,145	17,885,210	51,069,458	1,745,566	5,174,643	12,578,523	10,235,528
1827	27,948,592	4,568,297	17,724,192	50,244,081	2,118,560	6,327,758	13,727,274	10,808,244
1828	30,820,944	6,018,784	17,127,077	53,966,805	2,298,352	6,205,107	14,454,169	12,414,390
1829	32,703,280	8,417,021	13,925,701	55,046,002	2,474,750	6,411,998	15,172,164	15,011,352

* The actual amount of circulation is generally four-fifths of the gross amount, the rest being notes *in transitu*, or accumulated in offices where they are not payable.

Actual Circulation of the Bank of the United States aud Branches in September, 1830, and places where the Notes were payable.

WHERE PAYABLE.	NOTES IN CIRCULATI'N	WHERE PAYABLE.	NOTES IN CIRCULAN.
Bank United States	$1,367,180	Amount brought forward	$7,190,095
Portland	79,280	Mobile	940,825
Portsmouth	101,985	New Orleans	2,623,320
Boston	271,180	St. Louis	228,700
Providence	113,920	Nashville	1,235,275
Hartford	171,532	Louisville	662,375
New York	834,733	Lexington	908,625
Baltimore	528,638	Cincinnati	647,240
Washington	647,602	Pittsburgh	554,102
Richmond	469,440	Buffalo	258,130
Norfolk	532,400	Burlington	96,595
Fayetteville	713,760	Agencies Cincinnati and Chillicothe	2,375
Charleston	835,840		
Savannah	522,605		$15,347,657
Amount carried forward	$7,190,095		

NEW YORK SAFETY FUND LAW.

On April 2, 1829, the "Safety Fund Act," so called, was passed. Mr. Van Buren and his friends, then in the control of the State Government at Albany, exerted an important influence in procuring its passage. Banking under special charters was then a monopoly in that State.

It was very difficult to obtain new charters, and there was considerable hostility manifested at that early period to the United States Bank by those who controlled the State Government.

The Safety Fund Act of 35 Sections, contained provisions which gave considerable patronage and influence to the State Government. The United States Bank in Philadelphia, and its branches in the State of New York, came in competition with the State Banks. Mr. Van Buren, who had been elected Governor of New York, resigned that position, and became Secretary of State upon the inauguration of Gen. Jackson, in March, 1829, just previous to the final adoption of the Safety Fund Act, which was pending in the Legislature of New York.

HOSTILITY TO UNITED STATES BANK, 1829.

On the 8th of December, 1829, *more than six years before the expiration of the Charter* of the United States Bank, President Jackson, in his first Annual Message to Congress, manifested his hostility to it in these words: The Charter of the Bank of the United States expires in 1836, and its stockholders will most probably apply for a renewal of their privileges. Both the constitutionality and the expediency of the law creating this Bank, are well questioned by a large portion of our fellow-citizens; and it must be admitted by all that it has failed in the great end of establishing a uniform and sound currency!" The same views were repeated in his annual messages in 1830 and 1831. The Cabinet was not harmonious on the subject. Mr. Van Buren strongly supported President Jackson in the position he had taken in these messages. Hon. Lewis McLean, Secretary of the Treasury, was decidedly opposed to the President. In his annual report to Congress in December, 1831, he declared his conviction that the Bank was a necessary part of the plan for the improvement and management of the revenue, and for the support of the public credit. He said:

"The important charge confided to the Treasury Department, and on which the operations of the Government essentially depend, in the improvement and management of the revenue, and the support of public credit, and of transferring the public funds to all parts of the United States, imperiously requires from the Government all the facilities which it may constitutionally provide for these objects, and especially for regulating and preserving a sound currency. * *

"The authority of the present Government to create an institution for these purposes cannot be less clear. It has moreover the sanction of the executive, legislative, and judicial authorities, and of a majority of the people of the United States, from the organization of the Government to the present time.

"The indispensable necessity of such an institution for the fiscal operations of Government in all its departments for the regulation and preservation of a sound currency, for the aid of commercial transactions generally, and even for the safety and utility of the local Banks, is not doubted; and, as is believed, has been shown in the past experience of the Government, and in the general accommodation and operation of the present Bank.

"The present institution may, indeed, be considered as peculiarly the offspring of that necessity—springing from the inconveniences which followed the loss of the first Bank of the United States, and the evils and distresses incident to the excessive, and, in some instances, fraudulent issues of the local banks during the war—the propriety of continuing it is to be considered, not more in reference to the expediency of banking generally, than in regard to the actual state of things, and to the multiplicity of State Banks already in existence, and which can neither be displaced, nor in any manner controlled in their issues of paper by the general Government. This is an evil not to be submitted to; and the remedy at present applied, while it preserves a sound currency for the country at large, promotes the real interests of the local banks by giving soundness to their paper issues.

"If the necessity of a Banking institution be conceded or shown, that which shall *judiciously combine the power of the Government with private enterprise, is believed to be the most efficacious.* The Government would thus obtain the benefit of individual sagacity in the general management of the Bank, and by means of its deposits and share in the direction, possess the necessary power for the prevention of abuse.

"These considerations, and others which will be adverted to in a subsequent part of this Report,—the experience of the department in the trying periods of its history, and the convictions of his own judgment, concurring with those of the eminent men who have preceded the undersigned in its administration—induced him to recommend the expediency of chartering the present Bank at the proper time, and with such modifications, as, without impairing its usefulness to the Government and the community, may be calculated to recommend it to the approbation of the executive, and—what is vitally important—to the confidence of the people."

On the 9th of January, 1832, Mr. Dallas presented a memorial of the Bank petitioning for a re-charter, which was referred to a Select Committee. On the 13th of March, this Committee reported in favor of a renewal of the charter for fifteen years, with the following modification:

"First. No notes (under fifty dollars) were to be issued from the Bank or any branch, unless made payable at the Bank or branch whence issued, except at the request of the persons to whom they are delivered.

"Second. The notes of the Bank to be received by every branch in payment of balances due by any State Bank.

"Third. The corporation to be prohibited retaining any real estate, other than for Banking purposes, longer than two years, under a penalty of ten thousand dollars in each case.

"Fourth. Not more than two branches to be established or retained in any State; and not more than one, except in the States in which they now exist, without the assent of the legislature.

"Fifth. A bonus of $1,500,000 to be given to the Government, payable in three annual payments."

This bill was ordered to a second reading, and then laid upon the table of the Senate, until after the Report of the Committee appointed by the House to inquire into the affairs of the Bank.

The Committee appointed consisted of Messrs. Clayton, Camberling, Thomas, R. M. Johnson, McDuffie, Adams, and Watmough.

When the two reports were made it appeared that the investigation had not been confined to the alleged violation of the charter, but had been extended to all the affairs of the Bank. These reports were very lengthy, and attracted much attention at the time.

The conclusion at which the majority, consisting of Messrs. Clayton, of Ga., Camberling, of N. Y., Thomas, of Md., and R. M. Johnson, of Ky., arrived, from this investigation was, that Congress should not act upon the question of re-chartering the Bank until after the public debt was discharged, and the revenue adjusted to the expenditure of the Federal Government. They did not, however, give it as their opinion, that the Bank had violated its charter.

The minority, composed of Messrs. John Quincy Adams, of Mass., George McDuffie, of S. C., and Watmough, of Pa., made a counter report, vindicating the conduct of the Bank, and recommending a renewal of the charter, concluding as follows:

"Upon a review of the whole ground occupied in the examination they have made, the minority are of the opinion that the affairs of the Bank have been administered by the President and Directors with very great ability, and with perfect fidelity to all their obligations to the stockholders, to the Government, and to the country. They regard the Bank as an institution indispensable to the preservation of a sound currency, and to the financial operations of the Government, and should consider the refusal of Congress to renew the charter as a great national calamity.

"They will add in conclusion, that they are equally decided in the opinion that Congress is called upon by the most weighty and urgent considerations to decide this important question during the present session. The uncertainty which prevails on this subject, is calculated to exert a very pernicious influence over the industry, enterprise, and trade of the country. If the charter of the Bank is not to be renewed; if the tremendous operation of withdrawing from the community fifty millions of Bank accommodations, and twenty-two millions of its circulating medium, must take place, it is full time that it should be distinctly known, that the shock of this operation may be mitigated by timely arrangements on the part of the Bank, and that the community may have time to prove the necessary substitutes. Considering the immense extent of the operations of this institution, the time which its charter has yet to run will be scarcely sufficient for the winding up of its affairs."

GEO. McDUFFIE,
J. Q. ADAMS,
JOHN H. WATMOUGH.

These reports were ordered to be printed for general circulation, and on the 22d of May, the bill was taken up in committee of the whole in the Senate for consideration. The bill was very fully discussed and various amendments voted upon.

The bill was finally prepared by the 9th of June for a third reading, and after an unsuccessful effort to indefinitely postpone it, it was ordered to a third reading. Yeas 25—Nays 20; and on the 11th of June was passed. Yeas 28—Nays 20; as follows:—

Yeas—Messrs. Bell, Buckner, Chambers, Clay, Clayton, Dallas, Ewing, Foot, Frelinghuysen, Hendricks, Holmes, Johnson, Knight, Naudain, Poindexter, Prentiss, Robbins, Robinson, Ruggles, Seymour, Silsbee, Smith, Sprague, Tipton, Tomlinson, Waggaman, Webster, Wilkins.—28.

Nays—Messrs. Benton, Bibb, Brown, Dickerson, Dudley, Ellis, Forsyth, Grundy, Hayne, Hill, Kane, King, Mangum, Marcy, Miller, Moore, Tazewell, Troup, Tyler, White.—20.

Mr. Dallas said, that having been owner of stock in the Bank, he had sold it out as soon as he knew the subject of re-chartering the Bank would come before the Senate.

Mr. Silsbee said the same.

Mr. Webster said he had seen his name on the list of Stockholders, but it was altogether the mistake of a Clerk at the Bank in Philadelphia.

When it came into the House strenuous efforts were made to postpone its consideration, but that body having refused by a vote of 111 to 88 to lay the bill upon the table, the minority yielded to a motion of Mr. McDuffie, that it be made the special order of the day for the 18th of June. The House was then, however, engaged in the consideration of the Tariff, and it was not until the 30th of June that the subject was taken up in the Committee of the Whole. A motion then made for its postponement to the next session was negatived. Yeas 75—Nays 100; and Mr. McDuffie proposed an amendment to that section, which limited the number of branches in each State, providing the existing branches should not be interfered with. Various attempts were then made to alter this proposed amendment, so as to incorporate in the bill all the provisions with which its opponents sought to restrict the Bank.

The bill was then ordered to a third reading. Yeas 106—Nays 84. A motion was then made to suspend the rule of the House in order to permit the third reading of the bill the same day and carried. Yeas 124—Nays 61. The previous question was again called and ordered, 109 to 76, and the bill was then passed with Mr. McDuffie's amendment. Yeas 107—Nays 85.

The following are the yeas and nays on the final passage of the bill, viz: Yeas—Messrs. Adams, Chilton, Allen, H. Allen, Allison, Appleton, Armstrong, Arnold, Ashby, Babcock, Banks, Noyes, Barber, Baninger, Barstow, Isaac C. Bates, Boon, Briggs, Bucher, Bullard, Burd, Burgess, Choate, Collier, Lewis Condict, Silas Condict, Eleutheros Cook, Bates Cook, Corwin, Coulter, Craig, Crane, Crawford, Creighton, Daniel, John Davis, Dearborn, Denny, Dewart, Dodridge, Dayton, Ellsworth, G. Evans, Joshua Evans, Edward Everett, Horace Everett, Ford, Gilmore, Grennell, Hodges, Heister, Horn, Hughes, Huntington, Ihrie, Ingersoll, Irvin, Isaacks, Jenifer, Kendall, Henry King, Kerr, Letcher, Mann, Marshall, Maxwell, R. M'Coy, M'Duffie, M'Kennan, Mercer, Milligan, Newton, Pearce, Pendleton, Pitcher, Potts, Randolph, John Reed, Root, Russell, Semmes, William B. Shepherd, August H. Shepherd, Slade, Smith, Southard, Spence, Stanberry, Stephens, Stewart, Storrs, Sutherland, Taylor, Philemon, Thomas, Tompkins, Tracy, Vance, Verplanck, Vinton, Watmough, Wilkin, Elisha Whittlesey, Frederick Whittlesey, E. D. White, Wickliffe, Williams, and Young.—107.

Nays.—Messrs. Adair, Alexander, Anderson, Archer, Barnwell, Jas. Bates, Beardsley, Bell, Bergen, Bethune, James Blair, John Blair, Bouck, Bouldin, Branch, John C. Broadhead, Camberling, Carr, Chandler, Chinn, Claiborne, Clay, Clayton, Connor, Davenport, Dayan, Doubleday, Felder, Fitzgerald, Foster, Gaither, Gordon, Griffin, Thomas H. Hall, William Hall, Hammons, Harper, Hawes, Hawkins, Hoffman, Hogan, Holland, Howard, Hubbard, Jarvis, Cave Johnson, Kavanagh, Kendall, Kennon, Adam King, John King, Lamar, Lansing, Leavitt, Lecompte, Lewis, Lyon, Mardis, Mason, M'Carty, M'Intyre, M'Kay, Mitchell, Newman, Ruckolls, Patton, Pierson, Plummer, Polk, Edward C. Reed, Rencher, Roane, Soult, Speight, Standifer, Francis Thomas, W. Thompson, Ward, Wardwell, Wayne, Weeks, Wheeler, Campbell, P. White, Wilde, Worthington—85.

The Senate concurred in the amendment, and the bill July 4th, 1832, was sent to the President for his approbation and signature. It was by many apprehended, that the President would resort to the mode previously adopted by him to avoid the responsibility of rejecting bills that he disapproved of, and that he would retain it until after an adjournment of Congress.

To prevent this, the Senate declined acting on the resolution for an adjournment until the bill had been sent to him for concurrence, and then the 16th of July was inserted so as to leave ten full days exclusive of Sundays, by which he was compelled to return the bill to Congress, or permit it to become a law. Accordingly on July 10th, the next day after the Senate had fixed the time of adjournment a veto message was sent to that body, stating the reasons of the President for refusing his signature to the bill.

The great length of this Message prevents its entire insertion; the reasons assigned by the President are familiar, it is presumed to all, and were in substance as follows: That the act was unconstitutional because the law creating this Bank is not one of the necessary and proper means vested in Congress to carry into effect the *powers expressly* granted; that the bill granted exclusive privileges and was a dangerous "monopoly;" that it was not subject to State taxation; that it was ill-timed, inexpedient, and unnecessary for the public service.

This veto message having been received in the Senate, DANIEL WEBSTER, on the 11th July, 1832, proceeded to the consideration of the objections made by President Jackson to the re-charter of the Bank, and his reasons for not signing the bill. Mr. Webster said that the objections of the President " go against the whole substance of the law originally creating a Bank. They deny in effect that the Bank is constitutional; they deny that it is expedient; they deny that it is necessary for the public service."

"It is not to be doubted, that the Constitution gives the President the power which he has now exercised; but while the power is admitted, the grounds upon which it has been exerted become fit subjects of examination. The Constitution makes it the duty of Congress in a case like this, to reconsider the measure which they have passed, to weigh the force of the President's objections to that measure, and to take a new vote upon the question.

"Before the Senate proceeds to this second vote, I propose to make some remarks upon those objections. And, in the first place, it is to be observed, that they are such as to extinguish all hope, that the present Bank, or any bank at all resembling it, or resembling any known similar institution, can ever receive his approbation. He states no terms, no qualifications, no conditions, no modifications, which can reconcile him to the essential provisions of the existing charter. He is against the Bank, and against any Bank constituted in a manner known either to this or any other country. One advantage, therefore, is certainly obtained, by presenting him the bill. It has caused his sentiments to be made known. The bill is negatived; the President has assumed the responsibility of putting an end to the Banks; and the country must prepare itself to meet that change in its concerns which the expiration of the charter will produce. Mr. President, I will not conceal my opinion, *that the affairs of this country are approaching an important and dangerous crisis. At the very moment of almost unparalleled general prosperity, there appears an unaccountable disposition to destroy the most useful and most approved institutions of the Government.* Indeed it seems to be in the midst of all this national happiness, that some are found openly to question the advantages of the constitution itself.

"Within three years and nine months from the present moment, the charter of the Bank expires; within that period, therefore, it must wind up its concerns. It must call in its debts, withdraw its bills from circulation, and cease from all its ordinary operations. All this is to be done in three years and nine months; because, although there is a provision in the charter, rendering it lawful to use the corporate name for two years after the expiration of the charter, yet this is allowed only for the purpose of suits, and for the sale of the estates belonging to the Bank, and for no other purpose whatever. The whole active business of the Bank, its custody of public deposits, its transfers of public moneys, its dealings in exchange, all its loans and discounts, and all its issues of bills for circulation, must cease and determine on or before the third day of March, 1836; and within the same period, its debts must be collected, as no new contract can be made with it, as a corporation, for the removal of loans, or discount of notes or bills, after that time. * * *

"As to the *time* of passing this bill it would seem to be the last thing to be thought of, as a ground of objection, by the President; since from the date of his first message to the present time, he has never failed to call our attention to the subject with all possible apparent earnestness. So early as December, 1829, in his message to the two Houses, he declares, that he 'cannot, in justice to the parties interested, too soon present the subject to the deliberate consideration of the Legislature, in order to avoid the evils resulting from precipitancy, in a measure involving such important principles and such deep pecuniary interests.'"

Gen. Jackson was re-elected President in the fall of 1832, which settled the question that the second United States Bank must like the first go into liquidation and wind up its affairs.

REMOVAL OF GOVERNMENT DEPOSITS.

Without the authority of law the President assumed that the Secretary of the Treasury might select as many of the State Banks as he might deem necessary to receive the Government deposits, and perform the fiscal service of the Government. A large number were subsequently selected. But the 16th Section of the

United States Bank Act required, "that the deposit of the money of the United States, in places in which the said Bank and branches thereof may be established, *shall be made* in the said Bank, or branches thereof, unless the *Secretary of the Treasury shall, at any time, otherwise order and direct, in which case the Secretary of the Treasury shall immediately lay before Congress,* if in session, and, if not, immediately after the commencement of the next session, *the reasons of such order or direction.*"

The Secretary of the Treasury, in his report of December 5th, 1832, advised Congress that doubts were entertained *in some quarters* of the safety of the Bank as a depositary of the public revenues, and that, in consequence, he had appointed agents to examine into its condition. The President's Message of the same date expressed similar doubts, and indicated the propriety of removing the Government deposits from the Bank. A committee of investigation was appointed by Congress, and on the two reports, together with the statement of the Bank Directors, the House of Representatives declared, by a vote of 109 to 40, that the public deposits might safely be continued in the institution. The three examinations agreed so closely as to exclude all possibility of collusion or error. The Hon. Gulian C. Verplanck, of New York, chairman of the Congressional Committee, stated in his report, that they "had examined the report of the Treasury agents, and also the Directors of the Bank under oath, and that it appeared that the Bank had $80,866,000 of available resources, and that its liabilities, exclusive of its stock, amounted to only $37,800,000.

After this report was rendered, and after the vote of confidence by Congress, Secretary McLean expressed his final determination to take no part in changing the custody of the public revenues. Whereupon the President transferred him to the State Department, to make room for a more pliable officer; but his successor, the Hon. William J. Duane, of Pennsylvania, proved even less tractable. He declared his unwillingness to act in the matter without reasons that would justify him in the eye of the law. The President summoned a special meeting of the Cabinet for consultation, with no better result. He then announced that he would assume the responsibility of issuing a mandatory order of removal, which he expected the Secretary to obey. But that officer, like his predecessor, deeming the proposed action of the President illegal, would neither execute the order nor voluntarily retire from the office. The President had no alternative but to remove him by an arbitrary dismissal; and he appointed in his stead the Hon. Roger B. Taney, whose opinions were known to coincide with those of the President.

On the 18th of September, 1833, the President issued a peremptory order for the removal of the Government deposits, and on the first of October following, the order was executed by Mr. Taney, and such deposits transferred from the United States Bank to the "State Deposit Banks."

The amount of deposits thus transferred was about $11,000,000, and the State Banks thus favored were encouraged to expand their loans upon the faith of such deposits. Thus ended the services of the United States Bank as the Financial Agent of the Government.

Mr. Taney, in his report December 3d, 1833, stated that he had selected certain State Banks as depositaries and fiscal agents of the Government, and that the "deposit banks" so employed, were all institutions of high character and undoubted strength, and under the control of persons of unquestioned probity and intelligence. And to insure the safety of the public money, each one of them was required to give security whenever the amount of the deposits should exceed the half of the amount of its capital actually paid in." He also gave his reasons to Congress as required by law, for removing the deposits, which were deemed by the Senate as insufficient to justify such removal.

On the 5th of February, 1834, Mr. Webster, from the Finance Committee, made a lengthy and very able report on the subject which concluded as follows:

"The Committee cannot but regard the removal of the deposits, on the whole, as a measure highly inexpedient, and altogether unjustifiable. The public moneys were safe in the Bank. This is admitted. All the duties of the Bank connected with these public moneys were faithfully discharged. This, too, is admitted. The subject has been recently before the House of Representatives, and that House had made its opinion against the removal known by a very unequivocal vote. Another session of Congress was close at hand, when the whole matter would again come before it. Under these circumstances, to make the removal, with the certainty of creating so much alarm, and of producing so much positive evil and suffering, such derangement of the currency, such pressure and distress in all the branches of the business of private life, is an act which the Committee think the Senate is called on to disapprove."

In pursuance of the recommendation contained in the above

report of the Finance Committee, the Senate on March 28th, 1834, passed the following resolutions by decided majorities:

"*Resolved*, That the reasons assigned by the Secretary of the Treasury for the removal of the money of the United States deposited in the Bank of the United States and its branches, communicated to Congress the 4th day of December, 1833, are unsatisfactory and insufficient.

"*Resolved*, That the President, in the late executive proceedings in relation to the public revenue, has assumed upon himself authority and power not conferred by the Constitution and Laws, but in derogation of both."

It was not until near the termination of the United States Bank Charter when the act of June 23d, 1836, was passed, giving the authority of law, for using the State Banks as depositaries of the public monies belonging to the United States.

GOOD CONDITION OF UNITED STATES BANKS.

On November 1st, 1834, (after the removal of the U. S. Deposits.)

LIABILITIES.

Notes in circulation	$15,968,731.90
Deposit to the credit of the Treasury	429,465.07
do. Public Offices	1,837,168.66
Private Deposits	6,741,752.24
Capital Stock	35,000,000.90
Total liabilities	$59,977,117.87

RESOURCES.

To meet the foregoing, the Bank had the following resources, viz :

Discounts (Bills Receivable)	$34,667,828.24
Mortgages	87,591.29
Domestic Bills	11,086,373.07
Foreign Bills	2,727,782.11
Real Estate	3,024,788.45
Due from State Banks	427,102.89
Specie on hand	15,910,045.31
Total resources	$67,931,511.36
Showing a surplus over all liabilities of	$7,954,393.49

The immediate consequence of the defeat of the bill for renewing the charter of the United States Bank and the illegal removal of the Government deposits from that institution, was the incorporation by the several States of a great number of local Banks. Capital stock was authorized for each, but in most cases the stock was not *bona fide* paid up. The Banks in most cases went into operation upon an insecure basis upon fictitious capitals. In the seven years from 1830 to 1837 no less than 304 sprang into existence, with a nominal capital of $145,000,000, and paper circulation of $59,000,000, and the total circulation rose to $104,000,000. The mass of Bank loans increased from $200,000,000 to $525,000,000.

The Treasury balance in the "deposit banks" rose from $11,000,000 October 1, 1833, to over $49,000,000, on November 1, 1836. The Bank of the United States, instead of closing up on the expiration of its charters, obtained a new charter from the State of Pennsylvania, and transferred its assets to the new State institution, and maintained its proportion in the general expansion of credit. Speculation and overtrading increased to an alarming extent all over the country. The expansion of bank credit, the increase of State, corporate and individual indebtedness was far in excess of legitimate business. Reckless speculation in corner lots on paper, and running into debt generally was the order of the day. This kind of speculation extended to the public lands. Large quantities were taken up—not by actual settlers—but by large operators who paid for it in State Bank currency. "Wild-cat" banking became rampant in many of the Western States, which operated to swell the indebtedness enormously in that portion of the country.

The importations from foreign countries had been large and the specie in the country had been diminishing for some time previous. The duties paid on these large importations served to increase the revenues; the National debt was paid in full, and a surplus in paper money was accumulating in the United States Treasury which was then being deposited in the State deposit banks to the credit of the Treasurer in Bank ledgers.

SURPLUS MONEY DISTRIBUTED TO STATES.

On the 23d of June, 1836, an act was passed for distributing to the several States, the supposed surplus monies above $5,000,000, belonging to the Treasury of the United States, in proportion to their respective representation in the Senate and House. The sums to be thus deposited for safe keeping with the several States was to be made in the following proportions:—one-fourth part on the first of January, 1837, one-fourth part on the first of April, one-fourth part on the first of July, and the remaining fourth part on the first day of October, all in the same year. It was supposed that the whole amount to be thus distributed would be between $40,000,000 and $50,000,000.

CONDITION OF THE STATE DEPOSIT BANKS.

According to the returns made to the Treasury Department, April 1, 1836.

NAME.	PLACE.	CAPITAL.	SPECIE.	DEPOSITS Treasurer United States
		Dollars.	Dollars.	Dollars.
Maine	Portland	30,000.00	27,339.82	113,074.94
Commercial	Portsmouth	102,000.00	11,065.56	128,338.33
Commonwealth	Boston	500,000.00	209,064.54	1,009,731.52
Merchants'	"	750,000.00	295,546.30	931,105.79
Burlington	Burlington	127,912.00	12,082.35	52,893.48
Farmers' and Mechanics'	Hartford	410,496.00	10,763.80	67,560.89
Mechanics'	New Haven	472,970.00	153,546.38	41,315.06
Arcade	Providence	300,000.00	52,231.26	115,132.40
Mechanics' and Farmers'	Albany	442,000.00	114,032.33	217,430.22
Bank of America	New York	2,001,200.00	1,274,220.66	3,858,750.20
Manhattan Co	"	2,050,000.00	1,028,946.33	3,462,800.38
Mechanics'	"	2,000,000.00	1,271,593.00	3,985,083.72
Girard	Philadelphia	1,500,000.00	461,374.86	2,516,858.76
Moyamensing	"	174,950.00	93,030.32	502,042.25
Union, Md	Baltimore	1,845,562.50	107,943.24	906,491.54
Franklin	"	508,970.00	124,197.74	347,388.74
Bank Metropolis	Washington	500,000.00	217,219.39	200,394.40
Vir. and Branches	Richmond, &c.	3,240,000.00	633,700.07	358,230.56
North Carolina	Raleigh	1,206,100.00	292,018.15	38,471.07
Planters' and Mechanics'	Charleston	1,000,000.00	317,162.81	252,522.42
Planters', Georgia	Savannah	535,400.00	178,472.45	111,862.48
Augusta	Augusta	897,000.00	313,750.03	129,770.95
Branch of Alabama	Mobile	2,000,000.00	339,723.01	1,623,818.12
Commercial	New Orleans	2,945,430.00	202,533.17	1,119,314.50
Union Bank of Louisiana	"	7,051,000.00	955,559.01	1,961,116.73
Merchants' and Mechanics'	Pittsburgh	600,000.00	127,514.59	51,095.72
Franklin	Cincinnati	1,000,000.00	167,020.90	244,048.12
Commercial	"	1,000,000.00	266,803.87	395,175.82
Clinton	Columbus	289,225.00	121,143.47	328,127.52
Savings Institution	Louisville	96,512.00	50,807.58	494,842.26
Union Bank, Tennessee	Nashville	1,817,255.00	116,585.17	484,086.61
State	Indianapolis	1,279,857.78	964,758.34	1,379,949.98
Agency C. Bank, Cincinnati	St. Louis		513,859.06	1,978,383.94
Planters'	Natchez	4,143,940.00	438,324.32	2,732,319 38
Michigan	Detroit	448,200.00	62,139.34	1,070,820.03
Farmers' and Mechanics'	"	150,000.00	59,923.70	703,675.25
		43,690,980.28	10,885,996.92	33,294,024.08

RECAPITULATION OF DEPOSIT BANKS.

	Dollars.		Dollars.
Loans and Discounts	68,850,287.67	Capital	43,690,980.28
Domestic Exchange	32,775,529.42	Treasurer of U. S.	33,294,024.08
Real Estate	1,929,056.68	Public Officers	3,477,252.42
Due from Banks	15,931,916.22	Due to Banks	15,366,674.49
Notes of other Banks	11,107,447.78	Contingent Fund	1,102,763.15
Specie	10,885,996.92	Profit and Loss, &c	4,094,358.12
Foreign Exchange	532,450.96	Circulation	28,796,186.68
Expenses	184,901.22	Private Deposits	15,453,092.11
Other Investments	10,651,759.92	Other Liabilities	7,574,015.16
Total,	152,849,346.78	Total	152,849,346.79

SPECIE CIRCULAR.

To check speculation in the public lands, President Jackson, on the 11th July, 1836, issued the famous *Specie Circular*, in the form of an order from the Treasury Department, prohibiting the receipt of anything but gold and silver coin in payment of lands sold by the Government.

STATE BANKS FAIL IN MAY, 1837.

By the successive acts and proceedings just narrated, a train was skillfully laid for a general crash in the financial affairs of the government, the Banks and the people. The natural result of what had taken place during the last six years, led inevitably to a general smash up. The Bank, which President Madison, in his first annual message, after approving its charter, declared was "essential for the interests of the community at large, as well as for the purposes of the Treasury," was killed by the veto of President Jackson, and forced to wind up its affairs as a national institution; the government deposits were illegally removed to a great number of State deposit banks; the State Banks were increased, upon fictitious capitals, to an alarming extent; bank credits were extended in the form of paper currency and improper loans upon inadequate and unconvertible security; high prices, overtrading and extravagance in living followed as a natural consequence. The catastrophe resulting from this unnatural and reckless state of things could not long be delayed.

The specie circular issued by President Jackson, showed distrust of the State Bank currency; gold and silver was demanded. Failures became frequent in the latter part of 1836, and the early part of 1837. State Bank currency, in many cases, was not redeemed in coin when presented for that purpose, and very soon became uncurrent money. The Wild Cat and Red Dog Banks at the West first broke down; the Safety Fund of New York received a blow from which it never recovered, and finally went out of existence.

Each day developed some new case of insolvency on the part of Banks and individuals. Finally, the distrust extended to all classes of business; credit was destroyed; the panic became general, when in May, 1837, all the banks in the country suspended specie payments, and the "deposits" in the "Pet Banks" to the credit of the Treasurer of the United States became unavailable. The demoralization was complete and general in all private as well as governmental transactions. It was difficult for the Secretary of the Treasury to manage the fiscal affairs of the government.

EXTRA SESSION OF CONGRESS, 1837.

Martin Van Buren having been inaugurated President on the 4th of March of that year, issued a Proclamation for an Extra Session of Congress in the following words:

PROCLAMATION.

"Whereas, *great and weighty matters* claiming the consideration of the Congress of the United States from an *extraordinary occasion* for convening them, I do, by these presents, appoint the first Monday of September next for their meeting at the city of Washington; hereby requiring the respective Senators and Representatives then and there to assemble in Congress, in order to receive such communications as may be made to them, and to consult and determine on such measures as in their wisdom may be deemed meet for the welfare of the United States.

"MARTIN VAN BUREN."

It is a remarkable fact that in a time of profound peace the finances of the country should have been so badly managed as to "form an extraordinary occasion" for an extra session of Congress. Five years previously the public finances were in a remarkably good condition and a large surplus was accumulating in the Treasury. A uniform currency convertible in gold on demand, had been maintained for nearly twenty years, and the business of the country had greatly prospered. The great convulsion which made an extra session of Congress necessary was very annoying to the friends of the administration who had largely participated in bringing it about.

Mr. Van Buren was very much disgusted with the State Deposit Banks for their mismanagement in locking up and rendering unavailable the public deposits. His motto became "an entire divorce of the United States Treasury from all banks and banking transactions." The institutions which Mr. Taney declared in 1833, to be of "high character and undoubted strength," proved to be very weak in 1837. Many of them proved to be not only a failure but a fraud.

GENERAL JACKSON wrote from his retirement at the *Hermitage*. that "the history of the world never has recorded such base treachery and perfidy as had been committed by the deposit banks against the government."

THOMAS H. BENTON, a pronounced hard money man, familiarly known as OLD BULLION, said, at a subsequent date, "I am one of those who promised gold, not paper. I promised the currency of the constitution not the currency of corporations. I did not join in putting down the Bank of the United States to put up *a wilderness of local banks*. I did not join in putting down the paper currency of a National Bank, to put up a national paper currency of more than a thousand local banks. I did not strike Cæsar to make Antony master of Rome."

On the 4th September, 1837, the extra session of Congress opened its proceedings. President Van Buren sent in his special message, in which he stated that the object of the session was :—

"To regulate by law the safe keeping, transfer and disbursement of the public moneys ; to designate the funds to be received and paid by the Government ; to enable the Treasury to meet promptly every demand upon it ; to prescribe the terms of indulgence and the mode of settlement to be adopted, as well in collecting from individuals the revenue that has accrued, as in withdrawing it from former depositaries ; and to devise and adopt such further measures within the constitutional competency of Congress as will be best calculated to revive the enterprise, and to promote the prosperity of the country. * *

"A system," he said, "which can in a time of profound peace, when there is a large revenue laid by, thus suddenly prevent the application and the use of the money of the people in the manner and for the objects they have directed, cannot be wise, but who can think without painful reflection, that under the same unforeseen events might have befallen us in the midst of a war, and taken from us at the moment when most wanted the use of those very means which were treasured to promote the national welfare and guard our national rights."

The first act passed postponed the payment of the fourth instalment of surplus moneys to the States, providing, however, "that the first three instalments should remain on deposit with the States until otherwise directed by Congress," amounting to $28,101,645, which is still to the credit of the U. S. Treasurer on the books of the Treasury Department.

An act was also passed for the issue of ten million 6 per cent. *Treasury Notes*, redeemable after one year, which were intended to be circulated to some extent as a paper currency, by making them receivable in payment of "all taxes and duties laid by the authority of the United States, of all public lands sold, and for all debts due to the United States of any character whatsoever."

An act was also passed for *adjusting* the remaining claims against the late deposit banks, which were in default in making payment of the monies deposited with them.

NEW YORK IN A TIGHT PLACE.

The State of New York was also in a tight place, and had considerable difficulty in raising coin to pay the interest on its funded debt, falling due October 1st, 1837. In the month of August the Commissioners of the Canal Fund finally placed in the Bank of America, State Stocks issued for the Chenango Canal, to the amount of $545,000 at the par of gold and silver, and obtained from that bank an advance of $73,000 in specie with which the interest on the State debt was paid on the first of October, which prevented any default on the part of the State.

To aid in the resumption of specie payments, Canal Stock was also placed in the following banks:—

Bank of New York	$209,000.00
Merchants' Bank	310,000.00
Manhattan Company	426,526.55
Union Bank	209,000.00
National Bank	160,000.00
Bank of State of New York	416,000.00

These advances of Stock were made to the several banks amounting to $2,030,000, under a special agreement for "facilitating an early resumption of specie payments by the banks," and finally pay the State for the Canal Stock thus advanced to them.

FAVORABLE WINDING UP OF U. S. BANK.

At the time of closing the United States Bank after its charter expired, the stock was worth a premium of more than 15 per cent., and the stock in the Bank owned by the United States was paid back to it in full, and also a premium on the same exceeding 15 per cent., besides the previous regular dividends, so that the United States actually made money on its stock, and did not lose a dollar of the money deposited in the Bank. It fulfilled all its obligations to the Government, redeemed all its circulating notes, paid all its private depositors, and as a National institution went out of existence with a clean record.

BANK OF THE UNITED STATES OF PENNSYLVANIA.

When it was finally settled that no re-charter of the National Bank was to be obtained, a plan was projected to combine the advantages of the long established correspondence, name, and machinery of the former Bank, by incorporating its stock with a new institution under the name of " The President, Directors, and Company of the Bank of the United States of Pennsylvania," which was chartered on the 18th of February, 1836, by the Legislature of that State. The transfer of the funds of the old institution was made into the new State Bank. In consequence of the advantages to be derived from the new institution, the stockholders were generally content to subscribe anew in the new State Bank; and it is alleged that all of them might, at this juncture, have received their investments back, not only at par, but with a large advance. This, as before stated, the Government actually did, and no power was enjoyed by the Government that was not shared by every individual. Indeed, it was alleged by Mr. Nicholas Biddle (who held the administration of the affairs of the State Bank, as he had done in the National Bank), as recently as April, 1841, that the State institution was prosperous down to the end of his administration in March, 1839. But under the pressure of the revulsion which followed the panic of 1837, the stock of the State Bank declined from 116 to 17 per cent. in 1841, and finally failed along with a great number of other State Banks. The depression and hard times continued until 1843.

A bill for establishing a Fiscal Bank of the United States passed the House of Representatives, August 6th, 1841; vetoed by President Tyler, August 16th. Another bill for a Fiscal Corporation vetoed September 9th, 1841, followed by a resignation of all the Cabinet, except Mr. Webster, which ended for a time all efforts to obtain under any name a new National Bank.

On January 1, 1837, the Bank circulation of the country, according to the Treasury reports, was $149,000,000. By January 1st, 1843, it was reduced to $58,000,000. A ruinous fall of prices was the consequence, and wide-spread distress, attended by many failures. In the four years ending with 1842, the exports of specie exceeded the imports by $8,500,000; but under the favorable influence of the Tariff of 1842, in the nine months ending June 30, 1843, the imports of specie exceeded the exports by $20,000,000; as the Banks of New York and New England had paid specie regularly since 1838, they soon recovered from the effects of the revulsion of 1842–43. Those of the grain-growing States, from New Jersey to Missouri, did not fully recover till 1847, when the demand for breadstuffs in Europe gave a balance of specie in our favor of $22,000,000. The Banks in the South and West were not fully re-established until some years later, when an extraordinary demand for cotton replenished their coffers.

FREE BANKING LAW OF NEW YORK.

On April 18th, 1838, the monopoly of banking under special charters, was brought to a close in the State of New York, by the passage of the act "to authorize the business of Banking." Under this law Associations for Banking purposes and Individual Bankers, were authorized to carry on the business of Banking, by establishing offices of deposit, discount and circulation. Subsequently a separate Department was organized at Albany, called "The Bank Department," with a Superintendent, who was charged with the supervision of all the Banks in the State. Under this law institutions could be organized simply as Banks of "discount and deposit," and might also add the issuing of a paper currency to circulate as money. At first the law provided that State and United States stocks for one-half, and bonds and mortgages for the other half, might be deposited as security for the circulating notes to be issued by Banks and individual Bankers. Upon a fair trial, however, it was found that when a Bank failed, and the Bank Department was called upon to redeem the circulating notes of such Bank, the mortgages could not be made available in time to meet the demand. The mortgages when brought to the test of raising ready money proved to be unavailable, and by an amendment of the law the receiving of mortgages as security for circulating notes was discontinued.

This law with the various amendments that have been made, has proved to be a valuable and useful mode of carrying on the business of banking, and ultimately a very large majority of the banks in New York came under its provisions in the transaction of their business. Among them I may name a few of the most prominent.

THE BANK OF COMMERCE in the city of New York, organized under the provisions of this act, January 1st, 1839, with a capital of $5,000,000, which was afterwards increased to $10,000,000, and was among the first of the Free Banks in the State. It was a bank of "discount and deposit" mainly, and issued only a small amount of circulating notes until it came under the provisions of the National Bank Act in 1865.

THE AMERICAN EXCHANGE BANK is another of the large and prosperous banks which came early under the provisions of the free banking law of New York. Its capital is $5,000,000, and in 1865 it organized under the National Bank Act.

THE METROPOLITAN BANK of New York City, is another of the prominent banks which, at a later period, organized under the same law, with a capital of $4,000,000, and is uow doing business under the National law.

Many other banks ought to be specially mentioned for the ability and fidelity with which they have been managed, did time and space permit.

SUB-TREASURY ACT.

For more than ten years there was an earnest discussion in Congress and in the Treasury reports, for and against an Independent Treasury. Robert J. Walker, Secretary of the Treasury, in his annual report in December, 1845, said that "the only proper course for the Government was to keep its own money separate from all banks and bankers, in its own Treasury—whether in the mint, branch mints, or other Government agencies ; *and to use only gold and silver coin in all receipts and disbursements.* Various forms of *paper credit* have been suggested as connected with the operations of the Treasury, but they are all considered as impairing one of the great objects of the Independent Treasury, namely, an augmented circulation of specie." In other words a complete divorce of the Government from all banks and banking transactions.

On the 6th of August, 1846, the Sub-Treasury act was finally passed, and went fully into operation January 1st, 1847, upon the theory mainly of gold and silver in all the financial transactions of the Government; but with the expectation that Treasury notes might be resorted to if necessary.

THE SUB-TREASURY LAW NOT ADEQUATE TO THE EXIGENCIES OF THE WAR WITH MEXICO—NOT GOLD AND SILVER ENOUGH FOR THE PURPOSE.

In less than a year after the passage of the Sub-Treasury Act, it was found that very little gold was in the Treasury. It was easy to enact that "all disbursements" from the Treasury should be made in coin, but soon after the commencement of the war with Mexico, it was found very difficult to get the coin into the Treasury for "disbursement." The Army and Navy had to be supported, and material of war had to be provided. Coin in sufficient amount could not be obtained for that purpose. Resort was almost immediately had to the alternative of *paper* to carry on the war. The acts of July 22, 1846, and January 28th, 1847, authorized the issue of $28,000,000 6 per cent. Treasury notes, to be put upon loan, and paid to contractors and others who furnished supplies to carry on the war. A large part of the "disbursements" for the war were in Treasury notes instead of gold, showing the impracticability of the Sub-Treasury to carry on even a small war in gold and silver.

THE PANIC AND REVULSION OF 1857.

This crisis, like the revulsion of 1837, was caused by too great an expansion of credit. Debts in all forms became excessive. The Railway system had been largely extended upon borrowed capital. There had been excessive importations of foreign goods. The banks loaned too much of their funds on stocks, bonds and other securities that could not be readily converted into money to meet checks of depositors. The Ohio Life Insurance and Trust Company, which had a large branch office in the city of New York, was completely loaded down with unavailable securities, and on the 25th of August, 1857, failed with very large liabilities outstanding. This was the starting-point of the panic. Distrust very soon became general. Confidence was destroyed. It was soon ascertained that too much floating capital had been converted into fixed capital. Call loans were called in. A large part of the hundreds of millions of stock and bonds that had been created during the previous ten years, proved to be unavailable. Wall street and the Stock Exchange became greatly excited. A large number of the members of the Board of Brokers were unable to respond to their call loans, and failed. Stocks fell 50 per cent. At the height of the panic New York Central R. R. stock sold down to 48, Illinois Central, Michigan Central, and Rock Island at about 30, Michigan Southern at 5. Money so stringent that bankers were unable to borrow currency on gold bullion; the Michigan Southern sold at ten per cent. guaranteed stock at 50, and the Michigan Central, an eight per cent. mortgage bond, at the same price.

The panic continued about fifty days, until the middle of October, 1857, when all banks suspended specie payments.

The system of redemption of bank notes then in force by the Suffolk Bank in Boston, and the Metropolitan Bank in New York, operated unfavorably. This mode of requiring redemption of the interior bank currency which was sent in packages to these banks and then hurried back again to the interior, frequently in the same packages, greatly accelerated the panic. Finally the banks in New York, by common consent, ceased sending home good currency and finally took the *secured* currency of the State of New York, and made it a basis for Clearing House Certificates, which had an important influence in stopping the panic and restoring confidence. When the banks suspended, relief came, of course. Confidence gradually returned, money flowed into business channels, prices improved, and the banks were enabled to resume in December.

STATE BANKS—REBELLION—SUB-TREASURY.

At the breaking out of the Rebellion in 1861, the Government of the United States had no National institution to resort to, like the Bank of England or the Bank of France, for aid to sustain the Union Army and Navy. It had only a barren Sub-Treasury, which in every effort of the Government to make loans, was known to be antagonistic to the customary commercial operations of the State Banks. The Sub-Treasury was in no way connected with Clearing House operations, and could not check on the Banks for Government disbursements, and if the Government borrowed money on its bonds from the banks, the money had to be paid into the Sub-Treasury in gold and silver coin, or treasury notes, which at once weakened the bank reserves, and tended to disturb the whole financial business of the country. The Sub-Treasury law was a positive obstacle to a successful management of the finances in the great war then in progress to maintain the Union.

LOAN OF $250,000,000 AUTHORIZED.

Two important loan acts were passed at the extra session of Congress in July and August, 1861, authorizing a loan of $250,000,000. The first act was approved July 17th, and the second August 5th. By section six of the last mentioned act, the Sub-Treasury law passed in 1846, was so far suspended as to allow the Secretary of the Treasury

"To deposit any of the moneys obtained on any of the loans now authorized by law, to the credit of the Treasurer of the

United States, in such solvent specie-paying banks as he may select; and the said moneys, so deposited, may be withdrawn from such deposit, for deposit with the regular authorized depositaries, *or for the payment of public dues*, or paid in the redemption of the notes authorized to be issued under this act, or the act to which this is supplementary, payable on demand, as may seem expedient to, or be directed by the Secretary of the Treasury."

"After the battle of Bull Run, which occurred on the twenty-first of July of that year, the necessities of the Government in clothing, arming and feeding troops—in providing munitions of war, and building a navy—became so urgent that the banks in New York, Boston and Philadelphia, most patriotically came forward and made arrangements in several negotiations with Secretary Chase, to loan to the Government $150,000,000, under the provisions of the two loan acts passed at the extra session. Of this sum $105,000,000 was apportioned to the associated banks in the city of New York, payable by installments. The banks were then in good condition, transacting their business on a specie basis, and paid coin for all balances at the clearing house, and redeemed their circulating notes in coin, and the loan to the Government was made with the expectation that the money would be deposited in the banks, and be checked out under the direction of the Secretary, in pursuance of the sixth section above referred to. The Secretary of the Treasury refused to use the discretionary power conferred upon him by that section, and would not check on the banks for the expenses of the war, so that current bank notes could be paid or balances settled through the clearing house, but insisted that the banks should pay the money loaned into the Sub-Treasury in gold or gold treasury notes, and from thence it was distributed for war purposes and scattered in different parts of the country. By far the greater part of this loan was paid in gold coin, taken from the reserves of the banks, commencing on the nineteenth of August, 1861. This unnecessary mode of requiring the payment of the loans, so weakened the banks, that it brought on a general suspension of specie payments, during the last days of December, 1861. Mr. Chase in breaking the banks at the same time broke the Sub-Treasury, and both were discredited together." (See Spaulding's Financial History of the War, Second Edition, pages 2 and 3 of Introduction.)

HON. SALMON P. CHASE, Secretary of the Treasury, in his report in December, 1861, stated that there were about sixteen hundred local banks, and that the value of the then existing bank note circulation depended upon the laws of thirty-four States, and the character of those private corporations. He estimated the total circulation of all these banks, January 1st, 1861, to be $202,000,767. "Of this circulation, $150,000,000 in round numbers was in the loyal States, and $50,000,000 in the rebellious States."

The Government was without any National paper currency to circulate as money, and Mr. Chase was not then favorable to the issue of legal tender notes. He however was in favor of a National currency under the authority of the United States, and recommended the

NATIONAL BANK ACT.

Mr. Chase in his annual report in December, 1861, above referred to, said:

"It has been well questioned by the most eminent statesmen whether a currency of bank notes, issued by local institutions under State laws, is not, in fact, prohibited by the National Constitution. Such emissions certainly fall within the spirit, if not within the letter, of the Constitutional prohibition of the emission of 'bills of credit' by the States, and of the making by them of anything except gold and silver coin a legal tender in payment of debts.

"However this may be, it is too clear to be reasonably disputed that Congress, under its Constitutional powers to lay taxes, to regulate commerce and to regulate the value of coin, possesses ample authority to control the credit circulation which enters so largely into the transactions of commerce, and affects in so many ways the value of coin. In the judgment of the Secretary, the time has arrived when Congress should exercise this authority. The value of the existing bank note circulation depends on the laws of thirty-four States, and the character of some sixteen hundred private corporations. It is usually furnished in greatest proportions by institutions of least actual capital, circulation, commonly, is in the inverse ratio of solvency. Well-founded institutions, of large and solid capital, have, in general, comparatively little circulation, while weak corporations almost invariably seek to sustain themselves by obtaining from the people the largest possible credit in this form. Under such a system, or rather lack of system, great influctions and heavy losses in discounts and exchanges are inevitable, and not unfrequently, through failures of the issuing institutions, considerable portions of the circulation become suddenly worthless in the hands of the people. The recent experience of several States in the valley of the Mississippi, painfully illustrates the justice of these observations; and enforces, by the most cogent practical arguments, the duty of protecting commerce and industry against the recurrence of such disasters.

"The Secretary thinks it possible to combine with this protection a provision for circulation, safe to the community and convenient for the Government.

"Its principal features are: first, a circulation of notes bearing a common impression, and authenticated by a common authority; second, the redemption of these notes by the associations and institutions to which they may be delivered for issue, and third, the security of that redemption by the pledge of United States stocks, and an adequate provision of specie.

"In this plan the people, in their ordinary business, would find the advantages of uniformity in currency; of effectual safe-guard, if effectual safe-guard is possible, against depreciation; and of protection from losses in discounts and exchanges; while in the operations of the Government, the people would find the further advantages of a large demand for Government securities, of increased facilities for obtaining the loans required by the war, and of some alleviation of the burdens on industry through a diminution in the rate of interest, or a participation in the profit of circulation, without risking the perils of a great money monopoly.

"A further and important advantage to the people may be reasonably expected in the increased security of the Union, springing from the common interest in its preservation, created by the distribution of its stock to associations throughout the country, as the basis of their circulation.

"The whole circulation of the country, except a limited amount of foreign coin, would, after the lapse of two or three years, bear the impress of the nation, whether in coin or notes; which the amount of the latter, always easily ascertainable, and, of course, always generally known, would not be likely to be increased beyond the real wants of business.

"He expresses an opinion in favor of this plan with the greatest confidence; because it has the advantage of recommendation from experience. It is not an untried theory.

"In the State of New York, and in one or more of the other States, it has been subjected, in its most essential parts, to the test of experiment, and has been found practicable and useful. The probabilities of success will not be diminished, but increased by its adoption under national sanction, and for the whole country. * *"

This report of Mr. Chase was referred to the sub-committee of Ways and Means, consisting of myself as chairman, Mr. Hooper, of Mass., and Mr. Corning, of N. Y. After a careful examination of the report, I applied to Mr. Chase for the draft of a Bill to carry into effect the plan of a National Bank in accordance with his recommendations. He had not prepared any bill, and requested me to prepare one as soon as practicable. Hon. John J. Knox, the present Comptroller of the currency, in his last able report to Congress, says: "A National Bank bill was prepared by Mr. Spaulding, of New York, in accordance with the plan of Secretary Chase." This is true; I prepared the Bank Bill during the holidays in December, 1861, and had two hundred copies of it printed by the Public Printer for the use of the Committee of Ways and Means, with a view to have it considered, amended, and finally to be reported. (I here produce one of the original copies of the bill as prepared by me at that time, and which I have retained until now). Considerable opposition was manifested to the bill. It became certain that it could not at that time pass without a long discussion. The expenses of the Government were running on at a fearful rate, and the Treasury was nearly empty. It soon became apparent that the bank bill could not be passed and made available in time to meet the gigantic expenses of the war. It was, therefore, laid aside for future consideration. There was an imperative necessity for a National circulating medium, as well as immediate available means to sustain the Army and Navy in the prosecution of the war. The State Banks and Sub-Treasury suspended specie payments on the 28th of December, 1861. The notes of these banks became uncurrent money, and at best had only a local character and credit. Under these circumstances I immediately introduced into the House of Representatives

THE LEGAL TENDER ACT.

On introducing the bill, I stated that it was a temporary "War Measure"—a measure of necessity and not of choice, and that it would at once insure a *loan* to the Government without interest and a *national currency*. (For a full history of this measure see Spaulding's History of Legal Tender Act, commencing at p. 6).

The real purpose and object of the Legal Tender Act was to *fund* the debt incurred for war expenses. To do so it was necessary to quickly *create* a temporary National currency for disbursement to the Army and for other war expenses, and which should also be receivable for taxes and other dues to the Government, except custom duties. In order to prevent any redundancy it was also provided that it might at any time be converted into six per cent. gold bonds.

The act authorized the issue of $500,000,000 six per cent. gold bonds, into which these legal tender notes could be funded.

The title of the act was very expressive of its object, "An Act to authorize the issue of United States notes and for the *redemption and funding thereof*, and for *funding the floating debt of the United States.*"

In the opening remarks I made, I said "The demand notes put in circulation would meet the present exigencies of the Government in the discharge of its existing liabilities to the army, navy and contractors, and for supplies, materials and munitions of war.

These notes would find their way into all the channels of trade among the people; and as they accumulate *in the hands of capitalists they would exchange them for the six per cent. twenty years' bonds.*

"These circulating notes in the hands of the people would enable them to pay the taxes imposed, and would facilitate all business operations between farmers, mechanics, commercial business men and banks, and be equally as good as, and in many cases better, than the present irredeemable circulation issued by the State banks.

"The $500,000,000 six per cent. twenty years' bonds in the hands of the Secretary of the Treasury ready to be issued, would afford ample opportunity for funding the treasury notes as fast as the capitalists might desire to exchange treasury notes, not bearing interest, for coupon bonds of the United States, bearing six per cent. interest, and amply secured by a tax upon the people and all their property."

"In this way the Government will be able to get along with its immediate and pressing necessities without being obliged to force its bonds on the market at ruinous rates of discount; the people, under heavy taxation, would be shielded against high rates of interest; *and the capitalists will be afforded a fair compensation for the use of their money during the pending struggle of the country for national existence.* * * *

"Our army must have what is far more valuable to them then gold and silver. They must have food, clothing, and the material of war. Treasury notes issued by the Government, on the faith of the whole people, will purchase these indispensable articles, and the war can be prosecuted until we can enforce obedience to the Constitution and laws, and an honorable peace be thereby secured. This done, I will be the first to advocate a speedy return to specie payments, and all measures that are calculated to preserve the honor and dignity of the Government in the time of peace, and which I regret are not practicable in the prosecution of this war."

The first Legal Tender Act for $150,000,000 was passed and approved by President Lincoln, February 25, 1862.

The second Act for an additional $150,000,000 was passed and approved by Mr. Lincoln, July 11, 1862.

On the back of the notes issued under these two acts was printed the following words: "This note is a legal tender for all debts, public and private, except duties on imports and interest on the public debt, *and is exchangeable for U. S. six per cent. bonds redeemable at the pleasure of the United States, after five years.*"

These notes in the form of greenback currency, were immediately issued by Secretary Chase and disbursed for war expenses, and the Treasury of the United States was soon relieved of the pressing demand that was made upon it. The army and navy were paid, and supplies and materials of war obtained on these paper promises in sufficient quantity to prosecute the war with vigor. A further issue of $150,000,000 of *un*-fundable greenbacks was authorized in 1863.

This currency did not grow out of industry and production, and was not, therefore, a legitimate commercial currency. It sprang from the dire necessity of a gigantic civil war. It was debt created in the absence of ready means. It was the evidence of want, and the waste of war. The Government had no gold or other products of industry on hand with which to redeem it. It was simply a temporary war currency. During the war we were obliged to accept it, but with a view to get rid of it as soon as possible on the return of peace, it was by the original acts made convertible, as before stated, into a six per cent. gold bond, which was a practical redemption, and an easy and natural mode of getting rid of the evil effects of this redundant and unnatural currency.

THE GREAT MISTAKE OF THE WAR.

I said on another occasion and I reproduce it here: "The great mistake—greater than all other mistakes in the management of the war—was the abrogation of the right to fund the greenback currency into gold bonds, as provided for in the two preceding acts."

All the other mistakes, civil and military, which occurred during the war were of slight consequence when compared with the mischievous and grave consequences resulting from this one mistake. Taking away from the holder of this paper currency the right to redeem it on demand in gold bonds, besides being manifestly unjust to the holders, let the Government and the whole country—banks and people—down into the *slough* of an irredeemable paper currency, where we have remained for over eleven years. From 1864, to 1876, it has been a dead weight on the business and industry of the country, without elasticity, and without any provisions whatever being made for its redemption or payment. Its redundancy, and consequent depreciation, has operated very injuriously to the legitimate business of the country. It was an instrument of expenditure, a visible evidence of the waste of war, and not possessing the essential elements of a commercial currency. A majority of the people, however, have been deluded into the belief that those broken promises, mere evidences of debt, were money and a proper standard of value as a basis for doing business, and have plunged headlong into all sorts of speculation, unprofitable enterprises, extravagance in living, general abuse of credit, idleness and consequent demoralization.

If the right to fund the greenbacks into the six per cent. gold bonds had not been abrogated, no financier or practical business man, whose opinion is worth quoting, can doubt that we would have gone to specie payment within two or three years after the close of the war, in spite of ourselves. The individual indebtedness at the close of the war in 1865 was small. Every one was comparatively free from debt. The six per cent. gold bonds were sought for as an investment. They soon appreciated to par in gold, and if the right to fund had been continued, the greenback currency would have appreciated to par in gold along with bonds. The legal tender act would have served its purpose as a war measure, and we would have returned to the specie standard without material detriment to the legitimate business of the country. In this way we would have avoided a large part of the extravagance and demoralization that has been so reckless since the close of the war.

THE BANK BILL PASSED 1863.

On the 2d February, 1863, the National Currency Bank bill, as prepared by Mr. Spaulding, in December, 1861, after being altered and amended in several important particulars, was reported from the Finance Committee to the Senate by John Sherman, of Ohio. The debate upon it was opened on the 9th, and continued from day to day until the 12th, when it was passed by the following vote —yeas 23, nays 21, as follows:

Yeas—Messrs. Anthony, Arnold, Chandler, Clark, Doolittle, Fessenden, Foster, Harding, Harlan, Harris, Howard, Howe, Lane (of Kansas), Morrill, Nesmith, Pomeroy, Sherman, Sumner, Ten Eyck, Wade, Wilkinson, Wilmot, and Wilson of Massachusetts)—23.

Nays—Messrs. Carlisle, Collamer, Cowan, Davis, Dixon, Foot, Grimes, Henderson, Hicks, Kennedy, King, Latham, McDougal, Powell, Rice, Richardson, Saulsbury, Trumbull, Turpie, Wall, and Wilson (of Missouri)—21.

So the bill was passed.

The bill as it passed the Senate was sent to the House on the 12th. On motion of Mr. Hooper it was ordered to be printed, but was not referred to the Committee of Ways and Means. It remained on the Speaker's table until the 19th, when it was taken up for consideration in the House. A motion to refer it to the

Committee of the Whole having been defeated, Mr. Spaulding opened the debate in a lengthy speech in favor of the bill. The debate continued until the 20th, when the bill was passed without amendment by the following vote—yeas 78, nays, 64, as follows:

Yeas—Messrs. Aldrich, Alley, Ashley, Babbitt, Beaman, Bingham, Jacob B. Blair, Blake, Buffington, Calvert, Campbell, Casey, Chamberlain, Clements, Colfax, Conway, Covode, Cutler, Davis, Delano, Dunn, Edgerton, Eliot, Ely, Fenton, Samuel C. Fessenden, Thomas A. D. Fessenden, Fisher, Frank, Goodwin, Granger, Hahn, Haight, Hickman, Hooper, Hutchins, Julian, Kelley, Francis W. Kellogg, William Kellogg, Lansing, Leary, Lovejoy, Law, McIndoe, McKean, McPherson, Marston, Maynard, Moorhead, Anson P. Morrill, Noell, Olin, Patton, Timothy G. Phelps, Potter, Alexander H. Rice, John H. Rice, Sargent, Sedgwick, Segar, Shanks, Shellabarger, Sherman, Sloan, Spaulding, Stevens, Trimble, Trowbridge, Van Horne, Van Wyck, Verree, Wall, Wallace, Washburne, Albert S. White, Windom, and Worcester—78.

Nays.—Messrs. William Allen, Ancona, Baily, Baker, Baxter, Biddle, Cobb, Frederick A. Conkling, Roscoe Conkling, Cox, Cravens, Crittenden, Dawes, Edwards, English, Gooch, Grider, Gurley, Hall, Harding, Harrison, Holman, Horton, Johnson, Kerrigan, Knapp, Law, Lazaer, Loomis, Mallory, May, Menzies, Justin S. Morrill, Morris, Nixon, Noble, Norton, Nugent, Odell, Pendleton, Perry, Pike, Pomeroy, Porter, Price, Robinson, James S. Rollins, Sheffield, Shiel, John B. Steele, William G. Steele, Stiles, Stratton, Benjamin F. Thomas, Francis Thomas, Vallandigham, Wadsworth, Wheeler, Whaley, Chilton A. White, Wickliffe, Wilson, Woodruff, and Wright—64.

So the bill was passed and approved by President Lincoln, February 25, 1863.

No National Bank currency was issued until near the first of January, 1864. After that time it was gradually issued. On the first of July, 1864, the sum of $25,825,695 had been issued; and on the 22d of April, 1865, shortly after the surrender of General Lee, the whole amount of National Bank circulation issued to that time was $146,827,975.

FREE BANKING—NO MONOPOLY.

At first the act limited the amount of currency to be issued under it, to $300,000,000, but by a subsequent act this limitation was removed. Free Banking is now allowed to all the people who comply with its provisions. There is no longer a monopoly of banking under the laws of the United States. It is a system of National Banking and National Currency co-extensive with the boundaries of our National Union. It requires the circulating notes to be well secured by gold-bearing Government bonds, deposited with the Treasurer of the United States; requires each bank to redeem its circulating notes in lawful money on demand, and to keep an adequate reserve for that purpose; makes them a legal tender for all taxes and other debts to the Government, except customs, and for all debts owing by the Government, except principal and interest of the funded debt; it also makes them receivable by each National Bank for all ordinary debts due them, and each bank designated as a depositary, is also required to receive it on deposit from all public officers. These are important provisions in the law for *nationalizing* this currency, and it consequently obtains a wide circulation. Congress, by the act of March 3d, 1865, drove all State Bank circulation out of existence by the imposition of a tax upon it of ten per cent.

REDEMPTION OF PAPER MONEY.

Redemption is an essential requisite of paper money. To fulfil the functions of money it must be convertible into coin on demand. No other device which has been tried during the last hundred years by any Bank or any Government, to circulate its issues of paper currency on a par with gold has been successful, unless it could be immediately and conveniently converted into gold on demand. In regard to the truth of this proposition history repeats itself wherever and whenever it has been tried. The attempt to circulate the *Assignats* and *Mandats* of France without such convertibility, is a striking example of the folly of such an undertaking. They depreciated under excessive issues, until they possessed no value, and were finally repudiated. In the case of France there was no necessity or valid excuse for trying the experiment. In the case of the Thirteen Colonies, united in self-defence, there was some justification for the issue of Continental currency. The necessity of self-preservation and the ultimate aim of American Independence, were the reasons assigned for its excessive issue. It depreciated until it was valueless, and its final total loss operated as an unequal tax upon the people. It was irredeemable, and shared the same fate of all such currency.

REDEMPTION OF NATIONAL CURRENCY.

The National Bank Act requires that each National Bank which issues National Currency, shall redeem it on demand "in lawful money of the United States."

In a normal condition of the country this requirement means gold coin, the value of which is regulated by Congress.

Unfortunately eleven years after the close of the war, the temporary "war currency" issued in the form of greenbacks, still lingers as an evil element, and is declared by law to be "lawful money," so that the banks can and do redeem their circulating notes in this depreciated greenback currency. This is practically no redemption at all. It is merely swapping one kind of paper for another of about the same current value, and both of them depreciated about 13 per cent. below the price of gold.

There has been recently established a BUREAU in the Treasury Department at Washington, for the purpose of assorting and enforcing redemption of National Bank Currency. This operation furnishes clean notes for those that are worn and defaced, but it is in no sense an efficient redemption, and cannot be made so, until the Government takes out of the way its irredeemable greenback currency. When this is done the Banks will then be obliged to redeem their notes in gold or in funds on a par with gold. This redemption bureau will then have a real significance, and tend to hold in check excessive issues of Bank Currency.

PROGRESS MADE IN BANKING.

The refusal of Congress to re-charter the first United States Bank, and the arbitrary and illegal action of the Executive in regard to the second United States Bank, seriously retarded the progress of sound banking, under the authority of the United States. By these blunders the Government and people have been deprived of the great benefits they would have received from the stability given to business by the continuance of such an institution. In spite, however, of this incongruous and unwise action of Congress and the Executive there has been real progress made in the business of banking during the last hundred years. The Bank of North America in Philadelphia, the Bank of New York in New York City, the Massachusetts Bank in Boston, the first three banks organized in the United States, have always maintained a respectable position, and are to-day performing their duties to the public, and are favorably regarded for their high-standing and solidity. Having been re-organized, they are to-day doing a prosperous business under the present National Bank Act.

Most of the Banks organized in the principal cities since January 1st, 1790, have maintained their existence in some form; have increased their capitals, have done a successful business, and are now highly creditable institutions, and doing as good a business as the present state of trade will admit.

State Banks and National Banks are generally in a prosperous condition, and most of the old State Banks finally re-organized under the National Bank Act in 1865.

Hon. JOHN J. KNOX, Comptroller of the Currency, in his last report made to Congress in December, 1875, gives a detailed report of the condition of all the National Banks. It is a most valuable and interesting statement of the favorable condition of the business of banking in the United States. Those desiring further details in regard to the banks can study this report to great advantage.

Capital Stock of National Banks paid in is	$505,485,865
" " State Banks " "	164,366,669
Aggregate amount of deposits in Savings Banks	849,581,633
Capital Stock of Loan and Trust Companies	21,854,020
	$1,541,288,187

PRIVATE BANKERS do not report the amount of capital employed in their business. It is therefore difficult to make any approximate estimate of their aggregate capital. It is known, however, to be large, and their business transactions largely swell the banking operations of the country.

Bank officers and private bankers are generally men of high character. Their business is intimately interwoven with all the industrial and commercial operations of the country. Their customers are also generally men of the same high character. They have a common interest in the success of the trade transactions of the country. Bankers and customers are alike interested in maintaining a high standard of integrity, punctuality, and commercial honor.

CREDIT AND CLEARING HOUSE.

CREDIT is the essential element that underlies the business of banking. Banking in all its forms is dependent upon credit. Well organized banks, and the system of daily settlements through the clearing Houses in all the great commercial centers, and a weekly publication of the condition of the banks, has an important influence in keeping all credit transactions under due control, and confining them within proper limits. About one hundred years ago, the private banks in London organized the first Clearing House in that city. THE NEW YORK CLEARING HOUSE ASSOCIATION, composed of New York Bankers, went into operation October 1st, 1853, and its present constitution was adopted June 6th, 1854.

The system of Clearings by off-set is one of the most useful improvements of modern times. It economizes both time and money in the liquidation of debts, especially all the large commercial transactions of the world, amounting to several hundred millions daily, with only a very small resulting balance to be paid in money. Very little gold or paper money is required to do the business of any of the large cities.

When the economy of the check-system had caused the innumerable daily payments of the community to be carried on without any withdrawal of money from the banks, the next and culminating step in the process was to allow the payments among the banks themselves to be likewise effected without the use of money. This has been admirably accomplished by means of the clearing-house. To this establishment each bank sends the checks upon other banks which have been paid in by its customers, so that a balance of these check transactions is struck for each bank with each of the others.

The balance due to or by each bank being thus ascertained at the Clearing-House, the debtor bank in New York pays its balance in money. In London each debtor bank gives its check on the Bank of England, where the private banks keep accounts. In this way the balance is paid without using any money at all. This is effected simply by a transference of a certain amount from the credit of one bank to the credit of another, on the books of the Bank of England.

For the year ending April 30, 1875, the aggregate debts paid at the London clearing-house without the use of any money, was the enormous amount of £6,013,299,000. Mr. Hankey, former President of the Bank of England, says: "That all this has been effected without the use or employment of a single bank note, or one single sovereign."

In New York the currency exchanges of the year ending in October, 1875, amounted to $23,042,276,858.47; and the currency balance to $1,104,346,845.32. The gold exchanges amounted to $108,940,058.85, and the gold balance to $18,284,429.61. Thus the total transactions of the year at the Clearing-House amounted to $24,273,848,192.25, showing a daily average for the year of $79,326,301.28 of debts thus paid.

Clearing Houses have been established in Boston, Philadelphia, Baltimore, and the other principal cities of the United States, with useful and beneficial results.

THE PANIC OF 1873.

After the right to fund the greenback currency into 6 per cent. gold bonds was revoked in 1863, which rendered this currency irredeemable, credit became so expanded under the excessive issues of paper currency and other obligations during the war, that neither the banks, the Clearing House, nor any other human agency could restrain it within reasonable limits, especially under the vacillating course adopted by Congress. The *abuse* of credit became general in the creation of debts in all its forms—States, cities, counties, corporations, and individuals combined to swell the *paper bubble* until it finally burst in the great panic of 1873. The combination of the banks in the Clearing House in New York, exerted a most powerful influence in staying the calamity, and preventing the general suspension of all the banks. By an extra form of credit in the shape of clearing-house certificates, they continued to pay and liquidate a very large amount of debts each day, without paying money for even resulting balances. The Clearing House Associations in other cities exerted a favorable influence in the same direction. The panicy feeling passed away in due time, and the banks again resumed their former mode of settling balances. The Temporary Clearing House certificates, improvised during the panic, were soon after redeemed and taken off the market.

REVIEW AND CONCLUSION.

The lesson taught by the experience of the last hundred years may, if rightly comprehended, be of great advantage in the future. It clearly shows that we need more stability in financial legislation—more statesmanship—less passion and political partisanship. We have been on a high wave of financial uncertainty too long. It affects in too many ways the industrial interests of the country. Upon a review of the banking and financial legislation of the nation from 1791 to the present time, we are struck with the changes and uncertainty that has prevailed. In 1791, under the auspices of Washington and Hamilton, the first United States Bank was organized, to continue twenty years, with a capital of $10,000,000. After very careful examination and unusual deliberation, it was decided to base the bank upon the combined power of the government united to the private influence of its people; that the government and people had a common interest, and that the two interests combined in a national institution, was the best mode of carrying on the financial affairs of the country. Upon the organization of this bank, the finances were soon placed upon a specie basis, and the business of the country was steady and prosperous for nearly twenty years.

In 1811, this prosperous and useful institution was, by a very close vote in the Senate and House, refused a re-charter, and was obliged to wind up its affairs. This produced great confusion and uncertainty. The war with Great Britain, from 1812 to 1815, added to the embarrassments, until, in 1816, the second bank of the United States was organized, with a capital of $35,000,000, upon the same principles as the first, to continue for twenty years. As soon as this bank got fairly into operation, order was again restored to the finances of the government, and specie payments were again resumed in all parts of the country. This restored prosperity again to the business of the country, which continued, with but little interruption, down to 1832, when President Jackson, by his veto, prevented a re-charter of this bank. The next year he illegally removed the government deposits, which led to a panic and general crash in 1837, which depressed all the industrial interests of the country for nearly six years.

The sub-treasury law was finally passed in 1846, which was found to be wholly inadequate to meet even the exigencies of the small war with Mexico, and still more so to meet the requirements of the great war of the rebellion. The State banks have always been unfavorably affected by the uncertainty that attended the financial legislation of the national government.

It is remarkable to notice how frequently many of the leading statesmen of the country have changed their minds on this question. James Madison, in 1791, led the opposition, in the House, to the charter of the first United States bank, and voted against the act. In 1816, he being then President, recommended the second United States bank, approved the bill, and afterwards said that it was "essential for the interests of the community at large, as well as for the purposes of the treasury." Henry Clay, in 1811, voted against a renewal of the charter of the first bank, but afterwards changed his mind, and was a firm supporter of the second bank. Daniel Webster opposed the chartering of the second bank in 1816, but in 1830 he became its warm advocate.

In 1791, Thomas Jefferson gave a written opinion to President Washington against signing the first United States bank bill. Afterwards, and while he was President, the Territory of Louisiana having been acquired from France, he approved a bill to establish a *branch* of the same bank in the city of New Orleans.

General Jackson and Mr. Van Buren, in 1833, were very favorable to the State deposit banks, and in 1837, during the revulsion of that year, changed their minds and denounced them in very decided terms.

Many other similar cases might be named, of gentlemen, who, having become convinced of their error, did not hesitate to change their minds on this question, and it is highly creditable to them that they had the courage to do so.

The present national banking system—organized in the midst of civil revolution, and which could only be brought into existence under the pressure of a great public calamity, and amid the enthusiasm of the people determined to maintain the Union—has drawn to its support a very large majority of the banking capital of the country. Experience has shown that it is well adapted to the wants of American industry and progress; that it is a convenient and safe depositary of the public funds which can easily be transferred to any part of the country without any of the machinery or expense of the sub-treasury, and that when more fully perfected will be adequate to meet the demands of our anomalous situation in war as well as in time of peace. That it is not perfect, is not the fault of those who originated it; that it is not perfected and the sub-treasury discontinued, is the fault of the government itself. Let the government return to its integrity, re-adopt, at a lower rate of interest, the funding of the greenbacks, or in the mode prescribed in Senator Sherman's act of last year, retire its over-due indebtedness in the recognized money of the commercial world, and the national banks will be ready to redeem their circulating notes in the same kind of money. Meantime they loyally await the action of Congress, and will be ready to redeem in lawful money, whether it be greenbacks or gold, whatever shall be recognized by the government for itself, and by it prescribed to the people as the legal standard of redemption.

The causes which led to the panic of 1873, were too deep and far-reaching to be easily got rid of or overcome. Debt and taxation are heavy burdens; defaulted railroad bonds lie dormant in safes and drawers; irredeemable paper money is still in excess; industry and production languish; Congress still vacillates and fails to settle the financial problem on a firm basis; the depression and stagnation in business which commenced in the panic of 1873, still continues, and is likely to continue until the finances are finally settled on a specie basis, the question removed from political agitation, and the business of the country allowed to resume its normal condition free from the excesses and demoralization of the war. Then will be the time to complete the history of the paper bubble, which has been so demoralizing for the last twelve years. I await that time with a good deal of anxiety, and trust that the day is not very distant when we shall reach solid bottom, and again commence another era of general prosperity.

APPENDIX.

FIRST BANKS ORGANIZED IN UNITED STATES.

In Vol. III. of the American edition of the Edinburgh Cyclopedia published in 1813, the following table is given "to exhibit in one view the names of the Banks most deserving of notice, the time of their institution, and the amount of their capital." The table is not complete, but it shows the time in which the State Banking System was introduced in the different States:

Names.	Instituted.	Capital.
Bank of North America, Pa.,	1781	$ 400,000
Bank of New York,	1784	950,000
Massachusetts Bank, Boston,	1784	300,000
Bank of Maryland,	1790	300,000
Providence Bank, R. I.,	1791	400 000
Bank of Albany, N. Y.,	1792	260,000
Bank of South Carolina,	1792	640,000
Union Bank of Boston, Mass.,	1792	1,200,000
New Hampshire Bank,	1792	100,000
Bank of Alexandria, Va.,	1792	500,000
Hartford Bank, Conn.,	1792	930,000
Union Bank, N. London, Conn.	1792	500,000
New Haven Bank, Conn.,	1792	400,000
Bank of Columbia, N. Y.,	1793	160,000
Bank of Columbia, D. C.,	1793	500 000
Bank of Pennsylvania,	1793	2,000,000
Bank of Nantucket, Mass.,	1795	100,000
Bank of Delaware,	1795	110,000
Bank of Baltimore, Md.,	1795	1,200,000
Middletown Bank, Conn.,	1795	400,000
Bank of Rhode Island,	1795	100 000
Norwich Bank, Conn.,	1796	200,000
Manhattan Bank, N. Y.,	1799	2,000,000
Portland Bank, Me.,	1799	300,000
Essex Bank, Salem, Mass.,	1799	300,000
Washington Bank, Westerly, R. I.,	1800	50,000
Bank of Bristol, R. I.,	1800	120,000
Exchange Bank, Providence, R. I.,	1801	400,000
Farmers' Bank, Lansingburg, N. Y.,	1801	75,000
State Bank of South Carolina,	1801	800,000
Maine Bank, Portland, Me.,	1802	300,000
New Hampshire Union Bank,	1802	200,000
Lin. and Ken. Bank, Wiscasset, Me.,	1802	200,000
Kentucky Insurance Company,	1802	150,000
Merchants' Bank, N. Y.,	1803	1 250,000
Bedford Bank at N. B., Mass.,	1803	150,000
New York State Bank,	1803	460,000
Newburyport Bank, Mass.,	1803	550,000
Saco Bank, Mass.,	1803	100,000
Albany Merchants' Company, N. Y.,	1803	25,000
Plymouth Bank, Mass.,	1803	100,000
Boston Bank, Mass.,	1803	1,000,000
Stafford Bank, Dover, Mass.,	1803	150,000
Philadelphia Bank, Pa.,	1803	2,000,000
Miami Exporting Company, Cincinnati, Ohio,	1803	200,000
Salem Bank, Mass.,	1803	200,000
Roger Williams' Bank, R. I.,	1803	150,000
Newport Bank, R. I.,	1803	120,000
Warren Bank, R. I.,	1803	68,000
Exeter Bank, N. H.,	—	200,000
Union Bank of Maryland,	1804	1,258.775
Bank of Cape Fear, N. C.,	1804	350,000
Bank of Newbern, N. C.,	1804	300,000
Newark Banking and Ins. Co., N. J.,	1804	225,000
Trenton Bank, N. J.,	1804	300,000
Hallowell and Augusta Bank, Me.,	1804	200,000
Worcester Bank, Mass.,	1804	150,000
Nantucket Pacific Bank, Mass.	1804	100,000
Marblehead Bank, Mass.,	1804	100,000
Rhode Island Union Bank,	1804	150,000
Smithfield Union Bank, R. I.,	1805	50,000
Narragansett Bank, R. I.,	1805	60,000
Rhode Island Central Bank,	1805	60,000
Bank of Virginia, Va.,	1805	1,500,000
Mechanics' Bank, Baltimore, Md.,	1806	1,000,000
Bank of Chillicothe, O.,	1806	100,000
Bridgeport Bank, Conn.,	1806	200,000
Derby Bank, Conn.,	1806	200,000
Bank of Kentucky,	1807	1,000,000
Bank of Nashville, Tenn.,	1807	500,000
Bank of Marietta, Ohio,	1807	100,000
Farmers' Bank of the State of Delaware,	1807	500,000
New Brunswick Bank, N. J.,	1807	150,000
Farmers' & Mechanics' Bank, Pa.,	1807	1,250,000
Hagerstown Bank, Md.,	1807	250,000
Mohawk Bank, N. Y.,	1807	200,000
New London Bank, Conn.,	1807	200,000
Hudson Bank, N. Y.,	1808	300,000
Bank of Steubenville, Ohio,	1809	100,000
Chambersburg Bank, Pa.,	1809	250,000
Commercial Bank. R. I.,	1809	50,000
State Bank of North Carolina,	1810	1,600,000
Commercial & Farmers' Bank of Baltimore, Md.,	1810	1,000,000
Farmers' & Merchants' Bank of Baltimore, Md.,	1810	500,000
Franklin Bank, of Baltimore, Md.,	1810	600,000
Marine Bank of Baltimore, Md.,	1810	600,000
Elkton Bank, Md.,	1810	300,000
Farmers' Bank of Lancaster, Pa.,	1810	300,000
Mechanics' Bank, N. Y.,	1810	2,000,000

Names.	Instituted.	Capital.	Names.	Instituted.	Capital.
Bank of Troy, N. Y.,	1811	500,000	Camden State Bank, N. J.,	1812	800,000
Mechanics' & Farmers' Bank, Albany,	1811	600,000	Trenton " "	1812	300,000
State Bank at Boston, Mass.,	1811	2,000,000	New Brunswick State Bank, N. J.,	1812	400,000
Merchants' Bank at Salem, Mass.,	1811	200,000	Newark State Bank, N. J.,	1812	400,000
Cumberland Bank of Allegheny, Md.,	1811	200,000	Elizabeth " "	1812	200,000
Bank of Newburg, N. Y.,	1811	400,000	Morris " "	1812	200,000
Farmers' Bank of Wor. and Som., Md.,	1811	200,000	Utica Bank, N. Y.,	1812	1,000,000
Middle District Bank, N. Y.,	1811	500,000	Pittsburg Manufacturing Co., Pa.,	1812	1,000,000
Bank of New Orleans, La.,	1811	500,000	City Bank of Baltimore, Md.,	1812	1,500,000
Union Bank, N. Y.,	1811	1,800,000	Bank of Wilmington & Brandywine, Del.,	1812	120,000
Eagle Bank, Conn.,	1811	750,000	Farmers' & Mechanics' Bank of Delaware,	1812	75,000
Bank of America, N. Y.,	1812	2,000,000	Commercial Bank of Delaware,	1812	200,000
City Bank, N. Y.,	1812	1,000,000	Farmers' & Mechanics' Bank of Virginia,	1812	1,500,000
Farm. & Mechanics' Bank of Cincinnati, O.,	1812	500,000	Savannah Bank, Ga.,	—	1,000,000
Bank of Muskingum, Zanesville, O.,	1812	100,000	Union Bank, S. C.,	—	1,000,000
Monongahela Bank, O.,	1812	250,000	Planters' & Mechanics' Bank, S. C.,	—	1,200,000
New York Manufacturing Co., N. Y.,	1812	1,200,000			

NUMBER OF BANKS AND BANKERS IN THE UNITED STATES, FROM THE BANKER'S ALMANAC AND REGISTER FOR 1876.

STATE.	National	BANKS. Under State Charter.		Savings.	Private Bankers.	STATE.	National	BANKS. Under State Charter.		Savings.	Private Bankers.
			Capital.						Capital.		
Alabama	10	6	$1,600,000		19	Missouri	35	104	$14,437,124		105
Arkansas	2	1	200,000		10	Montana	5				6
Arizona					1	Nebraska	10	8	595,000		25
California	9	45	23,839,000	25	60	Nevada		2	150,000		18
Colorado	11	5	380,000		22	New Hampshire	44	2	150,000	68	4
Connecticut	81	14	2,700,000	81	17	New Jersey	67	18	2,925,750	40	10
Dacotah	1				6	New Mexico	2				3
Delaware	11	7	880,000		3	New York State	234	61	9,065,870	116	204
Dist. of Columbia	5	6	422,950		9	New York City	48	30	18,935,200	44	26
Florida	1				6	North Carolina	15	6	1,125,000		8
Georgia	13	31	16,336,700		41	Ohio	176	35	1,207,500		237
Idaho	1				3	Oregon	1				5
Illinois	146	23	6,111,000		282	Pennsylvania	232	132	18,336,672		324
Indiana	103	20	570,000		111	Rhode Island	62	16	3,727,880	37	5
Iowa	84	32	1,776,900		186	South Carolina	12	8	1,875,000		19
Kansas	20	27	934,617		76	Tennessee	26	15	1,400,000		12
Kentucky	51	52	12,363,025		37	Texas	10	16	2,225,000		80
Louisiana	7	9	4,500,000		9	Utah	2				6
Maine	71	3	175,000	58	7	Vermont	47	2	100,000	18	2
Maryland	31	24	4,408,724		26	Virginia	20	49	4,168,567		30
Massachusetts	236	5	1,300,000	179	55	West Virginia	17	14	856,000		7
Michigan	80	30	2,285,000		122	Wisconsin	42	27	1,118,000		69
Minnesota	35	14	500,200		40	Wash. Territory					2
Mississippi		8	685,000		16	Wyoming	2				4
						Forward			81,968,106		
			81,968,106						164,366,669		

		Capital.
Chartered State Banks	907	$164,366,669
National Banks	2,118	505,485,965
Savings Banks	666	
Private Bankers	2,375	
Total Banks and Bankers	6,066	

www.ingramcontent.com/pod-product-compliance
Lightning Source LLC
Chambersburg PA
CBHW020122020526
44111CB00049B/625